COLLECTING
TOY
SOLDIERS
No. 2

An Identification & Value Guide
by Richard O'Brien

BOOKS AMERICANA INC

ISBN 0-89689-089-9

Seen on the cover: Wounded doughboy by Manoil; surrendering German by Holt's Hobbies; 54th Massachusetts marcher by Thomas' Tin Soldiers (Tom Loback); Marine flagbearer by Combat Ready Collectibles, which also cast the airplane from a 1930s mold from C.A. Wood; Pointing Jones officer reproduced by Ed Poole; Guard by Britains.

To Gus (Augustus W.) Hansen, Hank Anton and
K. Warren Mitchell, for all they have given
back to the hobby.

TABLE OF CONTENTS

INTRODUCTION AND ACKNOWLEDGEMENTS

Well, a second miracle has occurred. The first was when publisher Dan Alexander allowed me to do a 500-page book on nothing but soldiers. The second happened when it sold out (for the statistics-minded: over 10,000 copies were gobbled up), allowing me to do this follow-up.

Dan had given some thought to letting me do two volumes - one on American and one on foreign. But after some thought he decided the market isn't strong enough for that. Thus, because of all the new information I wanted to get in, and because books can only get so big, some things have been dropped. Try your library for the first edition if you'd like information on homecasts (since people ask me from time to time, these molds sell for about $75), Kilia, more illustrations of German composition and extensive lists of the sets produced by some of the newer makers.

Dimestore collectors will find that, with the uncovering of H.B. Toys, all the significant dimestore makers have now been identified. Discoveries of various catalogs since the last edition have given a better sense of when these figures were first produced, and some company numberings and descriptions.

As before, to my bottomless gratitude, many people have contributed to this edition. K. Warren Mitchell, a dealer who thinks like a collector, gave up his vacation to completely overhaul the Britains section, both text and photos. I've offered him my house in token gratitude, especially because, as you will see, he didn't end his contributions with Britains. Donald P. Grant's gracious go-ahead on using his list of Mignots gave the book a major leap forward. Jack Matthews once again came through with his expertise on German composition. Also pitching in mightily on short notice were Bob Hornung on Courtenay and Bertel Bruun on Danish soldiers and the newly-discovered George Grampp, plus early toy soldier experts Bill Nutting and Will Beierwaltes.

Kudos to Bill Greenbaum, who put me onto former Lido owners Seymour and Effrem Arenstein. Thanks to them for all the information on their firm, and for putting me onto the owner of Ajax. In turn, thanks to Judy and the late Harry Sternberg for filling me in on Ajax, sending me materials from their company, and figures to photograph.

What fun it was to finally unravel the mystery that turned out to be named H.B. Toys! Thanks to former owners Frank, Walter and Patricia Helm, to Frank for additional information on early doings at Barclay, and to all three for the emergence of another possible manufacturer; Paul Paragine.

The father of us all, Gus Hansen, pitched in by allowing me to go through all of J. Edward Jones' files, which gave me information on not just Jones, but a number of other companies. Another dean of the hobby, Bob Bard, the toy soldier guru for most of us in the 1950s and 1960s, took the time to go through the teeniest portion of his files; the result was a welcome and major deluge of information.

Johillco fans will undoubtedly think kind thoughts about Ken Winterich, of the West Falls Toy Company. I wrote and asked Ken if he might have any photos of the figures he produces from his original Johillco molds. He didn't, so he merely expressed me over 100 castings, so I could shoot them.

Hank Anton and Phil Savino kept me up to date by keeping me on their auction lists, as did K. Warren Mitchell with his dimestore and Britains lists. John E. Bussjager dropped me info on Grey Iron, and William G. Floyd did the same on Jones. Dave Leopard provided prices on Auburn vehicles, Paul Stadinger gave me a choice tidbit on Peco, Ron Cherner made a neat discovery on a Barclay podfoot, Cliff Finkelstein filled me in on SAE's U.S. distributor, and Frank J. Burghart provided me with a later Authenticast list than I had, while Lou Sandbote and Vadis Godbey saw that Authenticasts in photos I sent them got identified.

Photographs are the heart of this book. In many cases, people dropped everything so they could shoot their soldiers and get the results to me in time for my deadline. Whole armies of thanks to the following: Gary Linden, Dave Mitchell, Bill O'Brien, Wayne Hill (actually, a formerly unseen Barclay catalog sheet), Albert W. Lane, Jerry Combs, Mike McAfee, Ron Steiner, Ed Poole, Phil Savino, Hank Anton, Perry R. Eichor, Craig A. Clark, Lester G. Saulsbury, Gordon Gee, Stan Alekna, Ron Hillman, Old Toy Soldier, Don Pielin, Don Patman, Harold Haseley, Bob Hornung, Jim Furstman, Jim Krakowiecki, Fred Wilhelm, Max Heiss, John Kurinsky, Charlie O'Brien, Bertel Bruun, Roy E. Bonjour, Edward Ryan (for patent drawings), Bill Cardiff (also for information on Wilton), Gene Parker, A.J. (Bob) Mergenthaler, Henry Kurtz of Phillips, Larry G. Alkire, Robert D. Worthen, John Alliston, Ken Butler, Ed Hyers, Fred Maxwell, Gary Franson, Bob West, Ron Fink, A.E. Hemminger, Vinnie Pugliese, Tony Diksa, Joseph Saine, Ronald L. Simkoff and Jim Casey. Great fun was the day when Charlie Breslow and Roger Johnson came over and let me photograph all their rarities.

Finally, thanks to everyone in the past who contributed, including the veterans of all the toy soldier companies I've interviewed (often over and over) during the past years, and anyone I've (gulp!) forgotten.

Richard O'Brien
May, 1992

CONDITION OF A TOY SOLDIER AND ITS RELATION TO PRICE

The price of a toy soldier depends not only on its desirability, but on its condition.

"Mint" means just that; the condition in which it was originally issued — perfect, regardless of age, not the slightest blemish. Needless to say this is a fairly rare state of affairs, but enough soldiers exist in mint condition to make it an employable term. Many people, hoping to dispose of toys, are tempted to term them "mint" when they are really "near mint", "very good" or sometimes even just "good". Inevitably this can result in unhappiness all around, and not infrequently, in a cancelled sale.

"Very Good" indicates a soldier which has obviously seen use; with signs of wear and aging, but with most of its paint remaining and in general having a freshness to its appearance that makes it seem attractive and collectible to all but the most discriminating.

"Good" signals a soldier that has seen considerable wear, but has at least one half to one third of its original paint, and is basically sound. A collector will collect it, but will often not be wholly satisfied with it as an example of his collection, and thus prices are well below that which the same item in mint can command.

Condition below good results in another drastic drop in price, and figures with missing parts, although otherwise in excellent condition, will usually fall into this lower-priced category. At present, a BARCLAY soldier minus its tin helmet (signalled by a large round hole in the top of its head) is worth about half of what it would otherwise bring. Rust, even small spots of it on the cast iron soldiers, can seriously lower their price, as can repainting of any of the soldiers. "Near-Mint", "Fine", "Very Fine", "Excellent" and similar terms often found in sellers' descriptions, denote conditions between Mint and Very Good, and are priced accordingly.

The key to grading is to avoid wishful thinking. Grading can sometimes be a problem for the uninitiated, but common sense will usually prevail, and when possible a consultation with an expert in the field can often clear up lingering doubts. A toy in its original box is worth up to 10 to 20% more if the box is in mint condition, with the price dropping as condition lessens.

* * * * * * * *

NOTE: As this book was going to press, the author learned that collector-soldiermakers Bill Holt (Holt's Hobbies), Ron Eccles (Eccles Brothers) and Edward H. Burley had manufactured a number of toy soldiers to be shown at the climax of "Toys", a major motion picture to be released during the 1992 Christmas season. These makers can be found in the "Newer Makers" and "Leading Collectors and Dealers" sections.

AMERICAN SOLDIER COMPANY-EUREKA

Charles W. Beiser seems to have been the first successful manufacturer of lead toy soldiers in America. His company was founded in 1898. It was Beiser's first venture into toy soldier-making.

Research by collector Bill Nutting suggests that Beiser became interested in soldiers through his earlier business. In an 1896-97 directory he is listed as a stationer at 75 York, Brooklyn, NY. The next year the listing changed to "inkstands". Quite probably Beiser carried a soldier line in his shop (German-made, as suggested by a 1903 article). In any event, in the 1898-99 directory his listing changed to "Eureka Mfg. Co. 482 Hamilton Ave." Box labels on his soldier sets suggest the precise name for the firm at the outset may have been Eureka Metal Co. The 1901-2 directory shows only Chas. W. Beiser *toys,* with the address 127 Wyckoff, still Brooklyn.

The American Soldier Company was mentioned in the first issue of *Playthings* Magazine, January, 1903; the firm's soldiers were available in both gilt and regular paint. The next month Beiser ran his first *Playthings* ad, as "American Soldier Co., Makers" of "Eureka American Soldiers". In March, there was a line about "a very neat catalogue" having been issued. In May it was announced that "The American Soldier Co. have moved their factory", apparently to Glendale, Brooklyn. The next month *Playthings* noted "C.W. Beiser of the American Soldier Co. says that his new factory is running along smoothly."

"Eureka" was dropped from the firm's ads beginning with the July, 1903 issue. This suggests that any boxed set found with the Eureka name dates from 1898-1903. Other things can be dated: Rough Riders first appeared in 1904; a running soldier with movable arms in 1907; cork-shooting rifles debuted in 1908, along with Indians and "Phillipine Warriors" (almost certainly Britains Zulus).

There was a marked tie between Beiser and Britains. The heart of it was a patented tray. The tray, judging by his ads, interested Beiser more than his figures. His invention of it seems to have propelled him into the business. The tray was designed so that soldiers could be kept in a lying position or stood up without removing them from the tray. This enabled them to be displayed as easily as they were shipped. Furthermore, any single soldier could be slipped out of the tray without disturbing the rest.

Today, Beiser's creation seems less than breathtaking, but back then, according to the July, 1903 *Playthings*, Mr. J.T. Doll of Wanamaker's (then a leading department store), when shown the first tray, rhapsodized that Beiser had discovered "the art of display" and "that in all his experience as a toy buyer he had never seen any toys put up in a similar manner." Furthermore, "his opinion was backed by a substantial order given on the spot."

The 1903 article also states that Beiser patented his tray in Germany, England and the U.S. In England he seems to have worked out a deal whereby Britains used his tray in some of its sets, in exchange furnishing him soldiers for his own sets (beginning about 1906). There is some evidence that it was Germany's Heyde who used the tray there. Beiser apparently patented his trays twice, probably when he changed from cardboard to metal, since the presently known patent dates are given as 1904 and 1905.

Because so many soldiers in American Soldier Company sets are Britains (and marked that way), collectors had long thought that Beiser never cast soldiers on his own. This is refuted by an article in the February, 1904 *Playthings*. While the piece never mentions the firm by name, there is no question that it is American Soldier, as it mentions the tray (and the only other soldiers advertiser in *Playthings* at the time was William Feix, whose ads were small and few).

Unfortunately, the account doesn't give any indication of the size of the factory, the number of workers, or where the designs and molds came from. What does get considerable attention is the process by which the soldiers were made. There was a melting pot, an alloy of antimony and lead (originally made by Beisser, later ordered in bulk from an outside source) and two-part molds, with wooden handles.

Occasionally one or more cores were required in the molds (evidently for more complex pieces). They had to be removed after each soldier was cast, then replaced. The soldiers were slush molded, with the metal poured into the mold, which was then dipped to "flush" it, after which the excess metal was poured out. Even in those days it was considered important, according to the article, that the soldiers be the proper weight; too much lead in one and some of the profit was lost.

The story goes on to say that the German-made metal horse of the day was modeled "more along the lines of a racer, with slim legs and body, and these goods are cast solid. The American horse, on the other hand, follows the lines of a charger or campaign horse, and even with the added bulk is lighter in weight."

After the soldier had been cast and the metal cooled, the "gate" (where the alloy had poured in and out, leaving a residue) was sawed off to make the bottom of the base smooth. A boy then pared away the "fins" as they called it (and a good description, too, of the flashing) with a knife. The guns, swords, flags, etc. were made of "half and half" - equal proportions of lead and "block tin" - and attached to the figure with solder. The "half and half" was deemed necessary because it allowed flexibility, helpful with the accessories but "not wanted in the soldier itself".

3

Paint was applied "by a boy or girl with a multitude of brushes and paint pots." Enamel paints were used, and after each color was brushed on the soldier was set aside to dry. Each figure went through "about fifteen handlings before it stands complete, a soldier, a sailor, a Rough Rider or whatever he may be." The remainder of the article devoted itself to the tray.

Beiser's Eureka soldiers were hollowcast and roughly 52mm scale, which matches with Britains figures of those years. They almost always have very nicely and distinctively painted faces. The eye consists of a white dot with a black pupil inside (rarely done by soldier-makers), plus an eyebrow. The horses' bases are round with two small tabs sticking out. (Eureka-*type* soldiers exist, but these seem to be from a different company. The painting is simpler, particularly in the face, and the casting is a bit cruder and thicker, so the figures are heavier. The likelihood is that after 1904, when Beiser no longer made the Eureka figures, someone continued with the molds, perhaps casting soldiers until the early 1920s).

The American Soldier Company figures came in several sizes and base shapes. 55mm fuller-bodied men were introduced around 1904 and almost certainly didn't last through 1906 in American Soldier Company sets. Somewhere between 1904-06, probably because of the new tray, oblong bases were changed to rectangular ones. Beiser's 54mm soldiers date from about 1906 into the 1920s. Some were hollowcast and some solid. There were also 68mm soldiers, at least three types, German in style and probably all solid cast. Another type of soldier is shown in a full-page *Playthings* ad in July, 1903. These are presumably in the 55mm range, but at present none of these particular figures is known to exist.

In the 1920s, when interest in toy soldiers waned, American Soldier Company tried a variety of ploys. The "American Heroes" series debuted in 1923. These featured sets of Indians, Cowboys, Sailors, "Young Americans" (Boy Scouts) and, very low profile, Soldiers. In February, 1924, it advertised the Audubon Bird Game, a shooting game that featured 3 ($1) or 6 (the $2 set) birds perched on a fence against a brightly-colored forest background. Little Auduboners could knock them off via a cork-shooting gun. In December, 1925, "Big Animal Shooting Games" were advertised, and in 1925, 1926 and 1928 the Meadowbrook Bird Game (the birds were celluloid). February, 1926 saw an ad for "The Buffalo Hunt" on hinged platforms. Here only distributor A.S. Ferguson's name was used, but presumably this was another of the firm's products. (Ferguson was one of several distributors for the company).

The last stab was in 1926, when, in February and April, "The Magic Theatre" was advertised. This was a theatre with 18 paper actors that could be moved via a magnet. There were three scenes; country, city and living room. None of the actors were soldiers.

Beiser's move to Glendale was presumably to Myrtle Avenue and DeBoo Place (apparently also, or later, Debevoise Place or Avenue). In 1922, the address remained the same, but there was also a Manhattan location: 48 East 21st Street. Presumably the latter was the showroom or sales office. At that time Wm. M. Ferguson was the owner and Beiser the treasurer, suggesting he had run into financial difficulties and stepped down a notch or two. Ferguson was the son of A.S. Ferguson, and had by then also taken over his father's firm. A 1925 address for American Soldier Company may simply have been a clarification: 2760 Myrtle Avenue.

Soldier-maker J. Edward Jones compiled two single-spaced pages of notes on the firm. Much of it was conjecture, but he did note that Beiser had been "deceased since 1924", and that William Ferguson, in a letter dated December 24, 1925 had offered to sell the assets of the firm. However, in 1927 Ferguson was still the company's distributor.

American Soldier Company last appears in the Winter 1928-29 phonebook, and not in the Summer 1929 book, which suggests it folded *before* the 1929 crash. In 1930 Selchow and Righter announced it had purchased rights to the firm's "American Hero" cowboy and Indian sets.

EUREKA SOLDIERS

C. W. BEISER.

	G	VG	M
EUR1 Soldier with Ramrod	10.00	15.00	20.00
EUR2 Soldier with Drum ..	4.00	6.00	8.00
EUR3 Soldier Flagbearer ..	10.00	15.00	20.00
EUR4 Soldier on Guard ...	4.00	6.00	8.00
EUR5 Sailor on Guard ...	5.00	8.00	10.00
EUR6 Officer on Rearing Horse, plumed helmet ...	22.00	33.00	45.00
EUR7 Mounted Officer in Militia Cap (NOT SHOWN)	No Price Found		
EUR8 Mounted Officer in Kepi (NOT SHOWN) ...	No Price Found		

AMERICAN SOLDIER COMPANY (POSSIBLY ALSO EUREKA) as shown in July, 1903 ad

AE1 Officer on Rearing Horse	No Price Found
AE2 Sailor, shoulder arms	No Price Found
AE3 Soldier, shoulder arms	No Price Found
AE4 Sailor Drummer	No Price Found
AE5 Soldier Drummer	No Price Found
AE6 Sailor with Ramrod	No Price Found
AE7 Sailor, empty-handed	No Price Found

AMERICAN SOLDIER COMPANY, circa 1904-1906 (Oblong-Round bases earliest)

BE1 Mounted Rough Rider, gilt paint, both hands on reins	12.00	18.00	24.00
BE1a Mounted Rough Rider, regular paint, both hands on reins	10.00	15.00	20.00
BE1b As above, but base rectangular, not round	10.00	15.00	20.00
BE2 Rough Rider with blanket roll, rifle, gilt paint	6.00	9.00	12.00
BE3 Rough Rider Foot Officer, gilt paint	6.00	9.00	12.00
BE4 Rough Rider with blanket roll, regular paint, rectangular base	4.00	6.00	8.00
BE4a As above, oblong base	4.00	6.00	8.00
BE5 Volunteer Officer or Rough Rider Officer (depending on paint), rectangular base	4.00	6.00	8.00
BE5a Same as above, oblong base	4.00	6.00	8.00
BE6 Rough Rider or Volunteer on Guard, rectangular base	4.00	6.00	8.00
BE6a Same as above, oblong base	4.00	6.00	8.00
BE7 Volunteer with Ramrod, rectangular base	5.00	8.00	10.00
BE7a Same as above, oblong base	5.00	8.00	10.00
BE8 Volunteer Flagbearer	5.00	8.00	10.00
BE8a Same as above, oblong base	5.00	8.00	10.00
BE9 Volunteer Drummer	4.00	6.00	8.00
BE9a Same as above, oblong base	4.00	6.00	8.00

AMERICAN SOLDIER COMPANY, c.1906 on. All solidcast, except where noted, and 54mm.

AS1 Shoulder Arms	2.00	3.00	4.00
AS2 Drummer	2.00	3.00	4.00
AS3 Officer	2.00	3.00	4.00
AS4 On Guard	2.00	3.00	4.00
AS5 Officer in Cap	2.00	3.00	4.00
AS6 Flagbearer	4.00	6.00	8.00
AS7 Officer, moving arm	5.00	8.00	10.00
AS8 Right Shoulder Arms, hollow, moving arm	7.00	11.00	15.00
AS9 Running Sailor, moving arm	5.00	8.00	10.00
AS10 Running Sailor	2.00	3.00	4.00
AS11 Running Sailor Bugler, moving arm	5.00	8.00	10.00
AS12 Running Sailor Officer with sword, moving arm	5.00	8.00	10.00
AS13 Running Bugler	2.00	3.00	4.00
AS14 Running Soldier	2.00	3.00	4.00
AS15 Officer on Rearing Horse	5.00	8.00	10.00
AS16 Running with Flag	No Price Found		
AS17 Hollowcast soldier with moving arm	7.00	11.00	15.00
AS18 Hollowcast Officer with moving arm, sword	7.00	11.00	15.00
AS19 Hollowcast Running Soldier	7.00	11.00	15.00
AS20 Indian Chief, arm raised	2.00	3.00	4.00
AS21 Indian Brave with rifle	2.00	3.00	4.00
AS22 Mounted Officer, Spanish-American War, right hand on hip, no rifle	10.00	15.00	20.00

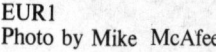

EUR1
Photo by Mike McAfee

EUR2

The label for a Eureka box.
Courtesy Mike McAfee

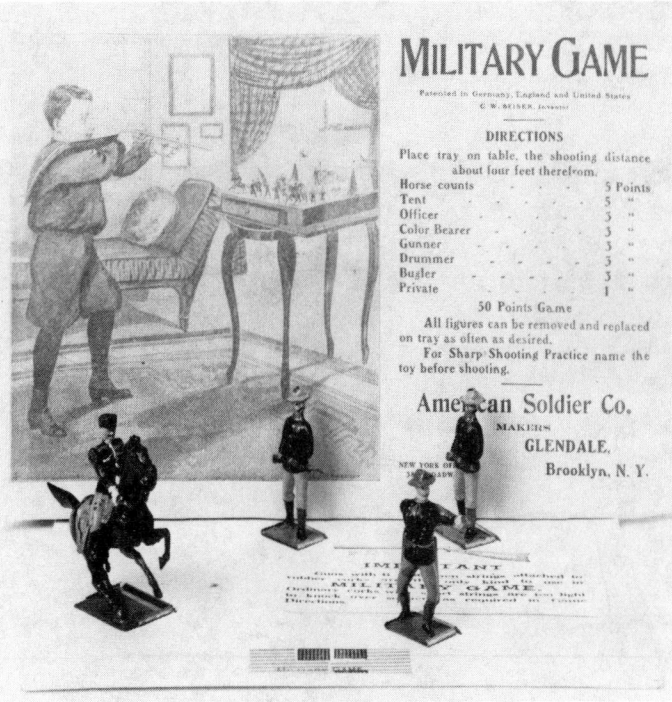

A four-piece American Soldier Co. game with Britains
soldiers sold June 1982 for $352 at Christie's
Courtesy Christie's New York

EUR3
Photo by Mike McAfee

Another four-piece American Soldier Co. game. Shown
are BE1b officer and three BE6's. One of these sets sold
in 1989 for $125.

EUR4   EUR5
Photo by Bill Nutting

EUR6
Photo by Bill Nutting

Crude versions of Eureka soldiers by an unknown maker. Value 3-8 dollars.
Photo by Bill Nutting

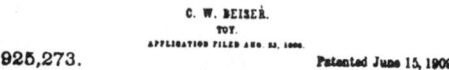

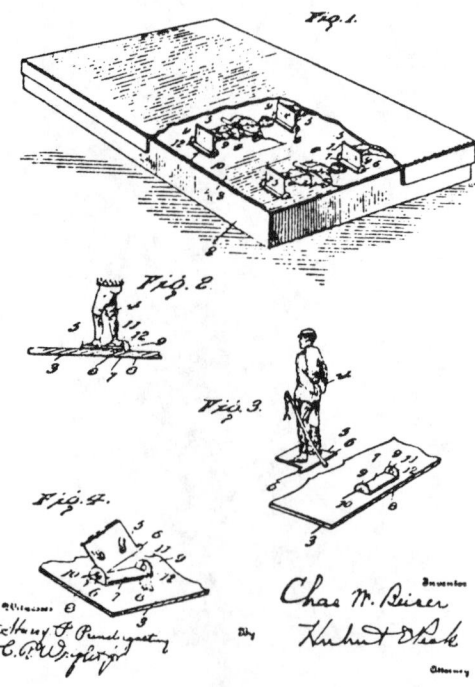

The patent drawings for Beiser's tray.

Crude versions of Eureka soldiers by an unknown maker. Value 3-6 dollars.
Photo by Bill Nutting

AE1 through AE7, as shown in the July, 1903 *Playthings*.
Courtesy *Playthings* Magazine

BE1
Photo by Bill Nutting

BE2   BE3
Photo by Bill Nutting

BE4   BE5   BE6
Photo by Bill Nutting

BE7   BE8   BE9
Photo by Bill Nutting

AMERICAN SOLDIER

AS1 AS2 AS3 AS4   AS5   AS6   AS7

AS8   AS9   AS10   AS11   AS12   AS13   AS14
Photo by Bill Nutting

A?40 A?41 A?42 A?43 A?44 A?45 A?46

A?47   A?48   A?49   A?50   A?51
Photo by Bill Nutting

A?52   A?53   A?54   A?55

A?56   A?57   A?58   A?59
Photo by Bill Nutting

**SEE NEXT PAGE FOR THE SET
ALL OF THESE CAME FROM**

AS16

AS15   AS17   AS18   AS19   AS20   AS21
Photo by Bill Nutting

AS22
Photo by Bill Nutting

Accessories and A?60 Sailor. The palm trees in the set are all three-dimensional.
Photo by Bill Nutting

This very large, wooden-boxed set sold in 1990 for an undisclosed price. The pieces it contains were all previously unknown to collectors. The box label tantalizingly discloses only some of the company's name. It seems to be American Soldier Co. The Broadway address isn't one known to be one of the firm's, but could be that of one of its several distributors.
Photo by Bill Nutting

The contents of the set
Photo by Bill Nutting

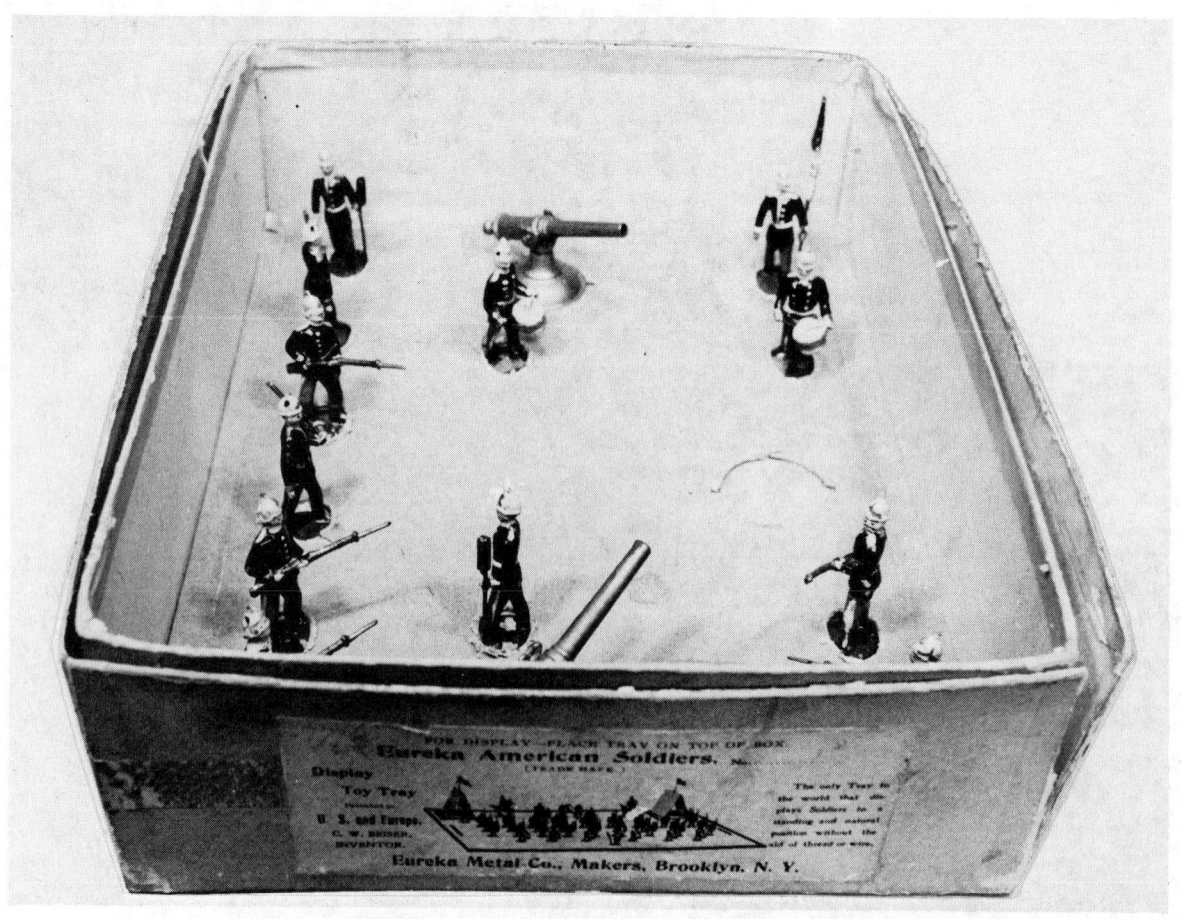

American Soldier Company's American Soldier Military Game, with Britains Soldiers and 4 American made figures (2 flagbearers, one drummer, one infantry officer with sword). It was auctioned for $880 at Christie's New York in March, 1982.
Courtesy Christie's New York

"Eureka American Soldiers" C.W. Beiser Inventor
Photo by Mike McAfee

Auctioned in 1988 for $1200; American Soldier Company's No. 118 Zulus Set. Britains figures.

Courtesy Phillips New York

An unusual American Soldier Company set, since the soldiers are solid, Germanic in style and 68mm, rather than 54. The rifle in the set establishes that this was sold no earlier than 1908. Auctioned in December, 1987 for $900.
Courtesy Phillips New York

WILLIAM FEIX

Until a few years ago, William Feix (probably pronounced "Fakes") was unknown to collectors. Today it appears that Feix followed C.W. Beiser as the second successful American maker of hollow lead toy soldiers.

The discovery of an ad in the June, 1903 Playthings magazine is what turned this around. It showed soldiers previously known (and attributed to McLoughlin). All look like copies of Britains, with the exception of a foot officer with sword. It is a distinctive and apparently original piece.

Feix was located in Brooklyn, at 58 Troutman Street. This wasn't far from Beiser, which suggests he was inspired by the latter's success. Feix was in business there from at least 1903 till 1927, and possibly longer. This means many years of toy soldier manufacturing. Whenever identified in publications as anything more than a toymaker, it was always as a maker of lead or pewter soldiers (in 1903, 1909, 1919, 1920, 1924 and 1925) or, in 1921, of "Soldiers and Sailors". A 1908 toy catalog, using the same illustration minus Feix's name, also lists Indians and Japanese.

It must be pointed out that this illustration was offered in 1907 by a New York company as a generic advertising cut. However, it wasn't unusual for a catalog company to sell customers cuts of illustrations in its catalog. Furthermore, the Japanese troop is considered by knowledgeable collectors to belong to the group of soldiers now considered to have been manufactured by William Feix. In addition, two illustrations in a 1910 Butler Bros. catalog show the Feix mounted officer crossing over into a second group of soldiers which collectors had already decided were from Feix, thus reinforcing their conclusion. The rest of the soldiers shown and listed here have been determined by collectors of early American soldiers to be from Feix because of their design and paint style. While remaining in that style, the modeling and painting of the Japanese and Russian soldiers are of particularly high quality. Oddly, though a few of the striking Russian officers have surfaced, there is as yet no evidence that William Feix produced an accompanying Japanese officer.

An investigation of the Troutman Street address by Achilles Papaliolios reveals an empty narrow lot, approximately 20' wide and 70' deep. According to architect Papaliolios, the remaining houses on the block, wood-framed and two-story, predate 1903. This of course suggests that Feix operated out of a two-story building that was also his house. This wouldn't have prevented him from producing huge amounts of soldiers, as the history of H.B. Toys, elsewhere in this book, attests.

Collector Bill Nutting's research has established that Feix was born in Austria in 1866. He immigrated in 1888. He was listed in the 1900 census as a "manufacturer of metal", and appears in a 1900-01 directory as "Feix, Wilhelm, pinmfr. (presumably pin manufacturer), 58 Troutman".

Since none of the known boxed sets of presumed Feix soldiers bears a manufacturer's name (nothing more than "American Soldiers; Set No. 9; Fine Enameled Pewter Figures"), discovery of catalogs or illustrated order sheets issued by the distributor Owens-Kreiser could remove any remaining uncertainty. In their listings of the toymakers they handled, from at least 1919 through 1925 Feix was their only toy soldier maker. A 1927 catalog could be enlightening, too, as that year the jobber listed the otherwise unknown J&G Scheuring and their "pewter soldiers", while dropping Feix.

Although Feix drops out of the phonebook by the summer 1927 issue, in January 1928 he was listed as being an exhibitor at the Toy Fair, and a 1928 catalog shows pieces that appear to be by Feix.
Listings after WF?21 are less clearly Feix.

	G	VG	M
(WF?1) Soldier on guard position	2.00	3.00	5.00
(WF?2) Officer with sword, free arm raised	4.00	6.00	8.00
(WF?3) Drummer	4.00	6.00	8.00
(WF?4) Marching with Rifle	7.00	11.00	15.00
(WF?5) Mounted Officer	7.00	11.00	15.00
(WF?6) Japanese Soldier	No Price Found		
(WF?7) Russian Soldier	No Price Found		
(WF?8) Russian Officer	No Price Found		
(WF?9) Sailor Marching with Rifle	2.00	3.00	5.00
(WF?10) Sailor Drummer	4.00	6.00	8.00
(WF?11) Indian on Rearing Horse	7.00	11.00	15.00
(WF?12) Indian Chief, arm raised	3.00	5.00	6.00
(WF?13) Indian Brave, rifle across waist	2.00	3.00	5.00
(WF?14) Cannon, American Flag on side	7.00	11.00	15.00
(WF?15) Volunteer on Rearing Horse	14.00	21.00	28.00
(WF?16) Volunteer Officer	4.00	6.00	8.00
(WF?17) Volunteer with Rifle	5.00	8.00	10.00
(WF?18) Rough Rider with Rifle	4.00	6.00	8.00
(WF?19) Volunteer Flagbearer	12.00	18.00	24.00
(WF?20) Rough Rider Drummer	11.00	16.00	22.00
(WF?21) Volunteer Fifer	11.00	16.00	22.00
(WF?22) Officer on Bowed-Head Horse	6.00	9.00	12.00
(WF?23) Mounted Cowboy	6.00	9.00	12.00
(WF?24) Cowboy on foot, rifle across waist	2.00	3.00	5.00

WF?1 WF?2 WF?3 WF?4 WF?5

WF?6 WF?7 WF?8 WF?9 WF?10

Photo by Bill Nutting

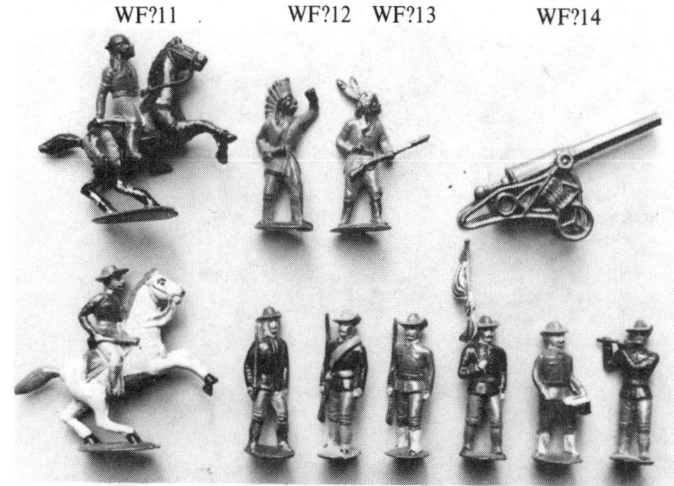

WF?11 WF?12 WF?13 WF?14

WF?15 WF?16 WF?17 WF?18 WF?19 WF?20 WF?21

Photo by Bill Nutting

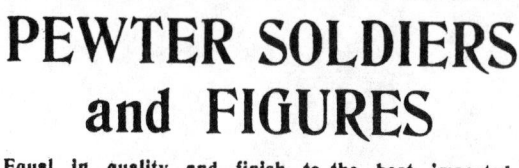

June 1903 Playthings ad
Courtesy Playthings Magazine

4F2860—6 pcs., 4 soldiers, mounted officer and folding canvas tent with flag. ½ doz. sets in pkg. Doz. sets, **$2.15**

4F2861—10 pcs., 5 soldiers, drummer, 2 mounted officers, mounted cannon and folding tent. ¼ doz. sets in pkg. Doz. sets, **$4.10**

4F2860 and 4F2861

4F2862—22 pcs., 13 soldiers, fife and drum corps, color bearer, 2 mounted officers, 2 tents, 2 mounted cannon. **1** set in pkg.............................Set, **72c**

4F2862 and 4F2863

4F2863—32 pcs., 21 soldiers, fife and drum corps, color bearer, 4 mounted officers, 2 tents, 2 mounted cannon. 2 sets in pkg. Set, **$1.15**

The crossover of the mounted officer in the top illustration into the one below helps tie one group of "Feix" soldiers to another. From a December, 1910 Butler Bros. catalog.

WF?22
Photo by Bill Nutting

WF?23
Photo by Will Beierwaltes

Two of these sets are known to have been sold, one at auction for $550, and another from a dealer, in better condition, for $275.
Photo by Jane Vail
Courtesy Mid-Hudson Auction Galleries

Feix Russian, cannon and tent. The flag and flagpole tip may be unique to Feix.
Photo by Will Beierwaltes

NOTE: There are many figures similar to the WF?5. As yet, no mounted officers thought to be by Feix are known to show anything in their right hand. They also have sloping shoulders. German-made cavalry officers of the same type have a slight rise at the shoulders.

William Feix may have produced this artillery team with officer.
Photo by Will Beierwaltes

WF?23   WF?23   WF?24

The two mounted cowboys seem to be from the same company, presumably William Feix. However, the one in the middle has no saddle markings on the back of the horse, and also bears the mark of an ejection pin on the horse's belly. If it was made by Feix, then so was the foot cowboy, as it has the same paint.
Courtesy Ken Wittenrich and Hank Anton

WF?12   WF?23   WF?5

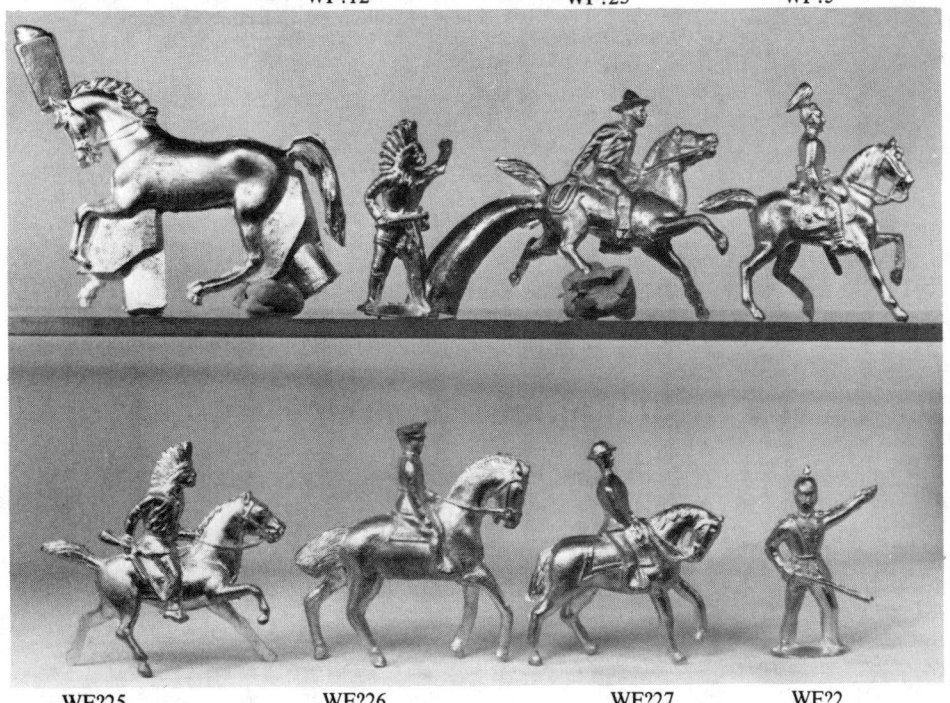

WF?25   WF?26   WF?27   WF?2

Two groups of molds have been found recently, sold by gun dealers in the area of upper New York State. They all seem to be from William Feix, based on the Feix ad and collectors' judgments. The large horse at upper left came out of the mold unfinished, as it lacked the necessary inserts. It may have been sold as a circus horse.
Courtesy Ken Wittenrich, West Falls Toy Company

WF?25 Mounted Indian
   Chief . . . .   No Price Found
WF?26 Mounted Officer in
   Cap . . . .   No Price Found
WF?27 Mounted Rough
   Rider, upturned hat brim   No Price Found

SCHOENHUT

Schoenhut was in business in Philadelphia beginning about 1872, manufacturing toy pianos. It made its mark in the toy world, however, in 1903, when it introduced a long-popular group of toys, the Humpty-Dumpty Circus. In May of that same year it introduced its new U.S. Armory in Playthings magazine. It included an officer and seven soldiers, which varied only in weapon. They were made of composition and stood about 4½" high. These may have been the only soldiers made by the company. To a Schoenhut fancier they might be worth more, but to a soldier collector about $25 in mint condition for the troop and $30 for the officer.

Schoenhut soldiers
Photo by Ed Poole

May 1903 ad in *Playthings* Magazine.
Courtesy *Playthings*

McLOUGHLIN

Collectors had long considered New York's McLoughlin Bros. the first important mass manufacturer of American-made metal soldiers. Recent and considerable research suggests otherwise.

McLoughlin dates from the 1850s, and may have been the maker of the first American *paper* soldiers, circa 1857. However, the earliest known appearance of McLoughlin's metal military is in the company's 1911 and 1914 catalogs (exactly the same page, even to printing defects and page number).

Bill Nutting, who found these pages, has checked about fifteen of the firm's catalogs from 1879 to 1920 (when it was bought by Milton Bradley) and discovered no other references to lead soldiers. In fact, McLoughlin seems to have taken no real interest in them. Though it frequently advertised a long string of its wares, it never included its metal soldiers, which are solid-cast 48mm types, Germanic in style. (They are not, however, from German molds, according to Patrick McCaleb, an expert on German-made soldiers. He also notes they are "grotesque" copies of Heydes).

What makes these pieces seem very early is their uniforms. But recently, similar uniforms have been found on soldiers that were produced here as late as World War One. The very attractive lithography on the boxtops also suggests an earlier era. Another legend among longtime collectors is that McLoughlin sold (though perhaps didn't manufacture) hollow lead soldiers, sailors, etc. To date nothing has turned up, but a possible clue is offered by Gus Hansen. He believes McLoughlin offered the mold of a 54mm hollowcast Rough Rider with rifle at side in a Popular Mechanics-type magazine in 1925. According to the knowledgeable Hansen, hollowcast McLoughlins can be recognized by a "cauliflower ear" (a hole in the side of the head with edges puffing outward). However, till the discovery of a boxed set, catalog or ad, this will have to remain in the realm of lore.

The five figures McLoughlin is known to have sold came in four color variations; red coat, white pants; gray coat, white pants; light blue or blue/gray coat, white pants; white coat, light blue pants. An identifying feature of McLoughlins is a thick base whose underside reveals two holes pushing up into the base. The company is known to have used a civilian figure in this style for one of its games. Another as yet unproved belief is that McLoughlin made none of its soldiers; that they were jobbed out.

	G	VG	M
(MC1) Mounted Officer	10.00	12.00	15.00
(MC2) Left Shoulder Arms	5.00	8.00	10.00
(MC3) Officer	5.00	8.00	10.00
(MC4) Flagbearer	10.00	15.00	20.00
(MC5) Drummer (plug-in drum)	5.00	8.00	10.00

MC1   MC2   MC3   MC4   MC5

(Drum missing on MC5)
Photo by Bill Nutting

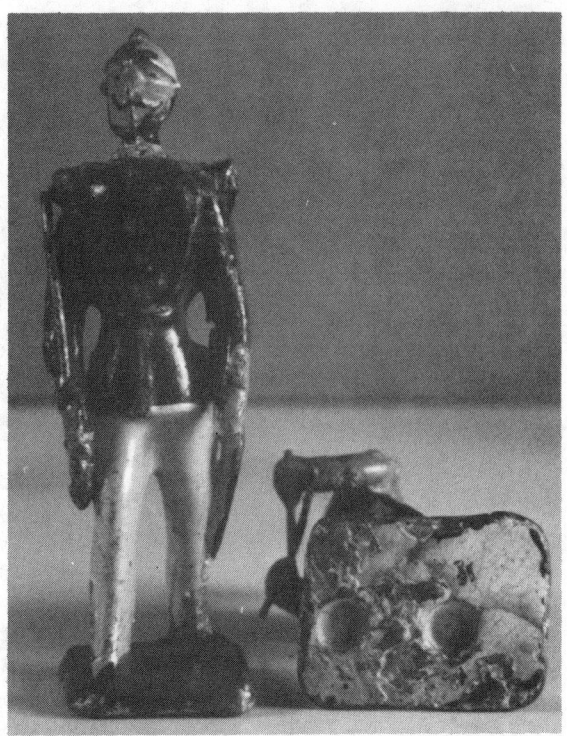

The McLoughlin MC3 Officer and alongside it the
distinctive McLoughlin underbase.
Photo by Bill Nutting

LEAD OR "TIN" SOLDIERS

60 CENT SETS
SET A

Contains 11 pieces, viz.: 1 horseman, 1 captain, 1 drummer, 1 flagman, and 7 privates.

SET B

Contains 6 horsemen.

$1.00 SETS
SET C

Contains 17 pieces, viz.: 1 horseman, 1 Captain, 1 flagman, 2 drummers, and 12 privates

SET D

Contains 9 horsemen.

$1.25 SET
SET E

Contains 23 pieces, viz.: 1 horseman. 1 captain, 2 drummers, 1 flagman, and 18 privates.

$1.25 SET
SET F

Contains 12 horsemen.

$1.75 SETS
SET G

Contains 27 pieces, viz.: 11 horsemen, 1 captain, 2 drummers, 1 flagman, and 12 privates.

SET H

Contains 18 horsemen.

SET I

Contains 37 pieces, viz.: 1 horseman, 1 captain, 2 drummers, 1 flagman, and 33 privates.

$2.50 SET
SET K

Contains 37 pieces, viz.: 11 horsemen, 1 captain, 2 drummers, 1 flagman, and 22 privates.

1911 and 1914 were the only known appearances of McLoughlin's soldiers in its catalogs. The same page ran each time.
Courtesy Bill Nutting

A distinctive McLoughlin boxtop. It contained Set A, according to the McLoughlin catalog, and sold for $125.
Photo by Bill Nutting

Photo by Mike McAfee   Boxed set of McLoughlin Gray Infantry, all solid-cast. Value about $250

Apparently set F, according to the
company's catalog. Value about $200

This appears to be set k, as seen in the firm's catalog. Value about $450.

Courtesy Christie's, New York

INDESTRUCTO

In 1915, Indestructo Specialties Co. advertised "Something New In Soldiers". They were of "unbreakable composition" and stood four inches high. Their uniforms were "careful copies of different national military costumes".

It was obvious why the company employed composition. The top half of one of the ads showed a doll with "flirting and sleeping eyes". Doll heads, of course, were often made of composition, as well as hands and sometimes bodies.

There was a large variety of figures in the two known ads. Among them were mounted and foot Highlanders, mounted and foot French (including a flagbearer), sailors (the officer possibly in a seated position), foot Americans (including a flagbearer; there also may have been a mounted officer), what may be mounted and foot Italians and finally what may be mounted and foot Germans, of two types.

In one of the ads it was mentioned that each set was packed in a "Large Armory" and could be retailed for a dollar. Whether any of these troops, which Indestructo proudly noted "weigh less than an ounce apiece" has surfaced is impossible to assess, because until now nothing has been written on Indestructo. No prices known, of course, but presumably in mint condition the foot figures would be worth about $25 and the mounted and flagbearers (with flags) $35 each.

According to collector Jack Matthews, these could be imports, made by Vienna's Pfeiffer (Tipple Topple) or its successor, O. & M. Hausser.

HERE THEY ARE ! SOMETHING NEW AGAIN !

THE INTERNATIONAL FORCES
of the
INDESTRUCTO SPECIALTIES CO.
136-142 WEST 52ND STREET
NEW YORK

These Soldiers are Four Inches High, <u>Unbreakable</u>, Weigh Less than <u>One Ounce</u> Each, the Costumes are Exact Reproductions of the <u>Real Army Uniforms</u> of the Different Nations and Each Set is Packed in a <u>Large Armory</u> and Can Be Retailed for <u>One Dollar</u>.

BEAT THIS IF YOU CAN!

We are now prepared to fill all orders promptly and invite the Trade to visit our sample rooms or write.

A March, 1915 ad, probably from *Toys & Novelties*.

FICHTMAN & ALEXANDER

All that is known about the possible look of Fichtman & Alexander's soldiers comes from a drawing in a 1915 ad. The art suggests they were, like virtually all American-made soldiers of the period, Germanic in style. If the drawing is accurate, their very thin, perfectly rectangular bases would be a possible way of identifying pieces from the firm.

Fichtman & Alexander, of 325 LaFayette Street in New York City, first turns up in the July, 1915 *Toys & Novelties* magazine. A story proclaims that the manufacturer of jewelry novelties had begun to make "very high grade lead soldiers...being in color, finish and design an exact duplicate of imported lines, which manufacturers have failed to imitate in the past."

In August the firm ran its illustrated ad, calling its troops "Boys of the U.S.A.", and claiming that "in workmanship and finish they are fully equal to the finest soldiers made in Germany". There was a "complete line" of infantry, cavalry, officers, musicians, etc., "in a variety of uniforms".

The last known mention is February, 1916, when it was announced the firm had prepared fifteen new models, including sailors, soldiers, Indians, mounted officers and "similar characters". Collectors presumably would pay about eight to ten dollars for these pieces in mint condition.

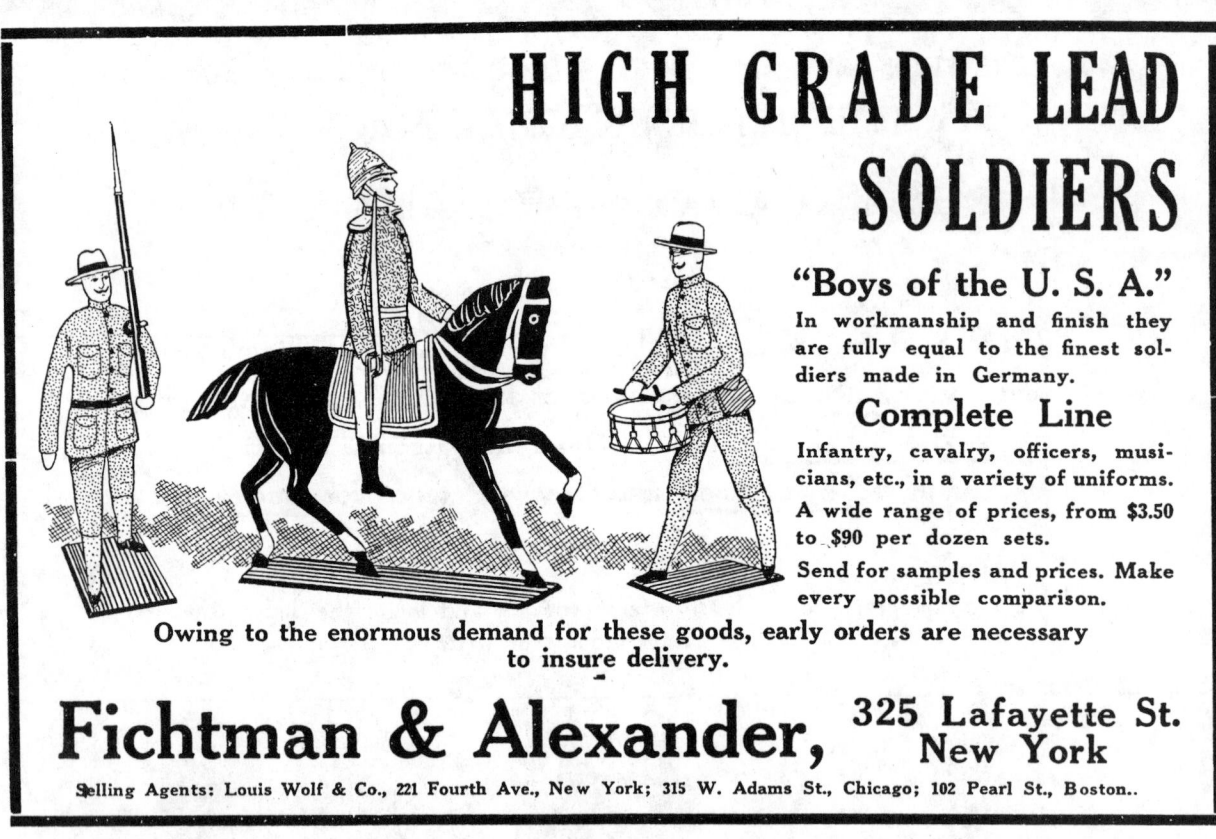

An August, 1915 *Playthings* ad for Fichtman & Alexander.
Courtesy *Playthings*

METAL TOY SOLDIER CO.

Metal Toy Soldier Co. was relatively long-lived. It was located at 156 Chestnut Avenue in Jersey City, New Jersey, and appears to have been in business from at least 1915 through 1923. A 1919 city directory lists the company and suggests the owner was Carl Dickmann.

In its first known ad (April, 1916) its soldiers appear to be demi-round homecast types, and thus of little interest to most collectors. However, in December, 1916, a new ad appeared. It is a drawing, and here the figures, cadets, appear to be fully dimensioned. There is a flagbearer, what appear to be empty-handed officers, and troops holding what seem to be rifles. All have the right arm held out away from the body, with the rifles, if they are rifles, gripped about a third of the way up the weapon.

None of these pieces is presently known, but a soldier in soft cap and another in a campaign hat have been found. The soft-capped figure greatly resembles the cadets, and the other piece resembles it in design and paint. They are about two inches high to the top of the head, and solidcast.

In April, 1916 a toy trade magazine stated, "because of the large demand for their products in 1915, the Metal Toy Soldier Co. was forced to enlarge their quarters this Spring and have recently moved into a two-story building in Jersey City, NJ. Sixty-five sets of lead soldiers representing every nationality are manufactured, besides a totally new line including mountain scenes, etc." The article went on to say that the firm employed a special artist to make window displays for dealers, and that a new catalog would soon be sent out, showing the complete lines.

In August, 1916 an article stated, "Metal Toy Soldier Company is about to market a new toy cannon that shoots." It would be ready by September and sell for 15 cents. The text isn't clear, but it also sounds as if the firm put out unpainted soldiers which were sold with watercolors. It was during this time that the company advertised: "We Do Any White Metal Casting Works."

Judging by ads and text, cannons seem to have been an obsession with the firm. In February, 1917 it was announced "The Metal Toy Soldier Co...are now making the toy cannon formerly manufactured by the Art Metal Toy & Novelty Works. This cannon is made of solid cast metal, attractively decorated." They also advertised, at various times, a "Big-Bang Cannon", "Topsy-Target Cannon" and "A New 10¢ Toy Cannon That Shoots."

The last known announcement ran in February, 1921 and stated "The Metal Toy Soldier Company are showing many sets of lead soldiers from ten to fifty in a box, 32 different sizes. Soldiers, marines, sailors, Indians, regular infantry, West Point cadets and aviators. Highly colored and complete in all details." The mention of the aviator is intriguing, and might furnish clues to some of the firm's other figures. Sets found with the cannon shown here might be another way of establishing the company's product.

	G	VG	M
(MT1) Cadet Officer.......	No Price Found		
(MT2) Cadet Flagbearer....	No Price Found		
(MT3) Cadet Soldier.......	No Price Found		
(MT4) Soldier in Cap......	4.00	6.00	8.00
(MT5) Soldier in Campaign Hat.................	4.00	6.00	8.00
(MT6) Marine (none known)	No Price Found		
(MT7) Sailor (none known).	No Price Found		
(MT8) Indian (none known).	No Price Found		
(MT9) Aviator (none known)	No Price Found		

MT4   MT5
Photo by Ed Poole

TOPSY-TARGET CANNON WITH PROJECTILES Retails 25 cts. a Box

You must see our **1917** Tin Soldier Line of highest finish. Trenches, etc. Ask for illustrated price list. Representatives wanted in all parts of the United States and America.

METAL TOY SOLDIER COMPANY
156 Chestnut Ave.   Manufacturers   JERSEY CITY, N. J.

MT1-MT3
A March, 1917 ad.
Courtesy *Playthings*

February, 1917 ad
Courtesy *Playthings*

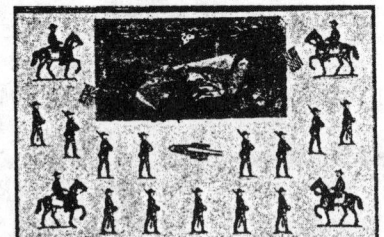
April 1916 ad of homecast types in *Toys and Novelties* magazine

LOEBEL, WIDMANN - MAIDEN AMERICA

Loebel, Widmann's (later Maiden America) soldiers were made in at least three different styles; homecast types using German, or German-derived, molds, hollowcasts of the types usually attributed to William Feix, etc., and solid-cast soldiers in the Heyde style.

The Germanic, Heyde-like soldiers appear in ads in December, 1916 and August, 1917. These are the most distinctive of the firm's known pieces. One huge, incomplete boxed set has survived. Although it bears no maker's name, it employs the same illustration on its boxtop as seen in the August, 1917 ad.

In December, 1917 *Playthings* ran a five-paragraph story on Loebel, Widmann. The occasion was its consolidation with the Maiden Toy Company. Loebel, Widmann was located in Hoboken, New Jersey. According to the report, "upon leaving the ferry one soon reaches the building where the cornerstone has been laid for this growing concern. Long since, however, this place had to be abandoned for larger quarters, as, in addition to the original manufacture of Lead Soldiers, they engaged in the manufacture of Doll Heads. One year of successful business has put them among the leading doll manufacturers in the East.

"And now we hear," the story continues, "that Loebel, Widmann, in order to expand their business still further, have consolidated with the Maiden Toy Company, Inc. of New York, the manufacturers of the country-wide known 'Maiden America'. This charming doll has unfortunately been out of the market for the last six months through the serious illness of the former manager of the Maiden Toy Company". Research by Bill Nutting discloses in 1917 the Maiden Toy Co., Inc. (also known as the Maiden Toy Shop, Inc.) was run by Joseph M. Kalvin, secretary, and Louis Kalvin, manager, both of whom lived on West 112th Street. Possibly it was Louis' illness which pushed the sale forward.

The article shows photos of two buildings, captioned "Doll Factory, New York" and "Soldier Factory, Hoboken". It went on to say that in the future the two combined concerns would do business as "The Maiden America Toy Manufacturing Company, Inc. with headquarters at 101-03 Varick Street, New York City" (a February, 1918 ad shows New York and Hoboken addresses). Representation was to be by the well-known jobber Riemann-Seabrey and the more obscure Tip Top Toy Company. Both of these were New York-based firms. The final line states that Arthur Loebel was the firm's president and general manager (the same title he was reported to have in 1916 at Loebel, Widmann) and "through his long experience, is known as an expert in the toy line."

LOEBEL WIDMANN

Ads indicate the firm may just have been in business from late 1916 through early 1918. The olive khaki-clad Americans coded LW1-LW8 are from the huge (24¾" x 33") boxed set, which is labeled, in part, "Lot No. 195. Nation-American." The LW9-LW13 are from a smaller box numbered "850 Scottish". These figures have red tunics and green kilts. LW20-LW28 are shown and listed because there seems little doubt they came from this company. The remaining listings come from the figures shown in the ads (homecast types not listed).

	G	VG	M
(LW1) Mounted flagbearer, campaign hat	4.00	6.00	8.00
(LW2) Mounted Officer, campaign hat	4.00	6.00	8.00
(LW3) Flagbearer, campaign hat	4.00	6.00	8.00
(LW4) Drummer, campaign hat	2.00	3.00	5.00
(LW5) Left Shoulder Arms, campaign hat	2.00	3.00	5.00
(LW6) Officer, sword raised, campaign hat	3.00	4.00	6.00
(LW7) Standing Firing, campaign hat	2.00	3.00	5.00
(LW8) Kneeling Firing, campaign hat	2.00	3.00	5.00
(LW9) Scot Flagbearer	4.00	6.00	8.00
(LW10) Scot Bugler, arm raised	4.00	6.00	8.00
(LW11) Scot Bugler, arm lowered	4.00	6.00	8.00
(LW12) Scot on guard position	4.00	6.00	8.00
(LW13) Scot standing firing	4.00	6.00	8.00
(LW14) Officer with sword, helmet (8/17 ad)	4.00	6.00	8.00
(LW15) Helmeted Soldier kneeling firing (8/17 ad)	4.00	6.00	8.00
(LW16) Bugler, campaign hat (3/17 ad)	2.00	3.00	5.00
(LW17) Mounted Rough Rider (like Barclay Bg; 3/17 ad)	2.00	3.00	4.00
(LW18) Rough Rider, blanket roll (3/17 ad)	2.00	3.00	4.00
(LW19) Sailor marching with rifle (3/17 ad)	2.00	3.00	4.00
(LW20) Mounted Officer, helmet	4.00	6.00	8.00
(LW21) Officer with sword, cap	3.00	4.00	6.00
(LW22) Flagbearer, cap	4.00	6.00	8.00
(LW23) Bugler, cap	2.00	3.00	5.00
(LW24) Drummer, cap	2.00	3.00	5.00
(LW25) Left Shoulder Arms, cap	2.00	3.00	5.00

	G	VG	M
(LW26) Kneeling Firing, cap	2.00	3.00	5.00
(LW27) Standing Firing, helmet	2.00	3.00	5.00
(LW28) Standing Firing, cap	2.00	3.00	5.00
Below are all from 12/16 ad			
(LW29) Marching Drummer, helmet	2.00	3.00	5.00
(LW30) Marching Flagbearer, helmet (flags different paint)	4.00	6.00	8.00
(LW31) Marching Trombonist, helmet	2.00	3.00	5.00
(LW31A) Marching Trumpeter, helmet	2.00	3.00	5.00
(LW32) Marching Officer with sword, helmet	2.00	3.00	5.00
(LW33) Marching Left Shoulder Arms, helmet	2.00	3.00	5.00
(LW34) Bugler on Horseback, helmet	4.00	6.00	8.00
(LW35) Officer Standing, large, helmet	4.00	6.00	8.00
(LW36) Marching Left Shoulder Arms, large, helmet	4.00	6.00	8.00
(LW37) Mounted Bugler, large	5.00	8.00	10.00

LW1 LW2 LW3 LW4 LW5 LW6

LW7 LW8 LW9 LW10 LW11 LW12 LW13
Photo by Bill Nutting

26

ON THE MARCH
TO A BIG LEAD SOLDIER BUSINESS
MADE IN THE U. S. A.

This year will be a banner one for lead soldiers.

Men in uniform are seen everywhere.

The effect will be to stir up the little boys and a set of lead soldiers will be an appreciated gift.

Our line is one of quality and finish.

Careful attention is given to details. Various Nationalities correctly represented.

Goods are carefully and properly boxed.

Wide range of prices. Suitable for all classes of trade.

Manufactured by **LOEBEL, WIDMANN & CO., Hoboken, N. J.**

SOLE DISTRIBUTERS

RIEMANN, SEABREY CO., SALESROOM AND OFFICE 11-15 UNION SQUARE WEST **New York**

Ad in August, 1917 *Playthings*. Shown are LW14, LW15. All the firm's ads noted that the soldiers were manufactured by them.
Courtesy *Playthings*.

PLAYTHINGS

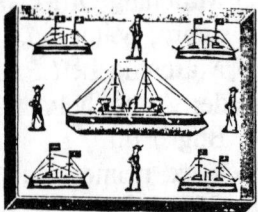
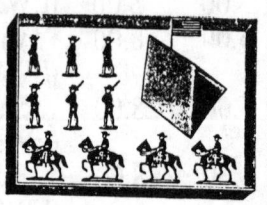

IT IS QUALITY THAT COUNTS IN LEAD SOLDIERS THESE DAYS

We have perfected a line, the QUALITY of which is UNSURPASSED—A FINISH that is DIFFERENT—and with EVERY DETAIL COMPLETE.

Among our Feature Numbers are:

UNCLE SAM'S REGULARS, ROUGH RIDERS, and BLUE JACKET Sets

FOR PATRIOTIC AMERICAN BOYS

Other Nationalities, too, correctly represented

SEE OUR LINE BEFORE YOU PLACE YOUR ORDER

Manufactured by

LOEBEL, WIDMANN & CO., Hoboken, N. J.

SOLE DISTRIBUTORS **RIEMANN, SEABREY CO.** 11-15 Union Sq. W. NEW YORK

Forts Trenches

Battlefields Sceneries

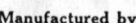
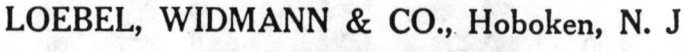

A March, 1917 *Playthings* ad. Shown are (at top, left, and bottom, right), LW17, LW18. At bottom, left, LW16, and at bottom, middle. LW19. Note that the company also sold Forts, Trenches, Battlefields and "Sceneries".
Courtesy *Playthings*.

LW20 (the ruler is metric)
Photo by Ed Poole

From the April, 1917 *Playthings*.
The mounted cowboys and buffalo are homecasts sold by a
number of American firms.
Courtesy *Playthings*.

JUST THE THING
FOR THIS YEAR'S

FOURTH OF JULY

LEAD SOLDIERS

UNCLE SAM'S REGULARS
UNCLE SAM'S ROUGH RIDERS
UNCLE SAM'S BLUE JACKETS

Largest and Most Complete Line.

MANUFACTURED BY

Loebel, Widmann & Co.
HOBOKEN, N. J.
SOLE DISTRIBUTORS
RIEMANN, SEABREY CO.
11-15 Union Sq. West, New York

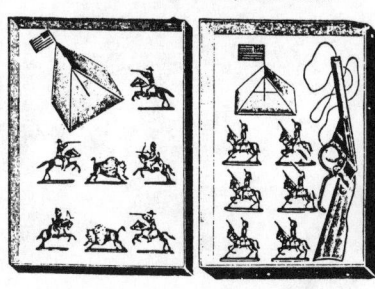

DO YOU BUY LEAD SOLDIERS?
See our line before you place order!
LARGEST AND MOST COMPLETE
LINE MADE IN THE U. S. A.
HOLIDAY SEASON 1917

AMERICAN
MADE

BIGGEST VARIETY OF DESIGN
AND COMBINATIONS:
Good or elaborate according to price.
The line that is different—
Right goods, properly boxed.
WIDE RANGE OF PRICES.
Goods to retail at 10c to $25.00.
Good low, medium and high priced values.
Suitable for all classes of trade.

LEAD
SOLDIERS

Correctly representing various nationalities

Manufactured by LOEBEL, WIDMANN & CO., Hoboken, N. J.
RIEMANN, SEABREY CO., Sole Distributers
SALESROOM AND OFFICE
11-15 Union Square, West   Broadway and 15th Street,   NEW YORK

A December, 1916 *Playthings* ad. Shown are
LW29-LW37. The large ship either comes
from a German mold or is a direct copy, as
collector Don Haberman has found one that
reads on the edge of its base below the water
line "SEEMANNSHILFE 1914-15" and
"S.M.S. - EMDEN". It is 5¾" long and 2½"
high.
Courtesy *Playthings*.

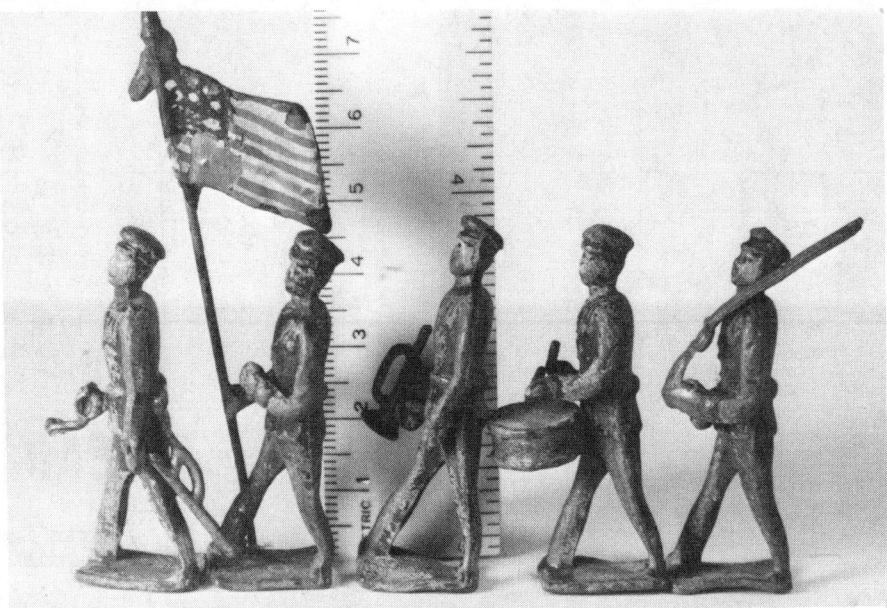

LW21   LW22   LW23   LW24   LW25
(Sword broken on LW21)
Photo by Ed Poole

Photo by Ed Poole   LW26   LW27   LW28

The large, incomplete Loebel-Widmann or Maiden America set
Photo by Bill Nutting

R. GRICKS - LIBERTY TOY SOLDIERS

Some odd, intriguing, and at present very obscure soldiers first appear in the December, 1917 *Playthings*.

They were featured in a full-page ad for "Camouflage Toys" and "Liberty Toy Soldiers", all manufactured by R. Gricks at 524-526 West 166th Street, New York City. This may have been the same firm mentioned in the September issue: Liberty Toy Co. of NY was featuring a "Modern Trench Warfare" set in white pine.

In January, 1918, there was another ad. This had the same art, but the text was different and far more extensive. The firm was now known as Liberty Toy & Novelty Co. Gricks' name was missing and in the same issue a text piece noted the "lead soldiers" were being produced under the "personal supervision" of Gricks, suggesting he may have stepped down from ownership. A "patent" is mentioned.

The Liberty Toy Soldiers, unfortunately, are dwarfed in the ads by the "Castle", "U.S. Signal Station", "Windmill" and "Fort & Battlefield" they're arranged on. The first ad states they're of lead and hand-painted. The second goes considerably further, headlining that they come with "interchangeable heads and arms". Furthermore, in addition to being "the acme of perfection in workmanship and finish", they were "as different from the old fashioned lead soldiers as a live man is from a corpse"!

They could be transformed into "288 different models" and "into an American, English, French or Italian soldier as quickly as you can say it. At your command he will present arms, swing a sword, wave a flag..." etc. Furthermore, Liberty seems to have designed its own molds, as the ad claims "we are the only manufacturer of these new, unique and epoch-making lines of toys mentioned above".

There is no mention in the ad that the soldiers (and the ones shown are the same as in the previous issue) are made of lead, and there's the curious statement that no "spirited American boy" would prefer the "old fashioned stiff pieces of metal" to the new Liberty brand. Were they using a soft, malleable lead, or had they dropped lead entirely?

A year later, in the February, 1919 issue of *Toys and Novelties* there is a mention of "Liberty Toy & Novelty Co. papier mache soldiers with moving arms and interchangeable heads". However, the last appearances known for Liberty Toy & Novelty are in the February and March, 1920 *Playthings*, each once more citing the firm's (still at the same address) "Lead soldiers of all nations with moveable heads and arms". Its "Camouflage toys" are also mentioned. The dim illustrations of the soldiers in the 1917 and 1918 ads suggest that some, and perhaps all of those pieces were demi-round homecast pieces.

A December, 1917 *Playthings* ad.
Courtesy *Playthings*

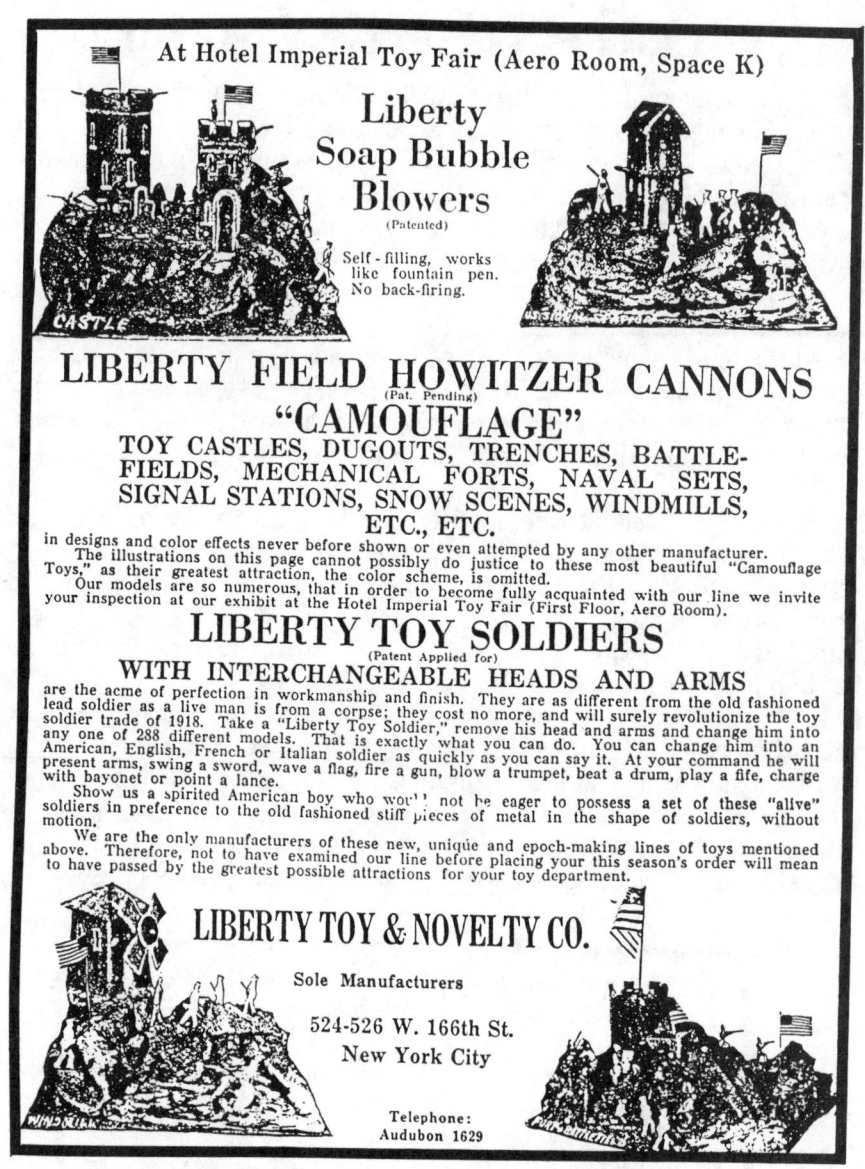

At Hotel Imperial Toy Fair (Aero Room, Space K)

Liberty Soap Bubble Blowers
(Patented)

Self-filling, works like fountain pen. No back-firing.

LIBERTY FIELD HOWITZER CANNONS
(Pat. Pending)
"CAMOUFLAGE"
TOY CASTLES, DUGOUTS, TRENCHES, BATTLE-FIELDS, MECHANICAL FORTS, NAVAL SETS, SIGNAL STATIONS, SNOW SCENES, WINDMILLS, ETC., ETC.

in designs and color effects never before shown or even attempted by any other manufacturer.
The illustrations on this page cannot possibly do justice to these most beautiful "Camouflage Toys," as their greatest attraction, the color scheme, is omitted.
Our models are so numerous, that in order to become fully acquainted with our line we invite your inspection at our exhibit at the Hotel Imperial Toy Fair (First Floor, Aero Room).

LIBERTY TOY SOLDIERS
(Patent Applied for)
WITH INTERCHANGEABLE HEADS AND ARMS

are the acme of perfection in workmanship and finish. They are as different from the old fashioned lead soldier as a live man is from a corpse; they cost no more, and will surely revolutionize the toy soldier trade of 1918. Take a "Liberty Toy Soldier," remove his head and arms and change him into any one of 288 different models. That is exactly what you can do. You can change him into an American, English, French or Italian soldier as quickly as you can say it. At your command he will present arms, swing a sword, wave a flag, fire a gun, blow a trumpet, beat a drum, play a fife, charge with bayonet or point a lance.
Show us a spirited American boy who won't not be eager to possess a set of these "alive" soldiers in preference to the old fashioned stiff pieces of metal in the shape of soldiers, without motion.
We are the only manufacturers of these new, unique and epoch-making lines of toys mentioned above. Therefore, not to have examined our line before placing your this season's order will mean to have passed by the greatest possible attractions for your toy department.

LIBERTY TOY & NOVELTY CO.

Sole Manufacturers

524-526 W. 166th St.
New York City

Telephone:
Audubon 1629

A January, 1918 *Playthings* ad; same art, very different text.
Courtesy *Playthings*

FERDINAND GUTMANN

A Novel Toy With Action and Pep. That was how Ferdinand Gutmann advertised his impressive line of tin, jointed soldiers in the December, 1918 *Playthings*. The ad's clarion call of **The Line Is Now Ready For Your Inspection** suggests these toys, with their eyecatching color lithography, were new in 1918.

New to the United States, that is. Collector-author Edward Ryan has found patent information showing that as early as 1915 a Johannes Gotthilf Dietrich, "a citizen of the German Empire residing at Berlin-Tempelhof, Germany" had filed for a patent. Unlike other toy soldier ads of the time, Gutmann's don't state that his toys were made in America. In addition, a boxed set of German-made figures that are indistinguishable from Gutmann's has been found (the two accessories in the set are also identical). The box for these "Gloria-Lino Soldiers - Marke Erhala" bears a logo that suggests the initials EHL. The company at this writing is otherwise unknown. Dietrich later (from Germany) filed a similar design in the U.S. on January 17, 1921. This patent was approved November 28, 1922.

A single Gutmann piece, because of its joining, offered a great deal of variety. With the proper adjustments it could march, run, present arms, stand and fire, kneel and fire, etc. The line seems to have consisted of a U.S. soldier, U.S. sailor, U.S. bugler, U.S. flagbearer, U.S. officer with sword, and British, French and Italian soldiers, possibly with the same variations. Also offered were thin cardboard tanks, cannons, trucks, bushes and apparently a tent. The bush is 3¼" high, the tank 3¾" high, and the soldiers 5" high, with "Pat. Pend." on the upper side of the tab on the figures' right foot.

Research by Bill Nutting has revealed that in 1917 and 1918 Gutmann was at the address shown in the first ad: 134-40 West 29th Street, New York City (in 1919 it was 55 Fifth Avenue). He was the president and seems to have been involved in several companies, including the Jam Perfecto Bottle Cap Co. (same address) with Jesse Gutmann as its vice-president.

GUTMANN

If Gutmann did any manufacturing of its soldiers it could be it used the same tin, and perhaps lithography, that it employed in its bottle caps.

The last known ad for the soldiers appears in October, 1919. This doesn't necessarily mean anything, as soldier company ads were erratic, and often nonexistent, but does at least suggest that with war's end the toy soldier fad was over, and possibly Gutmann's contribution to it.

These soldiers, in mint, would be worth $25-$35, with the foreign troops commanding the higher price.

Ferninand Guttman's first known soldiers ad. Since their ads that featured U.S. troops exclusively show only the campaign hat, the tin helmet presumably represents the British, and the kepi possibly both French and Italian, depending on uniform color. December, 1918 *Playthings* magazine. In 1991, the sailor, in excellent condition, with a missing base, sold for $21. Courtesy *Playthings*

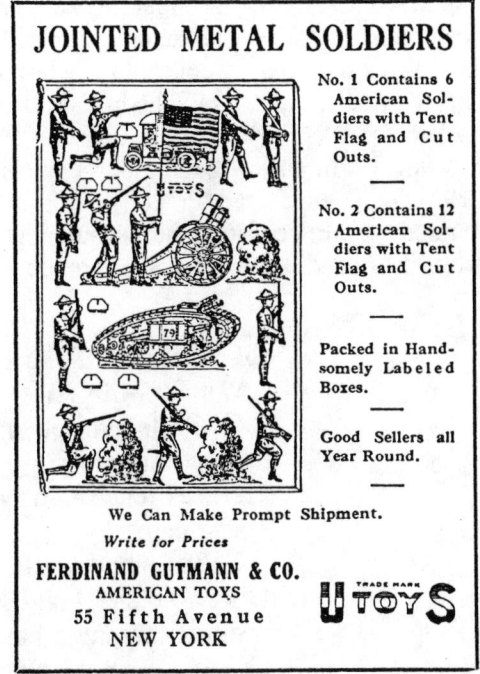

October, 1919 ad in *Toys and Novelties* magazine showing the accessories, officer, flagbearer.

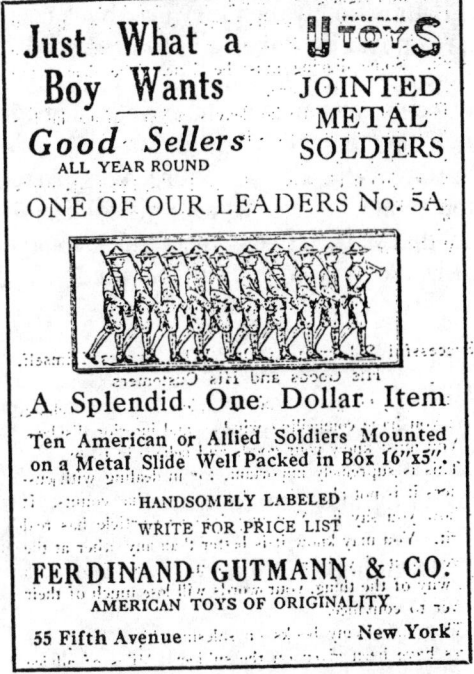

September, 1919 ad in *Toys & Novelties* magazine showing the bugler.

GEORGE GRAMPP & CO., Patchogue, NY
by Bertel Bruun

This company, the existence of which has only recently been discovered, is poorly known. The known facts are few, but tantalizing:

The factory (if the 2 outbuildings or sheds can be so called) was situated on East Oak Street in Patchogue, Long Island, New York. These two sheds were dismantled in 1972 by John Fetkovich of St. James, Long Island. He was at that time engaged in the construction business. In the outbuildings he found a large number of intact moulds and lead figures as well as an even larger number of unfinished lead soldiers and novelty items all of which he kept and still has. Correspondence was also found by him but not kept because of its deteriorated condition. It indicated the owner's name as Anthony Grumpp and that one of the company's customers was F.A.O. Schwartz. Intrigued by his find, Fetkovich did some research at the time, discovering that Anthony Grumpp was born in Germany, moved to Parsippany, NJ and from there to Manhattan, NY. Later he moved from there to Patchogue where he, according to his death certificate, died in 1903 (the only known date). He supposedly had only one daughter who lived in the main house on East Oak Street until the 1960's, but who was unable to furnish any meaningful information.

Richard O'Brien in 1990 discovered mention of a company named "George Grampp & Co., Patchogue, NY" in a review of the New York toy show in the February 1920 issue of *Playthings*. To quote: "George Grampp & Co., Patchogue, NY, manufacturers of lead soldiers and metal novelties, represented by Mrs. Grampp, are showing their usual large line of metal soldiers. A novelty box full of red metal deer is a new feature this year. It is provided with a real wooden gun air rifle." A photograph illustrating the article shows George Grampp & Co.'s booth at the exhibit. With the help of an enlargement of this photograph it is possible to identify the figures in the many boxes as being identical to the ones found on East Oak Street by Fetkovich.

A subsequent search through local telephone books and Chamber of Commerce archives as well as help from the town historian of Brookhaven, David Overton, failed to reveal any further clues. The connection between Anthony Grumpp and George Grampp & Co. remains obscure and the date of start-up and closure of the establishment unknown.

John Fetkovich, after acquiring the moulds, taught himself how to cast and tried, through an entrepreneur, John McCrone, to market new, painted castings through a company called Pembroke miniatures in the late 1970's. The venture was a failure, but figures from this reissue might possibly be in circulation. These reissued figures are recognizable by their poorer painting, harder lead mixture and different rifles and swords (new moulds were made for these items at the time of reissue).

Original George Grampp & Co. figures depicted U.S. Doughboys with Montana hats and in turn of the century blue dress uniforms, West Point cadets on parade, English troops with peaked caps, German troops with pickelhaub, Poilus with Adrian helmets, Austrian soldiers with caps and U.S. sailors in both summer and winter uniform. The size varies from 40 to 50mm and the footplate is either square or formed as a cross. The heads are cast with the bodies (the somewhat similar Heyde figures from which they may have been copied usually have plug-in heads) and the facial features are characterized by a large nose and rather well painted details. Mounted soldiers are on prancing horses with a stand under the rear legs. A motorcycle, U.S. airplane, cannon, machine gun and a battleship completes the military collection. A few Indians and cowboys were also made. The novelty items include the Statue of Liberty, a large variety of Elks in various positions as well as their mounted heads (presumably for B.P.O.E.), bears, rabbits and foxes.

Boxed sets have as yet not been discovered. (O'Brien: Since some unfinished moulds were found, the likelihood is that Grampp created at least some of its soldiers, if not all. The January, 1991 Smithsonian ran an ad by St. Louis' Armchair General that showed two soldiers which could have come from Grampp molds. No Prices found, but presumably foot figures in mint would average $10 and mounted $15. The very large motorcyclist, if full-bodied, might bring as much $45 in mint).

(GG1) U.S. Officer in dress uniform
(GG2) U.S. Soldier in dress uniform
(GG3) Doughboy marching with rifle
(GG4) Doughboy mounted officer
(GG5) Doughboy Flagbearer, cross base
(GG6) Doughboy Drummer
(GG7) Doughboy Officer with sword, on foot
(GG8) Doughboy Bugler

(GG9) Doughboy Flag Bearer, like (GG5), but flat base
(GG10) Rough Rider?, on guard position
(GG11) Cadet Drummer
(GG12) Cadet marching with rifle
(GG13) U.S. Soldier kneeling, firing, Heyde-like discharge at tip of rifle barrel
(GG14) British Soldier in cap, advancing

(GG15) British Soldier advancing with flag
(GG16) German Soldier, prone firing
(GG17) French Officer advancing
(GG18) Sailor Flag Bearer
(GG19) Soldier Flag Bearer, short, campaign hat
(GG20) Officer standing with sword
(GG21) Sailor Blowing Bugle
(GG22) Bugler in campaign hat, short, bugle at side

(GG23) Soldier with sword, short, in campaign hat

(GG24) Cowboy, pistol held high

(GG25) Cowboy, hand at holster

(GG26) Doughboy Flag Bearer, standing, larger size

(GG27) Doughboy Bugler, standing, larger size

(GG28) Doughboy Rifleman, standing, larger size

(GG29) Sailor Standing, rifle at side, larger size

(GG30) Indian holding rifle at angle, larger size

(GG31) Mounted Doughboy Officer, holding sword in air, larger size

(GG32) Mounted Indian, larger size, possibly holding rifle at side

(GG33) Motorcyclist, very large, probably semi-round

(GG34) Doughboy, kneeling firing, larger size

(GG35) Doughboy, standing firing, larger size

(GG36) Doughboy, advancing with rifle, larger size

(GG37) Officer on Rearing Horse

(GG38) Sailor marching with rifle, larger size

(GG39) Doughboy kneeling with binoculars

(GG40) Doughboy kneeling, arm extended

(GG41) Cadet Officer (NOT SHOWN; like G6, G7)

GG1
Photo by Bertel Bruun

GG2
Photo by Bertel Bruun

GG3
Photo by Bertel Bruun

GRAMPP

GG4　　　　　　　GG5
Photo by Bertel Bruun

L to R: GG10 and the Britains figure from which it seems to be copied
Photo by Bertel Bruun

GG6　　　GG7
Photo by Bill Nutting

GG11　　　GG12
Photo by Bill Nutting

GG8　　　　　　　GG9
Photo by Bill Nutting

GG13　　　GG14　　　GG4　　　GG15
Photo by Bertel Bruun

GG16　　　　　　　　　　　GG17
Photo by Bertel Bruun

35

GG18	GG18	GG19	G19	GG20	GG21	21	20	GG22	GG23	23	GG22

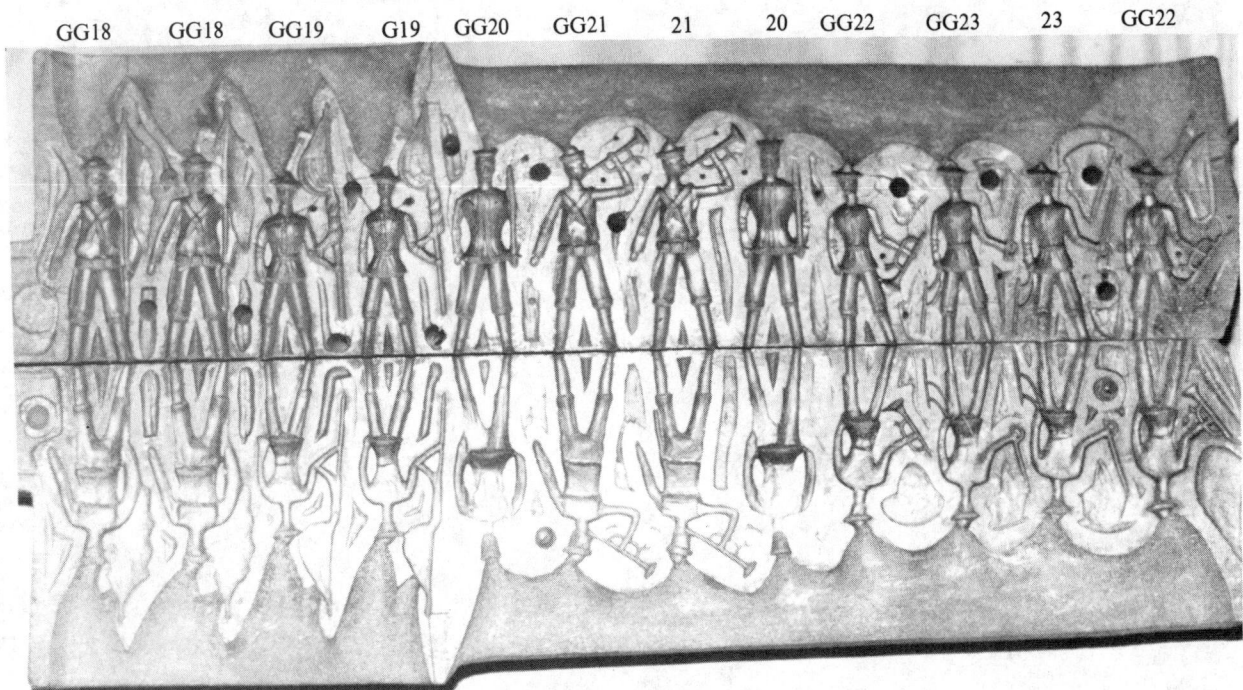

A George Grampp mold in two parts
Photo by Bertel Bruun

The large soldiers in this photo, are, from L to R, starting at the top, GG26, GG27, GG28, GG29, GG21, GG30, GG31, GG32, GG33
Photo by Bertel Bruun

GG24   GG25
Photo by Bertel Bruun

GRAMPP

The large soldiers in this photo are, from L to R, starting at the top, GG34, GG35, GG36, GG26, GG28, GG20, GG37, GG38. The cannon at bottom left appears to be the same as the ones sold by William Feix and the Christies. The infantry on the three bottom rows appear to be homecast types.
Photo by Bertel Bruun

Although this is an unfinished mold, some castings have been found of these figures. From L to R: GG36, (two), GG35 (two), GG39, GG34, GG40
Photo by Bertel Bruun

Ad in the January, 1991 *Smithsonian* magazine of what seem to be Grampp soldiers.
Courtesy Ed Poole

Mold for U.S. Plane
Photo by Bertel Bruun

Homecast type Battleship with three smokestacks
Photo by Bertel Bruun

Unfinished casting of two-stack Battleship. The casting was found at the Grampp site in Patchogue, LI.
Photo by Bertel Bruun

The Race Horse and Jockey Collection . . . Cast in Pewter . .
Bearing Famous Racing Colors . . . A Heirloom Collection
With a History Dating Back Almost 100 Years.

Racing enthusiasts . . . horsemen and women . . . you'll want to
have your own stable of race horses and jockeys carrying favorite
and famous racing colors. The originals of these exceedingly
life-like, detailed miniatures were created almost a century ago.
Hand cast following the care and detailing of their original
counterparts . . . in pewter, enhanced by meticulous hand
painting to achieve enduring realism. Sure to become increasingly
valuable and sought after. Each figure is 7" long, 2¼" wide,
6½" high. Specify Racing Colors: 1. Sea Blue & Blue. 2. Vivid Orange
& Ebony Black. 3. China & Dark Brown. 4. Jungle Green & Sun
Yellow. 5. Flame Red & Sun Yellow. 6. International Orange/
Flame Red/Fire Red/Ebony/Black. 7. Sea Blue & Dark Blue.
8. Royal Purple & Flame Red.

#49227   Each Race Horse, Jockey and Case
(Specify racing colors) **$125.00**
SAVE $100.00 . . . #49226 Buy the Entire Set of 8 Statues . . . **$900.00**

Each Race Horse & Jockey Is
Complete With A Handsome
Lucite Display Case with
Wood Base.

These large racehorses came from a Grampp mold. From an August, 1978
catalog offered by "The Gallery of Amsterdam", Amsterdam, NY.
Courtesy Ed Poole

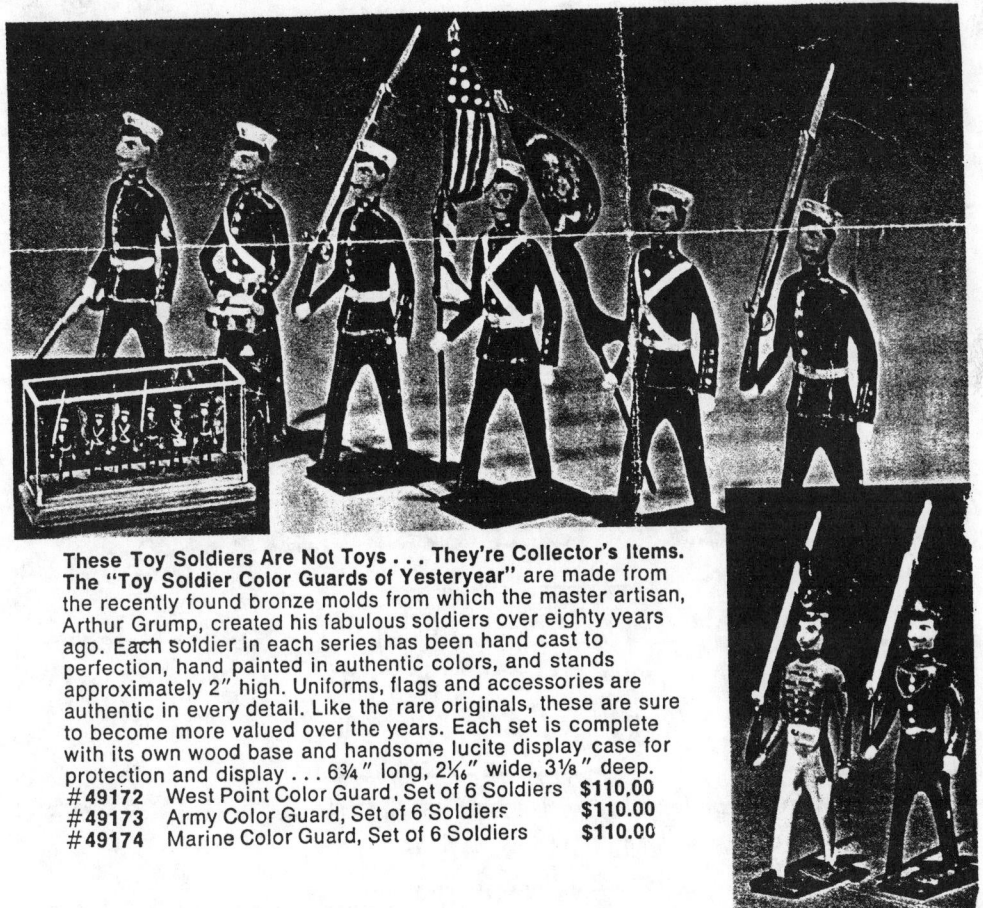

These Toy Soldiers Are Not Toys . . . They're Collector's Items.
The "Toy Soldier Color Guards of Yesteryear" are made from
the recently found bronze molds from which the master artisan,
Arthur Grump, created his fabulous soldiers over eighty years
ago. Each soldier in each series has been hand cast to
perfection, hand painted in authentic colors, and stands
approximately 2" high. Uniforms, flags and accessories are
authentic in every detail. Like the rare originals, these are sure
to become more valued over the years. Each set is complete
with its own wood base and handsome lucite display case for
protection and display . . . 6¾" long, 2 1/16" wide, 3⅛" deep.

#49172   West Point Color Guard, Set of 6 Soldiers $110.00
#49173   Army Color Guard, Set of 6 Soldiers $110.00
#49174   Marine Color Guard, Set of 6 Soldiers $110.00

These George Grampp soldiers were offered in the August, 1978 "The Gallery
of Amsterdam" catalog, Wallin's Corner Road, Amsterdam, NY. These were
the ones sold by John McCrone, who claimed the molds were then 80 years
old (more likely sixty) and from **Arthur Grump** (getting both names wrong).
Note the very high prices for the time.
Courtesy Ed Poole

OTHER WORLD WAR ONE ERA COMPANIES

A number of U.S. toy soldier companies sprang up during the First World War. Virtually all of the ones shown here employed molds of the type thought to be homecasts, many originating, one way or another, in Germany; the result was semi-round, solid-cast lead soldiers. Prices for these are not likely to bring more than three dollars apiece for foot troops, and about four dollars for mounted figures. However, boxed sets, particularly ones with interesting graphics and company names, would bring considerably more; probably a minimum of fifty dollars.

In addition to those shown here, there was the Otto Mfg. Company of Coopersburg, PA, which in July, 1916 ran an all-text ad for "Lead Soldiers Nuremburg Style - artistically hand painted". The company added, "Remember, we are manufacturers, not mere dealers".

Steiner Novelty Works, with a factory in Whitestone, NY, and office and showroom at 32 Union Square East in New York City, in February, 1916 advertised "Unique Mechanical Toys" and, in smaller print, "Also Lead Soldiers, Tents and Cannon - with springs". There was no illustration of any of its toys.

October, 1914 found a *Playthings* ad from John C. Loeffel of 535 Elizabeth Ave., Elizabeth, NJ. "Lead Soldiers Made in America, Infantry, Cavalry, Cowboys, Indians, Buffaloes, etc." stated the all-text ad. The inclusion of buffalo suggests these were all homecast types, as buffalo ran rife in that form.

German Style, Made in the U.S.A.
LEAD SOLDIERS
We Are the Largest American Manufacturers of These Fast Selling Toys and Make Complete Sets of Soldiers of All Nations, Cowboys, Indians, Animals, etc.

METAL TOY MFG. CO., Inc.
41 First Street,   New York City

N. Y. Selling Agents: The Strobel & Wilken Co.;
Louis Wolf & Co.; Adolph Straus & Co.

A June, 1915 *Playthings* ad for the Metal Toy Mfg. Co. of New York. These homecast types were also advertised in February, 1916, with the address of Metal Toy now 1409 Wilkins Ave. in NYC. They appear to come from molds of the Schneider/Schierke type.

There is a DIFFERENCE in
LEAD SOLDIERS !

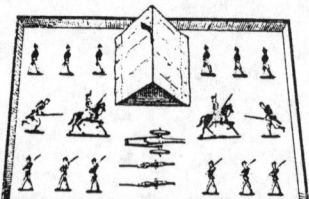

This is one of the 21 different styles and sizes we make

Retail Prices
10c to
$2.00

If you want to make a hit with Lead Soldiers write for samples of the
"AMERICAN MADE" LINE
MANUFACTURED BY
THE AMERICAN TOY MFG. CO., Inc.
FORMERLY KAHN & WIRTH
571 FOURTEENTH STREET   MILWAUKEE, WIS.

The soldiers of the American Toy Mfg., Co., Inc., "formerly Kahn & Wirth" were homecast types resembling those from the molds of Schalk (but not the cannon). The address of the firm in this May, 1916 ad was 571 Fourteenth Street in Milwaukee.
Courtesy *Playthings*

The North American Toy Co., Inc. of 223 East 80th Street in New York City advertised these homecast types, possibly from Schneider/Schierke molds, in December, 1916 and February, 1917. In 1920 it was still listed as making lead soldiers.
Courtesy *Playthings*.

TOY SOLDIERS

Imported Style

Large assortment of artistic models and new designs.

Let us explain the new features which will create a big demand for them.

We are enlarging our plant to take care of orders.

North American Toy Co., Inc.

223 East 80th Street
NEW YORK

SOLDIERS ARE GOING

This year hundreds of thousands of lead soldiers will be sold. Small boys instead of possessing but one set will own at least two and have each set arrayed against the other in battle.

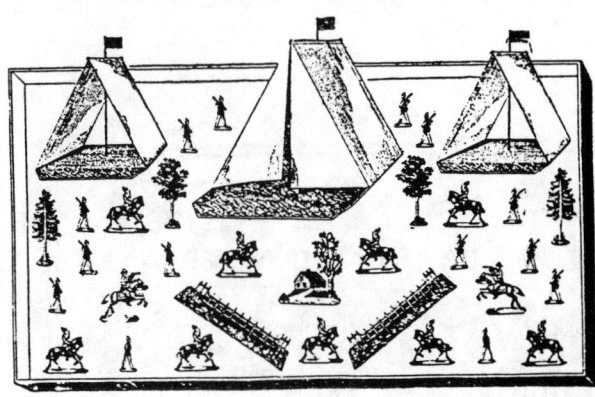

We are manufacturing a most extensive line. Soldiers of all nations in cavalry, infantry. etc. Beautifully painted and made of fine material. Prices very satisfactory.

Our line is shown by all leading factory agents.

NORTH AMERICAN TOY CO., Inc.

223 East 80th St.
NEW YORK, N. Y.

Another ad by North American Toy Co., this time in June, 1917. Some new types appear in this ad, all homecast types, some perhaps from Schalk.
Courtesy *Playthings*.

TOY SOLDIERS

Boxed, as Illustrated, to Retail at 25 Cents

Joy to Every Child

We have just taken over a factory specializing in the manufacture of these lead soldiers, and can make prompt deliveries. Each foot soldier is 1¾ in. high; mounted soldier, 2¼ in. They are handsomely finished in five colors—green, red, blue, black and gold—hand painted. Twelve foot soldiers and two mounted soldiers put up in special carton 10½x5¼ in. Carton retails at 25c. **Price per gross cartons, $24.00 f. o. b. Chicago.** This is one of the most attractive low priced toys offered this season. Sample carton on request.

SALESMEN AND JOBBERS
GET OUR LIBERAL OFFER

STANDARD MAP COMPANY

127 W. Ohio St.　　　Toy Dept.　　　CHICAGO

The Standard Map Company ran this ad in October, 1917 in *Toys and Novelties* magazine. It was located in Chicago at 127 W. Ohio St. It had "just taken over a factory" which made these lead soldiers. The mounted soldier is 2¼" high.

These "hand-made toy soldiers" appear to be from the WWI era. Semi rounds, they were produced at 1412 New York Avenue in Shegoygan, Wisconsin. No company name known. The soldiers are 54mm high. Photo by Ed Poole

This appears to be the mounted officer shown in the October, 1917 Standard Map Company ad. It is from a tray of five which overlaid a printed sheet reading "Our Army and Navy".
Courtesy Mike McAfee

Although B. Shackman made some toys, it was primarily a jobber, and a former owner of the firm states that it made no soldiers. This October, 1918 *Toys and Novelties* ad is shown here for dating purposes.

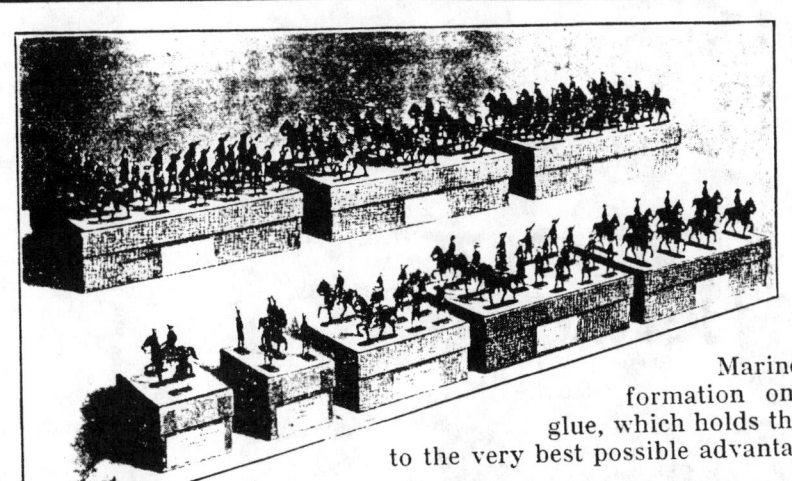

TOY SOLDIERS AND HORSES

Hand Painted, Finished in Marine and Khaki. Set up in parade formation on cards with special cement glue, which holds them upright and displays them to the very best possible advantage.

EACH SET IN INDIVIDUAL BOX. Handsome Label. Packed to withstand shipping. Will not tear loose from card.

Retail from 10c to $1.00 Per Set

Liberal Profit to Jobber and Retailer. Complete Sample Line as Illustrated, $2.75

Order Sample Line at Once. Stock deliveries will be made in 2 to 3 weeks after receipt of order.

WESTERN NEW YORK TOY CO., Inc.
JAMESTOWN, N. Y.

Bad timing department: Western New York Toy Co., Inc. of Jamestown, New York's homecast-type soldiers were advertised in September, 1919, a year after war fever had cooled down.
Courtesy *Playthings*

Popular Toy Soldiers, Water Pistols and Popguns

Your Choice of These Sets 19c

Here are two low priced sets of 2¼-in. full body Lead Soldiers, nicely made and brilliantly enameled in colors. There are two different assortments at the same low price, and each comes in a box 8x10 inches. They are very nice sets and unusually good quality. Shipping weight of each, 1¼ pounds.
37Y4706 Set consisting of 6 Infantry Soldiers.
37Y4707 Set consisting of 5 Infantry Soldiers and one Tent. Price, for either set.............**19c**

37Y5098 A complete Soldier Camp Outfit in a box 11x16 inches. Outfit consists of 13 full body 2¼-inch foot soldiers, 1 officer on horse, 1 gilded aeroplane, 1 gilded cannon and 1 collapsible tent with American flag. Soldiers, aeroplane and cannon made of lead, nicely painted. Shipping weight, 2 pounds.
Price, each.............**79c**

Rapid Fire Soldier and Gun Set **39c**

Our big Rapid Fire Soldier and Gun Set. This fine gun shoots ten wooden shells in five seconds. It is a wood cannon mounted on a strong iron stand. 8 inches long, 5½ inches high, and fitted with a powerful spiral spring, operated by the crank which shoots bullet shaped wooden slugs at the soldiers. Shipping weight, 2½ lbs.
37Y1925 Price, complete with four soldiers.........**39c**
37Y1926 25 extra shells. Shpg. wt., 10 oz. Price..**10c**

HEAVY ARTILLERY CANNON. Solid cast iron cannon. Screwed together. Can be taken apart. Mounted on large wheels and can be raised or lowered. Mechanism operated by turning crank. Outfit supplied with six hollow rubber balls and five soldiers. An unusually amusing toy that a boy will not tire of for a long time. Length, 13½ inches. Shipping weight, 5 pounds.
37Y1923 Price, complete.........**83c**
37Y1924 6 Extra Rubber Balls.........**9c**

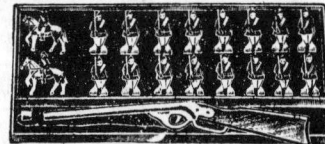

21c and 39c

37Y1951 A new Sharp Shooter Game with an improved lever loading gun, 16½ inches long, sixteen 3-inch lithographed flat metal foot soldiers and two mounted soldiers. This is a splendid new shooting game, better than any of its kind ever before offered at the price. Size of box, 20x9 inches. Shipping weight, 1¼ pounds.
Price, complete.............**39c**
37Y1952 Same but smaller, with 11-inch gun, eight foot soldiers and two mounted soldiers. Size of box, 12x9½ inches. Shipping weight, 1 pound. Price, complete....**21c**

Toy U. S. Battleships and Marines

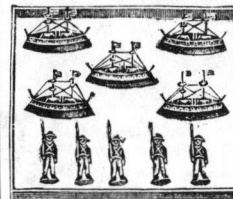

37Y5097 A fine Outfit of U. S. Battleships and Marines, in a box 9½x12 inches. Set consists of 5 battleships, that will float, fully rigged with flags, etc., and 5 U. S. Marines, height, 2¾ inches; made with full lead body and beautifully painted. Well balanced; will stand alone. A very novel outfit at a low price. Shpg. wt., 1¼ pounds.
Price, each.........**39c**

Soldiers advertised in 1916 by the Charles Williams stores, NYC. The figures in top left could be from William Feix. Those on the bottom left have the look of Japanese-made pieces.

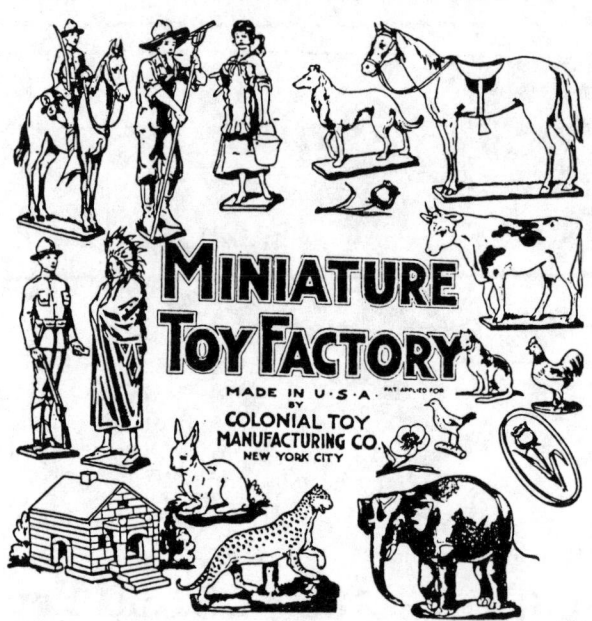

MORE THAN A CONSTRUCTION TOY

ALL THAT ITS NAME IMPLIES — A TOY FOR THE WHOLE FAMILY

"MINIATURE TOY FACTORY" is an educational toy for girls as well as boys, without the limitations of the construction toy.

With "Miniature Toy Factory" a child can make every toy his heart desires—animals, soldiers, Indians, building blocks, birds, ornaments and medallions without end.

To mold the toys is clean, easy work and every model is a work of art. No crude dabs of clay. No skeletons of sticks, but a regiment of perfectly made

soldiers, a whole band of Indians, a herd of animals and every piece the work of an experienced sculptor. To paint these toys is an added interest. Handsome boxes with dies, paints, color charts, etc., come complete in every detail to retail at from $1.00 up.

Dealers will be supplied with colored advertising matter and demonstrating outfits. A descriptive booklet with complete details will be sent on request and samples to rated concerns.

COLONIAL TOY MFG. CO. INC.

352-62 W. 13th St.   NEW YORK

The "Miniature Toy Factory", sold by the Colonial Toy Mfg. Co. Inc., 352-62 West 13th Street in New York City, allowed children to make toy soldiers and other pieces from "Multi-Make Flour", presumably a form of composition. This ad ran in June, 1916.
Courtesy *Playthings*

The Oriole Toy Co., located in the Hartje Building in Pittsburgh, produced these "Oriole Monumental Toy Soldiers", with ads running in January and March of 1919. The bases bore the names of the figures: the running sailor was B. Gray, the running soldier G. Baker, the top mounted officer Gen. Pershing, the lower one T. Brown, all "a recent war hero". They were "beautifully colored" and may have been tin, as Oriole's other toys seem to have been. They were, however, described as "perfectly cast". Unlike many soldier companies Oriole made them "entirely on machines operated by adults; no child labor or sweat shop methods employed."
Courtesy *Playthings*

THEODORE HAHN

Theodore Hahn is known only because of an ad that ran in 1921 in *Playthings* magazine. However, the soldiers shown in that ad suggest that Hahn was one of the more important of the early American toy soldier companies.

Hahn and the Christies' Metal Toy Soldier Co. seem to have been the first American makers to produce doughboys in steel helmets. The two contemporaneous firms may have purchased their molds from the same source; several of their soldiers, aside from paint, are probably exact duplicates.

Hahn's mounted officer and bugler, both with moving arms, resemble those by Barclay (and Britains). Collector Will Beierwaltes has found an unboxed set which appears to be from Hahn. It includes one of the trees, a circular tent, and a similar cannon. It also has a mounted soldier which resembles Barclay's Bg. This latter figure, like many of those sold by Hahn and the Christies, seems to have originated in France.

In addition to Hahn and the Christies, another as-yet-unidentified American firm cast similar steel-helmeted doughboys. However, these have flat bases (the Hahns and the Christies are mounted) and line and dot eyes. The Hahn soldiers appear to all be dot-eyed (no eyebrows) as are most of the Christies.

Theodore Hahn was located at 16-18 Hopkins Avenue in Jersey City, New Jersey. If its ad is accurate, it occupied all of a three-story building, with signs on its sides reading "Theodore Hahn White Metal Castings". Its approximate production span is 1921 to January, 1927, when it was listed as an exhibitor at the Toy Fair in New York.

In addition to soldiers and sailors (the latter not shown in the 1921 ad, but presumably like the Christies'), Hahn produced white metal (lead alloy) trains, automobiles, at least one airplane, one cannon and a canary whistle. The No. 187 Aeroplane was sold in assorted colors, and the No. 189 Cannon in Gold and Grey.

A 1922-23 city directory shows Theodore Hahn as the firm's president, Jack Pflug vice-president, Louis M. Schmidt secretary and John Slack treasurer. 1925-26 shows Hahn as both president and treasurer, Conrad Koegel vice-president and Slack secretary. Hahn's home was in South Orange, NJ.

Despite the similarity of some of their figures and the firms' proximity, there seems to be no connection between Hahn and Barclay, even to a transfer of molds.

	G	VG	M
(THA) Mounted Bugler(?) on rearing horse, moving arm	22.00	33.00	45.00
(TH1) Mounted Officer on rearing horse, moving arm	25.00	38.00	50.00
(TH2) Officer with Sword, movable arm, cap	5.00	8.00	10.00
(TH3) Flagbearer, campaign hat	No Price Found		
(TH4) Bugler, movable arm, cap	5.00	8.00	10.00
(TH5) Doughboy Charging, steel helmet	4.00	6.00	8.00
(TH6) Doughboy Advancing, rifle out at angle, steel helmet	4.00	6.00	8.00
(TH7) Doughboy Kneeling Firing, steel helmet	3.00	4.00	6.00
(TH8) Sailor (not known what it looked like, probably like Christies' I9)	No Price Found		
(TH9) Mounted soldier, like Barclay Bg	10.00	15.00	20.00
(TH10) Shoulder Arms, campaign hat	5.00	8.00	10.00
(TH11) Bare-handed, campaign hat	4.00	6.00	8.00
(TH12) Rifle at Trail, campaign hat	5.00	8.00	10.00

TH1   TH9
Photo by Will Beierwaltes

TH4 TH2 TH6 TH5 TH7
Photo by Will Beierwaltes

THEODORE HAHN

TH3   TH10
Photo by Will Beierwaltes

TH12
Photo by Ron Steiner

What is almost certainly a Theodore Hahn set.
Photo by Will Beierwaltes

Identical cannons. The broken one at right came in what seems to be a Theodore Hahn set. However, the spokes and barrel backs are different from the piece shown in the Hahn ad. Value about $25 in mint.
Photo by Will Beierwaltes

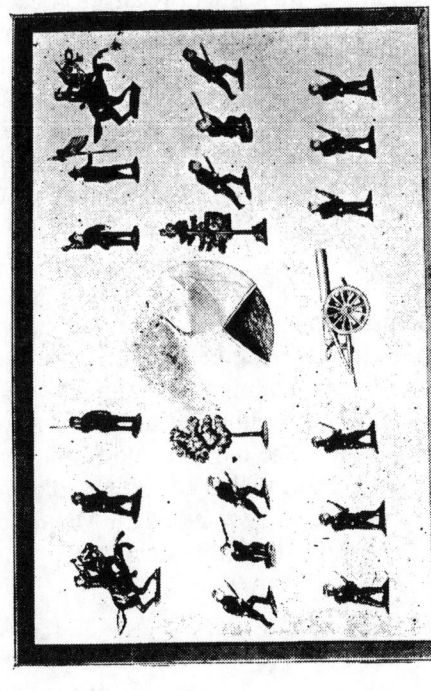
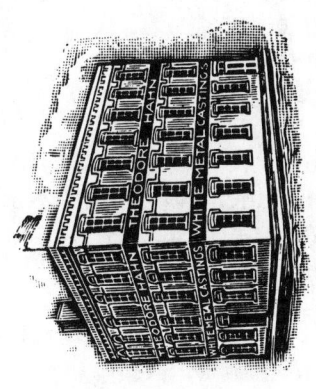

CHRISTIES' METAL TOY & SOLDIER CO.

Information supplied by a descendant of the Christies had led collectors to believe that the company's name was "Ideal" and that the firm was an important one that was in business for some years. Neither is true.

From 1917 through 1921 brothers Albert A. and Lewis D. Christie operated the Atlantic Metal Parts Company at 252 Middle Street in Bridgeport, Connecticut. Atlantic Metal did metal casting and had nothing to do with toys or even lead casting. A directory shows the Christies at the same address in 1922, now owning the Metal Toy Soldier Company. The 1923 directory reveals a different tenant at the address and each of the Christies employed elsewhere. They had sold the metal business to Warner Bros. Co. Corsets, and the two found they couldn't support themselves with the soldiers. After they gave up the firm, finished inventory was sold, but no casting was done. "Ideal" was not only not the company's name, it was also never a trademark.

The way to tell the Christies' products from others, according to early American soldier specialist Bill Nutting, is by the paint, a combination of very metalic paints, such as the blue tunics, and very flat paints, such as for the bases. Though these approximately 54mm soldiers do turn up despite their short production span, presumably most soldiers that appear at a quick glance to be from the Christies are from the much longer-lived Theodore Hahn, and at least one other company which also had the same, or similar molds (possibly the latter was also the producer of the crude Eureka copies).

Although a descendant says he was told the molds came from Germany, many of the Christies' (and Hahn's) pieces seem to have had their origins in France, as a number of similar soldiers turn up with that nation's name on them. A toy directory of 1923-24 lists the firm at the same address, calling it Metal Toy & Soldier Co. The date of the directory muddies matters, but toy directories of the time weren't terribly accurate.

	G	VG	M		G	VG	M
(I-1) Infantryman with campaign hat	5.00	7.00	10.00	(I-9) Sailor, rifle thrust out at angle	5.00	7.00	10.00
(I-2) Bugler, brown uniform	5.00	7.00	10.00	(I-10) Kneeling rifleman, steel helmet	3.00	4.00	6.00
(I-2a) Bugler, gray uniform	5.00	7.00	10.00	(I-11) Train figure, conductor?	No Price Found		
(I-3) Bugler, blue uniform	5.00	7.00	10.00	(I-12) Train figure, signalman	No Price Found		
(I-4) Officer with sword, grey uniform	5.00	7.00	10.00	(I-13) Train figure, woman	No Price Found		
(I-5) Officer with sword, blue uniform	5.00	7.00	10.00	(I-14) Indian, arm raised	3.00	4.00	6.00
(I-6) Infantryman with rifle, cap, blue uniform	5.00	7.00	10.00	(I-15) Indian, with rifle	3.00	4.00	6.00
(I-7) Officer, blue uniform, no weapons	5.00	7.00	10.00	(I-16) Charging soldier, steel helmet	4.00	6.00	8.00
(I-8) Sailor at slope arms	5.00	7.00	10.00	(I-17) Infantryman with campaign hat, rifle	4.00	6.00	8.00
				(I-18) Baseball Fielder	No Price Found		

I-1 I-2 I-4 I-5 I-6 I-3 I-7 I-8 I-9

I-10 I-11 I-12 I-13 I-14 I-15

I16   I17

Photo courtesy Bill Nutting

I-18

SAINT LOUIS LEAD SOLDIER COMPANY - LLOYD'S DE LUXE SOLDIERS

If not for J. Edward Jones, the Saint Louis Lead Soldier Company would almost certainly be unknown today. Jones, analyzing firms both preceding and competitive with him, compiled notes on a number of them. The most complete of these histories concerns Saint Louis Lead Soldier. All the following is based on Jones' work (Jones prepared the report March 22, 1930 after a March 18 visit to the maker).

S. Chichester Lloyd was the owner. The company probably began in 1925 and was still in business in 1930. However, it seems from first to last to have been a part-time venture, with Lloyd working as a salesman for the Elliot-Fisher Co. The address for the firm was originally Suite 309, 804 Pine Street, St. Louis, Missouri, but was changed to 7040 Elmhurst Avenue in Detroit when Lloyd was transferred by Elliott-Fisher.

Even before the move to Detroit the firm also styled its product as Lloyd's De Luxe Soldiers and S. Chichester Lloyd's De Luxe Soldiers. There was at least one catalog. Though Jones mentions one of ten pages, the 1927 catalog found with his notes runs twelve, and shows approximately 275 different figures, plus animals, vehicles, cannon, ships, etc.

Many of Lloyd's soldiers came from homecast molds sold by Schneider, Metal Cast, and another German firm, since established by the author as Ideal. Some came from C.E. Turnbull & Co. of London. Others may have come from Reka and even Heyde. In some cases Lloyd may have produced new molds using Britains figures. The German molds were in both slate and brass. The English hollowcast molds featured interchangeable heads. Jones' belief was that Lloyd didn't know how to hollow cast, though claiming he could. Lloyd also claimed to have spent $15,000 on the molds, thus leaving him short of capital. He told Jones he had "picked up his learning in the trade and sought the German consul for the information on which to get started and paid cash for his molds".

Though Jones heard of the company "from four different sources in 1929" he never saw Lloyd's product for sale, and believed distribution was very limited. Lloyd claimed orders from J.L. Hudson, Kresge and other outlets. Painting of the pieces varied from soldiers that showed "unusual painting ability" to those where both the "material applied and the finish" were "far from ideal". Soldering was necessary on many of the pieces. Because of this and the detailed painting, Jones felt the product couldn't be produced on a large scale. Despite many reservations about Lloyd's product, he did feel that it was second in quality only to Jones' own Metal-Art.

The boxes Jones saw at Lloyd's were plain, without labels or cover design, and with the numbers of the sets inked in. Lloyd claimed to pay a penny per piece to the workers who painted them. He expected ten cents each for many of the foot figures.

At present there is no established price on any of Lloyd's soldiers.

These knights, currently manufactured in the Netherlands by Frank Poeth (see Currently Made Soldiers) from molds by Germany's Ideal, were featured in Lloyd's catalog.
Photo by Frank Poeth

Two of these ships and the lighthouse, currently made by Frank Poeth in the Netherlands from molds by Germany's Ideal, were sold by Saint Louis Lead Soldier Company.
Photo by Frank Poeth

SOLJERTOYS-PEARLYTOYS

Both Pearlytoys and Soljertoys were New York firms owned by S. Rosenberg. Pearlytoys, probably founded in 1928, was the first. The company was still known by that name in the December, 1929 Butler Bros. catalog, but in March of 1930 *Playthings* magazine stated that Soljertoys had been established in 1929 (S. Rosenberg Toy Manufacturers was incorporated on January 14, 1930). Possibly the September, 1929 Crash, which had quick, devastating results, convinced Rosenberg to walk away from Pearlytoys and its creditors.

Essentially the two had the same product. In 1929 Pearlytoys was selling all of the Britains-sized soldiers, sailors, marines, cadets, cowboys and Indians (except possibly the mounted cowboy or Indian) later offered by Soljertoy. Some of the large Pearlytoys sets contained rifles (presumably cork-shooting), but none of the Soljertoys sets are known to.

Soldier-maker J. Edward Jones compiled notes on the two companies, saying that Pearlytoy's "goods were first seen on the market in 1928 in Chicago, where they seemed quite popular". He also mentions "two different poses of baseball players", presently unknown, and perhaps a Jones mistake. However, I-18, attributed by the less than reliable Gordon F. Christie to the Christie's Metal Toy & Soldier Co., could possibly be a Pearlytoy.

The March, 1930 *Playthings* announcement also revealed that Soljertoy's sets were retailed from 25 cents to $3.00, "with loose pieces obtainable at 10 retail". It further stated "The Jam Jar, a 25¢ item, was also shown". Obviously, this was a non-soldier toy, and as the years went on, Rosenberg seems to have stopped concentrating on soldiers, by 1933 veering to a marked degree into "soft dolls and animals".

In 1933 *Playthings* announced that S. Rosenberg had made its fourth move in three years, "each to larger quarters". Maybe, but this was the Depression, a time when many people moved into places that granted concessions of a month or more in rent. Making this seem likely is that in 1934 or earlier, a Mr. Illfelder became the president of S. Rosenberg, with the company becoming the Illfelder Corporation in 1934 (Rosenberg had previously worked for Illfelder), at 7 West 22nd Street (other addresses were 36 West 20th Street, 37 West 19th Street, 40 West 25th Street and 20 West 17th Street). A study of Manhattan phone books reveals that by 1936 or 1937 Rosenberg-Soljertoy-Illfelder appears to have bitten the dust.

But while it lasted, Soljertoys obviously had aspirations. In the August, 1930 *Playthings* it advertised "Paint-A-Toy" sets at $1.00 retail which contained 10 lead figures. In April it had added its first, and probably last, 3¼" pieces, an advancing doughboy and an Indian doing a war dance (SO11, SO10), apparently, in a bizarre juxtaposition, placing them in the same box. In 1932 it was still pushing its sets in *Playthings*, using the box with the nicely-done art shown here with the large soldiers set.

The not-always accurate "The World Encyclopaediea of Model Soldiers" states that in 1936 Soljertoys used the molds of Metal-Cast Products; a sorry end, if true.

	G	VG	M
(SO1) Officer with sword, approx. 2¼" high	10.00	15.00	20.00
(SO2) Marching left shoulder arms, approx. 2⅞" high	4.00	6.00	8.00
(SO3) On Guard with fixed bayonet, approx. 2¼" high	4.00	6.00	8.00
(SO4) Officer on horse, 2¼" high	20.00	30.00	40.00
(SO5) Mounted Indian Chief	7.00	11.00	14.00
(SO6) Indian on foot with rifle	3.00	4.50	6.00

	G	VG	M
(SO7) West Point Cadet	12.00	18.00	24.00
(SO8) Cowboy on foot	2.50	3.75	5.00
(SO9) Mounted Cowboy	7.00	11.00	14.00
(SO10) Indian doing war dance (3¼" type)	40.00	60.00	80.00
(SO11) Doughboy advancing with rifle (3¼" type)	40.00	60.00	80.00
(SO12) Sailor	12.00	18.00	24.00
(SO13) Marine	12.00	18.00	24.00
(SO14) Marine in White	15.00	22.00	30.00
(SO15) Nurse (Soljertoy?)	No Price Found		
(SO16) Doctor (Soljertoy?)	No Price Found		
(SO17) Indian doing war dance (3¼" type), knife	No Price Found		

A Pearlytoys boxed set of Cowboys. This sold in December, 1990 for about $65.
Photo by Bill Nutting

SOLJERTOYS-PEARLYTOYS

At left S04, and next to it a piece that seems to be Soljertoy, since the only difference appears to be the hat. Next to SO1 is an in-between size that bears many Soljertoy characteristics, suggesting the firm made soldiers in three sizes. Courtesy Tony Diksa

SO2   SO1   SO3
Photo by Ed Poole

SO11 Soljertoy doughboy with rifle.
Photo by Ed Poole

Cannon from Soljertoy set. This cannon was produced by a number of manufacturers both German and American.
Photo by Ed Poole

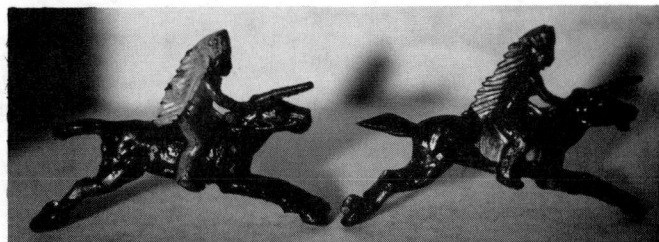

SO5 Soljertoy Indian on left, similar Indian on right (notice difference in horses' tails)
Photo by K. Warren Mitchell

Left, Soljertoy SO4, right Pearlytoy mounted officer. The only difference between the two figures is that the Soljertoy is less sharply defined in its details, and most of the "Pearlytoy" trademark found on the Pearlytoy horse's neck has been effaced on the Soljertoy.
Photo by Ed Poole

Incomplete boxed set of Soljertoys, circa 1932.
Photo by Ed Poole

A Soljertoys boxed set of Indians. Value about $65. Photo courtesy Perry R. Eichor

A probably incomplete boxed set of Indians that sold at auction for $121 in 1986. Set No. 101.
Courtesy Hank Anton

PEWTER SOLDIERS, SAILORS AND MARINES

2½ In.—Heavy pewter, bright enameled regulation uniforms.

20 enlisted men, 4 officers. 2 doz. in box.
1F2309—Infantry.
1F2310—Marines.
Gro $9.00   Doz 78¢

1F2315—Sailors, asstd. blue and white, 20 enlisted men, 4 officers. 2 doz. in box.
Gro $9.00   Doz 78¢

PEARLYTOYS

1F2323—Soldier and marine set, 6 pcs., 5 enlisted men, 1 officer. Asstd. 2 soldier and 1 marine set. ¼ doz. sets in pkg.
Doz sets **$4.00**

PEARLYTOYS

1F2324—Soldier set, 2 styles (1 with 12 infantry men, other with 6 infantry men and 4 mounted officers), each set in box. Asstd. ⅙ doz. sets in pkg.
Doz sets **$8.00**

Pearlytoys, as shown in a December, 1929 Butler Bros. catalog

SO8   SO6
Photo by Bill Nutting

SO15   SO16

These are thought to be Soljertoys, though there is no documentation.
Photo by Ed Poole

SOLJERTOYS-PEARLYTOYS

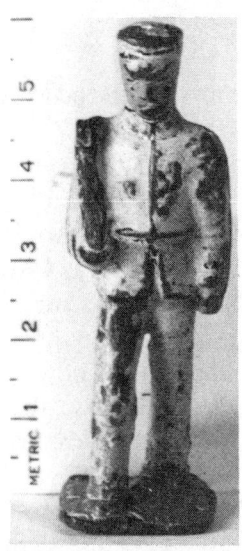

SO14
Photo by Ed Poole

SO7   SO13   SO12
Photo by Bill Nutting

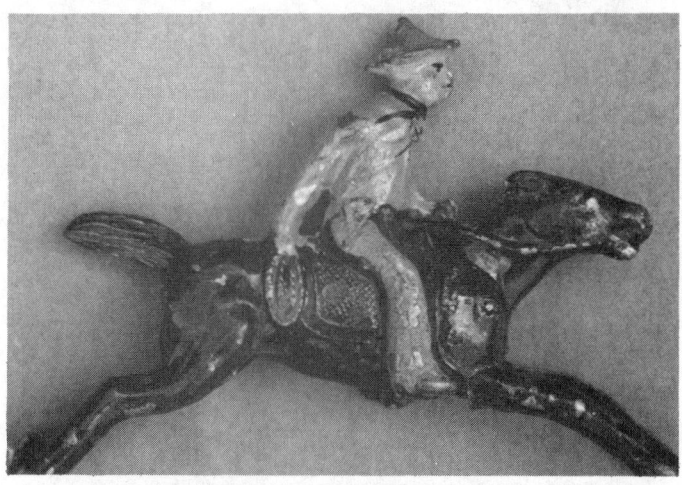

SO9
Photo by Bill Nutting

SO17   SO10
Courtesy Charlie Breslow

SO10   SO4
Courtesy Jacki and Tony Grecco

COSMO

Cosmo may have had the oddest beginning of any toy soldier company; it started out as a manufacturer of rhinestone souvenirs.

It was known variously as Cosmo Ornament Co. Inc. and Cosmo Novelty Co., and was listed as a toy soldier manufacturer as early as 1930. In March, 1931, Playthings Magazine reported it as selling lead soldiers – including sailors, cadets, Indians and cowboys, boxed in various sets to retail from 25¢ to $5.00.

The company's address was 44 West 36th Street in New York, and it appears to have been out of business by 1932.

The only Cosmos known are an infantryman and an officer, and even here there is some uncertainty, as in the March, 1931 Playthings photo the rifles are on the right shoulder, and it's hard to tell on which shoulder the officer's sword rests. In all likelihood, however, these are Cosmos, and the photo in Playthings was reversed. The figures are hollow lead, and slightly outsize; the officer is almost 3½" high. The bases are rather thick, a trait their other figures may share. The two known Cosmos appear to be copies of German composition soldiers.

Although Cosmo Ornament was listed as a corporation, New York State shows no papers on file, and no other information on the company has been found. Cosmo's soldiers are extremely rare, but since they are rather crude, and not attractively painted (the faces are a garish pink, the uniforms mustardy and the helmet a light blue-grey), it's likely they would command no more than $20-40 in mint condition.

Cosmo Officer and Infantryman
Courtesy Edward Szpond

BARCLAY

December 21, 1949: A party given by Barclay owner Michael Levy for employees with over twenty years with the company. The site is the Claridge, at 11th Street and Central Avenue in Union City, N.J. Seated, from right are: Mr. and Mrs. Frank Terminini, Harry Bogaty, Sally Newman, Michael Levy, Mr. and Mrs. Angelo Addeo, Mr. and Mrs. George Fall. Each of the veteran employees was presented with a gold Waltham watch.
Photo courtesy George Fall

UPDATE: Since the last edition, much information has turned up via interviews, Barclay order sheets and general catalogs. All three types of "early Barclays" have been confirmed as being from the company (see section following this history). A 1935 catalog reference to a Barclay "bugler on horseback" suggests the moving-arm Barclays were still in production at that date. 1935 also now seems to have been the starting date for Barclay's 3¼" soldiers, Barclay numbers 701-723. The Italians and Ethiopians were produced in late 1935 or no later than January, 1936. Numbers 728-741 followed in 1936. 743-746 would have been late 1936 or possibly early 1937. In 1937 long-stride variations of the earlier figures were introduced, as well as 747-760 and probably 761. The oriental soldiers, probably using the numbers formerly employed for the Italians-Ethiopians, seem to have first sold that year. The fact that both the Japanese and his opponent had villainous mouths suggests that a collector who remembers the latter as Mongols may be right, as the Mongols were communists, a group often frowned on by such capitalists as manufacturers.

1938 saw the emergence of 762-773 and the four Boy Scouts. In 1939 civilians 610-626 seem to have begun production, with the probable exception of B168, B188, B189. The tall soldiers, B10, B20, B76, 774, 775, 776 and 777 presumably also began that year. 1940 was probably the first year that the cast helmet soldiers were sold. Although collectors believe pod-foots emerged about 1950, the earliest confirmed date is via a Woolworth's catalog dated December, 1951.

For a few years in the 1930s and early 1940s, Barclay Mfg. Co. was the largest manufacturer of toy soldiers in the United States. At its zenith it employed 400 workers, a figure not approached before or since in this country, and produced about 20,000,000 toys a year.

Barclay's soldiers were made of antimonial lead (87% lead, 13% antimony) and, in the days prior to World War II, most were sold for a nickel apiece. In addition to soldiers, Barclay turned out vehicles, aircraft, ships, horse-drawn carriages, soldiers accessories and a number of novelty items, among them a Japanese village and a wheeled baby crib.

Unfortunately, despite the firm's prominence, few records were kept, and most of the information on the company has had to be gleaned from its former workers, who in turn, were drawing on memories that had to go back as far as six decades.

It's known Barclay was in business by 1924, and perhaps as early as 1922 or 1923. Before that, one of its founders, an elderly one-eyed Frenchman, Leon Donze (pronounced, at Barclay, DUN-zee), was listed as a toymaker in a 1922-23 business directory. His son, John, who later became a foreman at Barclay (remaining after his father left) was also listed, as was Adolph Donze, about whom nothing is known. The address given for the operation was 238 Bergenline Avenue, West Hoboken, New Jersey. (Leon died April 8, 1950, at the age of 84).

BARCLAY

Barclay was formed by Donze and Michael Levy (c. 1895-10/9/64), who, according to one account, had been working as a bookkeeper in the Brooklyn Navy Yard. Donze had the molds and the set-up, and Levy the cash (apparently $800, "borrowed from Household Finance"). The company was named after the street it fronted on in West Hoboken (there was a renaming of streets and town sometime later; the original Barclay Street address is now 316 10th Street in Union City).

According to Louis Picco, who joined the company in July, 1924, Barclay at that time had only "about five other employees" and just six or seven molds, all of them "crude" (a year later there were "30-50 employees"). The most prominent toy at the time was a cannon with a brass spring, modeled after a French 75. Whether there were also soldiers is also uncertain, but the consensus is that there were.

In addition to Donze and Levy, there was another important name associated with the company, a "Mr. Thompson" from Woolworth's. This was probably William J. Thompson, who had begun with Woolworth's in 1900, was a buyer from 1920 on, and died in 1954. According to Picco, Thompson "carried the company" in its early days (perhaps for that reason the company had about 100 workers by 1928). Thompson frequently traveled to Europe in search of new toys for the Woolworth's chain. Upon his return, he would bring some of them to Barclay, with instructions to "make them cheaper". Although Barclay seems to have sold to Kresge's too from the beginning, Thompson is remembered for buying from the company "practically everything they made". In time, Michael Levy also picked up other companies' toy soldiers in his travels and used some as the basis for new Barclays.

The earliest known Barclay soldiers, possibly not produced until the late 1920s, were 54mm-scaled mounted figures with moving arms. However, it's the company's 3¼" figures that attract most collectors. By all accounts, manufacture of these seems to have begun no earlier than 1934 and no later than 1935 (the first documentation of Barclay's 3¼" soldiers appears in the May, 1936 issue of Consumers Union magazine, showing B9 and B86).

Production must have been enormous from the start, as the soldiers issued only up until late 1935 or early 1936 have an eye that consists of a curved eyelid with a dot attached to the extreme end of it, giving all the figures a sideward glance. Despite the short production run, these figures turn up today in great numbers (the distinctive Barclay eye, the later version having the dot at the middle of the eyelid, was probably designed by Barclay's Dorothy Grisar, and most likely was a simplified version of the Elasolin-Lineol eyes, dispensing with the eyebrow). Certainly the company was geared for volume production, as by 1935 it had 300 employees.

Sculpting of these figures was done at first by Frank Krupp (see All-Nu) and later by Olive Kooken (see Tommy Toy). There are some indications Kooken also designed for the company in the late 1920s and early 30s, then was supplanted by Krupp from about 1930 or 31 to the end of 1937. Kooken then returned and designed the company's figures from 1937 till the end, with her friend, Margaret Cloninger, possibly assisting her from 1937-41.

Krupp initiated the 3¼" line with what collectors call "short stride" soldiers. These were rather stiff-looking items whose feet were close together. As early as 1937, the more realistic "long strides" were produced. All of Krupp's soldiers sported separate tin helmets. At first they were glued on, but because gluing was messy, and there were complaints from the 5&10s that the helmets fell off, they were redesigned with a clip that, inserted into the airhole in the soldier's head, held them fast. These also seem to have appeared by 1937, although blueprints for the clip are dated February, 1938.

By 1939 or 1940 (probably the latter) the company began to dispense with the separate tin helmet due to its expense and the time it took up (the helmets and pins were sub-contracted, but put together at Barclay), and made the helmet an integral part of the figure. These are known to collectors as "cast helmets". (An important part of the mold-making was the "chasing" of molds. This consisted of restoring, with the use of small hand tools, all the details lost in the mold-making process, and insuring that the parts of the mold – usually two, sometimes three, occasionally more parts – fitted perfectly. Chasing of a single mold would take about a week.)

Discovery in late 1984 of a trove of early order sheets and several pages of rough sketches suggests that Olive Kooken doodled out ideas on paper that she presented to Levy (Donze was gone by about 1930, reportedly selling out for $10,000; he later tried to come back to Barclay, without success.) It's also known that Krupp and later Bill Rucci (who took over the design of the company's toy vehicles after Krupp left) would go over new car ads with Levy, deciding on which the company would turn out in miniature.

For most of the pre-War years Barclay cast its soldiers by hand. A caster would pour molten lead into a mold and then rock the mold so that almost all of the lead poured back out. What remained was a shell that adhered to the cavity in the mold, resulting in a hollowcast figure. A good caster (Barclay had 40 at its peak) could turn out 2 gross an hour.

Later, about 1940, injection molds came into use. With these, a piston would push lead up into the automatically water-cooled mold and then suck most of it back out.

The day for most Barclay workers began at 8 a.m. (there was only one shift, ending at 4:45), with the lead pots lit two hours earlier, to insure their being ready when the casters arrived.

None of the excess lead was wasted. Flashing from the soldiers and excess from the dies went down a chute, onto a belt, and into a large remelting pot. Soldiers which had lost their sales value, such as the American Legionaires made for the large 1937 convention, were also melted down. Initially, pots were ladled from when casting was done, but later a faucet was used, with a flame kept on the pipe to keep it running. If a representative soldier from a batch weighed too much, the entire lot would go into the remelt pot, since anything above a certain weight would cause the company to lose money.

The slush molds quickly became too hot, and every three or four castings they'd have to be dipped in water, to cool them. Until die-casting machines came in, the flash was cleaned off with a knife, on a piece-work basis. With the introduction of die-casting (the first die-cast toy was a cannon, about 1934 or 1935), the soldiers were trimmed automatically in the die, with the trimmings dropping out on the other side of the mold. Once cleaned, the soldiers were painted.

The base coat was usually applied by laying the soldier face up on a two-foot square screen. This was brought into the spray booth, where the figures were sprayed with a quick-drying lacquer (usually the basic khaki color). They were than placed in a rack and taken out so girls could turn them over. The tray was returned to the painters, who would spray the unfinished side.

For a period in the late 1930s, dipping the soldiers in a base coat was tried. The soldiers had a clamp attached to their base and then were moved via a chain through the tub of paint, where they were fully immersed. However, the process wasted paint, as the lacquer in the tub dried too quickly, so the company returned to spraying. Even spraying had to be done quickly, with a rack of figures being completed in five or ten minutes, because the lacquer dried so quickly.

Finishing touches were added by women, and in the early years the factory used a table that revolved by hand. Later a conveyor belt was designed, and women would sit alongside the slow-moving belt, one painting the face and other flesh parts, another the green stand, another the rifle,etc. For many of the years, two sisters, Josephine and Mary Como, did the intricate work, such as the eyes.

After the toys dried, they were packed. The drying, which was usually done by air, would take about an hour. Moved to the shipping department, each soldier was individually wrapped in tissue, twelve to twenty-four to a box, then put in a flat truck and numbered for the stock bin. Mounted figures were placed in special cardboard crates and slid into the openings. Stores the toys were shipped to included Woolworth's, Kresge's, Lamston, Kress, E. C. Murphy, Ben Franklin Stores, Sears-Roebuck, W. T. Grant.

Barclay was a patriarchy, with all that implies, both good and bad. For some it was wholly good. There are memories of "a pleasant atmosphere. . . all the workers shared the sense of being one family – from the office to the factory and even to the maintenance men". On the other hand, workers who'd been with the company for decades received nothing in settlement pay or pensions when they were let go.

In the early days, many of Barclay's workers began at the age of fourteen, getting around the educational process by applying for their working papers and going to something called "continuation school," which meant turning up for classes just one day a week. Probably one of the reasons so many children were employed in the 1920s and early 1930s is because the wages then were too low for an adult to make a living. In 1928 the pay rate was 21 cents an hour. In 1933, just before the NRA took effect, pay was still only 25 cents per hour, or $10 a week. In addition to the NRA's raising the wage rate, there was a strike around 1938, which presumably pushed wages upward. (In 1938 a "B. Bogaty – Lead Toys" company at 34 Montgomery Street in Jersey City was listed with a workforce of three men. This was a subsidiary of Barclay, owned by Michael Levy – Bogaty was the original family name – and may have been set up in case of a long strike at the main plant.)

Some of the products Barclay sold were made outside the company. These included the mess tables, benches, stretchers and tents. The latter were sewn by neighborhood housewives, working in their homes.

Then on April 1, 1942, all production stopped, due to the War. Four workers were retained, the machine shop was expanded, and sub-contracting for companies involved in defense work was begun.

Production resumed in late 1945, but the company was never as successful after the War. Although a 1946-47 directory lists Barclay as employing 150 male and 126 female employees, there was gradual attrition. Warlike toys were no longer in vogue, and nothing the company tried could pick up the slack. In addition lead was becoming expensive, the company now had a union, and children could no longer be hired at the age of fourteen. Furthermore, competition from plastic became more and more of a force.

Then, too, Michael Levy had grown old, and was no longer the spark plug he had been. In 1961, his son-in-law, Stanley Goldsmith, joined the company, and on Levy's death in 1964, Goldsmith took over the reins. He made some innovations, painting the soldiers' uniforms a contemporary green, and introduced bottle-shaped blister packs for Barclay's line of vehicles and pressure-sensitive labels that enabled the company's trucks, etc. to have various insignia and brand names. It was Goldsmith, too, who got Sears to carry the line. He gave the company a sense of history for the first time, but got it wrong by a year or two, having some boxes stamped "Since 1925". But none of it was enough, and in 1971 Barclay went out of business, its workforce now down to 50-75 people.

Barclay moved a number of times. In 1927, it was still situated on Barclay Street, but now it was called 10th Street. About 1930 it was on Paterson Plank Road, around 12th or 13th streets. From at least 1931-1935 the address was 934-940 Hoboken Street in North Bergen, and from 1935 through 1946 or 1947 701-723 West 9th Street in West New York (a reorganization of the streets changed the address to 567 52nd Street – this was about 1941). In 1947 Barclay made its final move, to 316 Palisade Avenue, Union City, which stood empty from 1971 till it was torn down in 1982.

Barclay numbered its soldiers and issued illustrated catalogs or order sheets from the beginning, but until recently none of the pre-War ones could be found. Then, in the fall of 1984, it was discovered that Stanley Goldsmith had retained some of Barclay's illustrated order sheets, circa 1935-1938, establishing the numbering of almost the entire line of Barclay soldiers, and furnishing Barclay's own descriptions for many of them. Thus, all bold words and numbers are Barclay's own description. In addition some figures (mainly the early ones) are listed with a question mark after the number. These are based on the memory of longtime Barclay employee George Fall, whose recall, measured against known Barclay numbers, is usually accurate, but not infallible. All short stride soldiers have tin helmets.

B81   B81A

B83a
Courtesy Vinny Pugliese

L to R: B1-A, B1
Courtesy K. Warren Mitchell

B135a   B135
(shown here without skis)
Courtesy K. Warren Mitchell

B46   B46a

Variations noticed by Gordon Gee. The figure at left has a wider face and a pronounced right breast pocket. The pocket on the B46a is very faint. Gee also reports these soldiers were painted in at least four shades and colors: bright yellow, two mustard yellow shades, yellow-orange. Photo by Gordon Gee.

EARLY BARCLAYS

EB1 through EB20 have been confirmed as Barclays by Frank Helm, who worked at Barclay on and off from 1928. He believes they were the "first batch" of soldiers produced by Barclay, and their general crudeness suggests this is so. They seem to have been produced through at least 1931. They are about 2½" high, the same height J. Edward Jones noted for Barclays in an April, 1930 report.

2B1 through 2B21 have been confirmed as Barclays via a Barclay printing block which shows 2B19, 2B21, 2B11, and 2B10, as well as Bh. The others in this series have been agreed to by knowledgeable collectors as belonging to this group because of paint, sculpting and bases. They are about 54mm high.

	G	VG	M		G	VG	M
(EB1) Drummer	7.50	11.00	15.00	(2B11) Charging Soldier ...	8.00	12.00	16.00
(EB2) Fifer	7.50	11.00	15.00	(2B12) Machine Gunner ...	8.00	12.00	16.00
(EB3) Bugler	7.50	11.00	15.00	(2B13) Grenade Thrower ..	8.00	12.00	16.00
(EB4) Marching at slope				(2B14) Attention, right			
arms	8.00	12.00	16.00	shoulder arms	8.00	12.00	16.00
(EB5) Officer	6.00	9.00	12.00	(2B15) Sailor at Attention .	7.00	11.00	14.00
(EB6) At the Ready	7.50	11.00	15.00	(2B16) Marine at Port Arms	7.00	11.00	14.00
(EB7) Kneeling, firing	10.00	15.00	20.00	(2B17) Flag Bearer, flag at			
(EB8) Seated Machine Gun-				soldier's left	8.00	12.00	16.00
ner	9.00	13.00	18.00	(2B18) Officer Saluting	7.00	11.00	14.00
(EB9) Cadet marching at				(2B19) Indian, tomahawk in			
slope	7.00	11.00	14.00	left hand	6.00	9.00	12.00
(EB10) (Unused)				(2B20) Standing firing,			
(EB11) Marching at slope,				thicker-looking	8.00	12.00	16.00
foreign helmet	8.00	12.00	16.00	(2B21) Cowboy firing pistol,			
(EB12) Highlander, marching	8.00	12.00	16.00	right arm at waist	6.00	9.00	12.00
(EB13) Mountie	8.00	12.00	16.00				
(EB14) Cowboy firing	6.00	9.00	12.00				
(EB15) Sailor marching at							
slope	7.00	10.00	14.00				
(EB16) Marine marching at							
slope	9.00	13.00	18.00				
(EB17) Indian with Bow ...	6.00	9.00	12.00				
(EB18) Flagbearer	7.50	11.00	15.00				
(EB19) Doughboy, advanc-							
ing with rifle at upward							
angle (not shown)	7.00	11.00	14.00				
(EB20) Cadet marching, rifle							
held out front at angle ..	7.00	11.00	14.00				

EB1 EB2 EB3 EB4 EB5 EB6 EB7

EARLY BARCLAYS · SECOND SERIES

	G	VG	M
(2B1) Cowboy firing pistol,			
right arm high	6.00	9.00	12.00
(2B2) Cadet	7.00	11.00	14.00
(2B3) Bugler	7.00	11.00	14.00
(2B4) Sailor	7.00	11.00	14.00
(2B5) Officer	7.00	11.00	14.00
(2B6) Marine	7.00	11.00	14.00
(2B7) Marine Officer	7.00	11.00	14.00
(2B8) Marching Soldier	6.00	9.00	12.00
(2B9) Flagbearer, flag at			
soldier's right	8.00	12.00	16.00
(2B10) Standing firing, finer			
modeling	8.00	12.00	16.00

EB8 EB9 EB11 EB12 EB13 EB14 EB15
Photo by Ed Poole

EB16

EB17
Photo by Bill Kaufman

EB18
Courtesy Charlie Breslow

EB20
Courtesy Charlie Breslow

2B21

Top, L to R: 2B1 through 2B12 Bottom, L to R: 2B13 through 2B20, Bh
Photo by Ed Poole

PRE-1934

(All bold words and numbers are **Barclay's Own Description.**
Words in quotes are either descriptions from general catalogs,
which sometimes, but not always, were Barclay's own description or later Barclay catalog descriptions applied to earlier
figures that were similar.)

	G	VG	M
(Ba) 87? Mounted Officer, moving arm holding sword, on rearing horse .	25.00	38.00	50.00
(Baa) 87? Same as above on cantering horse	25.00	38.00	50.00
(Bb) 87? Mounted Officer, moving arm holding bugle, on rearing horse . .	25.00	38.00	50.00
(Bba) 87? Same as above, on cantering horse	25.00	38.00	50.00
(Bc) 87? Mounted Officer, moving arm holding pistol on cantering horse	32.00	48.00	64.00
(Bd) 88? Mounted Cowboy with lasso, none known .	No Price Found		
(Be) 89? Mounted Indian, moving arm holding rifle	40.00	60.00	80.00
(BeA) Same as above, holding pistol	40.00	60.00	80.00
(Bf) 90? Mounted Cowboy with pistol	40.00	60.00	80.00
(BfA) 90? Mounted Cowboy with moving arm, holding rifle (horse's tail missing in photo)	35.00	53.00	70.00
(Bfa) Indian chief on foot, 54mm high, blue and red-striped headdress, may look like Christie's I-14 . .	No Price Found		

	G	VG	M
(Bfb) Indian brave on foot, 54mm high, carrying rifle across stomach	No Price Found		
(Bg) 186? Cavalryman mounted, 2¾" high, no moving parts, modeled on French toy soldier, circa late 1920s-early 30s	11.00	16.00	22.00
(Bh) **486 Cavalryman,** approx. 2¼" high, circa early 30s, no moving parts .	10.00	15.00	21.00
(Bi) Baseball fielder, approx. 1⅞" high, circa 1920s . . .	42.00	63.00	85.00
(Bj) Baseball pitcher, circa 1920s	42.00	63.00	85.00
(Bk) Baseball batter, circa 1920s	42.00	63.00	85.00
(Bl) Mounted Indian on rearing horse (may not be Barclay	15.00	23.00	30.00
(Bm) **200 Jockey on Horse**	17.00	25.00	34.00
(Bn) **No. 87 Officer on Horse,** smaller size, circa 1931 (5 known), horses came brown, black and gray	No Price Found		
(BA) Paint Your Own Army Set No. 2003, circa 1934, boxed	125.00	188.00	250.00
(BAa) Paint Your Own Army Set No. 2003, larger size than above, same toys, with compartment for one more toy, only one known	No Price Found		

Ba   Baa   Bb   Bba   Bc

Be   BfA   Bg   Bh

1935 and After

	G	VG	M
(BAC) 89 Indian on Horse (on catalog sheet with Ethiopians)	17.00	26.00	35.00
(BAD) 90 Cowboy on Horse (on catalog sheet with Ethiopians)	17.00	26.00	35.00
(B1) 89 Indian on Horse ...	12.00	18.00	24.00
(B1-A) As above, Indian's head turned toward his right	No Price Found		
(B1a) 89 Indian on Horse two feathers (earlier)	22.00	33.00	44.00
(B1b) As above, small saddle, **Note: Some 90 Cowboys are marked "99"**	22.00	33.00	44.00
(B2) 90 Cowboy on Horse	12.00	18.00	24.00
(B2A) 90 Cowboy on Horse, variation, thinner bullets in gunbelt, saddle not as long	12.00	18.00	25.00
(B2AA) 90 Cowboy on Horse, variation, no bullets in gunbelt	No Price Found		
(B2AAA) 100 Masked Rider on Horse (may not have been produced; in the order sheet the figure faces forward)	No Price Found		

Bf
Courtesy Bill Conover

	G	VG	M
(B2B) 100? Masked Rider on Horse, horse's tail down .	21.00	32.00	42.00
(B2C) 100? Masked Rider on Horse, horse's tail up ...	18.00	27.00	36.00

BARCLAY

Bi   Bj   Bk

Bl   Bm

	G	VG	M
(B3) 187? Mounted, in grey, cap, intermediate size....	37.00	53.00	75.00
(B3A) **87 Officer on Horse,** in cap, khaki or grey, larger black, grey or brown horse..........	14.00	21.00	28.00
(B4) 87? Mounted in colored jacket and cap, may be Chinese or Japanese (horse's tail missing in photo)	19.00	28.00	38.00
(B5) **701 Flagbearer,** tin helmet, short stride......	11.00	17.00	22.00
(B6) **701 Flagbearer,** tin helmet, long stride......	7.00	11.00	15.00
(B7) **701** Flagbearer, cast helmet	8.00	12.00	16.00
(B8 **701** Flagbearer, Cuban flag variation painted for 10 Woolworth's in Cuba, cast helmet or pot helmet.	No Price Found		
(B9) **702 Machine-Gunner,** kneeling, short stride....	7.00	11.00	15.00
(B10) **702 Machine-Gunner,** kneeling, long stride.....	9.00	14.00	18.00
(B11) **702** Machine-Gunner, kneeling, cast helmet....	10.00	15.00	20.00
(B12) **703 Sniper,** kneeling, firing, short stride.......	7.00	11.00	14.00
(B12A) 703 Sniper, kneeling, firing, short stride, shorter rifle, in front of fingers fat portion of gun and thin portion of barrel about equal length..........	7.00	14.00	18.00

	G	VG	M
(B13) **703 Sniper,** kneeling, firing, long stride, tin helmet	10.00	15.00	20.00
(B14) **704 Soldier on Parade,** shoulder arms, short stride	7.00	11.00	15.00
(B15) **704 Soldier on Parade,** shoulder arms, long stride, tin helmet	8.00	13.00	17.00
(B16) **705 Soldier at Attention** (actually port arms)..	11.00	16.00	21.00
(B17) **705** Soldier at Attention (actually port arms), cast helmet............	10.00	15.00	20.00
(B18) **706 Soldier, charging,** ,short stride............	7.00	11.00	15.00
B18a) Same as above, with shorter rifle, sling around hand, slightly larger, one known	No Price Found		
(B19) **706** Tall, tin helmet, solid puttees, only 4 known................	300.00	450.00	600.00
(B20) **706** Soldier, charging, tin helmet, long stride...	50.00	75.00	100.00
(B21) **706** Soldier, charging, cast helmet............	11.00	17.00	22.00
(B22) **707** At Attention, cast helmet	9.00	14.00	19.00
(B23) **708 Officer** with sword, short stride......	12.00	18.00	24.00
(B24) **723 Marine Officer,** same as above, in blue...	14.00	21.00	28.00
(B25) **708 Officer,** with sword, tin helmet, long stride	9.00	14.00	18.00
(B25a) 708 Officer with sword, tin helmet, long stride, no chest strap....	60.00	90.00	120.00
(B25b) 723 Marine Officer with sword, tin helmet, long stride, no chest strap, in blue................	60.00	90.00	120.00
(B26) **723 Marine Officer,** with sword, tin helmet, long stride............	17.00	26.00	35.00
(B27) **708** Officer with sword, cast helmet......	25.00	38.00	50.00
(B28) **708** Marine Officer with sword, cast helmet..	27.00	41.00	55.00
(B29) **709 Bugler,** short stride	12.00	18.00	24.00
(B30) **709 Bugler,** long stride, tin helmet.......	8.00	12.00	16.00

BAC   BAD   B1   B1a

B2   B2A   B2AA

BA
Photo by Perry R. Eichor

Bn. Officer's jacket is light blue, pants red. Horses have been found in brown, black and gray.
Courtesy Bill O'Brien

Judging by the mold variations found, Barclay's B81 Doctor must have been a popular figure. Number 1 has very thick flat-bottomed base. Number 2 seems to be B81b. Numbers 3 and 4 each have "Made U.S.A." stamped on their belt backs, but there is a variation in the spacing of the words. Number 3 is also entirely missing the left crease on his back. Doctor 5 has a larger hat. Courtesy Ron Hillman - *Old Toy Soldier Magazine*

BARCLAY

B2B   B3   B3A   B4

B5   B6   B7   B9   B10   B11

B12   B13   B14   B15   B16

B12   B12A

Photo by K. Warren Mitchell

63

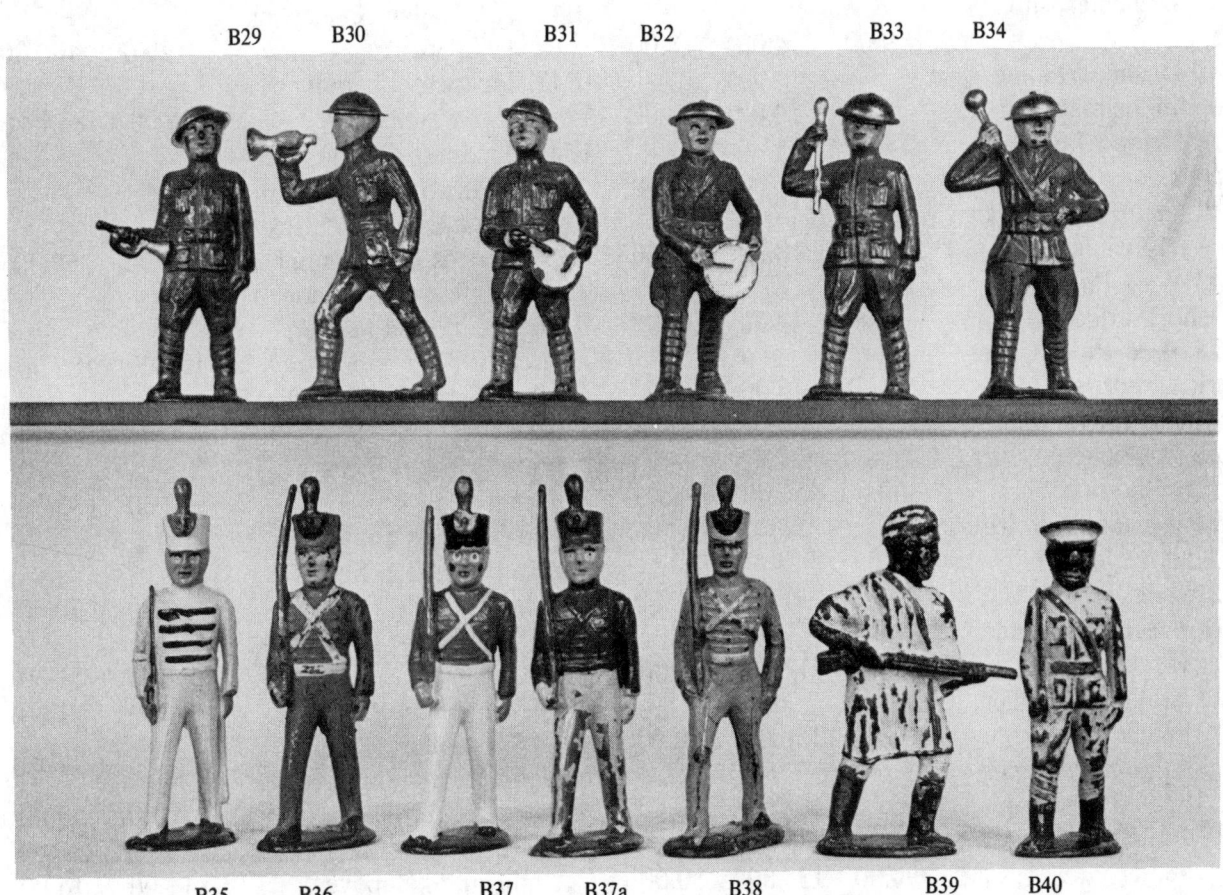

B17   B18   B18a   B19   B20   B21

B22   B23   B24   B25   B25a   B25b B26   B27 B28

B18a courtesy Don Pielin

B29   B30   B31   B32   B33   B34

B35   B36   B37   B37a   B38   B39   B40

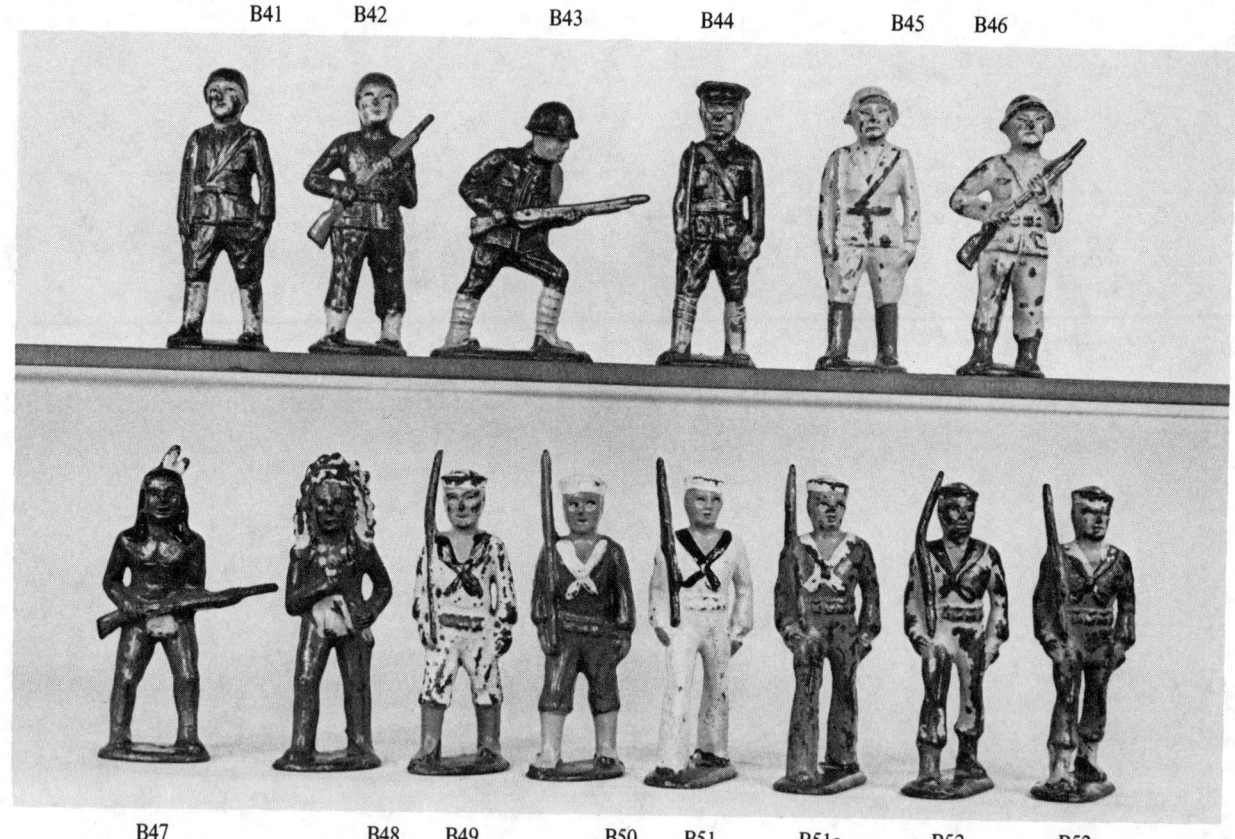

B41 B42 B43 B44 B45 B46

B47 B48 B49 B50 B51 B51a B52 B52a

	G	VG	M
(B31) **710 Drummer,** short stride	9.00	14.00	18.00
(B32) **710 Drummer,** long stride, tin helmet	9.00	14.00	18.00
(B33) **711 Drum Major,** short stride	11.00	17.00	22.00
(B34) **711** Drum Major, long stride, tin helmet	12.00	18.00	24.00
(B35) **743 West Point Officer,** short stride	8.00	12.00	16.00
(B36) **718 West Point Cadet** with rifle, short stride	10.00	15.00	20.00
(B37) Same as above, but painted as wooden soldier, only three known	300.00	450.00	600.00
(B37a) Same as above, with line-and-dot eyes, white pants, white gloves	10.00	15.00	20.00
(B38) **718 West Point Cadet,** long stride	8.00	12.00	16.00
(B39) **724 Ethiopian Soldier,** circa 1935-36	100.00	150.00	200.00
(B40) **725 Ethiopian Officer,** circa 1935-36	105.00	108.00	210.00
(B41) **727 Italian Officer,** circa 1935-36	90.00	135.00	180.00

	G	VG	M
(B42) **726 Italian Soldier,** circa 1935-36, ...	120.00	180.00	240.00
(B43) Japanese, charging with rifle, circa 1937	50.00	83.00	110.00
(B44) Japanese Officer circa 1937 (this is the original barefoot Ethopian officer, painted as a Japanese) . .	110.00	165.00	220.00
(B45) Chinese or Mongolian Officer in steel helmet, circa 1937	125.00	188.00	250.00
(B46) Chinese or Mongolian rifleman, circa 1937, pronounced right breast pocket	90.00	135.00	180.00
(B46a) Same as above, narrower face, faint right breast pocket	60.00	90.00	120.00
(B47) **717 Indian Brave,** rifle across waist	7.00	11.00	15.00
(B48) **716 Indian Chief**	7.00	11.00	14.00
(B49) **719 Sailor White Uniform,** marching, short stride	10.00	15.00	20.00
(B50) **720 Sailor Blue Uniform,** like above.	11.00	16.00	22.00
(B51) **719** Sailor White Uniform, long stride, bell bottoms	7.00	11.00	14.00

BARCLAY

B54a
Photo by Stan Alekna

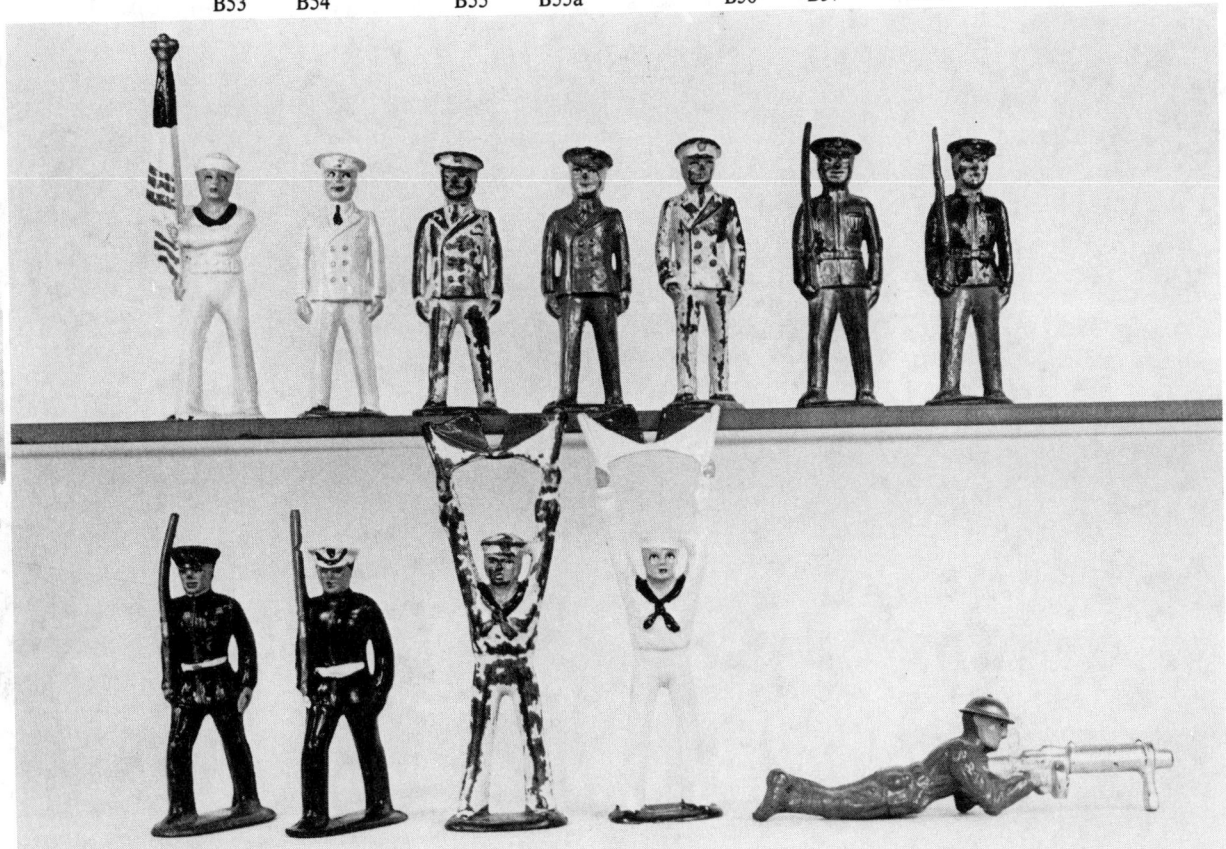

B53 B54 B55 B55a B56 B57 B58

B59 B59a B60 B60a B61

	G	VG	M
(B51a) 720 Sailor in Blue Uniform, long stride, bell bottoms	12.00	18.00	25.00
(B52) **719 Sailor in White Uniform,** in puttees	7.00	11.00	14.00
(B52a) **720 Sailor Blue Uniform,** in puttees	8.00	12.00	16.00
(B53) **756 Sailor, Flagbearer,** long stride	11.00	17.00	22.00
(B54) **721 Naval Officer,** short stride, tin top to cap	45.00	68.00	90.00
(B54a) Same as above, in blue	50.00	75.00	100.00
(B55) **721 Naval Officer,** short stride	11.00	17.00	23.00
(B55a) 721 Naval Officer, same as above, in blue . . .	100.00	150.00	200.00
(B56) **721 Naval Officer,** long stride	8.00	12.00	16.00
(B57) **722 Marine,** short stride, tin top to cap	45.00	68.00	90.00
(B58) **722 Marine,** short stride	11.00	17.00	22.00
(B59) **722 Marine,** long stride	8.00	12.00	16.00
(B59a) 722 Marine, long stride, white cap (probably post-War)	17.00	26.00	34.00

	G	VG	M
(B60) **757 Sailor with Signal Flags**	12.00	18.00	24.00
(B60a) 757 Sailor with Signal Flags, flat underbase, minor variation in cap . . .	13.00	19.00	27.00
(B61) **728 Machine Gunner Lying Flat**	8.00	12.00	16.00
(B62) **728 Machine Gunner** Lying Flat, cast helmet . . .	12.00	18.00	24.00
(B63) **728 Machine Gunner** Lying Flat, cast helmet, lip of base extends under gun barrel	7.00	11.00	15.00
(B64) **750 Soldier, Crawling** .	10.00	15.00	21.00
(B65) **730 Soldier Signal Man with Flag**	10.00	15.00	21.00
(B66) **731 Soldier Pigeon Dispatcher**	9.00	14.00	18.00
(B67) **732 Soldier Telephone Operator**	7.00	11.00	15.00
(B68) **733 Soldier Bullet Feeder** (actually a shell) . .	7.00	11.00	14.00
(B69) **734 Soldier Ammunition Carrier**	8.00	12.00	16.00
(B70) **735 Soldier Range Finder**	7.00	11.00	15.00
(B71) **736 Soldier Sentry**	7.00	11.00	15.00

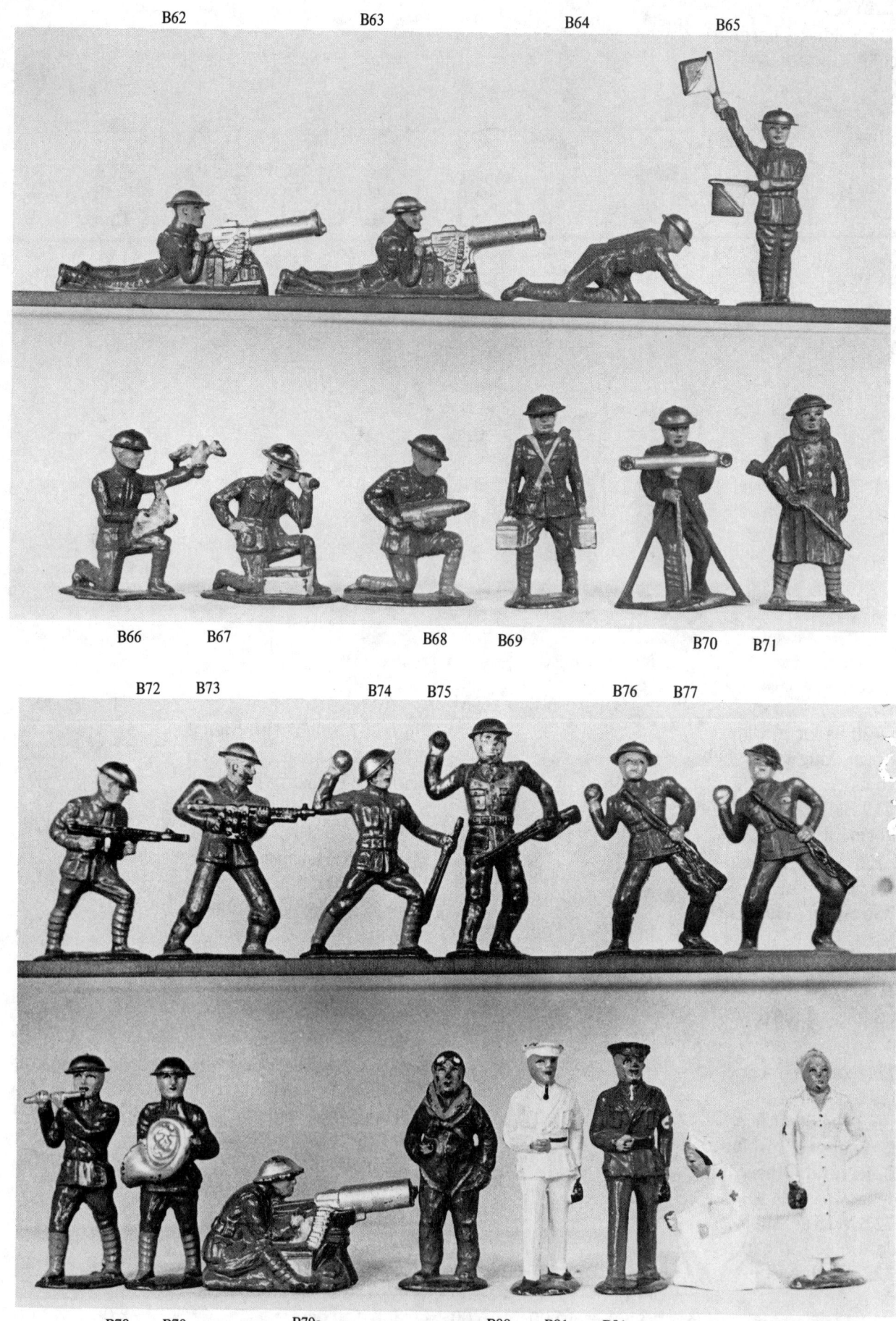

B62 B63 B64 B65

B66 B67 B68 B69 B70 B71

B72 B73 B74 B75 B76 B77

B78 B79 B79a B80 B81 B81a B82 B83

BARCLAY	G	VG	M
(B72) **737 Soldier Charging Machine Gunner,** tin helmet	6.00	9.00	13.00
(B73) **737 Soldier Charging Machine Gunner,** cast helmet	13.00	20.00	26.00
(B74) **738 Soldier Bomb Thrower**	7.00	11.00	15.00
(B75) **738** Soldier Bomb Thrower, tall, tin helmet, solid puttees	300.00	450.00	600.00
(B76) **738** Soldier Bomb Thrower, rifle off ground, tin helmet	11.00	17.00	22.00
(B77) **738**Soldier Bomb Thrower, rifle off ground, cast helmet	10.00	15.00	21.00
(B78) **739 Soldier Fifer,**	10.00	15.00	20.00
(B79) **740 Soldier French Horn**	8.00	12.00	17.00
(B79a) Machine Gunner, seated, cast helmet, bandage-type puttees	13.00	20.00	27.00
(B80) **741 Aviator**	8.00	12.00	17.00
(B81) **745 Navy Doctor,** in white, flat under base . . .	9.00	13.00	18.00
(B81a) **746 Army Doctor,** in brown, flat underbase . . .	9.00	13.00	18.00

	G	VG	M
(B81A&B) **746** Doctor, as above, inverted base, first version?	11.00	17.00	22.00
(B82) **767 Nurse,** kneeling . .	11.00	17.00	22.00
(B83) **744 Nurse,** hand on hip	7.00	11.00	15.00
(83a) Same as above, in blue	50.00	75.00	100.00
(B84) **751 Soldier, Sharp-shooter,** Prone Position .	10.00	15.00	20.00
(B85) **762 Wounded,** sitting, arm in sling	9.00	14.00	19.00
(B86) **707 Sharpshooter,** standing, firing, short stride	9.00	13.00	18.00
(B87) **747 Sharpshooter,** standing, firing, long stride	8.00	12.00	16.00
(B88) **747** Sharpshooter, standing, firing, cast helmet	9.00	14.00	18.00
(B89) **748 Soldier, Running,** with rifle, tin helmet	8.00	12.00	16.00
(B90) **748** Soldier, Running, with rifle, cast helmet	11.00	16.00	22.00
(B91) **749 Soldier, Gas Mask,** charging with rifle	8.00	12.00	16.00
(B92) **749** Soldier, Gas Mask, charging with rifle, cast helmet	13.00	20.00	26.00

B84 B85 B86 B87 B88

B89 B90 B91 B92

B93 B93b B93c

B93d B93A B93B

	G	VG	M
(B93) 310 Army Motorcyclist	20.00	30.00	40.00
(B93a) 310 Cop on motorcycle	20.00	30.00	40.00
(B93b) 310 Motorcyclist, head higher	20.00	30.00	40.00
(B93c) 310 Cop on motorcycle, head lower	20.00	30.00	40.00
B93d) 310 Motorcyclist, larger, markings on cycle like B93A and B93B but cruder	25.00	38.00	50.00
(B93A) 310 Army Motorcyclist, post-War, dot eyes, or none at all, larger, motor variation	25.00	38.00	50.00
(B93B) 310 Cop on Motorcycle, post-War, dot eyes, or none at all, larger, motor variation	22.00	33.00	45.00
(B94) 715 Cowboy with tin hat brim	5.00	8.00	11.00
(B95) 752 Cowboy with lasso	7.00	11.00	14.00
(B95A) 752 Masked Cowboy with lasso	8.00	12.00	16.00
(B95a) 752 Cowboy with lasso, Post-WWII version, lasso goes directly through hands	7.00	11.00	14.00
(B96) 753 Cowboy With Two Guns, pointing one	8.00	12.00	16.00

	G	VG	M
(B97) 754 Indian Chief, tomahawk and shield	5.00	8.00	10.00
(B97a) Same as above, flat base	5.00	8.00	10.00
(B98) 755 Indian, Bow and Arrow	5.00	8.00	10.00
(B99) 756 Indian Chief, long headdress, may only have been produced post-WW II	36.00	54.00	72.00
(B100) 757 Indian Brave, standing with bow and arrow, may only have been produced post WW II	11.00	16.00	22.00
(B101) 758 Camera Man, kneeling, tin helmet	15.00	23.00	30.00
(B102) 759 Soldier, Stretcher Bearer, open hand	36.00	54.00	72.00
(B102a) 759 Soldier, Stretcher Bearer, closed hand	8.00	12.00	16.00
(B103) 760 Surgeon, with stethoscope	10.00	15.00	21.00
(B104) 761 "Wounded", tin helmet	7.00	11.00	14.00
(B105) 763 Raiding, in crouch, tin helmet	8.00	12.00	16.00
(B106) 764 Advance, raised rifle, tin helmet	11.00	17.00	23.00
(B107) 765 Bayoneting, although no bayonet, thrusting with gun muzzle; tin helmet	20.00	30.00	40.00

BARCLAY

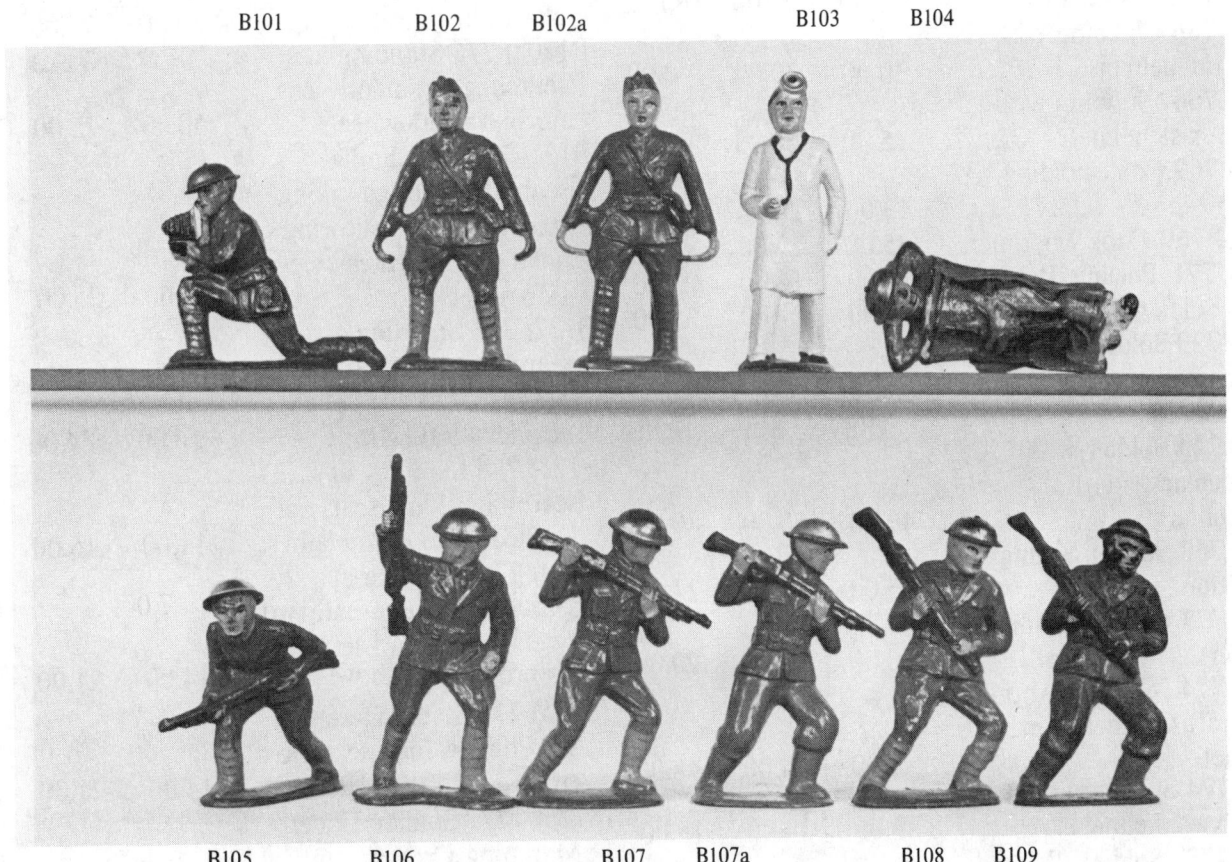

B94 B95 B95A B95a B96

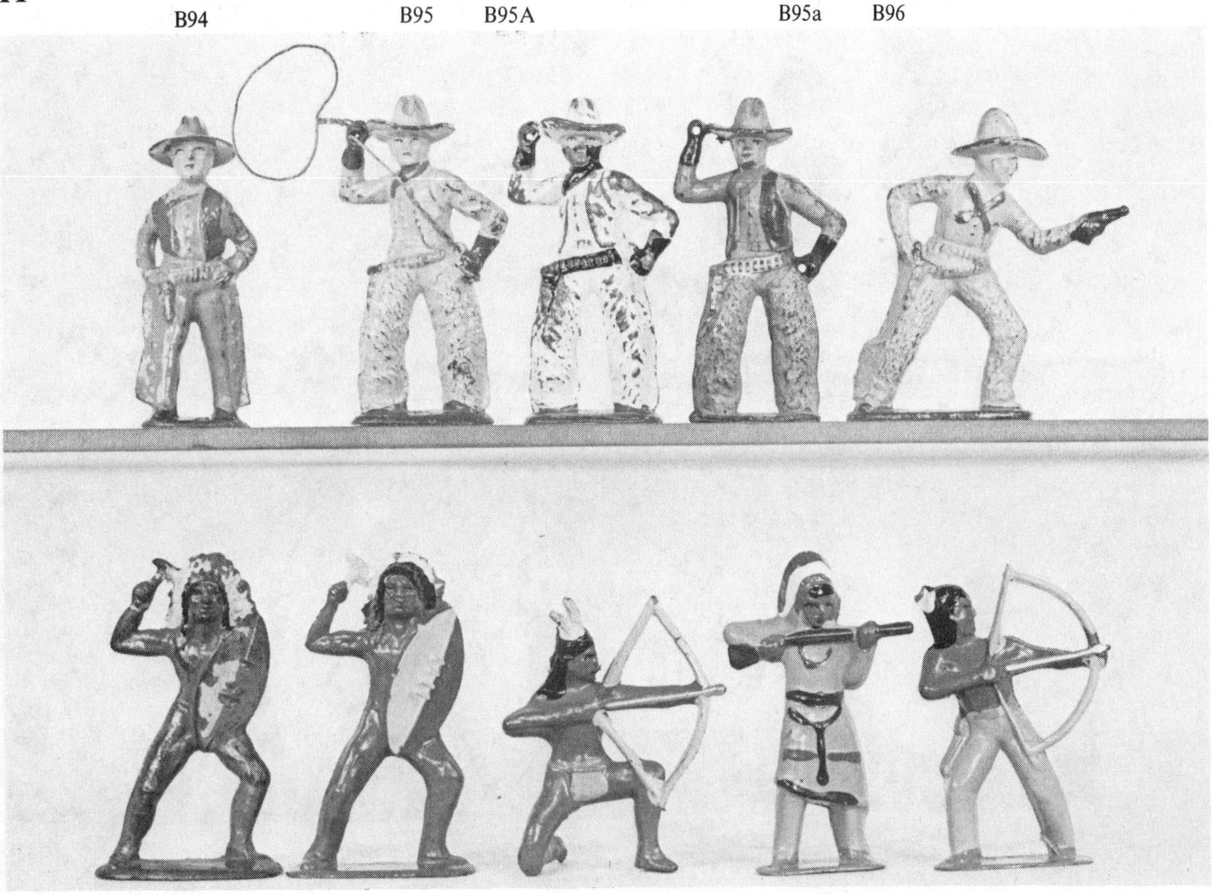

B97 B97a B98 B99 B100

B101 B102 B102a B103 B104

B105 B106 B107 B107a B108 B109

B110 B110a B111 B112 B113

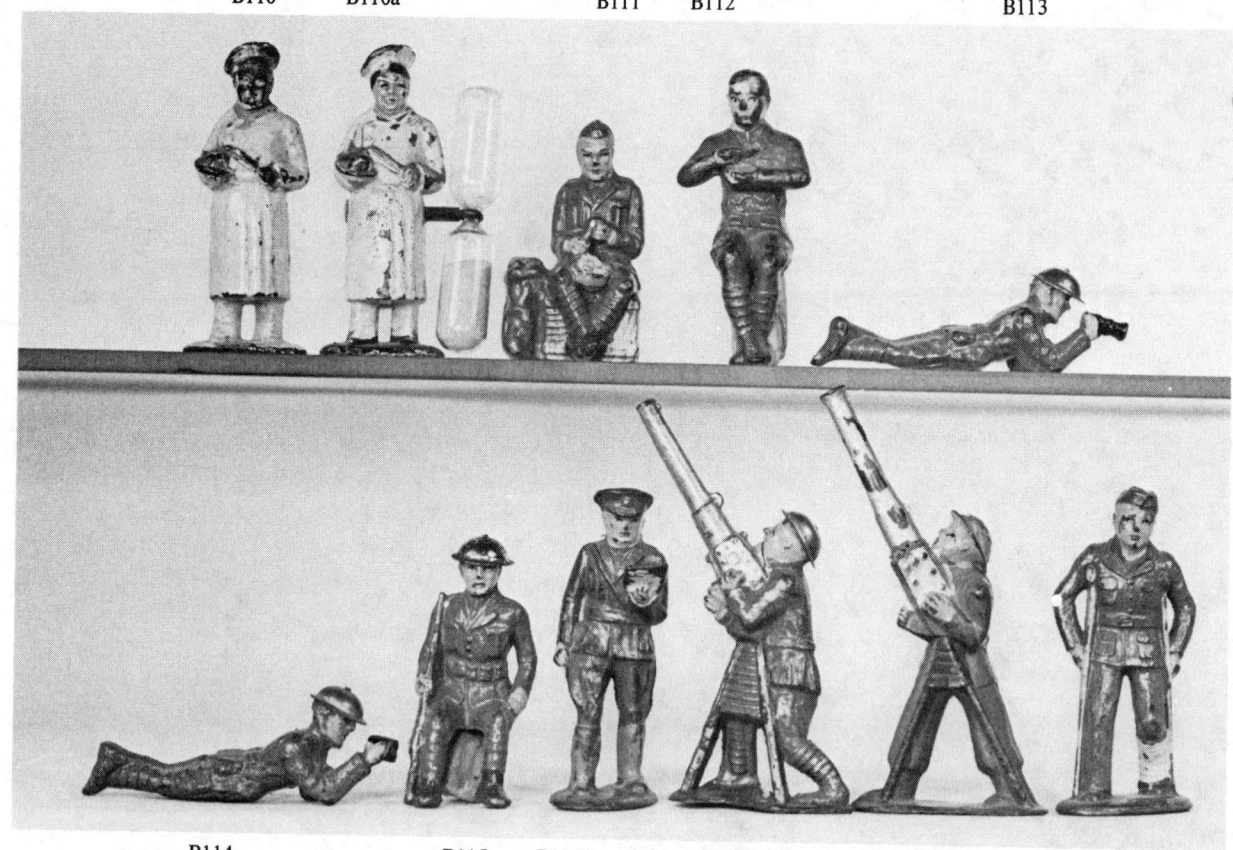

B114 B115 B116 B117 B118 B119

	G	VG	M
(B107a) **765** Bayoneting, same as above, no bayonet, cast helmet.....	80.00	120.00	160.00
(B108) **766 Clubbing** with rifle, tin helmet.........	20.00	30.00	40.00
(B109) **766** Clubbing with rifle, cast helmet........	45.00	68.00	90.00
(B110) **769 Cook** holding roast	13.00	20.00	26.00
(B110a) 769 Cook egg-timer.	35.00	52.00	70.00
(B111) **771 Peeling Potatoes**	11.00	16.00	22.00
(B112) Soldier eating.......	17.00	27.00	35.00
(B113) 729 Soldier with Binoculars, long binoculars	9.00	14.00	18.00
(B114) **729 Soldier with Binoculars**, short binoculars	40.00	60.00	80.00
(B115) **760 Soldier Sitting Position**	13.00	20.00	27.00
(B116) **773 Officer Reading Orders**..............	10.00	15.00	20.00
(B117) **774** "Soldier, Anti-Aircraft Gunner", tin helmet	9.00	14.00	18.00
(B118) **774** Soldier with AA gun, cast helmet........	9.00	14.00	18.00
(B119) **775** "Soldier, Wounded, with crutches"	10.00	16.00	21.00

	G	VG	M
(B120) **776** Standing at searchlight, smooth lens, elevation wheel.........	50.00	75.00	100.00
(B120a) **776** Standing at searchlight, smooth lens, no elevation wheel......	50.00	75.00	100.00
(B121) **776** Standing at searchlight, ridges along base (this and following have ridged lenses), elevation wheel)	17.00	25.00	34.00
(B122) **776** Standing at searchlight, smooth base connected to searchlight, no elevation wheel......	16.00	24.00	32.00
(B123) **776** Standing at searchlight, low seat, not connected to searchlight..	11.00	16.00	22.00
(B124) **776** Standing at searchlight, high seat, two rivets in front of left foot, no projection above lens	14.00	21.00	28.00
(B125) **776** Standing at searchlight, high seat, no rivets in front of left foot.	14.00	21.00	28.00
(B126) 777 "Soldier Under Marching Orders", tin helmet	8.00	12.00	16.00

71

BARCLAY

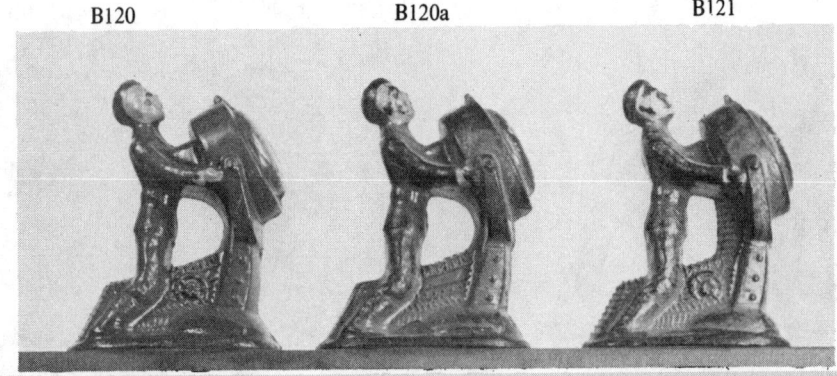

B120   B120a   B121

B122   B123   B124   B125

B126   B127   B128   B129   B130

	G	VG	M		G	VG	M
(B127) **777** Marching with pack, cast helmet.......	7.00	11.00	14.00	(B135) **785** Skier in white, cast helmet, 1940, with separate metal skis. (Meant to be Finn), no left breast pocket	12.00	19.00	25.00
(B128) **778** Officer with gas mask, cast helmet.......	10.00	15.00	20.00				
(B129) **779** Firing from behind wall, cast helmet..	30.00	45.00	60.00				
(B130) **780** Falling with rifle, cast helmet...........	16.00	24.00	32.00	(B135a) as above, has left breast pocket. Same value as above.			
(B131) **781** Digging, cast helmet..............	22.00	33.00	45.00	(B136) **785** Skier in white, no skis	9.00	14.00	18.00
(B132) **782** Leaning out, with field phone, antenna, cast helmet...........	31.00	46.00	62.00	(B137) **785** Skier in brown, no skis	26.00	34.00	52.00
(B133) **783** Crouching with binoculars, cast helmet...	16.00	24.00	32.00	(B138) **785** Skier in red, meant to be Russian, may not have been produced (listing based on memory)	No Price Found		
(B134) **784** Parachutist landing	10.00	15.00	20.00	(B139) **787** Diver with axe..	350.00	525.00	700.00

B131 B132 B133 B134 B135

B136 B137 B139 B140 B141

B142 B143 B144 B145

	G	VG	M
(B140) **788** "Soldier, marching with gun on back", cast helmet	7.00	11.00	14.00
(B141) **789** Soldier with AA gun, cast helmet, sitting .	10.00	16.00	21.00
(B142) **790** Two soldiers on raft, cast helmet.	30.00	45.00	60.00
(B143) **791** Two-man rocket team	11.00	17.00	22.00
(B144) **792** Mechanic with airplane engine, prop spins, brace on back of engine bulges.	17.00	26.00	34.00
(B144a) Same as above, brace on back of engine doesn't bulge.	17.00	26.00	34.00

	G	VG	M
(B145) Soldier kneeling with anti-tank gun, cast helmet	12.00	19.00	25.00
(B146) **960 Surgeon and Soldier**	50.00	75.00	100.00
(B147) **951 Soldier Wireless Operator**	15.00	23.00	31.00
(B148) **952 Soldier, Dispatcher with Dog**.	21.00	32.00	42.00
(B149) **953** American Legionaire in overseas cap, tall, made for 1937 Legion convention in New York, 12 known color combinations.	120.00	180.00	240.00
(B150) **954?** American Legionaire flag-bearer, tall, cloth flag, made in 1937,			

B146   B147   B148   B149   B150

B151   B151A   B152   B153

	G	VG	M		G	VG	M
as above, five known ...	300.00	450.00	600.00	(B162) **615 Engineer**	5.00	8.00	11.00
(B151) **961 At Typewriter,** with typewriter and table .	30.00	45.00	60.00	(B163) **616 Boy**	5.00	8.00	11.00
(B151A) **770 At Mess,** typist alone, apparently meant to sit at mess table	6.00	10.00	13.00	(B164) **617 Girl**	5.00	8.00	10.00
				(B165) **618 Elderly Woman** .	6.00	9.00	12.00
				(B166) **619 Old Man**	7.00	11.00	14.00
(B152) **374 Army Motorcycle,** with side-car	30.00	40.00	60.00	(B167) **620 Minister walking**	25.00	38.00	50.00
(B153) **45 "Machine Gunner and Driver"**	21.00	32.00	42.00	(B168) **620 Minister holding** hat	9.00	14.00	18.00
(B154) **714 Pirate**	7.00	12.00	15.00	(B169) **621 Newsboy**	6.00	9.00	12.00
(B155) **713 Knight** with pennant	7.00	12.00	15.00	(B170) **622 Shoeshine Boy** ..	6.00	9.00	12.00
(B156) **712 Knight** with shield	6.00	9.00	12.00	(B171) **623 Detective** with pistol, blue or gray suit ..	62.00	94.00	125.00
(B157) **610 Woman Passenger,** with dog	6.00	9.00	12.00	(B171a) As above, in tan suit, only one known ...	No Price Found		
(B158) **611 Man Passenger,** overcoat over arm	5.00	8.00	10.00	(B172) **624 Burglar**	39.00	60.00	78.00
				(B173) **625 Bride**	10.00	15.00	20.00
(B159) **614 Red Cap** with bags	6.00	10.00	13.00	(B174) **626 Groom**	10.00	15.00	20.00
				(B175) **627 Girl in Rocker** ..	8.00	12.00	16.00
(B160) **613 Porter,** with whisk broom	6.00	9.00	12.00	(B176) **628 Boy Skater**	5.00	7.00	11.00
(B161) **612 Conductor**	6.00	10.00	13.00	(B177) **629 Girl Skater**	5.00	7.00	11.00
				(B178) **630½ Man and Woman on Park Bench** .	13.00	20.00	27.00
				(B179) Seated man and woman in winter coats ...	10.00	15.00	20.00
				(B180) **635 Man Speed Skater**	6.00	10.00	13.00

BARCLAY

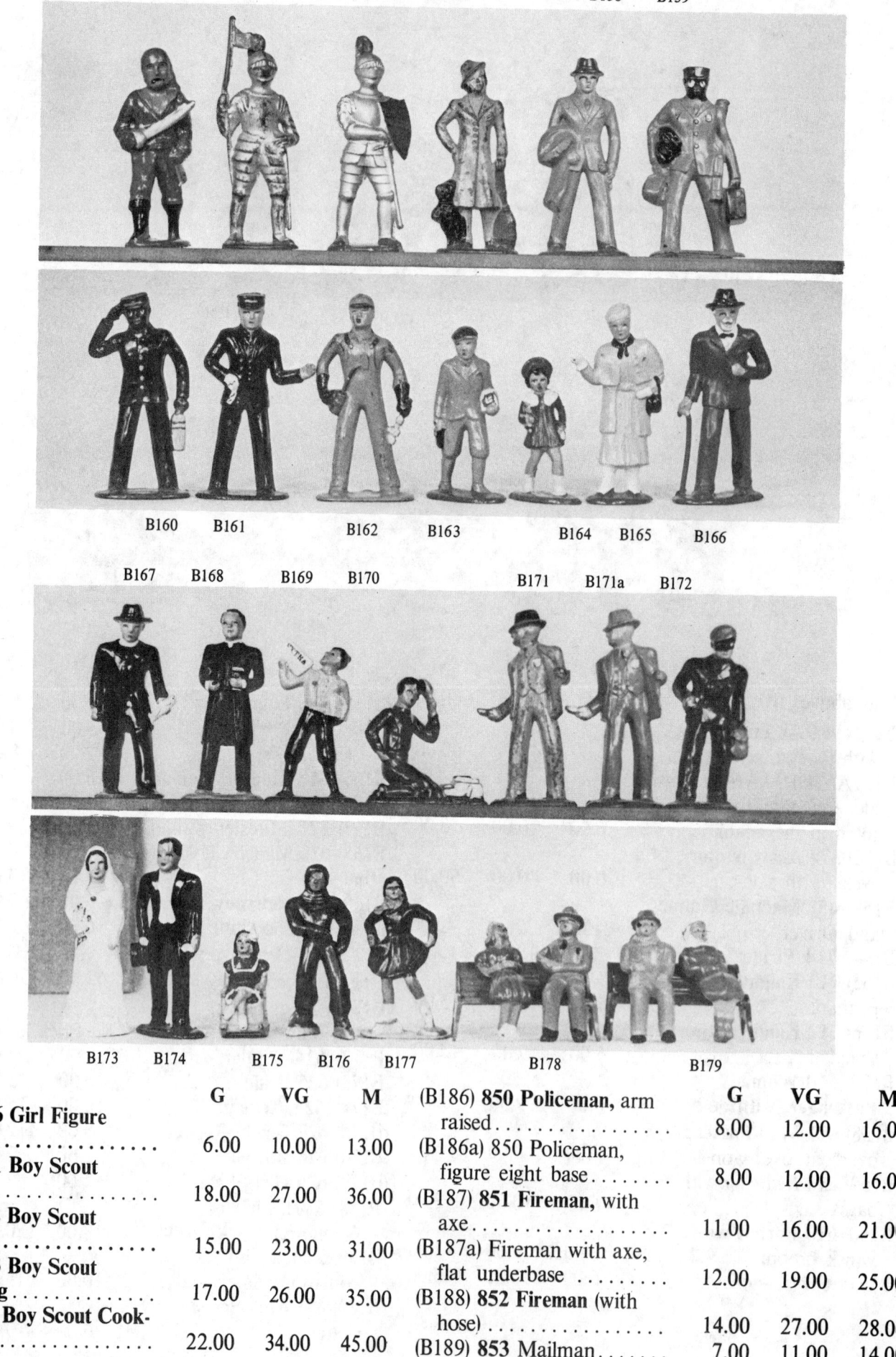

B154 B155 B156 B157 B158 B159

B160 B161 B162 B163 B164 B165 B166

B167 B168 B169 B170 B171 B171a B172

B173 B174 B175 B176 B177 B178 B179

	G	VG	M
(B181) **636 Girl Figure Skater**	6.00	10.00	13.00
(B182) **801 Boy Scout Hiking**	18.00	27.00	36.00
(B183) **802 Boy Scout Saluting**	15.00	23.00	31.00
(B184) 803 Boy Scout Signaling	17.00	26.00	35.00
(B185) **804 Boy Scout Cooking**	22.00	34.00	45.00

	G	VG	M
(B186) **850 Policeman**, arm raised	8.00	12.00	16.00
(B186a) 850 Policeman, figure eight base	8.00	12.00	16.00
(B187) **851 Fireman**, with axe	11.00	16.00	21.00
(B187a) Fireman with axe, flat underbase	12.00	19.00	25.00
(B188) **852 Fireman** (with hose)	14.00	27.00	28.00
(B189) **853 Mailman**	7.00	11.00	14.00

75

B180 B181   B182   B183   B184   B185

B186   B186a   B187   B187a   B188   B189

	G	VG	M		G	VG	M
(B190) **495 Man on skis**....	8.00	13.00	17.00	(B202) 703? Kneeling, firing rifle.................	17.00	26.00	35.00
(B191) **496 Girl on skis**....	8.00	13.00	17.00	(B203) **705** Port Arms.....	12.00	19.00	25.00
(B192) **497 Man on Sled**...	7.00	12.00	15.00	(B204) **707** Order Arms....	11.00	16.00	22.00
(B193) **498 Girl on Sled**....	7.00	12.00	15.00	(B205) 708 Officer with Sword...............	10.00	15.00	20.00
(B194) **499 Santa Claus on Sled**.................	19.00	29.00	38.00	(B206) **728** Prone Machine Gunner..............	9.00	14.00	18.00
(B195) **500 Santa Claus on Skis**................	23.00	35.00	46.00	(B207) 737 Tommy-Gunner.	9.00	14.00	18.00
(B195a) **500 Santa Claus on Skis,** no skis, or poles, and no holes for them.......	27.00	41.00	55.00	(B208) **747** Standing Firing Rifle................	13.00	20.00	26.00
(B196) Santa Claus with holly sprig..............	30.00	45.00	60.00	(B209) 774 AA Gunner....	7.00	12.00	15.00
(B197) Santa Claus seated, bag of toys at side, made to ride in sleigh.........	100.00	150.00	200.00	(B210) 777 Marching at Slope	10.00	16.00	21.00
(B198) **510 One Horse Open Sleigh** (Sleigh, horse, seated man and woman)..	25.00	38.00	50.00	(B211) **788** Marching, rifle slung.................	11.00	16.00	22.00
(B199) **530 Man Pulling Children on Sled**.......	25.00	38.00	50.00	(B212) **789** AA Gunner....	10.00	15.00	20.00
(B200) **535 Young Man Putting Skates on Girl Sitting on Bench**	50.00	75.00	100.00	(B212a) Cowboy, two pistols, one in air..............	26.00	39.00	52.00
Post-World War II				(B213) Drum Major.......	27.00	41.00	55.00
				(B214) Drummer.........	22.00	33.00	45.00
				(B215) Bugler...........	19.00	28.00	38.00
(B201) **701** Flagbearer, pot helmet...............	11.00	17.00	22.00	(B215A) Bugler, buttons run down front of uniform ..	22.00	34.00	45.00
				(B216) Clarinetist........	22.00	34.00	45.00
				(B217) Tubist...........	25.00	38.00	50.00
				(B218) Sailor, white......	17.00	26.00	35.00
				(B218A) **720 Blue Sailor**...	17.00	26.00	35.00

BARCLAY

B190 B191 B192 B193

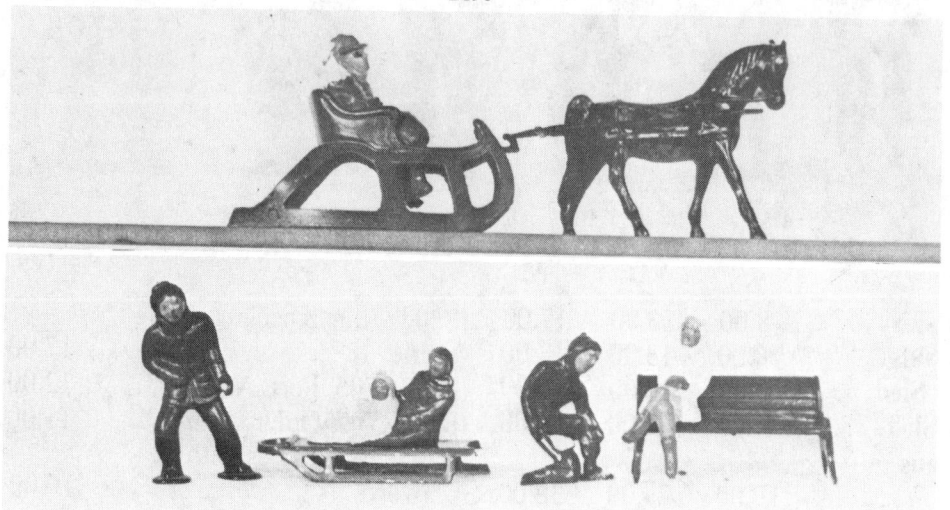

B194 B195 B196 B197

B198

B199 B200

BARCLAY POD FOOT SERIES, Circa 1950s to 1971

(Most podfoot soldiers came in khaki, and later, green.)

	G	VG	M		G	VG	M
(B219) 81 Two Soldier Crew at Radar Equipment	11.00	17.00	23.00	(B227) 190 Cowboy with Pistol on Horse........	8.00	12.00	16.00
(B220) 82 Three Soldier Crew at Range Finder...	12.00	19.00	25.00	(B228) 800 Black Knight w/Sword & Shield.......	11.00	17.00	23.00
(B221) 83 Two Soldier Crew at Searchlight..........	10.00	15.00	20.00	(B229) 801 Knight w/Red & Blue Shield & Sword....	15.00	23.00	30.00
(B222) 84 Two Soldier Crew at Mobile Cannon......	10.00	15.00	20.00	(B230) 802 Knight w/Orange & Black Shield & Sword.	7.00	11.00	14.00
(B223) 85 Two Soldier Crew at A.A. Gun...........	12.00	18.00	24.00	(B231) 803 Knight w/Red & Green Shield & Sword...	10.00	15.00	20.00
(B224) 187 Officer on Horse (pot helmet)...........	37.00	53.00	75.00	(B232) 901 Soldier Flag Bearer	6.00	10.00	13.00
(B225) 188 Cowboy on Horse (lasso)..........	11.00	16.00	22.00	(B232A) Same as above, in red (not shown)........	30.00	45.00	60.00
(B226) 189 Indian on Horse	10.00	16.00	21.00	(B233) 903 Soldier Sniper (kneeling).............	6.00	9.00	12.00
				(B233A) 903 same as above, in red................	20.00	30.00	40.00

B201 B202   B203 B204 B205

B206   B207   B208   B209

B210 B211   B212   B212a B213

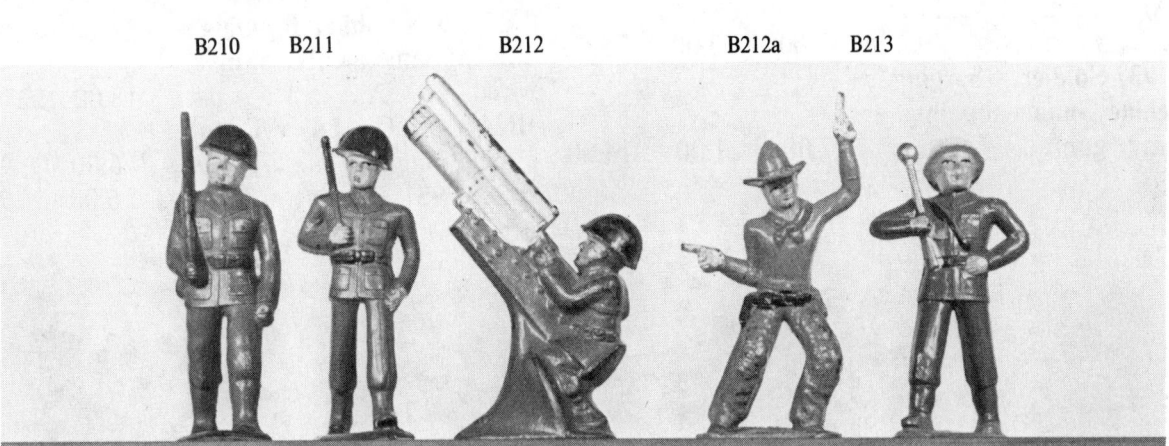

	G	VG	M		G	VG	M
(B234) **906 Soldier Charging**	6.00	10.00	13.00	(B237) **919 Sailor White**			
(B234A) Same as above, in				Uniform.............	5.00	8.00	10.00
red (not shown)........	16.00	24.00	32.00	(B238) **920 Sailor Blue**			
(B235) **908 Soldier Officer**..	5.00	8.00	10.00	Uniform.............	7.00	11.00	15.00
(B235A) Same as above, in				(B239) **922 Marine**........	7.00	11.00	14.00
blue................	32.00	48.00	64.00	(B240) **928 Soldier Machine**			
(B235B) Same as above, in				**Gunner Lying Flat**......	5.00	8.00	10.00
red..................	15.00	23.00	30.00	(B240A) Same as above, in			
(B236) **909 Soldier Bugler**..	5.00	8.00	11.00	red..................	18.00	27.00	36.00
(B236A) Same as above, in				(B241) **929 Soldier w/Pistol,**			
red (not shown)........	17.00	27.00	35.00	**Crawling**............	14.00	21.00	28.00

B214 B215 B216 B217 B218 B218a

B215 B215A
Courtesy Charles Breslow

	G	VG	M
(B241A) Same as above, in red	37.00	53.00	75.00
(B242) **937 Soldier, Charging Machine Gunner** (holding tommy gun)	7.00	11.00	14.00

	G	VG	M
(B242A) Same as above, in red	18.00	27.00	36.00
(B243) **938 Soldier Bomb Thrower**	5.00	8.00	11.00
(B243A) Same as above, in red	16.00	24.00	32.00
(B244) **941 Aviator**	6.00	9.00	12.00
(B244A) Same as above, in red	18.00	27.00	36.00
(B245) **947 Soldier Marksman**	5.00	8.00	10.00
(B245A) Same as above, in red	14.00	21.00	28.00
(B246) **948 Soldier Running**	6.00	9.00	12.00
(B246a) Same as above, in red	18.00	27.00	36.00
(B247) **950 Cowboy w/Pistol Shooting**	6.00	9.00	12.00
(B248) **951 Cowboy w/Rifle**	6.00	9.00	12.00

B219 B220 B221

B222 B223

B224   B225   B226

B227   B228   B229   B230   B231

B232   B233   B233A   B234

B235   B235A   B235B   B236   B237   B238

B239   B240   B240A   B241

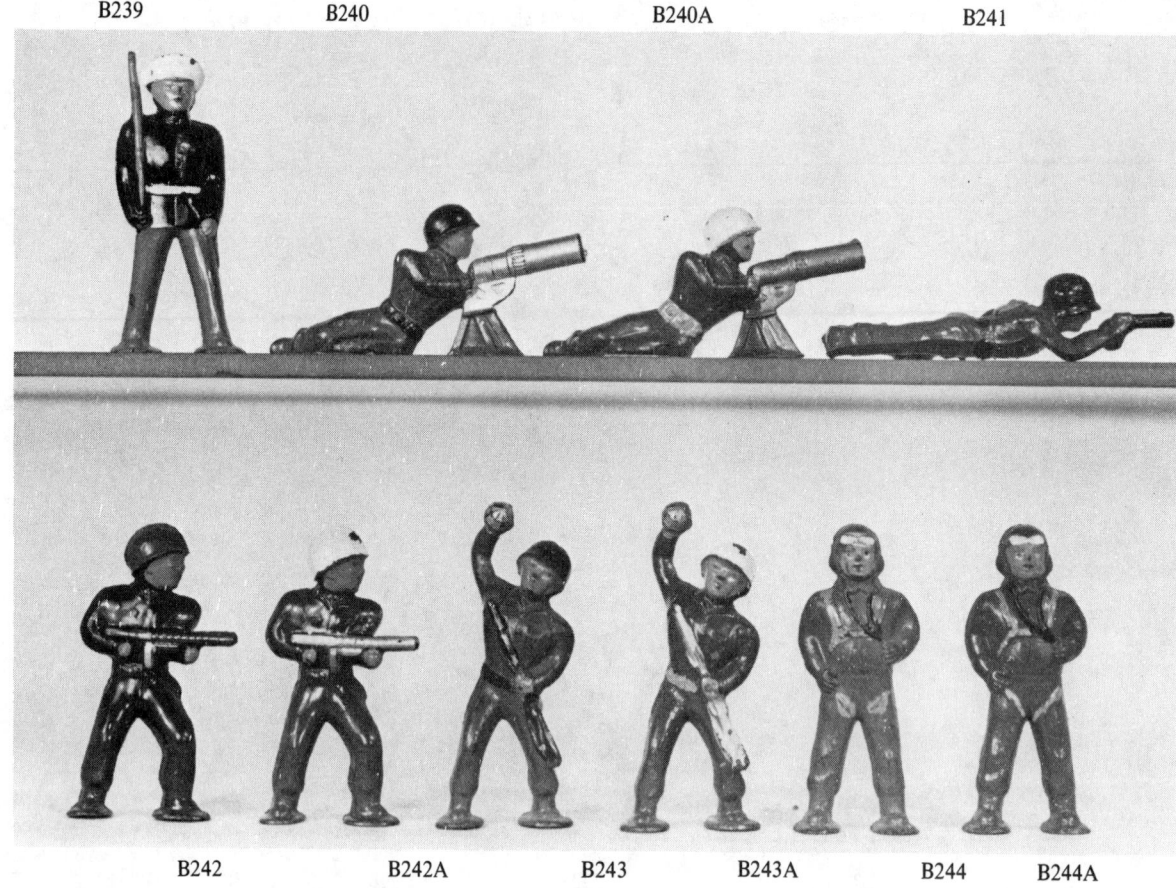

B242   B242A   B243   B243A   B244   B244A

B245   B246   B247   B248   B249

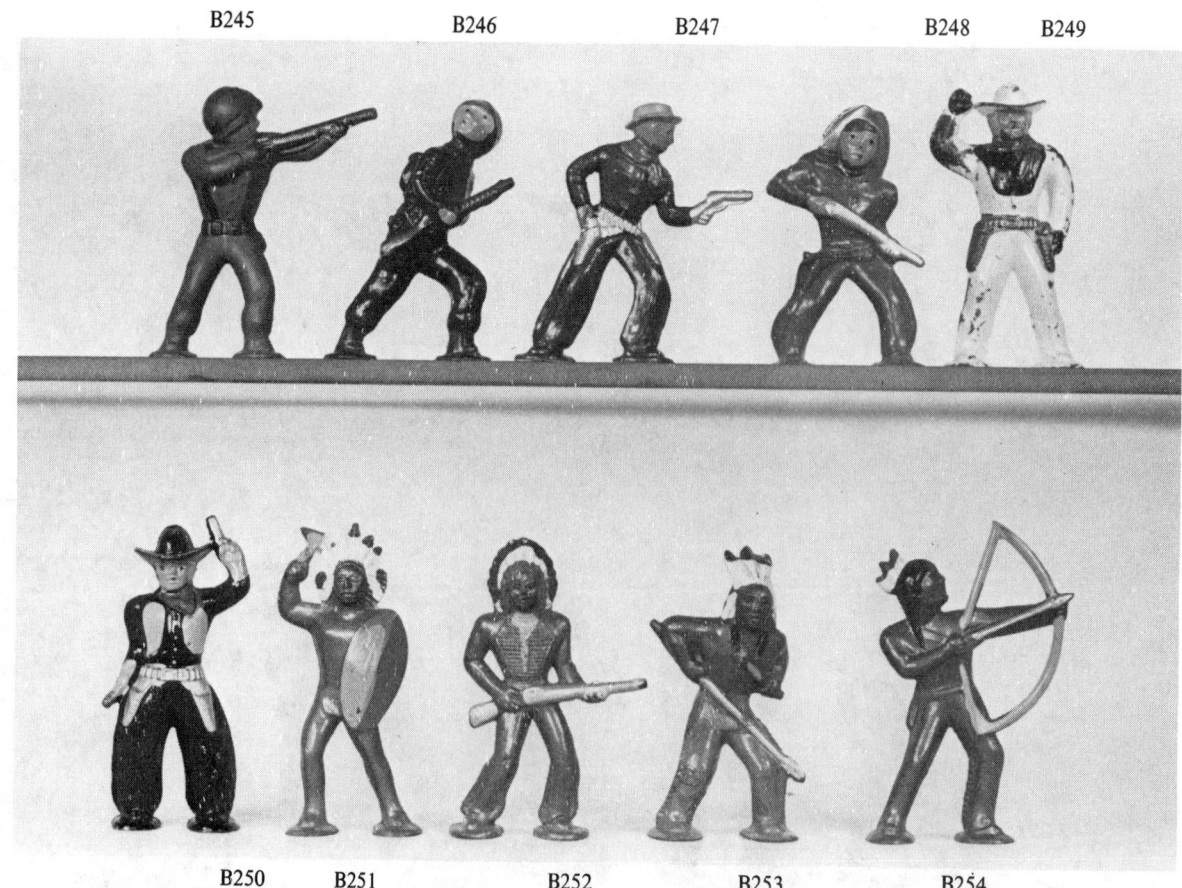

B250   B251   B252   B253   B254

BARCLAY	G	VG	M
(B249) **952 Cowboy w/Lasso**	4.00	6.00	8.00
(B250) **953 Cowboy w/Pistol** (upraised)	4.00	7.00	9.00
(B251) **954 Indian w/Shield & Tomahawk**	4.00	7.00	9.00
(B252) **955 Indian w/Rifle** . . .	4.00	7.00	9.00
(B253) **956 Indian w/Knife & Spear**	5.00	8.00	10.00
(B254) **957 Indian w/Bow & Arrow**	5.00	8.00	10.00
(B255) **960 Soldier, Wounded, w/Crutches**	11.00	17.00	23.00
(B255A) Same as above, in red	30.00	45.00	60.00
(B256) **961 Soldier, Wounded Head & Arm**	9.00	14.00	18.00

	G	VG	M
(B256A) Same as above, in red (not shown)	24.00	36.00	48.00
(B257) **962 Nurse**	15.00	23.00	31.00
(B258) **974 Soldier, Anti-Aircraft Gunner**	6.00	9.00	12.00
(B258A) Same as above, in red	20.00	30.00	40.00
(B259) **977 Soldier Under Marching Orders** (marching)	5.00	8.00	10.00
(B259A) Same as above, in red (not shown)	15.00	23.00	30.00
(B260) **988 Soldier, Marching w/Gun on Back (Gun slung over shoulder)**	5.00	8.00	10.00
(B260A) Same as above, in red	15.00	23.00	30.00
(B260B) Like B260, but longer legs. Shown in Barclay catalog, but none known	No Price Found		
(B261) **990 Soldier w/Bazooka**	6.00	10.00	13.00
(B261A) Same as above, in red	18.00	27.00	36.00
(B262) **991 Soldier Flame Thrower**	5.00	8.00	11.00

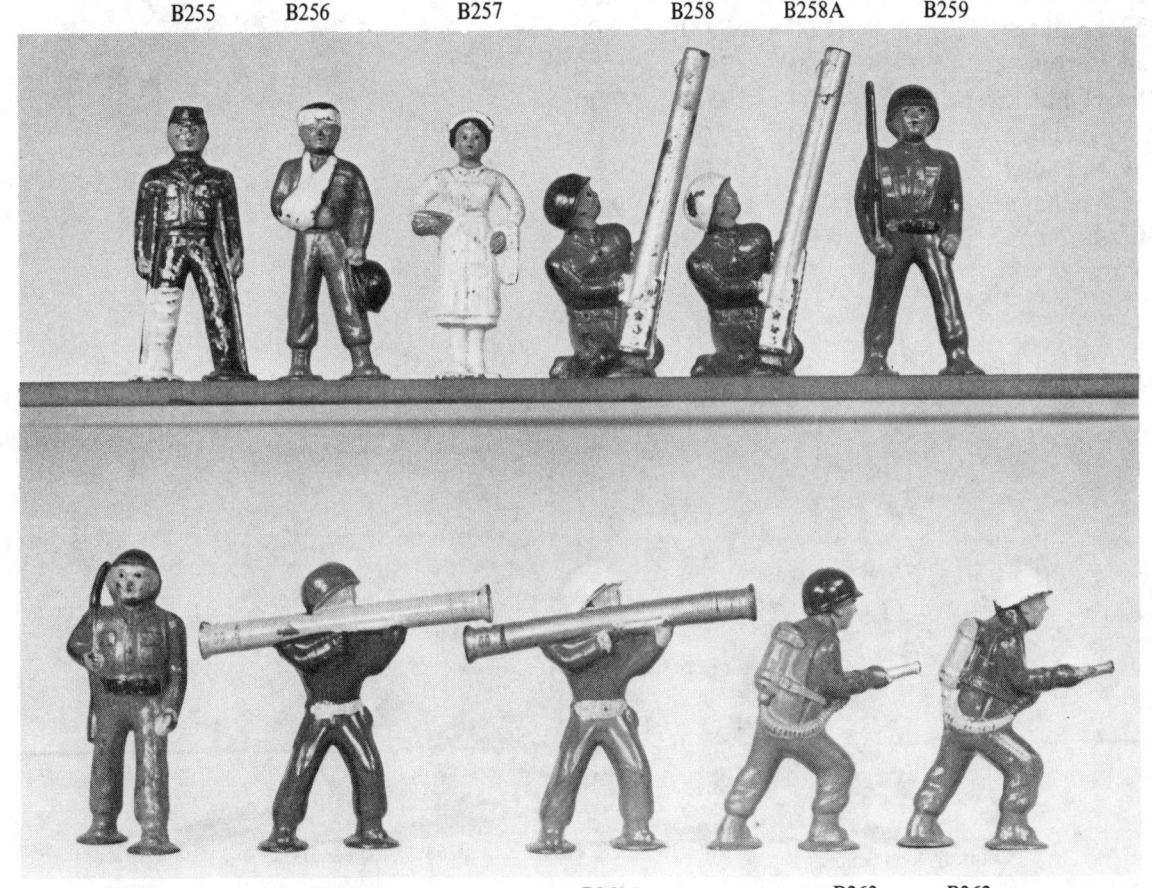

B260a   B241a

B255   B256   B257   B258   B258A   B259

B260   B261   B261A   B262   B262a

BARCLAY	G	VG	M
(B262A) 991, same as above, in red	14.00	21.00	28.00

"Midi" Size (Smaller Than Pod Foot)

	G	VG	M
(B263) Flame Thrower	30.00	45.00	60.00
(B264) Bugler	30.00	45.00	60.00
(B265) Officer With Binoculars	30.00	45.00	60.00
(B266) Talking on Field Phone	30.00	45.00	60.00
(B267) Advancing With Rifle	30.00	45.00	60.00
(B268) Marching, slung rifle	30.00	45.00	60.00
(B269) Firing Bazooka	30.00	45.00	60.00
(B270) Firing Tommygun	30.00	45.00	60.00
(B270a) Walking Forward, rifle at side, pointing down	30.00	45.00	60.00
(B271) Cowboy with Rifle	6.00	9.00	12.00
(B272) Cowboy with Pistol	6.00	9.00	12.00
(B273) Indian with Hatchet	6.00	9.00	12.00
(B274) Indian with Rifle	6.00	9.00	12.00

HO Figures for HO Trains

	G	VG	M
(B275) 350 Policeman	4.00	7.00	9.00
(B276) 351 Man	4.00	7.00	9.00
(B277) 352 Woman	4.00	7.00	9.00
(B278) 353 Conductor	4.00	7.00	9.00
(B279) 354 Redcap	4.00	7.00	9.00
(B280) 355 Oiler	4.00	7.00	9.00
(B281) 356 Brakeman	4.00	7.00	9.00
(B282) 357 Engineer	4.00	7.00	9.00
(B283) 358 Porter	4.00	7.00	9.00
(B284) 359 Dining Steward	4.00	7.00	9.00
(B285) 360 Hobo	4.00	7.00	9.00
(B286) 361 Newsboy	4.00	7.00	9.00
(B287) 362 Mailman	4.00	7.00	9.00
(B288) 363 Fireman	4.00	7.00	9.00

	G	VG	M
(B289) 366 Peg-Legged Gateman	6.00	9.00	12.00
(B290) 369 Woman Carrying Baby	4.00	7.00	9.00
(B291) 370 Little Boy	3.00	5.00	7.00
(B292) 371 Little Girl	3.00	5.00	7.00
(B293) 372 Bride	5.00	8.00	10.00
(B294) 373 Groom	5.00	8.00	10.00
(B295) Woman with Dog	6.00	9.00	12.00

B260B
From "The Barclay Catalog Book"

B271   B272   B273   B274
Photo by Don Pielin

B270   B269   B267   B268   B265

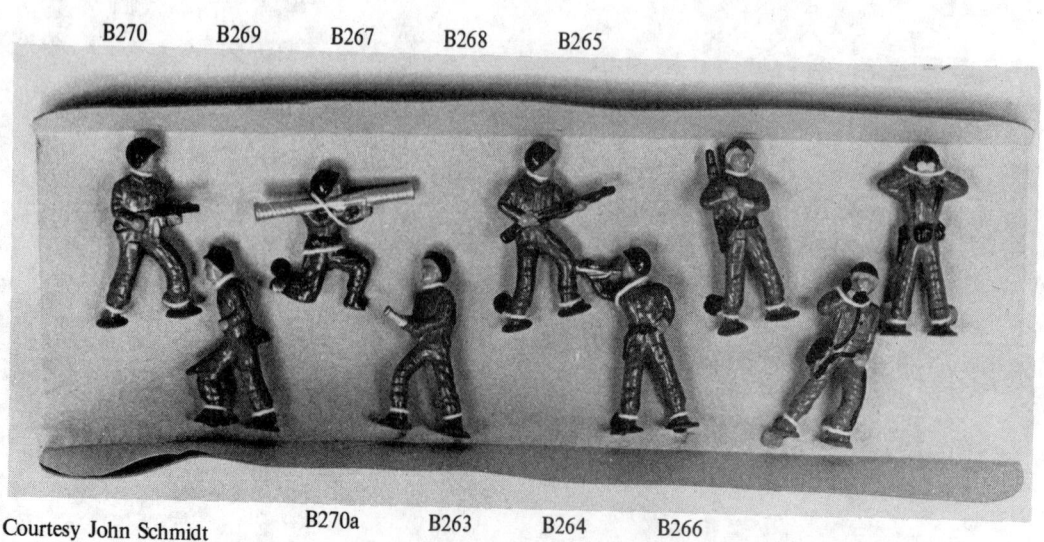

Courtesy John Schmidt   B270a   B263   B264   B266

BARCLAY

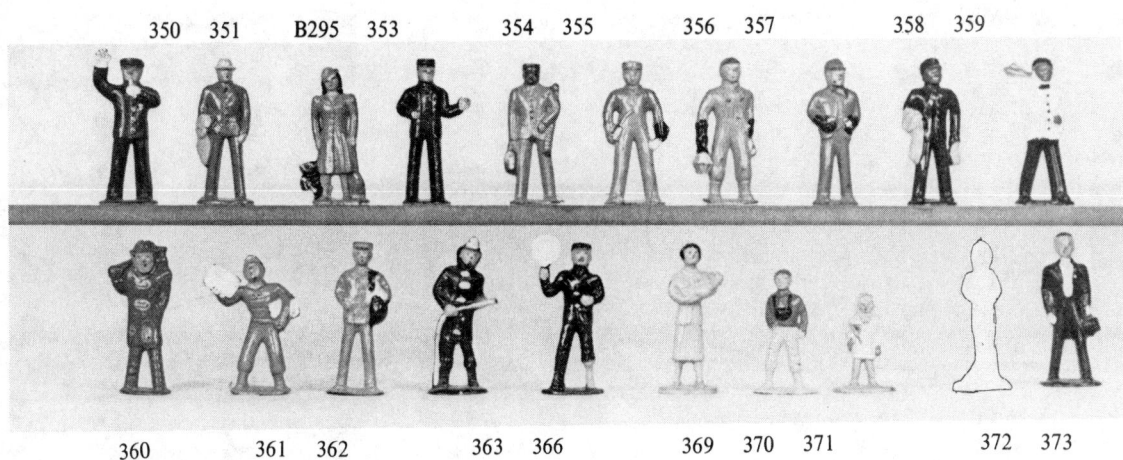

350 351 B295 353 354 355 356 357 358 359

360 361 362 363 366 369 370 371 372 373

352
Courtesy Charlie Breslow

	G	VG	M
BARCLAY Box only, circa 1939, 15"x4½"x2", 12 soldiers, coast gun, searchlight pictured, plus pictures of cowboys, Indians and Boy Scouts on sides of box. These boxes are known to have contained train figures, No. 50/08 7 pc. Marching Soldiers set and "No. 50/30 7-Piece Signal Soldier set. Box only	43.00	65.00	86.00
BARCLAY Boxed set of winter figures, post-war ..	100.00	150.00	200.00

BARCLAY Box, circa 1939, known to be used for Train Figures and a signal corps set.
Photo by Bill Kaufman

Blister pack of winter figures with sled, value $60 in mint. Blister pack of a Midi torn from a larger card. Value $22 in mint.

The cover of a late Barclay catalog. On all post-War boxed sets, add the value of the figures and then increase the total 30% to get the set's value.
Courtesy Terry Sells

BARCLAY

No. 400 blister pack of Barclay's HO figures. Value $40 in mint.
Courtesy Don Pielin

15R RAILROAD FIGURES is the legend on the box, which is post-WW II.
Photo by Hank Anton

A never-produced plaster prototype of the 360 tramp
Courtesy
Charlie Breslow

(BA1)   No number found

(BA10) **52**

(BA1a) **307**

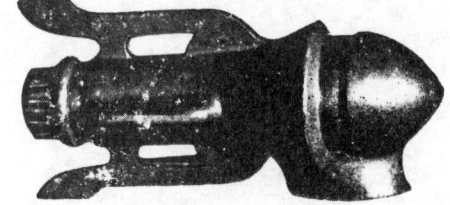

(BA8) This block is numbered "Old 307"

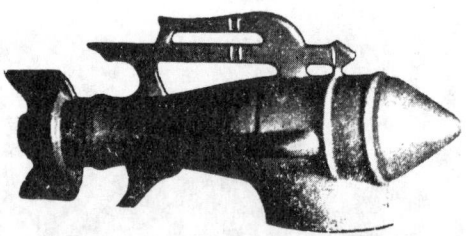

(BA5) **No. 610 Rocket Ship**

(BA4) **No. 57**

(BA6) **No. 611 Rocket Ship**

BARCLAY
BARCLAY AIRCRAFT

	G	VG	M
(BA1) **307** Lindy-type plane, wingspan approx. 4⅜" long, early-mid 30s	15.00	20.00	30.00
(BA1a) **307** Monoplane, single engine	15.00	20.00	30.00
(BA2) "Transatlantic Bremen," circa 1928	17.00	23.00	35.00
(BA3) Monoplane, single engine, high wing, Cracka-jack size, one-piece, sold with Aeroplane Carrier and piggy-backed on 195 Aeroplane	10.00	15.00	20.00
(BA4) **No. 57 Giant Zeppelin**	17.00	23.00	35.00
(BA4a) Dirigible, 4⅜" long, early - mid 30s	20.00	30.00	40.00
(BA5) **610 Rocket Ship**	25.00	38.00	50.00
(BA6) **611 Rocket Ship**	25.00	38.00	50.00
(BA7) **195 Aeroplane**, "U.S. Army" single engine transport, 3¾" wingspan	17.00	23.00	35.00
(BA7a) **195 Aeroplane** with BA3 monoplane piggy-backed on it	30.00	45.00	60.00
(BA7b) **195 Aeroplane,** with clip of bombs attached to it	25.00	35.00	50.00
(BA8) "Old 307"	12.00	18.00	24.00
(BA9) Thick-winged monoplane, approx. 2½" long with oversized wheels, in 1935 Butler Bros. catalog	17.00	23.00	35.00
(BA10) **52** Small Lindy-type plane	6.00	9.00	12.00

BA7   BA7a

Photo by Ed Poole

BA7B
Courtesy Hank Anton

BA1   BA4a
Photo by Bill Kaufman
Courtesy Evelyn Besser

BA2

BARCLAY ANIMALS
(Some were on sale by 1941, including 218)

	G	VG	M
209 Work horse	5.00	7.50	10.00
210 Horse	5.00	7.50	10.00
211 Grazing Horse	5.00	7.50	10.00
212 Standing Cow	5.00	7.50	10.00
213 Grazing Cow	5.00	7.50	10.00
214 Lying Cow	5.00	7.50	10.00
215 Bull	5.00	7.50	10.00
217 Standing Sheep	5.00	7.50	10.00
218 Resting Sheep	5.00	7.50	10.00
219 Ram	3.50	5.25	7.00
220 Pig	3.50	5.25	7.00
? Grazing Sheep (216?)	3.50	5.25	7.00

BARCLAY

Top: Barclay covered wagon, no "1849" marking. Neither version seems to be more rare. Bottom: Barclay Coach and two, no outrider. Value in mint is $50.
Photo by Craig A. Clark

Barclay Coach, single window on side, driver in flat-topped hat. Price in mint about $50.

Barclay Circus Wagon. Value in mint is $40. Note plumes on horses.
Photo by Stan Alekna

This milk wagon is almost certainly by Barclay. Bought in 1991 for $85.
Photo by Stan Alekna

The plane at right is Barclay's BA3, and is marked "Barclay". The one at left is a Tootsietoy. Early Barclay printing blocks show a vertical propeller, suggesting the Tootsietoy was used at first.
Photo by Ed Poole

BA9
Photo by Perry R. Eichor

A former Barclay employee remembers Barclay made "three or four different Buck Rogers airships". The rocket ship at left is Barclay's No. 610, and measures approximately 3⅜" long. The two at right don't seem to have been cast the same way, but the one in the middle very much resembles a Buck Rogers ship. It is painted red, white and blue and measures approx. 2⅞" long. The one at right is red and yellow and about 2¾" long.
Courtesy Tony Diksa

This tank and submarine were never produced by Barclay. Cast from unfinished Barclay molds by Ron Eccles.

Barclay covered wagon, worth $60 in mint.
Courtesy K. Warren Mitchell

Two Barclays which were never produced; the molds, in fact, were never finished, resulting in solid castings when these figures were made a few years ago. Presumably the War interrupted their release, and after the War they were outmoded. The sentry seems to have been planned to replace B71.

211   212

Courtesy K. Warren Mitchell

209   210   213   214

215   217   218   219   220   ?

Two castings by Ed Poole made from unproduced Barclay plaster figures. The ski troop was probably designed in 1940. The other piece is a fireman, made to climb a ladder.

Barclay's woman painters occasionally varied colors on slow days. It had long been rumored brides painted as bridesmaids had been seen. Collector Stan Alekna found these, painted, L to R: Green, Pink, White. The figure at right has a pink carnation, making him the groom's best man (grooms always have white).

The all-lead table on the left came out of the Barclay factory. Barclay's George Fall is sure it wasn't meant for the typist, but it fits perfectly and is far less ungainly than the wooden table the typist was sold with. The balsa wood mess table was sold with wooden benches, and is worth about $20 in mint. It was probably made by a subcontractor.

A number of Barclay's prewar soldiers seem to have been cast post World War II. The ones easiest to spot are those in the front row, with green helmets and brown bases. Pieces with whites painted in for the eyes (plus the usual Barclay eyelid and attached dot eye) are almost certainly also post-War.
Courtesy Ron Hillman and *Old Toy Soldier* magazine.

Barclay's BA2 Bremen and BA4 Giant Zeppelin, with their boxes. The Bremen set the East-West Atlantic crossing record in 1928. The zeppelin's box converted into a hangar.
Photo by Chic Gast from his collection

LEAD TOY SOLDIERS AND ACCESSORIES

No. 928 MACHINE GUNNER-15¢

No. 906 CHARGING SOLDIER-15¢

No. 903 SNIPER-15¢

No. 85 ANTI-AIRCRAFT CREW-25¢
(2½" x 3" long)

Soldiers approximately 2½" to 3½" high. Khaki color with contrasting colored details.

No. 988 MARCHING SOLDIER-15¢

No. 908 OFFICER-15¢

No. 909 BUGLER-15¢

No. 974 ANTI-AIRCRAFT GUNNER-15¢

No. 901 FLAG BEARER-15¢

No. 84 CANNON CREW-25¢
(3½" long)

No. 187 OFFICER ON HORSE-25¢
(3" x 3")

No. 938 BOMB THROWER-15¢

This is the earliest documentation yet found for Barclay's podfoot soldiers. From a Woolworth's Christmas, 1951 comic book-catalog. Prices are 15¢ and 25¢.

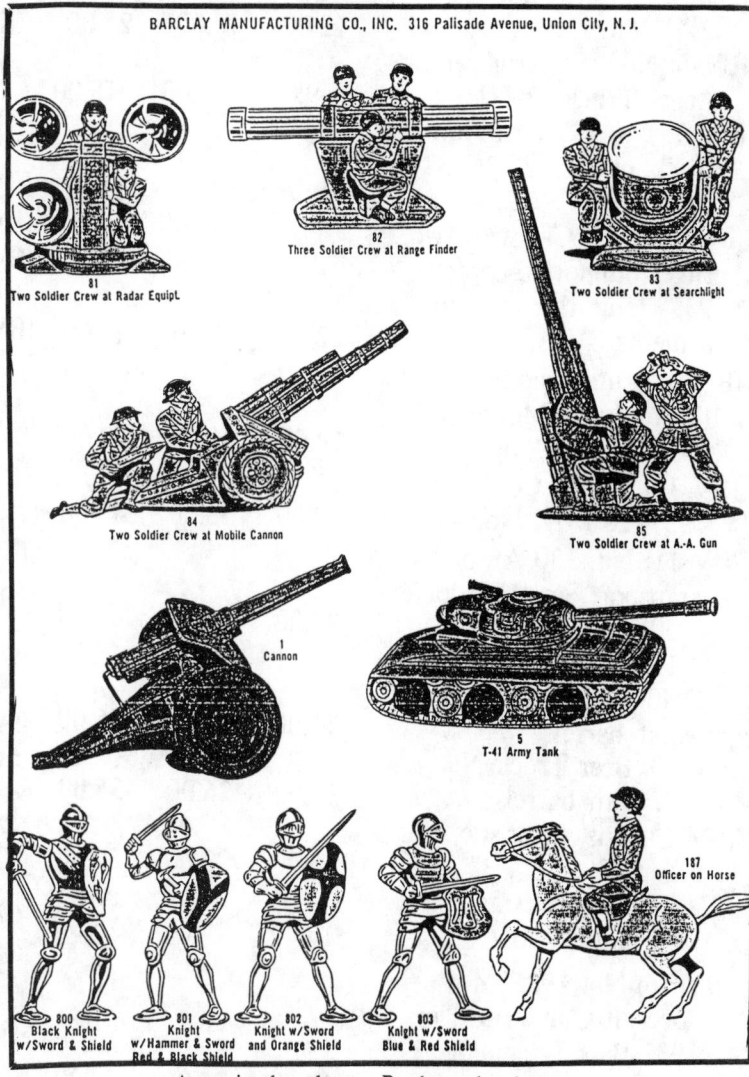

BARCLAY MANUFACTURING CO., INC. 316 Palisade Avenue, Union City, N.J.

81
Two Soldier Crew at Radar Equipt.

82
Three Soldier Crew at Range Finder

83
Two Soldier Crew at Searchlight

84
Two Soldier Crew at Mobile Cannon

85
Two Soldier Crew at A.-A. Gun

1
Cannon

5
T-41 Army Tank

800
Black Knight
w/Sword & Shield

801
Knight
w/Hammer & Sword
Red & Black Shield

802
Knight w/Sword
and Orange Shield

803
Knight w/Sword
Blue & Red Shield

187
Officer on Horse

A previously unknown Barclay order sheet.
Courtesy Wayne & Mary Hill - CRC Miniatures

BARCLAY VEHICLES

A number of unmarked vehicles were in the possession of the late Barclay-All Nu designer Frank Krupp. Most of these were too early to have been All-Nu and were checked with four early Barclay employees. The number of Xs in parenthesis after the toy's description indicate how many thought it had been Barclay. However, it is possible, since these are based on memories of several decades, that not all are Barclay. An X? indicates the employee believed it was Barclay but was not sure. These not marked with Xs have been identified in other ways.

	G	VG	M
(BV 1) Ambulance, **No. 194**, 3½" long, small cross . . .	20.00	30.00	40.00
(BV 2) Ambulance, **No. 194**, 3½" long, large cross . . .	20.00	30.00	40.00
(BV 3) Ambulance No. 50, 5" long	25.00	38.00	50.00
(BV 4) **No. 151 Army Truck with Gun,** 2¾" long	15.00	22.00	30.00
(BV 5) **No. 151 Army Truck with Anti-Aircraft Gun,** 2½" long	12.00	18.00	25.00
(BV 6) **No. 152 Armored Army Truck,** 2⅞" long . .	9.00	13.00	18.00
(BV 7) **No. 197** Army tank truck, circa 1935-36, 3⅛" long	15.00	22.00	30.00
(BV 8) Army Car with two silver bullhorns, approx. 2½" long (this may be same as BV86)	22.00	33.00	44.00
(BV 9) Army Tractor (Minneapolis-Moline "Jeep"), 2¾" long	14.00	21.00	28.00
(BV 10) Austin Coupe, circa 1931, 2" long, No. 43 . . .	22.00	33.00	45.00
(BV 11) No. 330 Auto Transport Set, 4½" long, 2 50's cars	30.00	45.00	60.00
(BV 12) "Beer" truck, circa 1940, **No. 376,** 4" long, wood barrels	17.00	26.00	35.00
(BV 13) Beer Truck **No. 377,** with barrels	17.00	26.00	35.00
(BV 14) Bus, futuristic, "Made U.S.A.", 3" long .	15.00	22.00	30.00
(BV 15) Cannon Car, 3⁵⁄₁₆" long, gunner low	13.00	19.00	26.00
(BV 16) **No. 198, Anti-Aircraft Gun Truck,** in 1931 Barclay catalog, 3⅛" long	17.00	25.00	34.00

	G	VG	M
(BV 17) Cannon Car, 3¼" long, slight casting differences from headlight version	17.00	25.00	34.00
(BV 18) Cannon Car, battery-powered headlight, 3½" long, in 1935 catalog	80.00	130.00	225.00
(BV 19) **No. 48 Anti-Aircraft Gun Truck,** 4" long, one man	17.00	26.00	35.00
(BV 20) **No. 48, Anti-Aircraft Gun Truck,** 4" long, two men	16.00	24.00	32.00
(BV 21) Cannon Truck, 4" long, with moveable cannon	20.00	30.00	40.00
(BV 22) (Unused)			
(BV 23) Chrysler Airflow, 4" long, circa 1936	15.00	22.00	30.00
(BV 24) "Coast to Coast" 2⅞" long diecast bus, "Barclay Toy," two-piece, **No. 405**	37.00	56.00	75.00
(BV 25) Coupe, 1930s, "Made in U.S.A." 3" long	15.00	22.00	30.00
(BV 26) Coupe, 2½" long, circa 1935 XXX	15.00	22.00	30.00
(BV 27) Coupe, 1934, 4¼" long, XXX	40.00	60.00	80.00
(BV 28) Coupe, 2-piece, 1930s 2⅞" long, "Barclay Toy"	32.00	48.00	65.00
(BV 29) Unused			
(BV 30) Coupe, 1934, 4¼" long, XXX	40.00	60.00	80.00
(BV 31) **No. 40 Cord Front Drive Coupe,** circa 1931, 3⅝" long	20.00	30.00	40.00

BV15   BV6   BV4   BV9

BV56   BV19   BV20

Photo by Ed Poole

91

BV1　　　　　　　BV2　　　　　　　BV3
Photo by Craig A. Clark

BV6a　　　　　　　　　BV6

BV6a has larger windows, no rivets up center, smaller front gun, no
headlights, etc.
Photo by Stan Alekna

BV10　　　　　BV11　　　　　　BV12　　　　　　BV13
Photo by Craig A. Clark

BV66　　　　　　　BV67　　　　　　　BV68
Photo by Craig A. Clark

BV63　　　　　　　BV64　　　　　　BV65
Photo by Craig A. Clark

BV69　　　　　BV70　　　　　BV71　　　　　BV71A
Photo by Craig A. Clark

BARCLAY

	G	VG	M
(BV 32) **No. 302, Streamline Car,** circa 1936, 3⅛" long?	25.00	38.00	50.00
(BV 33) "Delivery" Truck, **No. 309,** 2 15/16" long, XXX	14.00	21.00	28.00
(BV 34) Double Decker Bus, 4"	35.00	52.00	70.00
(BV 35) (Unused)			
(BV 36) (Unused)			
(BV 37) "Express" stake truck, 1930s, 2 15/16" long .	22.00	33.00	45.00
(BV 38) Fire Engine No. 390?, moveable ladder, circa 1950s............	15.00	22.00	30.00
(BV 39) Field Kitchen, 2¼" long	9.00	13.00	18.00
(BV 40) Fire Engine, 2 firemen, black metal wheels, 1930s, **No. 41,** 2¾"	12.00	18.00	25.00
(BV 41) Fire Engine, 4" long, French-looking (Barclay often copied foreign toys), XXX......	15.00	22.00	30.00
(BV 42) Ford, 1931, 2¼"...	15.00	22.00	30.00
(BV 43) "Golden Arrow Racer", 4½" long, X?X .	20.00	30.00	40.00
(BV 44) Mack Pick Up Truck, 3½"	15.00	22.00	30.00
(BV 45) "Milk & Cream" truck, stamped **No. 377,** 3⅝" long, white rubber trees	35.00	52.00	70.00
(BV 45A) Milk Truck, **No. 377,** 3⅝" long, black rubber tires	22.00	33.00	45.00
(BV 46) Motorcycle with flat rider, full-dimensioned sidecar, **No. 55,** 2¾" ...	25.00	38.00	50.00
(BV 47) "Oil-Fuel" truck, circa. 1936, 3 9/16" long	12.00	18.00	25.00
(BV 48) "Parcel Delivery", 3⅝" long, slush lead, **No. 45,** circa 1931	65.00	98.00	130.00
(BV 49) "Police" Car **No. 317,** slush mold, approx. 3⅝" long, circa 1930s (Radio Police), 1939 Packard	22.00	33.00	45.00
(BV 49A) Police Car **No. 317,** diecast, 3⅝" long ...	15.00	22.00	30.00
(BV 50) Race Car, 3"......	12.00	18.00	24.00
(BV 51) Racer, 5½", closed cockpit	17.00	26.00	35.00
(BV 52) Racer, closed cockpit, 7" long, circa 1939	30.00	45.00	60.00

BV57 BV21, cannon off BV39

BV16 BV18 BV17

Photo by Ed Poole

BV53 BV71 BV49 BV87 BV74

BV46 BV4 BV6 BV68

BV32 BV33 BV41

Photo by Bill Kaufman. Courtesy Evelyn Besser.

BV80-BV10 BV26 BV59

BV31 BV48 BV43

BARCLAY

	G	VG	M
(BV 53) Racer, **No. 53,** early slush lead, 1920s-30s, approx. 2" long	12.00	18.00	24.00
(BV 54) Racer, two passengers, 4¼" long, XXX	25.00	38.00	50.00
(BV 55) Racer with tail fin, "Made U.S.A.", 3½" long	17.00	25.00	35.00

BV67 BV66 BV70

BV68 BV5 BV69 Cannon 4" long, post WW II

Photo by Ed Poole

	G	VG	M
(BV 56) Renault Tank, circa 1937, **No. 47,** 4" long	20.00	30.00	40.00
(BV 57) Searchlight Truck, white rubber tires, circa 1940, 4 1/16" long	87.00	130.00	175.00
(BV 57A) Searchlight Truck, second version	87.00	130.00	175.00
(BV 58) Sedan, 4 door, approx, 5" long, maybe Chrysler, circa 1936	17.00	26.00	35.00
(BV 59) Sedan, two door, 3⅛" long, rubber wheels, slush lead, circa 1935, XX	17.00	26.00	35.00
(BV 60) Sedan, two-piece, **No. 401** 2-door, 1930s, "Barclay Toy", diecast, 2⅞" long	32.00	48.00	65.00
(BV 61) Sedan and "Tourist Trailer", Made in U.S.A.," 1930s, 6½" long	35.00	52.00	70.00
(BV 62) Silver Arrow Race Car, 5½"	22.00	33.00	45.00
(BV 63) Station Wagon, **No. 404,** diecast, 1930s, 2-piece "Barclay Toy", 2 15/16" long	37.00	55.00	75.00

	G	VG	M
(BV 64) Steam-Roller, 3¼" long, traction type, slush lead with tin roof, **No. 44**	30.00	45.00	60.00
(BV 65) **No. 363 Large Streamline Racer,** in 1935 catalog, 6⅞" long	25.00	38.00	50.00
(BV 66) Tank "4562" one man in turret, 3⅞" long	17.00	26.00	35.00
(BV 67) Tank "4562" two men in turret, 3⅞" long	17.00	25.00	35.00
(BV 68) Tank T41, 4¼" long	12.00	18.00	25.00
(BV 69) Tank, 2⅝" long, man in turret, diecast, black rubber tires	12.00	18.00	25.00
(BV 70) Tank 2½" long (based on US M2 light tank)	15.00	22.00	30.00
(BV 71) Taxi, 3¼" long, circa 1940s, slush	12.00	18.00	25.00
(BV 71A) Taxi, **No. 318,** diecast, 3¼" long	11.00	16.00	22.00
(BV 72) Tractor, approx. 2⅝" long, caterpillar type, slush lead, XX	17.00	26.00	35.00
(BV 73) (Unused)	5.50	7.75	11.00
(BV 74) Trailer Truck variously "Railway Express", or with Moving Company name, circa 1950s	5.00	8.00	10.00
(BV 75) **Transport Set No. 330,** 2 cars, 1960s, 4½" long	30.00	45.00	60.00
(BV 76) **No. 204 U.S. Army Truck,** 2½" long, no hitch, red wood hubs	7.00	11.00	15.00
(BV 77) "U.S. Army" truck, white rubber wheels, 2½" long, wire or peg hitch	10.00	15.00	20.00
(BV 78) Truck "U.S. Motor Unit", circa 1940, white rubber tires, came 3 ways; no hitch, wire hitch, peg hitch, 3¼" long	17.00	26.00	35.00
(BV 79) Wheel-A-Rific speedway track, two lead racers, black rubber wheels, 10' of plastic track, sold for $1.00 circa 1970	6.00	9.00	12.00
(BV 80) **No. 46** wrecker, 3½", circa 1931	17.00	26.00	35.00
(BV 81) Wrecker, 3 15/16" long, circa 1934, XXX	17.00	26.00	35.00

BARCLAY	G	VG	M
(BV 82) Wrecker, two-piece, **No. 403**, diecast 1930s, "Barclay Toy", 2⅞" long .	37.00	56.00	75.00
(BV 83) Cannon Truck, moveable cannon, 4" long	37.00	56.00	75.00
(BV 84) Milk truck in shape of bottle, No. 567......	40.00	60.00	80.00
(BV 85) "Milk" Van truck, 2⅞" long, bottle on side .	17.00	26.00	35.00
(BV 86) Officer's car, 2½" long with megaphone on top	22.00	33.00	44.00
(BV 87) Side dump, approx. 1½" long	2.00	3.00	5.00
(BV 88) Convertible with vacationers	17.00	26.00	35.00
(BV 89) **100/4 Build & Paint Auto Set,** 6 vehicles, parts, paints, 1930s	No Price Found		
(BV 89A) **No. 5004** Build and Paint Auto Set, circa 1934	No Price Found		
(BV 90) **2004 Build & Paint Set,** truck, coupe, sedan, parts, paints, early......	200.00	300.00	400.00
(BV 90A) **2004 Build & Paint Set** same number, only 2 vehicles	No Price Found		
(BV 91) "U.S. Mail" truck, 1960s, approx. 2"	4.00	6.00	8.00
(BV 92) Moving Truck, circa 1960s, approx. 2"	4.00	6.00	8.00
(BV 93) Log Truck, circa 1960s, approx. 2"	4.00	6.00	8.00
(BV 94) Dump Truck, circa 1960s, approx. 2"	4.00	6.00	8.00
(BV 95) Racing Car, circa 1968, approx. 2"	4.00	6.00	8.00
(BV 96) "Police" car (like BV86 and BV97), approx. 2" long	4.00	6.00	8.00
(BV 97) "Chief" police car (like BC86 and BV96), approx. 2" long	4.00	6.00	8.00
(BV 98) Vintage Car, approx. 2" long	3.00	4.50	6.00
(BV 99) Oil Truck, circa 1960s, approx. 2" long ..	4.00	6.00	8.00
(BV 100) Pepsi-Cola truck, 1960s, approx. 2" long ..	5.00	8.00	10.00
(BV 101) Racing car, circa 1968, no fenders, approx. 2" long	3.00	4.00	6.00
(BV 102) Volkswagen, 1960s, approx. 2" long ..	3.00	4.00	6.00

	G	VG	M
(BV 103) U.S. Army truck, circa 1968, approx. 2" long	6.00	9.00	12.00
(BV 104) Hospital Truck, circa 1968, approx. 2" long	6.00	9.00	12.00
(BV 105) Army truck, open bed, circa 1968, approx. 2" long	6.00	9.00	12.00
(BV 106) Army oil truck, circa 1968, approx. 2" long	6.00	9.00	12.00
(BV 107) **Double Transport Set No. 44,** 4½" long, four cars on upper and lower racks, 1960s, hinged for unloading	15.00	22.00	30.00
(BV 108) Two-door sedan, 1960s, 1⅝" long	3.00	4.00	6.00
(BV 109) **No. 203 Tractor,** 2⅛" long, peg hitch	11.00	16.00	22.00
(BV 110) Open coupe with driver in cap, early 30s ..	15.00	22.00	30.00
(BV 111) "Esso Gas" truck, 1930s, 5" long	20.00	30.00	40.00
(BV 112) **No. 361 Streamline Large Coupe** .	17.00	26.00	35.00
(BV 113) 1935 DeSoto AirFlow, 5³⁄₁₆" long	17.00	26.00	35.00
(BV 114) Car Carrier, two small cars, early 1930s ..	25.00	38.00	50.00
(BV 115) **No. 371** Racing Car, large, 1930s, 4¼" long	16.00	24.00	32.00
(BV 116) **No. 7** Tractor, circa late 20s- early 30s ...	15.00	22.00	30.00
(BV 117) **No. 1105** (or 1705) "Towing Service" truck, large	20.00	30.00	40.00
(BV 118) 1929 Buick Sedan? 3" long	15.00	22.00	30.00
(BV 119) **No. 312** "Towing" truck, in 1936 catalog, 3⅜" long	17.00	26.00	35.00
(BV 120) **No. 306 Racer,** in 1936 catalog	15.00	22.00	30.00
(BV 121) **No. 303 Streamline Racer,** 4⅜" long	15.00	22.00	30.00
(BV 122) **No. 208 Hook and Ladder,** in 1935 catalog, 3" long	16.00	24.00	32.00
(BV 123) **No. 301 Coupe Streamline,** 3¼" long ...	12.00	18.00	25.00
(BV 124) **No. 207 Stake Truck,** in 1935 catalog, 3⅛" long	17.00	26.00	35.00

BARCLAY

BV64   BV72   BV40

BV54   BV30   BV81

BV60   BV63   BV25   BV28   BV71

BV37   BV61   BV55   BV24

BV11   BV49   BV14   BV13

BV82   BV61 sedan   BV47

BV65   BV52

BV45. Photo from the Barclay files.
Courtesy Toy Soldier Review

BV83

Photo by Ed Poole

BARCLAY

BV84

Courtesy Larry Burke

BV88

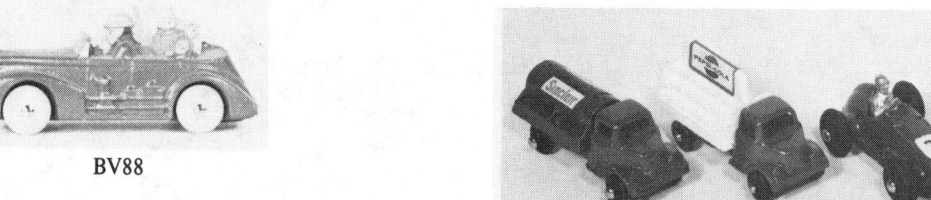

BARCLAY, top row, L to R: Howitzer, 4 wheels, loop hitch horizontal, Howitzer, 4 wheels, loop hitch vertical; BV78 with wire hitch; BV78 with peg hitch.
Bottom row, L to R: BV7; BV76, vertical hitch; BV76 wire hitch; BV76, no hitch.
Photo by Ed Poole

BV91. From the Barclay files.
Courtesy Toy Soldier Review.

BV92   BV93   BV94   BV87
From the Barclay files
Courtesy Toy Soldier Review

BV95   BV96   BV97   BV98
From the Barclay files
Courtesy Toy Soldier Review

BV99   BV100   BV101   BV102
From the Barclay files
Courtesy Toy Soldier Review

BV103   BV104   BV105   BV106
From the Barclay files.
Courtesy Toy Soldier Review

BV107
From the Barclay files.
Courtesy Toy Soldier Review

BV108
From the Barclay files
Courtesy Toy Soldier Review

BARCLAY	G	VG	M
(BV 125) **No. 362 Streamline Sedan Large,** in 1935 catalog	15.00	22.00	30.00
(BV 126) **No. 368** Fire Truck, 1930s, "Fire Dept. No. 99", 5¾" long	20.00	30.00	40.00
(BV 127) **No. 1703** 1935 Chrysler Airflow sedan, large	17.00	26.00	35.00
(BV 128) **No. 42** small tractor, in 1931 magazine, 2³⁄₁₆" long	12.00	18.00	25.00
(BV 129) **No. 39 Imperial Chrysler Coupe** circa 1931	15.00	22.00	30.00
(BV 130) **No. 5** Racer, in 1931 magazine, Golden Arrow	15.00	22.00	30.00
(BV 131) **No. 206** Delivery Truck "Bakery Fine Cake Pies", circa 1934, 3⅛" long	20.00	30.00	40.00
(BV 132) **No. 51** Coupe, circa 1931, 2³⁄₁₆" long	12.00	18.00	25.00
(BV 133) **No. 210** Fire, Truck, circa 1934, 3⅛" long	12.00	18.00	25.00
(BV 134) **No. 209 Fire Engine,** circa 1934, 3⅛" long	12.00	18.00	25.00
(BV 135) **No. 311** Sedan, circa 1936	12.00	18.00	25.00
(BV 136) **No. 309** "Delivery" truck, circa 1936, 3½" long	12.00	18.00	25.00
(BV 137) **No. 50** Fire Truck, circa 1931, 2⅜" long	22.00	33.00	45.00
(BV 137A) Like BV 137, but with gold hydraulics on both sides, wood hubs, rubber tires, 2⁷⁄₁₆" long . . .	No Price Found		
(BV 138) **No. 56** Double-Decker Bus, circa 1931, 3¼" long	22.00	33.00	45.00
(BV 139) **No. 58** Auburn Speedster, circa 1931 . . .	17.00	26.00	35.00
(BV 140) Sedan, circa 1934	15.00	22.00	30.00
(BV 141) **No. 205 Tow Car,** in 1935 catalog, 3¹⁄₁₆" long	20.00	30.00	40.00
(BV 142) **No. 338 Contractor Set,** approx. 6¼" long (has hole hitch for wire, unlike BV109's peg hitch), 1930s	No Price Found		

	G	VG	M
(BV 143) Large Streamline Coupe, 1930s	15.00	22.00	30.00
(BV 144) "Gasoline" Truck, small, circa 1931, 2⁵⁄₁₆" long, 3 tank top	12.00	18.00	25.00
(BV 144A) Gas Truck, circa 1935, 200 series? 4 tank top, 3" long	17.00	26.00	35.00
(BV 145) Coupe, cast rear tire, circa 1935, 200 series?, 3⅛" long	17.00	26.00	35.00
(BV 146) Coupe, removable spare tire, in 1935 catalog, 4½" long	25.00	38.00	50.00
(BV 147) Dump Truck, spring action, ratchet, in 1935 catalog, 4" long . . .	20.00	30.00	40.00
(BV 148) Sport Coupe, 2⅞" long, removable spare tire, in 1935 catalog	25.00	38.00	50.00
(BV 149) Racing Car, large, raised exhaust pipe, driver, in 1935 catalog . .	17.00	26.00	35.00
(BV 150) Race Car, open, driver, 4" long	70.00	105.00	140.00
(BV 151) Stake Truck, 4⅜" long, in 1935 catalog . . .	25.00	38.00	50.00
(BV 152) 2-Car transport set, approx. 4¾" long	42.00	63.00	85.00
(BV 153) 4-Car transport set, 10¼" long, open-cab Mack Truck, (4) 2½" cars, in 1935 catalog	No Price Found		
(BV 154) Roadster, 4½" long, open, driver, dummy spare tire on each side, in 1935 catalog	No Price Found		
(BV155) Streamline Coupe, 5" long, in 1937 catalog	No Price Found		
(BV 156) "White Horse" van, approx. 3" long (some have sticker reading "Welcome I.C.M.A. compliments THE WHITE MOTOR CO.") .	62.00	93.00	125.00

BV122   BV123   BV124
Photo by Craig A. Clark

Not shown is the Barclay **REINDEER**, which probably began production in 1949, as a bill by the New Jersey Art Foundry for "2 small deer cast in bronze from plaster model" is dated January 14, 1949. Two sleds are on the same bill. Value of the reindeer in mint about $20.

BV144   BV144A   BV145
Photo by Craig A. Clark

BV147   BV148   BV149
Photo by Craig A. Clark

BV151   BV152
Photo by Craig A. Clark

BV155   BV156
Photo by Craig A. Clark

BC7

Barclay small cannon with rubber wheels.
Value in mint $25
Courtesy K. Warren Mitchell

BC4   BC8   BC9

L to R: Barclay No. 2 Long Range Cannon, medium cannon, small cannon with wood wheels. Prices in mint respectively: $48, 30, 25.
Courtesy K. Warren Mitchell

BC?11

Possible Barclay howitzer. 6" long. Bought in 1991 for $75
Photo by Stan Alekna

Though Barclay's George Fall doesn't remember the small house, the shrine and the fisherman, knowledgeable collectors believe they belong to this group. L to R: Detachable woman on bridge, small house, torii, bird, shrine, fisherman, pagoda, large house. The houses go for about $45 in mint, and the other pieces for about half that. The Japanese issued a similar ceramic set.
Photo by Stan Alekna

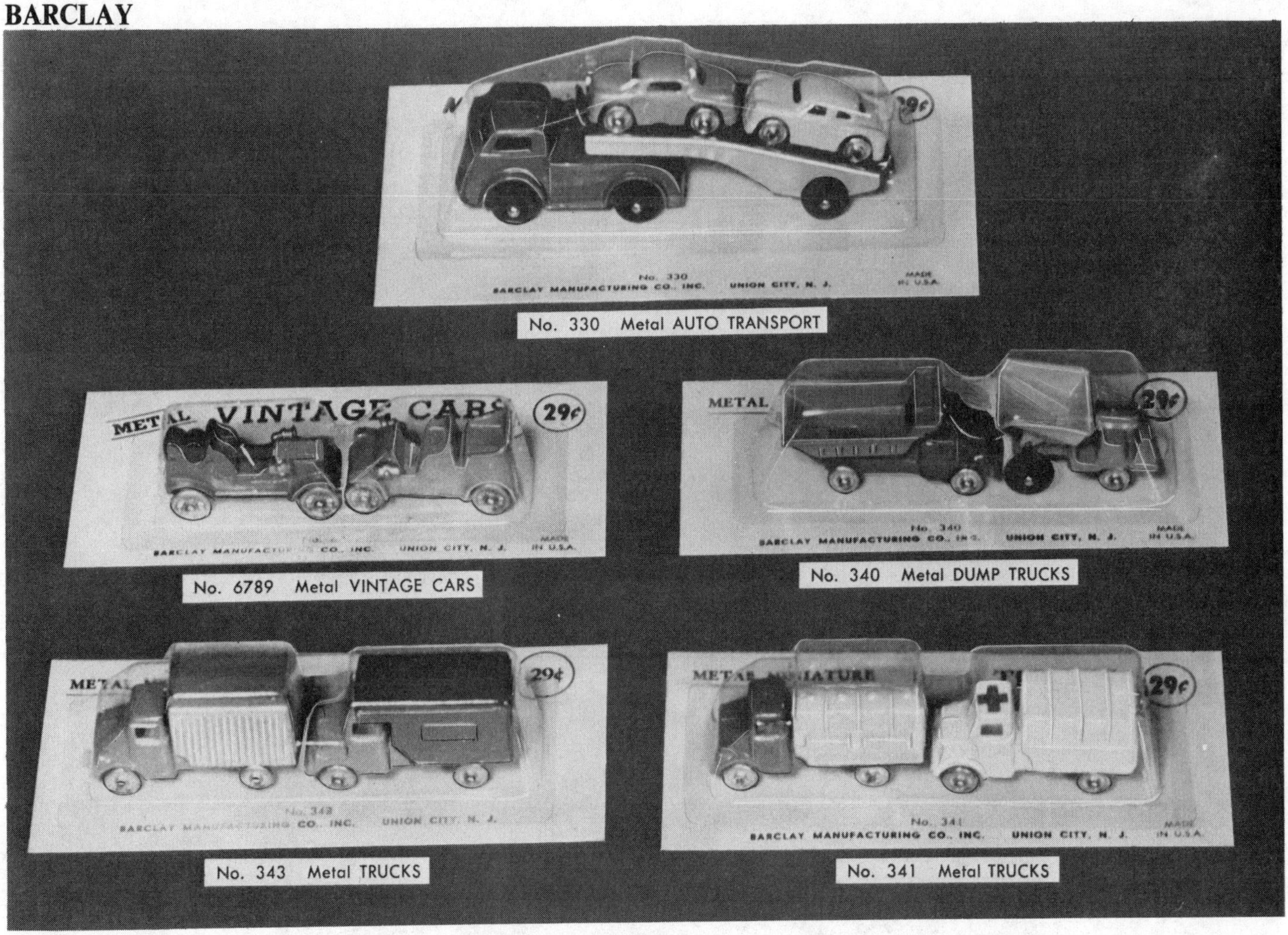

No. 330 Metal AUTO TRANSPORT

No. 6789 Metal VINTAGE CARS

No. 340 Metal DUMP TRUCKS

No. 343 Metal TRUCKS

No. 341 Metal TRUCKS

Barclay blister pack sets, circa 1968. The no. 330 Auto Transport (BV75) is worth about $35 in mint. The others are worth about $20 in mint. Photo from the Barclay files.
Courtesy Toy Soldier Review

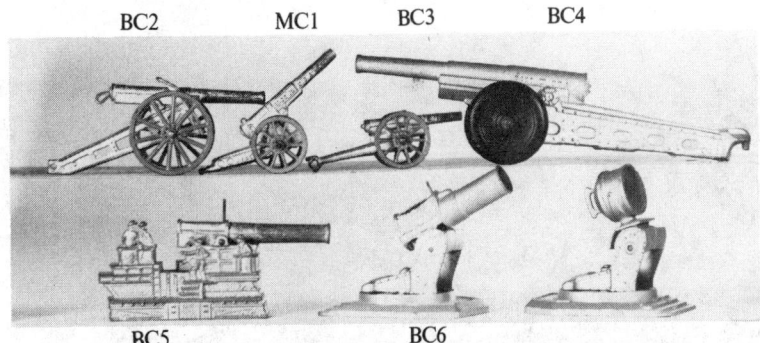

BC2   MC1   BC3   BC4

BC5   BC6

Top row, L to R: Cannon, spring-firing, spoke wheels, 4" long (value $25-38-50): Cannon, barrel elevated (value $6-9-12-): Cannon, spoked wheels, 3" long (value $6-9-12): No. 2 LONG RANGE CANNON (value $24-36-48): No. 4 COAST GUARD CANNON (value $45-68-90); No. 3 REVOLVING CANNON (value $20-30-40); No. 5 SEARCHLIGHT (value $25-38-50). MC1 may be Manoil.
Photo by Ed Poole

BC?12
Possible Barclay howitzer, 6" long. No price found.
Photo by Ed Poole

Top: 372 AEROPLANE CARRIER, which sold with two planes on its deck.
Value $25 good, $37.50 very good, $50 mint.
Bottom: 373 BATTLESHIP. Value $27 in good, $40 very good, $55 in mint.
Barclay veterans say these were the only two ships made by the company.
Photo by Ed Poole

Barclay loco 335, Tender 336 and passenger car 337. These were sold from at least the early 30s till about
the time of the firm's end. Value about $20 in mint for the set.

In 1984, 45 plaster castings retained by Barclay's chief of maintenance when he cleaned out the shut-down factory in 1971 were shown to the author
in the course of his research. Included were soldiers, Disney figures, vehicles and an autogiro, many never produced.

BARCLAY

BC10

BC1

Cannon, 4" long, Post-WWII, very large wheels. Value in good $20, very good $30, mint $40
Courtesy Holt's Hobbies

Barclay Cannon No. 1. This may be Barclay's earliest toy. Value in good $25, very good $38, mint $50.
Courtesy Ed Poole

BC2

Cannon, open and closed hitches.
Courtesy K. Warren Mitchell

Barclay coaches.
Photo by Don Pielin

BARCLAY Coach and Four, approx. 10¼" long.
Photo by Bill Kaufman. Courtesy Evelyn Besser
Value in good $30, very good $45, mint $60.

Barclay "Animal Cage" circus wagon, circa 1930s, lead and tin litho. Value in good $30, very good $45, mint $60

MANOIL

The four major dimestore toy soldier companies can be compared to the movie studios of their era. Barclay was a combination of MGM and Twentieth Century Fox; as monolithic as MGM, but not as stodgy, livelier in the sleek way that 20th was lively. Grey Iron was like Republic Pictures; near the poverty line but not quite, and poor Auburn Rubber's product was decidedly Monogram. Manoil? The Warner Brothers of its field; the most realistic, the most vivid, the most jaunty, the most down to earth.

What made Manoil was a combination of three men; Maurice Manoil (12/4/93–9/15/74), who handled the prosaic, but all-necessary production end, his brother Jack (1/29/02–9/1/55), who was far more interested in the creative area, and the man whose work defined Manoil; designer-sculptor Walter Baetz (1894-1978).

Maurice Manoil, circa 1969.
Courtesy Peter and Marjorie Ruben

Jack Manoil, circa 1945.
Courtesy Peter and Marjorie Ruben

The Manoils were from a family of eight and emigrated from Rumania in the early 1900s. They were essentially partners in the business, with Jack the driving force, but Maurice more often (though not always) billed as president of the company. Baetz was a Mennonite from Toronto, Canada.

Like many toy soldier companies, Manoil didn't begin as a toymaker. In its early days, and they go back to at least 1927, Manoil produced picture frames (a patent for one was granted to Jack Manoil in 1930), lamps, small containers, souvenirs, banks and ashtrays.

A combination of things may have prompted Manoil to turn to toys. Its major product just before the switch-over was a slush-cast still bank. These were sold largely to commercial banks which gave them out as premiums for savings accounts. But then a law was passed outlawing that practice. Another factor may have been the stir Tootsietoy caused in 1933 with its new Graham Series of toy cars. It's also possible that the creative instincts of Jack Manoil and Walter Baetz (who was with the company by now; collector-researcher Terry Sells has found three Manoil patents from 1933 which mention Baetz) would have propelled them in that direction anyway.

Whatever the impetus behind the change, in 1934 Manoil introduced a line of four 4½" long die cast cars. The distinctive Baetz-Manoil stamp was there from the first. The two sedans, the coupe and the wrecker are angularly attractive, strikingly original, and suggest a bent for exaggeration that became more and more evident in Baetz's work over the years.

Baetz was deeply artistic, as was his wife, who was a concert pianist. In his leisure time he worked in oils and acrylics and, in his last year, in India ink on white paper. According to Manoil relatives Arlene and Murry Bakel, who interviewed him a year or two before he died, this wasn't simply Sunday painting; Baetz sold his art.

Baetz worked very closely with Jack Manoil. The latter may have sketched out ideas for Baetz, but his drawings would have been crude; the likelihood is that most of his ideas were expressed verbally. Plaster molds show traces of plasticene clay, indicating this was the medium in which Baetz worked. According to the Bakels, Baetz and Jack loved the toy soldiers and the two often labored for long hours into the night, trying to come up with new designs, and improvements on the old.

"Improvements" is a key word with Baetz and Manoil. One of the sculptor's continuing concerns was to design a mold so that there'd be no structural weakness in the castings as a result of air bubbles. For this reason, many of Manoil's soldiers were redesigned a number of times, sometimes with subtle and sometimes with broad variations.

MANOIL

At left, a Manoil "Hollowbase", and to the right the normal underbase of a Manoil soldier. The "hollow base" figures were produced first, and according to the late Peter Ruben, who was a Manoil relative and worked with the company, were probably only produced exclusively for about six months, before the company changed to the two-hole base, which pours easier. Manoil's "hollow bases" probably stemmed from the fact that Manoil made lamps for years before it turned to toy soldiers (at one time being called Man-O-Lamp) and lamp bases are hollow.

Production of Manoil's soldiers began, according to the Bakels' records, in 1935. However, late 1935 ads suggest 1936 would have been the earliest date. The earliest documentation of Manoil's soldiers appears in the February, 1937 *Playthings*, in a display that also includes Barclays and Grey Irons. Manoil's first group of soldiers is known as "hollow base," because the underside of the base is pronouncedly concave. These figures are unmarked, as are the ones that followed immediately after, a group of soldiers, cadets, marines, sailors, cowboys, Indians, nurses and doctors who maintain the characteristic Manoil vigor despite an appearance that suggests a diet far too high in fats and sweets. The remaining pre-War line of soldiers, with few exceptions, was both leaner and more realistic, with a small group of figures (coded in this book as M62-M71) the most authentic-looking American combat soldiers ever produced. Everything about them suggests that they are deep in the middle of war.

Manoil never made any enemy soldiers, and the reason for this may have been Baetz. According to the Bakels, "he hated Japanese and other enemy soldiers," and did not want to model them.

Manoil's soldier line appears to have started off slowly – few collectors remember seeing Manoil soldiers much before 1939 – but by 1940 this situation had changed so greatly that Manoil found itself looking for a larger location. In 1927 Jack Manoil and Co. was located at 34 West Houston Street, Manhattan. By 1928 the company was called Man-O-Lamp, and in 1929 moved to 114 Bleecker Street. The next move I've been able to chart (the company changed its name to Manoil Manufacturing Co. in 1934) was in 1936, showing an address of 54 Bleecker Street. By that time Jack was living in Brooklyn, and thus the 1937 relocation to 346 Carroll Street in Brooklyn isn't surprising. According to a contemporary newspaper account, Manoil's move to Waverly, New York, in June, 1940 was because the brothers had decided Waverly offered "a supply of labor, good transportation facilities, nearness to the market for toys, and good living conditions."

Once in Waverly, the company employed 225 people, most of them young, and turned out an average of 80,000 toys a day. By 1940 Manoil had introduced virtually all of its pre-War soldier line (M105, with its solid puttees, suggests 1941 or even 1942 production), and in 1941 came out with its Happy Farm series, an arresting array of civilian figures which in particular displays Baetz's strong tendency toward caricature; some of them, the women in particular, have an almost Alice in Wonderland quality. (Let it be noted here that not once did Baetz come within miles of designing an attractive woman figure for Manoil).

With the end of toy soldier production on April 1, 1942, Manoil (pronounced MAN-oil) found itself floundering. Unlike other companies such as Barclay and Auburn, which turned to war production, Manoil was unable to land any defense contracts. It struggled throughout the War, trying first to make a go of it as a warehousing operation, and next as a poultry farm. Then, in December 1943, the company announced it had discovered "a new composition as a substitute for the metal formerly used in making toys" and that the plant would reopen after January 1.

The Bakels' records show that Manoil "manufactured composition toys from January 1, 1944 through Dec 31, '44", but my guess is that the run was shorter than that. I remember seeing them briefly in a 5 and 10 in 1944. I was excited, because I thought they were metal soldiers, the first in two years. But when I got them home, they broke almost immediately; they were made from a claylike substance which contained sulphur, and were extremely brittle. All of these pieces, which consist of five soldiers (one a mirror variation of the other) and a tank, have a distinctive inverted "V" underbase.

MANOIL

Manoil returned to toy soldier production by November or December of 1945, just a few short months after the end of World War II. Their first figures were slender, realistic, and unpainted, possibly rushed out to take advantage of pre-Christmas sales. The records of the New Jersey Art Foundry, which made Manoil's molds, show that their first job for Manoil after the War shut down production was on November 6, 1945 (or at least the billing was as of that date). Presumably this was for molds of Manoil's first post-WW II figures. (Pre-War pieces 14, 16, 20, 21, 17, 18, 22 18A, 65, 49, 13,, 15, 35, 52, 69, 73, 85 and 95 were also continued for a time.)

Production never reached the heights it had in the pre-War years; people were tired of war, and war toys, and there was increasing competition from the much cheaper plastic. But Manoil continued on, diminishing the size of its soldiers as lead prices increased, although unlike Barclay's bland podfoot troops, Manoil's remained distinctive to the end, and are quite attractive to collectors. By 1949 the firm began producing in plastic, selling millions of vehicles and airplanes, but its emphasis remained on metal.

In 1950 it added two new lines of toys. Its 500 series of soldiers was in the podfoot size. The My Ranch Corral pieces were planned as a group of 30, but only half were produced (though molds for the others survive). The gate for the corral bears the initials of Jack Manoil.

Then in 1953 Manoil shut down again, because of the shortage of materials caused by the Korean War. It reopened the same year, but in a smaller location, and as the Jack Manoil Company, Inc. Shortly after Jack's death in 1955, the company went out of business.

About 125 of Manoil's molds have been rescued, most of them post-War, as well as a quantity of post-war catalog sheets and box labels. Only one pre-War catalog, probably from 1939, is known to collectors. The Smithsonian has a number of the Happy Farm molds, and in the past has cast figures from them for sale to the public. It also has molds of the 716 sedan, the 718 convertible, the number 7 flagbearer and of the Empire State Building. The Margaret Woodbury Strong Museum in Rochester, New York, has the five-piece set of molds and trimming dies of the 710 tank truck, as well as advertising material.

Manoil also made things on special order, so there are one-of-a-kind Manoils out there (I've seen a horse, produced for an individual).

ALL NUMBERS AND WORDS IN BOLD PRINT ARE MANOIL'S OWN DESCRIPTION

	G	VG	M		G	VG	M
(M1) **7 Flag Bearer,** hollow base version	37.00	56.00	75.00	(M14) **11 Drummer,** stocky version	12.00	19.00	25.00
(M2) **7 Flag Bearer,** second version	10.00	16.00	21.00	(M15) **11 Drummer,** vertical drum	17.00	26.00	35.00
(M3) **7 Flag Bearer,** third version	10.00	15.00	20.00	(M16) **12 Machine Gunner (Prone),** grass on base	11.00	16.00	22.00
(M4) **8 Parade,** hollow base version	20.00	30.00	40.00	(M17) **12 Machine Gunner (Prone),** flat base, no grass	12.00	18.00	24.00
(M4a) as above, hollow base, bigger helmet	No Price Found			(M18) **12 Machine Gunner (Prone),** spaces under body	25.00	38.00	50.00
(M5) **8 Parade,** stocky version	8.00	12.00	16.00	(M19) **12 Machine Gunner (Prone),** no aperture between hands and gun	12.00	18.00	24.00
(M6) **8 Parade,** campaign cap straight on head	20.00	30.00	40.00	M20) **12 Machine Gunner (Prone),** no aperture, pack on back	9.00	14.00	18.00
(M7) **8 Parade,** number on back	32.00	48.00	64.00	(M21) **13 Cadet,** hollow base, no buckle on belt	22.00	33.00	44.00
(M8) **8 Parade,** fifth version	8.00	12.00	16.00	(M22) **13 Cadet,** second version	9.00	14.00	18.00
(M9) **9 Officer,** hollow base version	37.00	56.00	75.00	(M23) **14 Sailor,** hollow base	22.00	33.00	44.00
(M10) **9 Officer,** second version	9.00	14.00	18.00	(M23a) Same as above, in blue	25.00	38.00	50.00
(M11) **10 Bugler,** hollow base version	30.00	45.00	60.00	(M24) **14 Sailor,** second version	8.00	12.00	16.00
(M12) **10 Bugler,** second version	9.00	14.00	18.00				
(M13) **11 Drummer,** hollow base version	27.00	40.00	54.00				

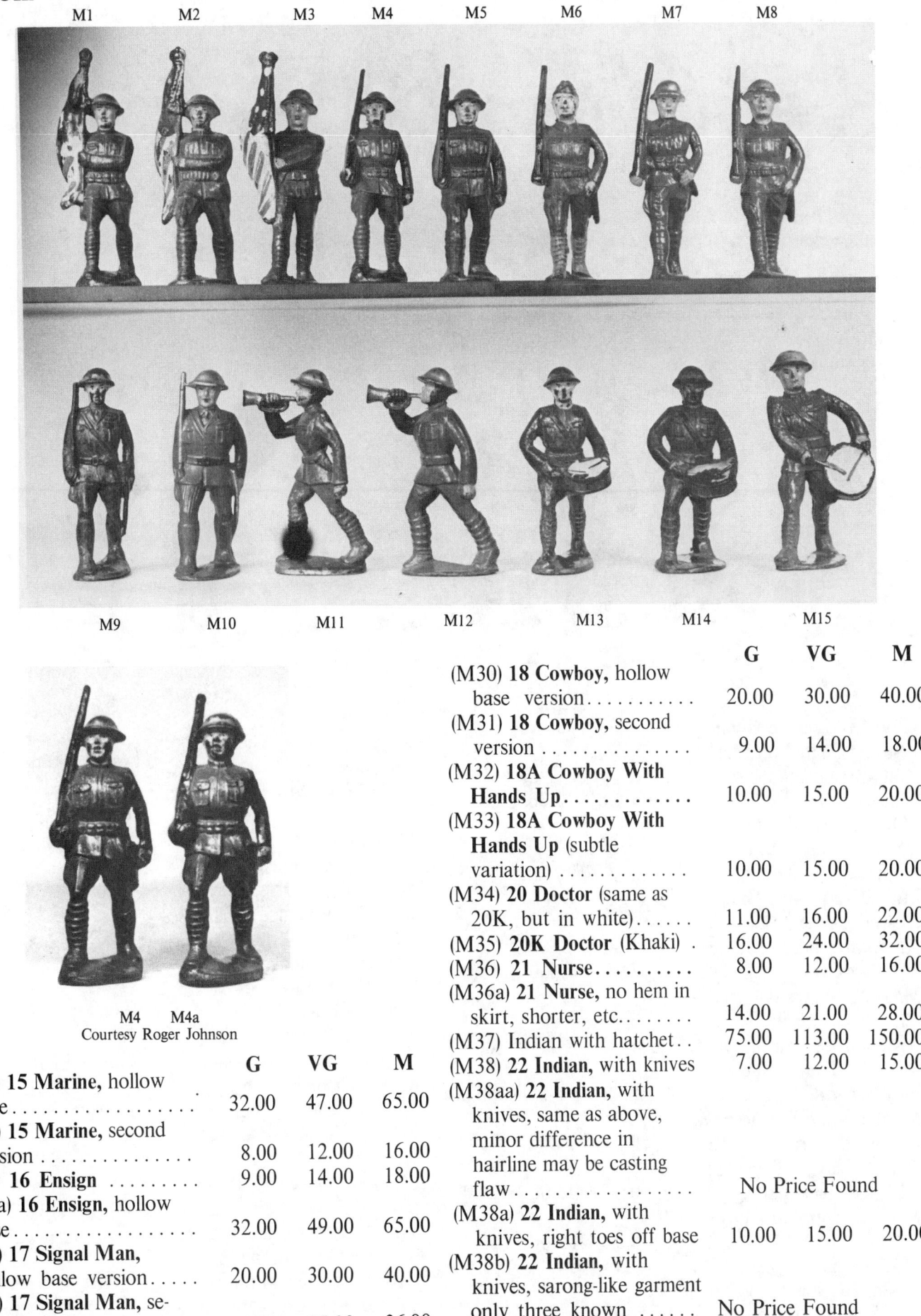

M1   M2   M3   M4   M5   M6   M7   M8

M9   M10   M11   M12   M13   M14   M15

M4   M4a
Courtesy Roger Johnson

	G	VG	M
(M25) **15 Marine,** hollow base	32.00	47.00	65.00
(M26) **15 Marine,** second version	8.00	12.00	16.00
(M27) **16 Ensign**	9.00	14.00	18.00
(M27a) **16 Ensign,** hollow base	32.00	49.00	65.00
(M28) **17 Signal Man,** hollow base version	20.00	30.00	40.00
(M29) **17 Signal Man,** second version	18.00	27.00	36.00

	G	VG	M
(M30) **18 Cowboy,** hollow base version	20.00	30.00	40.00
(M31) **18 Cowboy,** second version	9.00	14.00	18.00
(M32) **18A Cowboy With Hands Up**	10.00	15.00	20.00
(M33) **18A Cowboy With Hands Up** (subtle variation)	10.00	15.00	20.00
(M34) **20 Doctor** (same as 20K, but in white)	11.00	16.00	22.00
(M35) **20K Doctor** (Khaki)	16.00	24.00	32.00
(M36) **21 Nurse**	8.00	12.00	16.00
(M36a) **21 Nurse,** no hem in skirt, shorter, etc.	14.00	21.00	28.00
(M37) **Indian with hatchet**	75.00	113.00	150.00
(M38) **22 Indian,** with knives	7.00	12.00	15.00
(M38aa) **22 Indian,** with knives, same as above, minor difference in hairline may be casting flaw	No Price Found		
(M38a) **22 Indian,** with knives, right toes off base	10.00	15.00	20.00
(M38b) **22 Indian,** with knives, sarong-like garment only three known	No Price Found		

MANOIL

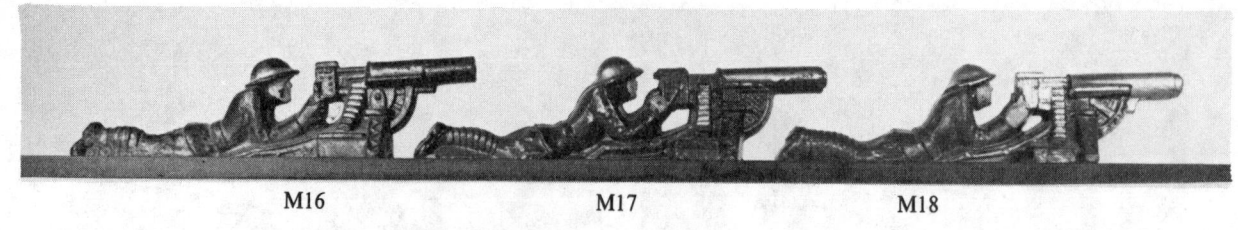

M16   M17   M18

M19   M20

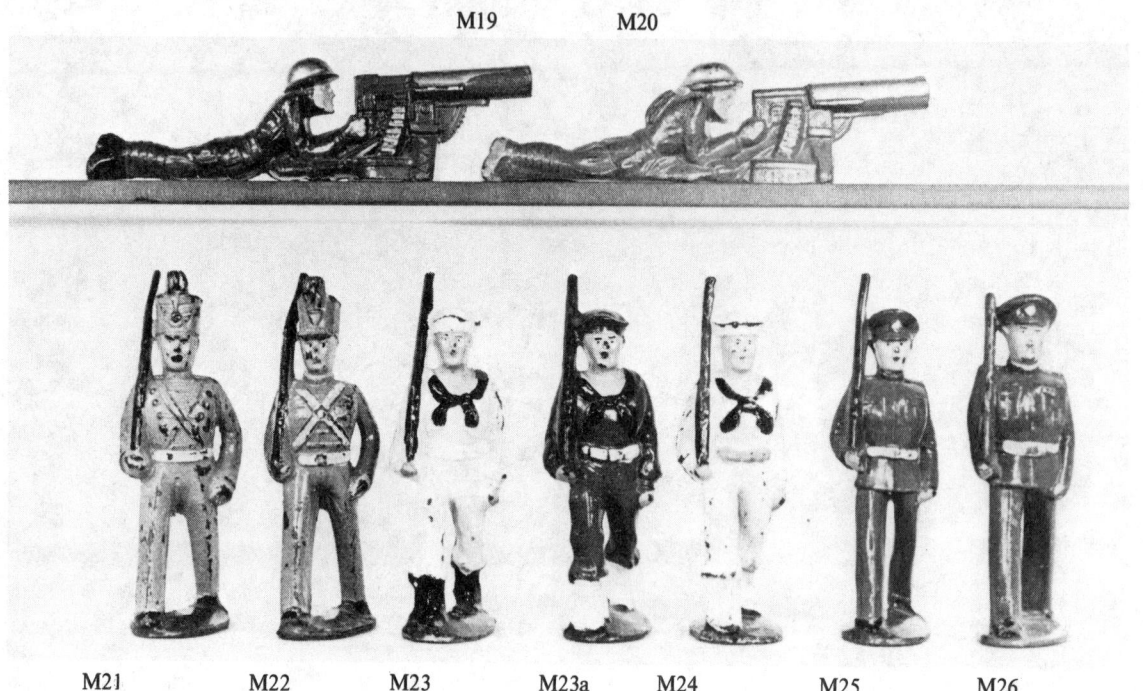

M21   M22   M23   M23a   M24   M25   M26

	G	VG	M
(M39) **23 Machine Gunner Sitting,** seated on four pillows, bullets feed from ammo box.	11.00	17.00	23.00
(M40) **23 Machine Gunner Sitting,** markings under base.	11.00	17.00	23.00
(M41) **23 Machine Gunner Sitting,** squarer-looking, markings near right leg. .	11.00	16.00	22.00
(M42) **24 Cannon Loader**. . .	7.00	12.00	15.00
(M43) **25 Sniper (kneeling)** hollow base, (probably not Manoil-see Paul Paragine)	40.00	60.00	80.00
(M44) **25 Sniper (Kneeling),** folding rifle.	150.00	225.00	300.00
(M45) **25 Sniper (Kneeling),** short thin rifle.	9.00	14.00	18.00
(M46) **25 Sniper (Kneeling),** longer, thicker rifle.	10.00	15.00	20.00
(M47) **26 Sniper,** folding rifle	130.00	195.00	260.00
(M48) **26 Sniper**.	9.00	14.00	18.00
(M48a) **26 Sniper,** shorter rifle, angle different on underside of rifle.	10.00	15.00	20.00

	G	VG	M
(M49) **27 Tommy Gunner,** bloated version.	15.00	23.00	30.00
(M50) **27 Tommy Gunner,** second version.	10.00	15.00	20.00
(M51) **28 Observer**.	9.00	14.00	18.00
(M52) **29 Wounded Soldier (Walking)**	9.00	14.00	18.00
(M53) **30 Wounded Soldier (Lying)**	8.00	12.00	16.00
(M54) **30 Wounded Soldier (Lying),** number on back, shorter head	9.00	14.00	18.00
(M55) **31 Bomb Thrower,** three grenades in pouch. .	8.00	12.00	17.00
(M56) **31 Bomb Thrower,** two grenades in pouch. . .	9.00	13.00	18.00
(M57) **32 Stretcher Carrier,** no medical kit.	8.00	12.00	16.00
(M58) **32 Stretcher Carrier,** medical kit.	9.00	14.00	19.00
(M58a) **32 Stretcher Carrier,** medical kit, number on back, buttons on uniform, different pockets and collar from above.	45.00	68.00	90.00

M27a   M27   M28   M29

M30   M31   M32   M34   M35   M36   M36a

M37   M38   M38aa   M38a   M38b   M39

M38aa and M38b courtesy Marjorie and the late Peter Ruben

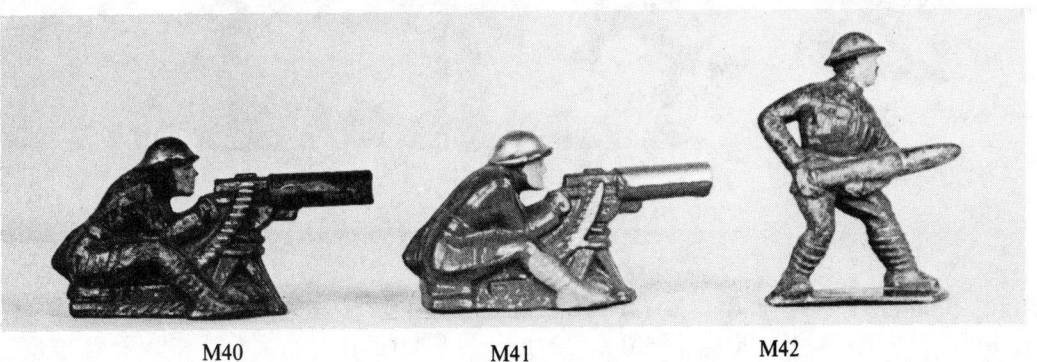

M40   M41   M42

M43   M44   M45   M46

M47   M48   M48a   M49   M50

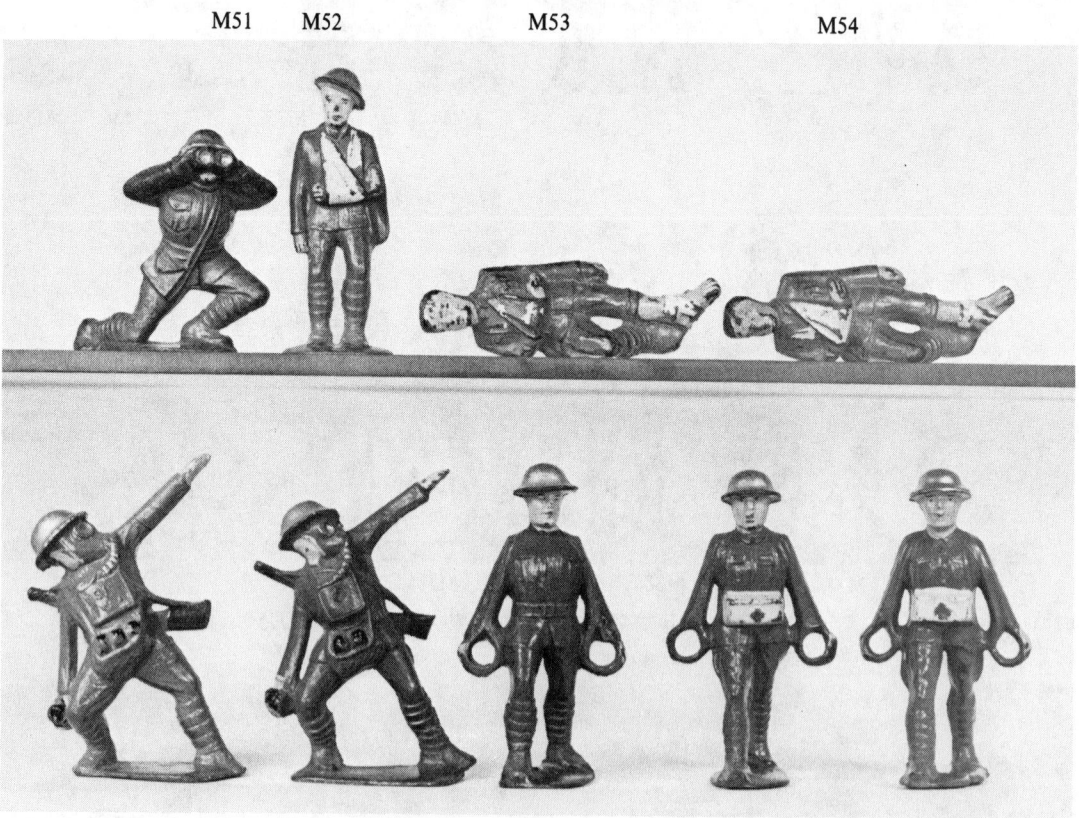

M51   M52   M53   M54

M55   M56   M57   M58   M58a

	G	VG	M		G	VG	M
(M59) **33 Sitting Soldier**...	20.00	30.00	40.00	(M63) **37 Soldier With Gun**			
(M60) **34 Aviator**........	10.00	15.00	20.00	**Charging**.............	22.00	33.00	44.00
(M61) **35 Hostess**, in white.	35.00	53.00	70.00	(M64) **38 Soldier With Gun**			
as above, in green.......	30.00	45.00	60.00	**Butting**..............	22.00	33.00	45.00
(M61a) **35 Hostess** in Khaki	150.00	225.00	300.00	(M65) **39 Soldier With**			
(M62) **36 Soldier With**				**Bayonet Jabbing**	25.00	38.00	50.00
Bayonet Charging......	17.00	26.00	35.00				

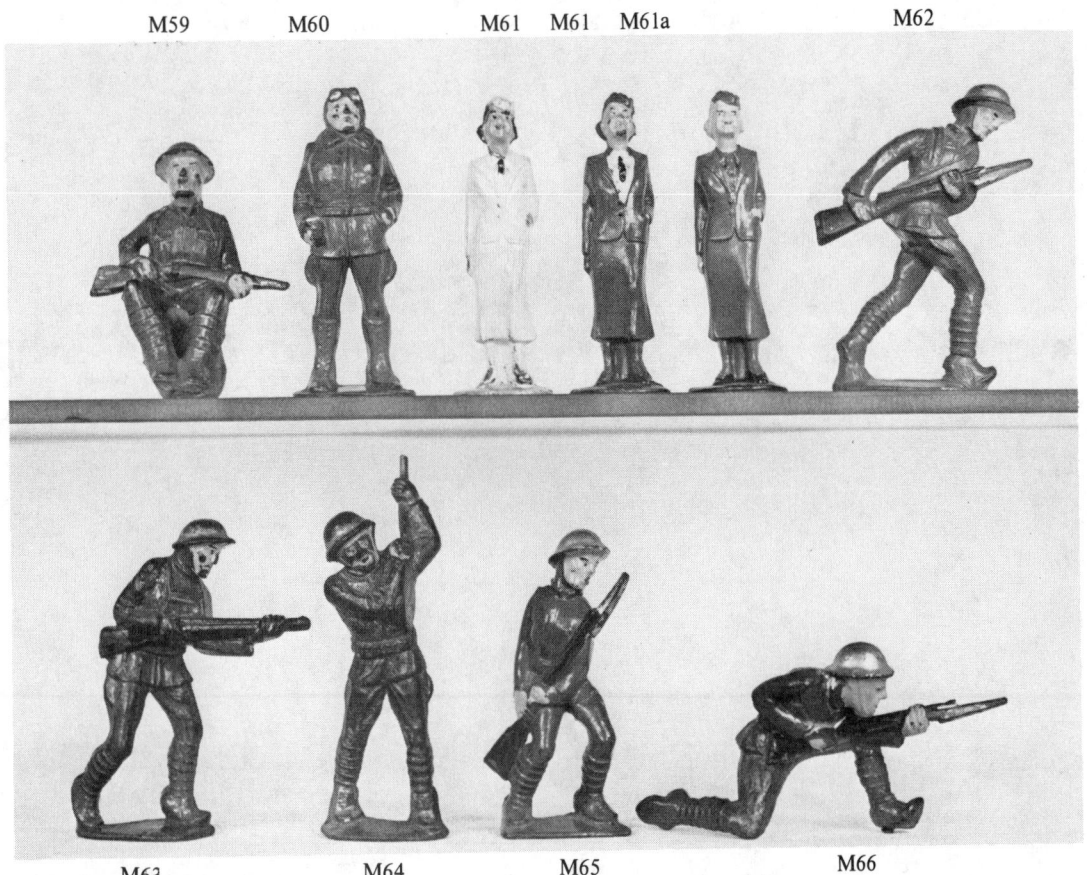

M59   M60   M61 M61 M61a   M62

M63   M64   M65   M66

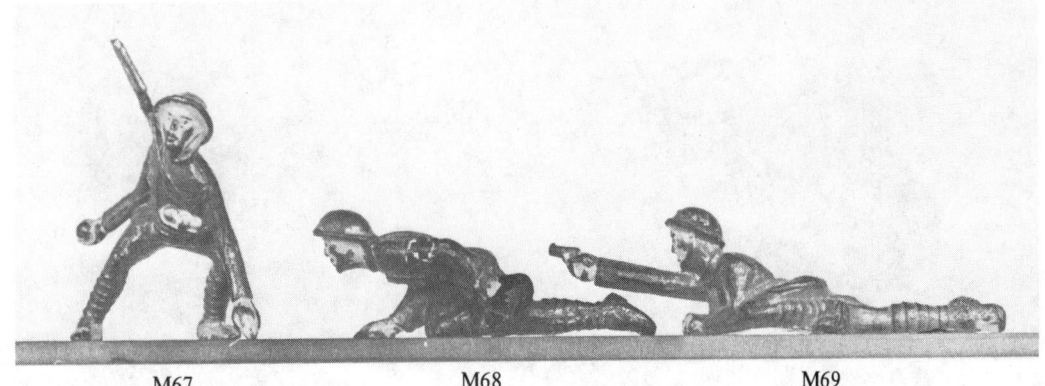

M67   M68   M69

M70   M71   M72

	G	VG	M		G	VG	M
(M66) 40 Soldier (Kneeling With Bayonet)........	31.00	47.00	62.00	(M68) 42 Field Doctor (Crawling)............	30.00	45.00	60.00
(M67) 41 Soldier (Crouching With Hand Grenade)....	30.00	45.00	60.00	(M69) 43 Officer (Lying Down - Shooting Revolver).............	27.00	41.00	54.00

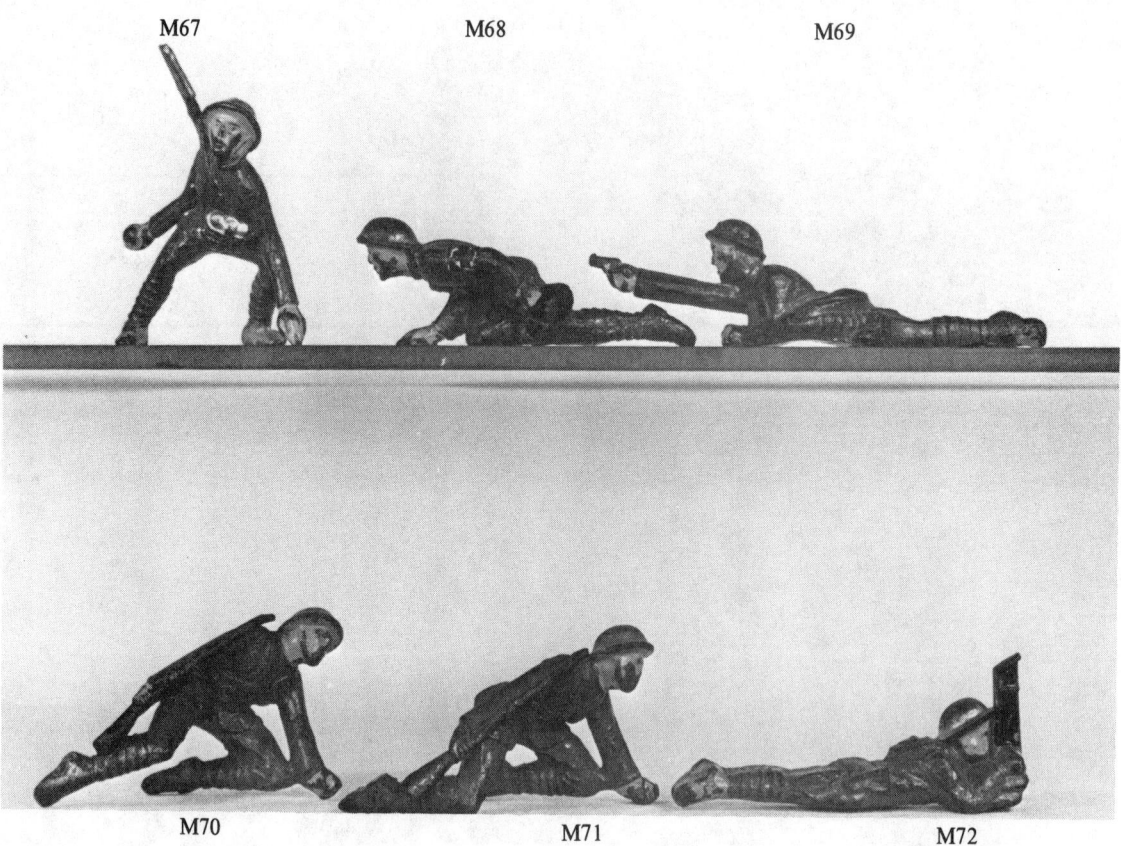

M67   M68   M69

M70   M71   M72

L to R: M79, M79a. M79a has no sprocket gears, its handlebars barely
clear the headlight, and its more rounded helmet suggests it is the earlier
version Courtesy Ron Hillman - *Old Toy Soldier*

L to R: M74a, M74
Photo by Harold Haseley

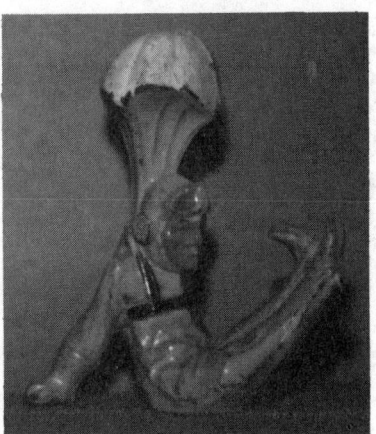

M88b, in gray
Photo by Jim Furstman

L to R: M89b, M89
Photo K. Warren Mitchell

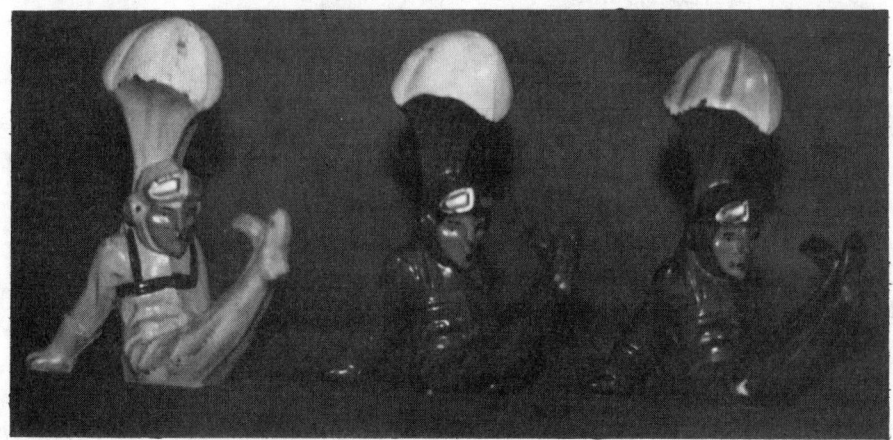

L to R: M88a, M88, M88 with what seems to be airbrushing. Not known
if the latter was painted by Manoil, but it appears to be legitimate.
Photo by Jim Krakowiecki

	G	VG	M
(M70) 44 Crawling Scout With Gun, left leg high when right leg on ground (only four known)	90.00	135.00	180.00
(M71) 44 Crawling Scout With Gun, left leg lower .	27.00	41.00	54.00
(M72) 45 Observer (With Periscope)	12.00	19.00	25.00
(M73) 46 Anti-Aircraft Gunner, barrel of gun drops below arm............	8.00	13.00	17.00
(M74) 46 Anti-Aircraft Gunner, barrel of gun ends at arm	10.00	16.00	21.00
(M74a) Like above, but stand under angled leg, barrel of gun longer, untapered	No Price Found		
(M75) 47 Anti-Aircraft Searchlight	10.00	15.00	20.00
(M75a) 47 like above, with tin lens	55.00	83.00	110.00
(M75b) 47 like M75, number on back, helmet looks as if it was adapted to look like WW II helmet......	11.00	17.00	22.00
(M76) 48 Navy Gunner	11.00	17.00	23.00
(M77) 49 Policeman.......	8.00	12.00	17.00
(M78) 49 Policeman, slightly larger version	8.00	12.00	17.00
(M79) 50 Bicycle Despatch Rider	13.00	20.00	26.00
(M79a) Like above, but no sprocket gear, more rounded helmet, handlebars barely clear headlight	No Price Found		
(M80) 51 Motorized Machine Gunner.......	21.00	32.00	42.00
(M81) 52 Motorcycle Rider, number over rear wheel, grass base.............	15.00	23.00	30.00
(M81a) 52 Same as above, motor variation	No Price Found		
(M82) 52 Motorcycle Rider.	20.00	30.00	40.00
(M83) 53 Sitting Soldier Without Gun..........	17.00	26.00	35.00
(M84) 54 Sitting Soldier Eating	23.00	35.00	46.00
(M85) 55 Sitting Soldier At Table With Phone & Map	17.00	26.00	34.00
(M86) 56 Paymaster.......	92.00	138.00	185.00
(M87) 57 Camouflage Sharpshooter Lying Down....	13.00	20.00	26.00
(M88) 58 Parachute Jumper	10.00	15.00	20.00

	G	VG	M
(M88a) Like above, painted white	110.00	165.00	220.00
(M88b) Like above, painted gray	No Price Found		
(M89) 59 Soldier Writing Letter	32.00	49.00	65.00
(M89a) Same as M89, foot not curled up, pencil is flat, helmet rounder, fuller	37.00	55.00	75.00
(M89b) Like M89, but no cigarette cast	28.00	42.00	56.00
(M90) 60 Cook's Helper With Ladle, normal helmet	21.00	32.00	42.00
(M91) 60 Cook's Helper with Ladle, helmet looks as if it was adapted to look like WW II helmet..	60.00	90.00	120.00
(M92) 61 Soldier With Camera	31.00	46.00	62.00
(M92a) 61 Soldier With Camera, thinner arm ...	31.00	46.00	62.00
(M93) 62 Soldier With Gas Mask & Gun..........	10.00	15.00	20.00
(M94) 63 Soldier With Gas Mask With Flare Pistol.	11.00	17.00	22.00
(M95) 64 Soldier Playing Banjo	50.00	75.00	100.00
(M96) 65 Deep Sea Diver..	15.00	23.00	30.00
(M97) 65 Deep Sea Diver with "65" on chest......	10.00	15.00	20.00
(M98) 66 Soldier With Gun on Parade with Overseas Cap	22.00	34.00	45.00
(M99) 67 Soldier With Gun And Pack Marching....	9.00	14.00	18.00
(M100) 68 Soldier Boxing..	37.00	53.00	75.00
(M101) 77 Lineman & Telephone Pole, pole comes with two different-shaped bases, oval or diagonal	43.00	65.00	86.00
(M102) 78 Anti-Tank Gun, round shield, all 4 variations based on Vickers 2.95 mountain gun......	15.00	23.00	30.00
(M103) 78 Anti-Tank Gun, squared shield..........	15.00	23.00	30.00
(M103a) 78 Anti-Tank Gun, angled shield	15.00	23.00	30.00
(M104) 78 Anti-Tank Gun, wooden wheels	30.00	45.00	60.00

M73   M74   M75   M75a   M75b

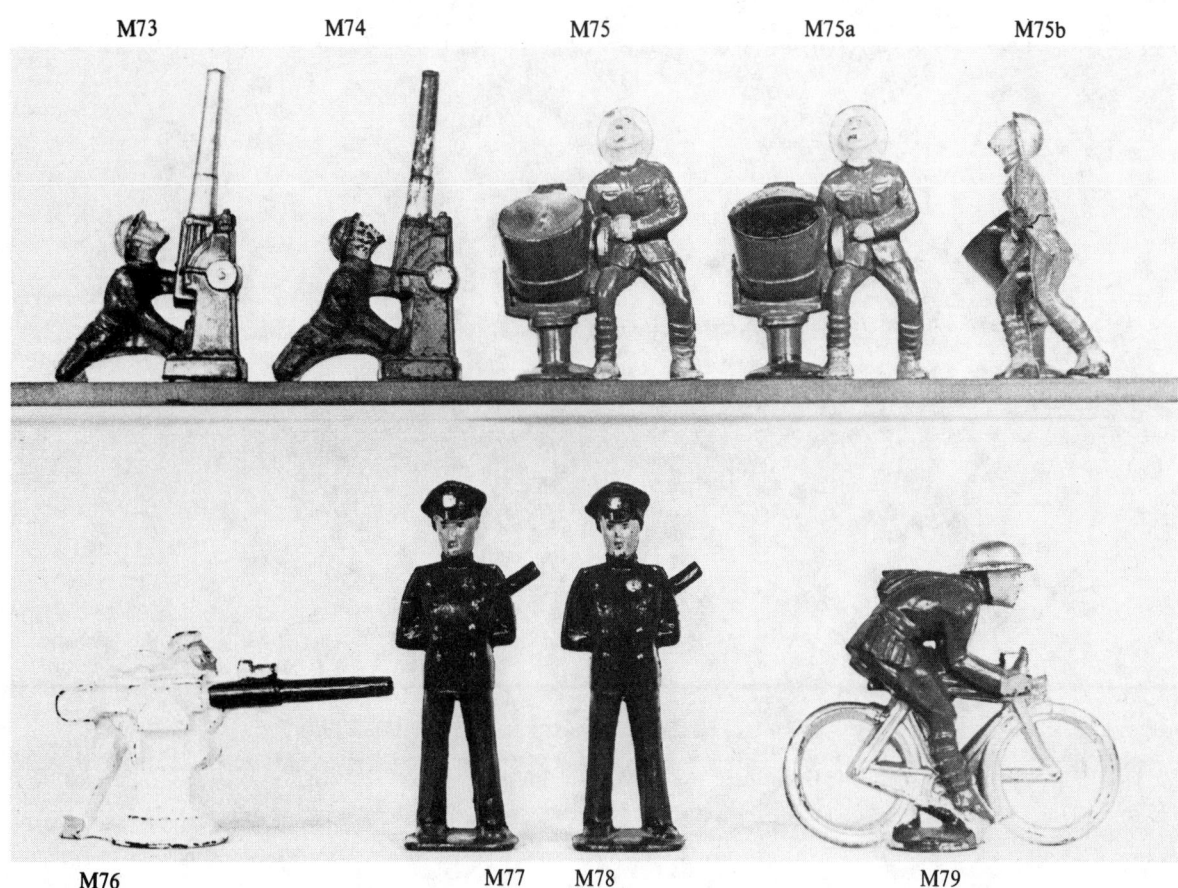

M76   M77 M78   M79

M80   M81   M81a

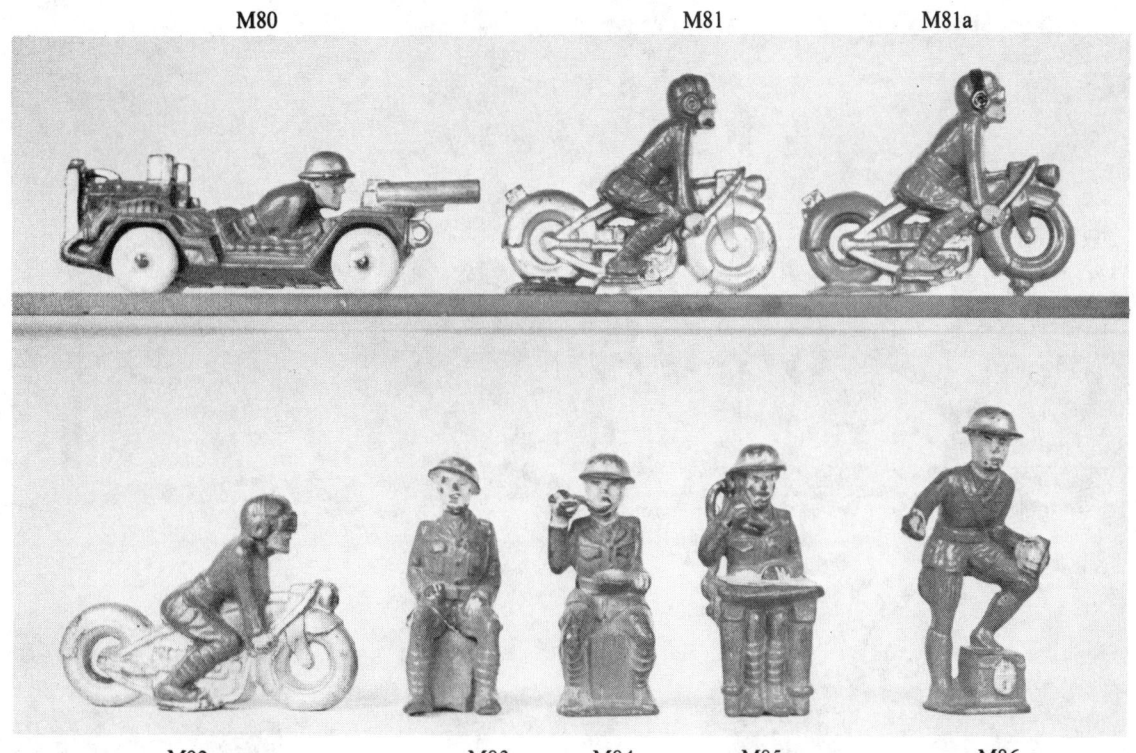

M82   M83 M84 M85   M86

M87　　　　M88　　　M89　　　M89a

M90　　M91　　M92　M92a　　M93　　　M94

M95　　　　M96　M97　M98　M99　　M100　M101

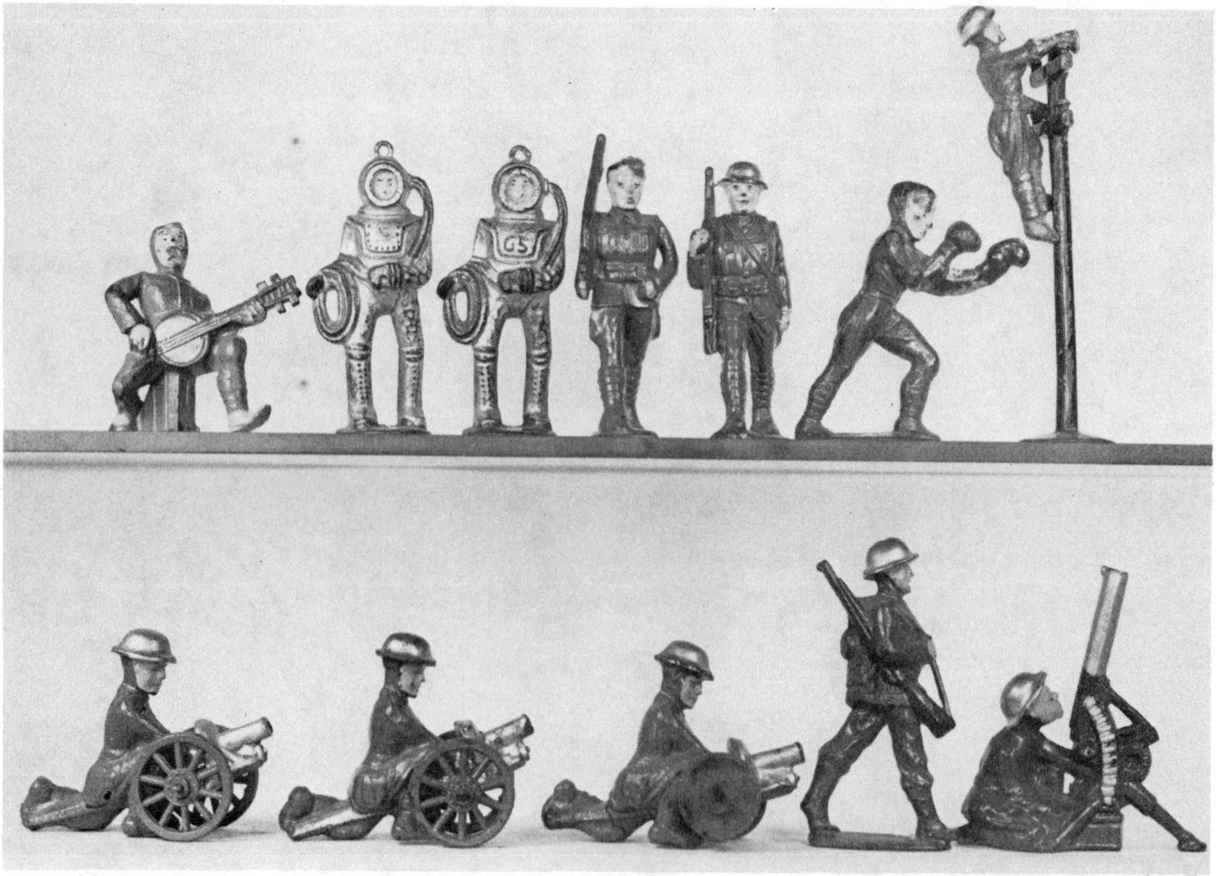

M102　　　　M103　　　　M104　　　M105　M106

MANOIL

This cowboy was never produced by Manoil. Cast from Manoil mold by Ron Eccles. Its main variation from M32 is the hat's longer crown.

L to R: M114b, M114, silver prop variation of M114b. On M114 the lower hand is flat against the propeller. With 114b it curves around the propeller.
Photo by Jim Krakowiecki

Original mold for Manoil's M179
Photo by Stan Alekna

Contents of a Manoil Happy Farm set (contents vary).
Photo by K. Warren Mitchell

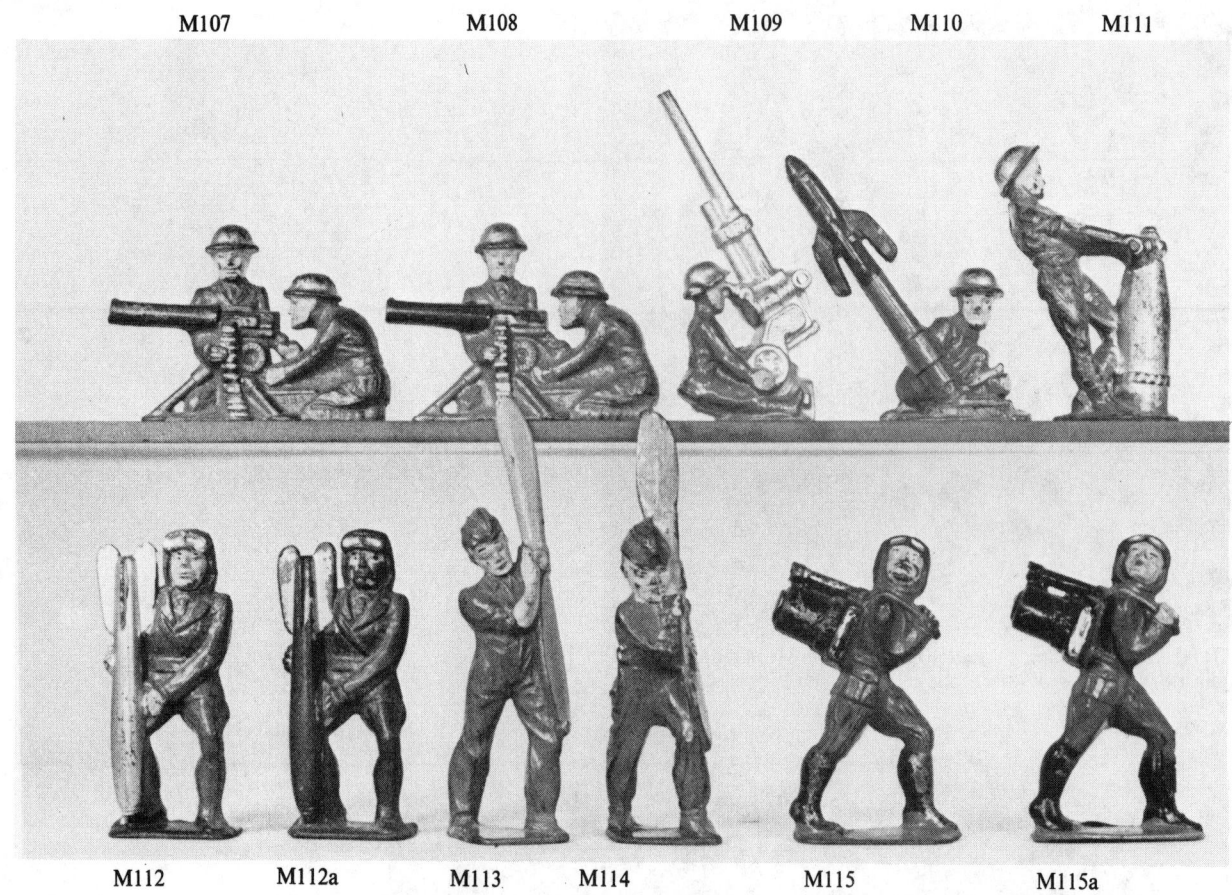

M107 M108 M109 M110 M111

M112 M112a M113 M114 M115 M115a

M116 M117 M118 M119 M120

M121 M121a M122 M123 M124

M123a   M123

M123a   M123

M125   M126

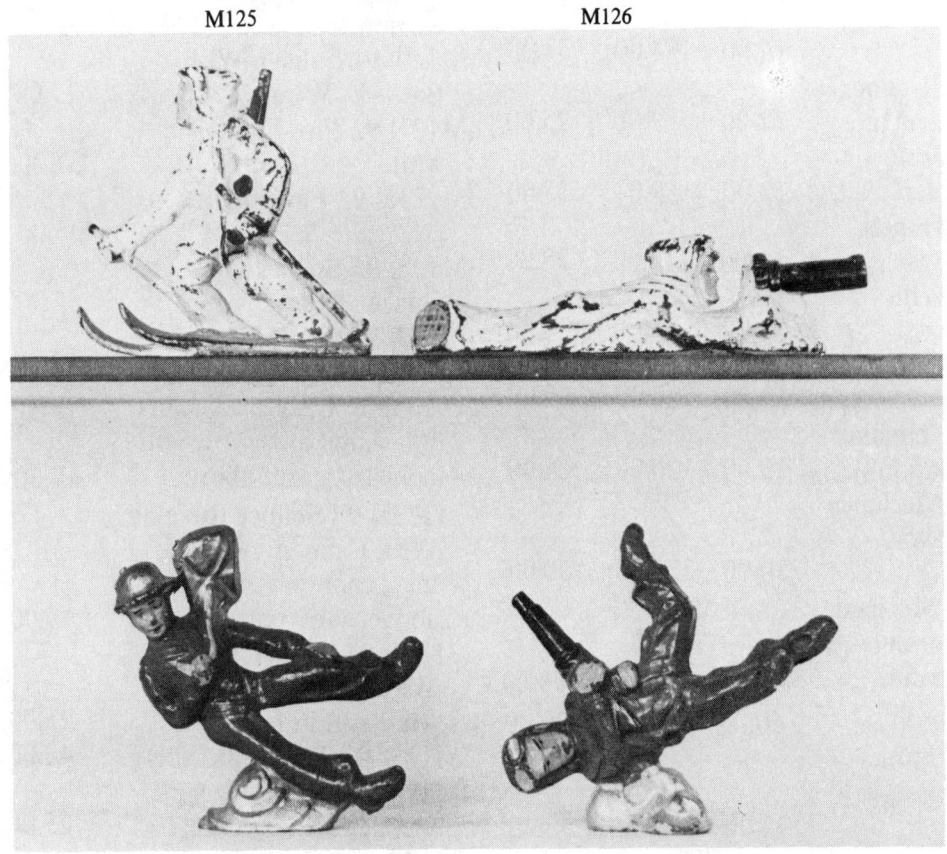

M127   M128

This is the Vickers 2.95 Mountain Gun, upon which Manoil based its M102-M104 figures.
Courtesy Ed Poole

Manoil anti-tank guns shown from the front to illustrate the difference in shields. Left to right: M102, M103, M103a.
Photo by Ed Poole

	G	VG	M
(M105) **79 Soldier marching with gun slung at angle**..	87.00	130.00	175.00
(M106) **80 Anti-Aircraft Machine Gunner**.......	9.00	14.00	18.00
(M107) **81 Machine Gunner and Helper,** aperture between hand and machine gun................	16.00	24.00	32.00
(M108) **81 Machine Gunner and Helper,** no aperture.	12.00	19.00	25.00
(M109) **82 Anti-Aircraft With Range Finder**.....	12.00	19.00	25.00
(M110) **83 Soldier Trench Mortar**...............	12.00	19.00	25.00
(M111) **84 Soldier With Shell**...............	14.00	21.00	28.00
(M112) **85 Aviator Holding Bomb**.............	13.00	20.00	26.00
(M112a) **85 Aviator Holding Bomb** (hand variation)...	13.00	20.00	26.00
(M113) **86 Aviator Mechanic With Propellor,** away from head.............	250.00	375.00	500.00
(M114) **86 Aviator Mechanic With Propellor, orange prop, flat lower hand.** ...	44.00	66.00	88.00
(M114a) **86 Silver prop**	60.00	90.00	120.00
(M114b) **86 orange prop, lower hand curves over prop**	44.00	66.00	88.00
(M115) **87 Aviator carrying bomb sight**............	20.00	30.00	40.00
(M115a) **87 Aviator carrying bomb sight, smaller base** .		No Price Found	
(M116) **88 Radio Operator Standing**	27.00	41.00	55.00

	G	VG	M
(M117) **89 Radio Operator (Lying Down)**	17.00	26.00	35.00
(M118) **90 Soldier Digging Trench**	22.00	33.00	45.00
(M119) **91 Soldier With Barbed Wire,** wide-faced version	20.00	30.00	40.00
(M120) **91 Soldier With Barbed Wire**..........	17.00	26.00	35.00
(M121) **92 Fire Fighter** in white	37.00	53.00	75.00
(M121a) **92 Fire Fighter** in grey..................	75.00	113.00	150.00
(M122) **93 Soldier On Guard Duty**...........	55.00	83.00	110.00
(M123) **94 Soldier Running With Cannon,** marked "Manoil USA", "1", cannon slants to right when looked at from above....	19.00	28.00	38.00
(M123a) **94 Soldier Running With Cannon,** no markings, cannon straight from above, face narrower....	19.00	28.00	38.00
(M124) **94 Soldier Running With Cannon,** wood wheels, thin face........	25.00	38.00	50.00
(M125) **99 Finn with Skis**..	40.00	60.00	80.00
(M126) **100 Finn Machine Gunner**	25.00	38.00	50.00
(M127) **101 Soldier Jumping with Chute**...........	50.00	75.00	100.00
(M127a) **Foot variation,** number in different place		No Price Found	
(M128) **102 Soldier Jumping With Machine Gun**	33.00	49.00	66.00

MANOIL

Happy Farm Series

According to the late Peter Ruben, a great number of color varieties and shades in this series exist, many of which can be related to the women who did the detail painting, and the season, as represented by 41/2 with long and short sleeve dresses. A number of Happy Farm figures were produced circa 1960 for the Smithsonian Museum, solid-cast with a patina or black finish.

	G	VG	M
(M129) 41/1 Bench	4.00	7.00	9.00
(M130) 41/2 Girl	4.00	7.00	9.00
(M131) 41/3 Young Man...	4.00	7.00	9.00
(M132) 41/4 Man Carrying Sack on Back..........	10.00	15.00	20.00

	G	VG	M
(M140) 41/12 Scarecrow With Top Hat	12.00	19.00	25.00
(M141) 41/13 Farmer Carrying Pumpkin..........	10.00	15.00	20.00
(M142) 41/14 Darky Eating Watermelon	37.00	53.00	75.00
(M143) 41/15 Scarecrow With Straw Hat........	10.00	16.00	21.00
(M144) 41/16 Watchman Blowing Out Lantern....	11.00	17.00	23.00
(M145) 41/17 Hod Carrier With Bricks	15.00	23.00	30.00
(M146) 41/18 Man Chopping Wood............	11.00	17.00	23.00

M129-M131   M132   M133   M134   M135

M136   M137   M138   M139   M140

	G	VG	M
(M133) 41/5 Farmer Pitching Sheaves............	10.00	16.00	21.00
(M134) 41/6 Farmer Sharpening Scythe......	10.00	16.00	21.00
(M135) 41/7 Blacksmith Making Horseshoes	12.00	19.00	25.00
(M136) 41/8 Farmer Cutting With Scythe..........	11.00	17.00	22.00
(M137) 41/9 Farmer Cutting Corn	12.00	18.00	24.00
(M138) 41/10 Farmer Sowing Grain.............	10.00	15.00	20.00
(M139) 41/11 Man Carrying Sheaves Under Arm.....	10.00	15.00	20.00

	G	VG	M
(M147) 41/19 Mason Laying Bricks	19.00	28.00	38.00
(M148) 41/20 Man Dumping Wheel Barrow.........	11.00	17.00	23.00
(M149) 41/21 Old Man Fixing Shoe.............	16.00	25.00	33.00
(M150) 41/22 Blacksmith With Wheel..........	12.00	18.00	24.00
(M151) 41/23 Carpenter Carrying Door........	18.00	27.00	36.00
(M152) 41/24 Hound	8.00	13.00	17.00
(M153) 41/25 Carpenter Sawing Lumber........	12.00	18.00	24.00

M141 M142   M143 M144   M145 M146

M147   M148   M149   M150   M151

M152   M153   M154   M155 M156

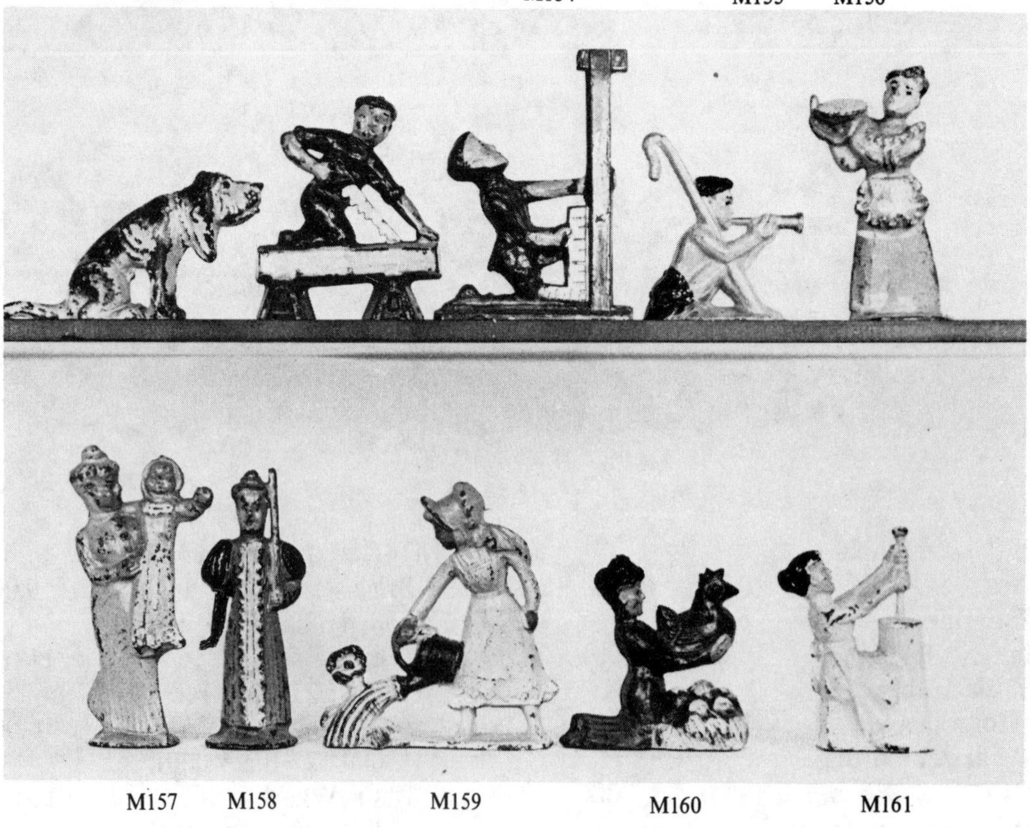

M157 M158   M159   M160   M161

MANOIL

M162 M163 M164 M164a M165

M166 M167 M168 M169

	G	VG	M		G	VG	M
(M154) 41/26 Carpenter With Square	22.00	33.00	45.00	(M168) 41/40 Boy Carrying Wood	12.00	18.00	24.00
(M155) 41/27 Sheperd With Flute	26.00	39.00	52.00	(M169) 41/41 Stacks of Sheaves	8.00	12.00	16.00
(M156) 41/28 Lady With Pie	14.00	21.00	29.00				
(M157) 41/29 Lady With Child	15.00	23.00	30.00				
(M158) 41/30 School Teacher	18.00	27.00	36.00				
(M159) 41/31 Girl Watering Flowers	9.00	14.00	18.00				
(M160) 41/32 Woman Lifting Hen From Nest	12.00	18.00	24.00				
(M161) 41/33 Woman With Butter Churn	11.00	16.00	22.00				
(M162) 41/34 Woman Laying Out Wash On Grass	14.00	21.00	28.00				
(M163) 41/35 Woman Sweeping With Broom	13.00	20.00	26.00				
(M164) 41/36 Man Juggling Barrel	15.00	23.00	30.00				
(M164a) As above, in khaki	28.00	42.00	56.00				
(M165) 41/37 Man Planting Tree	20.00	31.00	41.00				
(M166) 41/38 Girl Picking Berries	26.00	39.00	52.00				
(M167) 41/39 Farmer At Water Pump	11.00	16.00	22.00				

M169 41/41 **Haystack** is a rare variant, easily distinguished by the bottle and jug by its side. . . . . . No Price Found

(M169a) Boxed Happy Farm Set (10 pieces) mint with box, no standard contents   180.00   275.00   360.00

End Happy Farm Listing, Beginning Post-WW II

MANOIL

MC1   MC2

MC3   MC3a   MC4

Courtesy Marjorie and the late Peter Ruben

	G	VG	M		G	VG	M
MANOIL COMPOSITION				(MC3a) Motorcyclist, mirror			
(MC1) Prone machine-gunner	25.00	37.50	50.00	variation of above	24.00	36.00	48.00
(MC2) Seated machine-gunner	24.00	36.00	48.00	(MC4) Firing camouflaged AA gun	24.00	36.00	48.00
(MC3) Motorcyclist	24.00	36.00	48.00				

MANOIL "X" LINE

Recently, previously unknown Manoils were found in the collection of Manoil relatives Marjorie and Peter Ruben. Some of these are hollow, and perhaps were actually produced and sold. Others are solid lead, and presumably were prototypes which for one reason or another were never marketed. Those marketed with an "H" after the code number are hollow, and those with an "S", solid. Those in the 500 series are not the same size as the ones they resemble in that series, although it is these figures that are shown on order sheets of the period. That some "X" figures may have been produced has been underscored by the fact the tall cowboy has turned up at least twice in auctions.
Ron Eccles (see New Makers) is currently casting some of these from the original molds.

MXS1   MXS2 MXS3   MXS4   M23a

Photo by Norbert Schachter
Courtesy Marjorie and Peter Ruben

MXS1 Military School Cadet?	No Price Found
MXS2 Cadet	No Price Found
MXS3 Sailor	No Price Found
MXS4 Cowboy, gun raised	No Price Found
MXH50 Bicycle Dispatch Rider, WW II helmet	No Price Found
MXH57 Camouflage Sharpshooter Lying Down, WW II helmet	No Price Found

MXS62 Soldier with Gas Mask and Gun, WW II helmet	No Price Found
MXS82 Anti-Aircraft with Range Finder, WW II helmet	No Price Found
MXS83 Soldier Trench Mortar, WW II helmet	No Price Found
MXH88 Radio Operator Standing, one-piece puttees	No Price Found
MXH89 Radio Operator (Lying Down), one-piece puttees	No Price Found
MXS No Number Standing with Periscope, WW II helmet	No Price Found

123

MANOIL

MXS16　MXS24　MXH50　MXH57　MXS62　MXS82

MXS83　MXH88　MXH89　No. ?　MXH94
Photo by Norbert Schachter
Courtesy Marjorie and Peter Ruben

MXS521 through MXS530

MXS531 through MXS535
Photo by Norbert Schachter
Courtesy Marjorie and Peter Ruben

Unnumbered Manoil "X" line soldiers
Photo by Norbert Schachter
Courtesy Marjorie and Peter Ruben

	G	VG	M
MXH94 Soldier Running with Cannon, WW II helmet..............	No Price Found		
MXS16 Sailor...........	No Price Found		
MXS24 Cannon Loader, WW II helmet........	No Price Found		
MXS521 Flag Bearer......	No Price Found		
MXS522 Parade..........	No Price Found		
MXS523 Soldier in Poncho.	No Price Found		
MXS526 Observer........	No Price Found		
MXS527 Aircraft Spotter..	No Price Found		
MXS530 Machine Gunner (lying)..............	No Price Found		
MXS531 Machine Gunner Sitting..............	No Price Found		
MXS532 Sniper (kneeling)..	No Price Found		

	G	VG	M
MXS533 Soldier with gas mask and flare pistol....	No Price Found		
MXS534 Sniper.........	No Price Found		
MXS536 Anti-Aircraft Gunner..............	No Price Found		
MXS535 Soldier Throwing Hand Grenade.........	No Price Found		
MXS No Number Soldier with gas mask, gun, camouflaged helmet.....	No Price Found		
MXS No Number Tommy Gunner, leaning back....	No Price Found		
MXS No Number Tall cowboy, firing two guns.	16.00	24.00	32.00
M23a Sailor, hollow base, painted black, possibly for export to Cuba.........	No Price Found		

END OF "X" LISTING

According to the late Peter Ruben, M170 through M176 were the first new post WW II series (I bought one in November or December, 1945), and were produced only for a limited time. On a trial basis early production was also sold unpainted (as was the one I bought).

	G	VG	M
(M170) Flag Bearer (thin), circa late 1945........	13.00	20.00	26.00
(M171) Parade (thin), circa late 1945.............	16.00	24.00	33.00
(M172) Tommy Gunner (thin, circa late 1945)....	14.00	21.00	28.00
(M173) Machine Gunner Sitting (thin), circa late 1945	30.00	45.00	60.00
(M174) Machine Gunner Lying (thin), circa late 1945................	50.00	75.00	100.00
(M175) Sniper (thin), circa late 1945............	27.00	41.00	54.00
(M176) 45/6 Parade (thin), circa late 1945	14.00	21.00	28.00
(M177) 45/7 Flag Bearer...	17.00	26.00	35.00
(M178) 45/8 Parade.......	10.00	15.00	20.00
(M179) 45/9 Combat......	12.00	19.00	25.00
(M180) 45/10 At Attention (present arms).........	16.00	24.00	32.00
(M181) 45/11 Sniper......	17.00	26.00	34.00
(M182) 45/12 Tommy Gunner..............	13.00	20.00	27.00
(M183) 45/13 Soldier With Bazooka Cannon (some marked "45/18"........	15.00	23.00	30.00

M170　M171　M172　M173

M174　　　　M175　M176

M177　M178　M179　M180　M181　M182

M183　　M184　　　　M185　M186

MANOIL

M187   M188   M189   M190   M191   M192   M193

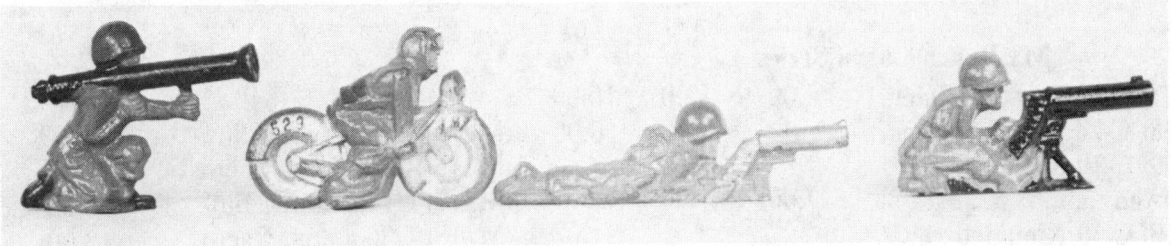

M194   M195   M196   M197

M198   M199   M200   M201   M202

	G	VG	M
(M184) **45/14 Soldier With Shell For Bazooka** (some marked "46/14")	15.00	23.00	30.00
(M185) **45/15 General** (some "46/15")	77.00	112.00	155.00
(M186) **45/16 Mine Detector** (some "46/16")	19.00	28.00	39.00
(M187) **521 Flag Bearer**, all 500s circa 1950	13.00	20.00	27.00
(M188) **522 Parade**	13.00	20.00	27.00
(M189) **523 Soldier in poncho**	19.00	28.00	39.00
(M190) **524 Combat**	15.00	23.00	31.00
(M191) **525 Aviator holding bomb**	15.00	23.00	30.00
(M192) **526 Observer**	18.00	27.00	36.00
(M193) **527 Aircraft spotter** .	19.00	29.00	38.00
(M194) **528 Soldier with bazooka**	12.00	18.00	24.00

	G	VG	M
(M195) **529 Motorcycle rider**	24.00	36.00	48.00
(M196) **530 Machine gunner (lying)**	16.00	24.00	32.00
(M197) **531 Machine gunner sitting**	15.00	23.00	30.00
(M198) **532 Sniper (kneeling)**	16.00	24.00	32.00
(M199) **533 Soldier with gas mask with flare pistol**	21.00	31.00	42.00
(M200) **534 Sniper**	17.00	27.00	35.00
(M201) **535 Soldier throwing hand grenade**	24.00	36.00	48.00
(M202) **536 Anti-Aircraft gunner**	18.00	28.00	37.00
(M203) **537 Soldier with tommy gun**	20.00	30.00	40.00
(M204) **538 Soldier firing up**	18.00	28.00	37.00
(M205) **539 Stretcher bearer**	55.00	83.00	110.00
(M206) **540 Wounded Soldier (lying)**	57.00	86.00	115.00

M203   M204   M205   M206

My Ranch Corral Series

	G	VG	M
(M207) **C-23 Cowboy Rider.**	5.00	8.00	10.00
(M208) **C-24 Cowgirl Rider.**	5.00	8.00	10.00
(M209) **C-29 Mounted Cowboy**	27.00	41.00	55.00
(M210) **C-30 Mounted Cowboy Shooting**	24.00	36.00	48.00
(M210a) Like above, but shorter pistol	No Price Found		
(M211) C2 Ranch fence, gate	37.00	53.00	75.00
(M212) C12 Blanket over Fence Section	16.00	24.00	32.00
(M213) C18 Small Calf	6.00	9.00	13.00
(M214) C20 Bull, head turned	7.00	11.00	15.00

	G	VG	M
(M215) C19 Cow feeding	6.00	9.00	12.00
(M216) C28 Short Cactus	7.00	11.00	15.00
(M217) C14 Brahma Bull	8.00	12.00	16.00
(M218) C26 Large Cactus	13.00	20.00	26.00
(M219) C1 Fence	4.00	7.00	9.00
(M220) C25 Small Horse	12.00	19.00	25.00
(M221) C22 Horse for Mounted Cowboy	10.00	15.00	20.00
(M222) C22 Horse for Mounted Cowgirl	11.00	17.00	22.00
(M223) Small Gate	15.00	23.00	30.00
(M224) Large Gate	14.00	21.00	28.00

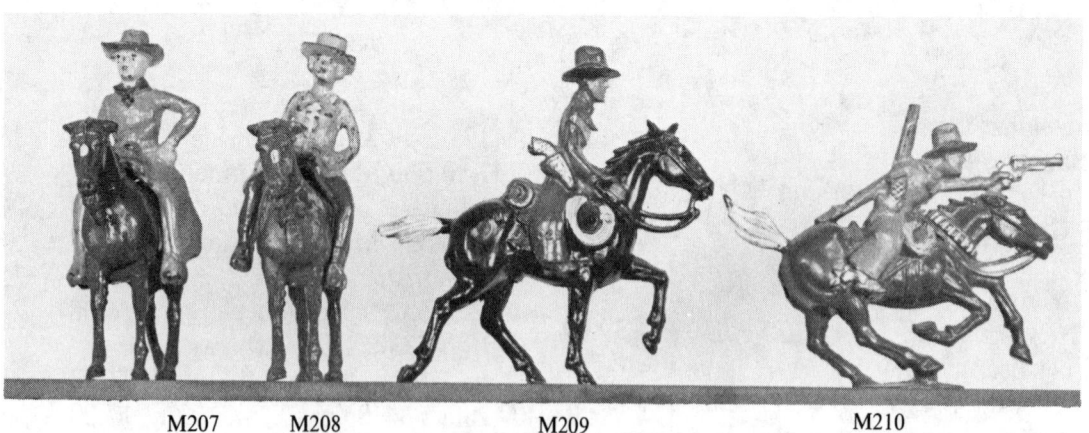

M207   M208   M209   M210

M212   M213   M214

L to R: M210, M210a
Photo by Bob Hornung

Box cover for a Happy Farm set.
Photo by K. Warren Mitchell

M222 Horse

M211

M215　　　　M216　　　　M217　　　　M218

M219　　　　M220　　　　M221　　　　M221

MRC2　MRC1　MRC3　MRC4　MRC5　MRC1a　MRC2a

Unproduced figures from the My Ranch Corral series.
Photo by Ron Eccles

MANOIL

MRC6   MRC7   MRC8   MRC9   MRC10   MRC11
Unproduced figures from the My Ranch Corral series.
Photo by Ron Eccles

MRC1   MRC2
Photo by Ed Poole

MANOIL CANNONS

	G	VG	M
Cannon, MANOIL 19 Metal Action Cannon, early version, "USA" ...	25.00	38.00	50.00
Cannon, MANOIL 69, metal spoked wheels	7.00	11.00	15.00
Cannon, MANOIL 69, early 2nd version, metal spoked wheels, marked "M" left side	7.00	11.00	15.00
Cannon, MANOIL 69, solid wood wheels.	9.00	13.00	18.00
Cannon, MANOIL 69, solid wood wheels variant. . . .	9.00	13.00	18.00
Cannon, MANOIL "Metal Action Cannon No. 200, later version of 19, "Made in USA".	7.00	11.00	15.00
Cannon, MANOIL 69, metal wheels, straight barrel, high angle, marked "USA", early version. . . .	7.00	11.00	15.00

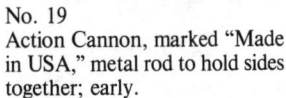

No. 19
Action Cannon, marked "Made in USA," metal rod to hold sides together; early.

No. 69. Cannon, metal wheels, marked M left side, early, 2nd version.

95   96   97   98

103   104   105   200

MANOIL 69 cannon, metal wheels, wood wheels, wood wheels variant. MANOIL Vehicles, top row, L to R; 70, 71. Middle row, 71 with variant on wheel support, 72, 73 with front tow loop, 74. Bottom row: 75, 75A with siren cast separately, 75A siren cast integrally.
Photo by Ed Poole

MANOIL VEHICLES

	G	VG	M
MANOIL 700 Sedan, futuristic	45.00	68.00	90.00
MANOIL 701 Sedan, futuristic	45.00	68.00	90.00
MANOIL 702 Coupe, futuristic	45.00	68.00	90.00
MANOIL 703 Wrecker, futuristic	45.00	68.00	90.00
MANOIL 704 Roadster, futuristic, Pat. No. 95791	45.00	68.00	90.00
MANOIL 705 Sedan, futuristic, Pat. No. 95792	45.00	68.00	90.00
MANOIL 706 Rocket, futuristic bus-like vehicle, Pat. No. 95793	60.00	90.00	120.00
MANOIL 70 Soup Kitchen, large number.	9.00	13.00	18.00
MANOIL 70A Soup Kitchen, small number.	9.00	13.00	19.00

MANOIL   705   708 early   708 later   713   716   P-7

707   710   709

Photo by Norbert Schachter
Courtesy Marjorie and Peter Ruben

714   P-10   P-11   P-9

Courtesy Peter and Marjorie Ruben

MC5

79
Submarine, colors silver, gray
Value $30 in mint.

	G	VG	M
MANOIL *71 Shell Carrier With Soldier On Shell Box,* has loop	11.00	16.00	22.00
MANOIL *71A* Same as above, no loop	10.00	15.00	20.00
MANOIL *72 Water Wagon,* large number	10.00	15.00	20.00
MANOIL *72A* Same as above, small number	9.00	13.00	18.00
MANOIL *72 B* No number	9.00	13.00	18.00
MANOIL *73 Tractor,* loop front	11.00	16.00	22.00
MANOIL *73A Tractor,* plain front	11.00	16.00	22.00
MANOIL *74 Armored Car with Anti-Tank Gun*	17.00	26.00	35.00
MANOIL *75 Armored Car with Anti-Aircraft Gun*	27.00	41.00	55.00
MANOIL *75A Armored Car with Siren,* siren cast separately	25.00	38.00	50.00
MANOIL *75A Armored Car with Siren,* siren cast with vehicle	32.00	48.00	65.00
MANOIL *95 Tank*	8.00	12.00	17.00
MANOIL *96 Large Shell on Truck*	9.00	13.00	18.00
MANOIL *97 Pontoon on Wheels*	18.00	27.00	36.00
MANOIL *98 Torpedo on Wheels*	10.00	15.00	20.00
MANOIL *103 Gasoline Truck*	10.00	15.00	20.00
MANOIL *104 Chemical Truck*	12.00	18.00	24.00

	G	VG	M
MANOIL 105 Five Barrel Gun on Wheels	11.00	16.00	22.00
MANOIL (MC5) Tank, composition	12.00	18.00	25.00

MANOIL Post War Vehicles

	G	VG	M
MANOIL *707 Sedan*	25.00	38.00	50.00
MANOIL *708 Roadster,* horizontal radiator	17.00	26.00	35.00
MANOIL *708A Roadster,* vertical radiator	25.00	38.00	50.00
MANOIL *709 Fire Engine*	15.00	22.00	30.00
MANOIL *710 Oil Tanker*	12.00	18.00	25.00
MANOIL *711 Aerial Ladder*	No Price Found		
MANOIL *712 Pumper*	No Price Found		
MANOIL *713 Bus*	12.00	18.00	24.00
MANOIL *714 Towing Truck*	10.00	15.00	20.00
MANOIL *715 Commercial Truck*	10.00	15.00	20.00
MANOIL *716 Sedan*	10.00	15.00	20.00
MANOIL *717 Hard Top Convertible*	12.00	18.00	24.00
MANOIL *718 Convertible*	10.00	15.00	20.00
MANOIL *719 Sport Car*	10.00	15.00	20.00
MANOIL *720 Ranch Wagon*	10.00	15.00	20.00

MANOIL Plastic Vehicles

	G	VG	M
MANOIL *P-7 Roadster*	2.50	3.75	5.00
MANOIL *P-8 Sedan*	2.50	3.75	5.00
MANOIL *P-9 Pick-Up*	2.50	3.75	5.00
MANOIL *P-10 Towing Truck*	2.50	3.75	5.00
MANOIL *P-11 Road Scraper*	2.50	3.75	5.00
MANOIL *P-12 Tractor*	2.50	3.75	5.00
MANOIL *P-13 Dump Cart*	2.50	3.75	5.00

MANOIL

P-8   P-12   P-13

712

Photo by Norbert Schachter   711
Courtesy Marjorie and Peter Ruben

517   518   519   520

Courtesy Peter and Majorie Ruben. Value each $20-30-40.

Unproduced Manoils. The nurse seems to have been planned as a replacement for 41/14 - Darky Eating Watermelon. The drummer may have been planned to take advantage of the Laurel & Hardy film, "Babes in Toyland," which was released November 12, 1934.

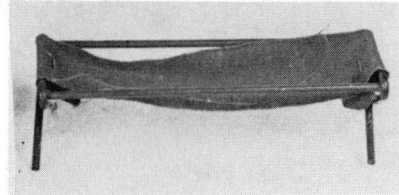

This cot was probably sold by Manoil. Value is $10 in mint.

Unproduced figure from the My Ranch Corral series.
Photo by Ed Poole

No. 76 Rifle Range targets "4-5-6" and "7-8-9". "1-2-3" doesn't appear to exist, except in a version produced in recent years by collectors Ed Poole and Ron Eccles. Prices are $40 in good, $60 in very good and $80 in mint.
Photo by Don Pielin

No. 700 - SEDAN

No. 701 - SEDAN

No. 702 - COUPE

No. 703 - WRECKER

MANOIL, circa 1935
Courtesy Peter and Marjorie Ruben

MANOIL

704 ROADSTER

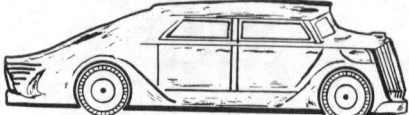

705 SEDAN

706 ROCKET

MANOIL Pre-World War II vehicles
Courtesy Peter and Marjorie Ruben

No. 716 - SEDAN

No. 717 - HARD TOP CONVERTIBLE

No. 718 - CONVERTIBLE

No. 719 - SPORT CAR

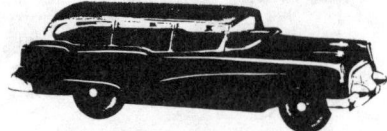

No. 720 - RANCH WAGON

MANOIL Postwar Vehicles
Courtesy Peter and Marjorie Ruben

No. 713   BUS

No. 710 - OIL TANKER

No. 709 - FIRE ENGINE

No. 707 - SEDAN

No. 715 - COMMERCIAL TRUCK has removable panels, as shown above

No. 714 - TOWING TRUCK

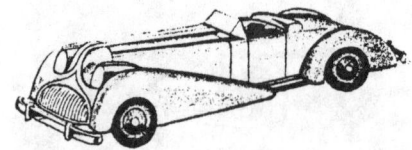

No. 708 - ROADSTER

MANOIL Post-War Vehicles
Courtesy Peter and Marjorie Ruben

GREY IRON

Grey Iron was the first of the major dimestore toy soldier makers. In late 1984, to everyone's surprise, it became known that it was also the last.

All indications had been that Grey Iron had permanently stopped manufacturing virtually all its figures in 1942, and that a factory fire in recent years destroyed the remaining molds. In fact, casting has been going on intermittently for years, sometimes in iron, sometimes in aluminum.

Grey Iron was the only company to produce 3" and 3¼" iron toy soldiers. In January, 1933, it introduced thirty-five different soldiers (four Revolutionary War soldiers – an infantryman, a foot officer, a mounted officer and a flagbearer – may have been introduced earlier, as they're numbered lower, but weren't a part of the 1933 announcement).

These soldiers tended to be slight in physique, and, though apparently successful, were superseded in July, 1936 by the firm's "Iron Men" series, a slightly larger, more robust model. These continued to be sold until World War II ended all toy production.

The molds at Grey Iron are more properly called "patterns", and the men who designed the figures and patterns appear to have been three; Samuel Eshlemann and Samuel S. Schmidt, who were full-time workers, and Edward Musser, who was part-time (Musser's son is sure Musser designed no soldiers for Grey Iron, but others disagree). But it's really of little consequence, as all the soldiers seem to have been turned out by the same hand, and they're also far less artistic than those that came out of Barclay and Manoil. However, they do have a charm of their own, and in addition some are unique, and a few dramatic.

Grey Iron's dimestore-style soldiers weren't its first. On August 14, 1917, the company was granted two patents for their 40mm solid cast iron Greyklip Armies, which they continued to manufacture through 1941 or early 1942. The last of this series emerged in 1938 as "Uncle Sam's Defenders", painted khaki rather than being nickel-plated, as the earlier versions were. The Greyklips weren't successful at first, but when a new distributor arrived on the scene, the figures took off, and the company was swamped with orders.

Grey Iron's origins go back to about 1840 when Harvey Bookmeyer, B. F. Mishey and a Mr. Brady formed the Brady Machine Shop. The location was West Main Street in Mount Joy, Pennsylvania. When it burned down in 1871, it was rebuilt on Mt. Joy St.

In 1881, it was organized as the Grey Iron Casting Company, Limited, with Brady out, and Bookmeyer and Mishey joined by H. S. Stauffer and William Sperra. Although it was subsequently owned by a variety of other companies – National Novelty Corporation (1903), Hardware & Woodenware Manufacturing Company (National Novelty's new name in 1907), A. A. Tisdale and H. T. Kingsbury (1912), Assets Realization Corporation (1913) and the Wrightsville Hardware Company (1914) – it was known continually as Grey Iron.

During those dizzying years of name-changing, the company also moved, to South Barbara Street and then East Donegal and South Jacob streets, which was its final location, although in 1899 there was another fire, and the greater part of the plant was rebuilt.

In 1926, a three-story office and showroom building was built adjoining the foundry. It was erected around the existing office building, and when the old two-story frame structure was torn down, the area was left as a courtyard in the middle of the office-foundry complex. Then in 1927 a one-story addition to the South Side of the Foundry Building and a two-story addition to the Mill Building were put up. In 1937 a two-story building was constructed to the east of the office building. This housed the machine shop and spray paint booths.

Grey Iron manufactured a variety of products; hinges, hammers, meat pounders, hooks, lamp brackets, etc. By 1903 it was also producing toys, such as banks, stoves, cap pistols, trains and wheeled toys.

Its Clever Clowns series was introduced in 1936, and in 1940 its American Family series was advertised as "new" with the On the Beach and On the Ranch sets introduced in April, 1940. Also new in 1940 were Takapart Buildings and "The Champions on the Diamond".

In 1942, the firm won a Navy Defense contract, and for the next four years Torpedo Trucks, Bomb Racks and Bomb Skids were among the war products turned out by the firm. The cupola (a vertical cylindrical furnace for melting iron in a foundry) was capped, and the molders were employed instead as welders, while the women ran the drill presses, assembled, and painted the bomb skids.

Because of the capping, when the War ended in 1945 toy production had to be done at first in aluminum. Products at the time were iron castings, cast iron hardware, and iron toys, with toys taking up the greater part of production.

In the early 1950s Grey Iron produced mechanical banks for Lee Howard Associates. The original banks were acquired through the Book of Knowledge, and patterns made from them.

From 1914 the company had been owned by the Coventry family. In 1958 the original owner, W. A. Coventry, died, and left the firm to C.W. and F. Coventry. C.W. had been with Grey Iron since 1929, so the transition was smooth. In 1960 he purchased the mechanical bank patterns, which continue to be used.

Grey Iron toys from a 1904 catalog.
Courtesy John Wright Company

On December 31, 1967, Grey Iron was purchased by Donald M. Smith, and on July 1, 1974 the name was changed to Donsco Inc., combining Grey Iron, Riverside Foundry, John Wright Co. and Keyco Inc., York Metalcrafters and Wrightsville Hardware Co. The Grey Iron arm of the company is now part of (and called) John Wright, which is located in Wrightsville, Pa. Today, almost all of the casting (which continues to be done in Mount Joy), is automated, but that of the soldiers is still done by hand.

Although no figures on employment seem to exist for the dimestore years, in 1921 Grey Iron had 70 employees, who were paid 19 to 37 cents an hour. During the 1930s and early 1940s the soldiers were hand-poured, and then clipped to a conveyor holder, which allowed them to be dipped in a base coat. After that they were hand-painted, on an assembly-line basis. Distribution was coast-to-coast, and in Canada.

Though the date of the start of dimestore production at Barclay is cloudy, the attitude of Grey Iron executives to their rivals is evidence enough that Grey Iron was there first. The people at Barclay and Manoil were blithely indifferent to their competitors, while Grey Iron violently regarded both companies as pirates and worse.

The surge of interest shown by collectors upon news that the old patterns are still available has persuaded John Wright to produce all, or nearly all, of the figures found on those patterns.

In early 1985 I visited the factory and inspected the patterns and pattern book. Patterns for all of Grey Iron's pieces, from the Greyklips through the Iron Men through the American Family series exist, except for the following, using the codes employed in this book: The GG5 airplane's wing, G3, G3a, G5, G7, G9, G16, G24, G25, G27, G33, G34, G37, G39, G41, G49, G57, G58, G60, G64, G68, G79, G81, G83, G85, G88, G90, G106, G107, T9, T11, H9, H11. Thus, with the exception of G85 (and I may have overlooked it), all of the larger-sized soldiers are available, while only one of the slighter figures (G12) seems to have survived. According to Larry Gilbert, currently in charge of the patterns at John Wright, originally the figures were produced from "loose master molds," and then sometime before the advent of World War II they were transferred to the patterns that now exist. Presumably the earlier line of Grey Iron soldiers, having been phased out of production, were not transferred. (It's also possible a few more patterns may exist; the photographs of the American Family series were particularly hard to figure out, and at least one mold wasn't photographed.)

Also available in the patterns are a Takapart Barn (which would fit into several of the American Family scenes) which can be built as either a single or double barn, fencing, tiny (about 1½" high) mounted jockeys, baseball players in fielding position, also about 1½" high (and possibly part, or the entirety of, "The Champions On The Diamond"), and the Treasure Chest that was sold with some of the pirate sets.

GREY IRON

Many of the patterns bear catalog numbers, pattern numbers and written descriptions of the figures. A random check of the pattern numbers indicates they don't seem to furnish any clues to the order of creation. The most intriguing written description is of the G91 infantryman, which all collectors think of as an Italian Infantryman, made to go with the Ethiopians that were produced about 1935-36. It's described as "British Soldier" (the corresponding officer's pattern bears no description). Whether this is correct or an error by the inscriber is unknown, as the two "Italians", along with the ski trooper and the Evzone, don't appear in any of the existing catalogs.

Although soldier production at John Wright is erratic and very slow (no one at the foundry is enthusiastic about hand casting, and the revenue from soldiers at this time doesn't compete with that earned by the other products), as this history was being written, the majority of the patterns were at the Mount Joy foundry, with production expected to begin in "about a month". This is happy news for some collectors, less so for those who are interested in figures readily identifiable as being produced only in "the olden days", or who paid stiff prices only to find the value of their figures possibly undercut by the new production (the unpainted castings are sold for a dollar apiece at the Wrightsville shop). However, since Grey Iron produced intermittently after the War, it's hard to be sure about the age of any of the pieces for which the patterns still exist. For instance, the Colonial soldiers may have only been produced, briefly, until 1933, and then at various intervals after the War, although most collectors assume their Continental pieces are pre-War.

Some years ago, at a Pennsylvania flea market, I saw some solid iron continental soldiers that were cruder and in a slightly smaller size than Grey Iron's. Figures G106 and G107 also don't appear in the company's existing catalogs, and are cruder than the similar ones that do. Samuel S. Schmidt, who was one of Grey Iron's designers, was a director of a company called Distinctive Products Inc., which was incorporated January 2, 1929. Most of the company's work was done at Grey Iron, and it's possible that the small continentals and the early horsemen were produced by Distinctive, and then, when they provoked interest from buyers, were put out by Grey Iron in newer and better-designed versions. In the ten or so years since I saw the Continentals, none has been known to surface. Presumably, if any do, they would be of value, at least to the completist.

Finally, there is the problematic palm tree. For years there had been rumors that one appeared in a set containing the Ethiopians and "Italians". In 1983, when one surfaced, it sold at auction for $560. Then in 1984 palm trees began popping up everywhere, and collector Gene Parker discovered they were being produced by Wilton Products, which is next door to John Wright. Interest immediately plummeted, but there are collectors who swear the 1¾" palm tree did appear in those sets. Possibly the pattern or mold originally was Grey Iron's or it simply purchased the trees from Wilton and used them in the sets during the brief period they were produced. Until a catalog or set turns up, collectors will have to continue to wonder.

All words and numbers in bold print are Grey Iron's own description.

Greyklip Armies

	G	VG	M
(GA) Set 1/Company A, at attention, consists of bugler, officer, flag-bearer, drummer, 6 riflemen, price per each	2.00	3.00	4.00
(GB) Set 2/Company B, marching, consists of bugler, officer, flag-bearer, drummer, 6 riflemen, price per each	2.50	3.75	5.00
(GC) Set 3/Company C, charging, consists of bugler, officer, flag-bearer, drummer, 6 riflemen, price per each	2.50	3.75	5.00
(GD) Set 4/Troop D, consists of four mounted troopers, one mounted officer, troopers all look alike, price per each..........	4.00	6.00	8.00

GREY IRON (GA) Set 1, Co. A
Courtesy the late Karl Zipple

	G	VG	M
(GE) Set 5/Battery E, two-piece set, led by officer from Troop D, second piece is a gun limber with four horses, several attached soldiers, price for second piece..........	6.00	9.00	12.00

GREY IRON

	G	VG	M
(GF) Set 6/Battery F, consists of shell stack, loader bending, loader standing, gunner, cannon, price per each, shells double......	3.50	5.25	7.00
(GG) Set 5/Aviation Corps, consists of pilot (two of the same figure in set) and plane with detachable wing. Price for set......	70.00	105.00	140.00
(GH) **Uncle Sam's Defenders,** consists of charging rifleman, machine-gunner, charging officer, rifleman at attention, flagbearer, officer saluting, price per each (double the price on saluting officer and flagbearer)............	6.00	9.00	12.00

Greyklips were sold on these illustrated cards. This is Company C. Value in mint $100.
Photo by Stan Alekna

End Greyklip Armies

GREY IRON (GD) Set 4, Troop D
Courtesy the late Karl Zipple

GREY IRON (GE) Set 5, Battery E
Courtesy Don Pielin

GREY IRON (GB) Set 2, Company B
Courtesy the late Karl Zipple

GREY IRON (GF) Set 6, Battery F
Courtesy Don Pielin

GREY IRON (GC) Set 3, Company C
Courtesy the late Karl Zipple

GREY IRON

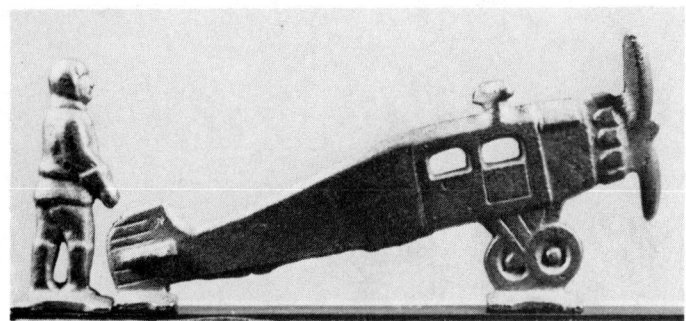

GREY IRON (GG) Set 5, Aviation Corps (Above two photos)
Courtesy the late Karl Zipple

	G	VG	M
(G10a) Same as above, no tie	No Price Found		
(G11) **3/1 U.S. Infantry, Port Arms**	10.00	15.00	21.00
(G12) **3A U.S. Infantry Officer,** early	8.00	12.00	16.00
(G13) **3A U.S. Infantry Officer**	7.00	11.00	15.00
(G14) **3AP Traffic Officer** (same as above, in blue)	11.00	17.00	22.00
(G15) **3AR Red Cross Officer** (same as above, with armband)	17.00	26.00	35.00
(G16) **4 U.S. Infantry, Port Arms,** early	8.00	12.00	16.00
(G17) **4A U.S. Doughboy Officer With Field Glasses**	11.00	17.00	22.00
(G18) **4/1 U.S. Doughboy Signaling**	12.00	19.00	25.00
(G19) **4/2 U.S. Doughboy Combat Trooper**	12.00	18.00	24.00

GREY IRON (GH) Uncle Sam's Defenders. These came with faces painted and unpainted.

	G	VG	M
(G1) **1 Colonial Soldier**	11.00	17.00	23.00
(G2) **1A Colonial Foot Officer**	12.00	19.00	25.00
(G3) **1B Colonial Color-Bearer**	175.00	263.00	350.00
(G3a) **1B Colonial Color-Bearer,** 1950s version, with rifle barrel drilled out for flag	25.00	38.00	50.00
(G4) **1MA Colonial Mounted Officer**	20.00	30.00	40.00
(G5) **2 Cadet,** early version	7.00	11.00	15.00
(G6) **2 Cadet**	11.00	17.00	22.00
(G7) **2A Cadet Officer,** early	9.00	14.00	18.00
(G8) **2A Cadet Officer**	12.00	19.00	25.00
(G9) **3 U.S. Infantry, Shoulder Arms,** early	8.00	12.00	16.00
(G10) **3 U.S. Infantry, Shoulder Arms**	7.00	11.00	15.00
(G20) **4/3 U.S. Doughboy With Range Finder**	40.00	60.00	80.00
(G21) **4/4 U.S. Doughboy Ammunition Carrier**	42.00	63.00	85.00
(G22) **4/5 U.S. Doughboy Sharpshooter**	12.00	18.00	24.00
(G23) **4/6 U.S. Doughboy With Bayonet**	11.00	17.00	22.00
(G24) **5 U.S. Infantry, Charging,** early	7.00	11.00	15.00
(G25) **6 U.S. Doughboy, Port Arms,** early	8.00	13.00	17.00
(G26) **6 U.S. Doughboy, Shoulder Arms**	5.00	8.00	11.00
(G27) **6A U.S. Doughboy Officer,** early	9.00	14.00	18.00
(G28) **6A U.S. Doughboy Officer**	7.00	11.00	15.00
(G29) **6/1 U.S. Doughboy Charging**	7.00	11.00	14.00

G1   G2   G3   G3a   G4

Photo by Ed Poole

G5   G6   G7   G8   G9   G10   G11

G12   G13   G14   G15   G16   G17   G18

G10   G10A

	G	VG	M
(G30) 6/2 U.S. Doughboy Sentry	11.00	17.00	22.00
(G31) 6/3 U.S. Doughboy Bomber, crawling	8.00	13.00	17.00
(G32) 6/4 U.S. Doughboy Grenade Thrower	15.00	23.00	30.00
(G33) 7 U.S. Doughboy Charging, early	6.00	10.00	13.00
(G34) 8M U.S. Cavalryman, early	17.00	25.00	34.00

139

G19   G20   G21   G22   G23

G24   G25   G26   G27   G28   G29   G30

	G	VG	M
(G35) **8M U.S. Cavalryman**.	15.00	23.00	30.00
(G36) **8M U.S. Cavalry Color Bearer With Silk Flag** (not shown, same as G34)	No Price Found		
(G37) **8MA U.S. Cavalry Officer**, early	18.00	28.00	37.00
(G38) **8MA U.S. Cavalry Officer**	17.00	26.00	35.00
(G39) **9 U.S. Marine**, early	6.00	10.00	13.00
(G40) **9 U.S. Marine**	8.00	12.00	16.00
(G41) **10 Royal Canadian Police**, early	11.00	17.00	22.00
(G42) **10 Royal Canadian Police**	16.00	24.00	32.00
(G43) **10M Royal Canadian Mounted Police** (same as G34)	21.00	31.00	42.00
(G44) **10M Royal Canadian Mounted Police** (same as G35)	22.00	33.00	45.00
(G45) **11 Indian,** with hatchet, early	7.00	11.00	14.00
(G46) **11 Indian Chief,** with knife	8.00	13.00	17.00
(G47) **11/1 Indian Brave,** shielding eyes	11.00	17.00	22.00
(G48) **11/2 Chief Attacking,** upraised tomahawk	50.00	75.00	100.00

	G	VG	M
(G49) **11M Indian Mounted,** early	17.00	25.00	34.00
(G50) **11M Indian Mounted,** lying on horse	37.00	53.00	75.00
(G51) **11/1M Indian Scout Mounted,** firing pistol rearward	100.00	150.00	200.00
(G52) **12 Cowboy,** early	6.00	9.00	13.00
(G53) **12 Cowboy**	6.00	9.00	13.00
(G54) **12/1 Hold-Up Man**	10.00	15.00	20.00
(G55) **12/2 Cowboy With Lasso,** with lasso price is 50.00 in mint	18.00	27.00	36.00
(G56) **12/3 Bandit,** surrendering	45.00	68.00	90.00
(G57) **12M Cowboy Mounted,** early	22.00	33.00	44.00
(G58) **12M Cowboy Mounted**	27.00	41.00	55.00
(G59) **12/1M Masked Cowboy Mounted**	110.00	165.00	220.00
(G60) **13 U.S. Machine Gunner,** early	7.00	11.00	14.00
(G61) **13 U.S. Machine Gunner**	7.00	11.00	14.00
(G62) **13/1 U.S. Machine Gunner**	8.00	13.00	17.00

GREY IRON

G31   G32   G33   G34

G35   G37   G38

G39   G40   G41   G42   G43   G44

G45   G46   G47   G48   G49

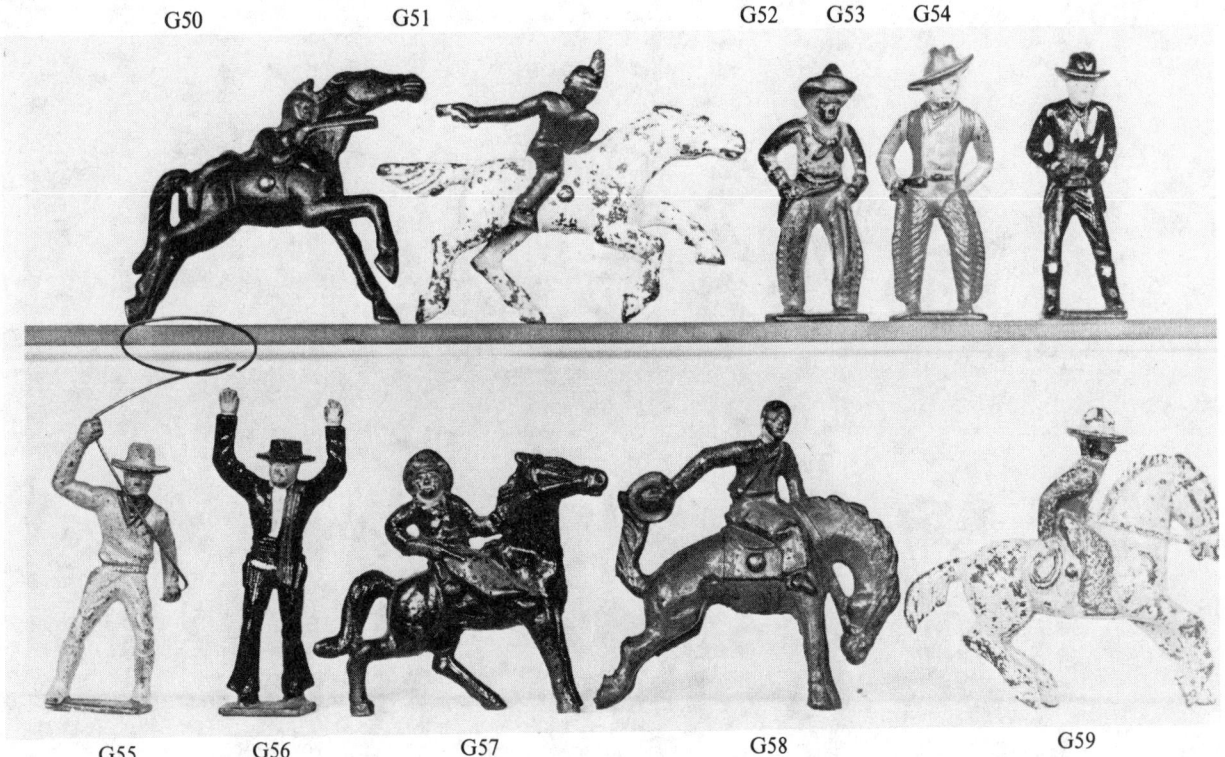

G50 G51 G52 G53 G54

G55 G56 G57 G58 G59

	G	VG	M		G	VG	M
(G63) **14 U.S. Sailor** in blue, early	8.00	13.00	17.00	(G76) **16/3 Pirate With Dagger**	11.00	17.00	22.00
(G64) **14 U.S. Sailor** in white, early	7.00	11.00	15.00	(G77) **16/4 Pirate With Hook**	10.00	15.00	20.00
(G65) **14 U.S. Sailor** in blue	7.00	11.00	15.00	(G78) **16/5 Pirate With Sword**	9.00	14.00	18.00
(G66) **14W U.S. Sailor,** in white	7.00	11.00	15.00	(G79) **17/1 Legion Drum Major,** early	21.00	32.00	42.00
(G67) **14A U.S. Naval Officer,** early, in blue	8.00	12.00	16.00	(G80) **17/1 Legion Drum Major**	10.00	15.00	20.00
(G68) **14AW U.S. Naval Officer,** early, in white	8.00	13.00	17.00	(G81) **17/2 Legion Bugler,** early	7.00	11.00	15.00
(G69) **14A U.S. Naval Officer,** in blue	7.00	11.00	14.00	(G82) **17/2 Legion Bugler**	8.00	12.00	16.00
(G70) **14AW U.S. Naval Officer** in white	6.00	10.00	13.00	(G83) **17/3 Legion Drummer,** early	9.00	14.00	18.00
(G71) **14/1W U.S. Sailor Signalman**	14.00	21.00	28.00	(G84) **17/3 Legion Drummer**	7.00	11.00	15.00
(G72) **15/1 Boy Scout Saluting,** early	9.00	14.00	19.00	(G85) **17/4 Legion Color Bearer**	7.00	11.00	15.00
(G73) **15/2 Boy Scout Walking,** early	8.00	13.00	17.00	(G86) **18/1 Ethiopian Tribesman,** circa 1936	26.00	39.00	53.00
(G74) **16/1 Pirate Boy** (all pirates circa 1935, were also sold as a Treasure Island set, with either tent or treasure chest included, pirates meant to represent Jim, Captain Flint, Long John, Blind Pew, Billie Bones)	12.00	18.00	24.00	(G87) **18/2 Ethiopian Chief**	28.00	43.00	57.00
				(G88) **18/3 Ethiopian Soldier, Shoulder Arms**	19.00	28.00	38.00
				(G89) **18/3A Ethiopian Officer**	25.00	38.00	50.00
				(G90) **18/5 Ethiopian Soldier, Charging**	30.00	45.00	60.00
(G75) **16/2 Pirate Chief**	10.00	15.00	20.00	(G91) Italian or English Desert Infantryman, "C2", "British Soldier" on pattern	125.00	188.00	250.00

G60   G61   G62   G63   G64

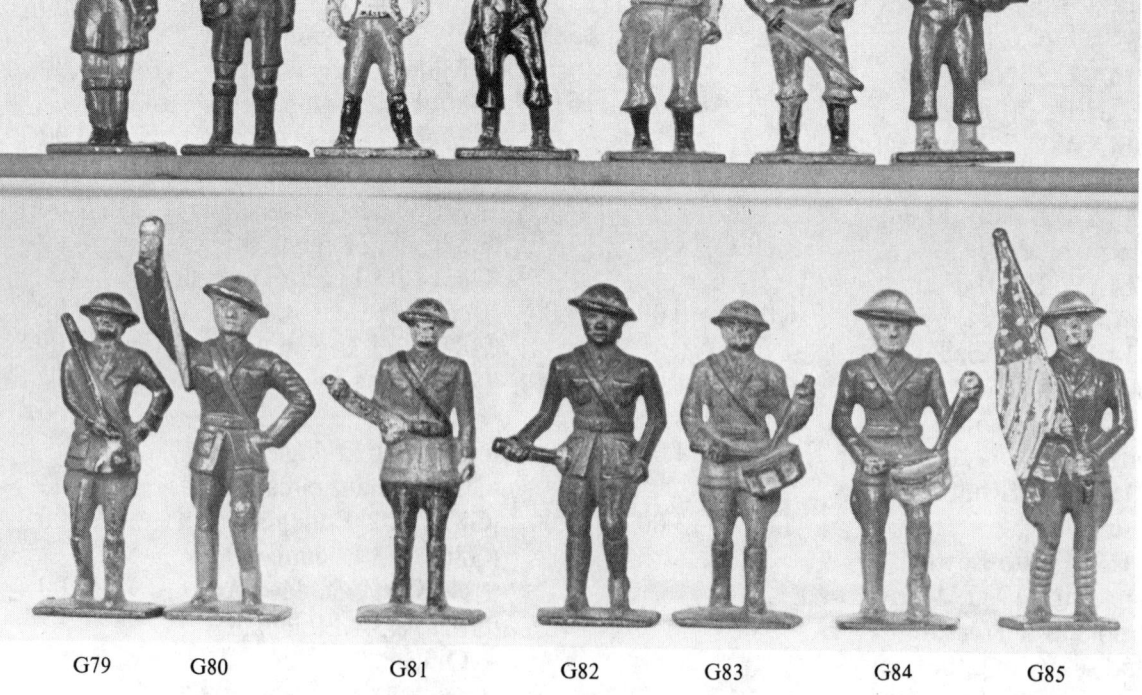

G65   G66   G67   G68   G69   G70   G71

G72   G73   G74   G75   G76   G77   G78

G79   G80   G81   G82   G83   G84   G85

GREY IRON

G86 G87 G88 G89 G90 G91 G92

G93 G94 G95   G96.   G97

	G	VG	M
(G92) Italian or English Desert Officer, "C1" on pattern	85.00	128.00	170.00
(G93) **19 Knight In Armor**	8.00	12.00	16.00
(G94) **20 Red Cross Doctor**	15.00	23.00	30.00
(G95) **21 Stretcher Bearer**	20.00	30.00	40.00
(G96) **22 Stretcher With Patient**	14.00	21.00	28.00
(G97) **22/1 Wounded Sitting**	48.00	72.00	96.00
(G98) **22/2 Wounded On Crutches**	20.00	30.00	40.00
(G99) **23 Red Cross Nurse**	12.00	18.00	24.00
(G100) **25 Aviator** (24 is a non-soldier)	19.00	29.00	39.00
(G101) Ski trooper, circa 1940, with skis four times the noted price	12.00	18.00	25.00
(G102) Greek Evzone	60.00	90.00	120.00
(G103) **75 Radio Set, Operator and two Aerials**	175.00	265.00	350.00
(G103A) **75 Radio Set, Operator Only**	48.00	73.00	95.00
(G104) **D26 Nurse and Wounded Soldier**	105.00	158.00	210.00
(G105) **D27 Doughboy Supporting Wounded Soldier**	125.00	188.00	250.00

	G	VG	M
*(G106) U.S. Cavalryman, probably Grey Iron, like G34, but horse's head and left leg up	70.00	105.00	140.00
*(G107) U.S. Cavalry Officer, probably Grey Iron, like G37, but horse's head and left leg up	60.00	90.00	120.00

*These may not have been produced by Grey Iron, but instead by Distinctive Products, Inc.

FOREIGN LEGION - All have blue uniforms

	G	VG	M
(G108) **6AF Foreign Legion Officer**	14.00	21.00	28.00
(G109) **6F Foreign Legion - Shoulder Arms**	14.00	21.00	28.00
G110) **6/1F Foreign Legion Charging**	14.00	21.00	28.00
(G111) **6/3F Foreign Legion Bomber**	19.00	29.00	38.00
(G112) **13F Foreign Legion Machine Gunner**	14.00	21.00	28.00
(G113) **8A/F Foreign Legion Cavalry Officer**	27.00	41.00	55.00
(G114) **8/F Foreign Legion Cavalryman**	27.00	41.00	55.00

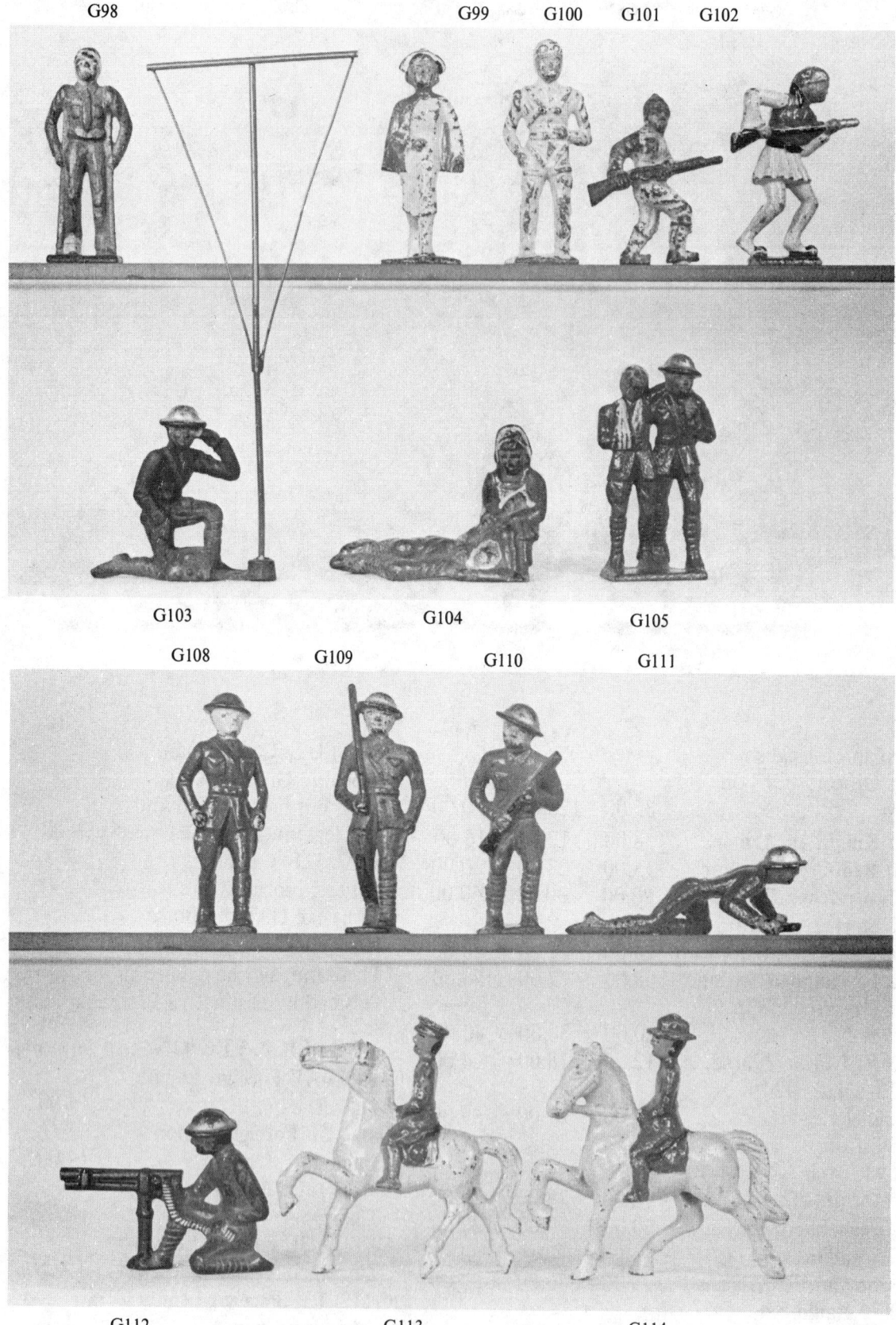

G98   G99   G100   G101   G102

G103   G104   G105

G108   G109   G110   G111

G112   G113   G114

GREY IRON

(G115) Foreign Legion
Stretcher Bearer, only one
known .... No Price Found

G   VG   M

One of Grey Iron's many sets, this one with a cardboard No. 400 Teepee.
Value about $120 in mint.

A very rare set of Grey Iron Ethiopians
Photo by Fred Wilhelm

Grey Iron No. 48 Large Shooting Cannon, 4½" long, value $25 in mint.
Courtesy K. Warren Mitchell

Grey Iron machine gun, 8" long, 6" high. In 1928 it was introduced with
a stationary platform, to be used as both a machine gun and an AA gun.
Value in mint $150
Photo by Stan Alekna

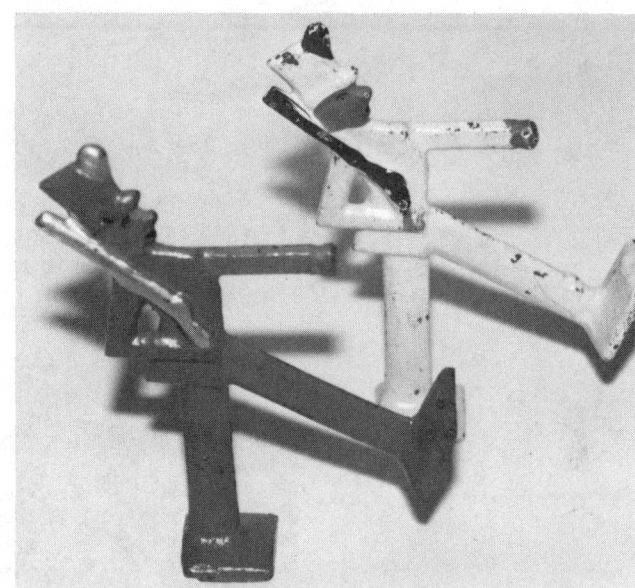

Grey Iron's The Royal Guard were introduced about 1940. Set No. 600
came with 18 pieces, in white, blue and scarlet. They can be stood on
either their left or their right foot. Value about $50 apiece in mint.
Photo by Stan Alekna

No. 24
Cannon
Nickeled Barrel,
Scarlet Wheels,
Khaki Carriage

Value $15 in mint

146

Greycraft Accessories

TENTS

**No. 100
U. S. Infantry**

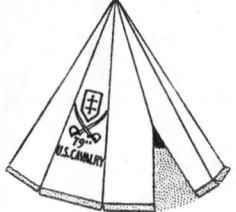

**No. 200
U. S. Cavalry**

White with insignia in blue and yellow. 7 in. diameter, 5½ in. high.

**No. 300
U. S. Marine Corps**

White with insignia in blue and yellow.
7 in. diameter, 5½ in. high.

**No. 400
Tepee**

Orange with Indian scenes in red and green
7 in. diameter, 6½ in. high.

Made of strong, Tough Cardboard. Base and Tent are collapsible.
Add greatly to realism of Army Groups.
1 dozen in a package. 1 gross, assorted numbers if desired, in a carton.
Shipping weight, 12 lbs. per carton.

TRENCHES

No. 900

Made of Heavy Tough Fibre-Board. Printed in appropriate colors.
18¾ inches long, 8¾ inches wide, 2 inches high.
Packed flat, 1 dozen in a package.
6 dozen in a carton. 26 lbs. per carton.

Grey Iron tents and trench.
From a circa 1940 Grey Iron catalog

GREY IRON

G107   G106   Courtesy Hank Anton

GX1   GX2   GX3   GX4   GX5

GX6   GX7   GX8   GX9   GX10

The soldiers in this photo came from the collection of a man who once worked for Grey Iron, and were sold, in 1984, to a collector through a succession of dealers. By the time I worked my way through the chain, both the father who'd amassed them, and the son who'd sold them, had died. Everything about them suggests Grey Iron; sculpture, paint, and even the stand of GX3, which is similar to some of Grey Iron's stands for its fowl. Only GX3, GX4 and GX8 are iron, but Grey Iron cast in other metals. Whether these are prototypes or were actually produced is unknown. In 1985 a Grey Iron employee showed me some soldiers he'd bought in the 1960s when the company sold off its pre-War pieces to employees for three cents apiece. Most were standard, though mint, but one was the GX7 Highlander, unpainted. He said he had three others also unpainted. Perhaps these foreign troops were planned to go with the Evzone and possibly the ski troop, who may have been a Finn. GX9 is Chinese, and has a queue hanging down his back. The figures on the bottom row are all in th 3¼" dimestore range, as is GX5.

					G	VG	M
			T-7	Porter	6.00	9.00	12.00
American Family Series			T-8	Policeman	5.00	8.00	10.00
(approximately 2¼" high)			T-9	Postman	5.00	8.00	10.00
The American Family Travels	**G**	**VG**	**M** T-10	Newsboy	6.00	9.00	12.00
T-1 Man in traveling suit	5.00	8.00	10.00 T-11	Preacher	6.00	10.00	13.00
T-2 Woman in traveling			**T-12 Old Colored Man —**				
costume	5.00	8.00	10.00	sitting	8.00	12.00	16.00
T-3 Boy in traveling suit	6.00	9.00	12.00 **T-13 Seat**		4.00	6.00	8.00
T-4 Girl in traveling suit	6.00	9.00	12.00				
T-5 Conductor	5.00	8.00	10.00				
T-6 Engineer	5.00	8.00	10.00				

GREY IRON

T1 T2 T3 T4 T5 T6 T7

F10 F11 F12

T8 T9 T10 T11 T12-T13

F13 F14

	G	VG	M
The American Family on the Farm			
F-1 Farmer	4.50	6.75	9.00
F-2 Farmer's wife	4.50	6.75	9.00
F-3 Girl	5.00	7.50	10.00
F-4 Hired Man digging	5.00	7.50	10.00
F-5 Horse	3.50	5.25	7.00

F1 F2 F3 F4 F5

	G	VG	M
The American Family At Home			
H-1 Man with watering can	5.00	8.00	11.00
H-2 Woman with basket	7.00	11.00	14.00
H-3 Boy flying kite	8.00	12.00	16.00
H-4 Girl skipping rope	10.00	15.00	20.00
H-5 Old man sitting	3.50	5.25	7.00
H-6 Old woman sitting	4.00	6.00	8.00
H-7 Colored cook	9.00	13.50	18.00

H1 H2 H3 H4 H5, H6 on H13

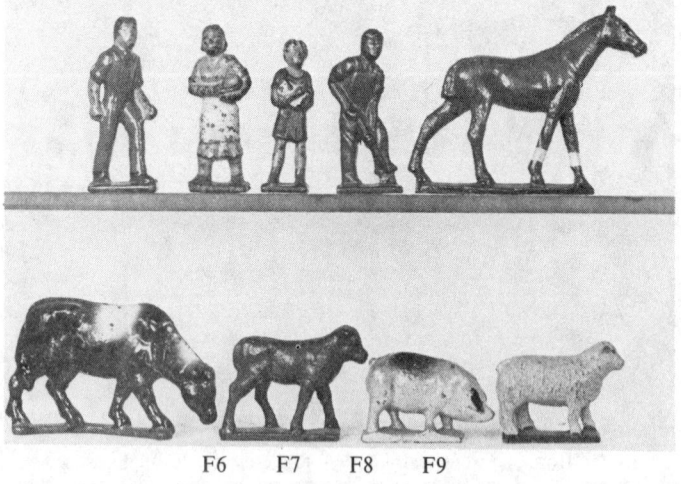

F6 F7 F8 F9

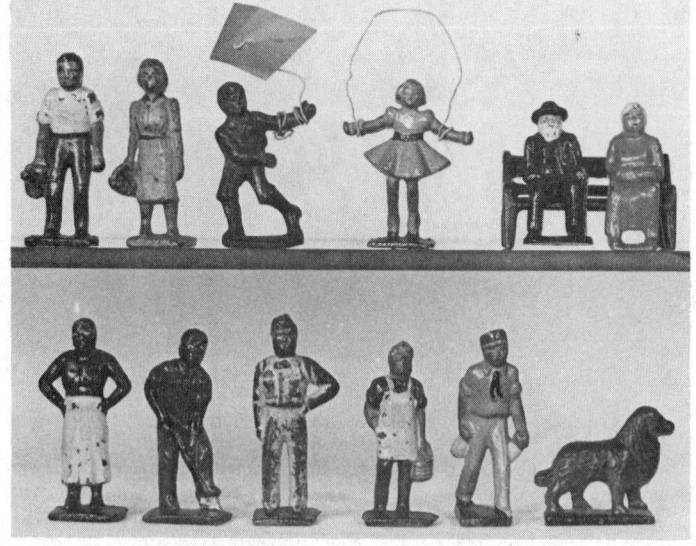

H7 H8 H9 H10 H11 H12

F-6 Cow	3.50	5.25	7.00
F-7 Calf	3.50	5.25	7.00
F-8 Pig	3.50	5.25	7.00
F-9 Sheep	3.50	5.25	7.00
F-10 Goat	3.50	5.25	7.00
F-11 Goose	3.50	5.25	7.00
F-12 Dog	3.50	5.25	7.00
F-13 Gate with Post	10.00	15.00	20.00
F-14 Fence	7.00	11.00	14.00

H-8 Colored man digging	16.00	24.00	32.00
H-9 Garageman	5.00	7.50	10.00
H-10 Delivery boy	5.00	7.50	10.00
H-11 Milkman	6.00	9.00	12.00
H-12 Dog	3.50	5.25	7.00
H-13 Lawn Seat	4.00	6.00	8.00

GREY IRON

The American Family On The Beach	G	VG	M
B-1 Man in bathing suit....	10.00	15.00	20.00
B-2 Woman in bathing suit.	10.00	15.00	20.00
B-3 Boy in summer suit....	6.00	9.00	12.00
B-4 Girl in slacks.........	9.00	13.50	18.00
B-5 Old Man Sitting......	3.50	5.25	7.00
B-6 Boy with Life Preserver.	9.00	13.50	18.00
B-7 Girl with Sand Pail....	9.00	13.50	18.00
B-8 Boy with Ball........	9.00	13.50	18.00
B-9 Girl Catching Ball.....	8.00	12.00	16.00
B-10 Life Guard..........	11.00	16.00	22.00
B-11 Life Guard's Chair....	12.00	18.00	24.00
B-12 Life Boat...........	12.00	18.00	24.00
B-13 Bench	4.00	6.00	8.00
B-14 Cabana.............	No Price Found		

The American Family On The Ranch	G	VG	M
R-1 Cowboy with lasso.....	9.00	14.00	18.00
R-2 Cowboy Rider........	19.00	28.00	38.00
R-3 Cowboy squatting.....	8.00	12.00	16.00
R-4 Boy in Cowboy Suit....	8.00	12.00	16.00
R-5 Girl in Riding Suit.....	7.00	11.00	15.00
R-6 Cowgirl Rider.........	11.00	16.00	22.00
R-7 Stallion..............	8.00	12.00	16.00
R-8 Bucking Broncho......	10.00	15.00	20.00
R-9 Colt................	6.00	9.00	12.00
R-10 Burro..............	7.00	11.00	15.00
R-11 Calf...............	5.00	8.00	11.00
R-15 Rooster and Chickens.	4.00	6.00	8.00
R-16 Three Ducks........	5.00	8.00	10.00

R1   R2, R8   R3   R4   R5   R6, R9

B1   B2   B3   B4   B5 on B13

B6   B7   B8   B9   B10, B11   B12

R10   R11   R15   R16

Grey Iron's pattern of the G56 surrendering bandit. The front of the figure is on one side of the pattern, and the back on the other. Fine-grained sand is then formed around the pattern, and then iron is poured into the sand mold. In this case, 18 figures are made per casting. Several hundred can be made before a new mold has to be formed.
Courtesy John Wright Co.

Grey Iron's "Clever Clowns." "Sailor Sam" is at right.
"Clever Clowns" came in 3 different sets. No. 100 sells for $300 in mint, No. 200 for $1000 and No. 300 for $800. The clowns come with both arched and straight backs.

R6 atop R7
Courtesy K. Warren Mitchell

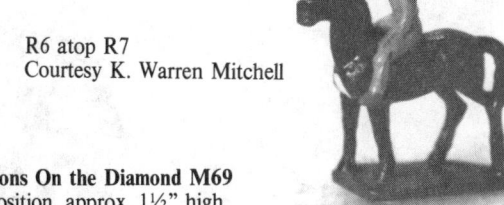

The Champions On the Diamond M69
Fielder in Position, approx. 1½" high
No Price Found

These unpainted figures were recently cast by the John Wright Company from old Grey Iron molds. Judging by their look, they were probably produced in the 1930's. The new unpainted figures sell for $1 each. Those produced in the pre-War period would sell for about $30 in mint.

150

Greycraft Models
THE AMERICAN FAMILY AT HOME

The American Family at Home set No. H113. None is known. From a circa 1940 Grey Iron catalog.

The American Family on the Beach set as shown in a 1940 Grey Iron catalog. A complete set in good condition, including the boardwalk, sold at auction in 1986 for $708.

The American Family Travels set No. T113. None is known. The station was made of heavy cardboard. From a circa 1940 Grey Iron catalog.

American Family on the Farm Set F114. In 1987 one of these sets was traded for an estimated value of $325. The illustration is from a circa 1940 Grey Iron catalog.

WILTON

The Wilton Company has been producing in cast iron and armetale (a very light alloy) for a number of years. Don Smith, owner of John Wright (Grey Iron's successor) has freely admitted to the author that Wright copied a number of Wilton's figures. Thus telling who made which is difficult, if not impossible, at least when it comes to those in iron.

According to collector Bill Cardiff, Loren "Red" Hancock was both the mold maker and caster of Wilton's figures. His initials, L.L.H., appear on the back of at least one of Wilton's products; its Colonial Soldier. Wilton is known to have produced (and Wright copied) a group of black music makers (value about $25 each in mint); the aforementioned colonial soldier; an Indian brave, squaw and bear as another set (presumably an Indian boy, who seems to belong to the set, as well); Union and Confederate troops and officers. Their iron worker seems not to have been copied by Wright. Wilton also produced the cast iron palm tree which some collectors believe appeared in Grey Iron's sets of Ethiopians and Italian or English soldiers. Perhaps Grey Iron wasn't above copying either.

Until recently, Wilton's cast iron division was located right next door to John Wright. The company is presently based in Columbia, PA.

At left, Grey Iron's G48 for size comparison. At right, the iron Indian Brave, either by Wilton or Grey Iron.

This impressive dimestore-sized piece stands about 4¼" high, has its pourhole in the base of the horse's tail and an airhole at the bottom of its nose. Despite being hollowcast lead, it is very heavy; about seven ounces. The cowboy is cast on the horse, but an identical separate horse was also sold, Two similar figures, obviously by the same company, were issued in 5¼" height, and another even taller. The 4¼" high figure was copied by the Japanese ("JAPAN" is on the underbelly), but as with most copies, it is slightly smaller. There are some indications this piece was produced by Wilton, but nothing has been confirmed.

A larger version of the hollowcast lead cowboy that may have been made by Wilton. Notice the differences in design.
Photo by Bill Cardiff.

Wilton iron worker
Photo by Bill Cardiff

Cast iron Indian Squaw with Papoose, Indian Brave, Indian Boy. By Wilton or John Wright.
Photo by Gene Parker

L to R: Wilton Colonial Soldier, Union Soldier, Confederate Officer, Union Officer. These are in armetale and were sold unpainted.
Photo by Bill Cardiff

Wilton Indian Brave, Indian Squaw with Papoose, Bear. These were cast in armetale and sold unpainted.
Photo by Bill Cardiff

AUBURN

UPDATE: The December, 1935 Fortune magazine mentions that W.T. Grant "is particularly proud of having scooped the chain-store field with Ethiopian soldiers. Until Grant could get ready-made Ethiopians, it colored up part of its regular stock of white soldiers with chocolate paint". This could apply to Barclay or Grey Iron as well as Auburn, but since Grant did it, and only one Auburn has been found painted "chocolate", it seems likely the soldiers were Auburns (it also means at least one dimestore company was producing Ethiopians in 1935).

Since the last edition, 1937 and 1940 color company catalogs have turned up, providing many new numbers and identifications. In 1988 a boxed set was found with a copyright line of 1935, and a 1939 general catalog shows the "skinny" early Auburns, suggesting they were still on sale at that point.

Avid collectors of Auburn Rubber soldiers are probably the kind who, when they look for a pet, tend to choose the runt of the litter.

For a number of reasons, many of Auburn's soldiers have a tendency to look a little . . . well, *silly*. Unlike their metallic counterparts, Auburn's figures frequently have problems with maintaining their dignity. Warped stands give many of them a precariously balanced, even drunken appearance. Their plain dot eyes invest them with a cartoony, simple-minded look. Finally, because of their medium, Auburn's men are not as finely detailed as Barclay's or Manoil's, or as smoothly cast as Grey Iron's.

Add to that the unsatisfactory lightweight "feel" in the hand of rubber as opposed to the more pleasurable weight of metal soldiers, and it's no wonder that most collectors begin to accumulate Auburn Rubber (also known as Aub-Rub'r and ARCOR) soldiers only after they've come close to completing their collections of Barclays, Manoils and Greys.

But I'm one of those who likes runts. From the beginning I've sought out Auburns, and am delighted whenever a new one is added to my collection. I think Auburn made some interesting soldiers. I also believe that about 1941 it added a few that are as arresting as any produced by its competitors.

Auburn's history is as skewed as some of its products. It began as a tire maker, added toys 25 years later, was bought by a town, and when the company met its death, it did so at the hands of organized crime.

Auburn was founded in 1910 as the Double Fabric Tire Corporation. Its line was auto tires and tubes, and about five years later it changed its name to Auburn Rubber Crown Cord. Around 1928 Auburn began molding rubber goods; stick-on soles and heels, fly swatters, stair treads, can openers, etc. Nothing of urgent concern to the readers of this book, but happily in 1935 A. L. Murray, Auburn's president and chief stockholder, went off on a trip to England.

He came back with a toy palace guard, and an idea that it could be turned out in rubber. The soldier was taken to a local artisan who made patterns from it; original molds were then produced in lead by Auburn, and sample toys molded for Murray. Subsequently these samples were taken to an artist and decorated per Murray's instructions. Presented to buyers, they immediately caught on, and Auburn quickly found itself very much in the toy business. Before long approximately 200 of Auburn's 400 employees were involved in toymaking on a two-shift basis.

The first toys were five soldiers, which were molded in 24" rubber presses. Each mold contained 40 to 60 soldiers, with cure time about 12 minutes. After removal from the mold, the excess rubber flash was trimmed off by hand, or in later days by "nipper" type dies.

Once trimmed, the soldiers were dipped in a base coat of lacquer (advertised as "pure vegetable dyes") and then sent down a conveyor belt for decorating. There women with small camel hair brushes added the finishing touches to uniforms, faces, belts, etc. After drying, the soldiers, which were sold for a nickel apiece, were individually wrapped in waxed paper and packed three dozen to a chipboard box and 12 dozen boxes to a corrugated carton for shipment.

The first known ad for Auburn Rubber's toys: April, 1936. Toy production had begun the year before.
Courtesy *Playthings*

An Auburn boxtop for one of its soldier sets. The copyright at line at bottom is 1935.
Photo by Stan Alekna

AUBURN

Shortly after the soldiers went into production Auburn began making wheeled toys. Since the company was located in Auburn, Indiana, its first choice was a natural; a Cord, which was one of the many cars built in Auburn. (With all those manufacturers one might assume Auburn was a big city, much like Gary, Indiana, but in 1940 the population was just 5415.) The cars were produced in much the same way as the soldiers, molded, trimmed, dipped with base coat laquer, and after the wheels were assembled, decorated by girls seated alongside a conveyor belt.

Design of Auburn's toys was by Edward McCandlish, a free-lancer, and unknown to all of the Auburn veterans I've queried. This may be the same Edward McCandlish who in 1920-21 drew a syndicated comic strip or panel titled "Folk Tales". In any event all indications are that he was, like so many of the dimestore sculptors, a trained artist.

Probably the most ubiquitous of Auburn's toys was its tractor, which sold in the millions, quite possibly even selling at stores that carried no other Auburn products. For though Auburn began with a bang, by 1939 it found itself running into problems.

My impression, as a toy soldier-buyer in the late 1930s, is that, of the major companies, Auburn at that time had more prestige than either Manoil or Grey Iron. Like Barclay, Auburn was found in the "class" 5&10s, like Woolworth's. Manoil was more likely to turn up in another good (but not *as* good) dimestore, Kresge's for example, while Grey Iron, at least in the New York area, was generally found only in the shadows of dimly-lit, unprepossessing candy stores. But by 1941 this had changed – in the New York area anyway – with Manoil beginning to command greater counter space than Barclay at Woolworth's, and Auburn's soldiers no longer on view.

Because of this, Auburn turned to New York's Martin Ullman, "internationally famous package designer". His fame seems to have been justified, as in 1940 Auburn's packaged set of eighteen baseball players won the Grand Prize at the 3rd National Toy Packaging contest, and according to publicity at the time, the company began recapturing many of its lost buyers.

Auburn's boxes, while prize-winning, were also models of how to advertise a product. The first issue of Consumers Union in May 1936 warned against metal toys such as soldiers since they were found to be "of a soft metal alloy containing a high percentage of lead" which was considered dangerous not only to younger childen, "who enjoy their toys with their mouths as well as their hands" but also to older children, since lead rubs off on the hands and can be "carried to the mouth."

A built-in boost for Auburn, and over the years Auburn boxes carried such messages as "Protect the Child While Playing," "Colored With Pure Vegetable Dyes", "Sanitary, Noiseless, Washable", "Will Not Scratch Fingers, Floors or Furniture", "Harmless, washable and will not scratch or mar furniture", "Will Not Cut, Scratch or Mar Furniture".

Auburn's pre-War soldiers went through three stages of development. The first were frail-looking, with long, thin bodies and small heads. (That is, the heads were small for a *toy soldier* – actually, the figures were more in proportion than most soldiers, which tend to approximate the body of an eight-year-old child.) The second version had a doughty, stocky look and the third, which evolved about 1940-41, was more well-proportioned and realistic than its predecessors, and contained the largest percentage of dashing action figures.

During the war, Auburn was unable to use any rubber for toys – up till that time it had been producing, aside from its soldiers and vehicles, "farm animals, airplanes, farm implements, sponge rubber blocks, streamlined car carrier, quoits, hammers, hatchets, knives, circus sets, bunnies, scotties and storybook characters."

While involved in war production of soles, gaskets, soling sheets, etc., the company experimented with non-critical materials that might be used in toy-making. Battery cases, sawdust and glue, excelsior and lime, and any other products that could possibly be molded into a toy were tried, but none worked out, and efforts to make toys were discontinued until the hostilities ended and proper materials became available.

For a time after the war, Auburn didn't have the space it wanted for toys, having added a great deal of new equipment to the plant, so the company bought a factory in Connellsville, Pennsylvania, and set it up just for rubber toy production. After four years buildings were added at Auburn and production of rubber toys resumed there about 1950, continuing until 1952, when Auburn bought its first plastic injection molding machine. From then on all its toys were converted to vinyl plastic and were injection molded. Among Auburn's post-war figures were farmers, cowboys, Indians, firemen, policemen and some Korean War-era soldiers, which are extremely well done, though as yet not deemed particularly collectible.

By 1959 Auburn had 16 molding machines, and a year later an offer from the city of Deming, New Mexico, to purchase its toy section only. Limited production began in Deming in February of 1960. By 1962 Auburn was producing 17 million toy items per year, as well as swim aids such as fins and masks.

However, despite all that action, in 1969 Auburn went out of business. According to the book "Vicious Cycles – The Mafia In The Marketplace" by Jonathan Kwitny, Auburn was taken over by labor racketeers and very quickly drained dry, thus providing what is almost certainly the darkest ending to any company in the history of toy soldiers.

AUBURN   All bold words and numbers are Auburn's own description.

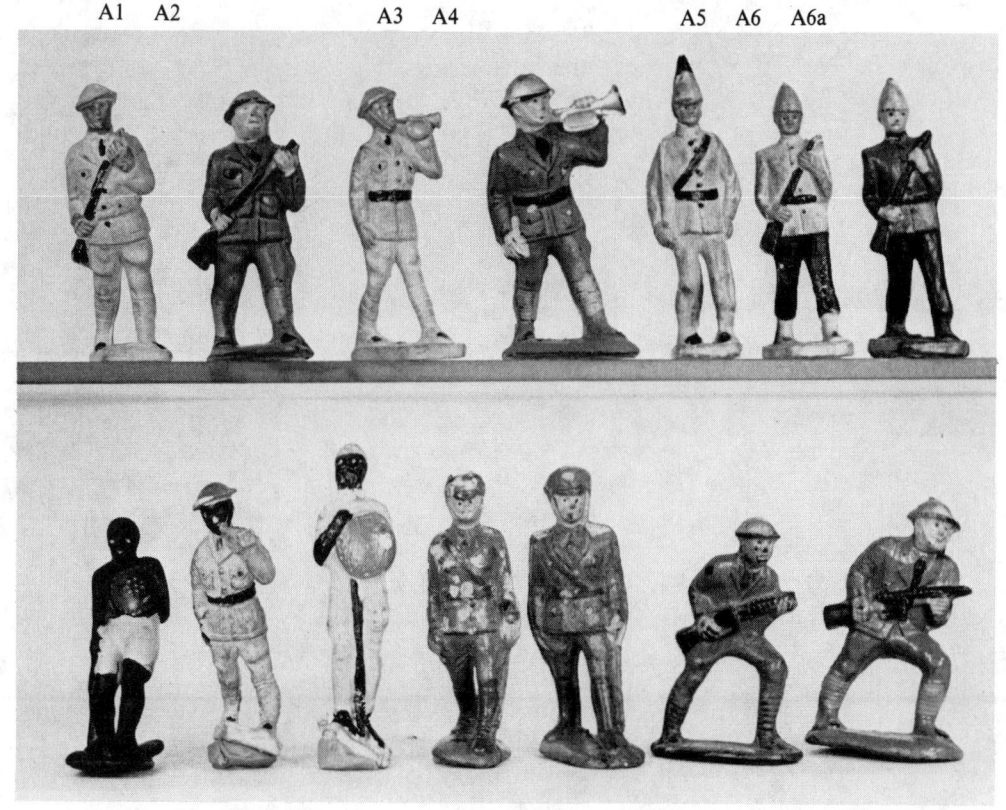

A1 A2   A3 A4   A5 A6 A6a

A7 A7a A7b   A8 A9   A10   A11

A14a
Photo by Ron Steiner

	G	VG	M		G	VG	M
(A1) 1200 Infantry Private .	6.00	10.00	13.00	**(A16) 206 Stretcher Bearer**	15.00	23.00	30.00
(A2) 200 U.S. Infantry				**(A17) 208 Wounded Soldier**	17.00	26.00	35.00
Private	5.00	8.00	11.00	**(A18) 216 Observer With**			
(A3) 1202 Infantry Bugler .	9.00	14.00	18.00	**Binoculars**	7.00	11.00	15.00
(A4) 202 Bugler, U.S. Infan-				**(A19) 236 Signalman**	30.00	45.00	60.00
try	9.00	14.00	18.00	**(A19a) Signalman**, early			
(A5) Foreign Legion, also				smaller size, only three			
White Guard officer, **No.**				known	100.00	150.00	200.00
220	11.00	17.00	22.00	**(A20) 222 Sniper**, crawling,			
(A6) 214 & 218 Foreign				rifle over shoulder	36.00	54.00	72.00
Legion Private	10.00	15.00	20.00	**(A21) 234 Bomb Thrower** .	12.00	18.00	24.00
(A7) Ethiopian with shield				**(A22) 242 Anti-Aircraft Gun**	15.00	23.00	30.00
and rifle	60.00	90.00	120.00	**(A23) 1546 Motorcycle Cop**,			
(A7a) Ethiopian bugler	No Price Found			blue or khaki as soldier .	25.00	38.00	50.00
(A7b) Ethiopian with rifle				**(A24) 240 Motorcycle**			
and shield, in robes	50.00	75.00	100.00	**Soldiers**, with sidecar . . .	25.00	38.00	50.00
(A8) Officer, early	7.00	11.00	14.00	**(A25) Aircraft Defender** . . .	15.00	23.00	30.00
(A9) 204 U.S. Infantry Of-				**(A26) Color Bearer**	22.00	33.00	44.00
ficer	7.00	11.00	14.00	**(A27) Marching Soldier** . . .	9.00	14.00	18.00
(A10) 1238 Charging Soldier	22.00	34.00	44.00	**(A28) Firing Soldier**	22.00	33.00	44.00
(A11) 238 Charging Soldier				**(A29) 272 Plane Shooter** . .	18.00	27.00	36.00
with tommy gun	7.00	11.00	15.00	**(A30) Sound Detector**	17.00	25.00	34.00
(A12) 232 Officer on Horse	18.00	27.00	36.00	**(A31) Searchlight**	18.00	27.00	37.00
(A13) 230 Machine Gunner	7.00	11.00	15.00	**(A32) 296 Trench Mortar** .	16.00	24.00	32.00
(A14) 224 Red Cross Doctor	17.00	26.00	35.00	**(A33) Tank Defender**	24.00	36.00	48.00
(A14a) Army Doctor, Khaki				**(A34) Tank Soldier**, running			
uniform	No Price Found			with box	17.00	26.00	35.00
(A15) 226 Red Cross Nurse				**(A35)** Pilot, running, looking			
white or khaki uniform .	17.00	26.00	35.00	skyward, in pilot helmet			
				and goggles	No Price Found		
				(A36) Motor Scout	20.00	30.00	40.00

A12 A13 A14 A15 A16

A17 A18 A19 A20

A19a
Courtesy K. Warren Mitchell

A21 A22 A23 A24

A25 A26 A27 A28 A29

AUBURN

Where Auburn may have found the idea for its A30 and A31 pieces. From a post card circa 1940.
Courtesy Ed Poole

Possible inspiration for Auburn's A33 "Tank Defender".

Auburn's Motor Scout, in the flesh.
Courtesy Ed Poole

	G	VG	M		G	VG	M
(A37) **258 Baserunner**	13.00	20.00	26.00	(A45) **260 Lineman**, football player	16.00	24.00	32.00
(A38) **252 Batter**	20.00	30.00	41.00	(A46) **266 Passer**, football player	21.00	32.00	42.00
(A39) **256 Fielder or Baseman**	14.00	21.00	29.00	(A47) Motorcycle Cop, large 5" high	25.00	38.00	50.00
(A40) **250 Pitcher**	21.00	31.00	42.00	(A48) **No. 100 Cowboy on horse**	30.00	45.00	60.00
(A41) **254 Catcher**	17.00	25.00	34.00				
(A42) **268 Carrier** football player	17.00	26.00	35.00				
(A43) **264 Center** football player	16.00	24.00	32.00				
(A44) **262 Backfieldman**, football player	15.00	23.00	30.00				

A30   A31   A32   A33

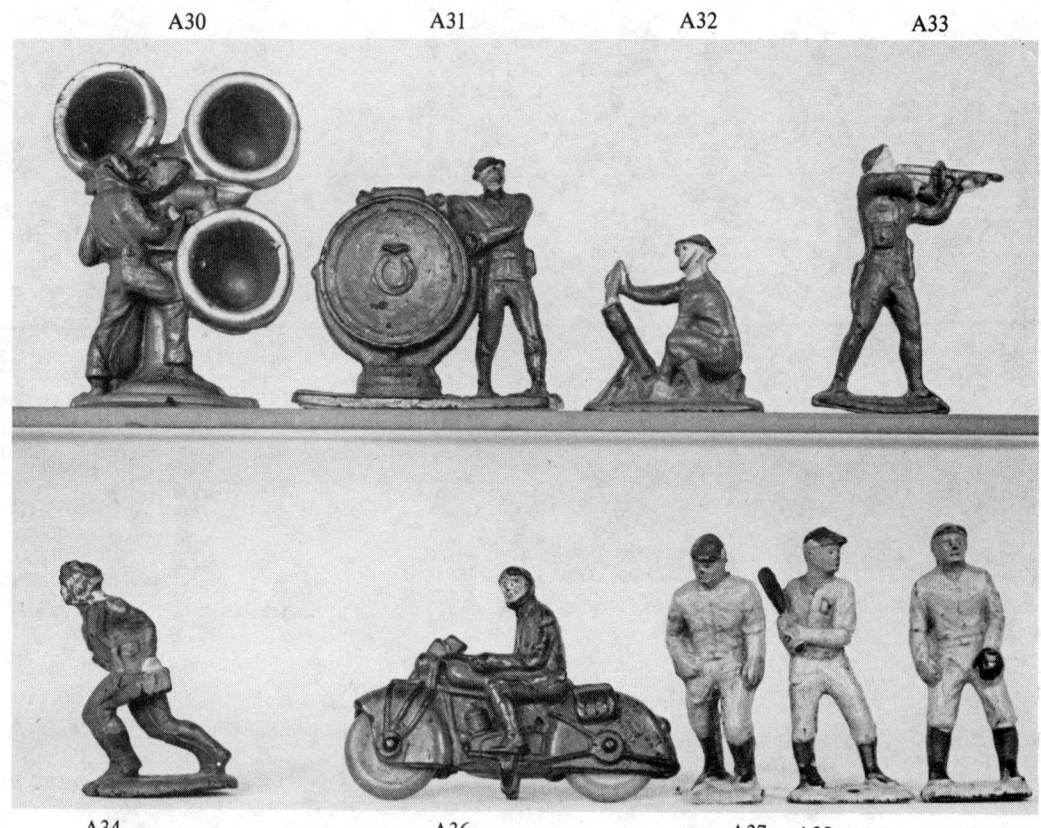

A34   A36   A37 A38 A39

A40   A41   A42   A43

A44   A45   A46

AUBURN

A48
No. 100 Cowboy on horse

A49
Fireman, possibly only
produced post-War
Courtesy Don Pielin

Auburn's soldiers seem to exist in a number of variations. Rectangular base at left and a much rarer round base at right.
Photo by Max Heiss

A35
Rough sketch from memory going back
40 years of A35. Note no box in hand,
head tilted up toward left, left hand
forward.
None known.

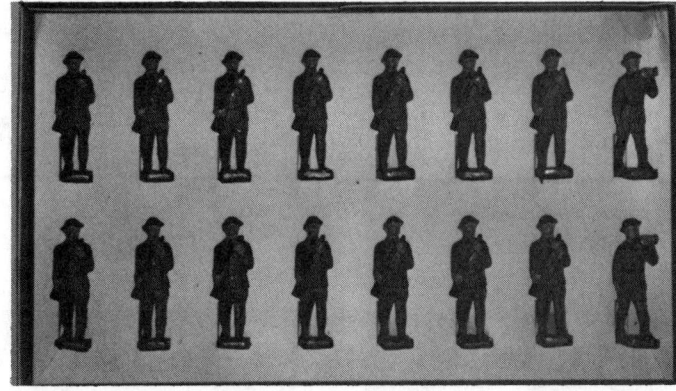

The soldiers in the set with the boxtop marked "Copyrighted 1935".
Photo by Stan Alekna

	G	VG	M
(A49) Fireman	15.00	22.00	30.00

A   B   C   D   E   F   G   H

P
Courtesy Charlie Breslow

I   J   K   L   M   N   O

Auburn's 3" high vinyl soldiers are attractive and well-sculpted, but at present don't seem to be collected. They sell for less than a dollar apiece. They appear in a 1958 Auburn catalog and apparently were introduced then.

AUBURN RUBBER FARM FIGURES

	G	VG	M
(ARA1) **110 Calf**	7.00	11.00	15.00
(ARA2) **112 Hen**	4.00	6.00	8.00
(ARA3) Collie, small	5.00	8.00	10.00
(ARA4) **116 Collie Dog** . . .	7.00	11.00	15.00
(ARA5) **104 Colt**	4.00	6.00	8.00
(ARA6) **108 Cow**	7.00	11.00	15.00
(ARA7) Duck	4.00	6.00	8.00
(ARA8) **102 Horse**	7.00	11.00	15.00
(ARA9) **106 Pig**	5.00	8.00	10.00
(ARA10) **126 Piglet**	4.00	6.00	8.00
(ARA11) **114 Sheep**	5.00	8.00	10.00
(ARA12) Turkey	4.00	6.00	8.00
(ARA13) **122 Rooster**	4.00	6.00	8.00
(ARA14) Farmer	7.00	11.00	15.00
(ARA15) Farm Wife	7.00	11.00	15.00
(ARA16) Team of horses (pulls wagon)	15.00	22.00	30.00
(ARA17) Watering Trough .	8.00	12.00	16.00

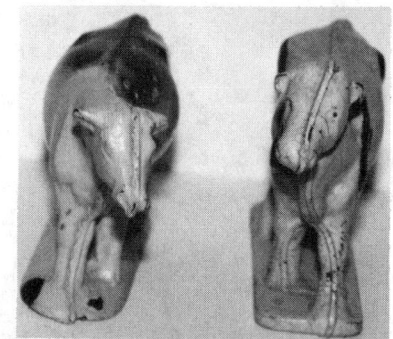

Variations in the ARA6 Cow: different leg and head positions, thickness. Photo by Stan Alekna

AUBURN CIRCUS FIGURES (sold 1936-37)

(AC1) **406 Circus Clown** . .	No Price Found
(AC2) **404 Circus Poodle** . .	No Price Found
(AC3) **402 Circus Elephant**	No Price Found
(AC4) **400 Circus Pony** . . .	No Price Found
(AC5) **408 Circus Ring**	No Price Found

ARA1   ARA2   ARA3   ARA4   ARA5

ARA6   ARA7   ARA8   ARA9   ARA10

Figures courtesy Clayton W. Nimtz and Tony Diksa

ARA11   ARA12   ARA13   ARA14   ARA15

ARA16   ARA17

Figures courtesy Clayton W. Nimtz and Tony Diksa

AC1   AC2   AC3   AC4

Courtesy Clayton W. Nimtz

AC1 AC2 AC3 AC4 AC5 AC6 AC7 AC8 AC9

AC10   AC11   AC12   AC13

Auburn plastic cowboys. Not shown is a mounted cowboy with lasso. Value foot $7 each, mounted $9 each. Photo by Jerry Combs

AUBURN AIRCRAFT

(AA1) **1548 Airplane** (Boeing C-98 "Clipper"), 8" wingspan	15.00	25.00	45.00
(AA2) **506 Small Airplane** (Consolidated A-11 light bomber), 4" wingspan . . .	10.00	20.00	35.00
(AA3) **586 Army Pursuit Plane** (Curtiss P-37), 4¾" wingspan	10.00	15.00	25.00
(AA4) **508 Large Airplane** (Douglas DC2 Transport), 6" wingspan	20.00	30.00	45.00

AUBURN

(AA5) "Jet 559" 10.00 15.00 25.00

AA1   AA2

AA3   AA4

Photo by Ed Poole

AA5
Photo by Max Heiss

AUBURN SHIPS

	G	VG	M
(AS1) **1582 Battleship**, 8¼" long, circa 1940	10.00	15.00	20.00
(AS2) Dreadnaught, 9⅛" long, new in 1941	10.00	18.00	25.00
(AS3) Freighter, 9¼" long, new in 1941	8.00	12.00	15.00
(AS4) Submarine, 6½" long, circa 1941	8.00	12.00	15.00

AS1

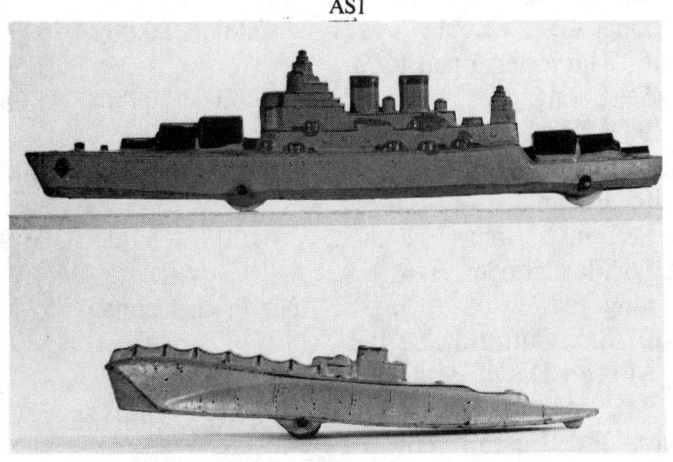

AS4

Photo by Ed Poole

AS3
Photo by Ed Poole

Auburn Vehicles
(List by Dave Leopard)

AA01 '36 Cord, four door coffin-nose sedan 6" long	No Price Found		
AA02 '37 Olds, 4 door sedan, 4½" long	15.00	18.00	22.00
AA03 '38 Olds, 4 door sedan, 5¾" long	20.00	25.00	30.00
AA04 '40 Olds, 4 door sedan, open fenders, 6" long	20.00	25.00	30.00
AA05 '40 Olds, 4 door sedan, fender skirts, 6" long ...	20.00	25.00	30.00
AA06 '48 Buick, 2 door sedanette, fastback, 7¼" long	30.00	35.00	40.00
AA07 '39 Buick, Y Job Experimental Roadster, 9¾" long	No Price Found		
AA08 '35 Ford Coupe, 4" long	20.00	25.00	30.00
AA09 '35 Ford 2 door slant-back sedan, 4" long	20.00	25.00	30.00
AA10 '50 Cadillac, 4 door sedan, 7¼" long	No Price Found		
AA11 '50 Cadillac, 4 door sedan, 5¾" long	No Price Found		
AA12 '39 Plymouth, 2 door trunkback sedan, 4¼" long	15.00	18.00	22.00
AA13 '46 Lincoln convertible, 2 door, square headlights, 4½" long ...	15.00	18.00	22.00
AA14 '46 Lincoln convertible, 2 door, round headlights, 4½" long ...	15.00	18.00	22.00
AA15 Late 40's Futuristic Sedan, fin down back, 5" long	15.00	18.00	22.00
AT01 '37 International cabover stake truck, 5⅜" long	20.00	25.00	30.00
AT01A Same as above, "U.S. Army" decal, khaki	15.00	18.00	22.00
AT02 Same as above with rounded bumper, minor variations	15.00	18.00	22.00
AT03 '37 International cabover stake truck, 4¼" long	15.00	18.00	22.00

AUBURN

Item			
AT04 Same as above with rounded bumper, minor variations	15.00	18.00	22.00
AT05 '37 International cabover stake truck, 3¾" long	15.00	18.00	22.00
AT06 Same as above with rounded bumper, minor variations	15.00	18.00	22.00
AT07 '37 International cabover stake truck, milk version, 4¼" long	No Price Found		
AT08 '37 International cabover stake truck, ambulance version	No Price Found		
AT09 Cab-Forward box truck, smooth sides, futuristic, 5½" long	15.00	18.00	22.00
AT10 Cabover box truck, smooth sides, futuristic 4⅛" long	15.00	18.00	22.00
AT11 '47 Chevy Cab Forward Box Truck, 5¾" long	15.00	18.00	22.00
AT12 c.'50 Pickup truck open fenders, 4½" long	15.00	18.00	22.00
AT13 c.'50 Pickup truck, fender skirts, 4½" long	15.00	18.00	22.00
AT14 '38 GMC "Carry Car" Auto Transport, 11½" long	40.00	50.00	75.00
AT15 '38 GMC Cab/Open Squared-off Trailer, 9" long	30.00	40.00	50.00
AT16 Updated Carry Car Transport, cab changed, trailer same, 11¾" long	No Price Found		
AT17 '35 Ford Stake Body Truck, 4¾" long	No Price Found		
AE01 Ahrens-Fox Fire Engine, 5½" long	No Price Found		
AE02 c.40s Fire Engine, hose and ladders, 7¾" long	25.00	30.00	35.00
AE03 c.40s Pumper, boiler, 7¾" long	25.00	30.00	35.00
AE04 c.40s Fire Engine, ladders, no hose, 7¾" long	25.00	30.00	35.00
AR01 Open racer, V-6, high fin, 10½" long	40.00	50.00	65.00
AR02 Open racer, V-6, low fin, 10½" long	35.00	45.00	55.00
AR03 Open racer, short, tapered tail, large tires, 10½" long	40.00	50.00	65.00
AR04 Open racer, short, boat tail, 6½" long	35.00	45.00	55.00
AR05 Open racer, boat tail, 4¾" long	20.00	27.00	35.00
AR06 Open racer, small fin, 6¼" long	20.00	27.00	35.00
AR07 Open racer short, boat tail, early, 6½" long	30.00	40.00	50.00
AR08 Open racer, no fenders, low fin, long back, 5¼" long	15.00	20.00	25.00
AR09 Open racer, boat tail, no side pipes, 4¾" long	30.00	35.00	40.00
AR10 Open racer, midget type, 5" long	40.00	50.00	60.00
AF01 Farm Tractor, John Deere "A", 5" long	20.00	25.00	30.00
AF02 Farm Tractor, John Deere, 4¼" long	20.00	25.00	30.00
AF03 Farm Tractor, Minneapolis-Moline "Z", 4" long	20.00	25.00	30.00
AF04 Farm Tractor, Minneapolis-Moline "R", early style, 7½" long	40.00	50.00	60.00
AF05 Farm Tractor, Minneapolis, Moline "R", later style, 7¼" long	40.00	50.00	60.00
AF06 Farm Tractor, Oliver Row Crop "70", 8" long	40.00	50.00	60.00
AF07 Farm Tractor, Oliver Row Crop "70", 6½" long	40.00	50.00	60.00
AF08 Farm Tractor, McCormick-Deering IH Farmall "M", 4" long	20.00	25.00	30.00
AF09 Farm Tractor, Graham-Bradley, 4¼" long	25.00	30.00	35.00
AI01 Trailer, 2 wheel, Graham-Bradley, 5¾" long	15.00	20.00	25.00
AI02 Trailer, 4 wheel, Graham-Bradley, 4¾" long	15.00	20.00	25.00
AI03 Harvester, open top, 5½" long	15.00	20.00	25.00
AI04 Manure Spreader, David Bradley, 4¾" long	10.00	15.00	20.00
AI05 Reliable Front-Lift Seeder, 5" long	10.00	15.00	20.00
AI06 Plow Seeder, 3½" long	No Price Found		
AI07 Side-Cutter Sickle Bar Mower, David Bradley, 3¾" long	No Price Found		
AI08 Two Furrow Plow, David Bradley, 4¾" long	10.00	15.00	20.00

AUBURN

AI09 Cultipacker (Disc Harrows?), David Bradley,
4⅜" long 10.00 15.00 20.00

AI10 Harrow, 4½" long . . No Price Found

AI11 Disc Harrows, 4½"
long 15.00 20.00 25.00

AI12 Plow with riding
farmer . . . . No Price Found

AM01 Tank, Marmon-
Harrington, 4½" long . . . 25.00 30.00 35.00

AM02 Tank, Marmon-
Harrington, 3¼" long . . . 15.00 20.00 25.00

AM03 Tractor and Cannon,
11½" long, olive green . . No Price Found

AAMI Ambulance, insert
top 25.00 35.00 45.00

AT101A & AT03A

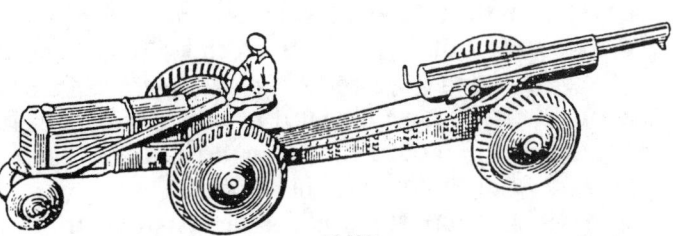

AM03

AAMI
Courtesy K. Warren Mitchell

AC1 Fieldpiece, 75mm, 7"
long 17.00 25.00 34.00

AC2 Howitzer, 155mm, 7"
long 17.00 25.00 34.00

AC2, AM01
AM02, AC1

No. 650 ARMY TANK   No. 652 ARMY RECON CAR

No. 654 JEEP AND GUN   No. 656 ARMY TRUCK
AUBURN vinyl vehicles, each worth about $2.50 in mint.

JONES

UPDATE: A large amount of Jones' own material has been found since the last edition. Though nothing emerged to tie him directly to the 3¼" dimestore manufacture, the appearance of J26 (bayoneting in gas mask) in a circa 1931 display of Metal-Art soldiers does provide a direct link. Listed but not shown in the Metal-Art order sheets are both a "German Infantry Kneeling with Rifle Aimed" and "German Gren. Inf. of 1918 charging" which were almost certainly J1 and J2, since those dimestore pieces, like J26, are in the three-inch range, rather than 3¼".

Also in Jones' files was a one-page listing of his Kingsart Products Company soldiers, with an address of 6650 South May Street in Chicago. In Jones' own handwriting on the listing is "1925". The amount of soldiers (129) and the variety of their positions is extraordinary. They were produced in "size 3" and some also in "size 2" (with no indication of just what those sizes were). Although there has been some belief that Kingsarts were large and full-sized soldiers, a June, 1929 ad in *Toys and Novelties* suggests instead that they were homecast types. The ad was by Metal-Art and said, in part, "we have obtained from our branch in Europe a number of semi-formed or flat figures made of solid metal. These are produced by Kingsart Ltd., in vast quantities..." Given Jones' personal history, it's more likely this was his way of disposing of old stock.

A 1939 variety store receipt suggests that Jones' dimestores sold as far west as Omaha.

"...seeing David Wark Griffith's 'America' has made such inroads on my mind that nothing seems able to eradicate it...Seeing that motion picture...gave yours truly a whirling thought that if historic figures, such as were portrayed in the battle scenes, could be made in miniature images, the viewer of the play could relive the scenes long after the movie had vanished."

That was how it began for J. Edward Jones, a man whose life was filled with contradictions. There are those who remember him as sweet-tempered, others who found him sour and rude. He was a man with a 4th grade education who was observed to make "grave mistakes" in his speech, and yet he wrote the paragraphs above, put out a publication on toy soldiers that was equally as literate, and served as editor of another. He considered himself an expert on the toy soldier business, and yet he continually failed. He "set the world on his daughter" and she rejected him. Finally, the one toy soldier line of his that he was ashamed of and "didn't like to talk about" is the group most prized by today's collectors. Or *did* he produce them? Even here there are contradictions; one group of collectors is sure Jones was the man behind them while others are equally certain he was not.

Longtime collector-dealer Gus Hansen knew Jones and states unequivocally that the 3¼" line of figures known as "Jones" was produced by him. It's Hansen who says Jones didn't like to talk about them. This is understandable, as Jones almost from the first was determined to produce American toy soldiers that would equal, perhaps even surpass those made by Britains. And until recently, there was no prestige involved in producing or collecting the 3¼" dimestore soldiers. Those who did were looked down upon.

According to Hansen, the 3¼" pieces were produced for wholesalers, with Jones not selling them directly. The three order sheets listing Jones figures that have surfaced were all published by Chicago distributors: N. Shure, Johnson & Smith and L. Gould. The sculptor for these pieces was Chicago's Henry Kasselowski. Hansen remembers watching him remove the tin helmet from a Barclay B61 prone machine gunner, shape a German helmet from red wax, place it on the piece's head, then make a plaster cast of the entire figure, from which a bronze mold was made. Which suggests yet another contradiction; while many of Jones' dimestore figures were original, even dramatically so, others were out-and-out copies.

Perhaps because of Jones' distaste for the line he was making, little is known about it. It probably began in the late 1930s, and seems to have cut off abruptly in September, 1941. According to Hansen, the soldiers were produced in a storefront, and in all likelihood when the company failed, Jones' investors seized the molds. There were two casters, a woman who worked part-time on the packing, the painting was farmed out to housewives and children, and Jones did all the rest. A big problem for Jones may have been the fact that his soldiers were much higher-priced than the Barclays, Manoils, Grey Irons and Auburns they competed with. The latter retailed for a nickel apiece. On L. Gould's list, the wholesale price is 92 cents a dozen. However, the N. Shure price was 42 cents a dozen, suggesting at least some were sold at a nickel apiece.

"America" was released on March 2, 1924. Some time later Jones got in touch with Harry A. Ogden (1856-1936) of Englewood, New Jersey. Shortly after being inspired to produce historical toy soldiers, Jones had realized the uniforms would have to be researched. While consulting a history, he'd come upon colored plates of U.S. and other costumes by Ogden. He consulted Who's Who, found Ogden was still alive, and wrote him. Shortly thereafter, Ogden began furnishing Jones with sketches of soldiers from American history.

JONES

Jones was in business by 1925, judging by his Kingsart order sheet and a rather hazy note in his publication, *The Prospector*, but at present his first important company seems to be the Metal-Art Miniature Co. of Chicago, which was in business from 1929-31 at 9339 Cottage Grove Ave. In June, 1931, there were 57 pieces in the line, in two and three-inch sizes. Ogden, 73 at the time, was the authority for the style and coloring of the uniforms. Of particular interest to dimestore collectors is one of the 3" figures; an officer in overcoat pointing with one hand and holding a pistol in the other. Jones in his dimestore line made a figure (J13) that was strikingly similar, but not exactly the same.

From 1932-39 Miniature Products Co. at 5 South Wabash Ave., Chicago, appears to be Jones' next enterprise, as in 1935 he was listed as its Founder and Partner. Even here, though, things get murky. In 1951 *The Prospector* stated "the Dimayos and McDonalds" had given up the company and "J. Edward Jones, who had worked with two soldiers firms, was able, with the assistance of Miss Ella Hume, to launch Metal Miniatures Co. in 1940."

There could be a simple answer to all the fog here. Jones, being a poor businessman, may have wanted to disassociate himself from enterprises that had failed; perhaps was even trying to throw creditors off the track.

Metal Miniatures Co. in addition to selling the Metal-Art soldiers, seems to have produced about 20 pieces, all in 54mm. We know what some of them were because, perversely, Jones listed them in a 1946 issue of *The Prospector*. According to Jones they were "acquired" by George Borgfeldt & Co. (a distributor) and Harry Barker. In actuality, they seem to have been seized when Jones wasn't able to fill an order he'd already been paid for. They consisted of a British 74th Foot captain of about 1777, running, British 93rd Ft. piper of about 1815, standing, British Kneeling Machine Gunner of about 1915, U.S. Seaman of about 1916 in pea jacket marching, U.S. Infantry of 1918 with full pack marching, British Royal Navy drummer of 1922, Italian Infantry of about 1936 running at trail, a standing un-saddled horse, a cannon of about 1780, and a French infantry sergeant, perhaps of 1781, standing at right support arms. According to *The Prospector*, "the first fully formed 54mm subject to be designed" by Metal Miniatures was an 1806 infantry private of the 1st Regiment of Infantry of the United States. This was one of the few Jones products to bear markings, and was inscribed "No. 1, MADE IN CHICAGO, U.S.A."

Metal Miniatures began in business on May 1, 1940, and was shut down April 30, 1942, by the restrictions of war-time. Jones was bitter about this, and complained in *The Prospector*, "We would cheerfully comply with the order had we believed it was necessary... Inasmuch as the government has already acquired a 3-year stockpile as planned, and the metal foundries are loaded with scrap beyond their desire, we contend that manufacturers should have at least 20% of their normal needs. Instead they must go bankrupt.

"We have continually received requests from army camps for certain of our figures, plus new designs required for tactical training purposes. The OPM refuses to let us make such items although both the British and Nazi utilize them.

"We close our factory then in protest...."

Jones wasn't the only toy soldier manufacturer unable to secure a government defense contract. The much-larger Manoil also floundered during the War years. But though Jones raged, his wife seems to have been happier. According to Michael Hitrovo in an account in the April 1972 "The Vedette", "Ed somehow obtained a job as an accountant at a rather meager salary, but even at this it was a 'better' period for his family. His wife told me later that this was one of the few times in their married life when she could have the security of a weekly check. Most of the time Ed was engaged in some 'project' or other, with no really steady income."

Even during this period, Jones was thinking about soldiers. According to Hitrovo, he "got in touch with a lady sculptor in Chicago's university section." From her he ordered several prototype figures, which were to be molded and produced after the war. Among them were "a British sapper carrying a bagion or a basket; a rifleman in hunting shirt, firing; another, walking; and many more – all of the American Revolution period. The figures were exquisitely done, with a wealth of detail". However there may have been too much detail – a number of undercuts that made the figures too difficult to cast – as none seem to have been produced, although Jones assured Hitrovo that the undercuts would present no problem; the figures would be cut and molded in several pieces.

On May 1, 1946, the 6th anniversary of the founding of Metal Miniatures Co., Jones began business again under the name Moulded Miniatures, at 7501 Cottage Grove Avenue, Chicago. About this this time Jones advertised that "Models have been created in clay, plaster and wood by experts of our time – Florence Gray, William Rauch, Don Ray and others. Moulds have been produced under the direction of Henry Kasselowski, known to be the most skilled die-maker of miniature items in America". Earlier, on December 8, 1938, Jones had advertised his "1806 Infantry private from Ray's modelers in London. Henri Castle, U.S., made mold." Presumably Henri Castle was actually Kasselowski, who also sculpted all of Lincoln Log's figures until the 1950s, when England's Crescent took over the Lincoln Log line.

Moulded Miniatures may have been Jones' most successful venture, though even it seems to have been far from a thriving, dependable enterprise. Figures that were advertised were not always made; substitutions were arbitrarily sent, and not infrequently they arrived broken. At one point, because of these problems, an organized group of toy soldier collectors came near to organizing a boycott against Jones. Still, whatever its problems, the company seems to have functioned without interruption from 1946 through at least 1955. The figures I have listed here are only those for which I've been able to obtain photos; Jones' order sheets show many more, but since he is known to have promised more than he delivered, I feel it's best to stay with those that are verifiable.

In addition to *The Prospector*, which came out in looseleaf form, Jones appears to have written two books. One was to be limited to 400 copies, published June 30, 1951, and titled "Fun With Lead Soldiers and Other Figures". The other, "Uniforms and Regiments", with "a brief sampling of information on Miniature Collecting" was scheduled for publication in 1955, with a run of 3000 copies.

In a 1950 or 1951 issue of *The Prospector*, Jones went into a bit of history about Britains Ltd., and then got into the following, taken from the 1951 book:

"The Crescent Toy Co. Ltd. of London was in existence at least during 1936, and probably much earlier. Mr. A. Schneider, one of the directors was employed many years ago by Reka, Ltd. This firm established in 1908 seems to have ceased operations about 1922. Exact date is unknown. A number of the subjects created by the firm of Reka, Ltd. now are part of the Crescent Toy Co. Ltd. range of designs. Others, often the same subjects, are found in those formerly marketed by the Metal-Art Miniature Co. of Chicago, which existed only during 1929-31.

"From the residue of this firm after the depression of 1931 had its fling, arose two other firms. John Lloyd Wright and Miniature Products Co. both lasted from 1932-1939. Wright is no longer in this enterprise but the designs created during his ownership are still being marketed with 'Lincoln Logs' construction set offered by The Playschool Co. of Chicago."

In connection with this, to me, rather muddled account, let me underline the fact that Kasselowski, who worked for Jones, also worked for Lincoln Log, until Crescent took over. To further add to the muddling, I'll take this opportunity to state that on the sheets that list Jones' 1931 Metal Arts soldiers, someone had hand-written, next to the pointing officer in greatcoat and the "German Infantry Charging" (not shown in the accompanying 1931 photo) "These subjects were reproduced without permission subs. by J.L. Wright In to 1931".

One more example of Jones' haziness: In 1948 he claimed (or did he?) that it was he who introduced hollow-casting in the U.S. with the statement "The title MOULDED MINIATURES represents the new firm as successor to an older organization which was the originator of the hollow-cast method in the United States".

Jones' end was a sad one. According to Michael Hitrovo, "the crowning misfortune came when his children (he had two) were grown and his wife left him, suing for divorce. All Ed's property, including the molds, were listed and "sealed off." With the molds inactive, Ed was paralyzed. He could not produce and he had no income. Emotional and mental illness overtook him, and he did not long survive this final failure. Thus ended the first real attempt to make American figures, comparable to, and competitive with, W. Britain's soldiers."

From his own account, Jones seems to have been in his twenties when he saw "America". Thus he must have been relatively young when he died in October, 1960.

Jones had this circa 1931 diorama of his 3" Metal-Art toy soldiers photographed, presumably for promotional reasons. Also present are what seems to be a Marx tank and Britains tree.

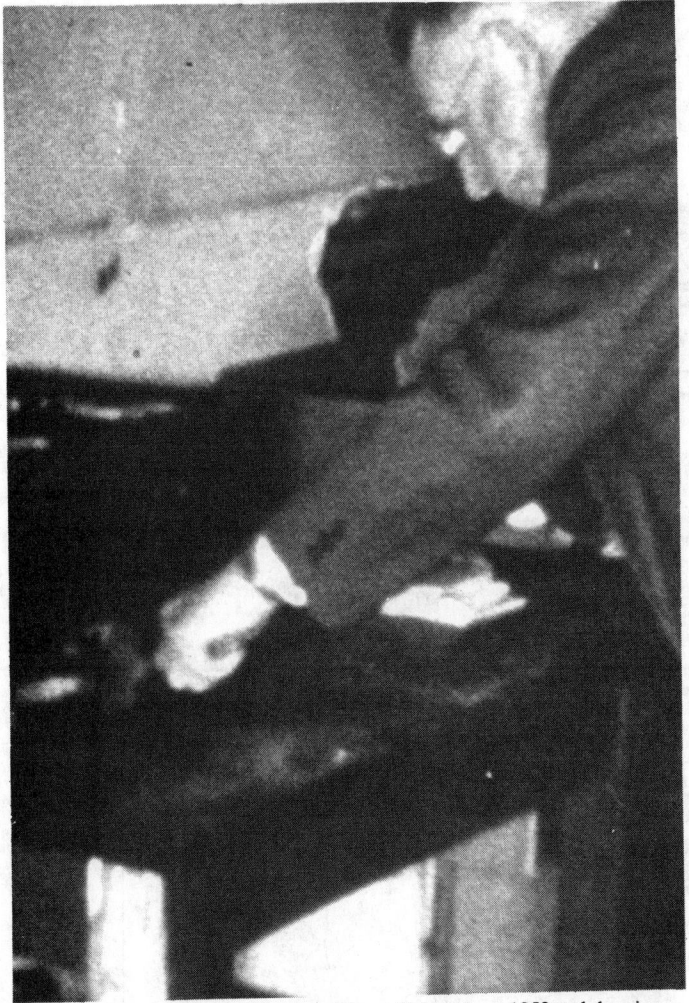

The only known photo of J. Edward Jones. Taken about 1952 and showing Jones casting with one of his molds (and in a suit!).
Courtesy Gus Hansen and *Old Toy Soldier*

Jones' Metal Arts 3" Soldiers, 1929-31

	G	VG	M
(MA1) Father Time with large wings	No Price Found		
(MA2) British Battalion Co. Marine	30.00	45.00	60.00
(MA3) British Dragoon with movable arm, 1775, mounted	62.00	93.00	125.00
(MA4) British Light Infantryman	20.00	30.00	40.00
(MA5) American Backwoodsman	No Price Found		
(MA6) Hessian Grenadier of 1777 Charging	62.00	93.00	125.00
(MA7) British Infantry Drummer	No Price Found		
(MA8) British Grenadier	75.00	112.50	150.00
(MA9) American Marine of 1812	62.00	93.00	125.00
(MA10) French Foreign Legion private of 1870, standing on guard	75.00	112.00	150.00
(MA11) French Foreign Legion, standing firing, with neckcloth (if it existed, same as MA14 with different paint)	No Price Found		
(MA12) Highlander Private Charging	75.00	112.00	150.00
(MA13) Highlander Piper Walking	No Price Found		
(MA14) British 1857 Marine	No Price Found		
(MA15) Cowboy Mounted on Standing Horse 1870	No Price Found		
(MA16) Indian lying on galloping horse with rifle aimed	No Price Found		
(MA17) Cowboy of 1870	6.00	9.00	12.00
(MA18) German Officer of 1915, binoculars	112.00	168.00	225.00
(MA19) German Infantryman of 1915, standing, firing	100.00	150.00	200.00

MA2
Courtesy Don Pielin - *Old Toy Soldier*

MA4
Courtesy Don Pielin - *Old Toy Soldier*

MA5

MA6
Courtesy Don Pielin - *Old Toy Soldier*

MA7

	G	VG	M
(MA20) American Cavalryman of 1918, mounted on standing horse, movable arm	No Price Found		

A box for Jones' 3" high Metal-Art figures. This was shown in a 1930
catalog.
Courtesy Gus Hansen

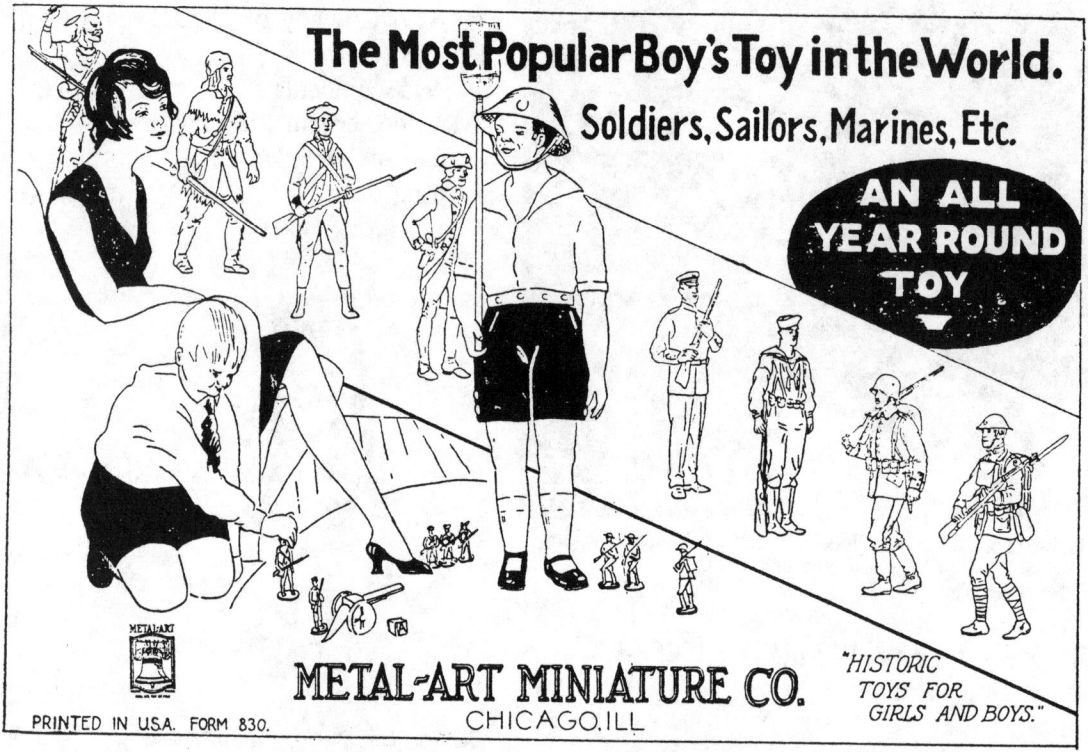

A Jones Metal-Art boxtop, circa 1931. It was made of heavy cardboard.
Courtesy Gus Hansen

JOMA8

MA9

MA10

MA12

MA13

MA14

Courtesy Don Pielin - *Old Toy Soldier*

Courtesy Don Pielin - *Old Toy Soldier*

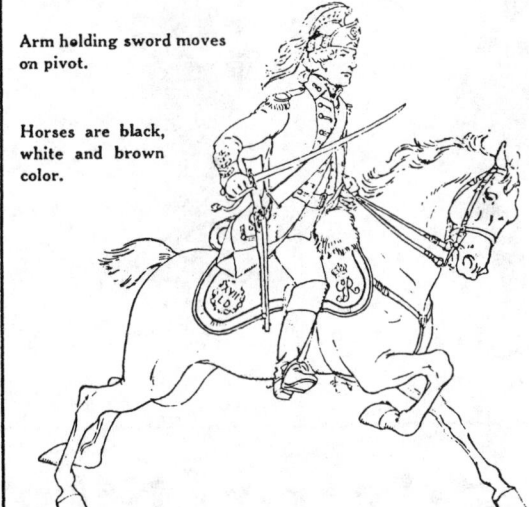

Mounted Cavalry Now Available!

(The 17th Light Dragoons)

Arm holding sword moves on pivot.

Horses are black, white and brown color.

Altho our full line of products will not be ready until August, we have another number ready for distribution. This is a companion piece to the red-coated British marines, advertised in February "Toys and Novelties." A 25c seller. Sample sent on request.

Watch for Later Announcements!

Many more numbers soon will be available. Put up in sets and in bulk.

Three Sizes—Being Prepared
Heights:
2 inch—3 inch—6 inch

Metal-Art Miniature Company
"Historic Toys for Girls and Boys"
9200 Cottage Grove Avenue, Chicago, Ill.

MA3
March, 1929 Jones ad in *Toys & Novelties*

MA17
Courtesy Don Pielin - *Old Toy Soldier*

German Infantry of 1915

Altho our full line of products will not be ready until August, here is another number that is a good seller.

Solid Castings

—

Natural Color

—

Retailed by single piece

Also in $1.00 Sets

Territory open to agents and jobbers in some sections of U. S.

METAL-ART MINIATURE CO.
"Historic Toys for Girls and Boys"
9200 Cottage Grove Ave.   CHICAGO

MA19
May, 1929 Jones ad in *Toys and Novelties*

MA19
Courtesy Gus Hansen and
Old Toy Soldier

MA18
(Ornament atop helmet missing)
Courtesy Don Patman and *Old Toy Soldier* newsletter

MA21
Courtesy Don Pielin - *Old Toy Soldier*

MA22
Drawing by the author from a murky circa 1931 photo. The biggest difference between this and Jones' J13 is the gas mask bag on the officer's chest. One MA22 is known to exist. Courtesy Gus Hansen

MA23
Drawing by the author
from two very murky
1931-era photos. The
uniform detailing is a guess.
Courtesy Gus Hansen

MA26
Courtesy Don Pielin- *Old Toy Soldier*

MA27
Courtesy Don Pielin - *Old Toy Soldier*

MA28
Courtesy Don Pielin - *Old Toy Soldier*

	G	VG	M
(MA21) American Engineer Bomber of 1918 (throwing grenade)	40.00	60.00	80.00
(MA22) American Infantry Major of 1918, standing in overcoat, holding pistol and pointing, resembles J13, but is not the same	No Price Found		
(MA23) American Infantry of 1918 in overcoat, at attention	No Price Found		
(MA24) Seaman 1918	No Price Found		
(MA25) Boy Scout	No Price Found		
(MA26) Boy Scout in Shorts	No Price Found		
(MA27) Boy Scoutmaster standing	125.00	188.00	250.00
(MA28) American 1929 Marine	12.00	18.00	25.00
(MA29) Midshipman of 1932	No Price Found		
(MA30) West Point Cadet of 1929	No Price Found		
(MA31) German Infantry of 1918 marching with movable arm	No Price Found		
(MA32) Indian Creeping . . .	No Price Found		
(MA33) American Marine of 1776 standing	No Price Found		
(MA34) British Artillery Gunner of 1776	No Price Found		
(MA35) British Light Co. Marines	No Price Found		
(MA 36) British 52nd Foot Light Infantry Captain, 1775, with sword, paint variation of MA41	No Price Found		
(MA37) Artillery Ensign Standing	No Price Found		

An April, 1929 *Toys and Novelties* ad. MA28.

(MA38) Indian running with rifle	No Price Found
(MA39) Indian with Tomahawk	No Price Found
(MA40) British Marine, 1775	No Price Found
(MA41) American Marine Captain of 1810	No Price Found
(MA42) American Infantry of 1920 with Flag	No Price Found
(MA43) American Infantry of 1920 with fixed bayonet marching	No Price Found

171

MA31
Courtesy Don Pielin -
Old Toy Soldier

MA38
Courtesy Charlie Breslow

MA39
Courtesy Don Pielin - *Old Toy Soldier*

MA40

MA41
Courtesy Don Pielin -
Old Toy Soldier

MA42
The original flag measured
2¾" x 2¹⁄₁₆"
Photo by Ed Poole

MA43
Rifle barrel and bayonet restored,
may not be accurate.
Photo by Ed Poole

Metal-Art soldiers in sizes of 6", 3", 2" and approximately 1¼". Courtesy
Don Pielin - *Old Toy Soldier*

Jones' Metal-Art 2" Soldiers, 1929-31

(M2-1) Mounted Cowboy, firing rifle	No Price Found
(M2-2) Foot Cowboy, firing pistol	No Price Found
(M2-3) Mounted Indian, firing arrow	No Price Found
(M2-4) Indian Walking with Rifle	No Price Found
(M2-5) Indian kneeling firing rifle	No Price Found
(M2-6) U.S. Officer, mounted	No Price Found
(M2-7) U.S. Soldier, marching	No Price Found
(M2-8) U.S. Soldier advancing in crouch with rifle . .	No Price Found
(M2-9) U.S. Soldier, prone machine gunner	No Price Found
(M2-10) Highlander, mounted	No Price Found

February, 1929 *Toys and Novelties* ad

HIBBARD, SPENCER, BARTLETT & CO.

MINIATURE METAL FIGURES

Two Inch Small Size Figures.   Each Set Packed in a Cardboard Box.

No. C131G—American Cowboys,
per dozen sets.............................$12.00

No. C132G—Indians...........per dozen sets $12.00

No. C148G—Hessian Soldiers..per dozen sets $12.00

o. C143G—Jockeys...........per dozen sets $12.00

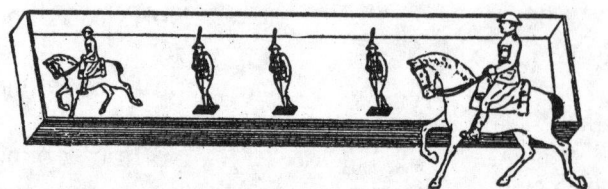

No. C163G—Cavalry and Infantry,
per dozen sets.............................$6.00

No. C189G—Combination Cowboys and Indians,
per dozen sets.............................$24.00

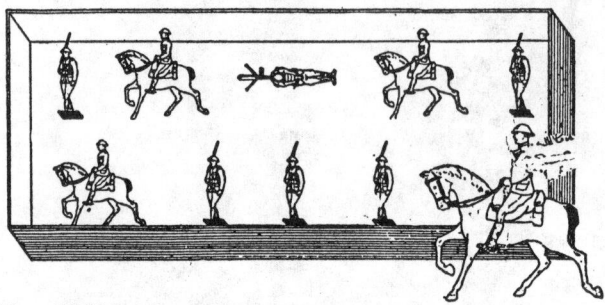

No. C133G—American Soldiers,
per dozen sets.............................$12.00

No. C139G—Farm Series.......per dozen sets $12

No. C162G—Cowboys...........per dozen sets $6.00

No. C159G—Indians.............per dozen sets $6.00

The hand-written date on this catalog is "Aug. 31st, 1931". With the possible exception of the Hessian Soldiers, these are the Metal-Art two-inch size. The cowboys, Indians, and farm sets also appear in a November, 1932 Butler Bros. catalog. Presumably they were sold through Jones' just-formed Miniature Products Co. Courtesy Gus Hansen

JONES

	G	VG	M
(M2-11) Highlander, marching with rifle		No Price Found	
(M2-12) U.S. Sailor? at attention (photo unclear)		No Price Found	
(M2-13) U.S. Ensign? at attention (photo unclear)		No Price Found	
(M2-14) U.S. Continental? marching with rifle (photo unclear)		No Price Found	
(M2-15) American Farmer of 1931		No Price Found	
(M2-16) American Farm Woman of 1931		No Price Found	

(There are at least two other 2" types, but the photo on which this list is partially based is too unclear to make them out)

Jones' 3¼" Soldiers, circa 1938-41 (virtually all also come in gray, as "Enemy". For those, add 30% in value). Some are copies of soldiers by Barclay, Manoil, etc. Jones' soldiers tend to have heavier eyes and eyebrows (dot and line), and the always-flat under bases often have one or two choked pourholes.

	G	VG	M
(J1) German, kneeling with rifle	102.00	153.00	205.00
(J1a) Same as above, short rifle	110.00	165.00	220.00
(J2) German, charging with rifle	95.00	143.00	190.00
(J3) German, prone machine-gunner	70.00	105.00	140.00
(J4) Observer with binoculars and rifle.................	37.00	53.00	75.00
(J5) Wire-cutter, prone	225.00	330.00	450.00
(J6) Soldier with rifle, gassed or shot in neck..........	175.00	263.00	350.00
(J7) Stretcher-bearer.......	50.00	75.00	100.00
(J8) Kneeling with AA Gun.	40.00	60.00	80.00
(J9) Charging, port arms ...	125.00	188.00	250.00
(J10) Firing machine gun on stump	40.00	60.00	80.00
(J10a) Same as above, No. 1 on pocket	100.00	150.00	200.00
(J11) Grenade thrower, no weapons	55.00	83.00	110.00
(J12) Seated with rifle	38.00	53.00	76.00
(J13) Officer in greatcoat, pointing, holding pistol ..	110.00	165.00	220.00
(J14) Prone with rifle, trunk upraised	75.00	113.00	150.00

	G	VG	M
(J15) Prone, firing double-barreled machine gun ...	50.00	75.00	100.00
(J16) Kneeling, firing anti-tank gun, 3 variations known	40.00	60.00	80.00
(J16a) Same as above with barrel brace, "23" on wheel	50.00	75.00	100.00
(J17) Cook with chef's hat, frying pan	30.00	45.00	60.00
(J18) Ammunition Carrier ..	200.00	300.00	400.00
(J19) Motorcyclist with machine gun mounted on motorcycle	70.00	105.00	140.00
(J20) Flagbearer (similar to Barclay B7)	90.00	135.00	180.00
(J21) Kneeling with search-light	37.00	53.00	75.00
(J21a) Kneeling with search-light, "27" "Made in USA" on sides of stanchion..............	50.00	75.00	100.00
(J22) Seated with phone ...	45.00	68.00	90.00
(J23) Kneeling, firing rifle, no stand	62.00	93.00	125.00
J23a Same as above, shorter rifle	70.00	105.00	140.00
(J24) Prone, body arched, firing machine gun	60.00	90.00	120.00
(J25) Bugler	82.00	123.00	165.00
(J26) Soldier with gas mask, plunging rifle down, slightly smaller in size ...	112.00	169.00	225.00
(J27) Nurse with bag, like Barclay B82	40.00	60.00	80.00
(J28) Doctor with bag, like Barclay B81	40.00	60.00	80.00
(J28a) Doctor in khaki	62.00	93.00	125.00
(J29) Standing, firing rifle ..	45.00	68.00	90.00
(J30) Wounded supine, like Manoil M53	45.00	68.00	90.00
(J31) Cowboy on rearing horse, firing backward ...	130.00	195.00	260.00
(J32) Marching with rifle ..	57.00	85.00	115.00
(J33) Cowboy Kneeling	30.00	45.00	60.00
(J33a) Like above, has base, is painted brown		No Price Found	
(J34) Indian on Rearing Horse	50.00	75.00	100.00
(J35) Indian with Bow (may resemble Beton's)		No Price Found	
(J35a) Indian kneeling, shooting		No Price Found	
(J36) Tramp	7.00	11.00	15.00
(J37) Farmer	6.00	9.00	13.00

JONES

	G	VG	M
(J38) Farmer's Wife	6.00	9.00	13.00
(J39) Cowboy on Prancing Horse, similar to Barclay B2		No Price Found	

(J40) Knight with shield, flat underbase .... No Price Found

(J41) Knight with pennant, flat underbase .... No Price Found

J1 J2 J3 J4

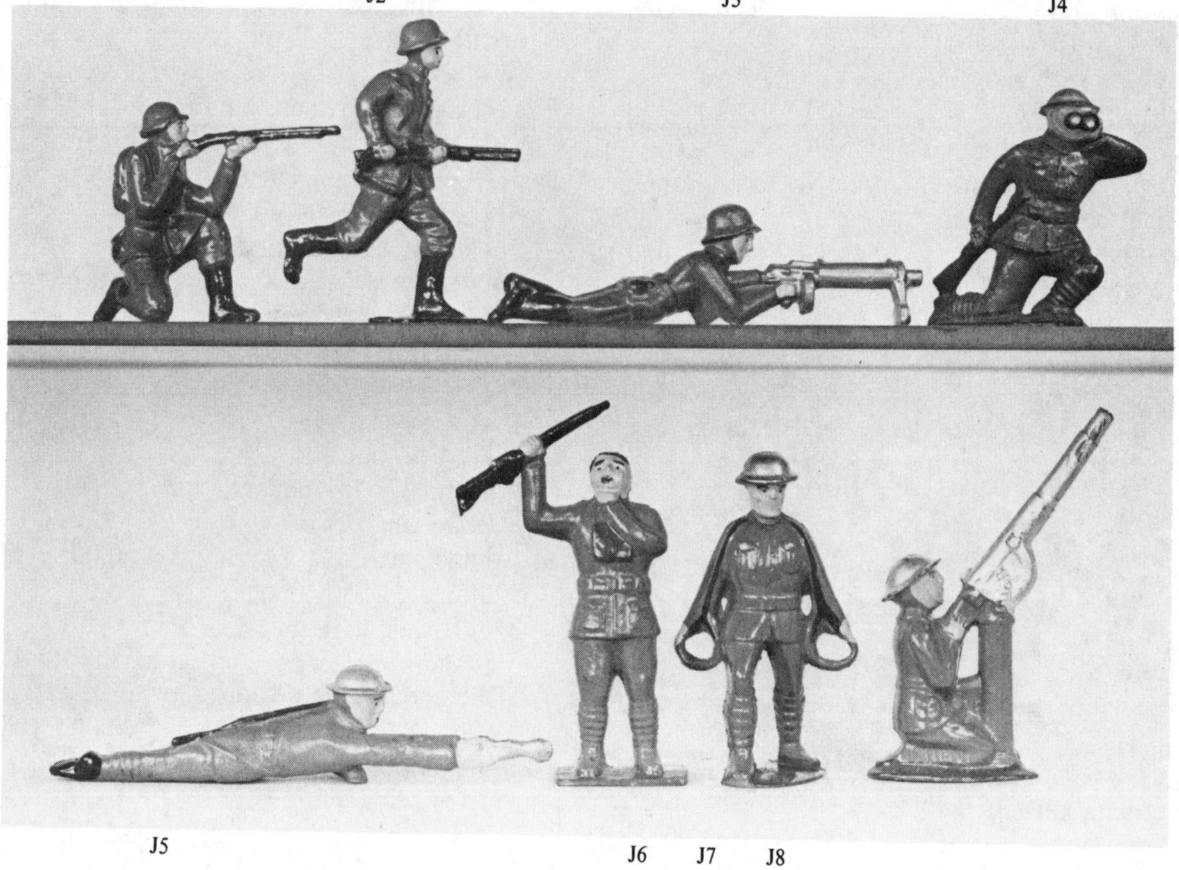

J9 J10 J11

J5 J6 J7 J8

J10a courtesy Gordon Gee

J12 J13 J14 J15

J16   J17   J18   J19

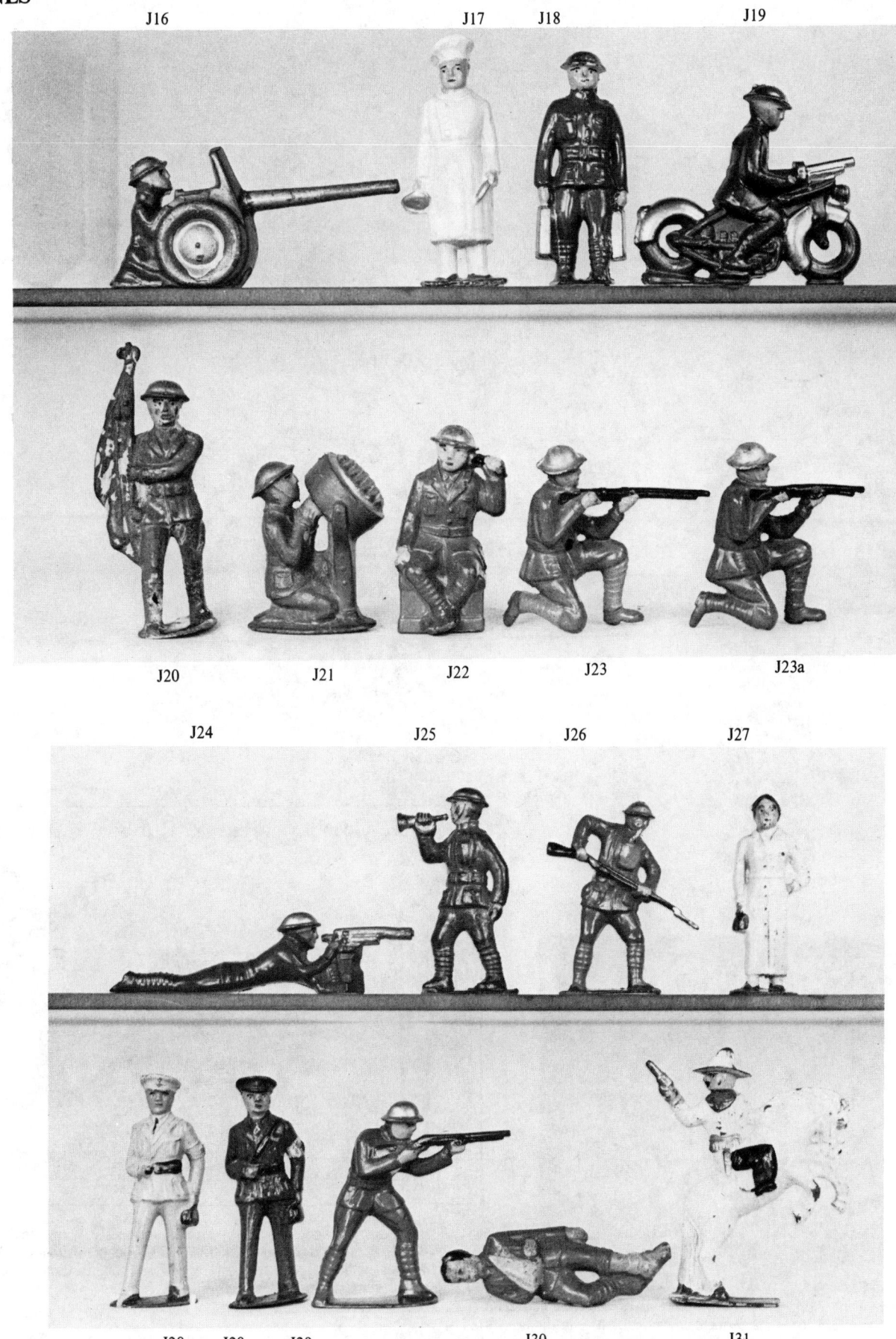

J20   J21   J22   J23   J23a

J24   J25   J26   J27

J28   J28a   J29   J30   J31

J32   J33   J34

J36   J37   J38

J35a
Collectors tend to agree this is the piece listed in two 1938 catalogs of soldiers presumably made by Jones.

J39
Courtesy Don Pielin

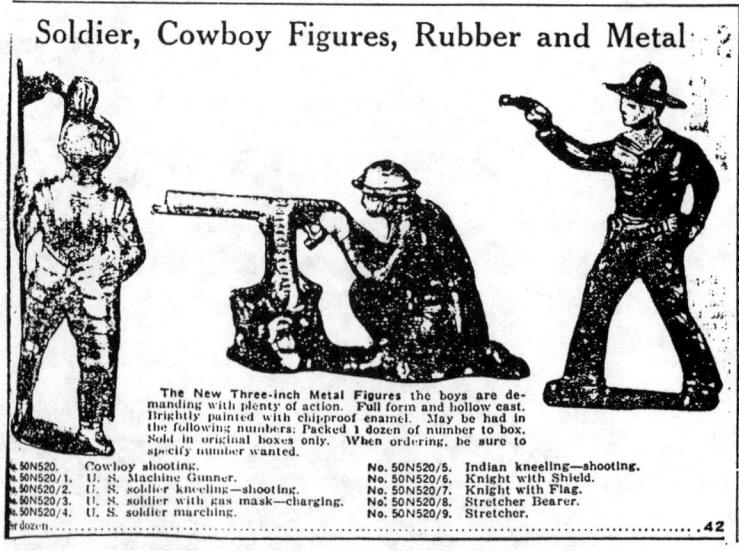

J40   J41
Courtesy Don Pielin

Two different collectors have suspected these pieces, which seem to share the same horse, are Jones. The roughly rectangular hole in the horse's stomach is the reason. Riders are separately cast, but in at least the Indian's case, soldered to the horse.
Photos by K. Warren Mitchell, Ron Steiner

Soldier, Cowboy Figures, Rubber and Metal

The New Three-inch Metal Figures the boys are demanding with plenty of action. Full form and hollow cast. Brightly painted with chipproof enamel. May be had in the following numbers. Packed 1 dozen of number to box. Sold in original boxes only. When ordering, be sure to specify number wanted.

50N520.	Cowboy shooting.	No. 50N520/5.	Indian kneeling—shooting.
50N520/1.	U. S. Machine Gunner.	No. 50N520/6.	Knight with Shield.
50N520/2.	U. S. soldier kneeling—shooting.	No. 50N520/7.	Knight with Flag.
50N520/3.	U. S. soldier with gas mask—charging.	No. 50N520/8.	Stretcher Bearer.
50N520/4.	U. S. soldier marching.	No. 50N520/9.	Stretcher.

r dozen .... .42

This is the earliest known catalog appearance of Jones' 3¼" high soldiers. N. Shure, Spring and Summer, 1938. A 1939-40 jobber's catalog added many soldiers but dropped the cowboy and two knights, though the illustration remained the same.

Metal and Rubber Soldier Sets, Children's Play Sets

U. S. Army Medical Unit. All 3-inch figures. Consists of two wounded soldiers, two stretcher bearers, stretcher, nurse and doctor. Packed in display box.

No. 50N525.   Per Set $0.70

3-inch Metal Soldier Set. An assortment of U. S. Soldiers in action. Machine gunner, officer, flag bearer. etc. Set of 7 packed in display box.

No. 50N523.   Per Set $0.70

Marching Soldier Set. All 3-inch figures. Cast metal. Consists of six U. S. Soldiers marching and one flag bearer. Packed in display box.

No. 50N524.   Per Set $0.70

U. S. Army Medical Unit with Red Cross nurse, doctor, stretcher, stretcher bearers, wounded soldiers and an assortment of U. S. Soldiers in action. Packed in display box.

No. 50N526.   Per Set $1.50

U. S. Soldiers and Opposition Soldiers. Opposition soldiers have olive green uniforms. An appealing set from a play value standpoint. Set of 14 pieces packed in display box.

No. 50N527.   Per Set $1.50

Boxed sets of Jones soldiers, as shown in Johnson Smith Catalog No. 152, apparently published in the fall of 1938. None has been found. They would be worth approximately the individual prices of the soldiers, plus 20 or 30%, depending on graphics and other information found on the box itself. The bayoneting soldier in gas mask is a link between these soldiers and Jones' 1929-31 Metal-Art figures.
Courtesy Don Pielin

Jones' Dimestore Vehicles and Accessories

	G	VG	M
(JV1) Tank, throwing flame, flame touching hull	40.00	60.00	80.00
(JV2) Tank, throwing flame, flame not touching hull . .	45.00	67.00	90.00
(JV3) Tank, throwing flame, "No. 25" (not shown) . . .	60.00	90.00	120.00
(JV4) Tank, "22" on side . .	50.00	75.00	100.00
JVA 5 Pillbox	60.00	90.00	120.00
(J42) "211" Lying Cow, "Made in USA".	4.00	6.00	9.00
(J43) "228" Small Horse, "Made in USA"	5.00	8.00	10.00
(J44) "270" Goat, "Made in USA"	4.00	6.00	9.00
(J45) "280" Fence, "Made in USA"	3.00	5.00	7.00
(J46) "300" Camel, "Made in USA"	5.00	8.00	10.00
	G	**VG**	**M**
(J47) Lying Sheep	5.00	8.00	10.00
(J48) Grazing Sheep	4.00	6.00	8.00
(J49) Pig	4.00	6.00	9.00
(J50) Horse	6.00	9.00	12.00
(J51) Work Horse	9.00	13.00	18.00
(J52) Mule	5.00	8.00	10.00
(J53) Duck	4.00	6.00	9.00
(J54) Rooster	No Price Found		
(J55) Chicken	4.00	6.00	9.00
(J56) Fox	10.00	15.00	20.00
(J57) Reindeer, (not shown)	No Price Found		
(J58) Bull (not shown)	No Price Found		
(J59) Standing Cow (not shown)	4.00	6.00	8.00
(J60) Calf (not shown) "236"	5.00	8.00	11.00
(J61) Donkey (not shown) . .	5.00	8.00	10.00
(J62) Walking Sheep "235" (not shown)	5.00	8.00	11.00
(J63) Dog (Fox?) Not shown	10.00	15.00	20.00

JV2   JV1
Photo by Don Pielin

JV4
Courtesy Gene Parker

JVA5   Jones Pillbox.

J42   J43   J44   J45

J46   J47   J48   J49

J50   J51   J52

J53   J54   J55   J56

MINIATURE TOY COMPANY — MOULDED MINIATURES METAL-ART · METAL MINIATURES

Both before and after World War II, at least into the 1950s, J. Edward Jones also made hollowcast 54mm figures. The following is a list of figures numbered to match the photos shown. Descriptions are provided where possible, with those in bold lettering Jones' own description. Since these photos have been matched against faint Xeroxes of Jones' sale lists, some may be identified incorrectly. Jones' numbers on its soldiers didn't remain constant. The 542 West Pointers, for instance, were sold as 2907 and 2908. The years given also could vary from catalog to catalog. Price is per figure, where found.

	G	VG	M
541 - Sailor, shoulder arms			
542 - **West Pointer** parade rest No. 2907	7.00	11.00	15.00
543 - Annapolis Cadet with Guidon			
544 - Annapolis Cadet at Port Arms			
545 - **U.S. Marine,** Shoulder Arms			
546 - Crawling with Rifle, in Snow Camouflage			
547 - German on Guard	8.00	12.00	16.00
548 - German Charging	9.00	13.00	18.00
549 - Charging in Pith Helmet, British			
5410 - Parade Rest with Fixed Bayonet, Chinese Nationalist No. 2901	7.00	11.00	15.00
5411 - **1942 U.S. Infantry**			
5412 - Highlander, WW I helmet, Shoulder Arms			
5413 - U.S. Infantry (?)			
5414 - **1948 U.S. Marine,** marching at shoulder arms			
5415 - **King's Royal Rifle Corps · Uni. King 1941 (BA0012)**	6.00	9.00	13.00
5416 - **1944 U.S. Cavalry**			
5417 - **1190 Herald**			
5418 - **1193 English Bowman**			
5419 - Robinson Crusoe (prototype, probably never produced)			
5420 - **1871 Cowboy**			
5421 - Indian Chief, running with rifle			
5422 - Indian Standing, Firing			
5423 - Right Carry Arms · Italian, WW II, running at trail			
5424 - WW I Infantryman, Marching Shoulder Arms			
5425 - **Pilot of the 17th Pursuit Squadron, 1937**	12.00	18.00	25.00
5426 - Officer with binoculars	9.00	13.00	18.00
5427 - Marching Highlander			
5428 - **1944 U.S. Aimer**			
5429 - Sailor Marching with Drum, British "Blue Jacket"			
5430 - **1921 British Guardsman,** shoulder arms	7.00	11.00	15.00

JONES	G	VG	M
5431 - Greek Evzone	6.00	9.00	12.00
5432 - Civil War (?) at attention	10.00	15.00	20.00

5433 - **1864 Militiaman**

5434 - **1861 Zouave of La.**   10.00   15.00   20.00

5435 - On Guard, circa 18th Century

5436 - U.S. Marine of early 19th century, no pigtail

         8.00   12.00   16.00

5437 - U.S. Marine of early 19th century, has pigtail

         25.00   38.00   50.00

5438 - 1775 Soldier, modified port arms

5439 **The Royal Highland Emigrants 1781:**
    American Loyalist Unit, Later British
    84th foot (DA0042)

5440 - Charging Highlander Officer, circa 1775

5441 - Officer circa 1775

5442 - Naval (?) Officer, circa 1775

5443 - Sailor circa 1775

5444 - French (?) soldier, circa 1775, modified port arms

5445 - Hessian (?) officer, marching

5446 - Hessian (?) soldier, on guard

         8.00   12.00   16.00

5447 - Highlander, at ready, 1757 Scotsman, No. 270118

5448 - French (?) soldier circa 1775 at attention

5449 - American Marine, circa 1775-1797

         15.00   22.00   30.00

5450 - **Highlander** of 1814, No. 1809GB

         7.00   11.00   15.00

5451 - **Scotchman,** at ready

5452 - Piper

5453 - Soldier, Wayne's Legion, 1802, on guard

         15.00   22.00   30.00

5454 - 1775 Officer, sword at side   8.00   12.00   16.00

5455 - 1776 **American Marine**

5456 - 1775 Officer, sword extended

5457 - 1775 Soldier, Rammer Drawn, British

         8.00   13.00   17.00

5458 - **1775 British Ranger,** shoulder arms, 2701LB

5459 - **1775 British Marine,** firing at upward angle, 2705MB

5460 - **1775 Colonial Woman,** deluxe finish is PL 1383 **Belle of Baltimore,** ordinary finish is PT2389 **1776 Belle of New York**

5461 - **1775 Colonial Man,** deluxe finish is PL1390 **Dandy of Charleston,** ordinary finish is PX2390 **Dandy of Philadelphia.**

5462 Tommy Gunner, 1944

5463 U.S. Marching with Pack, 1944

5464 U.S. Sailor 1919

5465 Irish Machine Gunner, 1918

5466 American Machine Gunner, 1918

5467 Marching in Flat Cap, marked "MADE IN CHICAGO"

5468 Kneeling machine gunner, marked "MADE IN CHICAGO"

5469 Sailor Firing (Jones?)

5470 Marine with Binoculars

541   542   543   544   545

Courtesy K. Warren Mitchell

546   547   548   549   5410

Courtesy K. Warren Mitchell

5411   5412   5413   5414   5415   5416

Courtesy K. Warren Mitchell

5417   5418   5419   5420   5421   5422

Courtesy K. Warren Mitchell

5423   5424   5425   5426   5427   5428

Courtesy K. Warren Mitchell

5429   5430   5431   5432   5433   5434
Courtesy K. Warren Mitchell

5435   5436   5437   5438   5439   5440
Courtesy K. Warren Mitchell

5450   5451   5452
Courtesy K. Warren Mitchell

5441   5442   5443
Photo courtesy K. Warren Mitchell

5453   5454   5455
Courtesy K. Warren Mitchell

5444   5445   5446   5447   5448   5449
Courtesy K. Warren Mitchell

5456   5457   5458   5459   5460   5461
Courtesy K. Warren Mitchell

5462   5463
Courtesy Don Pielin

181

5464
Courtesy Don Pielin
5465
5466

5470
Courtesy
K. Warren Mitchell

5467
5468
5469 (Jones?)

ALL-NU

When I was a child, the All-Nu figures I saw annoyed me. To my eye, they were out-and-out copies of Barclays and that made them contemptible. Today the only reason All-Nus annoy me is because they're so hard to find. It's perfectly natural that they look like Barclays; they came from the same hand.

Frank Krupp (1/24/98-8/30/65) was the man who originated and sculpted all of Barclay's tin helmet soldiers and related figures, and beginning in 1938 he performed the same work for his own company, All-Nu Products Inc.

Claude Frank Krupp (he never used the Claude) was born in New York City and moved when quite small to Eldred, New York. Creativity seems to have run in his family. His father, who'd been born in Essen, Germany, was a goldsmith. Krupp himself, like so many of the dimestore designers, was a trained artist. He studied modeling and design at New York's Beaux Arts for three years, and architectural drafting at Cooper Union in Manhattan for four years. Around 1916 he worked for New York's Museum of Natural History, constructing toy soldier-like dioramas, some of which may still be on display.

Krupp joined Barclay around 1930 or 1931, left in late 1937 or early 1938, and on February 16, 1938, incorporated All-Nu Products at 55-58 Main Street, Yonkers, New York. According to Louis Picco, who left Barclay at the same time to work with Krupp, All-Nu's first product was a souvenir horse, whose two halves were soldered together. Picco further states that when he left the company six months later, All-Nu had yet to produce any of its soldiers, cowboys or "Marching Majorettes". Another item Picco remembers Krupp working on was "a sailing ship", presumably the No. 600 Schooner, as it was described in a post-WWII catalog. Evelyn Besser, Krupp's daughter, also remembers Krupp being bitter about this time because he found Barclay was producing new soldiers he'd created while he was there. Mrs. Krupp was also unhappy; she didn't want him to leave Barclay, with its steady paycheck.

The majorettes seem to have come first, as I own a boxed set that has the Yonkers address. By the summer or fall of 1941 All-Nu had moved to a second-floor loft at 67 Irving Place in Manhattan. The first recorded sign of its soldiers appears in the April 1941 Toys and Novelties magazine.

Perhaps because he had no one to oversee him, and perhaps as owner, felt more pressed to turn out a product, Krupp's figures at All-Nu are considerably more variable in design quality than they were at Barclay. The majorettes were all well-made, but some of the soldiers and the souvenir cowboy and cowgirl appear to have been done hastily, with scant detail and some lack of symmetry. On the other hand, several, such as the grenadier, are outstandingly well done, and quite possibly the most coveted of all dimestore soldiers is the unique All-Nu newsreel cameraman.

For a short time David Reader, apparently the brother of Barclay salesman Irving Reader, was a partner in All-Nu, but basically the company was Krupp's. Well-liked by virtually all who knew him, Krupp was tall (5'11"), slender, his hair snow-white by the age of 30, and in his younger years said to have resembled actor Joseph Cotten. He was apparently able to fix anything, and although his first love was his creative work, he was known for his ability to improvise highly effective solutions to mechanical problems, at Barclay as well as at All-Nu.

All-Nu's figures were sold both singly and boxed. In the case of the majorettes, the box was an unmarked red one, with the numbers of the figures (and the name and address of the company) stamped onto the card that held them. The masked mounted cowboy firing straight up has turned up boxed several times, each time as a single figure in a small, totally unmarked box. Although All-Nu advertised "Action Soldier Sets", none has yet emerged.

All-Nu was never a large company. Six or seven women did the painting, five or six men the casting, and a few others were assigned to the remaining necessary jobs. When he sculpted, Krupp used red wax at Barclay, but plasticene clay, the kind found in the toy section of 5&10s, at All-Nu. Frank Cota, who was Krupp's assistant at Barclay, remembers it would take him a day and a half to sculpt a figure. According to both Cota and Evelyn Besser, Krupp's daughter, he never worked from sketches, but would simply set up an armature of wire and work from that, occasionally referring to anatomy books.

Frank Krupp, circa 1955

Krupp's family believes it was the Second World War that prevented All-Nu from becoming a success, and all evidence points to this being true. I remember the marching majorettes being on sale at Woolworth's in 1941, and of course an outlet like that was an enormous breakthrough for a small company. Unfortunately, shortly after December 7, 1941, the government impounded all shipments of lead. Krupp tried to surmount this by designing paper toys; drawing, painting and then producing 5" soldiers on heavy stock cardboard with an effective locking device to make them stand upright. He also manufactured one or more large cardboard weapons, but neither these nor the soldiers sold to any significant extent. All-Nu wasn't dissolved as a corporation until December 15, 1950, but in effect it was out of business a year or two after the War began, with Krupp going into bankruptcy around 1944 or 1945.

After the war, about 1946, Krupp resumed business as Faben Products Inc. at 47 Walker Street in Manhattan. However, of his prewar figures, only the horses, mounted hunters, jockeys and cowboy and cowgirl on bucking bronchos seem to have continued. All-Nu had advertised "we can also make toys to special designs . . . souvenirs, knick-knacks, premiums and advertising novelties. . . .", and it seems at Faben it was the knick-knacks and souvenirs that survived. Faben derived its name from two of the letters of Krupp's first name and the nickname of his partner (last name unknown).

After Krupp's work with Faben he seems to have given up any toy soldier-like activities. According to a resume he compiled, he worked from 1945-53 for Lee Mfg. Co. Inc. of River Edge, New Jersey, where as foreman he did original designs, modeling, plaster molds, plastic models, prototypes and plastic molds for clock cases, lamp bases and coin-operated rides. From 1953-56 he did similar work for U.S. Fiber Glass of Norwood, New Jersey, for auto bodies, play pools, planter boxes and baby carriages. Like most resumes, however, Krupp's was written for a purpose, and is not wholly accurate. Barclay and All-Nu, for instance, are not mentioned. Perhaps Krupp preferred to forget.

(Because All-Nu's military figures are so rare, I've indicated how many are known to me; of all the important American dimestore soldiers, All-Nu's are by far the rarest. All-Nu's soldiers, majorettes and mounted cowboy are marked "All-Nu Products Made in U.S.A." or "ANP".)

	G	VG	M
(AN1) "Newsreel" Cameraman in helmet, eleven known	875.00	1310.00	1750.00
(AN1b) like above, but helmet adapted to look like WWII, only one known	1000.00	1500.00	2000.00
(AN 2) Seated machine-gunner two, known	500.00	750.00	1000.00
(AN 3) Advancing with Tommy Gun, one known	No Price Found		
(AN 4) Grenadier, three known.	1000.00	1500.00	2000.00
(AN 5) Bugler three known.	300.00	450.00	600.00
(AN 6) Signalman, two known.	No Price Found		
(AN 7) Standing, firing rifle, seven known	40.00	60.00	80.00
(AN 8) Marching, slope arms, seven known	60.00	90.00	120.00
(AN 9) Advancing, fixed bayonet, three known . .	500.00	750.00	1000.00
(AN 10) Officer kneeling with binoculars, drawing pistol, only one known . .	No Price Found		
(AN 11) AA Gunner in campaign cap, only four known	250.00	375.00	500.00

AN 1   AN2   AN3   AN 4

AN5   AN6   AN7   AN8   AN9

The machine gun barrel on AN3 and the top flag on AN6 are replacements, and may not be correct. The gun stock on AN9 is a replacement and isn't correct.

AN10   AN11   AN13   AN14   AN15   AN16

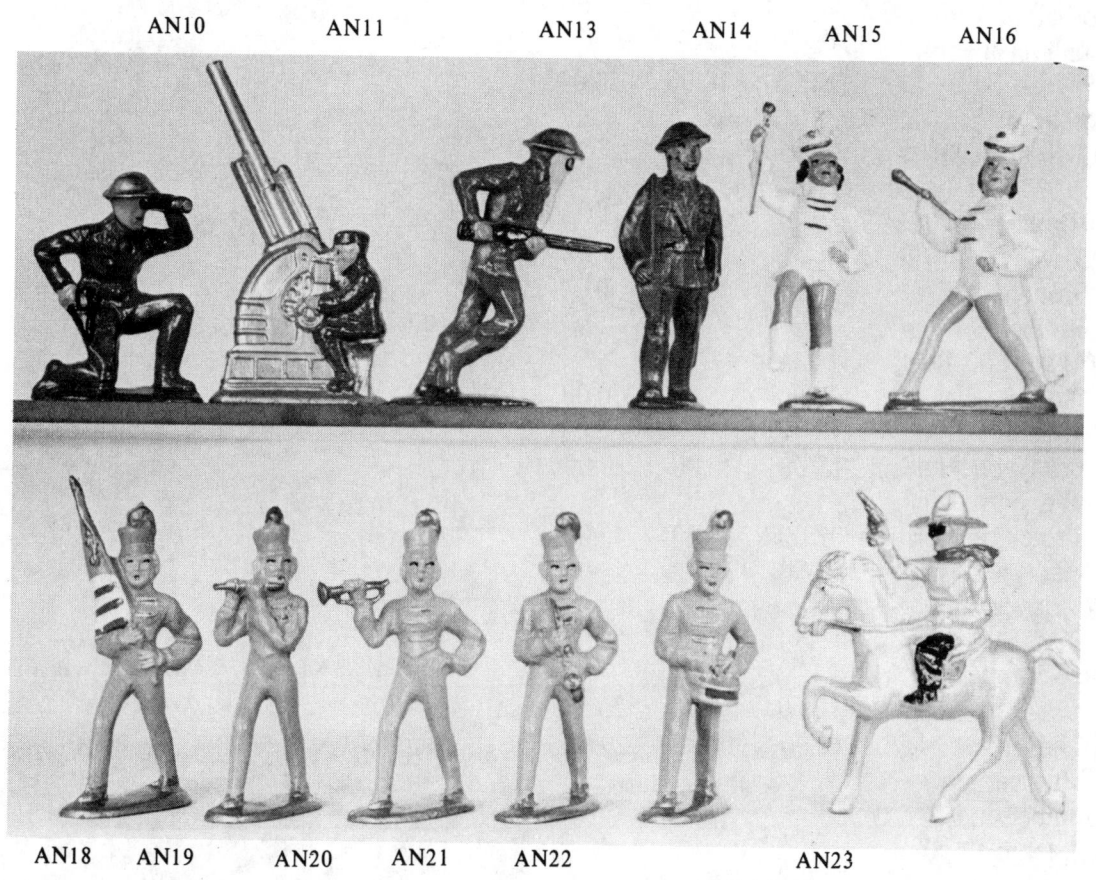

AN18   AN19   AN20   AN21   AN22   AN23

JONES

	G	VG	M
(AN 12) Prone, firing rifle, none known	No Price Found		
(AN 13) Running in Gas Mask, with Rifle, only one known	No Price Found		
(AN 14) Officer with sword, four known	50.00	75.00	100.00
(AN 15) 150? Majorette, baton in air	50.00	75.00	100.00
(AN 16) Majorette, baton held backward, cape-like cloth trailing behind, only one known (may be prototype, as underbase isn't finished)	No Price Found		
(AN 17) Majorette, ensign-type cap, with cape, three known	300.00	450.00	600.00
(AN 18) 151? Girl flagbearer	65.00	98.00	130.00
(AN 19) 152? Girl fifist. . . .	65.00	98.00	130.00
(AN 20) 153? Girl bugler . . .	65.00	98.00	130.00
(AN 21) 154? Girl saxophonist	65.00	98.00	130.00
	65.00	98.00	130.00
(AN 22) 155? Girl drummer	65.00	98.00	130.00
(AN 23) Mounted Cowboy masked, firing pistol straight ahead	50.00	75.00	100.00
(AN 24) Football player throwing ball (**probably** All-Nu	20.00	30.00	40.00
(AN 25) Football player running with ball (**probably** All-Nu	No Price Found		
(AN 26) 501 (Faben's number) Cowboy on Bucking Broncho	30.00	45.00	60.00
(AN 27) 502 (Faben's number) Cowgirl on Bucking Broncho	30.00	45.00	60.00
(AN 28) 521 (Faben's number) Jockey on Horse	15.00	22.00	30.00
(AN 29) 526 (Faben's number) Hunter on horse	22.00	33.00	45.00
(AN 30) Woman on horse . .	12.50	18.75	25.00
(AN 31) Polo Player on horse	12.50	18.75	25.00
(AN 31a) Male Jumper on Horse	12.50	18.75	25.00
(AN 32) Standing horse	10.00	15.00	20.00
(AN 33) **619 Prancer** (Faben's number and description), large 4-1/8" high	No Price Found		
(AN 34) Jockey on Prancer, large	No Price Found		

AN1b
Courtesy Monty Mitzelfeld

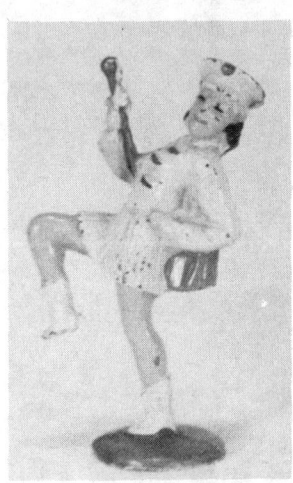

AN17
Courtesy Don Pielin

AN24　　AN25　　AN26　　AN27
Photo by Bill Kaufman　Courtesy Evelyn Besser

AN29　　AN30　　AN28　　AN32
Photo by Bill Kaufman　Courtesy Evelyn Besser

JONES

All-Nu jockey on standing long-tailed horse.
Courtesy Charlie Breslow

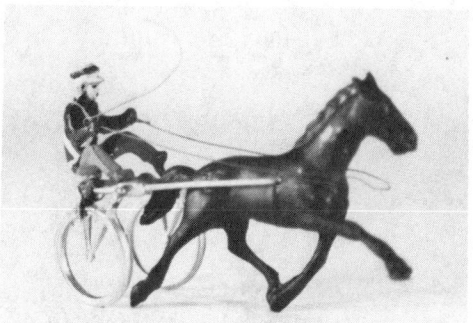

AN35
Photo by Bill Kaufman   Courtesy Evelyn Besser

AN31

AN33   AN34
Photo by Don Pielin

ALL-NU Searchlight, "Field Kitchen", Sound Detector, Tank.
No Prices Found. Photo by Bill Kaufman. Courtesy Evelyn Besser.

	G	VG	M
(AN35) Trotter	25.00	38.00	50.00
(ANV 1) "Field Kitchen", approx. 2½" long, "Made in USA" slush lead......		No Price Found	
(ANV 2) Searchlight, approx. 2¾" long, "Made in USA", slush lead........		No Price Found	
(ANV 3) Sound Detector, approx. 2¾" long, "Made In USA", slush lead........		No Price Found	
(ANV 4) Tank "USA", 3" long, "Made in USA", slush lead.............		No Price Found	

ALL-NU PAPER SOLDIERS

	G	VG	M
Decal sheet of soldiers, meant to be attached to heavy cardboard backing, circa 1942, by Frank Krupp	50.00	75.00	100.00

Soldiers, 5" high on heavy cardboard, circa 1942-3

	G	VG	M
100 Officer marching with sabre	3.00	4.50	6.00
101 Marching, slope arms, WW I helmet..........	3.00	4.50	6.00
102 Bugler, campaign cap...	3.00	4.50	6.00
103 Signalman, WW I helmet	3.00	4.50	6.00
104 Officer kneeling with binoculars	3.00	4.50	6.00
105 Kneeling, firing rifle with WW I helmet......	3.00	4.50	6.00
106 Throwing grenade, WW I helmet...............	3.00	4.50	6.00
107 Fixed bayonet, WW I helmet	3.00	4.50	6.00
108 Charging with gas mask, WW I helmet..........	3.00	4.50	6.00
109 Charging with rifle, port arms, WW I helmet.....	3.00	4.50	6.00

100   101   102   103   104   105

106   107   108   109   110

Figures courtesy Evelyn Besser

111   112   113   114   115

116   117   118

Figures courtesy Evelyn Besser

110 Seated machine gunner, WW I helmet	**G**	**VG**	**M**	111 Flag-bearer, WW I helmet	**G**	**VG**	**M**
	3.00	4.50	6.00		3.00	4.50	6.00

ALL-NU

	G	VG	M		G	VG	M
112 General MacArthur ...	5.00	8.00	12.00	119 Ski trooper..........	3.00	4.50	6.00
113 Nurse..............	3.00	4.50	6.00	120 Soldier advancing w/rifle, WW II helmet......	3.00	4.50	6.00
114 Men carrying wounded soldier on stretcher, WW II helmets............	3.00	4.50	6.00	150 3 men in jeep, WW I helmets	3.00	4.50	6.00
115 2 Men firing rifles from prone position, WW II helmets	3.00	4.50	6.00	151 5-man team with cannon, WW I helmets.....	3.00	4.50	6.00
116 Soldier on wireless radio	3.00	4.50	6.00	152 2 men manning wheeled AA gun, WW I helmets..	3.00	4.50	6.00
117 3 Soldiers w/rifles leaving boat, WW II helmets.	3.00	4.50	6.00	153 Tank with 3 men......	3.00	4.50	6.00
				154 Ambulance..........	3.00	4.50	6.00
118 2 paratroopers, one w/tommy gun, WW II helmets	3.00	4.50	6.00	155 Truck w/soldiers in rear, WW II helmets........	3.00	4.50	6.00
				ALL-NU Boxed Set of 24 of the above soldiers.......	No Price Found		

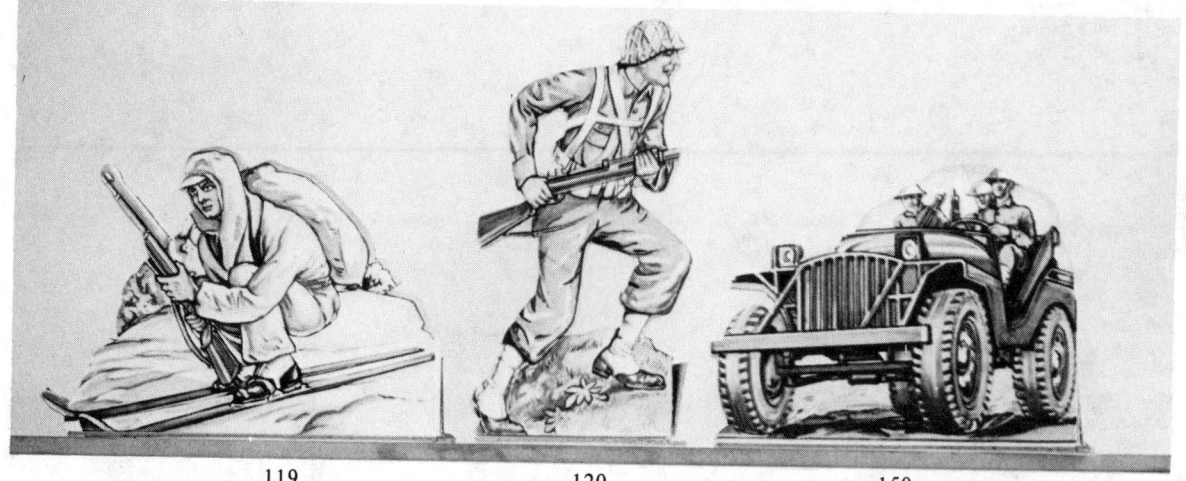

119   120   150

Figures courtesy Evelyn Besser

151   152   153

Figures courtesy Evelyn Besser   154   155

188

ALL-NU Dog Musicians. These sell for about $50 apiece in mint condition.
Photo by Bill Kaufman
Courtesy Evelyn Besser

AN31a

ALL-NU souvenir elephant. The alligator pencil-sharpener may be Faben.
The pencil is a black boy. The pair sold for $47 in 1988.
Photo by Bill Kaufman.
Courtesy Evelyn Besser

This goat was modeled by Frank Krupp, but probably for Faben.

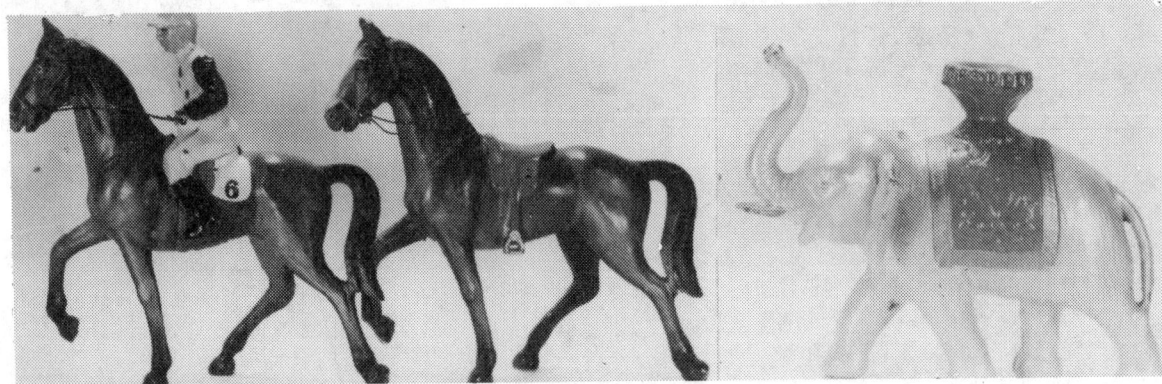

L to R: AN34, AN33, Al-Nu Elephant (missing glass globe on howdah).
Courtesy Don Pielin

TOMMY TOY

Girls? What do **girls** have to do with **toy soldiers?**

Not an unintelligent question. Soldiering, after all, is almost exclusively a male activity, and the figures it inspires don't deviate from that tradition. Toy soldiers are produced with boys in mind, and most of the buyers and collectors have been boys, and men. So why then **girls,** or **women?**

The answer is that at the production end, women have often been prominent, if not predominant. Nearly half the labor force of such companies as Barclay and Manoil consisted of women or teenage girls. It was the distaff side which almost exclusively did the painting, and they also packaged, clerked, and performed other duties. In that latter category is the key job of design. Here at least two women have figured, one of them quite prominently, and both of them did work for Tommy Toy.

Tommy Toy, located on the second story of 131 Palisade Avenue, Union City, New Jersey, had its first sale on November 13, 1935. The firm was owned as a sideline by Dr. Albert Greene (President) and Charles E. Weldon (Secretary-Treasurer, who at the time owned Towne Cabs, a fleet of 250 taxis, in New York City). Also associated were Joseph Maulbeck (Vice-President), George Ganzkow (Purchasing Agent and Manager) and John Zeman, who was in the holly berries business in Union City, and was either another partner or involved in the company's actual operation. There was another name involved too – though no one today remembers in what way – Leon Donze, the elderly, one-eyed

TOMMY TOY

Frenchman who had once been co-owner of Barclay. Donze had been edged out of Barclay, and presumably, as one of Dr. Greene's patients, had convinced him it would be financially worthwhile to get into the business of slush mold lead toys and novelties.

The company's first sale was of toys, and was recorded on a card marked "First Money Taken in Payment, one gross assorted toys – $6.30" (the buyer was Doctor Greene's father). It also made promotional banks for the Green River liquor company. Louis Picco, who got around, remembers working on a Popeye bank for Tommy Toy.

The company is best known for its soldiers and nursery rhyme figures, but it also made vehicles, which ones they are is uncertain. Only one, a Cord sedan, is known to have been marked "Tommy Toy". All the others that are identified as Tommy Toys were done so by Charles E. Weldon Jr., son of one of Tommy Toy's workers. Although he was sure they were all Tommy Toy, he admitted he might be mistaken about some of them, as he did own toys of other companies. In late 1984 I found a number of Barclay's printing blocks, and some of the "Tommy Toy" vehicles were shown on them. However, it's possible that Donze had taken the molds with him when he left Barclay, or that Barclay issued them as their own after it bought out Tommy Toy. It's not likely that anything will be definitely known, as Tommy Toy seems not to have had catalogs or order sheets. Several "Tommy Toy" vehicles look like the ones attributed to Savoye. Since the latter firm seems to have gone out of business in 1936, Tommy Toy could have bought the molds from the nearby company.

There are no problems with the soldiers or nursery rhyme figures, though. All are plainly marked "Tommy Toy" and most are also marked with a description of the toy, such as "Soldier Charging" or "Puss In Boots". In addition, the nursery rhyme figures were copyrighted, so that both the dates of their copyright and the names of their designers are known. They were sculpted by two women, Olive Kooken (pronounced KOO-ken) and Margaret Cloninger (pronounced KLAH-nin-jer).

Olive Kooken was born December 12, 1904 in Kansas. Margaret Ruth Cloninger (known as "Margo" to her friends) was born July 17, 1905 in Jackson, Tennessee, with the two becoming friends as early as high school in Wichita, Kansas. According to a long feature story in the March 31, 1929 Wichita Eagle Sunday Magazine, Miss Kooken became interested in sculpture when she was a young child. Her high school yearbook described her in part, "Brushes and pallettes and flats and sharps and naturals . . ." so she was obviously interested in painting and music as well. In 1927, when she was 22, she moved to New York City and attended the Art Students League from 1927-1928. According to my informant at the League, "In looking over the records it is obvious that Edward McCartan was her most popular teacher as she attended his class most often. He taught sculpture."

The young artist's return to Wichita in March, 1929 (where she had earlier studied art) and her old job at the Mid-Continental Map Company was an effort to save money to finance a trip to Europe, where she had hoped to work as an artist. Presumably, the 1929 Crash put an end to those hopes, and instead she returned to New York.

It is not known when Ms. Kooken began working for Barclay. Most of the company's workers didn't recall seeing her much before 1939, and two of her friends seem sure she did no work for Barclay during her first stay in New York. However, Sally Newman, longtime bookkeeper for Barclay, contradicts the others, saying that Olive Kooken did work for the company before 1929, when she lived in Greenwich Village, and Barclay's Harry Bogaty believes he saw her at the factory at about 1930-31.

A recent photo of the building which once housed Tommy Toy on its second floor.

Margo Cloninger in the 1930's

Olive Kooken, 1943

TOMMY TOY

Their memory does not square up with this account by Mildred Orr Hirth, a longtime friend of Olive Kooken and Margaret Cloninger: "You asked how she got started on the soldiers. She had some animals, lamps, bookends, etc., and they were expensive to cast. The steel foundries were close (she lived in Union City) and she started to do some of the casting herself. She met some of the toy manufacturers there, and Barclay's and another company asked her to do the soldiers." If this is true, then she couldn't have started with Barclay until 1936 or 1937, as she apparently moved to Union City around this time.

Presumably the other company mentioned by Mildred Hirth was Tommy Toy. It is at this point that Margaret Cloninger enters the scene. Miss Cloninger was an actress, and in 1935 had appeared on Broadway with Eva Le Gallienne in "L'Aiglon", and then remained with the company through their winter tour. However, according to Anna (Mrs. Hugh F.) Cloninger, "Because of hard times in the theatre, she took up sculpting and became outstanding in the art... The girls roomed together. Most of their work was done by Epplesheimer and Company – the company made molds for Hershey bars among other things – but much of their casting was with this company, and Margaret Ruth married the vice-president and general manager, John D. Warren, whose father was owner and president." John Warren subsequently founded the Warren Lines soldier company. (See Warren)

According to Mildred Orr Hirth, "I believe Margaret selected a subject to do, Olive helped her get started, corrected the figure when it was about half finished, and went over it at the end. She was trying to help her financially, but I think most of the work was Olive's." (Anna Cloninger remembers her relative also sculpted "zoo animals" in addition to her "figures of nursery rhyme characters, soldiers and horses.")

The fact that it may have been a collaboration of sorts makes separating just who did which work for Barclay and Tommy Toy difficult, if not impossible. Each artist did receive separate credits on the copyrights for Tommy Toy's nursery rhyme figures, but to my eye at least, the figures are in the same style, with, if anything, Miss Cloninger's work slightly superior. However, Miss Cloninger is said to have given up all toy soldier sculpting when she married on March 26, 1941, so it can safely be said that all postwar sculpting of Barclay's soldiers was done by Olive Kooken. (Before that time, however, Barclay's Harry Bogaty remembers seeing the two women arrive together at the plant when new figures were needed.)

At least two of the Tommy Toy soldiers would seem definitely to have been done by Miss Kooken, since they turned up again as Barclay podfoot figures – the wounded soldier holding his helmet, and the nurse with the towel over her arm. Olive Kooken's work was generally distinguished by a smooth, nearly wrinkle-free look, quite different from the more realistic figures produced by Frank Krupp, who preceded her at Barclay. Unless Sally Newman is correct and Olive Kooken did begin work for Barclay in the late 1920s, the sculptress's first work for Barclay appears to have been its civilian train figures, and then, around 1940, its cast helmet soldiers.

Margaret Cloninger, according to Warren expert Steve Balkin, was brought in to improve the look of Warren's horses in its toy soldier line, and she may have sculpted some of the soldiers as well. It is known that horses were her prime interest.

According to Jeannette Vrancken, who was a ward of Miss Kooken's, toys were the artist's "bread and butter", but the pay was low. She was never an employee of Barclay, just a free-lancer, and she "sometimes hated" working on the soldiers, since she was given so little time to do them.

Perhaps this was truer after the war than before, when detailing certainly deteriorated on the figures. Olive Kooken thus had to earn her living through more than soldier design. She sculpted jewelry, trophies, eight-foot tall angels and the rest of the altar for a modern Catholic Church in Newark, New Jersey, Beaut Manufacturing's toys from designs by its owner, modeled approximately half of the black model ID planes produced by Design Center of New York in 1942-43 for the armed services and the general public, did a sculpture in miniature for New York's Museum of Modern Art of its Sculpture Garden, and undoubtedly a number of other things. In addition, she had known the great American actress Minnie Maddern Fiske, and in 1955, her book, *Mrs. Fiske and the American Theatre,* cowritten with Archie Binns, was published by Crown.

Miss Kooken seems to have been liked by everyone I've been in touch with. She appears to have been a very kind and generous person. Like many artists, she was something of a nonconformist, wearing trousers most of the time, dungarees to the Metropolitan Opera in an era when virtually everyone dressed up for it, even getting up on the roof of her small stone home in Union City to make extensive repairs herself.

For a while, Margaret Cloninger Warren's life ran more smoothly. Her husband had money, and for a time they lived in a handsome home in the upper-class town of Bernardsville, New Jersey, but eventually the money ran out, and her later years seem to have been somewhat impoverished.

Unfortunately, both women died young. Miss Kooken died quite suddenly at the age of 59 on June 24, 1964, of arteriosclerotic heart disease. Neither of her obituaries mentioned her association with any toy company. Mrs. Warren died at age 61 on November 15, 1966, while visiting in Wichita from her home in Merritt Island, Florida. Her obituary,

TOMMY TOY

in the local Wichita paper, also made no mention of her connection with the toy industry.

Sadly, Olive Kooken never made it to Europe. According to Jeannette Vrancken, "...there was always a job someone was anxious to have done or somebody was sick that she had to help and one year melted into the next until it was too late." Presumably there was never the money, either.

The work the two women did for Tommy Toy is attractive, even charming. Oddly, it is the nursery rhyme figures that are robust, and the soldiers slight. After Barclay bought out Tommy Toy it tried casting the fairy tale figures with new, unmarked bases, but the effort seems to have confined itself to the factory. There is no indication that any of the soldiers were cast, but copies of two were made (presumably by Kooken and/or Cloninger) in a slightly larger size; the "Ground Arms" and "Officer Gas Mask" figures. To my eye, the latter, along with "Wounded", is the most eye-catching of Tommy Toy's soldiers.

Although their figures wear an air of success, Tommy Toy somehow never made the grade, perhaps because its owners didn't devote their full time to the business. In a 1938 New Jersey business directory it was listed as having just seven male and three female employees. There may have been a few more earlier (perhaps as many as 35), as Dr. Greene's son, Robert, who was about 15 at the time, remembers three or four casters, and three or four motorized assembly lines along which the toys were trimmed, sprayed with a base coat, and hand-painted.

No one is sure what the company's biggest seller was, although Marjorie Ross, Dr. Greene's daughter, believes it was the nursery rhyme toys. Those I spoke with doubt that Tommy Toy ever made it into the chainstores such as Woolworth's or Grant's, where the product would have had a much better chance.

Phone books of the time indicate that the firm went out of business between August 1938 and May 1939. Barclay's maintenance man, Charles Poretta, who cleaned out the Tommy Toy factory after the company was sold to Barclay, remembers that Dr. Greene lost $20,000 on the venture. "If I had only held on," Dr. Greene told his son in later years, and looking at these figures and knowing their attraction to today's collectors, one can understand, and sympathize with, his ruefulness. Sales should have been better, and perhaps as the Depression faded, they would have been.

Although it's not been possible to fix the date when Tommy Toy soldiers were first sold, it seems unlikely they came before mid-to-late 1937 at the earliest. Four of the thirteen basic figures are medical. It seems unlikely a small firm like Tommy Toy would have produced so large a percentage of this type if it didn't know they sold. Barclay's medical figures seem to have debuted in late 1936 or early 1937, Grey Iron's in 1937 or 1938 and Manoil's probably in 1937.

NOTE: All Tommy Toy soldiers not marked "Tommy Toy" were produced by American Alloy and Toy Creations.

TT1 TT2 TT3 TT4 TT5 TT6 TT7 TT8

TT9 TT10 TT11 TT12 TT13 TT14 TT15

Photo by Bill Kaufman

TOMMY TOY

TT18 TT19 TT20 TT21 TT22

Courtesy Tony and Jacki Grecco

TT23 TT24 TT25 TT26 TT27

Courtesy Tony and Jacki Grecco

	G	VG	M		G	VG	M
(TT1) "Officer"	100.00	150.00	200.00	(TT16) Nurse, white uniform, marked only "Tommy Toy", vinelike partition between the legs.	No Price Found		
(TT2) "Ground Arms"	125.00	188.00	250.00				
(TT3) "Soldier Marching"	80.00	120.00	160.00				
(TT4) "Port Arms"	100.00	150.00	200.00	(TT17) Nurse, brown uniform, same as above	No Price Found		
(TT5) "Soldier Charging"	80.00	120.00	160.00				
(TT6) "Hand Grenade"	100.00	150.00	200.00	(TT18) "Old Mother Hubbard" by Olive Kooken, copyright June 25, 1936	20.00	30.00	40.00
(TT7) "Soldier Firing", kneeling firing rifle	125.00	188.00	250.00				
(TT8) "Machine Gunner", standing firing tommy gun	150.00	225.00	300.00	(TT19) "Tom, Tom, The Pipers Son" by Kooken, copyright June 25, 1936	35.00	55.00	75.00
(TT9) "Officer Gas Mask"	150.00	225.00	300.00				
(TT10) "Stretcher-Bearer"	No Price Found			(TT20) "Humpty-Dumpty" by Margaret R. Cloninger, copyright June 25, 1936	32.00	48.00	65.00
(TT11) "Wounded"	150.00	225.00	300.00				
(TT12) "Doctor", brown uniform	200.00	300.00	400.00				
(TT13) "Doctor", white uniform	100.00	150.00	200.00	(TT21) "Little Bo Peep" by Cloninger, copyright June 25, 1936	22.00	33.00	45.00
(TT14) "Nurse", white uniform, marked this way, she has a fine-grained partition between the legs	90.00	135.00	180.00	(TT22) "Jack & Jill" by Kooken, copyright June 25, 1936 (much sought after by collectors)	400.00	600.00	800.00
(TT15) "Nurse" brown uniform, same as above	100.00	150.00	200.00	(TT23) "Puss In Boots" by Cloninger, copyright June 25, 1936	18.00	27.00	36.00

193

TOMMY TOY

	G	VG	M
(TT24) "Jack And The Bean Stalk", by Cloninger, copyright August 10, 1936	30.00	45.00	60.00
(TT25) "Old King Cole" by Cloninger, copyright August 10, 1936	35.00	52.00	70.00
(TT26) "Little Miss Muffet" by Kooken, copyright August 10, 1936	32.00	48.00	65.00
(TT27) "Old Mother Witch" by Kooken, copyright August 10, 1936	35.00	52.00	70.00

TOMMY TOY VEHICLES (Numbers TTV7, TTV10, TTV24 and TTV25 appear on Barclay's printing blocks)

	G	VG	M
(TTV1) Aerial Ladder Truck (like SAVOYE), late 20s type	20.00	30.00	40.00
(TTV2) Airflow type auto (like KANSAS TOY), circa 1935	32.00	48.00	65.00
(TTV3) "Ambulance", late 20s-early 30s type	16.00	24.00	32.00
(TTV4) "Beer Truck" with wooden barrels, late 1930s	14.00	21.00	28.00
(TTV5) Cannon Truck, like Barclay's	17.00	25.00	34.00
(TTV6) Convertible, no driver, mid-late 30s	8.00	12.00	16.00
(TTV7) Convertible with driver, mid-late 30s	10.00	15.00	20.00

TTV31 TTV33 TT13

TTV9 TTV29 TTV30

TTV27 TTV28

TTV2 TTV30 TTV32

TTV18 TTV17 TTV14 TTV16

TTV10 TTV11 TTV12

TTV24 TTV1 TTV15

TTV25 TTV26

TTV19

TTV20 TTV5 TTV7 TTV21

TTV4 TTV18 TTV6

TTV23 TTV22 TTV3

TOMMY TOY

	G	VG	M		G	VG	M
(TTV8) 1935 Cord 810	40.00	60.00	80.00	(TTV20) "Oil" tanker, "Cap 80000" (like METAL CAST, which has different capacity number), 1930s, attaches to TOMMY TOY Towing Car Coupe.	8.00	12.00	16.00
(TTV9) "Delivery Deluxe" delivery truck (like SAVOYE), late 30s......	18.00	27.00	36.00	(TTV21) "Packard", coupe, mid-30s	17.00	26.00	35.00
(TTV10) Double Decker Bus, closed top, early 30s.....	16.00	24.00	32.00	(TTV22) "Police Patrol", open windows, late 20s-early 30s type..........	40.00	60.00	80.00
(TTV11) Double Decker Bus, open top, extended hood (like SAVOYE), late 1920s	35.00	52.00	70.00	(TTV23) "Police Patrol", solid windows, late 20s-early 30s type..........	35.00	52.00	70.00
(TTV12) Double Decker Bus, open top, no hood (like BARCLAY), late 1930s..	16.00	24.00	32.00	(TTV24) Pumper, mid 1930s	12.00	18.00	25.00
(TTV13) Dump Truck, late 1930s (resembles KANSAS TOY, BEST TOY, MANHATTAN TOYS)..	16.00	24.00	32.00	(TTV25) Pumper, large, red hubs, late 30s..........	11.00	16.00	22.00
(TTV14) "General Trucking", late 30s..........	12.00	18.00	25.00	(TTV26) Pumper, small, late 30s	8.00	12.00	16.00
(TTV15) Ladder Truck, mid 30s.................	20.00	30.00	40.00	(TTV27) Racing Car, large, circa mid-30s..........	16.00	24.00	32.00
(TTV16) "Milk" truck, late 1930s...............	20.00	30.00	40.00	(TTV28) Racing Car, small, circa mid-30s..........	12.00	18.00	25.00
(TTV17) "Milk Truck", grilled window, circa late 1930s...............	20.00	30.00	40.00	(TTV29) Sedan, four-door, circa 1935..........	17.00	26.00	35.00
(TTV18) "Milk Truck", smooth window, circa late 30s..................	20.00	30.00	40.00	(TTV30) Sedan towing "Tourist" trailer, circa 1936-37	20.00	30.00	40.00
(TTV19) "Motorcoach", mid-30s (like SAVOYE)..	No Price Found			(TTV31) Towing Car Coupe (like SAVOYE), early 30s type	16.00	24.00	32.00
				(TTV32) Tractor..........	12.00	18.00	25.00
				(TTV33) Wrecker, late 1930s	10.00	15.00	20.00

TOMMY TOY TTV8
Courtesy C.B.C. Lee

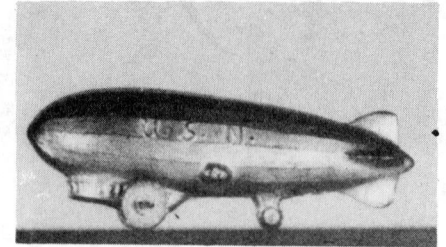

TOMMY TOY "U.S.N." Dirigible
Photo by Bill Kaufman, Courtesy Charles
E. Weldon, Jr.

AMERICAN ALLOY-TOY CREATIONS

Research in the dimestore toy soldier field can be difficult even when the principal figure is still alive. This is the case with a succession of companies called American Lead Toy & Novelty Co., American Alloy, and Toy Creations.

The ubiquitous Louis Picco was a key figure with all of these firms, but after forty years he doesn't remember everything, and some of those things he does remember vary from interview to interview. However, the essentials remain the same.

On August 19, 1939, American Lead Toy & Novelty Co. was entered in a new businesses directory. The officers were Charles Kremm, J. Bracco, Robert Bostwick, Louis Picco and George L. Miller. Unfortunately, Picco doesn't remember this company or ever being associated with Bostwick. Nevertheless, it appears to be either American Alloy or its forerunner, and Picco does remember another company, prior to American Alloy, which sold "six or seven" soldiers through Toy Creations. According to Picco these were not the ones produced by American Alloy, but the likelihood is they were.

Picco was a partner in American Alloy, and its president. This company's product was only soldiers, all of them copies of Tommy Toys, but with the underbase markings gone. The molds seem to have been made directly from the company's figures, and as a result the soldiers lack much of the detail that makes Tommy Toys appealing. The paint is also inferior. The company was listed in the August, 1941 North Bergen, New Jersey phone book, at 1015 Paterson Plank Road. It was not listed in the 1940-41 phone book or the May 1942 book.

American Alloy had six partners, but there were only four employees: Picco, Bracco and two women. According to Picco, some of the firm's soldiers were sold through Schranz & Bieber, but Picco, who lived over the shop, also remembers dealing directly with merchants on the lower East Side, orders being sought and placed under the shadow of the Manhattan Bridge, with the soldiers being sent C.O.D. to eliminate the need for bookkeeping personnel.

Only a few thousand American Alloy soldiers had been sold when the War broke out, and the government impounded 30 tons of lead that were waiting for American Alloy at a railroad siding. It's not known how many of Tommy Toy's figures American Alloy produced, and the discovery in late 1984 of a boxed set of Toy Creations soldiers makes it unlikely that they can ever be sorted out, as Toy Creations also copied Tommy Toys.

American Alloy seems to have resumed for a time after the War, but about 1946 Picco was approached by Toy Creations to set up a toy soldier department for them. Apparently all he did was provide some or all of American Alloy's molds, plus two additional figures; copies of the Barclay prone machine-gunner (B63) and soldier with field phone (B132). According to Picco, sculptress Olive Kooken was also hired by Toy Creations, but whether it was to make the new molds isn't known.

Again according to Picco, Toy Creations was a subsidiary of Schranz & Bieber, which was both a distributor and manufacturer of toys, games and dart and paint sets. Toy Creations also produced toys other than soldiers. In its incorporation papers, dated 11/24/37, the New Jersey company proposed to "manufacture, buy, sell, trade and deal in toy dolls."

Eugene Schwartz was the head man when Picco was involved, although the names on the incorporation papers in 1937 were Alton Gruenberg, Arthur J. Blake, David H. Stemer and Sylvia Mandell, and in 1959 when the company filed its last report, the officers seem to have been Rollin Shulberg, Donald P. Honig, Violet Shulberg and Nathan Armour.

While Picco was employed, the toy soldier arm of the firm was located in Jersey City. Picco remembers having been approached by Toy Creations in 1947 or 1948, and leaving about 1949, but he seems to be wrong about the dates. All he remembers at Toy Creations is the WW I-helmeted soldiers, but an ad in the March, 1947 Playthings shows a completely new set of figures (TC8-13) all in World War II pot helmets. Presumably all were sculpted by Olive Kooken. Although they don't look a great deal like her Barclay soldiers, they do have the same characteristic wrinkle-free appearance.

For the completists who'd like to own both American Alloy's and Toy Creations' versions of the same soldiers, there is only one reasonably sure way; finding a boxed set of Toy Creations soldiers and checking other figures against their paint jobs. However, another test can at least assure that a figure was produced by Toy Creations (while not at the same time assuring unlike figures were definitely produced by American Alloy). Some, perhaps the majority (but not all) of Toy Creations' soldiers, both WWI and WWII varieties, have a copper-colored underbase. In its July, 1942 issue, *Playthings* magazine announced that Toy Creations was selling three different boxed sets of composition soldiers. The figures shown in the illustrated boxed set were made by Molded Products.

Those figures listed with a "TC" coding are known to have been produced by Toy Creations, but probably all of them were at least sold by the company, since American Alloy was tied to the firm virtually from the beginning. TC7 has not been definitely identified as either as American Alloy or Toy Creations, but appears to be a transitional figure between Toy Creations' WW I and WW II figures.

AMERICAN ALLOY

AA1 TC1 TC2 TC3 TC4 AA2

TC5 TC6 TC?7 TC8

	G	VG	M		G	VG	M
AA1 Officer	22.00	33.00	44.00	AA2 Doctor	70.00	105.00	140.00
TC1 Wounded	80.00	120.00	160.00	AA3 Soldier Marching	20.00	30.00	40.00
TC2 Grenade Thrower	75.00	112.00	150.00	TC5 Soldier on field phone .	90.00	135.00	180.00
TC3 Tommy Gunner	75.00	112.00	150.00	TC6 Prone machine gunner .	30.00	45.00	60.00
TC4 Charging with rifle ...	70.00	105.00	140.00	TC?7 Charging with rifle, WW II helmet	No Price Found		

TC9 TC10 TC11 TC12 TC13

	G	VG	M		G	VG	M
TC8 Soldier with Walkie-Talkie, WW II helmet	42.00	63.00	85.00	TC12 Marching, WW II helmet	35.00	52.00	70.00
TC9 Soldier advancing with rifle, WW II helmet	40.00	60.00	80.00	TC13 Officer in gas mask with pistol, WW II helmet	68.00	102.00	135.00
TC10 Soldier with bazooka, WW II helmet	20.00	30.00	40.00	(TC14) Flag Bearer, copy of Barclay B7	No Price Found		
TC11 Grenade Thrower, WW II helmet	88.00	132.00	175.00				

A Toy Creations boxed set. This set was sold at auction in late 1984 for $777.00.   Courtesy Gene Parker

Toy Creations are offering U. S. Army approved soldiers moulded from wood flour composition. The figures, 3½" high, are unbreakable and attractively colored. There are three styles: one an action set containing anti-aircraft gunners, machine gunners, flame throwers, etc.; a second set contains infantry soldiers, while a third has soldier, sailor and Marine figures. Each set has 10 pieces and retails for $1.25.

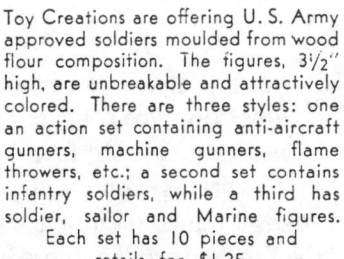

JULY, 1942—PLAYTHINGS

Molded Products soldiers sold by Toy Creations. From the July, 1942 *Playthings*.
Courtesy Jack Matthews

AA3   TC4
Photo by K. Warren Mitchell

Toy Creations TC14 Flag Bearer in the center, with Jones Flag Bearer at left and Barclay B7, on which the other two are based, on right.
Photo by Ed Poole

These soldiers came in a box marked "Toy Soldiers No." and "Trade Mark ANC". ANC could be an abbreviated acronym for American Lead Toy & Novelty Co., which may have preceded American Alloy or have actually been the original firm name. The soldiers look as if they could have come from early Barclay molds.
Photo by Tony and Jacki Grecco

METAL CAST

Metal Cast was not exactly an innovator.

Most of its dimestore-type soldiers were copies of Barclays and Manoils, and those that weren't were crude, and in a few cases, downright ugly. In fact, because most, and perhaps all, of these soldiers were turned out in the home by unskilled people working with cheap paints and very difficult molds, most original Metal Cast figures are unattractive. However, as Bill Lango's Vintage Castings company has shown, when the molds are modified to allow more air to escape, and the finished product is professionally painted, the majority of Metal Cast's pieces are presentable enough. (Naturally some collectors prefer the uglier but more historical "originals" which sell for far higher prices.)

Like American Alloy-Toy Creations, Metal Cast in 1946 was mystifyingly still offering its 3¼" soldiers with World War I helmets. However, by the following year it had updated its line and its helmeted soldiers now sported WWII headgear. (Its soldiers with WWI helmets were offered at least as early as 1941).

The company's pitch was to people who wanted to start their own businesses, and in its brochures it printed testimonial after testimonial from apparently satisfied customers. The most prominent of its patrons is Bergen Toy & Novelty Co. (Beton), which originally used its molds to cast hollow lead soldiers and then copied several of its pieces when it switched to production in plastic.

Metal Cast began in 1899 as S. Sachs Toy Soldier Manufacturing Company, selling hand-casting molds from the start. In 1920 it was advertised simply as The Toy Soldier Manufacturing Company, 32 Union Square, New York City. In 1928 it had moved to 1696 Boston Road, New York, which is its last known address. By 1929, under the hand of H. Sachs, it became Metal Cast Products Co., and had added molds for novelty items.

The firm's molds were originally for solid cast toys, but by 1933 it offered eight hollow cast molds for soldiers, cowboys and Indians about 2½" high. It is these figures and the later hollow-cast 3¼" soldiers that are presently considered the most collectible.

ALL BOLD WORDS AND NUMBERS ARE THE COMPANY'S OWN DESCRIPTION.

Courtesy Gene Coffman   21   22   23   24

Circa 1933

	G	VG	M
21 American Cavalry, mounted, wearing helmet, approx. 3" high	15.00	22.50	30.00
22 American Infantry Private, marching in helmet, rifle at slope, approx. 2½" high	12.00	18.00	25.00
23 American Infantry Officer, marching in cap, sword on shoulder approx. 2½" high	12.00	18.00	25.00
24 American Infantry Flag Bearer, wearing helmet	15.00	22.00	30.00

	G	VG	M
31 Broncho Bill, holding pistol, on bucking broncho	26.00	39.00	52.00
32 Cowboy holding rifle across waist	No Price Found		
33 Big Chief mounted Indian in war bonnet, holding bow	15.00	22.00	30.00
34 Indian, in war bonnet, holding hatchet and shield	11.00	16.00	22.00
Circa 1940-1946 in WWI Helmets			
21A Flag Bearer 3⅝" high	40.00	60.00	80.00
22A Aviator (very similar to Barclay's), 3" high	20.00	30.00	40.00

199

METAL CAST

21A 22A 23A 25A 24A

26A 27A 29A 30A

31

Photo by Bob Hornung

32A

	G	VG	M
23A Pilot With Bomb, 3⅛" high, similar to Manoil's.	100.00	150.00	200.00
24A Suicide Squad, 3" high, very similar to Barclay's officer with gas mask and pistol	39.00	52.00	70.00
25A Signal Corps, with Semaphore Flags	No Price Found		

	G	VG	M
26A Anti-Aircraft Soldier, with searchlight	15.00	22.00	30.00
27A Bomb Thrower, gas mask, slung rifle, throwing grenade	No Price Found		
28A Wounded, lying down, head on hand, arm in sling (none known)	No Price Found		
29A Machine Gunner, kneeling	No Price Found		
30A Motorcycle Officer on motorcycle, peaked cap . .	35.00	52.00	70.00
31A Cavalry Officer, 3¼" long	10.00	15.00	20.00

METAL CAST

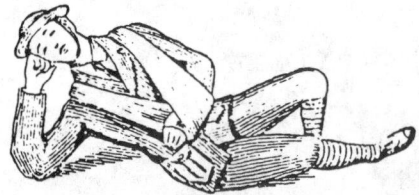

28A
This is the only Metal Cast shown in their catalogs that has yet to surface.

33A
Photo by Don Patman

METAL CAST No. 32
Courtesy Ron Steiner

33   34

31A   34A   35A

36A   37A   38A

This appears to be a Metal Cast, with a variation in the arms. All other known figures have their arms further from their sides.
Photo by Ron Cadieux

201

METAL CAST   Circa 1947, WW II Helmets

	G	VG	M
31A Cavalry Officer, in cap, 3¼" high	10.00	15.00	20.00
32A Flag Bearer, 3¼" high, in campaign cap	No Price Found		
33A Trumpeter, 3" high in campaign cap, one known	No Price Found		
34A Marching Private, 3" high, in campaign cap, no weapon	20.00	30.00	40.00
35A Infantryman, 3" long, similar to Manoil 44, pot helmet	6.00	9.00	12.00

	G	VG	M
36A Bomb Thrower, 2¾" high, similar to Manoil 31 and Metal Cast 27A, WW II pot helmet	6.00	9.00	12.00
37A Suicide Squad, 3" high, similar to Barclay 778 and Metal Cast 24A	40.00	60.00	80.00
38A Machine Gunner, 2½" high	25.00	38.00	50.00

METAL CAST NO. 66 Aeroplane, approx. 4½" wingspan, 2-engine, 1940s, lead. Price averages $12 in mint. Marked "Fred Green Toys." Photo by Norbert Schachter

Metal Cast tank, value $33 in good. $66 in mint condition. Photo by Ed Poole

This Indian and cadet may have been produced by Metal Cast, or, more likely, by Beton, before the company turned from lead to plastic. They are worth about $20 apiece in mint. The Indian stands 3" high, and could also be by Jones.

A soldier by an unknown maker (right) next to a Metal Cast (left). It is possible it is a Metal Cast or even a lead Beton, since Beton did cast in lead at first. Price in mint is about $20.
Courtesy Hank Anton   Photo by Ed Poole

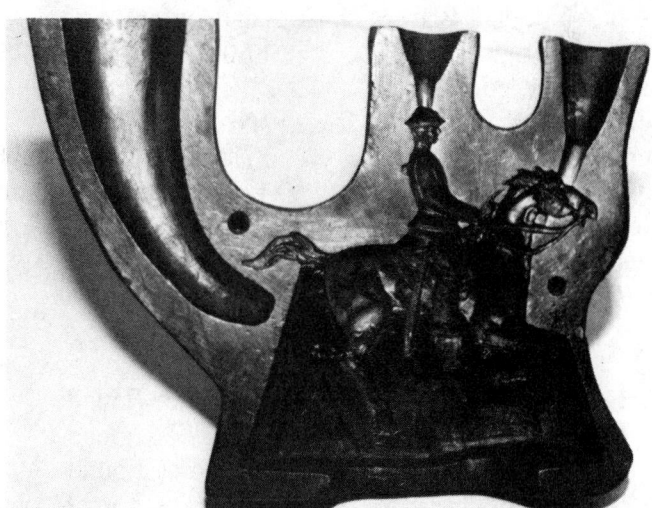

A Metal Cast mold
Photo by Max Heiss

Metal Cast Clown, approx. 3½" high. Value in Good $10.
Courtesy K. Warren Mitchell

SHEILA INC.

Sheila Inc. copyrighted its sports figures in 1937. Research by Orville C. Britton reveals the following: Sheila, of Cleveland, Ohio, was incorporated in 1936 as a cosmetics company. Edward Frantz was the president with the address 942 Prospect Avenue (in 1937 the address was 1104 Prospect, S.E.). In 1937 a directory listed the company as producing "toiletries". By 1938 the firm disappeared from the directories. The names listed in the copyrights of the figures were sculptors. Stephen Rebeck was a noted area sculptor and Jack Worthington was a student of sculpture at the Cleveland School of Art. Worthington has since become the sculptor for the Football Hall of Fame, doing their portrait busts (about 130 as of 1987). Worthington carved his Sheila figures out of blocks of plaster instead of wax, "thus their crudeness", he remembers. After the figures, Sheila made book ends and horse figurals, using Man-O-War and other race horses of the period as models. The only known Sheilas are two football players (back and lineman) which had labels marked "Sheila" pasted on them, and two other football players (center and passer), a baseball fielder, batter and pitcher, these three in gray uniforms with red trim.

Back   Lineman
Courtesy Hank Anton

The center and baseball fielder appear to be Sheilas. The kicker is iron and was made by Hubley.
Photo by Don Pielin

Football Players (Jack Worthington)

Back, copyright 7/8/37.....	17.00	25.00	35.00
Ball Carrier, copyright 7/8/37	No Price Found		
Center, copyright 7/8/37....	17.00	25.00	35.00
Lineman, copyright 7/8/37..	17.00	25.00	35.00
Kicker, copyright 7/17/37...	No Price Found		
Football Referee, copyright 7/17/37	No Price Found		

Baseball Players (Stephen A. Rebeck)
all copyright 7/7/37

A. Baseball Umpire.......	No Price Found
B. Baseball Catcher.......	No Price Found
C. Baseball Batter	No Price Found
D. Baseball Pitcher	No Price Found
E. Baseball Fielder	No Price Found
F. Baseball Fielder	No Price Found

Basketball Players (Jack Worthington)
all copyright 7/17/37

A. Guarding	No Price Found
B. Shooting	No Price Found
E. Passer	No Price Found
F. Pass Receiver	No Price Found
G. Pass Receiver	No Price Found

I. Punter (listed with basketball players)............ No Price Found

The above were found in the N.Y. Public Library copyright directory. Collector-writer Edward Ryan has found additional figures in the Washington copyright office attributed to Keith Frazine, presumably another sculptor.

Sports Figures (Keith Frazine)
All copyright 6/15/37

H. Baseball Batter	No Price Found
I. Baseball Batter	No Price Found
G. Baseball Catcher	No Price Found
M. Baseball Fielder	No Price Found
N. Baseball Fielder	No Price Found
J. Baseball Pitcher	No Price Found
K. Baseball Pitcher	No Price Found
L. Baseball Pitcher	No Price Found

H.B. TOYS

H.B. Toys was yet another soldier company inspired by Barclay. It was formed in 1947 in the bottom half of a two-story house at 208 63rd Street in West New York, New Jersey. Both the first floor and a loft-like structure behind it were used. H.B. stood for Helm Brothers: Frank (4/15/16- ————), Walter 1/27/22- ————) and silent partners Joseph and Charles.

Frank and Walter had previously worked at Barclay, and virtually all of H.B.'s pieces were copies of Barclays.

Moldmaking was done by New York's Facci Studio, who charged up to $250 per mold. Any changes from the original Barclay figures were worked by Facci. H.B.'s very rare Robe Man and Robe Boy, unauthorized copies of Captain Marvel and Captain Marvel Jr., were the idea of H.B.'s jobber, Al Farber. These are the only superheroes known to be produced by a dimestore company. They were designed by Facci and weren't successful, possibly because of their price, which may have been 50¢ and 25¢ each. Aside from its No. 1000 horse, soldiers were the firm's only product.

For a time H.B. was successful. It had twenty employees on eight-hour shifts. Four cast during the day and four at night (there were no other night workers). Each caster produced 16-17 gross of soldiers a day. Usually, the company was on a five-day week, but in busy seasons it went to six. This suggests the firm produced more than four million soldiers a year.

Frank and Walter had also previously worked at New Jersey's M&L toy company (which produced no soldiers). M&L copied many of Barclay's wheeled toys, which may have given the Helms their idea. It also used an alloy of 99% zinc, with a smidgen of aluminum, and the Helms went with the same material. This metal seems to have been prone to "explosions" as it aged, probably due to impurities. A number of H.B. figures have been found in varying sizes, while the Helms say that only one size of each soldier was cast.

Aside from the two superheroes, the soldiers were priced at ten cents for foot figures and fifteen for mounted. They never sold at Woolworth's but did reach the counters at such dimestore chains as Newberry's and W.T. Grant. They were also available, boxed, at Macy's in New York. The unmarked boxes came in two sizes. The larger could hold four mounted and nine foot figures; the smaller half that. Walter did some of the selling as well; in fact Newberry's was one of the many accounts he landed. Both brothers and their wives often pitched in on casting and painting, respectively.

H.B. never advertised and issued only one brochure. The Helms believe they sold a few soldiers not shown in the brochure; a cowboy on a rearing horse which rested on its tail, a mounted Indian with a headdress, and a mounted Indian with a rifle. At this writing none has surfaced. H.B. briefly tried to cut down on shipping costs, lightening the soldiers by sawing off parts of the bases after they were cast. The experiment was cut short when parents complained the resultant edges made the toys "too rough".

H.B. bought two batches of existing molds. One group it never used (see Paul Paragine). The other came from Tommy Toy, and explains the firm's Wounded Soldier and Soldier Doctor. The Helms believe they cast directly from the Tommy Toy molds.

There was no particular order to the company's releases. Walter Helm believes the first three or four pieces were the No. 1002 Cowboy, perhaps the No. 1016 Cowboy Shooting, and 1500 and 1501, the Mounted Cowboy and Indian. The soldiers were issued soon after the Western figures, well before the Korean War. Some of the figures were plated; the Helms bought a plating apparatus in an attempt to increase sales via souvenir shops, etc.

H.B. had been started on something of a shoestring. Though relatively prosperous, it remained economically vulnerable. The firm was using five tons of metal a week. When the Korean War came along, the Government cut them down to a quarter of a ton. There was no alternative; the company had to close, which it did in 1951 or 1952.

Happily, Walter Helm's wife Patricia prevented him from throwing out the firm's brochure, which is reproduced here. The gaps in the numbering are for soldiers the Helm brothers hoped to produce in the future from their extra molds. H.B. and American Alloy-Toy Creations produced look-alikes. Collector Tony Diksa has suggested a guide to tell them apart. First there is the paint, and probably the metal. Lead can be dug into with a knife, unlike zinc alloy. According to Diksa, all the H.B. Toys have bases that are slightly convex, and thus wobble. The Tommy Toy copies by American Alloy-Toy Creations have slightly concave bases, while their WWII figures' bases are perfectly flat.

	G	VG	M		G	VG	M
No. 1000 Horse	6.00	9.00	12.00	No. 1007 Mailman	10.00	15.00	20.00
No. 1002 Cowboy	10.00	15.00	20.00	No. 1011 Indian	10.00	15.00	20.00
No. 1004 Robe Boy	100.00	150.00	200.00	No. 1012 Kneeling Indian	10.00	15.00	20.00
No. 1005 Policeman	10.00	15.00	20.00	No. 1013 Kneeling Cowboy	10.00	15.00	20.00
No. 1006 Fireman	10.00	15.00	20.00	No. 1014 Indian with Gun	10.00	15.00	20.00

H.B. TOYS

	G	VG	M
No. 1015 Indian With Bow And Arrow	10.00	15.00	20.00
No. 1016 Cowboy Shooting	No Price Found		
No. 1030 Sailor	12.00	18.00	25.00
No. 1035 Marine	12.00	18.00	25.00
No. 1040 Machine Gunner	12.00	18.00	25.00
No. 1041 Marching Soldier	12.00	18.00	25.00
No. 1042 Marching Officer	12.00	18.00	25.00
No. 1043 Charging Soldier	12.00	18.00	25.00
No. 1044 Kneeling Soldier .	12.00	18.00	25.00
No. 1045 Drummer	12.00	18.00	25.00
No. 1046 Bugler	12.00	18.00	25.00
No. 1047 Flag Bearer	12.00	18.00	25.00
No. 1048 Wounded Soldier	12.00	18.00	25.00
No. 1049 Soldier Doctor ..	12.00	18.00	25.00
No. 1500 Mounted Cowboy	22.00	33.00	45.00
No. 1501 Mounted Indian .	22.00	33.00	45.00
No. 1502 Mounted Cowboy Shooting In Air	No Price Found		
No. 1504 Robe Man	No Price Found		
No.? Cowboy on rearing horse which rests on its tail	No Price Found		
No.? Mounted Indian with Headdress	No Price Found		
No.? Mounted Indian with Rifle	No Price Found		

No. 1004
Robe boy

No. 1005
Policeman

No. 1006
Fireman

No. 1007
Mailman

No. 1011
Indian

No. 1014
Indian With Gun

No. 1012
Kneeling Indian

No. 1013
Kneeling Cowboy

A large boxed set from H.B. Toys
Courtesy Hank Anton

No. 1015
Indian with Bow and Arrow

No. 1016
Cowboy Shooting

No. 1000
Horse

No. 1002
Cowboy

No. 1030
Sailor

No. 1035
Marine

No. 1040
Machine gunner

H.B. TOYS

No. 1041
Marching Soldier

No. 1042
Marching Officer

No. 1043
Charging Soldier

No. 1501
Mounted Indian

No. 1502
Mounted Cowboy
Shooting in Air

1044
Kneeling Soldier

No. 1045
Drummer

No. 1504
Robe Man

No. 1046
Bugler

No. 1047
Flag Bearer

No. 1048
Wounded Soldier

No. 1049
Soldier Doctor

No. 1500
Mounted Cowboy

PAUL PARAGINE

Circa the early 1950s Paul Paragine cast toys and "heraldics" in a small loft atop a Union City, New Jersey bakery in the vicinity of 27th Street and Center Avenue. He then sold his molds of soldiers to the Helms of H.B. Toys "for almost nothing". (Paragine is pronounced PARA-jean)

Paragine had worked at M & L, as had the Helms. According to Walter Helm, who visited the loft, he probably used the same alloy as those two companies. Frank Helm, who tried casting from those molds (H.B. sold none of the results) remembers they were "old molds" and that each soldier cast had "a little mound base - the top a little round", with the underside of the base "hollow".

Given all this, it seems likely that the soldiers shown here were cast by Paragine and sold by him in the late 1940s or early 1950s. The metal appears to be the same as that used by H.B. and M & L, the bases are mounded and the underbases hollow.

The soldiers are copies of Manoils or perhaps cast directly from old Manoil molds. Though they are larger than Manoils, much of this is due to the considerably higher base. The otherwise slightly larger size may be explained by an "explosion" of the metal similar to what seems to have happened to some of H.B.'s pieces.

Oddly, the Manoils these soldiers resemble were **not** hollow based. One possibility is that Manoil made hollow-based molds for these figures, then discarded them before production. The other is that Paragine made his own base molds. This theory would make more sense if the original Manoils had a company marking on the underbase, but they didn't. All attempts to track down Paragine have failed. The Helms believe he is dead.

	G	VG	M
PP1 Marching Officer	No Price Found		
PP2 Marching Soldier	No Price Found		
PP3 Kneeling Firing	40.00	60.00	80.00
PP4 Flag Bearer	40.00	60.00	80.00

M10   PP1   PP2   PP3

The Manoil M10 is shown for comparison
Photo by Ed Poole

HISTORICAL MINIATURES

When a group of these were discovered a few years ago by collector-dealer Steve Balkin of New York's Burlington Antique Toys, he turned to toy soldier expert Gus Hansen for information. Hansen thought he recalled an article had been written about the company that produced them. Recently, in the files of J. Edward Jones, Hansen found, and passed on to Balkin, an illustrated article from the New York Sunday Mirror magazine section of January 11, 1942. This revealed the company's name to be Historical Miniatures, Inc., and the sculptor Michael Gera (originally Gerashshenevsky, a Russian immigrant). Jones' accompanying penciled notes disclose that the firm was owned by Montgomery Evans, began "about June, 1941," and that the approximately 3¼" height of the figures was the same size as Jones himself made "back in 1932." The address of the company was 416 4th Avenue, New York City, and the soldiers were individually sold at fifty cents and seventy-five cents (the latter for drummers, flagbearers, etc.). Oddly, at almost the same time, James Miniatures of Garden City, New York began offering two representations of Winston Churchill which greatly resembled, in size and design, the Historical Miniatures figures. Historical Miniatures produced in composition during the second World War, and after the war sold at least a few metal G.I.s in pot helmets (first produced in composition). FAO Schwarz is known to have sold the G.I.s, which suggests this could have been a continuing outlet for Historical Miniatures. The following list is incomplete, and contains figures not yet found.

	C6	C8	C10		C6	C8	C10
HM1 Winston Churchill, with yachting cap, cane .	22.00	33.00	45.00	HM9 Napoleon	22.00	33.00	45.00
HM2 General MacArthur .	22.00	33.00	45.00	HM10 Abraham Lincoln ..	22.00	33.00	45.00
HM3 Majorette, with removable baton	22.00	33.00	45.00	HM11 Simon Bolivar	22.00	33.00	45.00
HM4 Florence Nightingale .	22.00	33.00	45.00	HM12 Josef Stalin	22.00	33.00	45.00
HM5 General Lafayette ...	22.00	33.00	45.00	HM13 Chiang Kai-shek ...	22.00	33.00	45.00
HM6 Nathan Hale	22.00	33.00	45.00	HM14 Ben Franklin	22.00	33.00	45.00
HM7 General DeGaulle ...	22.00	33.00	45.00	HM15 Steuben	22.00	33.00	45.00
HM8 Franklin Delano Roosevelt	22.00	33.00	45.00	HM16 Gold Miner of 1849	22.00	33.00	45.00
				HM17 George Washington, mounted, detachable	No Price Found		

HISTORICAL MINIATURES

	C6	C8	C10
HM18 George Washington, on foot, holding hat	22.00	33.00	45.00
HM19 Drummer Boy (Spirit of '76)	22.00	33.00	45.00
HM20 Fifer (Spirit of '76) .	22.00	33.00	45.00
HM21 Drummer (Spirit of '76)	22.00	33.00	45.00
HM22 Flagbearer (Spirit of '76)	30.00	45.00	60.00
HM23 Colonial Soldier circa 1776 charging, plug-in rifle barrel	22.00	33.00	45.00
HM24 Colonial Soldier circa 1776, walking	22.00	33.00	45.00
HM25 Charging Highlander, plug-in rifle	22.00	33.00	45.00
HM26 Black Watch with Flag	30.00	45.00	60.00
HM27 John Paul Jones ...	22.00	33.00	45.00
HM28 Martha Washington	22.00	33.00	45.00
HM29 Churchill with Derby	12.00	18.00	25.00
HM30 Pulaski	22.00	33.00	45.00
HM31 Lee	22.00	33.00	45.00
HM32 Baden-Powell	22.00	33.00	45.00
HM33 Martin Luther	22.00	33.00	45.00
HM34 Greek Evzone (charging)	22.00	33.00	45.00

	C6	C8	C10
HM35 Greek Evzone with flag	30.00	45.00	60.00
HM36 U.S. Legionnaire with Flag	30.00	45.00	60.00
HM37 Cossack, red uniform	27.00	38.00	55.00
HM38 Cossack, blue uniform	27.00	38.00	55.00
HM39 U.S. Soldier with Flag(s)	30.00	45.00	60.00
HM40 G.I. Charging with bayonet (composition) ...	27.00	38.00	55.00
HM41 G.I. Charging with bayonet (metal)	22.00	33.00	45.00
HM42 Stalin, composition .	22.00	33.00	45.00
HM43 General MacArthur, composition	22.00	33.00	45.00
HM44 Churchill (naval uniform), composition ...	22.00	33.00	45.00
HM45 Franklin Delano Roosevelt, composition ..	22.00	33.00	45.00
HM46 Dwight D. Eisenhower, composition	No Price Found		
HM47 Montgomery, composition	22.00	33.00	45.00
HM48 G.I. Marching with Rifle, composition	No Price Found		
HM49 G.I. Prone with Rifle, composition (wood dowel barrel covered by composition)	27.00	38.00	55.00
HM50 G.I. Officer Marching with Sword, composition	27.00	38.00	55.00
HM51 G.I. Kneeling with Rifle, composition (metal rifle barrel)	27.00	38.00	55.00
HM52 G.I. Officer Running with Pistol, composition .	27.00	38.00	55.00
HM53 Patton (?) composition	22.00	33.00	45.00
HM54 G.I. Flag Bearer, running, composition, paper flag	30.00	45.00	60.00

HM1   HM2   HM3   HM4

HM5   HM6   HM7   HM8   HM9   HM10   HM11   HM12   HM13   HM14   HM15

HISTORICAL MINIATURES

HM16   HM18   HM19   HM20   HM21   HM22

Courtesy Steve Balkin - Burlington Antique Toys, NYC

HM17
The horse used here is Elastolin.
Courtesy Bertel Bruun - Steve Balkin

HM23
Photo by Al Lane

HM24
Photo by Al Lane

HM25

HM27
Courtesy Bertel Bruun

HM29

HM56
Colonial Officer,
sword raised.
Photo by Al Smith

HM30
Courtesy Bertel Bruun

HM35   HM37-HM38
Courtesy Bertel Bruun - Steve Balkin

HM26   HM34   HM36
Rough sketch by the author of figures shown in 1942 newspaper article. Article courtesy Steve Balkin and Bertel Bruun.

209

HISTORICAL MINIATURES

HM41 (rifle tip not correct)
Photo by Ed Poole

HM42   HM45   HM44
Courtesy K. Warren Mitchell

HM43
Photo by Bertel Bruun

HM53   HM47
Courtesy K. Warren Mitchell

HM40   HM52   HM40
The plug-in barrel and bayonet on HM40 are metal,
Photo by A.J. Mergenthaler

HM55
G.I. officer running with
pistol (metal) No price found
Courtesy Charlie Breslow

HM40   HM54   HM40
Photo by Bertel Bruun

HM49   HM50   HM51

The figures here were bought by A.J. Mergenthaler in late 1946 or early
1947 at F.A.O. Schwarz. He remembers an extensive display with composition personality figures placed on a semi-circular tiered stand with composition G.I.s below.
Photo by A.J. Mergenthaler

JAMES MINIATURES

On August 5, 1941, Robert Elgin James, for James Miniatures, copyrighted a figure of Churchill. On October 30 of the same year he did it again. According to his second wife, he also sculpted Ingrid Bergman as Joan of Arc (this would have been about 1948, when the movie debuted) and a representation of Lincoln.

Bob James remembers his father worked in wax, then made bronze molds and did his casting in lead. He worked at it part-time, in his attic in Garden City, Long Island, in 1941, and sold the figures in little white boxes.

James says his father was very interested in English-American relationships, and worked for the maritime service during WW II. He believes about 500 of the Churchills were cast, with perhaps a few hundred sold (one was given to Churchill). There are still some castings left which James is painting and selling.

It's not surprising that Robert E. James was interested in producing historical soldiers. Before the Second World War he and his brother, Harrie A. James, owned a collection of approximately 15,000 pieces. About 1938 the James brothers got up a description and outline of their collection, in an attempt to "present dramatic scenes of various sizes, done to scale with authentic scenic effects and backgrounds, all of which will tell the story of World History. The Exhibition will include an interesting talk or lecture on the subject matter to supplement the actual scenes."

The Jameses believed their collection to be the largest in the country. According to their outline, the figures came from France, England, Germany and Sweden, and ran from 2000 B.C. "to the present era." They owned a large amount of "Portrait Figures," ranging from Tiglath Pileser IV – the King of Assyria – to George VI and Queen Elizabeth. Some of the pieces were as famous as Robin Hood, Napoleon, George Washington, Hitler and Mussolini, while others were such relative obscurities as Sir Nele Loring, Dunois and General Wartenberg.

On April 10, 1938, the Detroit Free Press's Rotogravure Magazine ran three photos of the James collection, one of which showed nine Britains boxes, and another which showed a figure being painted, presumably by one of the Jameses.

Oddly, James got the idea for his first figure about the same time that Historical Miniatures got under way, and there is a similarity to the sculpture. However, James' Churchill is shorter (about 2⅝" high), and has " © JAMES MINIATURES 1941" inscribed in the metal underneath the base. His other figures are also supposed to have been clearly marked with his name or initials.

JA1
Courtesy Bob James

MOLDED PRODUCTS

UPDATE: Since the last edition, a 1942-43 Christmas catalog has been found showing Molded Products soldiers. This is their only known catalog appearance, aside from undiscovered company catalogs. Since the art is different from anything else in the Butler Bros. pages, it's likely it's Molded Products' own catalog art. In addition a July 1942 *Playthings* shows a small illustration of a boxed set of Molded Products soldiers that were sold by Toy Creations. The caption mentions "flame throwers" but presumably is a mistake; none is known. The illustrated boxtop reads "American Soldiers Sailors", showing both, plus a marine.

Without a Mickey Mouse, there might never have been a Molded Products Inc.

During the Depression, Lionel Trains had helped bail itself out of near-bankruptcy by using extruding equipment to produce composition figures of Mickey for its wildly successful Mickey Mouse handcar.

By November 29, 1941, when Molded Products was incorporated, Leslie S. Steinau and his son, Leslie Jr., were hoping Lionel's old equipment would be just as effective in saving them from disaster.

The Steinaus owned a thriving advertising display business, but it was clear to them that approaching wartime shortages could quickly put them out of business, since there would be far fewer products needing their services. Consequently, when Lionel's old equipment became available to them, they snapped it up.

Without a Barclay Mfg. Co. there might not have been any Molded Products soldiers.

At the time, Leslie Jr.'s brother-in-law was the lacquer supplier to Barclay. He knew Barclay's salesman Irving Reader, and mentioned the purchase to him. Reader acted immediately.

Like the Steinaus, Reader sensed approaching problems. It was clear to him that the lead toy soldier business was doomed because of impending restrictions, and he quickly convinced the Steinaus to produce composition toy soldiers. They had the equipment; he had the dimestore contacts.

While in advertising, the Steinaus had employed a sculptor named Bill Zegel to produce display figures like Old Grand-Dad (for the liquor company). They now hired him to design their soldiers.

The company was successful from the first. "They grabbed everything we could send them!" Steinau Jr. recalls. It sold to all the five and tens except Penneys, which Steinau remembers objected to war toys of any kind. The factory was located at 203 East 12th Street in Manhattan, and employed about thirty people.

The soldiers (the company also made barnyard animals) were made from wood flour, starch, whiting and water. This material was kneaded in a dough mixture and then poured into the extruders, from which it emerged "like strips of baloney", and then went into molds under hydraulic pressure. The resultant soldiers were placed on nails (which were attached to strips of wood) to hold them upright – creating the distinctive holes that run through the center of the stand and into the crotch. They were then put in trays and dried by the warm air near the ceiling.

When the war ended, Irving Reader left, feeling there was no future in composition toys. However, the Steinaus were convinced otherwise by a toy distributor, who persuaded them to open a larger factory in Mamaroneck, New York. There, they produced pull-toys of Mother Goose, a duck family, and Easter rabbits.

"We just didn't know when to get out," Leslie Jr. recalled in later years. As Reader had feared, competitive materials gave them problems, and then a strike "broke our back." The company went into bankruptcy in 1945 or 1946.

But the legacy of Mickey Mouse had done its job; the Steinaus had survived the war. With shortages a thing of the past, they returned to the advertising display business, having made their contribution to the history of toy soldiers.

The descriptions in quotes are from the 1942-43 catalog, since general catalogs often (but not always) echoed the manufacturers' own designations.

	G	VG	M		G	VG	M
C1 "Cowboy"	3.00	4.50	6.00	C6 "Soldier with Gas Mask" and pistol, WWI helmet .	6.00	9.00	12.00
C2 "Indian"	3.00	4.50	6.00	C7 As above, with WWII helmet	5.00	8.00	10.00
C3 "Soldier with Parachute"	5.00	8.00	11.00				
C3a As above, larger, inside of chute painted white ..	6.00	9.00	13.00	C8 Soldier with machine gun, prone, pot helmet ..	5.00	7.00	9.00
C4 Aviator, "X" type front harness	6.00	9.00	12.00	C8a "Soldier with Machine Gun", prone, WWI helmet	6.00	9.00	12.00
C4a Aviator, square type front harness	6.00	9.00	12.00				
C5 Soldier with gas mask, tommy gun and grenade, pot helmet	4.50	6.75	9.00	C9 "Soldier with Anti-Aircraft Gun", WWI helmet	5.00	8.00	10.00

MOLDED PRODUCTS

	G	VG	M
C9a Soldier with anti-aircraft gun, WWII helmet	4.00	6.00	8.00
C10 "Sailor with White Uniform", large base, 3⅝" high	4.00	6.00	8.00
C11 "Marine", 3½" high, white, bent leg	7.00	11.00	14.00
C11A "Marine", blue, 3½" high, bent leg	5.00	8.00	11.00
C11a "Marine", 3¼" high, straight leg	7.50	11.00	15.00
C11b Marine, white, 3¼" high, straight leg	7.50	11.00	15.00
C12 "Flag Bearer", WWI helmet	5.00	8.00	10.00
C12A Flag Bearer, WWI helmet, bloused pants ...	6.00	9.00	12.00

	G	VG	M
C12a Flag Bearer, WWII helmet	6.00	9.00	12.00
C13 "Marching Soldier", WWI helmet	4.00	6.00	8.00
C13a Marching Soldier, WWII helmet	4.00	6.00	8.00
C13b Marching Soldier, WWII helmet, smaller ..	4.00	6.00	8.00
C14 Soldier on Horse, WWII helmet	12.00	18.00	24.00
C15 "Soldier on Horse", WWI helmet	13.00	19.00	26.00
C16 Horse	2.00	3.00	5.00
C17 Pig	2.00	3.00	5.00
C18 Cow	2.00	3.00	5.00
C19 Turkey	2.00	3.00	5.00
C20 Sheep	2.00	3.00	5.00

C1   C2   C3   C3a   C4   C4a   C5

C3b: All white except for face and blue goggles and gloves. No price found.
Photo by Stan Alekna

C6   C7   C8   C8a

Figures courtesy Clayton W. Nimtz, Tony Diksa, Ed Poole

C14   C15

C16   C17   C18

Courtesy Tony Diksa

MOLDED PRODUCTS

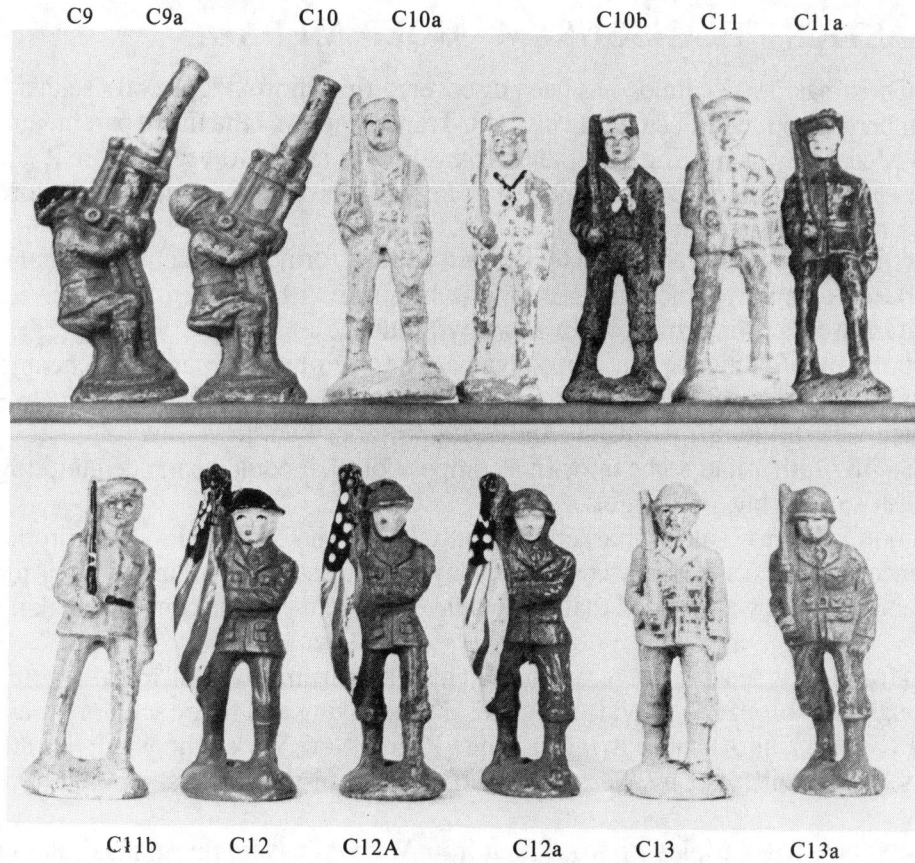

C9 C9a C10 C10a C10b C11 C11a

C11b C12 C12A C12a C13 C13a

C11 C11A

Photo courtesy Jim M. Morris

Photo by Jim M. Morris C13a C13b

C11 Paint variation (white cap). No Price found

Photo by Roy E. Bonjour

C20
Photo by Stan Alekna

Pressure-Molded Colorful Plastic Figures

Expertly molded wood plastic figures, formed under heavy pressure so that they are unusually durable. Splendid detail. Standing figures over 3¾ in. On oval base.

62-6463—Marching Soldier	
62-6464—Soldier With Anti-Aircraft Gun	
62-6465—Soldier With Machine Gun	
62-6466—Sailor With Blue Uniform	
62-6467—Sailor With White Uniform	2 Doz in Box
62-6468—Soldier With Parachute	
62-6469—Indian	60c
62-6440—Flag Bearer	Doz
62-6441—Soldier With Gas Mask	
62-6442—Marine	
62-6443—Cowboy	
62-6485—Soldier on Horse. 1 doz in box	Doz 83c

This Christmas 1942-43 Butler Bros. catalog is the only catalog that has been found with Molded Products figures. Aside from WWII-helmeted figures, the only one not shown or listed is the C4-C4a Aviator, suggesting it may have been produced later.

PLAYWOOD PLASTICS · TRANSOGRAM · GOLD MEDAL

UPDATE: Since the last edition a Christmas, 1942 catalog has been discovered that shows Playwood's soldiers. The company's Michael Weiss had remembered production beginning in 1943. Transogram was the firm's parent, and it's now known that via subsidiary Gold Medal, it was making toy soldier accessories at least two years before it got into toy soldier production. Several of its pieces appear in the December 9, 1940 *Life* magazine 2-page spread on dimestore soldiers. The accessories continued to be made during World War II.

In the spring or summer of 1942 Michael Weiss was approached by Reuben Roth, a former law school classmate. Weiss was with Transogram, a New York toy company which had been in business since 1915. When Roth arrived, with a client in tow, Weiss and Transogram were casting about for a new toy product.

A subsidiary of Transogram's, Anchor Toy of Coudersport, Pennsylvania, had been making papier mache and wood accessories to go with nativity scenes (barns, wells, campfires, nativity cribs, etc.), but the nativity figures themselves had been imported. With the war on, they were no longer available, and the accessories had little value.

Roth's client was a Mr. Smith, and Smith's father had come up with a composition that could be molded into toy soldiers. They owned a mold of an English soldier, but nothing else.

At the time, there was little competition in the toy soldier market, with only Beton and Molded Products prominent. The year before, Transogram had incorporated a subsidiary company, Playwood Plastics, intending to use it for something else; with the advent of Roth and Smith, it was decided that this would be the name of the company making its soldiers.

Weiss remembers scrambling around frantically, seeking out scrap metal. This was wartime, with all metal devoted to war purposes, but he finally found enough junk bronze to provide the molds. Moldmaking and figure sculpting were entrusted to Max Peinlich (pronounced PINE-lick), an Austrian living in White Plains, New York, who was in his 60s or 70s at the time. Weiss doesn't know where Peinlich got his ideas, but from the look of the soldiers, it could have been from his grandchildren's Manoils.

The composition of Playwood's soldiers consisted of triple zero wood flour from Wisconsin (very fine-grained, almost like talc), 20 Mule Team Borax, unbleached white flour (condemned by food inspectors who marked the inedible flour with chicken blood), and water. The flour and water provided the glue binder. The blend was churned in a high-speed dough mixer, and then extruded into bars 3" wide and about 1½" thick. These were cut into strips and fed through a hydraulic press which stamped out the soldiers, rather like cookies. The soldiers were then placed in wire trays and put into 8 foot high hot air bins, where they were cured. After their edges were buffed, they went into a centrifugal machine which coated them with khaki paint, and then onto a production line where the details were hand-painted. The soldiers were all marked with a P within a triangle, and numbered in a 400 series, but because of the crudeness of the material, not all the numbers are readable.

Although the selling office was located at 200 Fifth Avenue in Manhattan, the factory was at 133 Floyd Street, Brooklyn, formerly the home of Sklar surgical instruments. Originally Roth, Smith and Transogram went in on a 50-50 basis, but Roth and Smith had virtually no financing, and Transogram eventually took over completely, entering into an employment contract with Roth and Smith (Smith was later fired), with Weiss in full charge of production.

The company was successful while the War continued, employing 125 people. According to Weiss it never went beyond its original complement of soldiers because it was too busy meeting orders, and finding metal for the molds was so difficult. However, variations that have turned up in the figures suggest at least some additional mold-making was done.

Once the War ended, Playwood's days were numbered. There was less enthusiasm for soldiers among toy buyers, and also considerably more competition, in mediums more conducive to reproduction. The operation hung on for a while in the post-War days, making such items as composition fingers to be used with nail polish displays in cosmetics stores, but Transogram eventually closed it down.

Illustrated catalogs or order sheets were issued by the company. None has surfaced, but the art in that aforementioned 1942 catalog is different from anything else in the catalog, suggesting it could have come from Playwood's own order sheets. Descriptions of soldiers in quotes come from that catalog.

	G	VG	M		G	VG	M
401 "Parade Soldier With				to gun, helper's left knee			
Pack"	5.00	8.00	10.00	visible	9.00	13.00	18.00
402 "Flag Bearer"	5.00	8.00	10.00	404 "Stretcher Bearer"	7.00	11.00	14.00
403 "Machine Gun & 2				405 Later version of 405A,			
Gunners"	6.00	9.00	12.00	triangle base	9.00	13.00	18.00
403a As above, no mark-				405A "Anti-Aircraft Gun			
ings, gunner's head closer				and Gunner", plow base	9.00	13.00	18.00

PLAYWOOD PLASTICS

	G	VG	M
406 "Soldier with Gas Mask" holding Flare Gun	5.00	8.00	10.00
407? "Dispatch Rider on Cycle", oblong base, head down	7.00	11.00	14.00
407?a Round base, head higher, earlier version? ..	7.00	11.00	14.00
408 Later version of 408a? crossed legs	7.00	10.00	14.00
408a "Machine Gun and Gunner (in prone position)", legs spread	7.00	10.00	14.00
409 "Sniper with Tommy Gun"	7.00	11.00	14.00
410 "Anti-Tank gun & gunner", square shield, spoked wheels	5.00	8.00	10.00
410a Later version of 410?, more rounded shield, wheels not spoked	5.00	8.00	10.00
411 "Soldier with Overseas Cap"	5.00	8.00	11.00
412 "Paratrooper", pilot-type hat	7.00	11.00	14.00
412a As above, pot helmet .	7.50	11.00	15.00
413 "Machine Gun & Gunner"	4.00	6.00	9.00
414 Kneeling Firing	5.00	8.00	10.00
415 Advancing with Rifle .	22.00	33.00	44.00
438 or 436? Motorcyclist, Leather-type helmet (probably post-War)	No Price Found		

406 406a

Courtesy Charles Breslow

408   408a   409?

410   410a   411

Figures courtesy Clayton W. Nimtz

401   402   403   403a   404

405   405a   406   407?

Figures courtesy Clayton W. Nimtz and Tony Diksa

412   412a   413   414

Figures courtesy Clayton W. Nimtz and Tony Diksa

438 or 436? 407a?

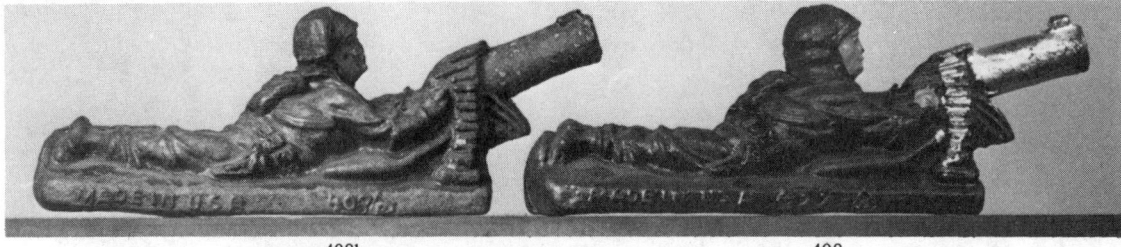

408b   408

Two versions of 408; one larger than the other. They seem to be mold variations, rather than variations due to shrinking or swelling. The projection under the gun barrel is the easiest way of distinguishing them from 408a.
Courtesy Charlie Breslow

415 Advancing with rifle

Courtesy K. Warren Mitchell

L to R: Gold Medal-Transogram Lookout Post and Sniper's Nest.
Courtesy John Schmidt

Playwood Plastics figures were susceptible to variations due to drying. Whether these four figures result from that process or are actual mold variations is unknown.
Photos courtesy Jim M. Morris

PLAYWOOD PLASTICS

Possible Playwood variations.
Photo by Jerry Combs

Possible Playwood variations.
Photo by Jerry Combs

Gold Medal-Transogram Artillery Emplacement, 7" x 6". Sold in
late 1990 in the above-shown condition for $40.
Courtesy K. Warren Mitchell

Gold Medal-Transogram Advance Sniper Post, 6" x 5½". This
was sold in late 1990 in the above condition for $28.
Courtesy K. Warren Mitchell

Gold Medal-Transogram Field Kitchen, 6" x 5½". This came with
table and two benches fixed in place plus open hearth with stove
pipe in corner. Sold in late 1990 in above condition (without the
Barclay soldiers shown) for $62.50
Courtesy K. Warren Mitchell

Gold Medal-Transogram Camouflage Airplane Shelter? 10" x 9".
Sold in late 1990 in above condition (without shown Barclay soldier)
for $36.50.
Courtesy K. Warren Mitchell

eal Gifts For The Little Fellow

"PLAYWOOD" PLASTIC

New . . . Fine Detail . . . Excellent Colors! Over 3 inches high with large substantial bases. One of the best lines of toy soldiers we have ever offered. Made of compressed wood-flour used for making doll heads.

od Profit For You!

this price up yo u e choice of o popular tres Fine details colors. 2 doz in

75¢ Dozen

421—Flag Bearer
431—Para-
oper. . . . . Doz 75c

Choice of 3 Soldier Figures

Cash-in on the big demand for toy soldiers. 2 doz in box.

62-6427—Machine Gun and Gunner (in prone position at top).
62-6432—Machine Gun and Gunner.
62-6424—Anti-Aircraft Gun and Gunner . . . . Doz 92c

92¢ Dozen

Choice of 3 Popular Figures

More detail and better subjects in this price group. Each item packed 2 doz in a box.

62-6422—Machine gun & 2 gunners.
62-6429—Anti-Tank gun & gunner.
62-6426—Dispatch Rider on cycle . . . . Doz 96c

96¢ Dozen

Low Priced Volume Group

This brand new line just added to this catalog will be one of your best sellers. Plan to feature these now. 2 doz in box.

62-6423—Stretcher Bearer . . . .
62-6425—Soldier With Gas Mask . . . . . .
62-6428—Sniper With Tommy Gun . . . .
62-6430—Soldier with Overseas Cap . . . .
62-6420—Parade Soldier with Pack . . . .

72c Doz

72¢ Dozen

The only known Playwood Plastic catalog appearance is in the one put out for Christmas 1942-43 by Butler Bros. Since the art shown here is different from anything else in that catalog, this could have been taken from Playwood's own catalog or order sheet. The only numbers not shown here are 414, 415 and 436 or 438, suggesting they were produced later. Note the Soldier with gas mask and flare gun, with his arm down, rather than raised. If any were produced in this variation, none is known.

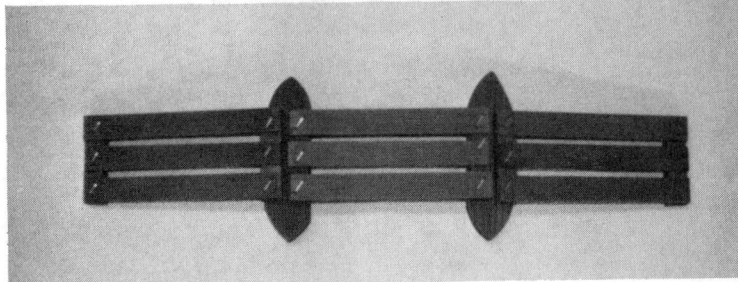

Gold Medal-Transogram Pontoon Bridge. This can be easily assembled and diassembled. No Price Found
Courtesy Charlie O'Brien
Photo by Kathy Paul

Gold Medal-Transogram Barbed Wire for dimestore soldiers. No Price Found.
Photo by John R. Kurinsky

Gold Medal-Transogram Campfire, 3½" x 2½". Sold in late 1990 in above condition for $29.50.
Courtesy K. Warren Mitchell

EMPIRE FORCES – UNITED NATIONS FORCES

Empire Forces' soldiers seem to have been made by the same company which manufactured United Nations Forces: Gardel Industries of 106 East 19th Street, New York City (later, 179 Wooster Street). The owner appears to have been F. Gardelle.

The Empire Forces soldiers came in both wood composition and plaster, and the machine gunners, both seated and prone, are copies of Manoils. United Nations Forces are plaster, to be painted by the buyer, and their prone machine gunner is also the same Manoil copy.

From at least April, 1943, through March, 1944, United Nations Forces was advertised in *Playthings Magazine*. Empire Forces (with United Nations Forces) appears in a Christmas, 1944 *Billy and Ruth* catalog. The plaster United Nations soldiers included "infantry, paratrooper, airman, RAF", a sailor, the prone gunner and a tank.

The Empire Forces pieces are painted medium green with occasional spots of dark green for camouflage effect. Straw, covered with thin paper, acts as a buffer between the top of the box and the figures. All but the machine gunners appear to be original designs. Gardel also sold a similar "Kiddie's Circus".

No current prices have been found on either the boxes or the original figures.

Empire Forces

E1 Seated Machine Gunner
E2 Prone Machine Gunner
E3 Prone Machine Gunner, smaller
E4 Paratrooper, 4" high
E5 Tank
E6 Tank, smaller

No. 125 Machine Gunner Set - contains 6 prone machine gunners, 1 seated machine gunner, two tanks of different size.

Paratrooper Set (no number found) - contains 2 prone machine gunners, 1 seated machine gunner, 2 different-sized tanks, 4 paratroopers

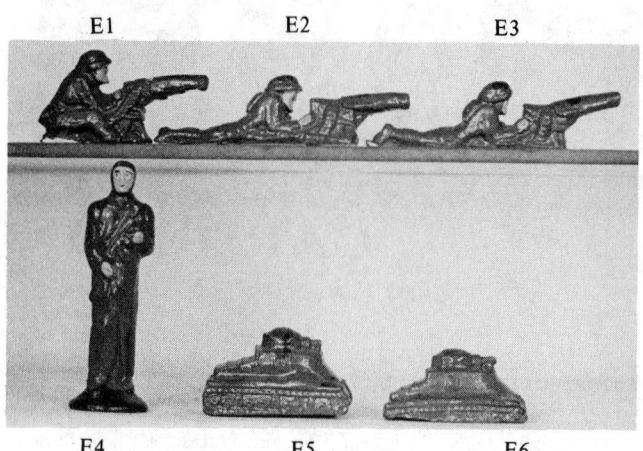

Figures courtesy Jim M. Morris

The contents of "Empire Forces" **No. 125 Machine Gunner Set.**
Courtesy K. Warren Mitchell

The top of an "Empire Forces" box.
Courtesy K. Warren Mitchell

UNITED NATIONS FORCES

UN1 **Infantry**
UN2 **Paratrooper**
UN3 **Airman**
UN4 **Machine Gunner** (prone)
UN5 **RAF**
UN6 Sailor
UN7 Highlander
UN8 Grenadier Guard
UN9 Tank

There were number 50, 100 and 200 United Nations Forces sets. The No. 100 contained 8 soldiers, one tank, pallete with 6 water colors, brush. The suggested retail price in a September, 1943 ad was $1.19

A September, 1943 ad in *Playthings*. Notice the similarity of some of the United Nations Forces soldiers to those in the Empire Forces sets.

MILLER

Most collectors who lived through World War II and the Korean War are surprised to hear that there were shortages during the latter conflict. In World War II they were evident on almost a daily basis; in the time of the Korean police action, the only noticeable difference in routine was that there was a section of the front page that one passed up every day (one disgruntled editor even ran the same Korean War report for several days in a row; only one reader gave evidence of noticing).

But the restrictions on lead during that period must have been very noticeable to John H. Miller, or at least to the buyers for dimestores, who may have urged him to begin producing toy soldiers to help keep their toycases filled. Consequently, plaster soldiers marked "Miller" 1950" and "Miller 1951", selling at 19¢ apiece began turning up at five and and dimes across the country. The following history of Miller is based on information furnished by Gary Moritz to collector-author Don Pielin.

The J.H. Miller Company got its start in Chicago, in 1938. Miller worked for a company that used latex rubber, and got the idea it could be used for casting molds. When his employer expressed no interest, Miller decided to experiment at home, where he created molds for a nativity scene. With his wife Shirley's help, Miller began selling them locally, and in three months, the couple produced and painted over 1500 pieces in their cellar. This early success prompted Miller to rent a 10x30 foot storeroom in early 1939 for $18 a month.

Until Miller came on the scene, all nativity sets were imported, mainly from Germany and Japan. The imported figures were only available in sets, and thus the easily chipped and broken figures could only be replaced by buying another complete set. This gave Miller an edge, as he sold all his figures individually, wholesaling them two dozen in a box.

The burgeoning success of his company prompted five moves within the next two years, each time to a larger location. With the outbreak of the War, Miller found himself with a monopoly. He wanted to move to a small town where he and his family could enjoy an outdoor life, and now he could afford it. An old family friend, W. W. Bower, convinced Miller that Quincy, Illinois was the place to settle home and firm.

In February, 1943 J.H. Miller Company was ensconced at 225 Hampshire Street in Quincy. One hundred ten people were employed, only four of them men.

MILLER

The figures were made by mixing two tons of plaster and water at one time, which was then poured into the firm's latex molds, which were kept on the building's third floor, where it was warmer. It would take 15 minutes for a figure to harden in the mold, after which it was removed, and the mold refilled. The castings were then sorted by type and moved to a drying room, where they remained overnight. The next day they were dipped in a basic color and then sent down a conveyor belt where girls and women painted in details. Quality control was strict, and any missing details were remedied before packing. Production varied from 400 to 2000 figures per day, depending on size and paint-detailing. 90,000 went out a week during the height of the pre-Christmas season.

In the early 1950s employment doubled as the soldier line was added. The soldiers were nicely modeled, though in a five-inch size that was far out of scale with the usual dimestore soldiers. Because they chipped and broke so easily, they must have proved disappointing as playthings, and this may be why no Millers of this type have turned up with a date later than 1951.

But in July, 1958, Miller was producing soldiers of various countries, as well as nativity scenes in two sizes, a line of dinosaurs (10,000 a week went out), Santas, animals and a "Purple People Eater" based on a novelty tune of the period. Around this time Miller, with the aid of H. H. Hanlon of Kenilworth, Illinois, who was a financial backer, partner and salesman, decided to produce a bust of Fidel Castro and sell it in American chain stores in Cuba. Since it sold for $1.98, a large amount for virtually all the Cubans who hadn't escaped, it proved a disaster. This may have led to the July 1959 bankruptcy of the company, although foreign competition in plastic was probably the underlying factor.

Miller's soldiers came with bronze-colored plastic weapons, which are frequently missing when the pieces turn up.

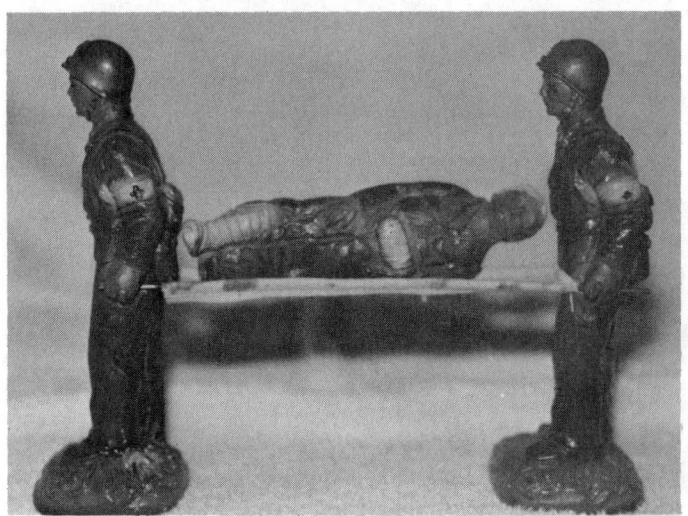

ML1   ML2   ML1
Photo by James Furstman, Jr.

ML6   ML7   ML8
Photo by James Furstman, Jr.

ML3   ML4   ML5
Photo by James Furstman, Jr.

ML8   ML11   ML14

ML15   ML13   ML16   ML6
Photo by Don Pielin.

ML18
Courtesy Charles Breslow

ML19

ML9   ML10   ML11
Photo by James Furstman, Jr.

ML12   ML13   ML14
Photo by James Furstman, Jr.

ML16   ML17   ML19   ML20
Photo by James Furstman, Jr.

MILLER

	G	VG	M		G	VG	M
(ML 1) Stretcherbearer.....	6.00	9.00	13.00	(ML 13) Soldier advancing with rifle (possibly also with tommy gun)......	7.00	11.00	15.00
(ML 2) Wounded man on separate cloth and wire stretcher	15.00	22.00	30.00	(ML 14) Soldier throwing Grenade..............	7.00	11.00	15.00
(ML 3) Nurse with Plasma.	18.00	27.00	36.00				
(ML 4) General MacArthur.	20.00	30.00	40.00	(ML 15) Soldier charging with Machine Gun......	No Price Found		
(ML 5) Officer with Binoculars............	9.00	13.00	18.00	(ML 16) Soldier planting flag	9.00	13.00	15.00
(ML 6) Soldier Kneeling with Sentry Dog........	No Price Found			(ML 17) Soldier marching with rifle.............	9.00	13.00	15.00
(ML 7) Soldier Kneeling with Flame-Thrower....	32.50	48.75	65.00	(ML 18) Kneeling with Bazooka.............	10.00	15.00	20.00
(ML 8) Soldier Kneeling with Walkie-Talkie	10.00	15.00	20.00	(ML 19) Kneeling with sub-machine gun	No Price Found		
(ML 9) Soldier Prone with Bazooka	7.00	11.00	14.00	(ML 20) Standing on Guard with rifle	No Price Found		
(ML 10) Soldier Prone with Rifle	8.00	12.00	17.00				
(ML 11) Soldier in Foxhole Firing Rifle............	8.00	12.00	16.00				
(ML 12) Soldier Walking with Flag.............	9.00	13.00	18.00				

Miller nativity figures. These aren't marked but have a typical Miller paper tab protrusion. Some nativity figures have been found marked " © Miller '47". Animals about $4 mint , figures about $10 mint.
Photo by Roy E. Bonjour

Miller nativity figure. Value about $14 mint.
Photo by Roy E. Bonjour

Miller plaster Easter Rabbits, value $35 each in mint. Miller also made Halloween witches, pumpkins and a No. 903 Witch (the boxed set for the latter is dated Sept. 17 1948)
Photo by Stan Alekna

SLIK-TOY

Slik-Toys first surfaced when collector Jim M. Morris found some in 1984. A year later another collector, John R. Kurinsky, was able to track down their history. He interviewed John Brophy, the company's former president, and Robert Kester, its past production manager.

Slik-Toys were manufactured by the Lansing Co., Inc. of Lansing, Iowa. The firm had started in business as a button manufacturer. It was located on the Mississippi River in Northeast Iowa. Clam shells from the river were stamped into buttons and sold nationwide. In 1940, deciding to diversify, the company began to manufacture steel and aluminum farm toys (tractors, graders, wagons, etc.)

World War II curbed the company's toy production significantly, but after the war Lansing resumed full production and eventually added a line of plastic toy cars. Then in 1950, when the Korean War began, a decision was made to begin manufacturing soldiers.

Eugene Silverburg, a nephew of one of the company's executives, designed and carved six figures in early 1951. Because of the wartime scarcity of metal, flexible synthetic rubber-latex type mold forms were made, and a plaster-like material (U.S. Gypsum Industrial Hydrocal white gypsum cement) employed. Production began in mid to late 1951.

At the height of production eighteen women turned out hundreds of figures daily. After molding the soldiers were air-brushed in shades of green, yellow, brown earth tones and flesh. They were advertised as "steel reinforced" and the No. 9310 Walkie Talkie had a metal antenna. All have "Slik-Toy (T)" cut into the base. They were wholesaled at $1.25 a dozen in 1951, and retailed at twenty-nine cents each in five and tens across the country.

Slik-Toy soldiers are attractively sculpted, contain considerable detail, and are quite dramatic in appearance. They are large-sized, with the tallest soldiers standing five inches high. Most have their numbers and descriptions cut into the base. Prices presumably would be comparable to Miller, but in a somewhat higher range, due to the fact that they are both attractive and considerably more scarce.

Lansing also produced a smaller series of soldiers under the Slikite name. These were described as the No. 9203 Fighting Men set, which consisted of four 2½" to 3¼" figures. They wholesaled at nine dollars per set.

The Lansing Co. ended all toy production in 1956.

ST1 - **No. 9305 Flame Thrower**
ST2 - **No. 9306 Grenade Thrower**
ST3 - **No. 9307 Machine Gunner**
ST4 - **No. 9308 Recoilless Rifle**
ST4a - **No. 9309 Mortar man**
ST5 - **No. 9310 Walkie Talkie**
ST6 - Slikite Port Arms
ST7 - Slikite Marching, slung rifle
ST8 - Slikite Bazooka Man
ST9 - Slikite Crouching with gun

ST1   ST2   ST3

ST4   ST5

Figures courtesy Jim M. Morris

ST4a

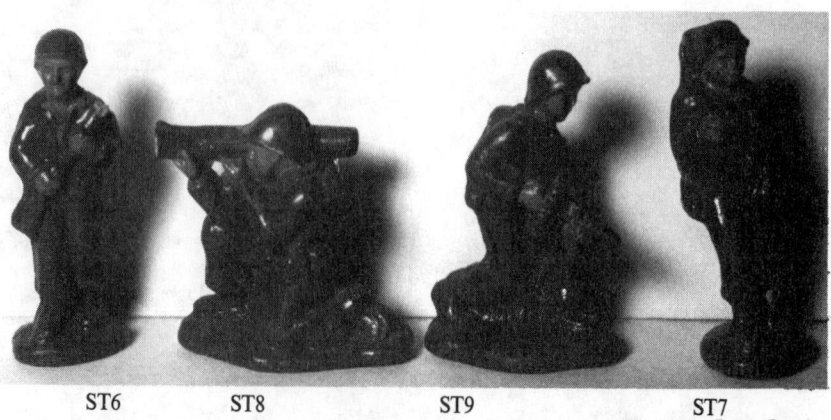

ST6   ST8   ST9   ST7

Photo by Jerry Combs

225

BETON

UPDATE: Beton's original name may have been Marcak Toy & Novelty Co. A 1938 Metal Cast catalog prints a testimonial from that firm. Since Metal Cast's testimonial letters ran for years, it could be that this letter was written before 1935. The letter reads as follows:

> "Please enter our order for the following: 10,000 American
> Infantry; 2000 American Officer; 2000 American Flag;
> 10,000 Indians; 10,000 Cowboys; 5000 Big Chief; 5000
> Broncho Bill; 5000 Cavalry. We would appreciate your rushing
> this order as fast as you can as we are very much in need
> of it. Marcak Toy & Novelty Co."

Soldiers with the usual Beton markings have been found in soft plastic (most Betons are hard plastic). The earliest base is the glue-on oval. The next is the glue-on rectangular. The earliest documented date for these is 1942. However, very rare flesh-colored Indians have been found, all with rectangular bases. The author still owns a flesh-colored Indian (minus its base) which he received in 1940, and his memory has always been that the base was rectangular.

Variations have been found by collector Ron Steiner in the galloping horse (among them, double reins and a sword on one; single rein and no sword on the other) and the bucking boncho (among them thin and thick pommels; flying mane and longer mane lying on the body, a lasso near the pommel and no lasso).

It was competition from plastic that put the lead toy soldier companies out of business. In 1938 Bergen Toy & Novelty Co. (better known as Beton) became, according to a newspaper account, "the first to begin acetate plastic figurine toy manufacture". Ironically, when Beton went out of business, it was because of competition from plastic.

Bergen Toy & Novelty Co. was established at least as early as 1935 under the ownership of Charles Marcak (pronounced MAR-sak). At that time it manufactured lead toy soldiers, using molds purchased from another toy soldier company, Metal Cast. The firm was located at 417 Third Street in Carlstadt, New Jersey, but William Nussbaum, the son of the outfit's accountant, remembers working in a corner of a shop in East Rutherford, New Jersey, when, in the summer of 1935 he got his first job, with Bergen Toy.

As one of the company's two casters, he turned out slush lead soldiers, cowboys and Indians. The figures were then transferred to the Carlstadt address, where approximately ten workers trimmed, painted and packed the figures.

Beton issued its first known catalog in 1938, the year it moved into plastics. Unfortunately, none of its figures were illustrated, and its descriptions were general, listing only, non-specifically, "Infantry, Cadet, Indians, Cowboys" and mounted "U.S. Cavalry, U.S. Cadet, Big Chief, Broncho Bill". The latter two descriptions were also employed by Metal Cast, from whom Beton copied several of its early figures. A 1938 business directory lists the employees as one male, eight females. That was also the year that the company was first known as Beton. The name was simply a contraction of the longer appellation (which continued to be used as well) and was pronounced BEE-ton.

When Beton turned to plastic, it stopped doing its own casting, which it farmed out to another Carlstadt firm, Columbia Protektosite, which spent most of its time manufacturing sunglasses. Once cast, the soldiers were transported to 9 Rose Street in Wood Ridge, New Jersey, where workers finished, painted and packed them. By 1940, the firm had about twenty employees.

In Wood Ridge from August, 1938 through 1940 or 1941, the firm was listed again in May, 1942 at Carlstadt, although Beton is known to have moved to Rutherford in early 1942. Perhaps, as in its early days, it worked out of two locations.

The coming of World War II was the making of the company. From April, 1942 through the late fall of 1945 its only real competition came from two firms which manufactured composition soldiers; Molded Products and Playwood Plastics.

If Beton had produced all its figures in the three-inch scale that its early Indians came in, it might have had no competition at all, as Beton's product was far superior in design and detail. But its soldiers were about a half inch shorter than their lead brothers. This put them enough out of scale when grouped with Barclays, etc., to make them vaguely unsatisfactory, and prompted occasional defections to the composition soldiers, which, though clumsy and unattractive (and total disasters when sufficiently moistened by rain or bathwater), were at least the right size. In 1940-41 Beton was listed as having just two male and five female employees. At the height of the War in 1943, "Orders exceeded manufacturing possibilities for the year". (In a 1946-47 directory, with the figures from 1945, Beton, at 49 Meadow Road, Rutherford, lists six male and seventy-five female workers).

BETON

Anyone seeing the rows upon rows of Betons in five and tens during the War years would have assumed the manufacturer had money coming out of his ears. Barclay's and Manoil's owners had become wealthy from toy soldier-making, but Marcak, according to those who knew him, was at best middle class. Perhaps it was because Beton didn't do its own manufacturing or distribution. It may also be because, unlike Barclay and Manoil, the company didn't diversify into vehicles and airplanes.

In a contemporary account, Harold Frutchey, who was Beton's general manager from January 1951 through September 1957, explained, "the firm follows the example of English manufacturers in concentrating its production on figures rather than expanding to other varieties of plastic toys." Thus, for all of its existence, Bergen made only people and animals. (Although there is no evidence to support this, my memory is that shortly before World War II ended, Beton began producing its soldiers in World War II helmets, perhaps easing of wartime restrictions allowing it to create new molds.)

On March 11, 1944, Marcak and his wife Elsie bought a small stone home in Hackettstown, New Jersey, where he hoped to do "a little farming" on the five or six acres of land that came with the house. On July 23, 1946, Beton moved from Rutherford to a one-story building "little bigger than a diner" on Stiger Street in Hackettstown, where the city hall now stands.

There, perhaps for the first time, Beton did its own plastics casting. It employed no more than 20-25 workers, running two eight-hour shifts a day. No workers were added during the busy season; overtime sufficed.

The company issued catalogs every year, according to Frutchey, and in 1952 it had ten national sales representatives, and shipped 500,000 figures a week. 1952 was also the year it added its circus line.

The plastic it used in 1940 was Tenite, produced by Tennessee Eastman Corp., Kingsport, Tennessee. An account of the 1950s describes the casting process as follows, "...the material from which the toys are made is an acetate substance in the form of chips resembling the colored stones used in goldfish bowls. As much as 50 pounds of the material may be dumped into the hoppers of the moulding machines. The acetate material enters a heating chamber where it is converted into liquid form by four 400-degree heating units and is then forced into the channels of the solid steel molds which weigh from 400-1000 pounds...For most of the toys, the actual moulding process takes about 25 to 30 seconds, after which the mould opens automatically, the jointed figures are removed and immediately immersed in water to retain their shape and then separated from the stem."

Beton sold its figures painted and unpainted, probably from the start (I bought both types in 1940). Nussbaum remembers that finding a paint that would adhere gave the firm many problems, with DuPont probably the company that provided the solution. According to Nussbaum, one of the reasons some of the figures were painted was because every scrap of plastic, both from the trimming and the mold gates, was reground and recast, with some of the figures thus emerging in a varicolored state that necessitated a cover-up. For a time in the 1950s, the company also sold electroplated figures, at higher prices.

It's not known who Beton's sculptor was, although evidence points to a Carl Holsthammer as the company's designer in its Hackettstown days. Frutchey does remember that the sculptor at that time was a man from New York who'd been born around 1900. He would be paid from $200 to $1000 per sculpture, depending on its size, and seems to have done a lot of his work from life, studying animals in the field. The moldmaker was R.A. Koegel of Newark, New Jersey.

Frutchey recalls that Charles Marcak, who was born around 1896, died about 1960, and that Beton "almost certainly" closed in 1958 after Marcak attended the New York Toy Fair at the McAlpin Hotel in March to take orders for Christmas sales. The Japanese had been "copying his toys" and selling them at a much lower price. When Marcak saw the Japanese product displayed at the show, utilizing the material he'd introduced twenty years before, he realized there was no way he could match their prices. Shortly thereafter, he sold out to Rel Plastics of East Paterson, New Jersey.

BETON (The following illustrations are from Beton's own catalogs and order sheets).

BT1 No. 501
Machine Gunner

BT2 No. 502
Infantryman charging

BT3 No. 503
Hand Grenade Thrower

BT4 No. 504
Munitions Carrier

BT5 No. 505
Infantryman with gas mask

BT6 No. 506
Machine Gunner
in prone shooting position

BT8 No. 508
Bugler

BT11 No. 511
Infantryman with field
glasses

BT7 No. 507
Signaller

BT9 No. 509
Rifleman, shooting position

BT10 No. 510
Rifleman, marching position

BT12 No. 512
Rifleman, marching position

BT14 No. 514
Signaller

BT16 No. 516
Drummer

BT13 No. 513
Infantryman, saluting

BT15 No. 515 Infan-
tryman, charging

BT17 No. 517
Machine Gunner, kneeling

228

BT19 No. 727
Indian with Arrow

BT18 No. 726
Indian Leader

BT20 No. 728
Indian with Spear

BT21 No. 729
Indian Chief

BT22 No. 730
Indian Warrior

BT23 No. 731
Indian with Drawn Bow

BT24 No. 830
Masked Bandit

BT25 No. 831
Cowboy with Lasso

BT26 No. 832
Highwayman

BT27 No. 833
Cowboy, Hand on Holster

BT28 No. 620

BT29 No. 621

BT30 No. 622

BT31 No. 625

BT32 No. 901
Fireman

BT33 No. 907
Traffic Officer

BT34 No. 908
Patrolman

BETON

BT35 No. 950
Shoe Shine Boy

BT36 No. 951
Engineer

BT37 No. 952
Conductor

BT38 No. 953
Porter

BT39 No. 954
Red Cap

BT40 No. 955
Salesman

BT41 No. 956
Business Man

BT42 No. 957
Secretary

BT43 No. 58
Debutante

BT44 No. 959
Matron

BT45 No. 960
School Girl

BT46 No. 961
School Boy

BT47 No. 962
Newsboy

BT48 No. M400
U.S. Cavalry mounted on
trotting horse

BETON

BT49 No. M405
U.S. Cadet mounted on
trotting horse, asst. colors

BT50 No. M411
Indian, mounted on Bronco

BT51 No. M412
Cowboy
mounted on Bronco

BT52 No. M413
Road Agent
mounted on Bronco

BT53 No. M416
U.S. Cavalry Officer,
mounted on trotting horse

BT54 No. M417
Royal Mounted, mounted
on trotting horse

BT55 No. M418
Traffic Officer
mounted on trotting horse

PRE-1945	G	VG	M
(BT1) **501 Machine Gunner** .	2.00	3.00	5.00
(BT2) **502 Infantry man, charging,** with bayonet . . .	2.00	3.00	5.00
(BT3) **503 Hand Grenade Thrower**	2.00	3.00	5.00
(BT4) **504 Munitions Carrier**	2.00	3.00	5.00
(BT5) **505 Infantryman with gas mask**	2.00	3.00	5.00
(BT6) **506 Machine Gunner in prone shooting position**	2.00	3.00	5.00
(BT7) **507 Signaller,** left hand down	2.00	3.00	5.00
(BT8) **508 Bugler**	2.00	3.00	5.00
(BT9) **509 Rifleman, shooting position**	2.00	3.00	5.00
(BT10) **510 Rifleman marching position**	2.00	3.00	5.00
(BT11) **511 Infantryman with field glasses**	2.00	3.00	5.00
(BT12) **512 Rifleman, marching position** (somewhat heavier than 510)	2.00	3.00	5.00
(BT13) **513 Infantryman, saluting**	2.00	3.00	5.00

	G	VG	M
(BT14) **514 Signaller,** left hand across body	2.00	3.00	5.00
(BT15) **515 Infantryman, charging,** no bayonet	2.00	3.00	5.00
(BT16) **516 Drummer**	2.00	3.00	5.00
(BT17) **517 Machine Gunner, kneeling**	2.00	3.00	5.00
(BT18) **726 Indian Leader,** tomahawk away from head	2.00	3.00	5.00
(BT19) **727 Indian With Arrow,** carrying bow	2.00	3.00	5.00
(BT20) **728 Indian With Spear,** mohawk haircut . .	2.00	3.00	5.00
(BT21) **729 Indian Chief** with spear and headdress .	2.00	3.00	5.00
(BT22) **730 Indian Warrior,** hatchet touching head . . .	2.00	3.00	5.00
(BT23) **731 Indian With Drawn Bow**	2.00	3.00	5.00
(BT24) **830 Masked Bandit,** left hand pointing rearward	2.00	3.00	5.00
(BT25) **831 Cowboy With Lasso**	2.00	3.00	5.00

BETON	G	VG	M
(BT26) **832 Highwayman**, pointing pistol, left hand on hip..............	2.00	3.00	5.00
(BT27) **833 Cowboy, Hand On Holster**...........	2.00	3.00	5.00
(BT28) **620 Cadet**, red coat, white pants...........	2.00	3.00	5.00
(BT29) **621 Cadet**, all grey coat and pants........	2.00	3.00	5.00
(BT30) **622 Cadet** all blue coat and pants........	2.00	3.00	5.00
(BT31) **625 Cadet** blue coat, white pants...........	2.00	3.00	5.00
(BT32) **901 Fireman**.........	2.00	3.00	5.00
(BT33) **907 Traffic Officer**, hand raised............	2.00	3.00	5.00
(BT34) **908 Patrolman**, walking his beat............	2.00	3.00	5.00
(BT35) **950 Shoe Shine Boy**.	2.00	3.00	5.00
(BT36) **951 Engineer**......	2.00	3.00	5.00
(BT37) **952 Conductor**.....	2.00	3.00	5.00
(BT38) **953 Pullman Porter**.	2.00	3.00	5.00
(BT39) **954 Red Cap**.......	2.00	3.00	5.00
(BT40) **955 Salesman**, coat over arm............	2.00	3.00	5.00
(BT41) **956 Business Man**..	2.00	3.00	5.00
(BT42) **957 Secretary**, case in right hand..........	2.00	3.00	5.00
(BT43) **958 Debutante** in coat, purse in left hand ..	2.00	3.00	5.00
(BT44) **959 Matron** in coat, purse dangling from right hand	2.00	3.00	5.00
(BT45) **960 School Girl**....	2.00	3.00	5.00
(BT46) **961 School Boy**....	2.00	3.00	5.00
(BT47) **962 Newsboy**......	2.00	3.00	5.00
(BT48) **M400 U.S. Cavalry**, mounted on trotting horse, steel helmet......	3.00	5.00	7.00
(BT49) **M405 U.S. Cadet** mounted on trotting horse, assorted colors....	3.00	5.00	7.00
(BT50) **M411 Indian**, mounted on Broncho, with bow.............	3.00	5.00	7.00
(BT51) **M412 Cowboy** mounted on Broncho, with lasso............	3.00	5.00	7.00
(BT52) **M413 Road Agent** mounted on Broncho, with pistol...............	3.00	5.00	7.00
(BT53) **M416 U.S. Cavalry Officer**, mounted on trotting horse, peaked cap...	3.00	5.00	7.00

	G	VG	M
(BT54) **M417 Royal Mounted** mounted on trotting horse............	3.00	5.00	7.00
(BT55) **M418 Traffic Officer** mounted on trotting horse	3.00	5.00	7.00
Post-War Betons, with Copyright Dates (some pieces were in production long before these dates)			
(BT56) **52 Baby Goat**, September 1, 1949......	2.00	3.00	4.00
(BT57) **Bear**, January 2, 1952	2.00	3.00	4.00
(BT58) **2000 Broncho**, bucking..............	2.00	3.00	4.00
(BT59) **Buffalo**, June 5, 1952	2.00	3.00	4.00
(BT60) **508 Bugler**, WW II helmet, October 1, 1949..	2.00	3.00	5.00
(BT61) **10 Bull**, September 1, 1949................	2.00	3.00	4.00
(BT62) **620 Cadet, White**...	2.00	3.00	5.00
(BT63) **621 Cadet, Grey**....	2.00	3.00	5.00
(BT64) **622 Cadet, Blue**....	2.00	3.00	5.00
(BT65) **623 Cadet, Red-and-White**	2.00	3.00	5.00
(BT66) **624 Cadet, Grey-and-White**	2.00	3.00	5.00
(BT67) **625 Cadet, Blue-and-White**	2.00	3.00	5.00
(BT68) **M453 Cadet** on running horse............	3.00	5.00	7.00
(BT69) **13 Calf**, September 1, 1949	2.00	3.00	4.00
(BT70) **Camel**, January 2, 1952	2.00	3.00	4.00
(BT71) **42 Chick**..........	2.00	3.00	4.00
(BT72) **41 Chicken**, September 1, 1949......	2.00	3.00	4.00
(BT73) **Clown**, February 25, 1952 (See BT169)	2.00	3.00	5.00
(BT74) **1003 Colt**.........	2.00	3.00	4.00
(BT75) **Combat** Infantryman, January 15, 1952, holding rifle, butt upward.......	2.00	3.00	5.00
(BT76) **11 Cow**, standing...	2.00	3.00	4.00
(BT77) **12 Cow**, running, July 1, 1949............	2.00	3.00	4.00
(BT78) **M401 Cowboy** on broncho, waving hat.....	3.00	5.00	7.00
(BT79) **M454 Cowboy** on running horse, with lasso.	3.00	5.00	7.00
(BT80) **M412 Cowboy** on broncho, with lasso......	3.00	5.00	7.00
(BT81) **M4027 Cowboy** Rider with hat in hand, May 1, 1950..........	3.00	5.00	7.00

BETON

BT56 No. 52
Baby Goat

BT57

BT58 No. 2000
Bronco

BT59
Buffalo

BT60
Bugler

BT61
Bull

BT62 No. 620
White

BT63 No. 621
Gray

BT64 No. 622
Blue

BT65 No. 623
Red and White

BT66 No. 624
Gray and White

BT67 No. 625
Blue and White

No. 68 No. M453
Cadet on running horse

BT69 No. 13
Calf

233

BETON

BT70
Camel

BT71 No. 42
Chick

BT72 No. 41
Chicken

BT74
Colt

BT75
Combat

BT76
Standing Cow

BT77
Running Cow

BT78 No. M401
Cowboy on Bronco,
waving hat

BT79 No. M454
Cowboy on running horse,
with lasso

BT80 No. M412
Cowboy on bronco with
lasso

BT81
Cowboy w/hat

BT82
Alligator

BT86 No. 72
Duck

BT84
Dancing Girl

BT84
Z-5 Dancing Girl

BT85
Drummer

BT87 No. 73
Duckling

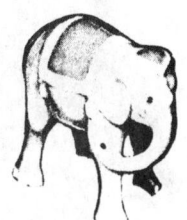

BT88
Elephant

234

BETON

BT89 No. 22
Farm Boy

BT90 No. 23
Farm Girl

BT91 No. 20
Farmer

BT92 No. 21
Farmerette

BT93
Gentleman Rider

BT94
Giraffe

BT95 No. 50
Goat, male

BT96 No. 51
Goat, female

BT97 No. 70
Goose

BT98 No. 71
Gosling

BT99
Hand Grenade Thrower

BT100
Hippopotamus

BT101′ No. M452t
Indian with tomahawk on
running horse

BT102 No. M452b
Indian with bow on
running horse

BT103 No. M452s
Indian with spear on
running horse

BT104
Indian with flag

BETON

BT105
Indian with lasso

BT106
Marching w/Flag

BT107
Paratrooper

BT108
Walkie-Talkie

BT109
Flame Thrower

BT110
Infantry Charging

BT111
Infantry w/Bayonet
Charging

BT112
Bazooka

BT113
Infantry Saluting

BT114
Gas Mask and Automatic

BT115
Observer

BT116
Infantry w/Gas Mask

BT117
Kangaroo

BT118
Machine Gunner Kneeling

BT119 No. 62
Lamb

BT120
Running Horse

BT122
Lion

BT123
Machine Gunner Standing

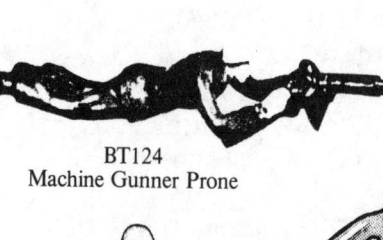

BT124
Machine Gunner Prone

BT128 No. 31
Pig

BT125
Moose

BT127
Panther

BT126
Munitions Carrier

BT129
Polo Player

BT131 No. 60
Ram

BT132
Reindeer

236

BETON

	G	VG	M
(BT82) Crocodile, April 15, 1952	2.00	3.00	4.00
(BT83) Dancer, Standing on one foot, May 2, 1955 (pg. 242)	2.00	3.00	5.00
(BT84) **Z-5 Dancing Girl,** January 15, 1952	2.00	3.00	5.00
(BT85) **516 Drummer,** WW II helmet, October 1, 1949	2.00	3.00	5.00
(BT86) **72 Duck,** September 1, 1949	2.00	3.00	4.00
(BT87) **73 Duckling**	2.00	3.00	4.00
(BT88) **Z-2 Elephant,** February 1, 1952	2.00	3.00	4.00
(BT89) **22 Farm Boy,** July 1, 1949	2.00	3.00	5.00
(BT90) **23 Farm Girl**	2.00	3.00	5.00
(BT91) **20 Farmer,** July 1, 1949	2.00	3.00	5.00
(BT92) **21 Farmerette,** July 1, 1949	2.00	3.00	5.00
(BT93) **M4036 Gentleman Rider,** large size	4.00	6.00	8.00
(BT94) Giraffe, January 15, 1952	2.00	3.00	4.00
(BT95) **50 Goat,** September 1, 1949	2.00	3.00	4.00
(BT96) **51 Goat, Female**	2.00	3.00	4.00
(BT97) **70 Goose,** September 1, 1949	2.00	3.00	4.00
(BT98) **71 Gosling,** September 1, 1949	2.00	3.00	4.00
(BT99) **503 Hand Grenade Thrower,** WW II helmet, October 1, 1949	2.00	3.00	5.00
(BT100) **Hippopotamus,** February 2, 1953	2.00	3.00	4.00
(BT101) M452 Indian with tomahawk on running horse	3.00	5.00	7.00
(BT102) M452b Indian with bow on running horse . . .	3.00	5.00	7.00
(BT103) M452s Indian with spear on running horse . . .	3.00	5.00	7.00
(BT104) Indian Warrior holding Flag and Shield, 5" high, January 2, 1952.	4.00	6.00	8.00
(BT105) Indian Warrior holding lasso, 4" high, January 2, 1952	4.00	6.00	8.00
(BT106) Infantryman Flagman **(Marching W/Flag),** WW II helmet, July 16, 1951	2.00	3.00	5.00
(BT107 Infantry Parachute Jumper **(Paratrooper),** July 16, 1951	2.00	3.00	5.00

	G	VG	M
(BT108) Infantry with **Walkie-Talkie,** July 16, 1951	2.00	3.00	5.00
(BT109) Infantry **Flamethrower** (Soldier), August 10, 1951	2.00	3.00	5.00
(BT110) **502 Infantryman, Charging,** facing forward, rifle across waist, October 1, 1949	2.00	3.00	5.00
(BT111) **515 Infantryman, Charging,** facing sideways, rifle held out, October 1, 1949	2.00	3.00	5.00
(BT112) Infantryman Holding **Bazooka,** September 17, 1951	2.00	3.00	5.00
(BT113) **513 Infantry Saluting,** WW II helmet, October 1, 1949	2.00	3.00	5.00
(BT114) Infantryman wearing **Gas Mask and** holding **Automatic,** August 10, 1951	2.00	3.00	5.00
(BT115) **511 Infantryman with Field Glasses,** kneeling, October 1, 1949	2.00	3.00	5.00
(BT116) **505 Infantryman with Gas Mask,** carrying rifle, October 1, 1949	2.00	3.00	5.00
(BT117) **Kangaroo,** April 15, 1952	2.00	3.00	4.00
(BT118) **517 Machine Gunner Kneeling,** October 1, 1949	2.00	3.00	5.00
(BT119) **62 Lamb,** head turned, September 1, 1949 . . .	2.00	3.00	4.00
(BT120) **4002** Large Running Horse with Saddle, October 2, 1950	2.00	3.00	4.00
(BT121) **Leopard, January 15, 1952 (Not shown)**	No Price Found		
(BT122) **Lion,** September 24, 1951	2.00	3.00	4.00
(BT123) **501 Machine Gunner,** holding gun at waist, WW II helmet, October 1, 1949	2.00	3.00	5.00
(BT124) **506 Machine Gunner in Prone Shooting Position,** WW II helmet, October 1, 1949	2.00	3.00	5.00
(BT125) **Moose,** February 1, 1952	2.00	3.00	4.00

BETON

	G	VG	M
(BT126) **504 Munitions Carrier**, WW II helmet, October 1, 1949	2.00	3.00	5.00
(BT127) **Panther,** January 15, 1952	2.00	3.00	4.00
(BT128) **31 Pig,** September 1, 1949	2.00	3.00	4.00
(BT129) **M4037 Polo Player, August 24, 1951, large**	4.00	6.00	8.00
(BT130) **4000 Prancing Horse, large, no saddle, January 1, 1950 (Not Shown)**	2.00	3.00	5.00
(BT131) **60 Ram, September 1, 1949**	2.00	3.00	4.00
(BT132) **Reindeer,** February 1, 1953	2.00	3.00	4.00
(BT133) **M4029-33 Rider, Cadet,** February 1, 1951.	5.00	8.00	10.00
(BT134) **M4030 Rider, Canadian Mounted Policeman,** February 1, 1951	5.00	8.00	10.00
(BT135) **M4031 Rider, Cavalry Officer,** February 1, 1951	5.00	8.00	10.00
(BT136) **M4033 Rider, Cowgirl,** July 16, 1951	4.00	6.00	8.00
(BT137) **M4027 Rider, Cowboy** Holding Hat, February 1, 1951	4.00	6.00	8.00
(BT138) **M4026 Rider, Hunter (Gentleman Rider)** February 1, 1951 (see BT 93)	4.00	6.00	8.00
(BT139) **M4024 Rider, Huntress (Lady Hunter),** February 1, 1951 See BT171	4.00	6.00	8.00
(BT140) **M4028 Rider, Jockey,** 3" high, February 1, 1951	4.00	6.00	8.00
(BT141) **510 Rifleman, marching position,** WW II helmet, October 1, 1949	2.00	3.00	5.00
(BT142) **M468 Rider, Jockey** 2" high, February 1, 1951	2.00	3.00	5.00
(BT143) **M4032 Police,** mounted, large. See BT135 .	5.00	8.00	10.00
(BT144) **509 Rifleman, shooting position,** WW II helmet, standing firing, October 1, 1949	2.00	3.00	5.00
(BT145) **M455 Road Agent on running horse, with pistol**	3.00	5.00	7.00
(BT146) **40 Rooster,** September 1, 1949	2.00	3.00	4.00
(BT147) **Running Horse**	2.00	3.00	4.00
(BT148) **1001 Saddled Standing Horse,** March 4, 1950	2.00	3.00	4.00
(BT149) **Seal,** April 15, 1952	2.00	3.00	4.00
(BT150) **61 Sheep,** September 1, 1949	2.00	3.00	4.00
(BT151) **514 Signaller,** WW II helmet, October 1, 1949	2.00	3.00	5.00
(BT152) Sitting Down Cow, August 21, 1950	2.00	3.00	4.00
(BT153) **M455 Small cowboy, holding pistol (mounted)**	3.00	5.00	7.00
(BT154) **M467 Small Cowboy Holding a Rifle (Mounted),** September 20, 1950	3.00	5.00	7.00
(BT155) **M454 Small Cowboy mounted holding lasso**	3.00	5.00	7.00
(BT156) **M466 Small riders, Cowboy holding a Guitar,** September 20, 1950	3.00	5.00	7.00
(BT157) **M452s Small Rider, Indian with Spear,** mounted	3.00	5.00	7.00
(BT158) **M452t Small Rider, Indian with tomahawk**	3.00	5.00	7.00
(BT159) **M465 Small Riders, Cowgirl,** 3" high, September 20, 1950	3.00	5.00	7.00
(BT160) **1000 Small Running Horse,** 4" long, September 1950 (See BT147)	2.00	3.00	4.00
(BT161) **1001 Small standing horse** (See BT148)	2.00	3.00	4.00
(BT162) **4001 Large standing horse,** February 21, 1950.	2.00	3.00	4.00
(BT163) **30 Swine,** September 1, 1949	2.00	3.00	4.00
(BT164) **Tiger,** January 15, 1952	2.00	3.00	4.00
(BT165) **Trainer,** Holding a Whip, February 25, 1952.	2.00	3.00	4.00
(BT166) **1002 Trotting Horse**	2.00	3.00	4.00
(BT167) **80 Turkey,** September 1, 1949	2.00	3.00	4.00
(BT168) **Zebra,** February 15, 1952	2.00	3.00	4.00
(BT169) **Clown**	2.00	3.00	4.00
(BT170) **Rhinoceros**	2.00	3.00	4.00
(BT171) **M4025 Lady Rider**	4.00	6.00	8.00

BETON

BT133
U.S. Cadet

BT134
Canadian Royal Mounted

BT135
Officer

BT136
Cowgirl

BT140
Jockey

BT141
Marching w/Rifle

BT142
Jockey

BT137
Cowboy

BT144
Infantry Firing

BT145 No. M455
Road Agent on running
horse

BT146 No. 40
Rooster

BT147
Running Horse

BT148
Standing Horse

BT149
Seal

BT151
Signalman

BT152
Sitting Cow

BT153
Cowboy w/gun

BT154
Cowboy w/shotgun

BT150
Sheep

BT155
Cowboy w/lasso

BT156
Cowboy w/guitar

BETON

BT157
Indian w/Spear

BT158
Indian w/Tomahawk

BT159
Cowgirl

BT162
Standing Horse

BT163
Swine

BT164
Tiger

BT165
Trainer

BT166
Trotting Horse

BT167 No. 80
Turkey

BT168
Zebra

BT169
Clown

BT170
Rhinoceros

BT171
Lady Rider

	G	VG	M
(BT172) Soldier in soft cap, saluting	5.00	6.00	7.00
(BT173) Soldier in soft cap, signaling	5.00	6.00	7.00

BETON ACCESSORIES (Circa 1940)

1004 Flagpole with Flag and Halyard, 12" high (Military Encampment and Cowboy Ranch). . . . . No Price Found

1012 Bridge, Sand Covered . No Price Found

1013 Trench, Sand covered . No Price Found

1014 6 Pup Tents (Military Encampment) . . . . No Price Found

1015 Trench, Grass covered No Price Found

1030 4 Machine Gun Towers (Military Encampment) . . . . No Price Found

1032 5 straight Sections, grass fence (Military Encampment) . . . . No Price Found

1033 Field Hospital (Military Encampment). . No Price Found

BT172   BT173
Photo by Ed Poole

Left: Soft plastic. Right: Hard plastic. Both are marked with the Beton logo.
Photo by Ed Poole

240

BETON

	G	VG	M
1034 2 Trees (Military Encampment)	No Price Found		
3000 Fence Section (Indian Village)	No Price Found		
3001 2 Tepees (Indian Village)	No Price Found		
3003 Tower (Indian Village)	No Price Found		
3005 Hut (Indian Village) . .	No Price Found		
3006 Tepee (Indian Village).	No Price Found		
3007 Well (Indian Village) . .	No Price Found		
3009 Tree (Indian Village and Cowboy Ranch)	No Price Found		
3019 Indian Lodge (Indian Village)	No Price Found		
3020 Barn (Cowboy Ranch)	No Price Found		
3021 Bunk House (Cowboy Ranch).	No Price Found		
3023 Tripod & Kettle (Cowboy Ranch).	No Price Found		
3025 Ranch Fence (Cowboy Ranch).	No Price Found		

BETON SETS

(When no prices are given, add up worth of figures and add 20% for the box to give an approximate value)

	G	VG	M
100 Unity Fortress Infantry Marching	No Price Found		
101 U.S. Cadets (foot and mounted).	No Price Found		
118 Indians-Assorted (foot and mounted).	No Price Found		
119 Cowboys - Assorted (foot and mounted).	No Price Found		
120 Cowboys & Indians - Asstd. (foot and mounted)	No Price Found		
121 9-Piece Fort.	No Price Found		
121A Landing Barge.	30.00	45.00	60.00
150 Railroad-Civilian Asst. (foot and mounted).	No Price Found		
160 Firemen and Policemen-Asstd. (foot & mounted).	No Price Found		
165 Dancing Girls - Asst. (foot and mounted).	No Price Found		
171 Dairy Farm-Asst. Farm Figures & Animals.	30.00	45.00	60.00
172 14-pc. Dairy Farm Set - Cows, farm figures & Animals	No Price Found		
173 26-pc. Dairy Farm Set - Assorted Farm Figures, Animals	No Price Found		
181 Cattle Ranch - Asstd. Cowboys & Animals.	No Price Found		
182 14-pc. Cattle Ranch - Cows, Cowboys & Animals	No Price Found		

	G	VG	M
183 23-pc. Cattle Ranch - Cows, Cowboys, Indians, Animals	No Price Found		
191 Assorted Farm Animals			
192 Two Cowboys on Horses, 16 assorted animals	No Price Found		
193 30-pc. Farm Set - Cowboys, Horses, Assorted Animals.	No Price Found		
261 Asst. Farm Figs. & Poultry	No Price Found		
262 22-pc. Poultry Set-Assorted Farm Figures, Animals	No Price Found		
263 34-pc. Poultry Set-Assorted Farm Figures, Animals	No Price Found		
500 Infantry In Action (foot and mounted).	15.00	22.50	30.00
4001 Indian Stockade Village	No Price Found		
4002 Military Encampment.	No Price Found		
4003 Cowboy Ranch.	No Price Found		
M124 12-Piece Wild West Set . . . Mounted	No Price Found		
M200 Mtd. U.S. Cav., Royal Mtd. & Cadets - Asstd. Horses.	No Price Found		
M204 Mounted U.S. Cadets Running Horse.	No Price Found		
M212 Mtd. Indians, Asstd. Horses	No Price Found		
M213 Mounted Indians Broncho Horse.	No Price Found		
M214 Mtd. Cowboys & Indians Asstd. Horses.	No Price Found		
M215 Mounted Cowboys Asstd. Broncho Horse. . .	No Price Found		
M216 Mtd. Cowboys - Asst. Horses	No Price Found		
M217 Mounted Cowboys Lasso Broncho Horse. . .	No Price Found		
M218 Mounted Cowboys Lasso Running Horse. . .	No Price Found		
M219 Royal Mounted.	No Price Found		
M222 Mounted Jockeys - Assorted Horses.	No Price Found		
M300 Lady Hunter & Gentleman Hunter (6 large riders, 6 large horses)	No Price Found		
M301 Cowboy (6 large riders, 6 large horses)	No Price Found		
M302 Jockey (6 large riders, 6 large horses).	No Price Found		

BETON

	G	VG	M
M303 Cadet-U.S. Cavalry Officer (6 large riders, 6 large horses)	No Price Found		
M304 Police (6 large riders, 6 large horses)	No Price Found		
M305 Canadian Royal (6 large riders, 6 large horses)	No Price Found		
M306 Cowboy & Cowgirl (6 large riders, 6 large horses)	No Price Found		
M307 Cowgirl (6 large riders, 6 large horses)	No Price Found		
M308 Lady & Gentlemen (6 large riders, 6 large horses)	No Price Found		
M309 Polo Player (6 large riders, 6 large horses)	No Price Found		
M380 Assorted Large Rider & Horses (6 large horses, 6 large riders)	No Price Found		
M381 Asstd. Large Horses - Extra Rider	No Price Found		
M382 Asstd. Large & Small Horses - Extra Rider	No Price Found		
M383 Asstd. Small Horses - Extra Rider & Footmen . .	42.00	63.00	85.00
MZ-252 Asstd. Mtd. - Circus Performers	No Price Found		
MZ350 Assorted Circus Horse and Riders	No Price Found		
MZ-351 Asstd. Mtd. Circus Performers on Horses & Elephants	No Price Found		
MZ-353 Asstd. Large Circus Animals & Figures . . .	No Price Found		
MZ-354 Asstd. Small Circus Animals & Figures	No Price Found		
PT 45 Infantry in Patrol Boat	30.00	45.00	60.00
Z-250 Asstd. Small Circus Animals & Figures	60.00	70.00	80.00
Z-251 Asstd. Large Circus Animals & Figures	No Price Found		
Z-252 Assorted Circus Horses, Elephant and Riders	No Price Found		
Z-353 Large Circus Animals	No Price Found		
Z-354 Small Circus Animals	No Price Found		
ZT-151 Circus Tent-Animals & Figurines	No Price Found		
NO NUMBER - Horse leaping hurdle	No Price Found		

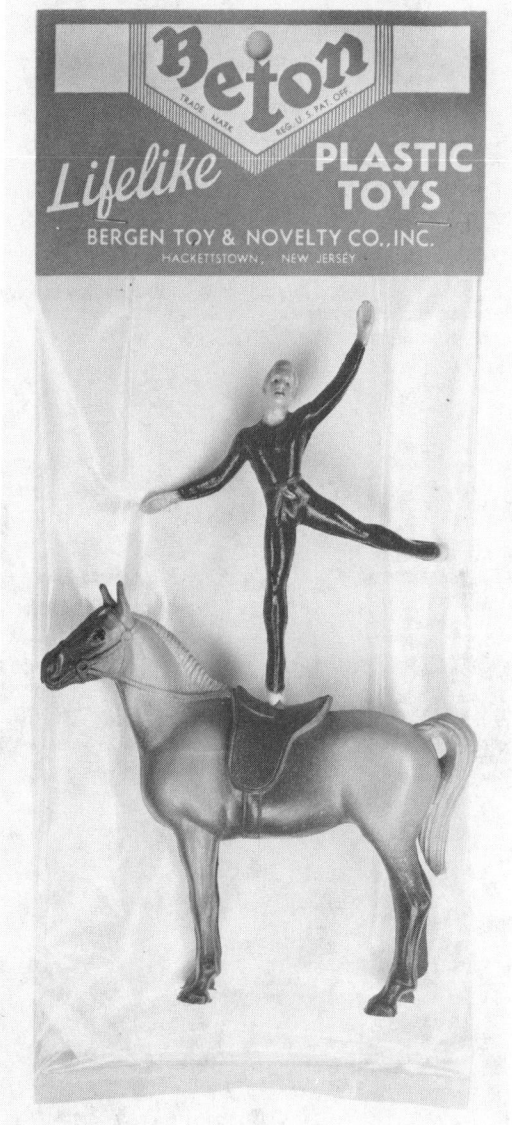

BT83

NO NUMBER (last figure on listing) - Horse Leaping Hurdle. Photo from Beton Archives

Another Beton variation. The right knee on the cowboy at left turns inward, unlike the figure at right.
Photo by Ron Steiner.

BT105   BT104

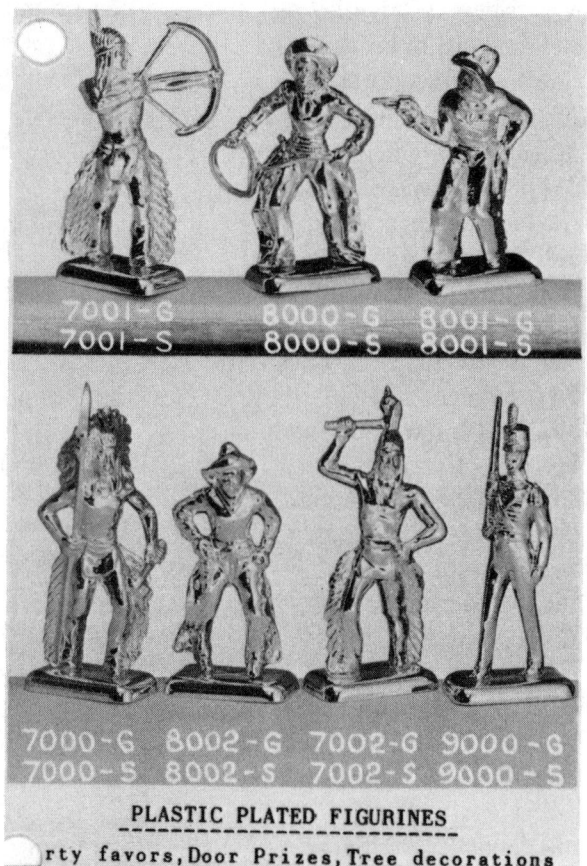

PLASTIC PLATED FIGURINES

...rty favors, Door Prizes, Tree decorations
...r Knick-Knack shelf ornaments, Packed 2 doz
of a color to a carton
BERGEN TOY & NOVELTY CO.   HACKETTSTOWN, N.J.
Telephone: 312

Beton also electro-plated its figures for sale in novelty and souvenir shops.
From the Beton archives

BETON

Plastic Soldier Set. Consists of 13 figures of soldiers in various action poses, mounted in attractive display box simulating a fort. Each figure is realistically hand painted and is perfectly lifelike model. Size of box 20x5x3½ inches. No. 50N525. Per doz. sets **10.80**

Indian Lodge With Plastic Indians. A set of 13 figures of Indians made of washable, unbreakable plastic material. Carefully hand painted. Each in a lifelike position. Mounted in a cardboard container lithographed to resemble a Lodge. Size of box 20x5x3½ inches. No. 50N526. Per dozen sets **10.80**

"Ranch" With Cowboy Figures. Set of 13 pieces. Made of washable, unbreakable Plastic. Each figure is a realistic model, and is colorfully hand painted. Packed in a cardboard box made to resemble a ranch. Size of box 20x5x3½ inches. No. 50N527. Per dozen sets **10.80**

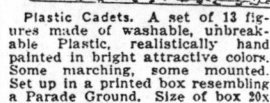

Plastic Cadets. A set of 13 figures made of washable, unbreakable Plastic, realistically hand painted in bright attractive colors. Some marching, some mounted. Set up in a printed box resembling a Parade Ground. Size of box 20x 5x3½ inches. No. 50N528. Per dozen sets **10.80**

Plastic Soldier Set. Consists of 9 figures of soldiers infantry in action, mounted in attractive display box simulating a fort. Each figure is realistically hand painted and is a perfectly lifelike model. Size of box 20x5x3½ inches. No. 50N516. Per dozen sets............. **8.25**

Plastic Soldiers Infantry Marching. A set of 9 figures made of washable, unbreakable Plastic, realistically hand painted in bright attractive colors. Set up in a printed box resembling a Parade Ground. Size of box 20x5x3½ inches. No. 50N517. Per dozen sets.................. **8.25**

Plastic Cowboy Figures. Set of 9 pieces. Made of washable, unbreakable Plastic. Each figure is a realistic model, and is colorfully hand painted. Packed in a cardboard box made to resemble a ranch. Size of box 20x5x3½ inches. No. 50N518. Per dozen sets.............. **8.25**

Indian Lodge With Plastic Indians. A set of 9 figures of Indians made of washable, unbreakable plastic material. Carefully hand painted. Each in a lifelike position. Mounted in a cardboard container lithographed to resemble a Lodge. Size of box 20x5x3½ inches. No. 50N519. Per dozen sets............. **8.25**

Beton Sets, shown in a 1942-43 N. Shure catalog. The cardboard boxes became forts, Indian lodges, ranches and parade grounds.

Beton

PT45

Tremendously popular . . . thrills that never dull . . . and so powerfully realistic!

WORLD WAR II saw the introduction of many new "weapons" . . . none more sensational than the spectacular PT45 which supplemented the offensive operations of our Army and Navy. Here BETON has succeeded in creating a very convincing version of the original. The colorful set, including businesslike infantrymen ready to carry the war to enemy ships, comes in a handsome individual carton that will multiply your sales. Here's PLENTY of play-action for all!

Beton PT45 Set
From the Beton archives

No. **PT45**

retail at . . . . $**1**⁰⁰

····· *for Modern Girls and Boys*

244

Beton

LANDING BARGE

Down goes the ramp . . . off go the soldiers!

NO DOUGHBOY ever experienced a more dramatic moment than that fateful instant when, crouched tense below the gunwale of a chugging cockle-shell landing craft, he felt and heard the grating of its bottom beneath his knees and realized it was time to UP-and-AWAY . . . down the swaying ramp onto a hostile beach! This colorful Landing Barge in attractive individual carton, creates a perfect illusion, even for seasoned veterans.

No. **121A**

retail at . . . . **60¢**

Beton No. 121A Landing Barge.
From the Beton archives   *Lifelike* **PLASTIC TOYS**

245

Beton

9-PIECE FORT

1^{00}

No. 121 ———— retail at

Beton No. 121 9-Piece Fort
From the Beton archives.

*B*RILLIANTLY DESIGNED to furnish a maximum of lifelike action and PLAY-value to energetic youngsters...this thrilling FORT SET will give the kids plenty to do on many a rainy day when they can't go outside to play. There are seven foot-soldiers and one exciting mounted figure...all sculptured as from actual life and smartly colored to look "the real thing". The carton itself is the Fort, in full colors, easily set up, a joy to ACTION-minded tots!

Lifelike PLASTIC TOYS................................ *for Modern Girls and Boys*

PLASTIC TOYS, INC.

I'd love to know if O.J. Sharpe was a scalawag, or a man who had his former employer's blessing.

In the March, 1944 issue of Toys and Novelties Magazine, ads appear for a company that made toy soldiers which look exactly like Betons. The company was named Plastic Toys, Inc., and was located in Cambridge, Ohio. An article in the same issue at least partially explains the situation.

O.J. Sharpe, the executive vice president of Plastic Toys, Inc. after serving as a department store representative for Auburn Rubber, had become the sales manager for Bergen Toy and Novelty Co. (Beton). While Sharpe was with the firm, the article explains, "their line of toys was revamped — a proper merchandising plan mapped out — and a definite policy established." Sales went up almost 400% the first year "and the company was launched into the 'leader' class." The article continues, "Early in 1942, greatly increased quarters were required...and a complete building was obtained in Rutherford, New Jersey. By the end of that year, Bergen Toy and Novelty Co., Inc. had become just about the acknowledged leader in its field, and by April, 1943, orders received exceeded manufacturing possibilities for the year."

This unmet demand apparently put a bee in Mr. Sharpe's bonnet, and on January 4, 1944, he submitted his resignation, effective February 1, to become connected with Plastic Toys, Inc. As I recall, in some areas (and this might include toys) manufacturers during the War were allowed only a specified amount of materials. This might have been Beton's problem, and may have convinced Sharpe that a new company, allotted a reasonable amount of materials, could fill up the holes that Beton couldn't. Since Beton could produce only so much, and no more, perhaps Beton owner Charles Marcak bestowed a benevolent pat or two on the head of Sharpe as he headed in the direction of Ohio, but not likely.

The only real difference between Beton's soldiers and those of Plastic Toys' are the latter's integrally cast round base without any manufacturer's markings. Neither of the two people I've spoken to who were connected with Beton were employed by the company during the WW II period, and knew nothing about Plastic Toys, Inc. Neither did Mr. Sharpe's widow when I called her, so this may be a mystery that will never be solved. One thing is certain; Sharpe was hardly keeping a low profile, with both the article and an ad in Toys and Novelties establishing his previous tie to Beton. Certainly, as its sales manager, he would have known that Beton also advertised in Toys and Novelties, and therefore Charles Marcak would quickly spot any ads for the fledgling company. In fact, the two firms' ads sometimes ran in the same issue.

Plastic Toys, Inc. was housed in a brick building in Cambridge that contained over 15,000 square feet of floor space on two floors. By the middle of 1945 it had moved to Byesville, Ohio. The Toys and Novelties article explains that the line had been planned carefully, "not simply allowed to 'grow up' as many toys do — and although the company is prepared to ship a tremendous volume in 1944, its schedule calls for shipments on farm animals and barnyard fowl from May 1, and on military toys from July 1." Just a few months later, in March, 1945, the company claimed that "several million" of its toys had been delivered.

Plastic Toys, Inc. also made plastic ships by 1945, which were either direct or modified copies of the vessels by Wannatoys, which had been sold since 1941. Later, Plastic Toys produced cowboys and Indians of its own design.

O.J. Sharpe died September 1, 1977, and his widow seemed to know little about her husband's business when we spoke. She did state that Sharpe was the owner of the company, which eventually—she didn't know when—turned from toymaking to custom molding (such as car parts) for other companies "because there was more money in that". Perhaps there had also been "more money" in piracy. Perhaps not.

In 1990 collector David W. Francis reported in Old Toy Soldier Newsletter that O.J. Sharpe's first and middle names were Otho James, and that he is remembered in Byesville, where he was twice elected mayor, as a "little, baldheaded fireball". He was born September 10, 1900 in Alexander County, North Carolina, and was educated at both the University of North Carolina and Georgia Tech.

Sharpe began working for Auburn Rubber in 1926, at various times selling for Auburn and Beton in all 48 states, Cuba and Mexico. It was while selling for Beton in 1943 that he arrived in Cambridge, Ohio and decided to go into manufacturing on his own. The principal stockholders were Sharpe, Elizabeth Ruby and Frank C. Leyshon. According to Francis, it was Leyshon who convinced Sharpe to headquarter in Ohio. Possibly because of Korean War restrictions, Sharpe ran into trouble in the early 1950s, and tried to get military contracts for plastic parts, but failed. Toy production seems to have come to an end in 1953 or early 1954. Sharpe closed down all production in the early 1970s and sold all of the property in 1977.

Prices are equivalent to Betons

PLASTIC

Plastic Toys Inc. soldiers
Photo by Bill Kaufman

Plastic Toys Inc. soldier set
Photo by Bill Kaufman

248

PLASTIC

Plastic Toys Inc. Cowgirl with lasso
Photo by Gary J. Linden

A September, 1949 ad in *Toys and Novelties*.

Ships by Plastic Toys Inc. as shown in a March, 1945 *Toys and Novelties* ad.

AUSLEY

Ausley Industries, Inc. began in 1943 in Atlanta, Georgia, and later moved to Thomasville, Georgia. Robert C. Ausley, its owner, founded it as a way of earning extra income. Its original soldiers were lead, and produced from home casting sets. However, in 1948, when lead became too expensive, and soldiers no longer were as popular, Ausley turned to plastic figures, sculpting the company's single cowboy and Indian himself. The cowboys and Indians, which had movable arms, were produced in plastic injection molds, and sold well until the outbreak of the Korean War, when sales slackened drastically due to a renewed demand for soldiers. Ausley's other business precluded his putting any more time into the company, and it ended production in 1950. All told, Ausley produced about 250,000 lead and plastic figures. The cowboys and Indians retailed at a dime apiece. Today, their value is about $2.00 each.

AUS 1 - Cowboy with two moving arms
AUS 2 - Indian with two moving arms

Ausley's plastic cowboys and Indians, flanked by two of the Homecast lead soldiers Ausley sold earlier.

Before turning to plastic, Ausley turned out a number of figures using home-casting molds. Here is one of their boxed sets. Photo by Elizabeth Ausley

A boxed set of Ausley plastic cowboys and Indians. Photo by Elizabeth Ausley.

LIDO

Lido was formed in October, 1947 by the Arenstein brothers, Seymour (4/16/16 —) and Effrem (12/7/20 —) with the purchase of Elite Toy Co. from David Krotman (now deceased). Krotman made plastic bubble pipes, scissors and a horn. Since his firm was near the Lido country club, he also used that name. For $6800 the Arensteins bought the molds and the name.

They opened Lido at 321 Rider Avenue in the Bronx and about 1960-61 moved to a 200,000-foot building at 1340 Viele Avenue, also the Bronx.

Seymour originally got into the toy business when, going to rabbinical school, he asked his millionaire uncle, the country's biggest importer of toys, William Shaland, for work. His first job was selling for Shaland, who wholesaled the toys. At Lido he was in charge of sales, while Effrem managed.

Among Lido's toys were cars, soldiers, cowboys, knights, Civil War figures, farm animals, jeeps, pinball games and a pool table. Their toys were small, always plastic and eventually the Arensteins were known as "the Louis Marxes of low-end". At peak they employed close to 1000 people. In the years after the 1950s they employed several thousand indirectly in Hong Kong, Japan and Taiwan.

Their basic policy was to copy items cheaper. As might be expected, they have no specific memories of their figures. Production of their soldiers may have begun in 1951, as suggested in a magazine ad. Neither brother remembers their being sold earlier. Lido's models were made by various people: Standard Tool in Leominster, Mass., Aaron Hirschkowitz in the Bronx and others the Arensteins no longer remember.

In 1964, due to disagreements, Lido was sold to the Bala Corporation of Philadelphia. Bala liquidated a year later, and what was left was eventually bought by Gabriel Industries. All but fifty of the molds were melted. In 1973 Seymour Arenstein formed Joy Toy, naming it after his daughter Joy. He used the remaining fifty molds, most of which were soldiers. In 1990 he sold the molds to Strombecker.

Lido Boxed SOLDIER SET

No. 900 — It's Lido's newest! Has authentic features and styling. Year 'round sales for you with this wonderful NEW boxed set of 20 plastic toy soldiers. Eight different action poses. Official O. color. Packaged in a colorful sale display box with cellophane window. Cut-outs on back of each box for additional play value. Size of box approximately 14½" x 11" x 1". Also available in bulk.

Tie in with LIDO'S popular and fast moving line. Write Dept. PM for new catalog, fully illustrated in color.

Lido TOY CORPORATION
N. Y. OFFICE
200 5th AVE. • ROOM 206
Plant: 781 E. 135th St., N. Y. 54, CYpress 2-4942-3-4

A November, 1951 ad in Plastics Merchandising magazine for Lido's new line of plastic toy soldiers.

FL1   FL2   FL3

AR1   AR2   AR3   AR4

Lido Foreign Legionaires and Arabs. Not shown is the legion officer with sword and the Arabs' mounts. Value about $5 each.

A boxed set of Lido Knights
Photo by Gary J. Linden

Small plastic planes, circa 1942, by Lido Toy Corp., NYC. No Price Found. This presumably was the original Lido, owned by David Krotman. Courtesy Roger Johnson.

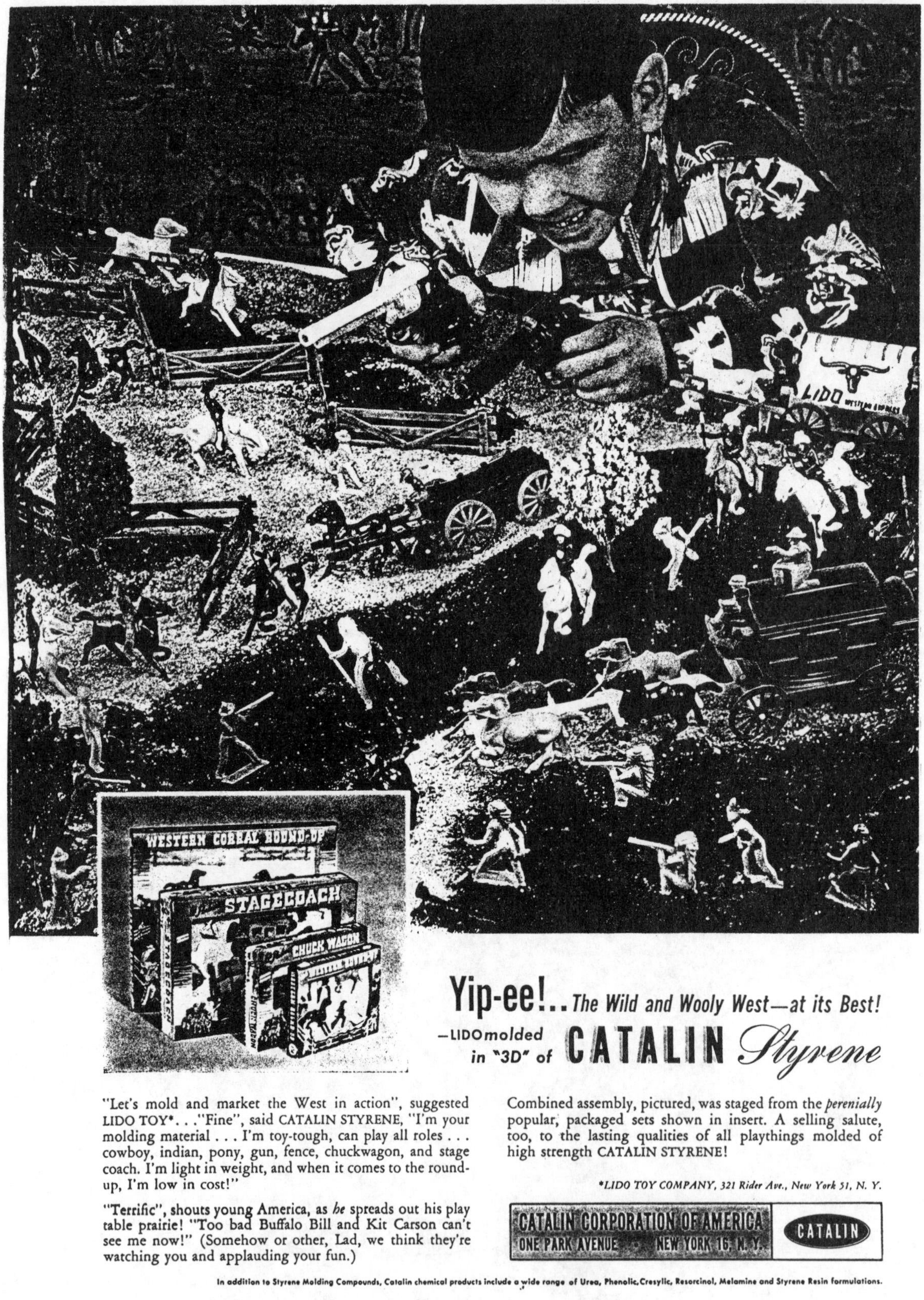
WESTERN CORRAL ROUND-UP
STAGECOACH
CHUCK WAGON
LIDO
Yip-ee!... The Wild and Wooly West—at its Best!
—LIDO molded in "3D" of CATALIN Styrene
"Let's mold and market the West in action", suggested LIDO TOY*. . ."Fine", said CATALIN STYRENE, "I'm your molding material . . . I'm toy-tough, can play all roles . . . cowboy, indian, pony, gun, fence, chuckwagon, and stage coach. I'm light in weight, and when it comes to the round-up, I'm low in cost!"
"Terrific", shouts young America, as *he* spreads out his play table prairie! "Too bad Buffalo Bill and Kit Carson can't see me now!" (Somehow or other, Lad, we think they're watching you and applauding your fun.)
Combined assembly, pictured, was staged from the *perenially* popular, packaged sets shown in insert. A selling salute, too, to the lasting qualities of all playthings molded of high strength CATALIN STYRENE!
*LIDO TOY COMPANY, 321 Rider Ave., New York 51, N. Y.
CATALIN CORPORATION OF AMERICA
ONE PARK AVENUE • NEW YORK 16, N. Y.
CATALIN
In addition to Styrene Molding Compounds, Catalin chemical products include a wide range of Urea, Phenolic, Cresylic, Resorcinol, Melamine and Styrene Resin formulations.

A March, 1954 Chain Store Age ad showing Lido toys.

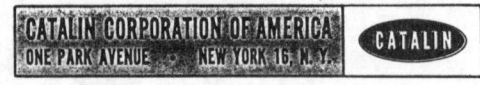

A March, 1954 Chain Store Age magazine ad for Lido.

AJAX

Ajax Plastic (also Plastics) Corporation was founded about 1950 (it was incorporated 12/15/49) by Harry Sternberg (9/6/11-9/23/91). He was a CPA whose father-in-law was William Shaland, a major toy jobber. It was Shaland who influenced Sternberg's getting into the business.

The firm's first items were cowboys and Indians. Presumably they were copies of Betons. Ajax did copy Beton and seems to have originated few, if any, of its toys. In 1951 Ajax showed its wares at a trade show. As a result, Standard Brands decided to use its soldiers (mainly copies of Barclays) as a Royal Desserts premium offer. Four soldiers could be obtained by sending in three Royal package fronts and a quarter. An extra 25¢ would insure the "9-Man Full Combat Team".

The firm, at 380 Lafayette St. New York City, had forty employees at its peak. Among its products were soldiers, cowboys, Indians, baseball players, football players, animals, dinosaurs, loving cups, a Happy Birthday form for cakes (the figures were often used on cakes) and spacemen, the latter produced very late in the firm's history.

Ajax's moldmaker was Standard Tool of Leominster, Mass. The model makers, names unknown, were either there or in Fitchburg. Ajax sold almost entirely to chain stores. Its products were offered both loose and boxed. Sternberg, who had kept up his accounting practice to some extent and didn't like manufacturing, gave up the business somewhere between 1967 and 1971. The firm's last outlet was Woolworth's.

The descriptions given for AJ1-AJ9 are those found in the Royal offer.

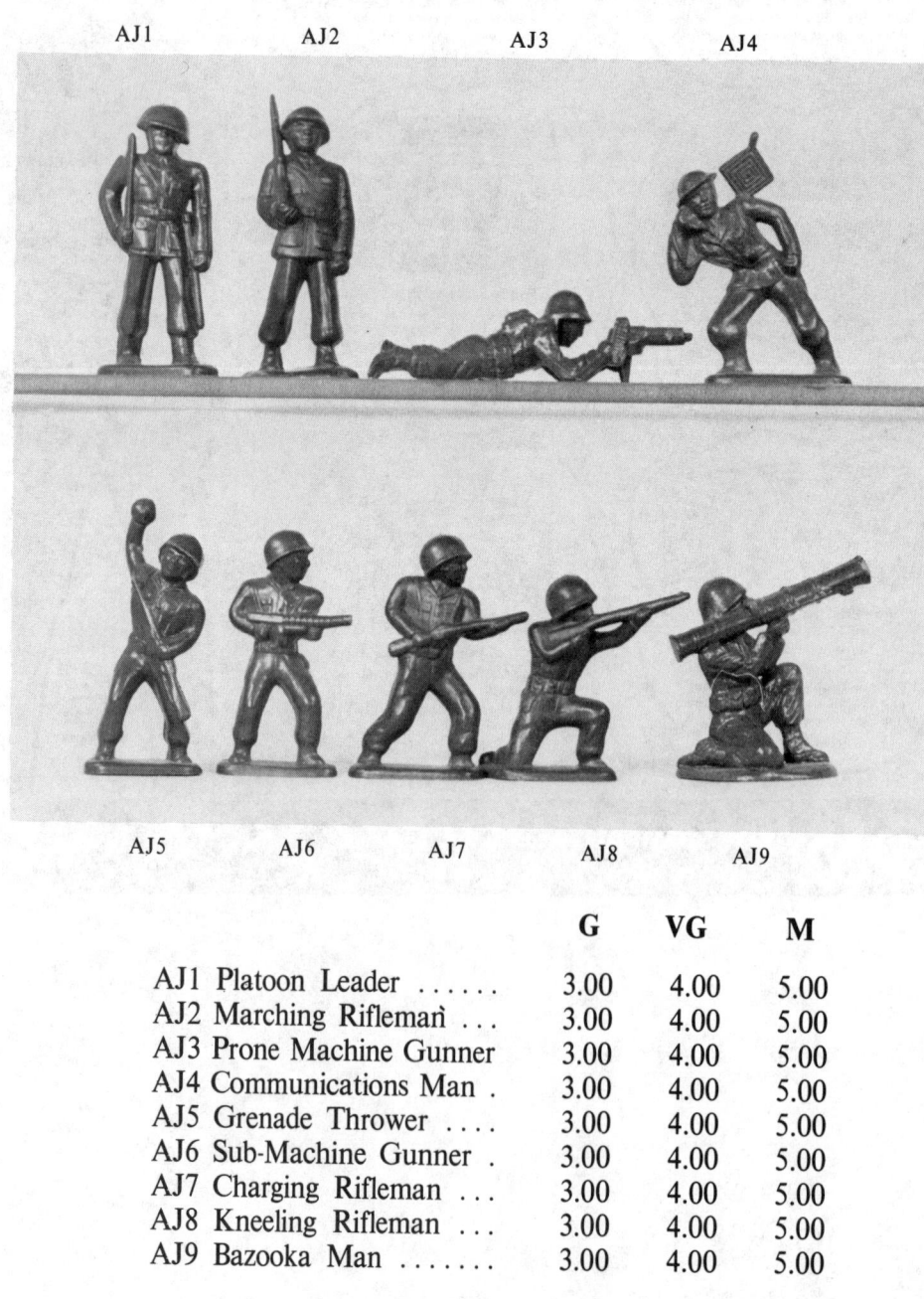

AJ1   AJ2   AJ3   AJ4

AJ5   AJ6   AJ7   AJ8   AJ9

	G	VG	M
AJ1 Platoon Leader	3.00	4.00	5.00
AJ2 Marching Rifleman ...	3.00	4.00	5.00
AJ3 Prone Machine Gunner	3.00	4.00	5.00
AJ4 Communications Man .	3.00	4.00	5.00
AJ5 Grenade Thrower	3.00	4.00	5.00
AJ6 Sub-Machine Gunner .	3.00	4.00	5.00
AJ7 Charging Rifleman ...	3.00	4.00	5.00
AJ8 Kneeling Rifleman ...	3.00	4.00	5.00
AJ9 Bazooka Man	3.00	4.00	5.00

Large-sized pieces by Ajax.
Courtesy Harry and Judy Sternberg

Harry Sternberg, with second son Gerald in a photo taken around 1950.
Courtesy Harry and Judy Sternberg

Ajax's copies of Beton's cowboys and Indians in the foreground. Behind the Ajax fence is the firm's large horse and cowboy.
Courtesy Harry and Judy Sternberg

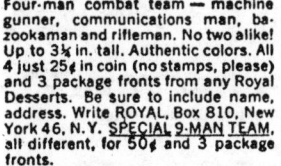

Send for this set of
PLASTIC TOY SOLDIERS

4 for 25¢ and 3 pkg. fronts from any ROYAL Puddings Gelatin Desserts Lemon Pie Filling Custard Flavor Dessert Mix

Four-man combat team — machine gunner, communications man, bazookaman and rifleman. No two alike! Up to 3½ in. tall. Authentic colors. All 4 just 25¢ in coin (no stamps, please) and 3 package fronts from any Royal Desserts. Be sure to include name, address. Write ROYAL, Box 810, New York 46, N.Y. SPECIAL 9-MAN TEAM, all different, for 50¢ and 3 package fronts.

This offer void wherever taxed, prohibited or otherwise restricted. Subject to availability of goods.

CUT OUT SOLDIER AND THIS FLAP.
FOLD FLAP TO MAKE SOLDIER
STAND UP.

No. 2 - Communications Man

The Royal offer. This ran on the back of a box of Royal Lemon Flavor gelatin dessert.
Courtesy Harry and Judy Sternberg

The mounted Indians are Beton copies. The football players, which are hard plastic, may have been produced in Hong Kong for Ajax.
Courtesy Harry and Judy Sternberg

One of Ajax's spacemen, surrounded by some of Ajax's Hong Kong-made novelty items.
Courtesy Harry and Judy Sternberg

147—8 Asst. FOOTBALL PLAYERS. Bright plastic colors.
Packed: 3 dozen to a box, 15 gross to carton. Weight: 35 lbs.

413—PEDESTRIANS. Realistic figures of people as they appear in every day life.
Packed: 4 dozen to box, 18 gross to carton. Weight: 50 lbs.

305—COWBOY AND INDIAN FIGURES. Each figure masked for more realistic look. 3"-3½" tall.
Packed: 3 dozen to box, 10 gross to carton. Weight: 35 lbs.

301 — COWBOY AND INDIAN FIGURES. Six poses out of the old west. 3"-3½" tall.
Packed: 3 dozen to box, 10 gross to carton. Weight: 35 lbs.

17 — LARGE HORSE AND RIDER. Asst. colors — Asst. figures. Horses, Cowboys and Indians in realistic poses. Excellent value.
Packed: 2 dozen to box, 6 gross to carton. Weight: 50 lbs.

17B—Same as No. 17 but one Horse and one Rider in polyethylene bag.
Packed: 2 dozen to box, 6 gross to carton. Weight: 55 lbs.

420—LARGE HORSE and RIDER. Asst. riding figures with horses.
Packed: 1 dozen to box, 4 gross to carton. Weight: 50 lbs.

79—HORSE, RIDER AND STANDING FIGURE. In Poly bag. Assorted riders and Cowboy and Indian figures in bright colors with horses in natural colors.
Packed: 4 dozen to box, 6 gross to carton. Weight: 45 lbs.

77—HORSES and RIDERS. Asst. color horses with Cowboy and Indian riders in assorted poses.
Packed: 2 dozen to box, 8 gross to carton. Weight: 50 lbs.

137—GOLD HORSE and RIDER: Cowboy and Indian figures that can be mounted on horses. Gold Plated.
Packed: 2 dozen to box, 8 gross to carton. Weight: 50 lbs.

88D — HORSE AND TWO RIDERS. In cello bag. Each package contains: Horse and two interchangable riders. Bright colors.
Packed: 4 dozen to box, 6 gross to carton. Weight: 45 lbs.

WILLIAM SHALAND CORPORATION • 401 PARK AVENUE SOUTH • NEW YORK 16, N.Y.   7

Toy Figures

73—SATELLITE EXPLORERS. 6 Astronauts with detachable helmets. Bright plastic colors. Colorful Header.
Packed: 1 dozen to box, 1 gross to carton. Weight: 45 lbs.

102B — ASTRONAUTS. 6 asst. Astronauts. Detachable helmets. Bright metallic colors. Colorful Header.
Packed: 2 dozen to box, 6 gross to carton. Weight: 50 lbs.

53—9 Asst. REALISTIC ACTION SOLDIERS. Various poses make these soldiers almost lifelike.
Packed: 3 dozen to box, 12 gross to carton. Weight: 50 lbs.

407/8 — Asst. SOLDIERS. Polyethylene — 12 Real action poses.
Packed: 4 dozen to box—16 gross to carton. Weight: 50 lbs.

155—8 Pc. SOLDIER SET. In Poly bag with descriptive header. Action soldiers in various poses.
Packed: 1 dozen to box, 2 gross to carton. Weight: 55 lbs.

403 — FIREMEN AND POLICEMEN. Asst. figures of our civil servants.
Packed: 4 dozen to box, 18 gross to carton. Weight: 50 lbs.

All but the ballerina and civilians were definitely produced by Ajax, and probably they were too.

424 — BALLERINA. Flesh colored dancer with skirt and crown. In matching colors.
Packed: 2 dozen to box, 20 gross to carton. Weight: 30 lbs.

110 — ASSORTED BASEBALL PLAYERS. 10 Asst. players in natural action poses.
Packed: 1 gross to box, 20 gross to carton. Weight: 35 lbs.

165—Asst. BASEBALL PLAYERS. 6 assorted Natural Action Poses. Bright plastic colors.
Packed: 3 dozen to box, 15 gross to carton. Weight: 35 lbs.

6   WILLIAM SHALAND CORPORATION • 401 PARK AVENUE SOUTH • NEW YORK 16, N.Y.

THOMAS TOYS

Thomas Toys produced some of the same G.I.'s that Ajax sold. However, Thomas' debut in the company's catalogs long after 1951, when Ajax was already selling these pieces. Islyn Thomas (5/27/12- —), who founded Thomas Toys in 1944 after leaving his post as general manager of the Ideal Toy Company, says there was no tie between the two firms, and has no idea how both could have produced the same pieces. Otherwise, Thomas Toys' figures appear to be its own.

Thomas Manufacturing began producing its first toys—jeeps, planes and vinyl dolls—in 1944. Soldiers (in World War II helmets) were introduced in 1946, according to Thomas, and he remembers their being cast in PVC plastic. They were never sold singly; only in sets. The early G.I.'s may have simply been the sitting figure used as a driver and gunner in various Thomas sets.

The company's molds, and perhaps some of its sculpting, were provided by Richard Koegl (perhaps Koegel), whose Koegl Stampworks were in Newark (Conrad Koegel, an executive of Theodore Hahn, considering the similar name and professions, could have been a relative). Koegl also did mold work for Beton, whose owner, Charles Marcak, in need of a job, joined Thomas Toys in 1958. Sculpting of some of Thomas' finer-detailed toys, such as its lines of small babies, dolls and civilians, were done by a Mr. Kaiser.

The firm was located from first to last at 80 Clinton Street, Newark, New Jersey, made only toys, and at its peak had 350 employees. In 1960 Thomas saw the handwriting on the wall in the form of low-priced Japanese imports, and sold out to Banner Plastics (Charles Marcak moving over there for a brief period). Thomas then became an international plastics consultant, which remains his profession.

Islyn Thomas was made a member of the Plastics Hall of Fame in 1977 (the presentation made by President Ford). He was also made an Officer of the British Empire by Queen Elizabeth. He had served as chief engineer for the plastic parts in the Spitfire's Merlin engine (which was made in the U.S.) and in the immediate post-War period, heading Thomas Engineering Company, he had helped restore the ravaged European community by setting up a number of companies in England and the Continent. One of these was the toy company Popular Playthings in Wales, of which he was half owner for a while. This was founded in 1945 and continues in business today. Thomas is also the author of the book *Injection Molding of Plastics* (Reinhold Publishing Corp.) and many technical articles.
(Note: Plastic "Barclays" were also produced and/or sold in Brazil, according to James Opie's Book, *Toy Soldiers*).

Following is a list of known Thomas Toys soldiers, using the Ajax codings, and the soldier-related sets described in the company's 1960 catalog, which was dated November 15, 1959. Prices are comparable to Ajax on the soldiers.

SOLDIERS: AJ3, AJ5, AJ6, AJ8, AJ9. A figure similar to AJ7 was also made, but it appears to be more deeply bent at the knees.

SETS:

No. 554 Roman Chariot (3-pc. set). Chariot and two horses.

No. 651 Marching Roman Centurions (new in 1959), 7 pieces, including one horse and its rider.

No. 642 Roman Legion on Parade (new in 1959), 9 pieces, 2 horses, driver, horse, rider, 3 marchers - two swordsmen, one spearman.

No. 643 Chariot Race (new in 1959), 8 pieces, pair of chariots with drivers, two pairs of horses.

No. 526 Western Set, stagecoach and covered wagon, each with a pair of horses.

No. 587 Large Stage Coach, coach, driver, 4 horses

No. 546 Stage Coach, coach with two white horses

No. 547 Covered Wagon, wagon with pair of white horses.

No. 627 Twisting and Turning Rider Set. This was new in 1959, consisted of 4½" high Legionnaires, Arabs, Cowboys and Indians, four riders and two horses to a set. In the catalog illustration, the riders are an Arab,

a cowboy, an Indian chief with rifle and and Indian brave with hatchet. Presumably the Legionnaire was a French Foreign Legionnaire.

No. 628 Horse and Rider, two pieces (new in 1959) which consisted of a horse and, variously, cowboy, Indian, Legionnaire, Arab.

No. 451 Army Maneuver Set, 11 pcs. Four soldiers with Searchlight Jeep, Anti-Aircraft Jeep, Howitzer Field Gun, Trailer, Fighter Plane, shells.

No. 452 Army Scout Set, 6 pcs. Jeep, Howitzer, four soldiers.

No. 457 Intercontinental Missile and Launcher (two pieces)

No. 603 Missile Shooting Space Gun. Gun with dart, four 2½" "Martian Space Figures."

No. 608 Combat Jeep Patrol. Sold either with AA jeep or Searchlight jeep plus soldier driver and trailer.

No. 188 Military Jeep. 4½". Three military policemen, radio antenna and siren, jeep.

No. 579 Authentic 8" Jeep. One piece, has spare tire and movable windshield.

Thomas Toy also made at least 8 sets of airplanes; fighters and passenger planes, most of them jets. It also produced ships.

Islyn Thomas

Thomas Toys' No. 627 Twisting and Turning Riders

No. 297 Roman Legion
Courtesy Islyn Thomas

Courtesy Islyn Thomas

"Swamp Buggy" set, no number known.
From the Thomas Toy archives, courtesy Islyn Thomas.

No. 447 Thomas Mobile Guided Missile Unit
From the Thomas Toys archives, courtesy Islyn Thomas

No. 525 Pontoon Bridge.
From the Thomas Toys archives, courtesy Islyn Thomas

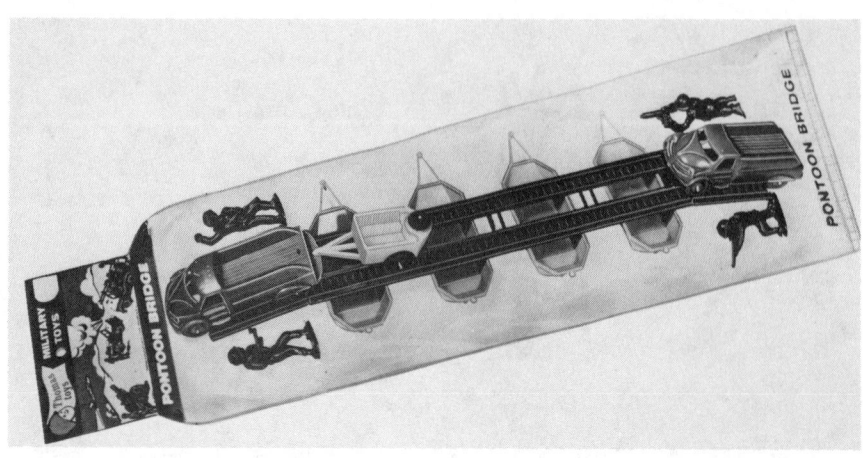

No. 186 ARMY ATTACK BOMBER
Length 4½", Width 5½", Height 1¼"
Colors: Olive Drab with Contrasting
   Colored Wheels and Propellers
Pack: 2–6–12 dozen per carton
Weight: 12 dozen—5¼ lbs.

No. 106 MILITARY DRIVER
Height 2½", Width 1½"
Color: Khaki
Pack: 3–6 dozen per carton
Weight: 6 dozen—2 lbs.

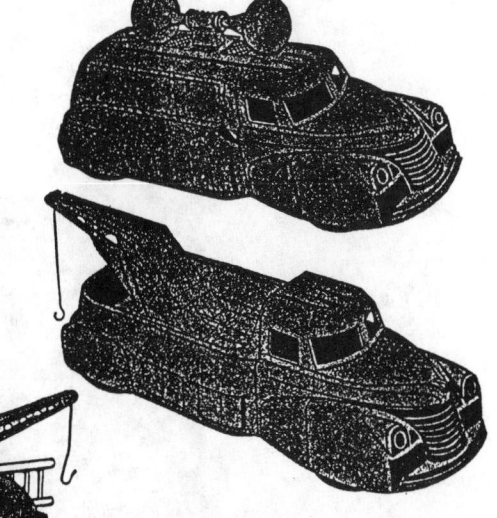

No. 184-5 ARMY RADAR & TOW TRUCKS
(50% each model)
Length 4", Width 1⅜", Height 1¾"
Color: Olive Drab
Pack: 3–6–12 dozen to a carton
Weight: 12 dozen—5½ lbs.

No. 189 ARMY MAINTENANCE TRUCK
(with detachable ladders)
Length 5½", Width 2⅛", Height 2⅛"
Colors: Olive Drab with Contrasting
   Colored Ladders
Pack: 2–6 dozen to a carton
Weight: 6 dozen—7 lbs.

No. 107 MILITARY POLICEMAN & MOTORCYCLE
(with detachable Policeman)
Length 4", Width 1¾", Height 2¾"
Colors: Olive Drab Motorcycle with Yellow
   Wheels & Khaki Military Policeman
Pack: 3–6 dozen to a carton
Weight: 6 dozen—5½ lbs.

No. 187 AIR FORCE HELICOPTER
(Patented—Action Toy)
Length 6¾", Width 1¾", Height 2",
   Propeller 5"
Color: Olive Drab with Contrasting Colored
   Wheels and Three-Colored Decals
Pack: 2–6 dozen to a carton
Weight: 6 dozen—4½ lbs.

No. 188 MILITARY POLICE JEEP
(with 3 Policemen)
Length 4¼", Width 1¾", Height 1¾"
Colors: Olive Drab with Contrasting Colored
   Accessories
Pack: 2–6 dozen to a carton
Weight: 6 dozen—6¾ lbs.

No. 196 ARMY ROAD ROLLER (Self Winding)
Length 4½", Width 2⅜", Height 2¾"
Colors: Olive Drab with Contrasting
   Colored Driver and Steering Wheel
   and 2-Colored Decals
Pack: 2–6 dozen per carton
Weight: 6 dozen—7½ lbs.

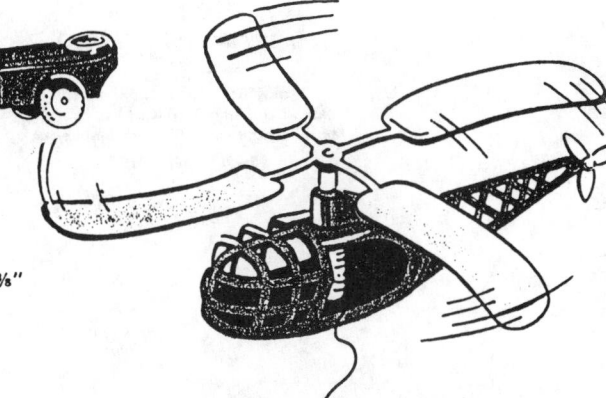

No. 183 ARMY JEEP AND TRAILER
(with Driver)
Length 8¾", Width 1⅝", Height 1⅜"
Colors: Olive Drab with Contrasting
   Colored Wheels & Driver
Pack: 2–6 dozen to a carton
Weight: 6 dozen—9½ lbs.

No. 205 FLYING RESCUE HELICOPTER (Boxed)
(Action Toy—it really flies)
Height 2", Length 8"
Colors: Olive Drab with Contrasting
   Colored Accessories
Pack: 2–4–6 dozen to a carton
Weight: 6 dozen—14 lbs.

Courtesy Islyn Thomas

THOMAS MANUFACTURING CORP. 80 Clinton St., Newark 5, N. J.

THOMAS' LINE OF
HISTORICAL TOYS

ITEM
NO.
337

ROMAN CHARIOT
with DRIVER

it's a
THOMAS
toy!

MARK
OF
QUALITY

No. 297 ROMAN LEGION
(Boxed)

Display Box: 13" x 10⅜" x 2⅝"
Colors: Gold Chariot, Black Horses, Silver
Metallic Figures. Multi Color Display Box

Sug. Retail $1.98

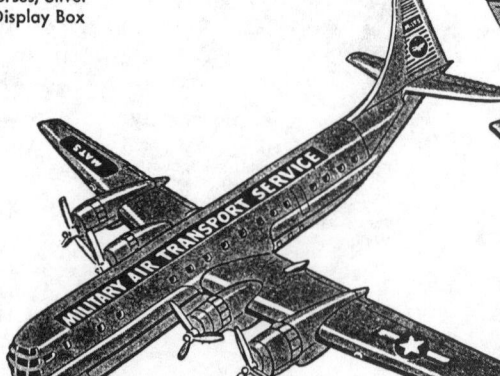

Courtesy Islyn Thomas

No. 204 MILITARY TRANSPORT PLANE
Wing Spread: 9½"
Colors: Plastic Silver Metallic with Contrasting
     Colored Accessories
Pack: 2–4–6 dozen to a carton
Weight: 6 dozen—12 lbs.

No. 15 ASSORTED 5½" PLASTIC BOATS (4 Styles)
(Queen Mary, Aircraft Carrier, Freighter, Battleship)

Length 5½", Width 1⅛", Height 1¼"
Asst. Colors: Red & Blue Decks with
     Contrasting Colored Hulls
Pack: 3–6–12 dozen to a carton
Weight: 12 dozen—5 lbs.

MARX

By the 1950s, Louis Marx was the largest manufacturer of toys in the world; six large factories in the U.S., and ownership of interest in factories in seven other countries. Marx, born in Brooklyn in 1896, was working for "Toy King" Ferdinand Strauss when he was in his teens, and by the age of twenty his energy and enterprise had made him a director of that company. A falling out with Strauss persuaded him to go into business for himself, and in 1921 he and his brother began making their own toys, including some adaptations of items by the now-defunct Strauss. Marx's watchword seems to have been quality at the lowest possible price, and he was such a favorite with toy buyers that he had virtually no need for salesmen or advertising. Marx made almost every type of toy but dolls, with the tin wind-ups and toy soldier playsets considered the most collectible. He eventually sold his company to the Quaker Oats Company, who in 1976 sold it to Europe's Dunbee-Combex-Marx. The company went into bankruptcy in 1980, with Marx dying in 1982 at the age of 85.

In 1982, American Plastics bought much of the Marx assets and in 1990 began producing toys from the original molds. However, as a result of the earlier break-up of the firm, certain rights and molds were retained in Mexico. These continue, and the total result is that many reissues reach the market, especially the plastic toy soldiers and accessories from the playset series.

Marx produced a large number of 3½" flat tin lithographed soldiers in the 1930s and after which are attractive to collectors. The following list was compiled by Gene Parker.

	G	VG	M		G	VG	M
(1MA) U.S. Cavalry	5.00	7.50	10.00	(22MA) Indian Sikh	4.00	6.00	8.00
(2MA) Infantry Private, marching	4.00	6.00	8.00	(23MA) Uhlan (Prussian Cavalry Soldier)	4.50	6.75	9.00
(3MA) Infantry Private, attention	3.00	4.50	6.00	(24MA) Russian Infantry	4.00	6.00	8.00
(4MA) Infantry Private, lying prone, fixing bayonet	4.50	6.75	9.00	(25MA) German Infantry	4.00	6.00	8.00
(5MA) American Infantry "Doughboy"	4.00	6.00	8.00	(26MA) Infantry First Lieutenant	5.50	8.25	11.00
(6MA) Air Force Mechanic	4.00	6.00	8.00	(27MA) American Indian, standing	4.00	6.00	8.00
(7MA) American Cowboy standing	4.00	6.00	8.00	(28MA) Bandit, on horse	4.00	6.00	8.00
(8MA) American Cowboy on horseback	4.00	6.00	8.00	(29MA) Howitzer	4.50	6.75	9.00
(9MA) Infantry Private, kneeling firing rifle	4.50	6.75	9.00	(30MA) Ski Trooper on patrol	12.00	18.00	24.00
(10MA) Infantry Sergeant	4.50	6.75	9.00	(31MA) Marine Corps Private	4.50	6.75	9.00
(11MA) Gordon Highlander	4.50	6.75	9.00	(32MA) Radio Operator	4.50	6.75	9.00
(12MA) Italian Bersaglieri	4.00	6.00	8.00	(33MA) Red Cross Nurse	4.00	6.00	8.00
(13MA) Kings Royal Rifle Corps	4.00	6.00	8.00	(34MA) Machine Gun Unit, private w/30 cal m/g	4.00	6.00	8.00
(14MA) Royal Scots Greys	4.50	6.75	9.00	(35MA) Tank Commander, standing	4.00	6.00	8.00
(15MA) Seaman Equipped for landing force	4.00	6.00	8.00	(36MA) Infantry Captain	4.00	6.00	8.00
(16MA) Signalman, Navy	4.00	6.00	8.00	(37MA) Chief Petty Officer	4.00	6.00	8.00
(17MA) Infantry Private, charging, two versions	4.50	6.75	9.00	(38MA) Parachute Trooper	4.00	6.00	8.00
(18MA) Infantry Private w/automatic rifle, lying prone, brown uniform	4.00	6.00	8.00	(39MA) 3-inch Anti-Aircraft Gun	5.50	8.25	11.00
(19MA) Infantry Private w/automatic rifle, lying prone, blue uniform	4.50	6.75	9.00	(40MA) Marine Corps Officer	4.00	6.00	8.00
(20MA) Sharpshooter w/rifle, green uniform	4.00	6.00	8.00	(41MA) Motorcycle Messenger	4.50	6.75	9.00
(21MA) French Infantry	4.00	6.00	8.00	(42MA) Wounded Soldier	4.00	6.00	8.00
				(43MA) Flame Thrower	4.00	6.00	8.00
				(44MA) Pilot, with papers	5.50	8.25	11.00
				(45MA) Pilot, adjusting gloves	4.00	6.00	8.00
				(46MA) Sniper, camouflaged	4.00	6.00	8.00

MARX

(47MA) Infantry Colonel	4.00	6.00	8.00
(48MA) Captain Commands Battleship	4.00	6.00	8.00
(49MA) Officer in full dress uniform	4.00	6.00	8.00
(50MA) General	6.00	9.00	12.00
(51MA) 50 cal. machine gun	6.00	9.00	12.00
(52MA) Fireman, sold with fire truck	4.00	6.00	8.00
(53 MA) Fireman with hose, sold with fire truck	6.00	9.00	12.00
(54MA) Fireman with saw, probably sold with fire truck	No Price Found		

MARX Soldiers of Fortune, set of eight with pop gun.	125.00	188.00	250.00
MARX Soldiers of Fortune, set of eight with cannon.	125.00	188.00	250.00
MARX Soldiers of Fortune, Fort Dix Barracks	100.00	150.00	200.00
MARX Soldiers of Fortune, set of 24 with pop gun . . .	125.00	188.00	250.00
MARX Anti-Tank set, anti-tank gun, exploding tanks, soldiers, circa 1940	500.00	750.00	1000.00

MARX Anti-Tank Set, open box.
Photo by Ed Poole

MARX Anti-Tank Set, box top.
Photo by Ed Poole

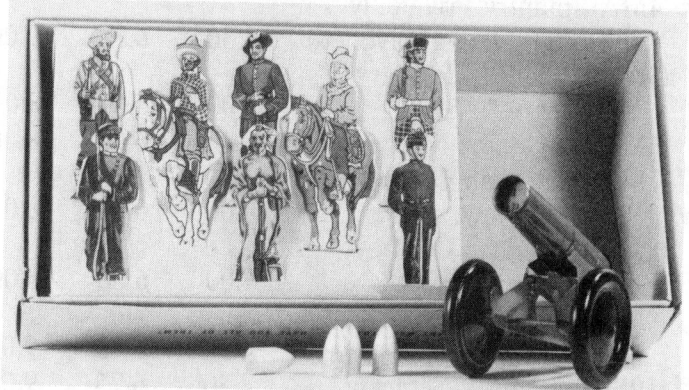

MARX Set with cannon, "Soldiers of Fortune."
Photo by Ed Poole

MARX Set with popgun, "Soldiers of Fortune".
Photo by Ed Poole

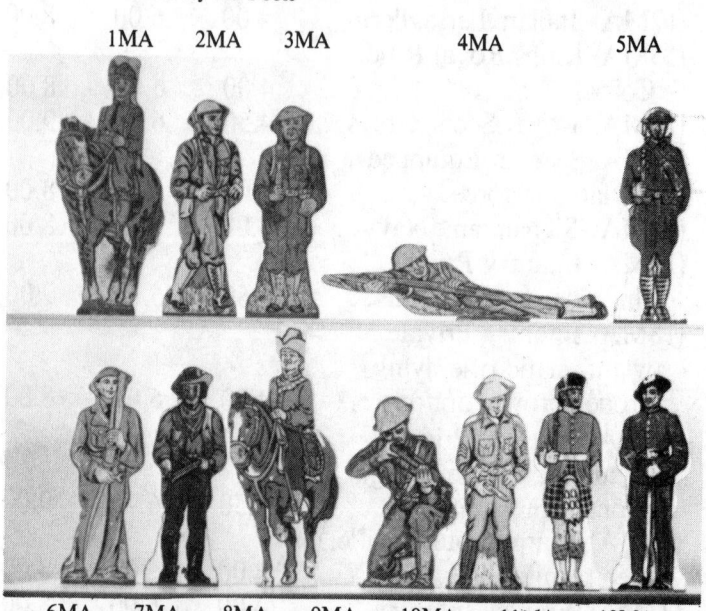

1MA   2MA   3MA   4MA   5MA

6MA   7MA   8MA   9MA   10MA   11MA   12MA

Photo by Ed Poole

13MA 14MA 15MA 16MA 17MA 17MA

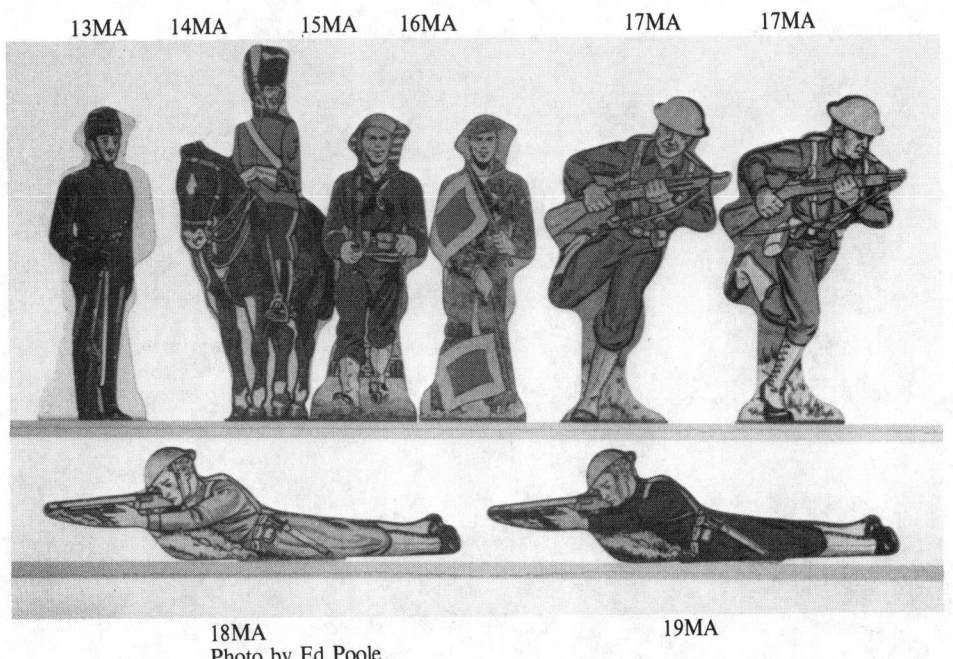

18MA
Photo by Ed Poole

19MA

20MA 21MA 22MA 23MA 24MA

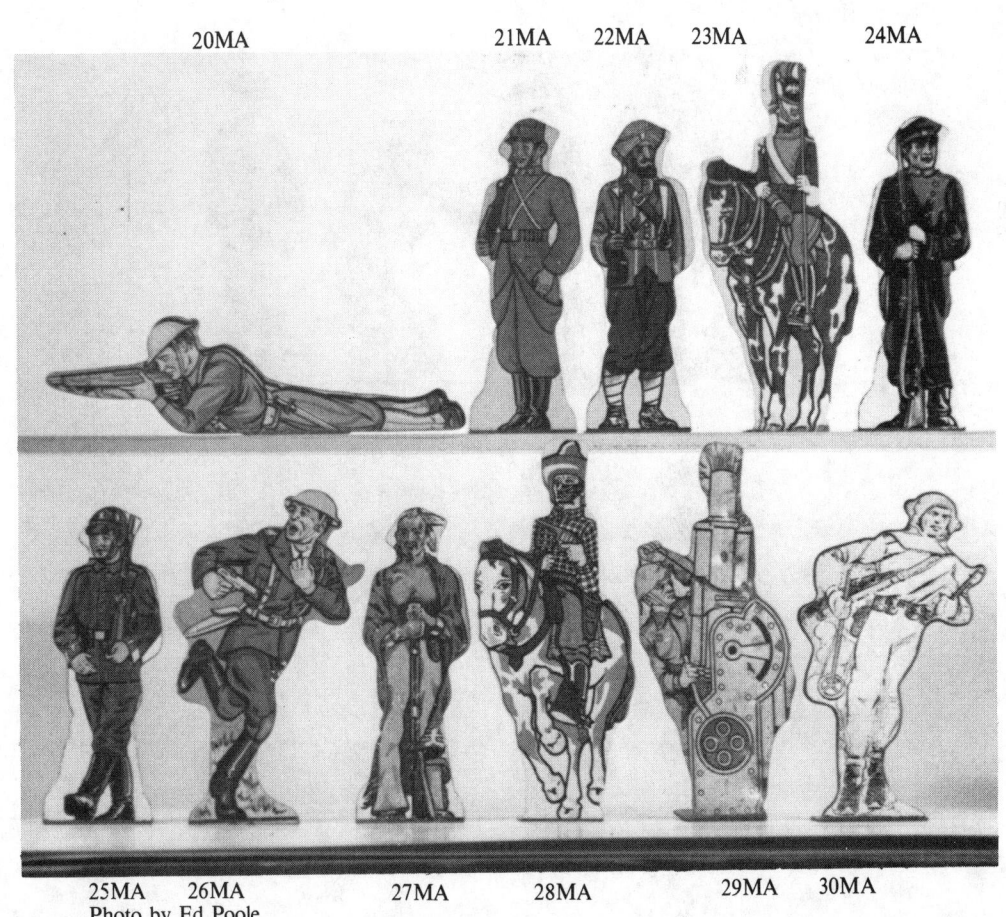

25MA 26MA 27MA 28MA 29MA 30MA
Photo by Ed Poole

31MA 32MA 33MA 34MA 35MA 36MA 3 7MA

38MA 39MA 40MA 41MA 42MA 43MA
Photo by Ed Poole

44MA 45MA 46MA 47MA

48MA 49MA 50MA 51MA
Photo by Ed Poole

52MA

53MA

54MA

Courtesy Jim Casey

MARX PLAYSETS

These sets, with plastic figures and buildings in metal or plastic, were produced from the late 1940s through 1976, and have become increasingly popular in the last few years. Many of the figures are beautifully sculpted, displaying striking detail that can't be matched in metal, and a number of the sets contain an enormous amount of accessories. The Marx Miniature Playsets, with considerably smaller figures (most of the others are 54mm. high), were manufactured from 1963-67. According to Ferriot Bros. of Akron, Ohio, about 90% of the sculpture was by Joe Ferriot. The sets are listed here alphabetically, rather than by number, and where sets begin with the word "Official", that word is dropped to the rear. Mint with the Playsets means a boxed set that hasn't been opened, or if opened, the building hasn't been put together, and all the parts are in their original paper bags. Very Good signals that the building has been put together, that all the parts are there, and that everything is in excellent condition. In Good, the building shows wear, and some parts are missing. Because of continuing reissues from original molds, caution is required. Most and perhaps all of the reissues can be spotted as such, but it takes a practiced eye.

Photo by Ed Poole   Marx Medieval Castle Fort.

Photo by Ed Poole   Marx Medieval Castle Box.

MARX

	G	VG	M
Adventures of Robin Hood (Richard Greene tv series) 4722	No Price Found		
Alamo 3442	225.00	338.00	450.00
Alamo 3534	No Price Found		
Alamo 3539	250.00	375.00	450.00
Alamo 3540	No Price Found		
Alamo 3543	200.00	300.00	400.00
Alamo 3546	375.00	563.00	750.00
Alamo 59091	225.00	338.00	450.00
Alaska 3708	500.00	750.00	1000.00
Allstate Blue and Grey 5959	No Price Found		
Allstate Centennial Blue & Grey 5929	No Price Found		
Allstate Farm Set 6020	72.00	108.00	145.00
Allstate Fort Apache 5951	No Price Found		
American Airline Astro Jet Port 4822	200.00	300.00	400.00
American Airlines International Jet Port 4810	No Price Found		
American Airlines International Jet Port 4811	No Price Found		
American Airlines International Jet Port 4812	No Price Found		
American Patrol 4165	No Price Found		
American Patrol 6007	325.00	488.00	650.00
American Patrol 6058	No Price Found		
Arctic Explorer 3702	500.00	750.00	1000.00
Army Barracks 3740	No Price Found		
Army Barracks 3742	No Price Found		
Army Combat Set 4148	No Price Found		
Army Combat Set 6017	No Price Found		
Army Combat Set 6018	No Price Found		
Army Combat Set 6019	No Price Found		
Army Combat Training Center 2654	175.00	265.00	350.00
Army Combat Training Center 4150	No Price Found		
Atomic Cape Canaveral	200.00	300.00	400.00
Auto Center Friction Cars 6002	No Price Found		
Babyland Nursery 3379	175.00	263.00	350.00
Babyland Nursery 3380	175.00	263.00	350.00
Babyland Nursery 3980	175.00	263.00	350.00
Bar-M Ranch 3956	45.00	68.00	90.00
Bar-M Ranch 3963	No Price Found		
Bar-M Ranch 3964	No Price Found		
Bar-M Ranch 3965	45.00	68.00	90.00
Battle of the Alamo 59091C	300.00	450.00	600.00
Battle of the Blue & Grey 2646 (small set, no house)	No Price Found		
Battle of the Blue & Grey 4658, large set	475.00	715.00	950.00
Battle of the Blue & Grey 4744	475.00	715.00	950.00
Battle of the Blue & Grey 4745	375.00	563.00	750.00
Battle of the Blue & Grey 4761, (small set, no house)	No Price Found		
Battle of the Blue & Grey 4762	450.00	675.00	900.00
Battle of the Blue & Grey 59098C (Sears)	No Price Found		
Battle of the Little Big Horn 4679	300.00	450.00	600.00
Battleground 2718, Montgomery-Ward	162.00	245.00	325.00
Battleground 3745	No Price Found		
Battleground 4169 (U.S. & Nazi troops)	No Price Found		
Battleground 4202	30.00	45.00	60.00
Battleground 4204	90.00	135.00	180.00
Battleground 4752	125.00	188.00	250.00
Battleground 4754	250.00	375.00	500.00
Battleground 4756	125.00	188.00	250.00
Battleground 4757	150.00	225.00	300.00
Battleground 4781	No Price Found		
Battleground 5934	No Price Found		
Battleground 48-2718m	No Price Found		
Battleground Convoy Set 3746	150.00	225.00	300.00
Battleground Terrain Set 4184	No Price Found		
Beachhead Assault 0641	125.00	188.00	250.00
Beachhead Landing 4638	125.00	188.00	250.00
Beachhead Landing 4639	No Price Found		
Beachhead Landing Set 4939 (U.S., Nazi troops)	No Price Found		
Ben Hur 4701 (largest set)	No Price Found		
Ben Hur 4702	700.00	1050.00	1400.00
Ben Hur 3696 (smallest set, but sought-after because of colors of plastic)	1250.00	1875.00	2500.00
Big Inch Pipeline 4445	200.00	300.00	400.00
Big Inch Pipeline 6008	No Price Found		
Big Top Circus 4310	No Price Found		
Big Top Circus 48-2714	250.00	375.00	500.00
Blue and Grey 2258, small set	No Price Found		
Blue and Grey 3000	225.00	338.00	450.00
Blue and Grey 4528	350.00	525.00	700.00
Blue and Grey (Sears) 4765	No Price Found		
Blue and Grey 5959	No Price Found		
Blue and Grey H.O. set	150.00	225.00	300.00
Blue and Grey (Sears) 59098	325.00	490.00	650.00
Boot Camp Playset 4645	65.00	98.00	130.00
Boy's Camp (number unknown), Boy Scout figures, etc.	450.00	675.00	900.00
Cape Canaveral, no number, 1960, larger box	162.00	243.00	325.00

MARX

54mm, L to R: Johnny Ringo, Lucas McCain, Mark McCain, Tonto, Lone Ranger. Value Ringo $125, McCains $25 each, others $15 each. Photo by Gary J. Linden

60mm hard plastic, top, L to R: Sitting Bull, Davy Crockett, Daniel Boone. Bottom, L to R: Kit Carson, Custer, Buffalo Bill. Value $15 each. Photo by Gary J. Linden

Wyatt Earp. Value $25 Photo by Gary J. Linden

54mm StageCoach with Driver and Bandit. Value $100 Photo by Gary J. Linden

3" soft plastic Cowboys. Value $2 each. Photo by Gary J. Linden

60mm soft plastic Cowboys. Value $3 each Photo by Gary J. Linden

3" soft plastic Indians. Value $5 each
Photo by Gary J. Linden

The rare six vinyl frontiersmen from the Fort Apache set, 60mm. Value $5 each.
Photo by Gary J. Linden

60mm 7th Cavalry from Fort Apache sets.
Value $10 each
Photo by Gary J. Linden

The rare five mounted 7th Cavalry figures from carryall sets. 54mm. Value $7 each.
Photo by Gary J. Linden

The nine rare 54mm frontiersmen from the Daniel Boone set. Value $30 each.
Photo by Gary J. Linden

MARX

60mm soft plastic WWI Doughboys, L to R: Officer, Charging Gas Mask, Grey Grenadier, Marching in Campaign Hat, Marching in Overseas Cap. Value $8 each.
Photo by Gary J. Linden

60mm soft plastic Union Army Value $6 each
Photo by Gary J. Linden

60mm soft plastic West Point Cadets. Value $2.50 each. Overcoat $4
Photo by Gary J. Linden

Falling Rider on shot horse, 54mm, from the Civil War Set. Value $75. In gray $150.
Photo by Gary J. Linden

60mm hard plastic U.S. Army Marching Band
No price found
Photo by Gary J. Linden

60mm soft plastic, U.S. Army, Mexican War. Value $12 each
Photo by Gary J. Linden

272

MARX

	G	VG	M
Cape Canaveral 2656......	125.00	188.00	250.00
Cape Canaveral 4522......	125.00	188.00	250.00
Cape Canaveral 4524......	No Price Found		
Cape Canaveral 4525	100.00	150.00	200.00
Cape Canaveral 4526	125.00	188.00	250.00
Cape Canaveral 4528	175.00	263.00	350.00
Cape Canaveral 5935......	No Price Found		
Cape Canaveral 5963......	162.00	245.00	325.00
Cape Canaveral missile Center 2686..........	No Price Found		
Cape Canaveral Missile Center 4525..........	175.00	265.00	350.00
Cape Canaveral Missile Center 4526..........	No Price Found		
Cape Kennedy 4625.......	No Price Found		
Captain Gallant of the Foreign Legion 4729....	500.00	750.00	1000.00
Captain Gallant of the Foreign Legion 4730	500.00	750.00	1000.00
Captain Space Solar Academy 7020........	No Price Found		
Captain Space Solar Academy 7026........	125.00	188.00	250.00
Captain Space Solar Port 7018	300.00	450.00	600.00
Castle and Moat Set 4734..	No Price Found		
Castle Fort 4709	182.00	275.00	365.00
Castle Fort 4710.........	175.00	265.00	350.00
Cattle Drive 3983 (mid 1970s)	No Price Found		
Charge of the Light Brigade	225.00	338.00	450.00
Church 3850.............	No Price Found		
Church 3852.............	No Price Found		
Colonial Service Station 3450	100.00	150.00	200.00
Commanche Pass 3416	175.00	263.00	350.00
Complete Army Battle-ground 9574	No Price Found		
Complete Jet Port 5945....	No Price Found		
Complete U.S. Army Train-ing Center 4124........	No Price Found		
Complete U.S. Army Train-ing Center 4144........	No Price Found		
Complete Happitime Dairy Farm (Sears)..........	No Price Found		
Complete Happitime Farm 5957	No Price Found		
Construction Camp 4439 ..	225.00	338.00	450.00
Construction Camp 4442...	No Price Found		
Construction Set 4436.....	No Price Found		
Construction Set 4440.....	200.00	300.00	400.00
Cowboy and Indian Camp Set 3949..........	No Price Found		

	G	VG	M
Cowboy and Indian Camp Set 3950.............	No Price Found		
Cowboys and Indians 2660.	No Price Found		
Cowboys and Indians Set 3162	No Price Found		
Crop Duster Plane Set 0796	50.00	75.00	100.00
Custer's Last Stand 4779 (has Sitting Bull)	325.00	485.00	650.00
Custer's Last Stand 6014...	No Price Found		
D-Day Army Set (U.S., Nazi troops) 6027...........	250.00	375.00	500.00
D-Day Invasion 6012	350.00	525.00	700.00
D.E.W. Defense Line Arctic Satellite Base 4802......	No Price Found		
Daktari 3717.............	No Price Found		
Daktari 3718.............	275.00	363.00	550.00
Daktari 3720 (large set)....	350.00	525.00	700.00
Daniel Boone 0631.......	No Price Found		
Daniel Boone Frontier Playset 1393..........	400.00	600.00	800.00
Daniel Boone Frontier Playset 1396..........	400.00	600.00	800.00
Daniel Boone Wilderness Scout Playset 0670, nine 54mm. frontiersmen (rare)	No Price Found		
Daniel Boone Wilderness Scout Set 2640, 54mm. figures	225.00	338.00	450.00
Davy Crockett at the Alamo, Official 3520....	No Price Found		
Davy Crockett at the Alamo, Official 3530....	300.00	450.00	600.00
Davy Crockett at the Alamo, 3534...........	No Price Found		
Davy Crockett at the Alamo, 3540	425.00	638.00	850.00
Davy Crockett at the Alamo 3544	425.00	638.00	850.00
Desert Fox 4177.........	No Price Found		
Desert Fox 4178..........	600.00	900.00	1200 00
Desert Patrol 4174 (U.S., Nazi troops)...........	175.00	265.00	350.00
Diner 3770..............	No Price Found		
Diner 3772..............	No Price Found		
Disneyland Playset 4368...	300.00	450.00	600.00
Disneyland Playset 5995...	1000.00	1500.00	2000.00
8 Miniature Sports Cars 5930	No Price Found		
Enchanted Village 3249....	No Price Found		
Enchanted Village 3252....	No Price Found		
Farm Set 3942 (100 pieces).	No Price Found		
Farm Set 3923...........	No Price Found		
Farm Set 3937...........	No Price Found		
Farm Set 3943...........	No Price Found		
Farm Set 3952...........	No Price Found		

MARX

MARX Alamo Playset figures and gate. Value gate $35.00
Photo by Paul Stadinger

MARX Rin Tin Tin Playset figures. Value Rip $15.
Value Rin Tin Tin $7
Photo by Paul Stadinger

MARX Robin Hood figures. Richard Greene Value $85. Others $14 each.

MARX Captain Gallant Playset figures. Value $6 each. Cuffy, Captain
Gallant $25. Arabs $30 each.

MARX Warriors of the World, a sampling of them shown here, are valued
by collectors. They were made in the U.S., West Germany and Hong Kong.
Value about $10 in mint.
Courtesy Hank Anton

MARX 70mm spacemen and robot, circa 1950s. Robot is worth $15 in mint,
as are spacemen with helmets. Spacemen worth $10 without helmets. The
figures, probably the best of the 1950s spacemen, originally sold for 10¢ apiece.
Photo by Bill Hanlon

MARX 70mm Spacemen, circa 1950s. Value $10 apiece in mint. $15 with
helmet.
Photo by Bill Hanlon

Some of Marx's "Warriors of the World."
Prices average $10 in mint.   Photo by Ed Poole

MARX

MARX made a number of individual soldiers. This one is marked "WW II Canadian Soldiers ... Louis Marx & Co." and is one of Marx's larger soldiers. Courtesy John Schmidt
Courtesy John Schmidt

MARX Gallant Men character figures.
Value $35 each

MARX Jungle Jim figures, L to R: Hunter, Jungle Jim, Kolu. Photo by Paul Stadinger Value $15 each on Jim, Kolu.

MARX Untouchables Playset figures. Capone and Ness $12 each. Others $10.00

Long Ranger Set
Courtesy J. Schmidt

MARX Gunsmoke character figures. Value $150 each.

Top, L to R: Barracks "CO A T7-34," 11½" wide, "Headquarters U.S. Army Training Center T3-21," 11" wide. Value $15 each.
Bottom - "Post Exchange, Company C Supply, Headquarters T30, 31 & 32" block 20" long. No price found.
Photo by Ed Poole

MARX L to R: Wagon Train (two figures), Lone Ranger, Tonto, Wyatt Earp, Jim Hardy (Tales of Wells Fargo). Wagon Train $50 each, Lone Ranger, Tonto $15 each, Earp $25, Jim Hardy $85.

MARX

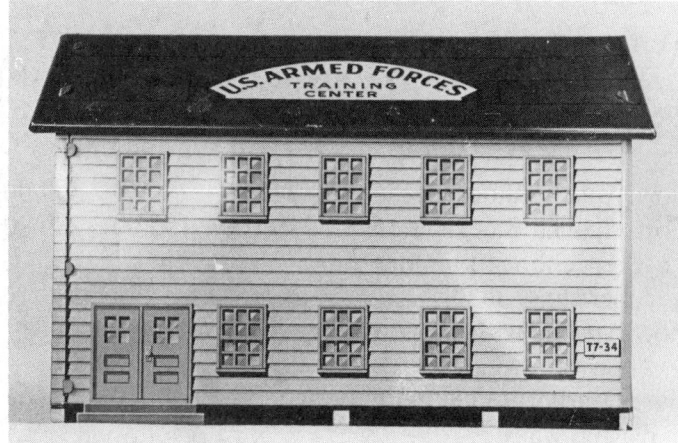

Tin litho barracks marked "T7-34" from a U.S. Armed Forces Training Center Set. Value in Very Good $30.
Courtesy John Schmidt

60mm soft plastic, United Nations, L to R, U.S. troops: Pilot, Soldier, Marine, Sailor. Value $20 each.
Photo by Gary J. Linden

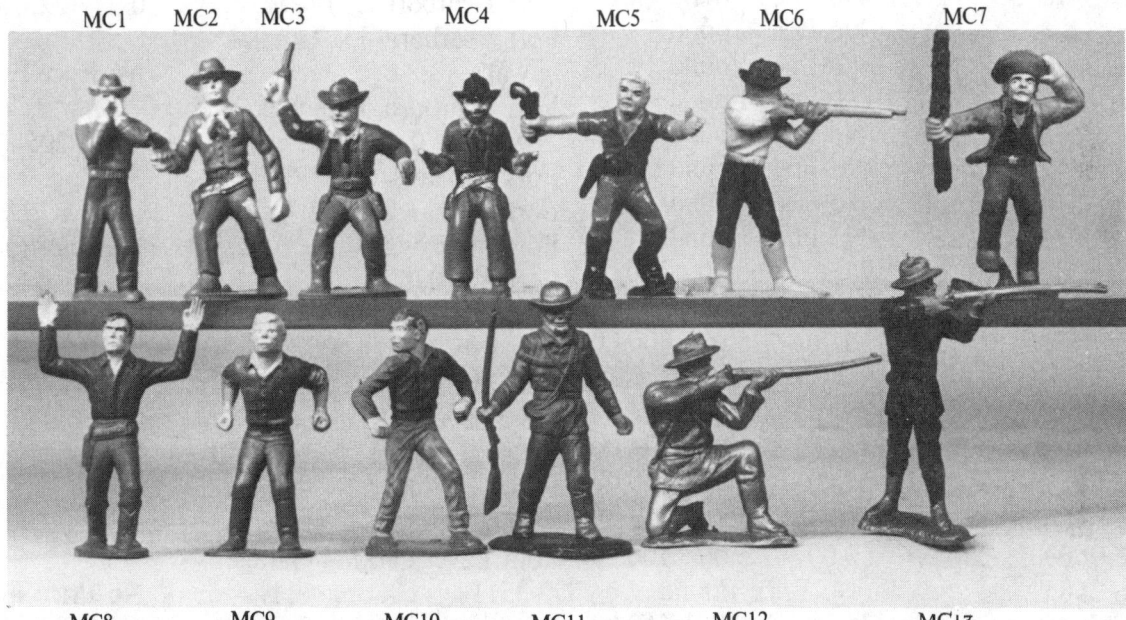

Marx Cowboys and Frontiersmen. These were sold unpainted (painted by the author). Value $6 each.

Marx Alamo figures. They were sold unpainted (painted by the author). Value $8 each.

MARX

	G	VG	M
Farm Set 3953	150.00	225.00	300.00
Farm Set 3964	No Price Found		
Farm Set 3970	No Price Found		
Farm Set 5942	No Price Found		
Farm Set 6006	225.00	335.00	450.00
Farm Set 6050	No Price Found		
Farm Truck Set 0977	7.00	11.00	15.00
Fighting Knights 4635	30.00	45.00	60.00
Fire House 3779	No Price Found		
Fire House 3780	No Price Found		
Fire House 3782	No Price Found		
Fire House 4819	900.00	1350.00	1800.00
Fire House 4820	No Price Found		
Flintstones Set 2670	175.00	265.00	350.00
Flintstones Set 4672	275.00	365.00	550.00
Flintstones Set 5948	No Price Found		
Fort Apache 3516	No Price Found		
Fort Apache 3606	No Price Found		
Fort Apache 3607	No Price Found		
Fort Apache 3609	No Price Found		
Fort Apache 3610	No Price Found		
Fort Apache 3612	No Price Found		
Fort Apache 3614	No Price Found		
Fort Apache 3616	No Price Found		
Fort Apache 3647	175.00	263.00	350.00
Fort Apache 3654	No Price Found		
Fort Apache 3660	150.00	225.00	300.00
Fort Apache 3675, over 300 pieces	No Price Found		
Fort Apache 3680	115.00	175.00	235.00
Fort Apache 3681	125.00	188.00	250.00
Fort Apache 3682	No Price Found		
Fort Apache 3683	50.00	75.00	100.00
Fort Apache 3685	No Price Found		
Fort Apache 3686	125.00	188.00	250.00
Fort Apache 3692, over 300 pieces	No Price Found		
Fort Apache 3694	No Price Found		
Fort Apache 3698	No Price Found		
Fort Apache 4102	No Price Found		
Fort Apache 4202	125.00	188.00	250.00
Fort Apache 4208	50.00	75.00	100.00
Fort Apache 4681	No Price Found		
Fort Apache 4685 carryall	100.00	150.00	200.00
Fort Apache 6059 (Sears)	No Price Found	.00	
Fort Apache 6063	No Price Found		
Fort Apache 6068	No Price Found		
Fort Apache 59093C (Sears)	100.00	150.00	200.00
Fort Apache Rin Tin Tin 3512	No Price Found		
Fort Apache Rin Tin Tin 3616	No Price Found		
Fort Apache Rin Tin Tin 3627	No Price Found		
Fort Apache Rin Tin Tin 3628	200.00	300.00	400.00

	G	VG	M
Fort Apache Rin Tin Tin 3658	300.00	450.00	600.00
Fort Apache Rin Tin Tin 3957	No Price Found		
Fort Apache Stockade 3612	175.00	263.00	350.00
Fort Apache Stockade 3678	100.00	150.00	200.00
Fort Apache with famous Americans 3630	No Price Found		
Fort Apache with Famous Americans 3636	No Price Found		
Fort Dearborn 3504 (with plastic walls)	No Price Found		
Fort Dearborn 3509 (metal walls)	200.00	300.00	400.00
Fort Dearborn 3510 (metal walls)	190.00	285.00	380.00
Fort Dearborn 3514	150.00	225.00	300.00
Fort Dearborn 3519 (metal walls)	No Price Found		
Fort Dearborn 3688 (plastic walls)	135.00	205.00	275.00
Fort Mohawk 3751	No Price Found		
Fort Mohawk 3752	250.00	375.00	500.00
Fort Mohawk 3757	No Price Found		
Fort Pitt 0750	No Price Found		
Fort Pitt 3741	No Price Found		
Fort Pitt 3742	No Price Found		
Fort Pitt 3750	No Price Found		
Four Level Allstate Service Station 6004	No Price Found		
Four Level Parking Garage 3502	No Price Found		
Four Level Parking Garage 3511	No Price Found		
Four Level Parking Garage & Service Station 3501	No Price Found		
Freight Terminal, no number	122.00	185.00	245.00
Freight Trucking Terminal 5220	60.00	90.00	120.00
Freight Trucking Terminal 5420	70.00	105.00	140.00
Freight Trucking Terminal 5422	185.00	280.00	375.00
Frontiersmen and Indians 3172	No Price Found		
Galaxy Command 4206	No Price Found		
Gallant Men Army Playset 4623 (U.S. troops)	No Price Found		
Gallant Men Army Playset 4632 (U.S. troops)	50.00	75.00	100.00
Giant Battleground 4768 (U.S., Nazi troops)	No Price Found		
Giant Martian Landing 4306	125.00	188.00	250.00

MARX	G	VG	M
Glendale Railroad Station 4410	No Price Found		
Gunsmoke 4268 (with gold mine)	No Price Found		
Happitime Army and Air Force Training Center 4159	200.00	300.00	400.00
Happitime Farm Set 3480 . .	No Price Found		
Happitime Farm Set 3951 . .	No Price Found		
Happitime Farm Set 5937 . .	No Price Found		
Happitime Farm Set 6020 . .	No Price Found		
Happitime Fort Apache, no number	175.00	265.00	350.00
Happitime Fort Apache 5915	No Price Found		
Happitime Fort Apache 5962	No Price Found		
Happitime International Jet Port 5931	No Price Found		
Happitime Roy Rogers Rodeo Ranch 3990	125.00	188.00	250.00
Happitime Roy Rogers Rodeo Ranch 3992	200.00	300.00	400.00
Happitime Service Station 3461	No Price Found		
Happitime Service Station 3480	200.00	300.00	400.00
Happitime Service Station 3484	No Price Found		
Happitime Service Station 3596	No Price Found		
Heliport Service Station 3487	No Price Found		
History in the Pacific 4164 .	175.00	265.00	350.00
Holiday Turnpike 5230, battery-operated	No Price Found		
Hugh O'Brien Wyatt Earp Dodge City Western Town Official, 4228	400.00	600.00	800.00
Indian Warfare 4748	No Price Found		
Indian Warfare 4778	No Price Found		
International Airport Set 4806	300.00	450.00	600.00
International Geophysical Year Arctic Satellite Base 4800	No Price Found		
International Jet Port 4808 .	75.00	112.00	150.00
Irrigated Farm Set 6021 (working pump)	No Price Found		
Irrigation Farm Set 612 . . .	20.00	30.00	40.00
Iwo Jima 4147	150.00	225.00	300.00
Iwo Jima 6057	No Price Found		
Iwo Jima 6062 (Sears)	No Price Found		
Johnny Apollo Moon Launch Center 4630	No Price Found		

	G	VG	M
Johnny Ringo Western Frontier Set 4784	No Price Found		
Johnny Tremaine Revolutionary War 3401	No Price Found		
Johnny West Ranch 4194 (may not have been produced)	No Price Found		
Jungle Animal 3714	150.00	225.00	300.00
Jungle Jim Playset, Official 3706	400.00	600.00	800.00
Jungle Playset 3705, Metal Trading Post	300.00	450.00	600.00
Jungle Playset 3716	No Price Found		
Knight and Viking 4733 . . .	175.00	263.00	350.00
Knights and Vikings 4743M	150.00	225.00	300.00
Large Allstate Service Station 6003	No Price Found		
Large Happitime Dairy Farm 3972	No Price Found		
Large Service Station 5941 .	No Price Found		
Large Service Station 5954 .	No Price Found		
Lazy Day Farm Set 3945 . . .	200.00	300.00	400.00
Little Red School House 3381	No Price Found		
Little Red School House 3382	225.00	375.00	450.00
Lone Ranger Ranch 3967 . .	200.00	300.00	400.00
Lone Ranger Ranch 3968 . .	No Price Found		
Lone Ranger Ranch 3969 . .	150.00	225.00	300.00
Lone Ranger Ranch 3980 . .	No Price Found		
Lone Ranger Rodeo Set 3696	175.00	265.00	350.00
Lone Ranger Rodeo Set 9392	200.00	300.00	400.00
Marine Beach Landing 4734	No Price Found		
Marine Beachhead 4731	75.00	112.00	150.00
Marine Beachhead 4732	No Price Found		
Marine Beachhead 4734	No Price Found		
Marx Masterbuilder Kit, the White House and 35 Presidents	30.00	45.00	60.00
Medieval Castle 4700	200.00	300.00	400.00
Medieval Castle 4704	No Price Found		
Medieval Castle with Knights and Vikings 4707	200.00	300.00	400.00
Medieval Castle 4708	212.00	318.00	425.00
Medieval Castle 4709	150.00	225.00	300.00
Medieval Castle 4710	125.00	188.00	250.00
Medieval Castle with Knights and Vikings 4733	No Price Found		
Medieval Castle with Knights and Vikings 4753	No Price Found		
Medieval Castle with Knights and Vikings 6053	No Price Found		
Metal Service Station 3449 .	No Price Found		
Metal Service Station 3453 .	No Price Found		

MARX

MAL9   MAL10   MAL11   MAL12   MAL13

MAL14   MAL15   MAL16   MAL17   MAL18   MAL19

Marx Alamo figures. Mexicans worth $8 each.
Frontiersmen worth $8 each.

MB1   MB2   MB3   MB4   MB5   MB6   MB7

MB8   MB9   MB10   MB11   MB12   MB13   MB14

Marx Battleground figures. Value $10 each

MB15   MB16   MB17   MB18   MB19   MB20   MB21

MB22   MB23   MB24   MB25   MB26   MB27   MB28   MB29   MB30

Marx Battleground figures. Value $10 each

279

MARX

MG1 MG2 MG3 MG4 MG5 MG6

MG7 MG8 MG9 MG10 MG11 MG12 MG13

Marx Germans. Not shown are the motorcyclist with sidecar and sitting soldier. Value about $1 each.

60mm soft plastic, United Nations, L to R: Great Britain, Republic of Korea, France, Canada, Turkey. Extremely rare. Value $30.00 each.
Photo by Gary J. Linden

60mm soft plastic U.S. Army. Value $20 each. L to R: Pilot walking, soldier carrying wounded buddy, paratrooper.
Photo by Gary J. Linden

40mm common U.S. Army. Value $1 each
Photo by Gary J. Linden

MARX

	G	VG	M
Metal Service Station 3459.	No Price Found		
Metal Service Station 3480	150.00	225.00	300.00
Metal Service Station 3490	150.00	225.00	300.00
Mid Town Shopping Center 2644	No Price Found		
Midtown Service Station 3420	No Price Found		
Midtown Service Station 3495	No Price Found		
Military Academy 4716	250.00	375.00	500.00
Military Academy 4718	No Price Found		
Modern Farm (number not known)	105.00	158.00	210.00
Modern Farm Set 3925	50.00	75.00	100.00
Modern Farm Set 3926	135.00	200.00	275.00
Modern Farm Set 3927	No Price Found		
Modern Farm Set 3930	No Price Found		
Modern Farm Set 3931	150.00	225.00	300.00
Modern Farm Set 3932	No Price Found		
Modern Farm Set 3933	No Price Found		
Modern Farm Set 3938	No Price Found		
Modern Farm Set 3940	No Price Found		
Modern Farm Set 3971	No Price Found		
Modern Farm Set 4734	No Price Found		
Modern Service Station 3436	100.00	150.00	200.00
Modern Service Station 3450	No Price Found		
Modern Service Station 3452	100.00	150.00	200.00
Modern Service Station 3457	No Price Found		
Modern Service Station 3469	150.00	225.00	300.00
Modern Service Station 3471	90.00	135.00	180.00
Nativity Set (number not known)	No Price Found		
Navarone Mountain Battleground Set 3412	92.00	138.00	185.00
Navarone Mountain Battleground Set 4302	50.00	75.00	100.00
New Car Sales and Service 3465	No Price Found		
New Car Sales and Service 3466	55.00	82.50	110.00
Noah's Ark 48	150.00	225.00	300.00
Noah's Ark 3720	No Price Found		
Noah's Ark 3960	No Price Found		
Noah's Ark 48-243399	175.00	265.00	350.00
Operation Moonbase 4654	250.00	375.00	500.00
Pet Shop 4209	175.00	265.00	350.00
Pet Shop 4210	175.00	265.00	350.00
Police Station 3719	No Price Found		
Prehistoric Animals 3399	125.00	188.00	250.00
Prehistoric Dinosaurs 4208.	112.00	165.00	225.00
Prehistoric Men and Animals	100.00	150.00	200.00
Prehistoric Mountain 3414 .	140.00	210.00	280.00
Prehistoric Times 2650	140.00	210.00	280.00

	G	VG	M
Prehistoric Times 3388	No Price Found		
Prehistoric Times 3390	275.00	412.00	550.00
Prehistoric Times 3391	No Price Found		
Prehistoric Times 3392	175.00	265.00	350.00
Prehistoric Times 3398	100.00	150.00	200.00
Prince Valiant Castle 4706 (has figures)	125.00	188.00	250.00
Private Hedge Set 0260	No Price Found		
Prize Livestock Set 0911	30.00	45.00	60.00
Project Apollo Cape Kennedy 4523	No Price Found		
Project Apollo Moon Landing 4521	No Price Found		
Project Apollo Moon Landing 4646	No Price Found		
Project Mercury Cape Canaveral 4524	No Price Found		
Ranch Set 3792	No Price Found		
Ranch Set 3936	No Price Found		
Ranch Set 5950	No Price Found		
Raytheon Missile Test Center 603A	No Price Found		
Real Life Western Wagon 4998	No Price Found		
Red River Gang 4104 (Cowboys)	No Price Found		
Revolutionary War Set 3402	350.00	525.00	700.00
Revolutionary War Set 3404	450.00	675.00	900.00
Revolutionary War Set 3408	No Price Found		
Rex Mars Planet Patrol 7040	275.00	410.00	550.00
Rex Mars Planet Patrol 7042	No Price Found		
Rex Mars Space Dome 7014	No Price Found		
Rex Mars Space Dome 7016	No Price Found		
Rhine River Battle 4187	No Price Found		
Rifleman Ranch, The 3997.	375.00	565.00	750.00
Rifleman Ranch, The 3998.	No Price Found		
Rin Tin Tin 3657	200.00	300.00	400.00
Rin Tin Tin at Fort Apache 3658	275.00	410.00	550.00
Riverside Service Station 3489	200.00	300.00	400.00
Robin Hood Castle Set 4717 (60 mm. figures)	No Price Found		
Robin Hood Castle Set 4718 (54 mm. figures)	225.00	338.00	450.00
Robin Hood Castle Set 4719 (60 mm. figures)	350.00	525.00	700.00
Robin Hood Castle Set 4723	212.00	318.00	425.00
Roman Gladiator Set 3385.	No Price Found		
Roman Gladiator Set 3386.	No Price Found		
Roy Rogers Double R Bar Ranch 3982	No Price Found		

MARX

	G	VG	M		G	VG	M
Roy Rogers Double R Bar Ranch 3989	No Price Found			Silver City Western Town Set 4220 (has Custer, Boone, Carson, Buffalo Bill, Sitting Bull)	350.00	525.00	700.00
Roy Rogers Mineral City 4227	350.00	525.00	700.00	Skyscraper 5449 (working elevator)	No Price Found		
Roy Rogers Ranch 3980	125.00	188.00	250.00	Skyscraper 5450 (working elevator and light)	No Price Found		
Roy Rogers Ranch 3981	No Price Found			Small Farm Set 3924	No Price Found		
Roy Rogers Ranch 3985	162.00	245.00	325.00	Small Farm Set 3925	No Price Found		
Roy Rogers Rodeo 3689	No Price Found			Sons of Liberty (Sears) 4170	175.00	263.00	350.00
Roy Rogers Rodeo 3690	No Price Found			Space Patrol Rocket Port Set, Official 7020	500.00	750.00	1000.00
Roy Rogers Rodeo Ranch 3979	112.00	165.00	225.00	Stagecoach 1395	100.00	150.00	200.00
Roy Rogers Rodeo Ranch 3986	150.00	225.00	300.00	Stagecoach 3814	50.00	75.00	100.00
Roy Rogers Rodeo Ranch 3988	175.00	265.00	350.00	Stock Farm Set 6005	62.00	93.00	125.00
Roy Rogers Rodeo 3990	175.00	265.00	350.00	Strategic Air Command 6013	No Price Found		
Roy Rogers Rodeo 3992	170.00	255.00	340.00	Suburban Colonial Doll House 4097	50.00	75.00	100.00
Roy Rogers Rodeo Ranch 3996	250.00	375.00	500.00	Super Circus 3920	200.00	300.00	400.00
Roy Rogers Western Town 4216	500.00	750.00	1000.00	Super Circus 4220	900.00	1350.00	1800.00
Roy Rogers Western Town 4258 (large set)	500.00	750.00	1000.00	Super Circus 4319	300.00	450.00	600.00
Roy Rogers Western Town, Official 4259	No Price Found			Super Circus 4320	300.00	450.00	600.00
Satellite Launching Station 2664	No Price Found			Tactical Air Command 4106	No Price Found		
School House 3819	No Price Found			Tales of Wells Fargo 4262	No Price Found		
School House 3820	No Price Found			Tales of Wells Fargo 4263	375.00	525.00	750.00
School House 3821	No Price Found			Tales of Wells Fargo 4264	1000.00	1500.00	2000.00
School House 3822	No Price Found			Tales of Wells Fargo 54762	500.00	750.00	1000.00
Sears Allstate 6003 Service Station	No Price Found			Tank Battle 4172 (U.S., Nazi troops)	No Price Found		
Sears Automotive Center & Store 5490	No Price Found			Tank Battle 6056 (U.S., Nazi troops)	No Price Found		
Sears Automotive Center & Store 5953	No Price Found			Tank Battle 6060 (U.S., Nazi troops)	No Price Found		
Sears Happitime Complete Dairy Farm 5944	No Price Found			Tank Battle 6061 (Sears - U.S., Nazi troops)	No Price Found		
Sears Parking Garage 3432	No Price Found			Tank Battle 6556 (U.S., Nazi troops)	No Price Found		
Sears Store 5980	No Price Found			Three Level Service Station 3505	No Price Found		
Service Station 3451	No Price Found			Three Level Service Station 6049	No Price Found		
Service Station 3454	No Price Found			Tom Corbett Space Academy 7010	325.00	490.00	650.00
Service Station 3455	No Price Found						
Service Station 3456	No Price Found			Tom Corbett Space Academy 7012	No Price Found		
Service Station 3462	No Price Found						
Service Station 3468	No Price Found			Tom Corbett Space Academy 7041	No Price Found		
Service Station 3470	No Price Found						
Service Station 3472	No Price Found			Tom Corbett Space Academy 7102	No Price Found		
Service Station 3486	135.00	205.00	275.00				
Service Station 3508	No Price Found			Toy Factory (Playset?)	32.00	48.00	65.00
Service Station 5459	No Price Found			Treasure Cove Pirate Set 4597	No Price Found		
Service Station 5952	No Price Found						
Shopping Center 3755	No Price Found			Treasure Cove Pirate Set 4598	No Price Found		
Shopping Center 3756	No Price Found						

MARX	G	VG	M
Trucking Terminal 5422...	225.00	338.00	450.00
Trucking Terminal 5424...	150.00	225.00	300.00
Untouchables, Official 4676.	1000.00	2000.00	4000.00
U.S. Airforce Playset 4807..	No Price Found		
U.S. Armed Forces 4149...	225.00	338.00	450.00
U.S. Armed Forces 4151...	No Price Found		
U.S. Armed Forces Training Center 4140..........	No Price Found		
U.S. Armed Forces Training Center 4141..........	No Price Found		
U.S. Armed Forces Training Center 4144 (Marines, soldiers, sailors, airmen, tin litho bldg., etc.)......	No Price Found		
U.S. Armed Forces Training Center 4149	225.00	338.00	450.00
U.S. Armed Forces Training Center 4151	235.00	310.00	475.00
U.S. Armed Forces Training Center 4163..........	No Price Found		
U.S. Army Mobile Set (number unknown, flat figures)	No Price Found		
U.S. Army Training Center 3146	No Price Found		
U.S. Army Training Center 3378	No Price Found		
U.S. Army Training Center 4120	185.00	282.00	425.00
U.S. Army Training Center 4122	No Price Found		
U.S. Army Training Center 4123	225.00	338.00	450.00
U.S. Army Training Center 4131	No Price Found		
U.S. Army Training Center 4133	No Price Found		
U.S. Army Training Center 4134	100.00	150.00	200.00
U.S. Army Training Center 4137	No Price Found		
U.S. Army Training Center 4139	No Price Found		
U.S. Army Training Center 4143?	No Price Found		
U.S. Army Training Center 4153	No Price Found		
Vikings and Knights 6053..	60.00	90.00	120.00
Wagon Train 4785........	No Price Found		
Wagon Train 4788........	350.00	525.00	700.00
Wagon Train, Official 4777.	No Price Found		
Wagon Train, Official 4805.	No Price Found		
Walt Disney Television Playhouse 3452........	No Price Found		

	G	VG	M
Walt Disney TV Playhouse 4232	No Price Found		
Walt Disney TV Playhouse 4349	No Price Found		
Walt Disney TV Playhouse 4350	350.00	525.00	700.00
Walt Disney TV Playhouse 4352	No Price Found		
Walt Disney Zorro, Official, 3753	450.00	675.00	900.00
Walt Disney Zorro, Official, 3754	500.00	750.00	1000.00
Walt Disney Zorro, Official 3758	No Price Found		
Wards Service Center 48-2405M	No Price Found		
Wards Service Station 3473.	No Price Found		
Wards Service Station 3476.	No Price Found		
Wards Service Station 3488.	No Price Found		
Warner Brothers Gallant Men 4634.............	No Price Found		
West Gate Service Station 3485	75.00	112.00	150.00
Western Mining Town 4266	No Price Found		
Western Ranch Set 3954...	100.00	150.00	200.00
Western Stagecoach Playset 1395	62.00	93.00	125.00
Western Town 2652.......	250.00	375.00	500.00
Western Town 4229.......	No Price Found		
Western Town 4230.......	No Price Found		
Western Town Miniature Playset 48-24398	100.00	150.00	200.00
White House, number unknown, house had 8 figures	25.00	38.00	50.00
White House & Presidents 3920 (House & Figures)..	No Price Found		
White House & Presidents 3921 (House & Figures)..	No Price Found		
Wild Animal Jungle Play Set (large animals) 3716.....	No Price Found		
World War II European Theatre 5949..........	No Price Found		
World War II Set 5938 (U.S., Nazi Troops)......	No Price Found		
World War II Set 5939 (Sears - British, French, Russian Troops)........	No Price Found		
Yogi Bear Jellystone National park 4364.......	290.00	435.00	580.00

MARX

Series 098, 60mm soft plastic War of 1812 Sailors. Value $20 each
Photo by Gary J. Linden

40mm common U.S. Army. Value $1 each
Photo by Gary J. Linden

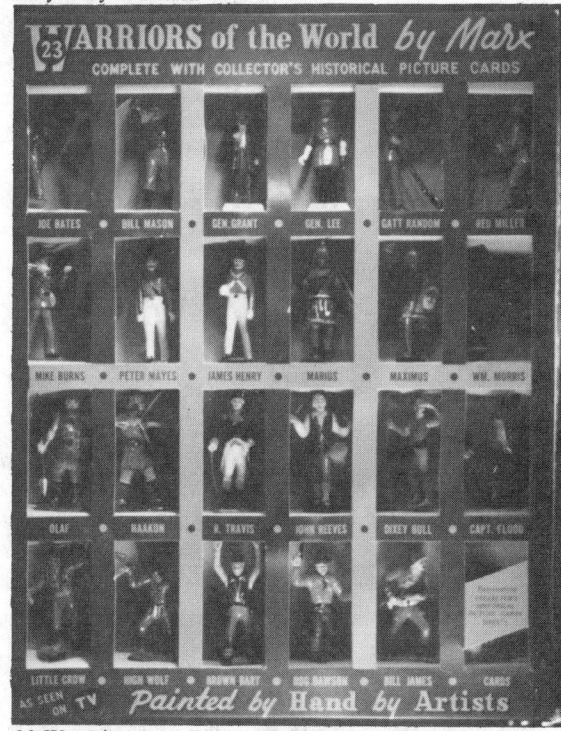

23 Warriors of the World, 60mm hard plastic
Photo by Gary J. Linden Value about $275.

6" high Marines (USMC on shirt). Value $15 each
Courtesy Roger Hocking

6" high Marines (USMC on shirt)
Value $15 each
Courtesy Roger Hocking

Back of 23 Warriors of the World
Photo by Gary J. Linden

284

MARX

American Heroes Set No. 11 of General Vandergrift and WWII Marines.
American Heroes sets sell for about $55 with the box.
Courtesy Robert Worthen

34 Disneykins, hard plastic, hand painted. Value about $9 each.
Photo by Gary J. Linden

4" soft plastic Spaceman. Value $4 each.
Photo by Gary J. Linden

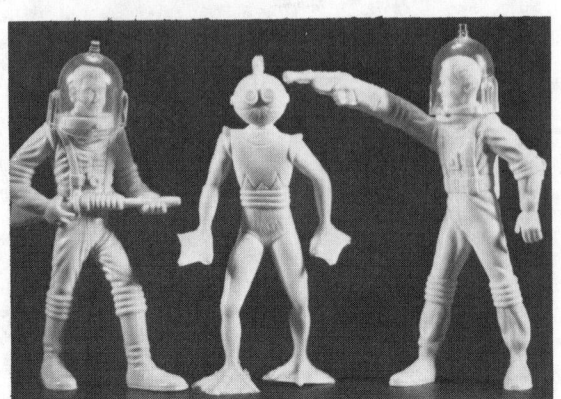

4" soft plastic Spacemen. Alien $8, others $4 each.
Photo by Gary J. Linden

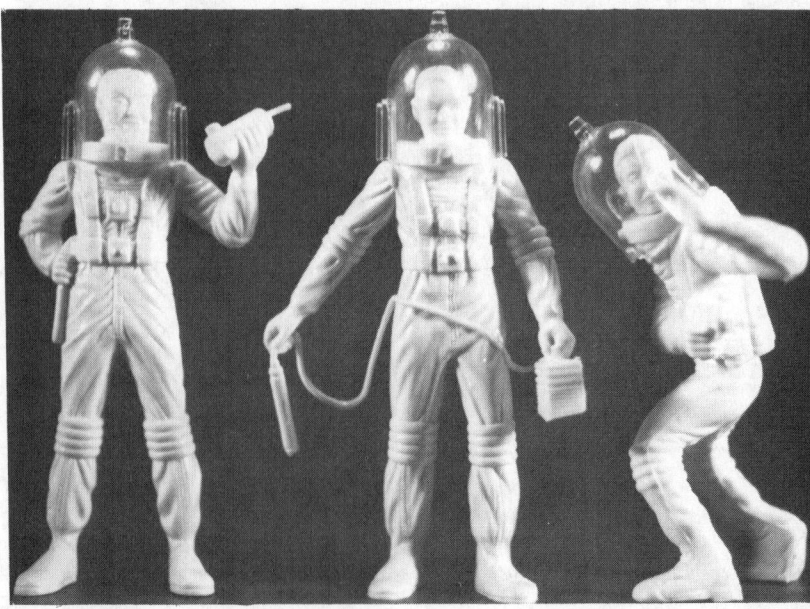

4" soft plastic Spaceman. Value $4 each.
Photo by Gary J. Linden

285

MARX

54mm soft plastic, 8 of the 16 non-character Ben Hur figures. Value $6 each.
Photo by Gary J. Linden

54mm soft plastic, 8 of the 16 non-character Ben Hur figures. Value $6 each.
Photo by Gary J. Linden

54mm accessories, hard and soft plastic, from Ben Hur. Value $6-$15

MARX

Ben Hur chariot. Value $75. Ben Hur, Emperor, Empress sell for $45 each.
Photo by Gary J. Linden

60mm hard plastic. Captain Kidd. Value $30.
Photo by Gary J. Linden

60mm hard plastic Telephone Booth (from Skyscraper), Superman. Value Superman $65.
Photo by Gary J. Linden

60mm hard plastic Babes in Toyland marching soldiers. Value $12 each.
Photo by Gary J. Linden

Series 0838 Royal Canadian Mounted Police, 60mm soft plastic. Value $15 each, with binoculars $30.
Photo by Gary J. Linden

54mm soft plastic from Johnny Tremain set, L to R: Samuel Adams, James Otis, Johnny Tremain, Rab Silsbee. Value $25 each
Photo by Gary J. Linden

40mm soft plastic from Super Circus, L to R: Ringmaster Claude Kirchner, Mary Hartline, Nickey, Cliffy, Scampy. Value $12 each
Photo by Gary J. Linden

287

60mm hard plastic, L to R: Jackie Gleason, Louis Marx, Jackie Gleason
(Ralph Kramden), Pinky Lee. Value $50 each.
Photo by Gary J. Linden

60mm soft plastic from Lassie bag: Gramps, Timmy, Lassie. $16 each.
Photo by Gary J. Linden

3" soft plastic Construction Workers. Value $8 each
Photo by Gary J. Linden

60mm hard plastic, four of eight American Beauties. A set of eight sells
for about $150.
Photo by Gary J. Linden

60mm hard plastic, four of eight American Beauties
Photo by Gary J. Linden

54mm soft plastic Cape Canaveral workers. Value $2.50 each
Photo by Gary J. Linden

MARX

3" soft plastic Fireman. Value $4 each
Photo by Gary J. Linden

3" Freight Station Figures. Value $6 each.
60mm soft plastic Freight Station figures.

60mm Kid Baseball Players. Value $2 each
Photo by Gary J. Linden

60mm soft plastic Freight Station figures Value $6 each.
Photo by Gary J. Linden

54mm soft plastic Race Track figures (5 of 6 shown). Value $15 each.
Photo by Gary J. Linden

3" soft plastic Telephone
Lineman. Value $5.00
Photo by Gary J. Linden

289

MARX

54mm soft plastic Skyscraper figures. Value $12 each.
Photo by Gary J. Linden

60mm hard plastic hand-painted Inaugural Set, L to R: George & Martha Washington, Abe and Mary Lincoln, Dwight and Mamie Eisenhower. Value $75. Photo by Gary J. Linden

60mm hard plastic, Marshal Zhukov, Montgomery, Mendes-France, Napoleon I. Value $40 each, except Montgomery $25.
Photo by Gary J. Linden

60mm hard plastic, L to R: Pope Pius XII, right-hand Jesus, left-hand Jesus, Francis Cardinal Spellman. Value $8 each.
Photo by Gary J. Linden

Famous Canadians, thought to be Marx, sold in Canada with tea. Value $10 each.
Photo by Gary J. Linden

Famous Canadians, thought to be Marx, sold in Canada with tea. $10 each
Photo by Gary J. Linden

60mm hard plastic hand-painted Ancient Chinese Warrior - Ma Chao
Photo by Gary J. Linden

60mm hard plastic hand-painted Ancient Chinese Warrior - Chao Yun
Photo by Gary J. Linden

50mm hard plastic hand-painted Ancient Chinese Warrior - Chang Fei.
Photo by Gary J. Linden

60mm hard plastic hand-painted Ancient Chinese Warrior - Lue Po
Photo by Gary J. Linden

60mm hard plastic hand-painted Ancient Chinese Warrior - Huang Chung
Photo by Gary J. Linden

60mm hard plastic hand-painted Ancient Chinese Warrior - Yau Fei
Photo by Gary J. Linden

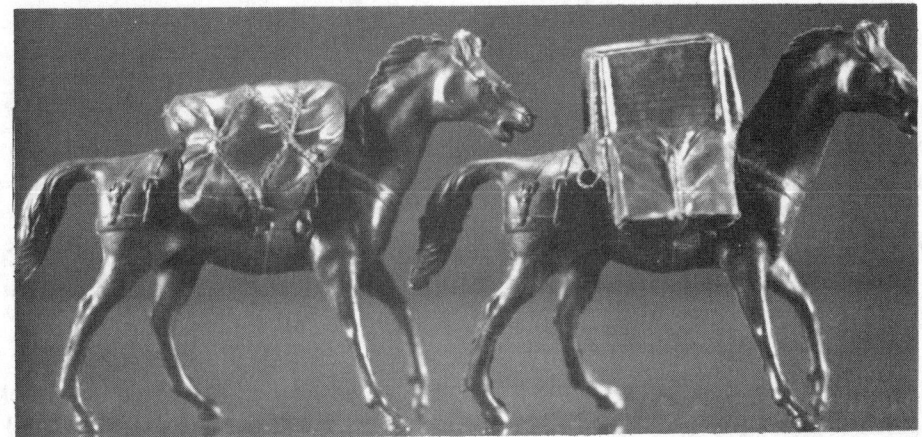

54mm Pack Horses with packs. Value $12 each
Photo by Gary J. Linden

Approx. 3" long soft plastic Wild Animals. Value $3 each
Photo by Gary J. Linden

Approx. 3" long soft plastic Wild Animals. Value $3 each.
Photo by Gary J. Linden

Approx. 3" long soft plastic Wild Animals. Value $3 each
Photo by Gary J. Linden

PECO FIGURES

By Bill Hanlon

An unbreakable toy figure with detachable equipment doesn't seem like a very revolutionary idea today, but back in 1952 it was just that. These highly detailed 88mm figures were conceived and sculpted by John Benneth of Tigard, Oregon.

Having spent most of his youth on a farm in Ada, Minnesota, John and his brother David often enjoyed making their own toys out of modeling clay.

In 1939, at the age of twelve, John and his family moved to Portland, Oregon where he continued sculpting as a hobby.

In 1952, while working in Public Relations for the City of Portland he presented his first figure, a walking GI with separate accessories, to Product Engineering Company, a nearby manufacturing firm.

PECO, short for Product Engineering Company, did custom die casting and produced and marketed their own line of golf carts. They had made only one previous toy, a die cast cap gun called the "Frontier Smoker". This gun was so well received it sold out the first day of the 1950 New York Fair (1 million pieces in 10 hours!).

Given the popularity of rubber and vinyl figures at the time and anxious for another success, the company decided to produce a line of oversized figures with detachable accessories.

John did all the sculpting himself. The first figure, the walking GI, was actually made of modeling clay, but all subsequent figures were made from "PYROCON", a clay-like substance that could be hardened in the oven and proved to be much more durable for die making.

All figures were sculpted actual size and were later cast in four cavity molds using a substance called "VINYLITE", PECO's name for vinyl.

Four sets of four figures each were produced: soldiers, cowboys and Indians, pirates, and little women. In addition, there were probably five other figures produced. These included four soldiers and a Davy Crockett figure which was not licensed by Walt Disney Productions.

John states he was very careful not to make the figure look anything like Fess Parker.

According to former National Sales Manager Al French, the figures were introduced at the 1953 New York Toy Fair, where they were an instant success. Despite their cost of $ .25 each, Al was able to place the figures in most major chains, including Woolworths.

Originally, production was farmed out, but later was done in-house to prevent delays. Oddly enough John Benneth only worked full-time for the company in 1954 when supply and demand required his full attention.

With success in the toy business comes the fear of being knocked off, and Al French constantly asked management to reduce the size and cost so they could maintain their strong position in the Toy Figure Market.

Despite this warning the company procrastinated and soon companies like Multiple Products and Lido introduced smaller figures with detachable accessories at a fraction of PECO's now high price of $ .29 per figure.

While there was no comparison as far as detail or the number of different accessories you received it was hard to compete with figures costing one-sixth the price. Production ceased in 1956 and these remarkable figures faded into history.

For the record Al French says the cowboys and Indians were the most popular, with the little women being the least favorite. My personal favorites were the pirates, which were so life-like you'd swear they could talk.

Today John Benneth is Regional Manager of the American Forest Institute and Al French is retired. Both are residents of Oregon. (NOTE: Paul Stadinger of Stad's says there is also a "Hattie the Hatter").

Codings in bold letters are PECO's own. All the figures listed have bases, except for P19 and P20. Good means figure only, not painted, cracked or overly distorted. Very Good means at least half the accessories included, including the major weapon and headpiece. Mint as above, including all the accessories. Add $10.00 for the original card.

	G	VG	M		G	VG	M
P1 **CS-4M** Combat Soldier walking with rifle.......	5.00	10.00	15.00	P6 **IA-4** Chief Wild Horse crouching with spear....	5.00	10.00	15.00
P2 **CS-3R** Combat Soldier charging with rifle......	5.00	10.00	15.00	P7 **GM-2** Battling Gold Miner standing with carbine	5.00	10.00	15.00
P3 **CS-2K** Combat Soldier kneeling with machine gun	5.00	10.00	15.00	P8 **COB-1** Cowboy walking with six-shooters	5.00	10.00	15.00
P4 **CS-1S** Combat Soldier Standing firing rifle.....	5.00	10.00	15.00	P9 Famous Pirate Blackbeard	10.00	15.00	20.00
P5 **IT-3** Chief Redhawk standing, shooting bow & arrow................	5.00	10.00	15.00	P10 Famous Pirate Captain Kidd	10.00	15.00	20.00
				P11 Famous Pirate Long John Silver with pegleg..	10.00	15.00	20.00

PECO	G	VG	M
P12 Famous Pirate Morgan	10.00	15.00	20.00
P13 **LS-1** Little Women Mother	7.00	12.00	17.00
P14 **CL-4** Little Women Rally Queen.............	7.00	12.00	17.00
P15 **LF-2** Little Women Debutante............	7.00	12.00	17.00
P16 **GD-3** Little Women School Girl with Dog....	7.00	12.00	17.00
P17 U.S. Infantryman kneeling with bazooka	5.00	10.00	15.00
P18 U.S. Infantryman crouching with rifle	5.00	10.00	15.00
P19 U.S. Infantryman lying with 50 cal. machine gun, no base.	5.00	10.00	15.00
P20 U.S. Infantryman kneeling with machine gun, no base.	5.00	10.00	15.00
P21 Davy Crockett walking with flintlock..........	15.00	25.00	40.00

P4

P1

P2

P3

P5

Photos by Bill Hanlon

PECO

P6

P7

P8

P9

P10

P11

P12

P13

P17

P18

Photos by Bill Hanlon

295

PECO

P19

P20

P21

Top to Bottom: P15, P16, P14

Photos by Bill Hanlon

296

ARCHER PLASTICS

By Bill Hanlon

Archer Plastics (New York, New York) was probably the most prolific of all hard plastic space toy manufacturers of the early 1950s.

The company's major effort seems to have been a wide variety of 95mm spacemen and women that were the standard for space play. Available in no less than five metallic colors, they were produced in 20 different types.

Some figures had detachable helmets, of which there were two different types. The round base helmets fit the five male figures from Series I and the square base helmets fit the Captain Video figures. The round base helmets are often missing or cracked, as they fit very snugly and often split when applied.

Series II figures came without detachable helmets and instead had detachable weapons and shoulder bags. There appears to have been six different figures in this series, and six different weapons and shoulder bags.

The scarcest figures are the spacewoman and the spaceboy (whose antenna that loops his head is almost always broken). One can only guess that when given a choice, a child of that time would have preferred a figure holding a weapon, not a baby! This would account for far fewer women being sold.

The figures were sold in boxed sets and loose. In addition, Archer made at least seven different cars and trucks of the future, and a large 13" rocket that only came in a boxed set and a very rare War of the Worlds playset.

Certain Series I and II figures appear to have also been produced in a softer vinyl plastic toward the end of production. This may possibly have been due to the brittleness of the earlier hard plastic pieces, which often broke the first time they were dropped on a hard surface. These figures, which lack the charm of their hard plastic counterparts, are scarcer and thus have a slightly high value. (NOTE: An Archer Spaceport Set has turned up dated 1949. It contained ten figures, one large car and two rocketships).

A1   A2   A3

Photo by Bill Hanlon

A4   A5   A6

Series I - Round Base Helmet (Mint includes helmet, if called for)

	G	VG	M
A1 Spaceman standing with bomb	3.00	5.00	7.00
A2 Spaceman standing with radio	3.00	5.00	7.00
A3 Spaceman marching with rifle	3.00	5.00	7.00
A4 Spaceman walking with raygun in holster	3.00	5.00	7.00
A5 Robot standing, both arms in air	5.00	7.00	10.00
A6 Spaceman standing with raygun in hand	3.00	5.00	7.00
A7 Spaceboy standing with hands on hips	10.00	15.00	20.00
A8 Spacewoman standing with hands at side	15.00	20.00	25.00
A9 Spacewoman standing with baby	15.00	20.00	25.00
A10 Spacewoman standing with hands on hips	15.00	20.00	25.00

Series II with detachable weapons and shoulder bags (one of each per figure)

	G	VG	M
A11 Spaceman walking with arms at sides	5.00	10.00	15.00
A12 Spaceman standing facing his left	5.00	10.00	15.00
A13 Spaceman standing with both arms overhead	5.00	10.00	15.00
A14 Spaceman standing with one hand on hip	5.00	10.00	15.00
A15 Spaceman standing facing his left and leaning to his right	5.00	10.00	15.00
A16 Spaceman standing facing his right	5.00	10.00	15.00

Series III Captain Video (square base helmets – mint includes helmet, if called for)

	G	VG	M
A17 Video Ranger standing with rifle across chest	10.00	12.00	15.00
A18 Tobor the Robot standing with one arm in air	10.00	15.00	20.00

ARCHER PLASTICS

	G	VG	M
A19 Captain Video standing with ray gun and wearing football type helmet.....	10.00	12.00	15.00
A20 Video Ranger standing with rifle across hips....	10.00	12.00	15.00

Series IV Vehicles

	G	VG	M
A21 Rocket, Red, Yellow and Black, 13".........	20.00	35.00	50.00
A22 Futuristic Convertible, 10"	10.00	15.00	20.00
A23 Futuristic Truck, 10"..	10.00	15.00	20.00
A24 Futuristic Coupe, 10".	10.00	15.00	20.00
A25 Futuristic Coupe, 5"..	5.00	8.00	10.00
A26 Futuristic Sedan, 5"	5.00	8.00	10.00
A27 Futuristic Truck, 5"...	5.00	8.00	10.00
A28 Futuristic Convertible, 5"	5.00	8.00	10.00

OTHER

A29 Raymobile...........	No Price Found
A30 Scopemobile........	No Price Found
A31 Searchmobile	No Price Found
A32 Rocketship Kit, boxed, mint in box price	125.00

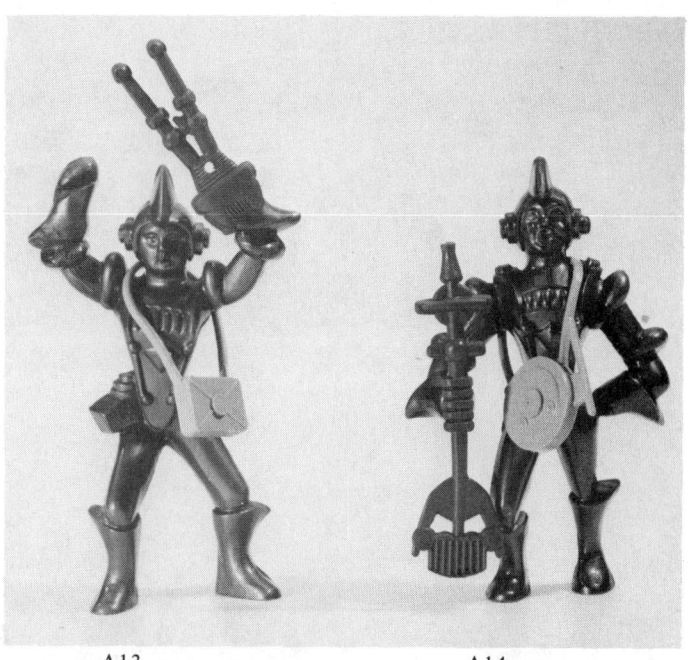

A13   A14

Photo by Bill Hanlon

A15   Photo by Bill Hanlon   A16

A7   A8   A9   A10

Photo by Bill Hanlon

A17   A18   A19   A20

Photo by Bill Hanlon

A11   A12

Photo by Bill Hanlon

A22   A23   A24

Photo by Bill Hanlon

ARCHER PLASTICS

A25   A26   A27   A29

Photo by Bill Hanlon

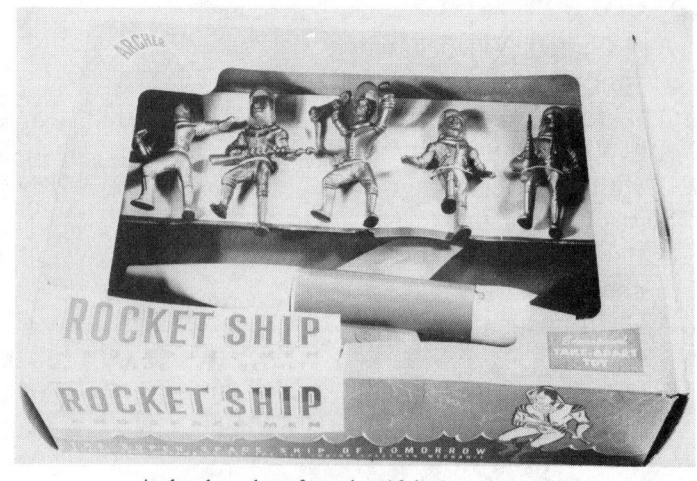

Archer boxed set featuring 13 inch rocket (A21)
Photo by Bill Hanlon

A50   A51   A52   A53   A54

Archer Plastics soldiers, worth $6 each in mint.
Photo by Stan Alekna

A55   A56   A57   A58   A59

Archer Plastics soldiers, worth $6 each in mint.
Photo by Stan Alekna

Top, L to R: A22, A23, A24
Bottom, L to R: A28, A26, A27

Photo by Bill Hanlon

An Archer Plastics set of soldiers. Value about $25 in mint. They also
came in a box of 5.
Photo by Stan Alekna

Boxed Set. For its value, total the worth of the figures and add 20% for
the box.
Photo by Bill Hanlon

Boxed set with rare A21 rocket. For price, total value of the pieces and
add 20% for the box.
Photo by Bill Hanlon

PREMIER PRODUCTS CO.

BY Bill Hanlon

Premier Products Co. of Brooklyn, New York, was the second-largest producer of hard plastic space toys in the early 1950s.

While their rival, Archer, cornered the market on figures, Premier locked up the spaceship category with two classics, each available in three sizes. Their three and five-inch spaceships usually account for over 75% of all hard plastic rockets found from this period. Oddly, the nine-inch size are two of the rarer rockets to be found.

Colors varied from metallics to basics, and most sizes seem to have been made with and without wheels.

It appears that Premier made only four different figures, all men, and judged by their availability, all were very popular. These were produced in metallic and basic colors, and even a few chrome-plated ones have turned up. All figures were about 75mm high, and all had their helmets attached.

The spacemen and rockets must have been sold separately, as no known boxed sets have turned up to date. Premier did, however, produce a carded set called Flash Gordon Solar Commando. This set included one 5" rocket and three different spacemen.

Several 3" and 5" vinyl rockets have turned up and probably represent Premier's last effort in a dying market.

	G	VG	M
PP1 Spaceman standing with raygun in air.........	4.00	5.00	6.00
PP2 Spaceman standing with one hand on hip......	4.00	5.00	6.00
PP3 Spaceman standing with rifle across chest......	4.00	5.00	6.00
PP4 Spaceman standing with both hands on hip and air hose or radio loop......	4.00	5.00	6.00
PP5 Rocket 9" thin fuselage	20.00	25.00	30.00
PP6 Rocket 5" thin fuselage	7.00	9.00	12.00
PP7 Rocket 3" thin fuselage	6.00	8.00	10.00
PP8 Rocket 9" bulbous fuselage................	20.00	25.00	30.00
PP9 Rocket 5" bulbous fuselage................	7.00	9.00	12.00
PP10 Rocket 3" bulbous fuselage................	6.00	8.00	10.00

PP1   PP2   PP3   PP4

Photo by Bill Hanlon

L to R: PP5, PP6, PP7

Photo by Bill Hanlon

L to R: PP8, PP9, PP10

Photo by Bill Hanlon

MISCELLANEOUS AMERICAN PLASTIC

Although Marx is by far the most-collected, more and more soldiers produced in plastic by American makers are becoming collectible. Here is a sampling.

Aurora made this attractive "Camelot" ten-figure set. Value mint on the card $90.
Courtesy Continental Hobby House

S1   S2   S3

Ideal, three of the figures from the sailor set, plastic. Value $8 each, mint.
Photo by Gary J. Linden

ID1   ID2   ID3   ID4   ID5   ID6

IP1   IP2   IP3   IP4   IP5   IP6

The Ideal 3" knights at top were sold about 1959. They are worth about $6 each. The Ideal pirates were sold with a pirate ship beginning in 1953. Their value is about $15 each. All these figures were sold unpainted (painted by the author).

Early plastic horses, made in a 54mm range. They were sold circa 1942-43, by an unknown U.S. maker. No price found.

MISCELLANEOUS

RC1   RC2   RC3

Ideal, 3 of the figures from the RCMP set, plastic. Value $8 each, mint.
Photo by Gary J. Linden

CW10 & 11
Ideal, Rider & Horse from the
Civil War Set, plastic

CW1   CW2

Ideal, two of the eleven Civil War figures, 60mm plastic (may be Andy
Gard), value $15 each.   Photo by Gary J. Linden

7C1   7C2   7C3

Ideal, three of the four figures from the 7th Cavalry set, 3" high plastic.
Value $9 each.
Photo by Gary J. Linden

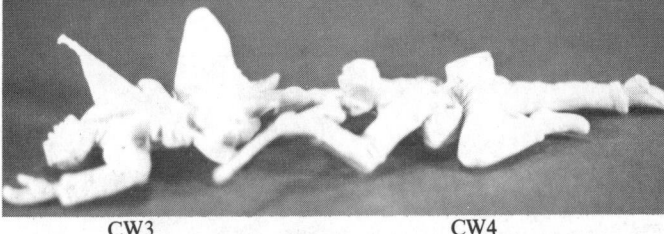

CW3   CW4

Ideal, two of the eleven Civil War figures, 60mm plastic (may be Andy
Gard), value $15 each.
Photo by Gary J. Linden

D1   D2   D3

Ideal, all three Detectives from the set, plastic. Value $15 each, mint.
Photo by Gary J. Linden

CW5   CW6   CW7   CW8   CW9

Ideal, five of the eleven Civil War figures, 60mm plastic (may be Andy
Gard), value $15 each.
Photo by Gary J. Linden

VF9   VF10   VF11   VF12

Ideal Valley Forge figures, 60mm plastic. Value $8 each, mint.
Photo by Gary J. Linden

302

VF1   VF2   VF3   VF4

Ideal Valley Forge figures, 60mm plastic. Value $8 each, mint.
Photo by Gary J. Linden

VF5   VF6   VF7   VF8

Ideal Valley Forge figures, 60mm plastic. Value $8 each, mint.
Photo by Gary J. Linden

Kilty soldiers were produced by Bonnie Built, Inc. of Inwood, New York. About 2" in height, Kilties were made of un-painted olive drab plastic. They came attached to a half box with a background battle scene. The No. 103 Medical Squad set shown here is worth about $70 in mint. Set No. 102 Machine Gun Squad has a similar value. They are semi-round.
Photo by Phil Savino

J1   J2   J3   J4   J5   J6 foreground   J7

R1   R2   R3   R4   R5   R6   R7

MPC Russians and Japanese. Not shown are the Japanese standing firing and the Russian prone machine gunner. Value about $2 each.

P1   P2   P3   P4

MPC Pirates with accessories. Value $4 each.
Photo by Gary J. Linden

MPC Beetle Bailey figures from Camp Swampy set, L to R: General, Sarge,
Beetle, Zero, Killer. Value $15 each, mint.
Photo by Gary J. Linden

Payton Stagecoach. Value $10.
Photo by Gary J. Linden

A boxed set of Plasticraft soldiers. Value in mint about $40.
Photo by Phil Savino

MPC Pirate Ship with Pirates. Value $125 mint.
Photo by Gary J. Linden

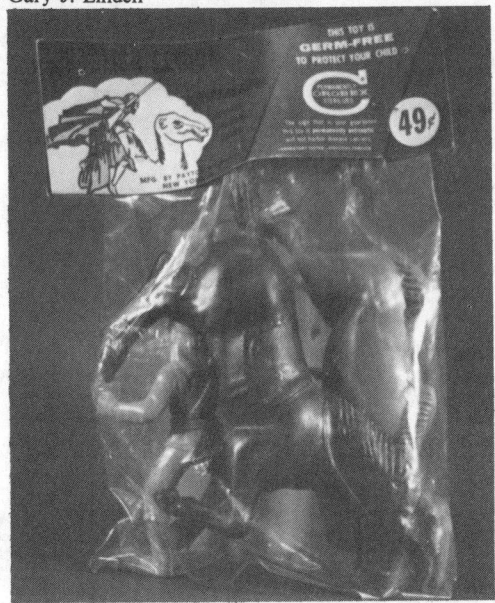

Payton Foreign Legion set with Legionaire, Horse, pink Camel (probably
the same Legionaire as Thomas Toys') Value in bag about $15
Photo by Gary J. Linden

Plasticraft was located at 287 Laurel Avenue, Kearny, New Jersey. Its
soldiers are worth about $4 each in mint condition. Missing in this photo
is the GI running with the rifle across his waist.
Photo by Bill Holt

MISCELLANEOUS

Rel stagecoach with driver, bandit, sheriff. Value $10.
Photo by Gary J. Linden

Sky King tv show cereal giveaways. L to R: Sky King, Sheriff, Penny, Clipper, plane (The Song Bird), horse (Yellowfury). Value $25 each.
Photo by Gary J. Linden

UN1   UN2
Plastic Indians by unknown maker
Photo by Gary J. Linden

Rel blister pack with Indian braves. Value out of the bag about $2 each.
Photo by Gary J. Linden

Superior produced a Captain Video Spaceport which included figures of GIs, Aliens and Spacemen. Not all of them are shown here. Value per figure in mint $9.
Courtesy Rex and Richard Gray

These baseball players, by an unknown maker, were found in the Beton factory, but weren't made by Beton. It's hard to tell if the pitchers at left are mold or casting variations. No prices found

The GI at left is by Airfix. The beautifully designed group at right were sold circa the 1960s, probably unpainted, were made of a soft plastic and stand just under 2" high. No prices found.

305

BUILT-RITE

BUILT-RITE began in 1922 as a manufacturer of cardboard boxes. Somewhere along the line, at least as early as 1934, it began to produce cardboard construction toys, and appears to have manufactured them into the 1950s, with its greatest period of success probably enjoyed during and just prior to WW II. The company remains in business as Warren Paper Products Co., making card games, games and puzzles. Numbers and words in bold print here are Built-Rite's own descriptions.

BUILT-RITE No. 20 Army Battery Set. Value $37.50 in Good, $56.25 in Very Good and $75.00 in Mint condition.
Photo by Ed Poole

BUILT-RITE Fort No. 25, with box-top and Barclay soldiers.
Photo by Ed Poole

"BUILT-RITE ARMY CAMP"

1 FORT
4 TRENCHES
6 PUP TENTS
108 SOLDIERS

No. 16 fort.

1936 BUILT-RITE ad. The same illustration appears in a 1950 Johnson Smith catalog.

	G	VG	M
No. 1 Toy Soldiers, WW I helmets, per each......	1.50	2.25	3.00
No. 2 Toy Trench........	20.00	35.00	40.00
No. 7 Private Garage, brick.	30.00	40.00	50.00
No. 7 Army Plane Hangar .	40.00	45.00	55.00
No. 8 House, brick........	65.00	75.00	85.00
No. 9 House, stucco and brick	65.00	75.00	85.00
No. 10 House, two story, brick and shingle.......	65.00	75.00	85.00
No. 14 "Front Line" Trench and soldier set, with trench, 6 WW II soldiers.	30.00	40.00	45.00
No. 15 Commercial Garage.	65.00	70.00	80.00
No. 16 Fort, no ramp......	65.00	70.00	80.00
No. 17 Service Station.....	65.00	70.00	80.00

	G	VG	M
No. 18 Airport..........	60.00	65.00	75.00
No. 19 Railroad Station....	50.00	60.00	70.00
No. 20 Railroad Tunnel....	8.00	15.00	20.00
No. 20 Army Battery Set...	80.00	100.00	125.00
No. 22 Army Outpost.....	40.00	50.00	60.00
No. 24 Union Station	No Price Found		
No. 25 Fort, one ramp.....	80.00	100.00	120.00
No. 25A-26-piece Fort and Soldier set same fort as 25, WWII soldiers, 2 sandbag foxholes and fibreboard pistol, sold through 1954	90.00	125.00	150.00
No. 26 United Airlines Airport Hangar	55.00	65.00	75.00
No. 27 Barn with Animals .	25.00	35.00	45.00
No. 28 Garage and Super Service Station	65.00	75.00	85.00
No. 29 Three Car Set	25.00	35.00	45.00
No. 33 Lokdwood Dolls, late 1940s, paper dolls.......	18.00	25.00	40.00
No. 33 House, Tudor type..	65.00	75.00	85.00
No. 34 House, two story...	65.00	75.00	85.00
No. 35 Modern Doll House	65.00	75.00	85.00
No. 36 House	65.00	75.00	85.00
No. 36F 3-Room Furnished Doll House...........	65.00	75.00	85.00
No. 37 Farm Machinery Set	25.00	35.00	45.00
No. 40 Manger with Nativity Figures	No Price Found		
No. 45 Living Room Furniture...............	45.00	55.00	65.00

BUILT RITE

	G	VG	M		G	VG	M
No. 46 Dining Room Furniture	45.00	55.00	65.00	No. 201 26 Piece Guardsman Set, 2 trenches, artillery base, cannon, pistol, WW II soldiers	40.00	75.00	80.00
No. 47 Bedroom Furniture	45.00	55.00	65.00				
No. 48 Bathroom Furniture	45.00	55.00	65.00				
No. 49 Kitchen Furniture	45.00	55.00	65.00	No. 202 Train Scenery (28 pieces, Terminal, Scenery, etc)	45.00	65.00	75.00
No. 50 Army Raiders' Victory Unit, 28 pieces, truck, tank, AA gun, jeep, semitrack truck, 20 soldiers, WW II	65.00	75.00	85.00	No. 204F Furnished Country Estate	55.00	65.00	75.00
No. 55 5 Miniature cardboard houses	30.00	55.00	60.00	No. 210 Railroad Station and Accessories	25.00	35.00	45.00
No. 56 5 Miniature buildings, church, school, RR station, firehouse, drugstore	30.00	55.00	60.00	No. 212 Station and Railroad Accessories	25.00	40.00	50.00
No. 57M 8 Piece Farm Set	25.00	35.00	45.00	No. 245 Miniature Village	25.00	35.00	45.00
No. 60 Navy Battle Fleet and Coast Artillery Gun	20.00	45.00	60.00	No. 252 Fort Set, 26 pcs., No. 25 fort, post-war	90.00	125.00	150.00
No. 66 3-Piece Kitchen Set	No Price Found			No. 298 Train Accessory Set	25.00	35.00	45.00
No. 75 Living Room Furniture	45.00	55.00	65.00	No. 300 Stock and Grain Elevator	25.00	35.00	45.00
No. 76 Dining Room Furniture	45.00	55.00	65.00	No. 375 Station and Railroad Set	25.00	35.00	45.00
No. 77 Bed Room Furniture	45.00	55.00	65.00	No. 415 House, circa 1943, 13 x 20" boxed set with 19" house and garage, 27 pieces of furniture, sedan, baby buggy, shrubbery, etc	75.00	90.00	100.00
No. 77 American Ranger Fighters, 8 vehicles, WW II soldiers	65.00	75.00	85.00				
No. 78 Kitchen Furniture	45.00	55.00	65.00				
No. 100A Fortress, circa 1938, two ramps	110.00	135.00	150.00	No. 459 - 5 Rooms of Toy Furniture	25.00	35.00	45.00
No. 105 Farm Set with 20 plastic animals	30.00	40.00	45.00	No. 460 Pocket Size Series of Minatures Paperdoll Set	15.00	20.00	25.00
No. 111 Railroad Accessory Set	20.00	25.00	30.00	No. 498 Train Accessory Set	25.00	35.00	45.00
No. 112 American Fighters - Includes 100A fortress with soldiers, cannons, etc, 55 pieces, no flag on tower	100.00	125.00	150.00	No. 556 Village	40.00	50.00	60.00
				No. 1001 Modern Stock Farm	45.00	55.00	75.00
No. 115 Doll House, Garage Set (with car)	65.00	75.00	85.00	No. 1027 Stock Farm	45.00	55.00	75.00
No. 119 Farm Set	40.00	50.00	60.00	No. 1033 Doll House	45.00	55.00	65.00
No. 120 Five Room Suburban Doll House	65.00	75.00	85.00	No. 1422 Fort and Soldiers (94 pieces, 2-ramp fort)	100.00	135.00	150.00
No. 127 Large Barn with Animals	25.00	35.00	45.00	No. 2050 Country Estate, house, bushes, dog, cat, baby buggy	65.00	75.00	90.00
No. 128 Miniature Village and Scenery Set	25.00	35.00	45.00	Built-Rite Ranch, over 108 pieces	150.00	185.00	200.00
No. 148 Train Accessory Set	25.00	35.00	45.00				
No. 156 Miniature Houses and Buildings	55.00	65.00	70.00				
No. 178 Train Accessory Set	25.00	35.00	45.00				

Built-Rite's earliest soldiers. Note the facial differences in the two officers at the left. L to R: Captain, Lieutenant, First Sergeant, Line Sergeant.
Photo by Ed Poole

Built-Rite's earliest soldiers, from L to R: Corporal, Private First Class, Private
Photo by Ed Poole

Top to Bottom: No. 84 Armored Car, No. 83 Weapons Carrier. Collector A.E. Hemminger contributed this Xerox as this book went to press. These seem to be extremely rare, and no price was found.

BUILT-RITE, #100-A.
Photo courtesy of Ed Poole

Built-Rite No. 22 Army Outpost
Courtesy Jack Matthews

1937.   D. M. WARREN   2,097,267
                        TOY FIGURE
                    Filed March 30, 1936

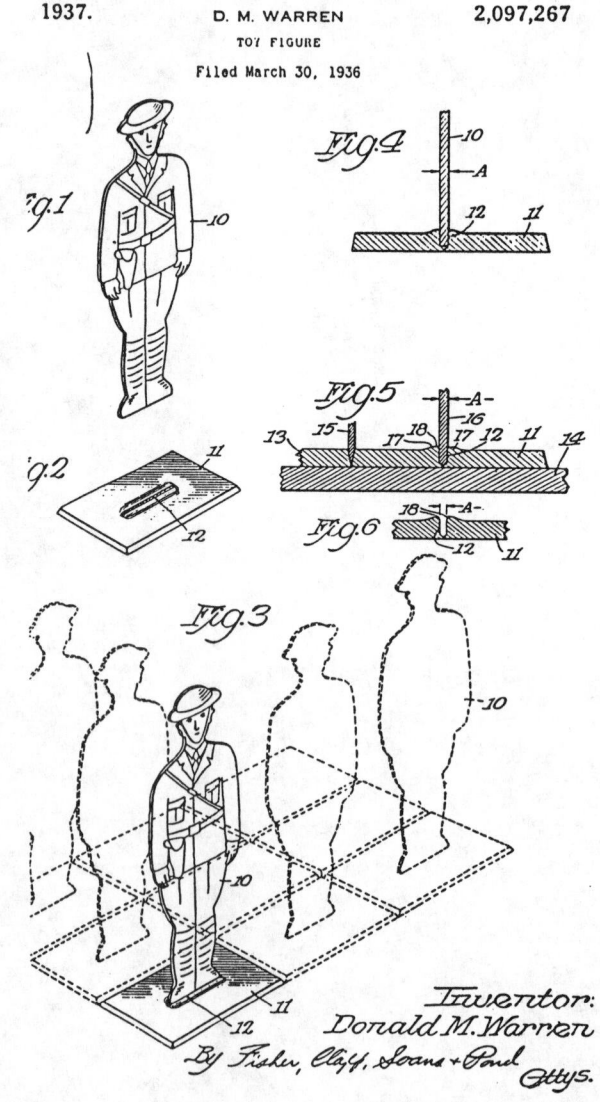

Patent drawings for Built-Rite's soldiers. The application was made March 30, 1936 by Donald M. Warren. Courtesy Edward Ryan

AMERICAN PAPER SOLDIERS
by Bill Nutting
(See also Built-Rite and All-Nu)

Paper toy soldiers truly come in all shapes and sizes. Since the late 1800s American publishers have turned out thousands of paper soldiers. Remember - all it takes to create a new figure is to sketch one out and paint it up.

The first real boom in the American paper soldier industry occurred between the late 1890s and about 1920. Typically the figures were paper, glued to cardboard, then nailed to (or slotted into) wooden stands. Most were in a 6" scale - that is, an infantryman measures 6" from head to feet, while cavalry figures would be accordingly taller. Three companies dominated the scene: McLoughlin Bros., Milton Bradley and Parker Bros.

Bradley and Parker were, and still are, well known for their board games; McLoughlin was a leading children's book as well as game publisher. Incidentally, Bradley acquired McLoughlin in 1920. In February 1991, Hasbro Inc. (which today owns Milton Bradley) purchased Tonka Corp. (which owned Parker Bros.) So today the three great rivals are all under one roof!

The second "Golden Age" of paper soldiers arrived in the World War II era, fueled by wartime restrictions which forced toy makers away from metal and wood toward paper. A great variety of patriotic sets appeared - in many different formats: punchout sets, construction sets, battle sets, target sets, etc. The best of these sets are dramatic and colorful, often accurately depicting up-to-date troops and equipment.

In the current market, boxed sets of 1890s - 1920 era cardboard soldiers sell at prices calculated at up to $5 per figure, in the boxed sets with attractive lithographed labels. Loose cardboard figures fetch about $2.50 each. Cut paper figures, almost always damaged, are worth about $1.00 each.

The World War II-era sets have proved increasingly popular with toy soldier collectors. Many of today's enthusiasts grew up playing with these pieces; their nostalgia has spurred demand. This is the same phenomenon which has given rise to the mania for dimestore soldiers.

The term "paper soldiers" is used to include types of figures which are not paper per se. One example is the omnipresent cardboard soldier (discussed above) which, because of its sturdiness, often survives better than its paper brethren. "Paper-litho-on-wood" soldiers are often early and collectible; prices for these range from about $10 for 6" tall figures to $20-25 for 12" tall pieces. Another type that turns up regularly is "newspaper supplement sheets"; these average $15.

McLOUGHLIN

McL1 Circa 1880s mounted figures including hussars, cowboys and Indians, 4" high, price per cut figure   3.50

McL1a Uncut strip of five of these figures 30.00

McL2 Circa 1880s infantry including zouaves and colonials. 4" high. Price per cut figure 3.50

McL2a Uncut strip of ten of these figures 40.00

McL3 Circa 1890s (and reissued 1905-10) infantry including colonials, marching infantry in campaign uniforms (Spanish-American War) and American Indians firing. Average 5" high. Per cut figure 2.00

McL3b Circa 1890s bands of the same type 4.00

McL4 Circa 1890s boxed sets "Paper Soldiers with Tents" including 60 uncut soldiers, tents and metal stands 150.00

(NB: The following several items are from what collectors call the "Glossy" series, so named because of the rich chromolithography. Whether in the cardboard or paper versions, these figures are arguably some of the finest paper soldiers ever made in America. However, these figures are quite common and are accordingly still inexpensive, although the colorful labels on the larger boxed sets bring these items up in price).

McL5 Circa 1898-circa 1920 boxed set "100 Soldiers on Parade" containing 6" tall cardboard soldiers on wood blocks 400.00

McL6 Circa 1898-circa 1920 boxed set "50 Soldiers on Parade" with 6" tall cardboard soldiers on blocks . 125.00

McL7 Circa 1898-1920 6" tall cardboard soldiers on blocks of various types: Spanish-American War infantry; Zouaves; U.S. Infantry in dress blue with helmets; highlanders; band; colonials. Prices are per individual figure.

AMERICAN PAPER

Soldier (any type) with rifle	3.00
Officer	5.00
Band Figure	5.00

McLouglin circa 1898-1910 paper soldiers in two scales: 6" tall and 5" tall. Prices are per cut figure.

McL8 Highlander, British Infantry, Zouave	3.00
McL9 Artillerymen and cannon	6.00
McL10 Nurses and Red Cross	6.00
McL11 Teddy Roosevelt . .	8.00
McL12 Spanish-American War infantry	4.00
McL13 Sailors in Blue	5.00
McL14 Uncut strip of 10 "British Regulars"	40.00
McL15 Circa 1915 - 5" tall cardboard doughboys and sailors, including officers	2.00
McL16 Circa 1915 5" tall cardboard flag bearers, signallers, and aviators . .	5.00
McL17 Cardboard folding tent with cloth flag, patented April 7, 1914 . .	15.00
McL18 Circa 1915 - 5" tall paper doughboys and sailors in paper. Per cut figure	1.00
McL19 Circa 1915 Boy Scouts holding rifles across chest. 6" or 5", cardboard	6.00
McL19a As above, paper . .	4.00
McL20 Circa 1916 Series No. 4026, 10½"x10½". Paper soldiers on sheet, seven soldiers plus officer. 1. Belgium 2. France 3. Italy 4. Britain - Price per sheet	20.00
McL21 "Playtime Soldiers on Parade", 175 paper pieces. Copyright 1937. (NB - by this time McLoughlin was a division of Milton Bradley) . .	95.00

Top: McL1. Bottom: McL2
Photo by Bill Nutting

McL 2a
Photo by Bill Nutting

McL3
Photo by Bill Nutting

McL3
Photo by Bill Nutting

AMERICAN PAPER

McL3b
Photo by Bill Nutting

McL4
Photo by Bill Nutting

McL7
Photo by Bill Nutting

McL9, McL10
Photo by Bill Nutting

McL6
Photo by Bill Nutting

McL7
Photo by Bill Nutting

L to R: McL11, McL12
Photo by Bill Nutting

McL7
Photo by Bill Nutting

McL14
Photo by Bill Nutting

L to R: McL17, McL15 and McL16
Photo by Bill Nutting

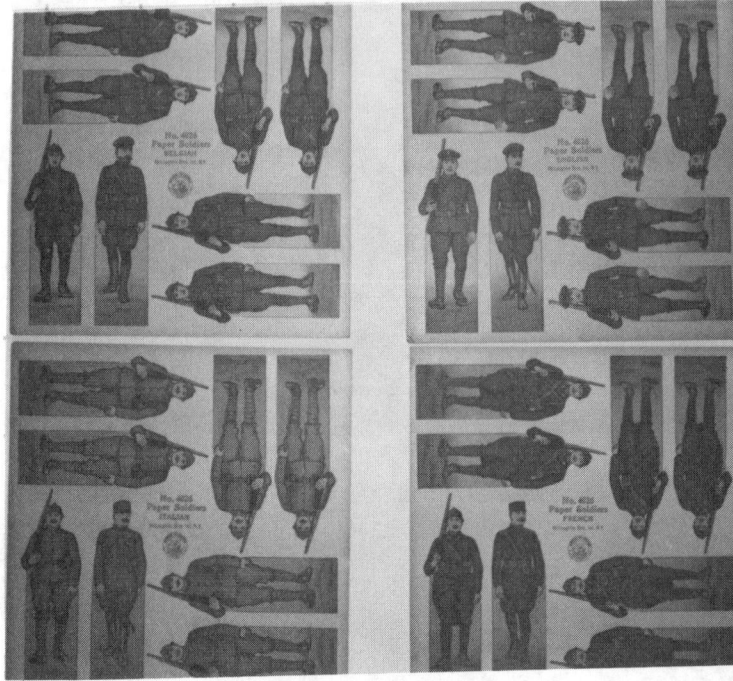

McL20
Photo by Bill Nutting

McL21
Photo by Bill Nutting

AMERICAN PAPER

MILTON BRADLEY, Springfield, Mass.: Best known for the **Game of Life,** Milton Bradley has produced games since the 19th century. Their cardboard figures often compare favorably with those of McLoughlin.

MB1 "Bradley's Infantry" with 25 6" tall cardboard soldiers as on the cover. c.1900-1910 .... 110.00

MB2 "Soldiers on Parade" No. 4518 with 10 - 6" cardboard pieces in an attractive box 95.00

MB3 "Game of Siege" containing 25 - 6" cardboard doughboys and pistol. c.1910 .... 75.00

MB4 Doughboy marching, each 3.00

MB4a Individual cardboard 6" pieces depicting figures with machine gun, cannon, and truck. Each ... 15.00

MB5 Highlander 6" tall, circa 1915, per figure 4.00

MB6 "Bradley's Cavalry - 50" with 6" tall figures .. 125.00

MB7 "Bradley's Cavalry - 25" with 6" tall figures .. 50.00

MB8 Individual Cavalry pieces, 6", cardboard, most types 2.50

MB9 Arabs 4.00

MB10 "Game of War" with 20 - 6" tall cavalry figures 90.00

MB11 "Soldiers Five with Pistol" No. 4518, 1920s . 80.00

MB12 "Sharp-Shooters" with 11 - 6" tall cavalry figures and 2 pistols 100.00

PARKER BROS., Salem, Mass: From the 1890s into the 1920s, Parker proved to be one of McLoughlin's main rivals on the cardboard soldier battlefield.

PA1 Infantry in red, 6" cardboard figure circa 1900-1920s, per piece ... 2.50

PA2 Infantry in light blue, 6" cardboard figure circa 1900-1920s, per piece ... 3.00

PA3 Cavalry in red, on extra-thick cardboard for target sets. Circa 1900-1920s 4.00

PA4 Doughboys charging, 6", circa 1910-20s, per piece 2.50

PA5 "The Battle Game, with Soldiers, Pistol and Ammunition" with unusually attractive box showing Boer War scene. 30 figures 170.00

SAMUEL GABRIEL SONS & CO., NY

GA1 "U.S.A. Band and Infantry, Cut Outs" boxed set 55.00

GA2 "U.S.A. Calvary, cutouts" boxed set 55.00

GA3 Cardboard figures on wood stands, per piece .. 2.00

GA4 Paper figures, per cut out piece 1.00

GA5 "Rocking horse" cavalry, of various types including Indians and Russian cossacks, Per piece 30.00

MB1
Photo by Bill Nutting

MB2
Photo by Bill Nutting

MB3
Photo by Bill Nutting

MB8
Photo by Bill Nutting

L to R: MB4, MB4a
Photo by Bill Nutting

MB8 and MB9
Photo by Bill Nutting

MB5
Photo by Bill Nutting

MB10
Photo by Bill Nutting

L to R: PA1, PA2
Photo by Bill Nutting

PA5
Photo by Bill Nutting

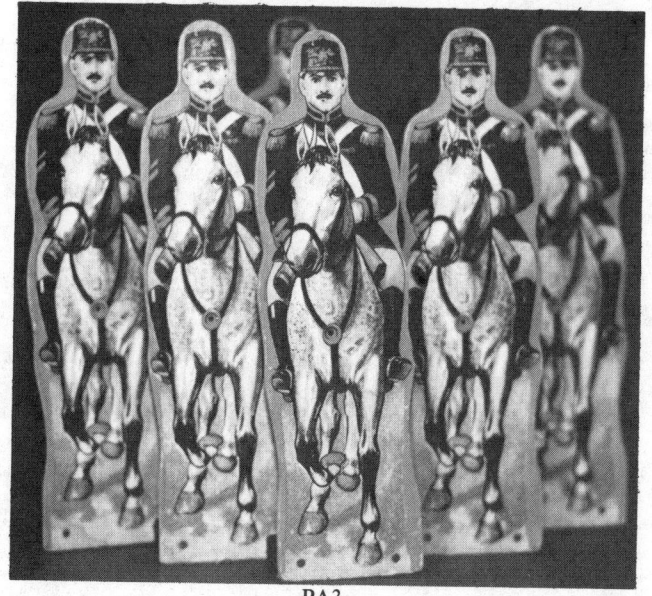

PA3
Photo by Bill Nutting

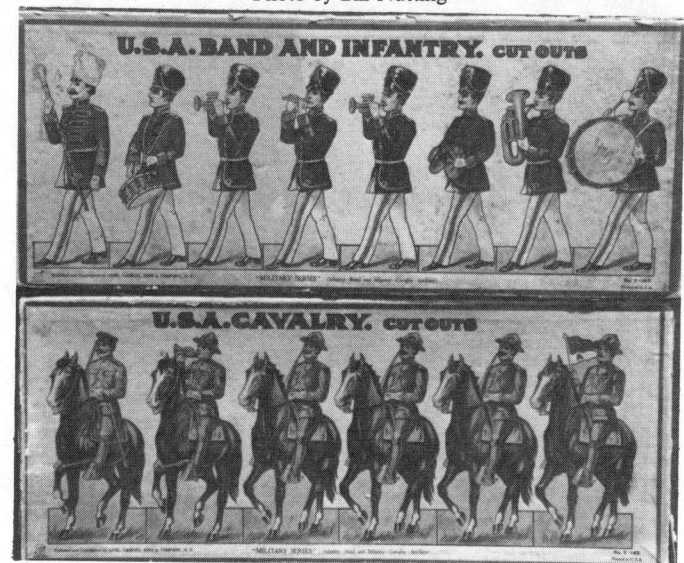

Top: GA1 Bottom: GA2
Photo by Bill Nutting

PA4
Photo by Bill Nutting

GA3
Photo by Bill Nutting

AMERICAN PAPER

MARKS, Boston
"Mickey Mouse Soldier Set",
   1930s 175.00
Price per individual figure .   20.00

POST TOASTIES, cereal soldier premiums, 1930s
Uncut piece 20.00
Cut figures 3.00

W.G. YOUNG, CO.,
  Chicago. "Spear-Em"
  game with 6 cardboard
  soldiers and darts.
  Copyright 1916 ....   45.00

ALL-METAL PRODUCTS (WYANDOTTE), Wyandotte, Michigan
"Wyandotte Indian Game"
  with Indians, Americans
  and jungle animals and
  pop-gun 24.00

CONCORD TOY CO.
"Soldiers", circa 1940, boxed
  set contains 9 press-out
  soldiers, 3½" each,
  wooden cannon and am-
  munition 50.00   60.00   75.00

J. PRESSMAN AND CO., NY
"Soldier Set" No. 1551 circa
  1940, contains five cardboard soldiers, 4½" high
  and marbles 30.00   40.00   50.00

WHITMAN
"100 Soldiers Punch-Out
  Book", No. 999, 1943 ...   50.00   55.00   60.00

MERRILL
ME1 Cut and Stick - Our
  Army and Navy in Ac-
  tion 30.00   40.00   50.00

LOWE
LO1 Service Kit of
  America's Armed Forces -
  on Land on Sea in the
  Air 40.00   50.00   55.00

JAY LINE
JL1 Camouflage Defense
  Force No. 431 - Airplane,
  soldiers, AA guns all hid-
  den within farm buildings   55.00   75.00   90.00

GA5
Photo by Bill Nutting

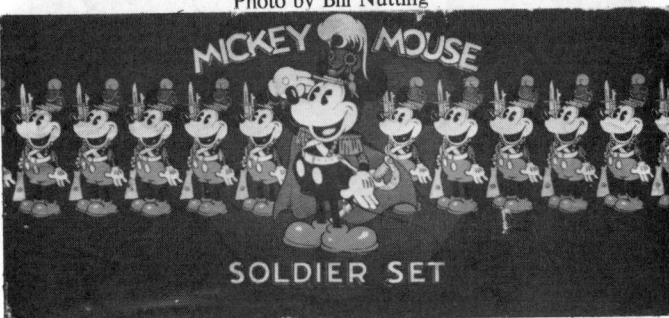

Marks "Mickey Mouse Soldier Set" boxtop
Photo by Bill Nutting

Marks "Mickey Mouse Soldier Set" box contents.
Photo by Bill Nutting

Post Toasties 1930s premiums
Photo by Bill Nutting

317

These solid-cast aluminum figures are probably French. The value in the condition shown is probably $12 apiece for the foot figures and perhaps $25 for the very dynamic mounted Arab. The trees were cast by Ron Eccles (see Leading Collectors and Dealers). Courtesy Joseph Saine.

Barclay's extremely rare (Bn) No. 87 Officer on Horse, with the horses in the three known color variations. Courtesy Bill O'Brien.

Toy Creations boxed set.
Photo by Don Patman.

Except for
the mounted figure these are
metal copies of Beton cowboys,
made in occupied Japan.
The same firm produced a
boxed set of metal Indians,
one of the three types being
a copy of Beton's BT21.
Value of each set, mint in
the box, about $50.
Photo by Don Patman.

Marks "Mickey Mouse
Soldier Set" boxtop (see Paper).
Photo by Bill Nutting.

Ferdinand Gutmann's "Active Sammy On The Firing Line". This is the only boxed Gutmann set known. Price not established. Courtesy Franc Isla.

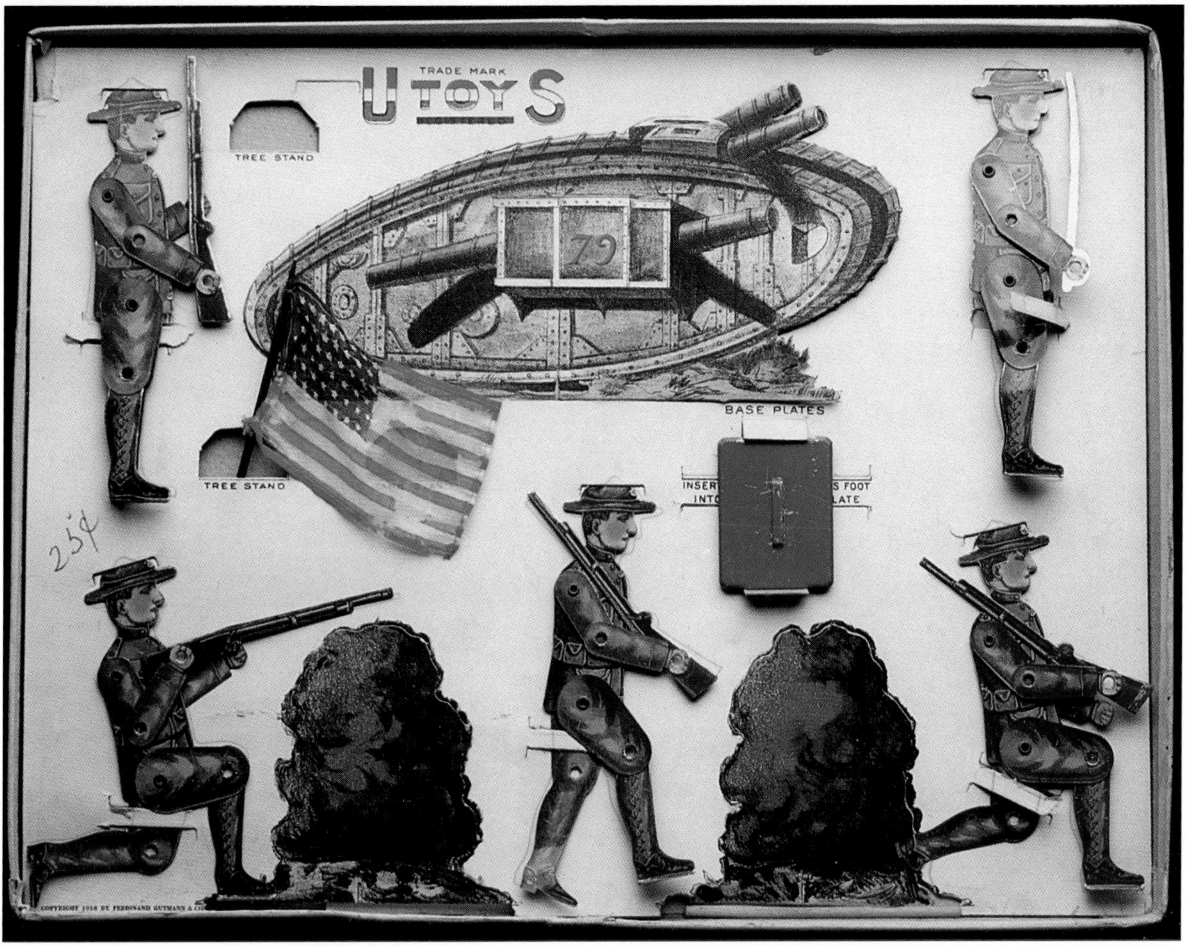

Jones' copies of Barclay's knights.
Flat underbases with choked pourholes
are the easiest way of telling them from
the Barclays. They're also shorter.
The earliest catalog appearance of these
knights is in a Spring and Summer 1938
N. Shure catalog.
Photo by Don Patman.

Barclay podfoots.
It's thought by collectors that
the red uniforms represent the
Korean War enemy, but to
date no corroborating
evidence has surfaced.
Photo by Don Patman.

What seems, apart from
minor variations, to be the entire
line of Tommy Toy soldiers.
Courtesy Charles E. Weldon Jr.
Photo by Bill Kaufman.

Lineol and Elastolin personality figures. Courtesy Jack Matthews.

Post-WW II Elastolin British Guards and country regiments. Value $100 each in mint condition. Courtesy Jack Matthews.

H.B. Toys' extremely rare Robe Boy, unpainted here. This was an unauthorized version of the comic books' Captain Marvel Jr. Photo by Don Patman.

Dimestore figures by All-Nu, Barclay and Manoil, fort by Built-Rite.
Photo by Ed Poole.

Jones' Metal-Art MA18, German Officer of 1915. This is the only one known (ornament atop helmet missing).
Photo by Don Patman.

Britains sets 318, 146A, 1331. Courtesy Edward H. Ruby.

Conversions of
Barclay figures by Ed Poole.
Photo by Ed Poole.

These oversized toy soldiers were made by
Lincoln Logs, and probably produced for the
first time in 1940, as they can be seen in a Playthings
magazine of that year, featured in a Lincoln Logs display.
They resemble the dimestore figures attributed to
J. Edward Jones, and in fact, according to Gus Hansen,
Jones did try to market them for Lincoln Logs, but was
unsuccessful. The flagbearer, from bottom of the stand
to top of the flag, measures 6" high.
Photo by Dave Mitchell.

Russians (left) and
Japanese, believed to
have been made by
Brooklyn's William Feix.
Photo by Will Beierwaltes.

New AUB-RUBR Toys
AUBURN RUBBER

No. 1202 Infantry Bugler No. 1200 Infantry Private No. 1212B Marine Bugler No. 1210B Marine Private No. 1212W Marine Bugler No. 1210W Marine Private No. 1238 Charging Soldier

U. S. SOLDIERS — 3" High

1 dozen weight ⅝ lb. Packed 2 dozen to carton.

No. 220 Officer No. 218 Private No. 214 Private

FOREIGN LEGION — 3¼" High

1 dozen weight ½ lb. Packed 2 dozen to carton.

No. 232
Soldier on Horse — 3⅞" high
1 doz. weight 2¼ lbs. Packed 1 doz.

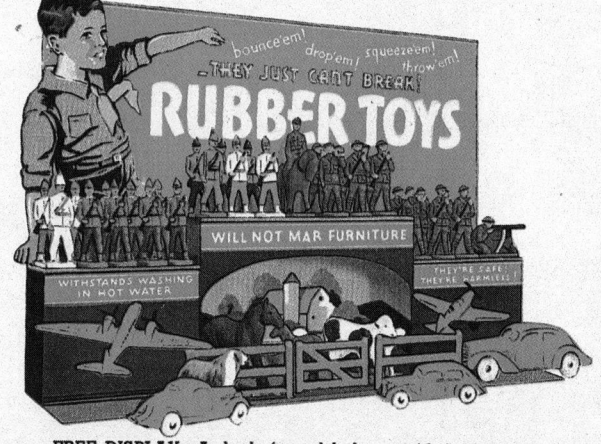

FREE DISPLAY—A dealer's real help — with initial order.

Aub-Rubr TOYS

These NATURAL HITS maintain

YEAR AROUND SALES with

quick PROFITABLE turnover

Light weight makes shipping cost low—

Pre-WW II catalogs of American-made soldiers are extremely hard to find.
Just two of Auburn Rubber's have emerged; from 1940 and this one, from 1937. For some reason, the
seated machine gunner, visible at right in the bottom display and in a boxed set on another catalog page, is the only
Auburn soldier then in production not to be shown individually. Both the 1937 and 1940 catalogs are all color.
Courtesy Anthony Annese.

These 6" lithographed/American troops came from Edgar O. Clark, the successor to Clark and Sowdon, a small but fine game and novelty company operating in New York City in the 1890s. Circa 1905.
Photo by Bill Nutting

W.G. Young & Co. "Spear-Em" game
Photo by Bill Nutting

JL1
Courtesy Jack Matthews

All Metal Products "Wyandotte Indian Game"
Photo by Bill Nutting

L01
Courtesy Jack Matthews

Whitman "100 Soldiers Punch-Out Book"
Courtesy Jack Matthews

ME1
Courtesy Jack Matthews

318

JUNIOR COMMANDER, contains Flying Fortress, Pursuit Plane, Tank, Jeep, Torpedo Boat, Machine Gun, Anti Tank Gun, Antiaircraft Gun, Transport Truck, Aircraft Carrier, Submarine, 25 Army, Navy, Air Force figures, decals. Offered for sale in mint condition in 1985 $95 (some wear on box).
Photo by Bo Hornung

MB11

Photo by Jonathan A. Newman
Courtesy Barbara and Jonathan Newman

1943, LOWE No. 140.
        G - 30.00 ; VG - 45.00 ; M - 50.00
Photo by Jonathan A. Newman
Courtesy Barbara and Jonathan Newman

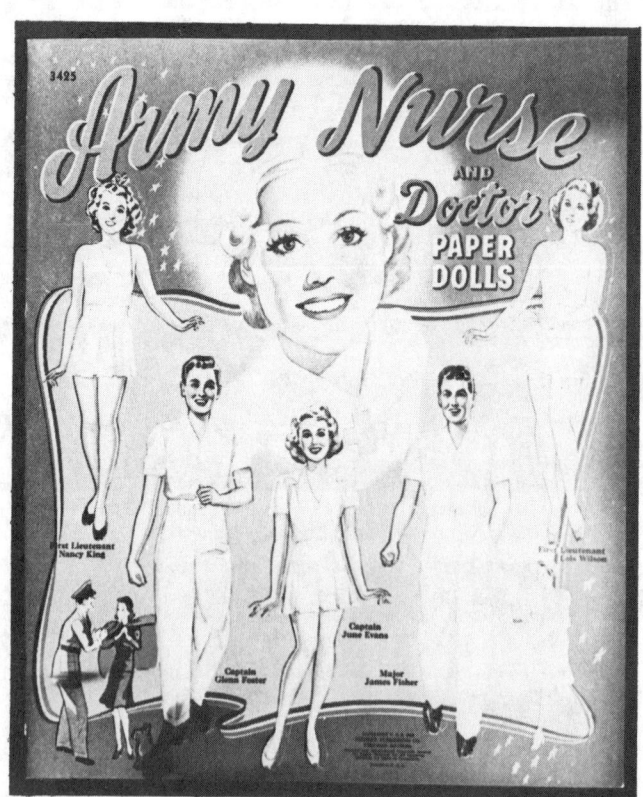

1942, MERRILL No. 3425.
        G - 40.00 ; VG - 50.00 ; M - 75.00
Photo by Jonathan A. Newman
Courtesy Barbara and Jonathan Newman

Circa 1942, HANDI-KRAFT.
        G - 25.00 ; VG - 35.00 ; M - 40.00
Photo by Jonathan A. Newman
Courtesy Barbara and Jonathan Newman

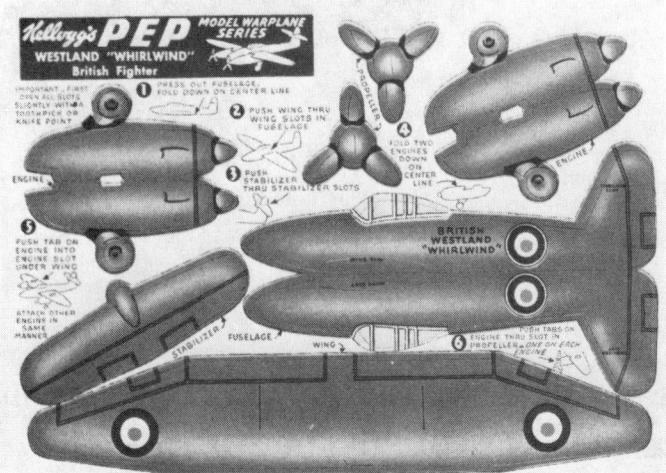

Circa 1944, KELLOGG'S PEP.
        G - 7.00 ; VG - 11.00 ; M - 15.00
Photo by Jonathan A. Newman
Courtesy Barbara and Jonathan Newman

McL5

Photo by Jonathan A. Newman
Courtesy Barbara and Jonathan Newman

1942, LOWE No. L535.
        G - 35.00 ; VG - 45.00 ; M - 50.00
Photo by Jonathan A. Newman
Courtesy Barbara and Jonathan Newman

Circa 1943, LOWE No. 848.
        G - 45.00 ; VG - 55.00 ; M - 60.00
Photo by Jonathan A. Newman
Courtesy Barbara and Jonathan Newman

1942, LOWE No. 265.
        G - 40.00 ; VG - 50.00 ; M - 55.00
Photo by Jonathan A. Newman
Courtesy Barbara and Jonathan Newman

TOOTSIETOY

The linotype machine was responsible for the birth of one of this country's most respected toymakers.

The machine was introduced at the Columbian Exposition in Chicago in 1893. Samuel Dowst, a trade journal publisher, after obtaining one, found he could adapt it to make small promotional miniatures related to one of the journals he published.

By the turn of the century, die-casting had become his principal business, and by 1911 he produced a small car with free-turning wheels. When he brought out a line of doll furniture in 1922 he called it Tootsietoy, after a relative, Tootsie Dowst.

Under the Dowst name, the company made toy soldiers, many, perhaps all of which, were sold for years, even after WWII.

In 1938 Tootsietoy introduced a line of four semi-flat, 1½" high soldiers that are better known to collectors. They consist of a Seated Machine-Gunner, a Charging Soldier, a marching Rifleman, and a Colorbearer. At the time they were sold 10 on a card for a dime. Although attractive and not easy to find, they have yet to prove real collector's items, and sell today for about $5.00 apiece in mint condition.

Midget die-casts. Top - Tootsietoy military vehicles and planes. Middle - none marked, but all are either Tootsietoy or pre-Tootsietoy era Dowst. Bottom - 3 on right unmarked, but probably Tootsietoy.
Photo by Ed Poole

TOOTSIETOY Jeep CJ3, 3", 1950.
G - 6.00; VG - 9.00; M - 12.00
Photo by Ed Poole

TOOTSIETOY, top L to R, Midget series: Battleship, Destroyer, Carrier, Cruiser, Tug, Submarine. Second row from top: 129 Tender, 1039 Tanker, 127 Destroyer. Middle row, L to R: 1037 Transport, 1034 Battleship, 128 Submarine. Second row from bottom: 1036 Carrier, 130 Yacht. Bottom row: 1037 Liner, 1035 Cruiser.
Photo by Ed Poole

TOOTSIETOY top row, L to R: 4649 Tri-Motor Plane, 04460 Aero-Dawn, 4675 Wings, no # High-Wing Floatplane. Middle row: 04650 Autogyro, 718 Waco Bomber, 719 Crusader. Bottom row, L to R: 119 Army Plane, 125 Lockheed Electra, 0717 TWA Douglas Airliner, DC4 Super Mainliner.
Photo by Ed Poole

TOOTSIETOY

	G	VG	M
TOOTSIETOY 106 Low-Wing Monoplane, 1932 .	20.00	25.00	30.00
TOOTSIETOY 119 Army Plane	15.00	20.00	25.00
TOOTSIETOY 125 Lockheed Electra	10.00	15.00	20.00
TOOTSIETOY 718 Waco Bomber	25.00	35.00	50.00
TOOTSIETOY 719 Crusader	25.00	35.00	45.00
TOOTSIETOY 721 Curtis P 40	50.00	80.00	125.00
TOOTSIETOY 722 Transport Plane, 1941	30.00	45.00	60.00
TOOTSIETOY 0001 P-38	20.00	30.00	40.00
TOOTSIETOY 0003 F9F-2 Panther, 1-piece casting	5.00	10.00	15.00
TOOTSIETOY 0008 S-58 Sikorsky Helicopter	20.00	30.00	40.00
TOOTSIETOY 0009 Navy Jet Cutlass	10.00	15.00	20.00
TOOTSIETOY 0717 Douglas DC-2 TWA Airliner	20.00	25.00	35.00
TOOTSIETOY 0720 Fly-N-Gyro, 1938	25.00	40.00	75.00
TOOTSIETOY 4482 Bleriot, 1910	20.00	30.00	40.00
TOOTSIETOY 4491 Bleriot, 1910 (smaller)	15.00	20.00	25.00
TOOTSIETOY 4649 Tri-Motor Plane	25.00	40.00	75.00
TOOTSIETOY 4650 Biplane	30.00	40.00	70.00
TOOTSIETOY 4659 Autogyro	25.00	45.00	65.00
TOOTSIETOY 4675 Wings	25.00	35.00	45.00
TOOTSIETOY 4675 Wings seaplane	30.00	40.00	50.00
TOOTSIETOY 4850 Shooting Star	10.00	15.00	20.00
TOOTSIETOY 04659 Autogyro	25.00	45.00	65.00
TOOTSIETOY 04660 Aero-Dawn	15.00	25.00	35.00
TOOTSIETOY 04660 Aero-Dawn seaplane	20.00	30.00	45.00
TOOTSIETOY "Atlantic Clipper," approx. 2" long	5.00	10.00	15.00

	G	VG	M
TOOTSIETOY Beechcraft Bonanza	5.00	10.00	15.00
TOOTSIETOY DC 4 Super-mainliner	20.00	30.00	40.00
TOOTSIETOY Navion	5.00	10.00	15.00
TOOTSIETOY Piper Cub	5.00	10.00	15.00
TOOTSIETOY "Tootsietoy Airport," hangar and two planes	300.00	450.00	600.00
TOOTSIETOY U.S. Moon Rocket, 3 types, all have 2 wheels to run on string, mid-1960s, replicas of original Buck Rogers spaceships	40.00	75.00	100.00
TOOTSIETOY "U.S.N. Los Angeles" dirigible, two grooved wheels on top to run on string (also was sold as part of Buck Rogers set)	37.00	56.00	75.00

TOOTSIETOY SHIPS

	G	VG	M
1034 Battleship, 6" long, 1939 on	9.00	14.00	18.00
1035 Cruiser, 5½" long, 1939 on	8.00	12.00	16.00
1036 Carrier, 6" long, 1939 on	9.00	14.00	18.00
1037 Transport, 6" long, 1939 on	6.00	9.00	12.00
1038 Freighter, 6" long, 1940 on	6.00	9.00	12.00
1039 Tanker, 6" long, 1940 on	6.00	9.00	12.00
127 Destroyer, 4" long, 1939	7.00	11.00	14.00
128 Submarine, 4" long, 1939 on	7.00	11.00	14.00
129 Tender, 4" long, 1940 on	6.00	9.00	12.00
130 Yacht, 4" long, 1940 on	6.00	9.00	12.00

TOOTSIETOY

TOOTSIETOY Airport Hangar with planes. Not shown in other planes photo are P38 (in front of hangar) and Sikorsky amphibian (front right).
Photo by Ed Poole

Top, L to R: 4635 Armored Car, value $40 in mint, 4634 Supply Truck, value $100 in mint. Bottom, L to R: 4674 Renault Tank, value $45 in mint, 4642 Long Range Cannon, value $12 in mint. 4646 Caterpillar Tractor, value $25 in mint.
Photo by Ed Poole

Post-War Tootsietoy military vehicles and cannon, with WWI soldiers. The ambulance is worth $40 in mint, the half track truck is worth $45 in mint. No other prices found.
Photo by Ed Poole

Top L to R: 4640 Mack, value $60 in mint, 4643 Mack AA Gun Truck, value $50 in mint, 4644 Mack Searchlight truck, value $55 in mint. Bottom, L to R: 4654 tractor, 4662 Mortar, 4642 long range cannon.
Value of three in mint set $130.
Photo by Ed Poole.

TOOTSIETOY Soldiers & Ambulance
Ambulance value in mint $40.00
Photo by Ed Poole

No. 1400 "Over The Top". No price found.
Courtesy Roger Johnson

No. 1401 "Movin Up".
No Price Found
Courtesy Roger Johnson

No. 1402 "Machine Gun Nest"
No price found
Courtesy Roger Johnson

No. 1404 "Uncle Sam's Soldiers"
No price found
Courtesy Roger Johnson

ARCADE

Arcade was incorporated in 1885, after an early start in 1869 as the Novelty Iron and Brass Foundry. Located in Freeport, Ilinois, it began making toys around 1893.

Its soldiers were first advertised in 1939, and presumably made their debut in that year. Arcade's slogan for its toys was "They Look Real," but their cast iron soldiers looked anything but. They are oddly streamlined, in an art deco style, and more **symbols** of soldiers than they are representations of them.

They came in at least two finishes, nickel and light bronze, as a way of forming separate armies. A set of 56 pieces included, in addition to the soldiers, an ambulance, an anti-aircraft gun and three airplanes, two with two engines, and one with four. In 1939, the set sold for $1.00.

Despite their presumed indestructability, Arcade's soldiers turn up rarely, but so far aren't much sought-out. Current price per piece is about $5.00 in mint condition. The numbers and descriptions that follow are Arcade's own.

7721 Soldier "Sentry", 1-5/8"
  high
7722 Soldier "Skirmisher",
  1-5/8" high

7723 Soldier "Sniper", 1¼"
  high
7724 Soldier "Marksman",
  1-5/8" high

7725 Soldier "Grenadier",
  1-¾" high

7721   7722   7723   7724   7725

New Soldier and Warfare
SET OF 56 PIECES

Arcade tank and cannon, cast iron with rubber wheels, spring firing, each 4" long. The tank is worth about $150 in mint, the cannon about $24 in mint condition.
Photo by Ed Poole

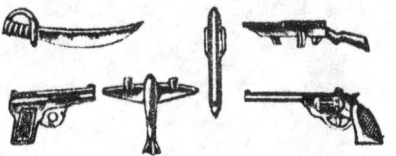

Arcade weapons and airplane, value $5.00 each in mint.

Arcade antiaircraft gun. No price found.
Courtesy Roger Johnson

Ad from the June 1939 Playthings Magazine.
Courtesy Playthings Magazine

LINCOLN LOGS

Since Lincoln Logs' most famous product was miniature wooden timbers that could be formed in the shape of buildings, it seems logical enough that its owner, John Lloyd Wright, was the son of America's most famous architect, Frank Lloyd Wright.

Although the company was in business from about 1910, its hollow lead 54mm soldiers didn't make their appearance till 1928. Sculpture is said to have been by Henry Kasselowski, who also designed for Jones (Lincoln Logs' soldiers and Jones' dimestore pieces look very much alike). In 1933 Wright introduced "a new series of figures known as 'Noveltoy Miniatures'". They were made from an alloy of aluminum, copper and zinc, with eight foot figures in a box retailing for fifty cents, and sixteen in a box for a dollar. In the 1920s two brothers, Henry N. Cooper Jr. and Kenneth L. Cooper formed or bought the Noveltoy Corp. They sold or lost Noveltoy in the 1933-35 period (probably 1933, which seems to be when Lincoln Logs took over). In 1939 Henry Cooper's son Kenneth, then 14, had a summer job at Noveltoy. He remembers the company occupying the entire premises of a three or four-story building, about 200'x600'. There were over a dozen women employed as painters. Cooper, who believes he was paid $6 a week, had the job of taking the painted soldiers in trays and baking them in an oven. He remembers only cowboys and Indians, and that it's likely Noveltoy employed at least one hundred people.

The Washington at Valley Forge figures, the U.S. Soldiers of 1918 and all of the Royal Canadian Police were introduced in 1932.

There was a fair variety to the figures, in both types and eras, possibly sparked by J. Edward Jones' approach to the field (Both Lincoln Log and Jones were located in Chicago). The figures were sold both separately and with Lincoln Logs. World War II put a stop to their production for a time, and the post-War soldiers were painted with less attention to detail, finally being replaced by plastic.

Lincoln Logs' most unusual figures are its "Og, Son of Fire" group. They were based on a Libby's Milk radio show of the 1930s, and were issued as premiums; Libby's bottle lids plus a few cents "for postage and handling" was all it took to have the postman bring them. The set came with a color map, about the same size as the Orphan Annie and Amos & Andy premium maps.

LINCOLN LOGS
Words in bold type are Lincoln Logs' own description.

	G	VG	M		G	VG	M
LL1 **Foot Soldier of 1812, No. 201**	6.00	9.00	12.00	LL18 **Machine Gunner, No. 204** (prone)	5.00	8.00	10.00
LL2 **Indian with Gun**	3.00	4.50	5.00	LL19 **Mounted Officer No.314**	7.00	11.00	14.00
LL3 **Indian with Gun, No. 225** (warbonnet)	3.50	5.00	7.00	LL20 **Royal Canadian Police, No. 280** (foot)	8.00	12.00	16.00
LL4 **Indian with Bow**	3.50	5.00	7.00	LL21 **Mounted Officer, No. 381** (Mountie)	17.00	25.00	34.00
LL5 **Indian with Bow, No. 226** (warbonnet)	3.50	5.00	7.00	LL22 **American Sailor at Attention No. 206**	5.00	8.00	10.00
LL6 **Indian Crawling No. 227**	3.50	5.00	7.00	LL23 **West Point Cadet, No. 205** (foot)	5.00	8.00	10.00
LL7 **Cowboy - Foot** (with lasso) **No. 261**	5.00	7.50	7.00	LL24 **Og**	16.00	24.00	32.00
LL8 **Cowboy - Foot** (firing pistol) **No. 262**	3.50	5.00	7.00	LL25 **Nada**	30.00	45.00	60.00
LL9 **Indian - Mounted** (with rifle)	7.00	11.00	14.00	LL26 **Big Tooth**		No Price Found	
LL10 **Indian - Mounted, No. 331** (with bow)	7.00	11.00	14.00	LL27 **Three Horn**	9.00	13.00	18.00
LL11 **Cowboy - Mounted, No. 372** (firing pistol)	7.00	11.00	14.00	LL28 **Ru**	37.00	56.00	75.00
LL12 **Foot Soldier of 1776. No. 202**	6.00	9.00	12.00	LL29 **Rex**		No Price Found	
LL13 **Mounted Officer of 1776, No. 432**	9.00	13.00	18.00	LL30 **No. 276 Rail Splitter**	17.00	26.00	35.00
LL14 **Mounted Officer of 1776** (larger casting)	10.00	15.00	20.00	LL31 **Farmer No. 282**	3.50	5.00	7.00
LL15 **Pioneer - Foot No. 275**	3.00	4.50	6.00	LL32 **Farm Wife No. 283**	3.50	5.00	7.00
LL15a Pioneer, thinner version	3.00	4.50	6.00	LL33 **Conductor No. 293**	5.00	7.50	10.00
LL16 **Foot Soldier of 1918, No. 203,** (marching)	5.00	8.00	10.00	LL33a Conductor, later, thinner base	5.00	7.50	10.00
LL17 **Foot Soldier of 1918, No. 207** (charging)	5.00	8.00	10.00	LL34 **Engineer No. 295**	6.00	9.00	12.00
				LL35 **Red Cap No. 294**	5.00	7.50	10.00
				LL36 **Telegraph Messenger No. 290**	6.00	9.00	12.00
				LL37 **Policeman No. 291**	6.00	9.00	12.00
				LL38 **Traveling Man No.292**	5.00	7.50	10.00
				LL39 **Oxen Team**	6.00	9.00	12.00
				LL40 **Poplar Tree No. 324**	7.00	11.00	15.00

LL1   LL2   LL3   LL5   LL6   LL7   LL8

LL9   LL10   LL11
Courtesy Lou Steinberg
Photo by Stefan Steinberg

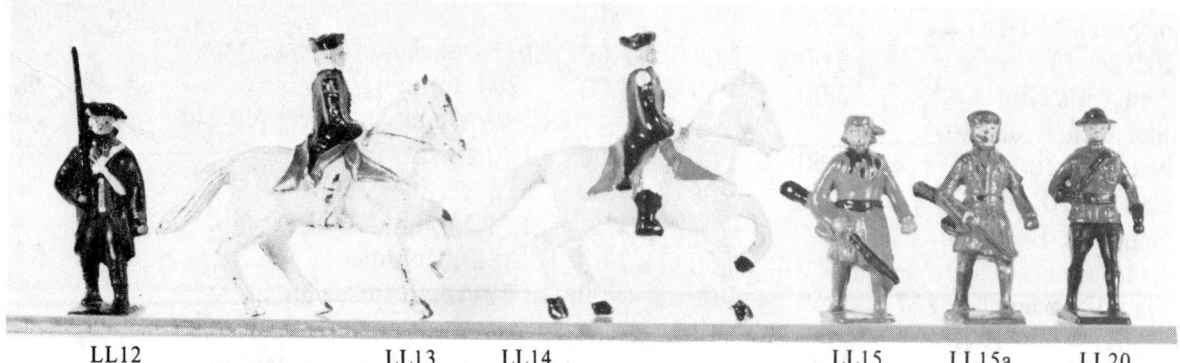

LL12
Courtesy Lou Steinberg
Photo by Stefan Steinberg

LL13   LL14   LL15   LL15a   LL20

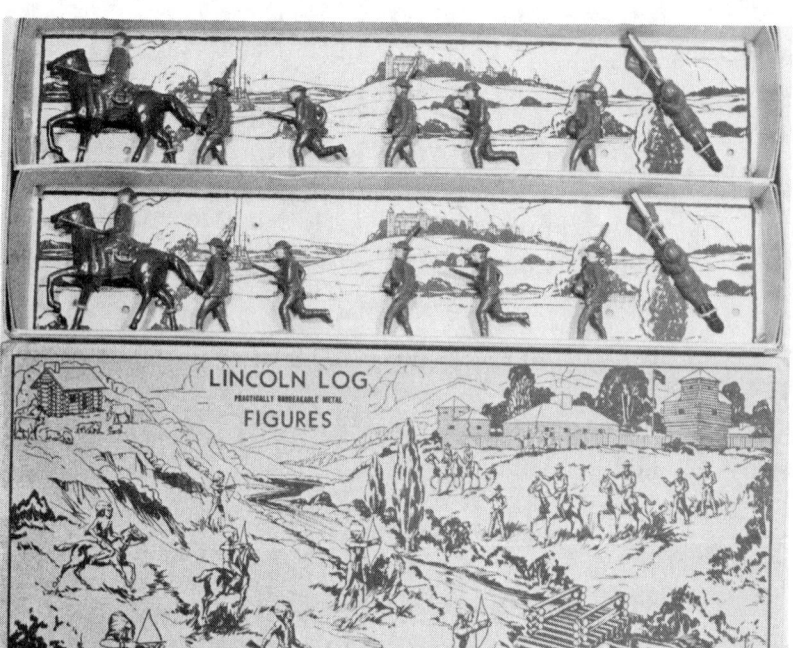

LL16 through LL19
Set NM-110 U.S. Soldiers 1918.
Courtesy Lou Steinberg
Photo by Stefan Steinberg

LL18
The figure at left appears to be Lincoln Logs LL18, but has an inverted under-
base. Perhaps a well-painted homecast, or simply a variation.
Courtesy Charles Breslow

LL21

LL22 and LL23
Courtesy Lou Steinberg
Photo by Stefan Steinberg

LL24   LL25   LL26   LL27   LL28
Courtesy Lou Steinberg
Photo by Stefan Steinberg

LL30   LL31   LL32
Courtesy Lou Steinberg
Photo by Stefan Steinberg

LL39   LL40   LL41
Courtesy Lou Steinberg
328 Photo by Stefan Steinberg

LINCOLN LOGS

LL33   LL33a   LL34   LL35   LL36   LL37   LL38

Courtesy Lou Steinberg
Photo by Stefan Steinberg

LL42 LL43 LL44 LL45   LL46   LL47
Photo by Don Pielin

LL50

Courtesy G. Ogden Nutting

LL48   LL49   LL7   LL8   LL50   LL11   LL51   LL52   Courtesy Don Pielin

Set No. 30 Railroaders Metal Figures.
Courtesy Lou Steinberg   Photo by Stefan Steinberg

Set NM80 Lincoln Station Figures $100 for mint set.
Courtesy Lou Steinberg   Photo by Stefan Steinberg

329

LINCOLN LOGS

Set 50 CI Settlers Cabin

Set NM13 American Sailors and West Point Cadets.
Courtesy Lou Steinberg   Photo by Stefan Steinberg

	G	VG	M
LL42 **Sheep No. 299**	3.00	4.50	6.00
LL43 **Pig No. 502**	2.00	3.00	4.00
LL44 **Cow No. 316**	3.00	4.50	6.00
LL45 Cow feeding........	3.00	4.50	6.00
LL46 **No. 315 Horse** feeding	No Price Found		
LL47 Horse feeding, short tail	No Price Found		
LL48 Large Cowboy, NOVELTOY	No Price Found		
LL49 Large Indian, NOVELTOY	No Price Found		
LL50 Cowboy on Rearing Horse................	No Price Found		
LL51 Cowboy waving hat..	No Price Found		
LL52 Masked Rider.......	21.00	31.00	42.00
LL52 As above, variation in horse's tail	25.00	38.00	50.00
LL53 Tall Marching Doughboy	175.00	263.00	350.00
LL54 Tall Standing Firing Doughboy	150.00	225.00	300.00
LL55 Tall Kneeling Firing Doughboy	150.00	225.00	300.00
LL56 Tall Signalman Doughboy	225.00	338.00	450.00
LL57 Tall Flagbearer Doughboy, 6" high, flag is cast with figure, only one known	No Price Found		
LL58 Tall Machine Gunner, prone, 5" long, only one known	No Price Found		

SNOW WHITE FIGURES (Snow White 6½" high, Dwarfs 3½"-4" high)

	G	VG	M
No. 1 Dopey	50.00	75.00	100.00
No. 2 Doc	50.00	75.00	100.00
No. 3 Grumpy	50.00	75.00	100.00
No. 4 Sneezy	50.00	75.00	100.00
No. 5 Bashful	50.00	75.00	100.00
No. 6 Sleepy	50.00	75.00	100.00
No. 7 Happy	50.00	75.00	100.00
No # Snow White	100.00	150.00	200.00

LL52 Variation. Notice horses' tails.
Courtesy K. Warren Mitchell

LL58

The rifle on LL55 is repaired, and far too long. The LL53 rifle tip is broken off. However, the LL54 rifle tip is unbroken. The LL55's should be about the same length.
J. Edward Jones tried to market these soldiers for Lincoln Logs but with no success.
Photo by Dave Mitchell

LINCOLN LOGS

LL56
(Replacement flags, not necessarily correct)
Courtesy K. Warren Mitchell

No.1

No.2
Photo by Bill Nutting

No.3   No.5   No. 4
Photo by Marvin Sussman

No.6   No.7
Photo by Bill Nutting

Lincoln Logs Royal Canadian Mtd.
Police Set No. NM-65, LL20, LL21.
Photo by Gary J. Linden

No. 20 Cowboys and Indians with Wigwam
Photo by Bill Nutting

This No. 32 Ox Cart boxed set sold in 1990 for $100.
The similar No. 31 - Load of Logs also sold for $100.
Courtesy Ogden Nutting

WARREN

Of the U.S. soldiers made in the Britains tradition, those of Warren are probably the most prized by collectors. Warren's are slightly larger (60mm rather than 54mm), and the paint doesn't compare to Britains' (instead being more like Authenticast's) but there is no question that they were meant to be a quality product and in a couple of instances they are superior to Britains. Most of the figures have **two** moving arms, and because they have plug heads they afford a variety Britains doesn't. In addition to meaning that any figure can have either a helmet or a peaked cap, a face that is particularly pleasing to a collector can be put on the body of his choice. An additional plus to some collectors is the vitality of Warren's figures in comparision to the rather sedate Britains.

Warren authority Steve Balkin has reported in the Old Toy Soldier Newsletter that as a child John Warren Jr. was very interested in toys, and had a large collection of toy soldiers as well as trains. Since his father's business, Epplesheimer and Company, made candy molds (for Hershey Bars, etc.), his experience as its vice-president and general manager made his deciding to go into the toy soldier business a logical step.

Warren's company, The Warren Lines, seems to have begun business in 1936 and gone into bankruptcy in 1939, or at the latest 1940. Warren, which was based in Manhattan, produced only American soldiers; infantry, cavalry and horse artillery. At the beginning, the line was mainly U.S. Cavalry and light field artillery, with the infantry added in 1937. In 1936 the individual soldiers sold for fifty cents up, and the boxed sets from $2.50 to $20.00. These were extraordinarily high prices for the era, and no doubt contributed greatly to the firm's short life, although in 1937, one-dollar boxed sets were added. Because of their high price, Warren's soldiers were probably confined to the better department stores (in New York, they sold at Macy's, in Brooklyn at Abraham & Straus).

Warren also offers the one touch of romance to have surfaced in the history of toy soldier-making. Although Warren may have done much of the sculpting himself, it is known that Margaret Cloninger, one of Tommy Toy's two sculptresses, was brought in to improve the look of Warren's horses, and she may also have designed some of its soldiers. Cloninger had sculpted for Epplesheimer, and presumably Warren knew her from her work for that company. In any event, her working for Warren must have brought them into close proximity, and they were married on March 26, 1941.

In 1941, after the company had ceased production, Comet bought Warren's remaining stock of horses, 3000 in all, intending to produce riders for them. But the advent of World War II resulted in the horses instead being melted down to make military identification models. Whether Warren's molds also were bought by Comet and then melted down for new models is not known, although Balkin has hope that some still exist.

Warrens are rare, and prices are accordingly high. In 1990 a boxed set of foot infantrymen in the wrong Warren box sold for $1000. The same year, a set of Warren field artillery set on a diorama base sold for $3000. Warren's Scout Car and Staff Car were in very limited production, and are each worth a minimum of $600.00 in mint. Foot figures average $100 apiece and mounted $200 apiece. The horses designed by Margaret Cloninger were all solidcast and presumably are considered more valuable than the early hollowcast models. The numbers in bold in the following list are Warren's own.

(W1) **No. 1** Horse Standing (hollowcast)
(W2) **No. 1** Horse Standing (solidcast)
(W3) **No. 2** Horse Striding (hollowcast)
(W4) **No. 2** Horse Striding (solidcast)
(W5) **No. 3** Horse Walking (hollowcast)
(W6) **No. 3** Horse Walking (solidcast)
(W7) **No. 4** Horse, head up, mouth open (hollowcast)
(W8) **No. 4** Horse, head up, mouth open (solidcast)
(W9) **No. 5** Horse Galloping (hollowcast)
(W10) **No. 5** Horse Galloping (solidcast)
(W11) **No. 6** Horse Cantering (hollowcast)
(W12) **No. 6** Horse Cantering (solidcast)
(W13) **No. 7** Horse Prancing (hollowcast)
(W14) **No. 7** Horse Prancing (solidcast)
(W15) Rider, upright, holding sword, peaked cap
(W16) Rider, upright, holding sword, helmet
(W17) Rider, upright, holding pistol, peaked cap
(W18) Rider, upright, holding pistol, helmet
(W19) Rider, upright, holding rifle, peaked cap
(W20) Rider, upright, holding rifle, helmet
(W21) Rider, upright, holding cavalry guidon, peaked cap
(W22) Rider, upright, holding cavalry guidon, helmet
(W23) Rider, upright, holding artillery guidon, peaked cap
(W24) Rider, upright, holding artillery guidon, helmet
(W25) Rider, upright, holding regimental standard, peaked cap
(W26) Rider, upright, holding regimental standard, helmet
(W27) Rider, upright, holding U.S. flag, peaked cap
(W28) Rider, upright, holding U.S. flag, helmet
(W29) Rider, upright, empty-handed, peaked cap
(W30) Rider, upright, empty-handed, helmet
(W31) Rider, upright, holding bugle, peaked cap
(W32) Rider, upright, holding bugle, helmet
(W33) Rider, leaning forward, holding sword, peaked cap
(W34) Rider, leaning forward, holding sword, helmet

WARREN

W16   W22

W30

W32   W22   W17

W131   W59   W59   W51

(W35) Rider, leaning forward, holding pistol, peaked cap
(W36) Rider, leaning forward, holding pistol, helmet
(W37) Rider, leaning forward, holding bugle, peaked cap
(W38) Rider, leaning forward, holding bugle, helmet
(W39) Rider, leaning forward, holding rifle, peaked cap
(W40) Rider, leaning forward, holding rifle, helmet
(W41) Rider, leaning forward, holding cavalry guidon, peaked cap
(W42) Rider, leaning forward, holding cavalry guidon, helmet
(W43) Rider, leaning forward, holding artillery guidon, peaked cap
(W44) Rider, leaning forward, holding artillery guidon, helmet
(W45) Rider, leaning forward, holding regimental standard, peaked cap
(W46) Rider, leaning forward, holding regimental standard, helmet
(W47) Rider, leaning forward, holding U.S. flag, peaked cap

W18

WARREN

(W48) Rider, leaning forward, holding U.S. flag, helmet

(W49) Officer at attention, sword to shoulder, peaked cap, green base

(W50) Officer at attention, sword to shoulder, peaked cap, groundwork base

(W51) Officer at attention, sword to shoulder, helmet, green base

(W52) Officer at attention, sword to shoulder, helmet, groundwork base

(W53) Soldier at attention, shoulder arms, peaked cap, green base

(W54) Soldier at attention, shoulder arms, peaked cap, groundwork base

(W55) Soldier at attention, shoulder arms, helmet, green base

(W56) Soldier at attention, shoulder arms, helmet, groundwork base

(W57) Soldier at attention, rifle at side, peaked cap, green base

(W58) Soldier at attention, rifle at side, peaked cap, groundwork base

(W59) Soldier at attention, rifle at side, helmet, green base

(W60) Soldier at attention, rifle at side, helmet, groundwork base

(W61) Bugler at attention, peaked cap, green base

(W62) Bugler at attention, peaked cap, groundwork base

(W63) Bugler at attention, helmet, green base

(W64) Bugler at attention, helmet, groundwork base

(W65) Drummer at attention, peaked cap, green base

(W66) Drummer at attention, peaked cap, groundwork base

(W67) Drummer at attention, helmet, green base

(W68) Drummer at attention, helmet, groundwork base

(W69) At attention with regimental flag, peaked cap, green base

(W70) At attention with regimental flag, peaked cap, groundwork base

(W71) At attention with regimental flag, helmet, green base

(W72) At attention with regimental flag, helmet, groundwork base

(W73) At attention with guidon, peaked cap, green base

(W74) At attention with guidon, peaked cap, groundwork base

(W75) At attention with guidon, helmet, green base

(W76) At attention with guidon, helmet, groundwork base

(W77) At attention with U.S. flag, peaked cap, green base

(W78) At attention with U.S. flag, peaked cap, groundwork base

(W79) At attention with U.S. flag, helmet, green base

(W80) At attention with U.S. flag, helmet, groundwork base

(W81) Officer charging with pistol, peaked cap, green base

(W82) Officer charging with pistol, peaked cap, groundwork base

(W83) Officer charging with pistol, helmet, green base

(W84) Officer charging with pistol, helmet, groundwork base

(W85) Officer charging with sword, peaked cap, green base

(W86) Officer charging with sword, peaked cap, grounwork base

(W87) Officer charging with sword, helmet, green base

(W88) Officer, charging with sword, helmet, ground work base

(W89) Doughboy charging, left foot forward, peaked cap, green base

(W90) Doughboy charging, left foot forward, peaked cap, groundwork base

(W91) Doughboy charging, left foot forward, helmet, green base

(W92) Doughboy charging, left foot forward, helmet, groundwork base

(W93) Doughboy charging, right foot forward, peaked cap, green base

(W94) Doughboy charging, right foot forward, peaked cap, groundwork base

(W95) Doughboy charging, right foot forward, helmet, green base

(W96) Doughboy charging, right foot forward, helmet, groundwork base

(W97) Doughboy charging with bugle, peaked cap, green base

(W98) Doughboy charging with bugle, peaked cap, groundwork base

(W99) Doughboy charging with bugle, helmet, green base

(W100)Doughboy charging with bugle, helmet, groundwork base

(W101) Doughboy charging with guidon, peaked cap, green base

(W102) Doughboy charging with guidon, peaked cap, groundwork base

(W103) Doughboy charging with guidon, helmet, green base

(W104) Doughboy charging with guidon, helmet, groundwork base

(W105) Officer marching with sword, peaked cap, green base

(W106) Officer marching with sword, peaked cap, groundwork base

(W107) Officer marching with sword, helmet, green base

(W108) Officer marching with sword, helmet, groundwork base

WARREN

W92　W104　W104　W100　W104　W162　W84
Courtesy Bob Kneale
Photo by Mary Cassavant

(W109) Infantryman marching right shoulder arms, peaked cap, green base

(W110) Infantryman marching right shoulder arms, peaked cap, groundwork base

(W111) Infantryman marching right shoulder arms, helmet, green base

(W112) Infantryman marching right shoulder arms, helmet, groundwork base

(W113) Infantryman marching rifle slung, peaked cap, green base

(W114) Infantryman marching rifle slung, peaked cap, groundwork base

(W115) Infantryman marching, rifle slung, helmet, green base

(W116) Infantryman marching, rifle slung, helmet, groundwork base

(W117) Bugler marching, peaked cap, green base

(W118) Bugler marching, peaked cap, groundwork base

(W119) Bugler marching, helmet, green base

(W120) Bugler marching, helmet, groundwork base

(W121) Marching with regimental flag, peaked cap, green base

(W122) Marching with regimental flag, peaked cap, groundwork base

(W123) Marching with regimental flag, helmet, green base

(W124) Marching with regimental flag, helmet, groundwork base

(W125) Marching with guidon, peaked cap, green base

(W126) Marching with guidon, peaked cap, groundwork base

(W127) Marching with guidon, helmet, green base

(W128) Marching with guidon, helmet, groundwork base

(W129) Marching with U.S. flag, peaked cap, green base

(W130) Marching with U.S. flag, peaked cap, groundwork base

(W131) Marching with U.S. flag, helmet, green base

(W132) Marching with U.S. flag, helmet, groundwork base

(W133) Officer at ease with binoculars, peaked cap, green base

(W134) Officer at ease with binoculars, peaked cap, groundwork base

(W135) Officer at ease with binoculars, helmet, green base

(W136) Officer at ease with binoculars, helmet, groundwork base

(W137) Officer at ease with pistol, peaked cap, green base

(W138) Officer at ease with pistol, peaked cap, groundwork base

(W139) Officer at ease with pistol, helmet, green base

(W140) Officer at ease with pistol, helmet, groundwork base

(W141) Doughboy standing firing, peaked cap, green base

(W142) Doughboy standing firing, peaked cap, groundwork base

(W143) Doughboy standing firing, helmet, green base

(W144) Doughboy standing firing, helmet, groundwork base

(W145) Doughboy kneeling firing, peaked cap

(W146) Doughboy kneeling firing, helmet

(W147) Doughboy prone firing, peaked cap

(W148) Doughboy prone firing, helmet

(W149) Doughboy crawling with rifle, peaked cap

(W150) Doughboy crawling with rifle, helmet

(W151) Doughboy kneeling with binoculars, peaked cap

(W152) Doughboy kneeling with binoculars, helmet

(W153) Doughboy kneeling with guidon, peaked cap

(W154) Doughboy kneeling with guidon, helmet

(W155) Doughboy prone empty-handed, peaked cap

(W156) Doughboy prone empty-handed, helmet

(W157) Doughboy prone with binoculars, peaked cap

(W158) Doughboy prone with binoculars, helmet

(W159) Doughboy sitting empty-handed, peaked cap

(W160) Doughboy sitting empty-handed, helmet

(W161) Machine gun on pod

(W162) Machine gun on cart

(W163) Artilleryman horse rider, with whip, peaked cap

(W164) Artilleryman horse rider, with whip, helmet

(W165) Artilleryman horse rider, with rifle, peaked cap

(W166) Artilleryman horse rider, with rifle, helmet

(W167) Artilleryman seated, arms across chest, peaked cap

(W168) Artilleryman seated, arms across chest, helmet

(W169) **No. 34** Three Inch Gun, seats on the trail only

(W170) Three Inch Gun, seats on the trail and shield

(W171) Gun Limber

(W172) Ammunition Caisson

(W173) Scout Car (conversion of a Kenton Toys auto)

(W174) **No. 42 Officer's Car** (conversion of a Kenton Toys auto), with flagstaff holders

(W175) Seated soldier with rifle, peaked cap

WARREN

(W176) Seated soldier with rifle, helmet
(W177) Seated soldier, empty-handed, peaked cap
(W178) Seated soldier, empty-handed, helmet
(W179) **250** Cavalry Band, 8 instruments
(W180) **450** Infantry Band, 12 pieces
(W181) **451** Infantry Band, 17 pieces

W169
(W170 was offered M1B for $400 in 1992).

Courtesy Bob Kneale
Photo by Mary Cassavant

W174 and W175

Courtesy Bob Kneale
Photo by Mary Cassavant

Above two photos: Warren Horse Artillery.
Photo courtesy Sotheby's

(W2) No. 1 Standing
(solidcast)

(W3) No. 2 Striding
(hollowcast)

(W4) No. 2 Striding
(solidcast)

(W6) No. 3 Walking
(solidcast)

(W7) No. 4 Head Up
(hollowcast)

(W8) No. 4 Head Up
(solidcast)

(W10) No. 5 Galloping
(solidcast)

(W12) No. 6 Cantering
(solidcast)

(W13) No. 7 Prancing
(hollowcast)

(W14) No. 7 Prancing
(solidcast)

Courtesy Ron Steiner

L to R: W173, 174
Courtesy Phillips

COMET

It's not known who sculpted Comet's toy soldiers, but one could say they came, by proxy, from the hands of Britains' artisans; they tended to be close, and in some cases even exact, copies of William Britains' soldiers.

Although one English writer has stated Comet began around 1938 or 1939 as a soldier-maker, the consensus is that 1940 was the year. "Brigadiers for Metal Soldiers" was copyrighted on July 25, 1940. Some and perhaps all of the company's sales were to department stores (I saw an extensive display on sale at Brooklyn's Abraham & Straus in 1941 and early 1942), and presumably were meant to compete with and perhaps eventually replace Britains when the events of World War II stopped all soldier-making in England.

According to the September 13, 1959 New York Times, Comet Metal Products Company Inc. was located in an ivy-covered, red brick plant in Richmond Hills, Queens, New York (91-04 132nd Street). It was founded as a die-casting operation in 1919 by Abraham Slonim. He was joined in 1935 by his sons, Joseph and Samuel. By the time of the Times article, Abraham was dead, Joseph was the president of the company, and Samuel its secretary-treasurer. (The 1940 copyright was in Samuel's name).

Although the tendency among collectors has been to sneer at Comet's output, the fact is that some of their sets are extremely attractive, particularly those of the American Revolution. That's not to say Comet figures didn't have their problems. The heads tended to be too small, which made it hard to paint in the eyes and eyebrows attractively. Also, because the 54mm. figures were solid-cast of lead, they tended to break easily. (A set of English Royal Guards I bought as a child were all headless by the second day; each time one fell over, the weight of the bearskin cap was too much for the figure's tiny neck. The legs of many Comet figures were nearly as vulnerable.)

Comet's soldiers came six to eight to a set, at a price of (as I recall) $1.00. The boxes, which seem to have come in several sizes, were colored yellow, red and blue, employed the same illustration, and were marked "The Brigadiers".

Most of the listing that follows comes from what appears to be a summer 1941 catalog, and its extensiveness suggests Comet was doing well, or felt itself on the verge of doing well. There may have been other sets produced; I recall copies of Britains' marching French Foreign Legionaires, with black-painted faces (possibly meant to be Senegalese) which were almost certainly produced by Comet. The company's soldiers are easily identified by their bases, which look like this:

When the War came, Comet switched over to making military models for the Government, and after the War its toy soldiers were produced under the far better known Authenticast trademark. In 1954 the firm's address was 132-09 91st Avenue in Richmond Hill.

Comet's soldiers have recently begun to attract collectors; a boxed set in mint condition averages $90.00. Individual figures sell for about $9.00. The number in parentheses indicates the amount of soldiers in the box.

COMET

C1 Chinese Infantry Charging (8)
K10 Knights in Armor w/Shields (8)
K11 Knights in Armor w/Shields (better painting) (7)
K12 Knights in Armor w/Shields & Lances (6)
GR50 Greek Evzones Marching (7)
GR51 Greek Infantry Charging (8)
GR52 Greek Evzones Marching (field uniform) (8)
T70 Turkish Infantry Charging (8)
T71 Turkish Machine Gun Set
D75 Danish Infantry Marching (7)
D76 Danish Royal Guards Marching (8)
A100 Arabs Running w/Swords (6)
A101 Arabs Running w/Rifles (6)
M200 Mexican Volunteers Marching (8)
EG450 Egyptian Infantry Charging (8)
G500 German Infantry Charging (8)
G501 German Infantry (SS Troops) Charging (8)
G502 German Infantry Marching (8)
G503 German Machine Gun Set
G504 German Infantry Running (8)
G505 German Infantry (SS Troops) Running (8)
G506 German Sailor Marching (8)
G507 German Infantry (SS Troops) Marching (8)
G508 German Machine Gun Set (SS Troops)
G509 Austro-German Alpine Troops (7)
G511 German-Alpine Troops (7)
G513 German Shock Troops (same as G514 but
     painted as German Infantry)
G514 German (SS) Shock Troops (6)
FR650 French Infantry Charging (8)
FR652 Turcos Charging (8)
FR654 Zouaves Charging (8)
FR656 Moroccans Charging (8)
FR658 Tunisians Charging (8)
FR661 French Machine Gun Set
FR662 French Foreign Legion Charging (8)
FR664 French Infantry (Maginot Line) Chg. (8)
FR665 French Infantry (Maginot Line) Mchg. (8)
FR666 French Infantry Marching (8)
SP700 Spanish Infantry Charging (7)
E800 Black Watch Marching (7)
E803 Indian Troops Charging (7)
E804 British Navy Marching (8)
E805 Australian Anzacs Charging (8)
E806 New Zealand Infantry Charging (8)
E807 English Infantry Charging (8)
E808 British Marines Charging (8)
E809 English Machine Gun Set
E810 English Royal Guards Marching (8)
E811 English Infantry w/Gas Masks (8)
E812 English General Staff (6)
E813 R.A.F. w/Aeroplane (7)
E814 R.A.F. without Aeroplane (8)
E815 English Infantry Running (8)
E816 English Infantry Marching Route Step (8)

E817 New Zealand Machine Gun Set
E818 Canadian Infantry Marching Overseas Caps (8)
E821 Sikhs Marching (8)
E822 Indian Frontier Troops Marching (8)
E823 Indian Malaca Troops Full Dress w/Lance (6)
E824 Indian Troops Full Dress Marching (7)
E827 Indian Army Marching (8)
E828 Australian Machine Gun Set
I1000 Italian Colonial Troops Charging (7)
I1001 Italian Infantry Charging (8)
I1002 Italian Machine Gun Set
I1003 Italian Infantry Marching (8)
I1004 Italian Infantry, Dress Uniform
J1050 Japanese Infantry Charging (8)
USSR1100 Russian Infantry Charging (7)
USSR1101 Russian Infantry Marching (8)
USSR1102 Siberian Troops Marching (7)
USA1250 U.S. Infantry Charging Steel Helmets (8)
USA1251 U.S. Natl. Guard Charging Campaign Hats (8)
US1252 U.S. West Point Cadets Marching (8)
US1253 U.S. Marines Marching (8)
US1254 U.S. Sailors Marching (white uniforms) (8)
US1255 U.S. Sailors Marching (blue uniforms) (8)
US1256 U.S. Infantry Marching Steel Helmet (8)
US1257 U.S. Infantry Marching Overseas Caps (8)
US1258 U.S. Panama Troops Charging (8)
US1259 U.S. Philippine Troops Charging (8)
US1260 U.S. Inf. Route Step Marching Steel Helmets (8)
US1261 U.S. Inf. Route Step Marching Overseas Caps (8)
US1262 U.S. Machine Gun Set Steel Helmets
US1263 U.S. Natl. Guard Machine Gun Set Campaign Hat
US1264 U.S. Infantry Crawling w/Gas Masks (8)
US1265 U.S. Marine Band (7)
US1266 U.S. Infantry Band (8)
US1267 American Indians w/Spears (6)
US1267 U.S. Inf. Marching (Cap).
US1268 U.S. Infantry Marching Overseas Cap (8)
US1269 American Indians w/Tomahawks (6)
US1270 American Anti-Tank Set (5)
US1274 U.S. Machine Gun Set Overseas Caps
US1275 U.S. Infantry Crawling Steel Helmets (8)
US1276 U.S. Confederate Army
US1277 U.S. Confederate Army (Hat).
US1278 U.S. Northern Army (Civil War)
S1300 Swedish Royal Guards Marching (7)
US1776 "Spirit of 1776" (Price $8.40 dz.) (6)
US2000 Colonial Infantry Marching (Revolution) (6)
US2001 Colonial Infantry Marching (Revolution) (6)
E2050 British Red Coats Marching (Revolution) (6)
E2051 British Red Coats Charging (Revolution) (6)
H2150 Hessian Troops Marching (Revolution) (6)
H2151 Hessian Troops Charging (Revolution) (6)
L2050 Lafayette's Troops?
L2051 Lafayette's Troops?
DH 300 - Unknown Dahomey?

COMET

DH 301 - Unknown Dahomey?
B750 - Unknown

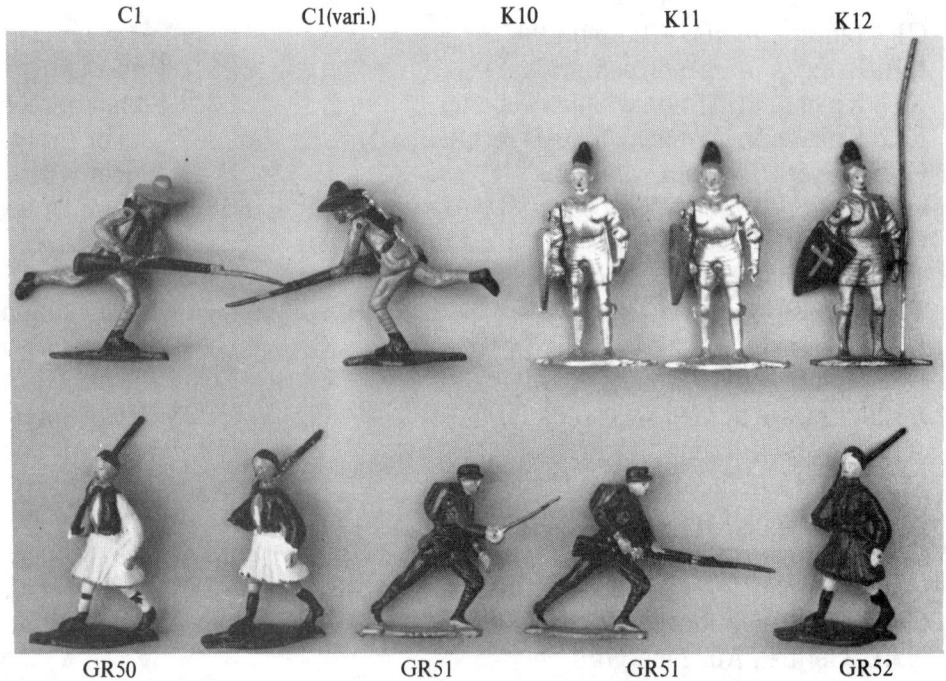

C1   C1(vari.)   K10   K11   K12

GR50   GR51   GR51   GR52
Photo by Bill Nutting

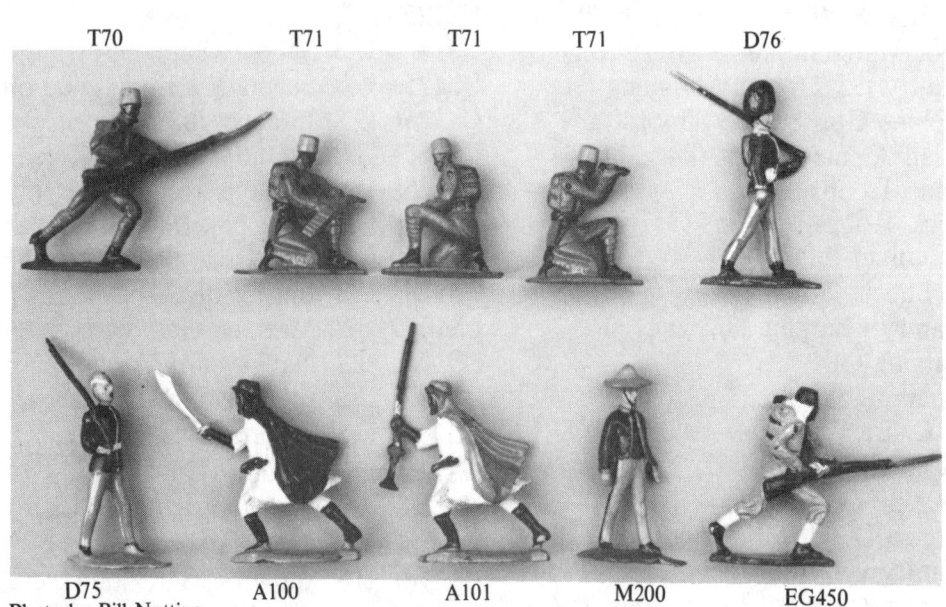

T70   T71   T71   T71   D76

D75   A100   A101   M200   EG450
Photo by Bill Nutting

G500   G500   G501   G501

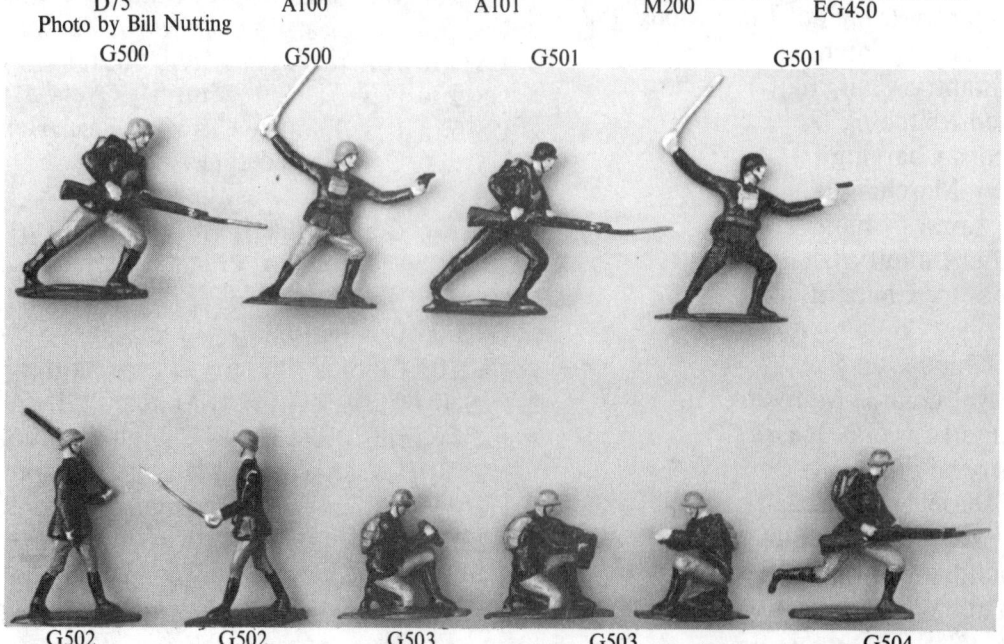

G502   G502   G503   G503   G504

Photo by Bill Nutting

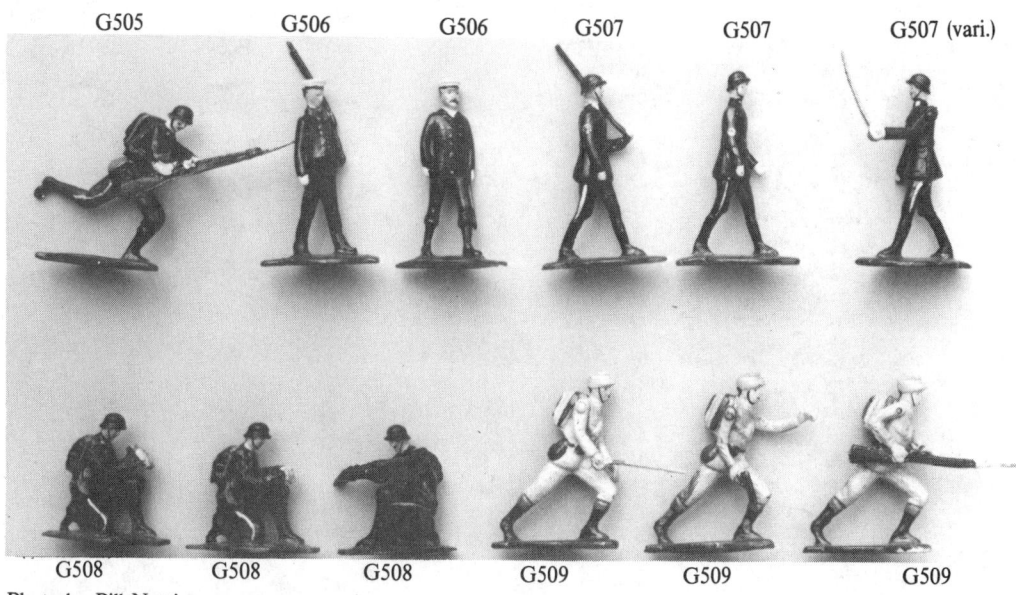

G505 G506 G506 G507 G507 G507 (vari.)

G508 G508 G508 G509 G509 G509

Photo by Bili Nutting

G513
Photo by Vadis Godbey

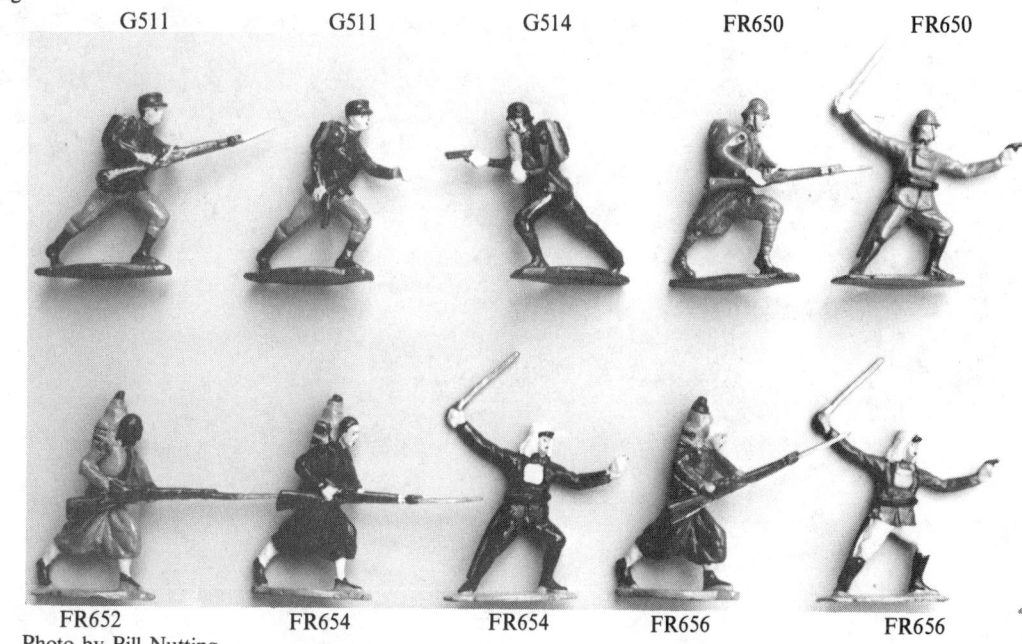

G511 G511 G514 FR650 FR650

FR652 FR654 FR654 FR656 FR656

Photo by Bill Nutting

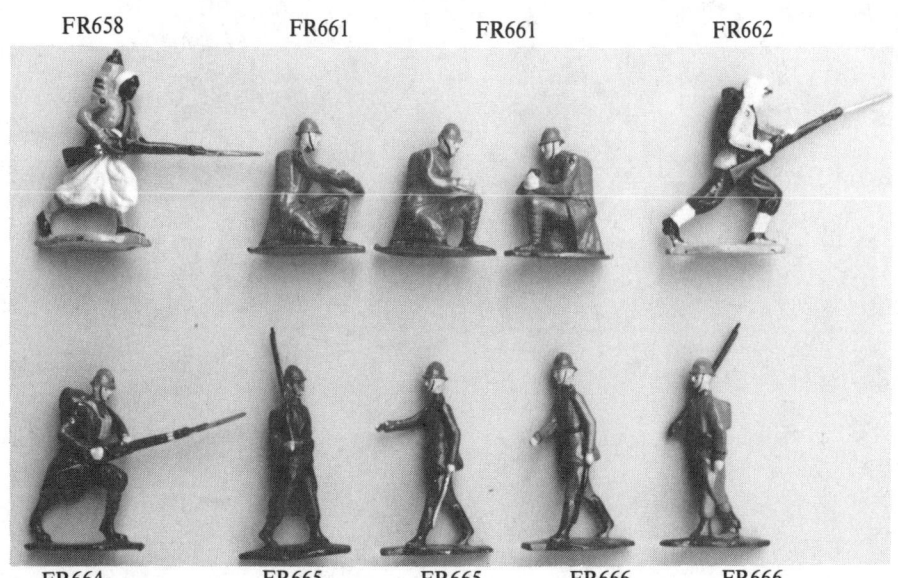

FR658 FR661 FR661 FR662

FR664 FR665 FR665 FR666 FR666

Photo by Bill Nutting

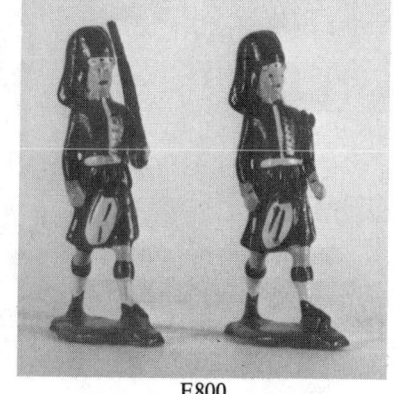

E800
Photo by Vadis Godbey

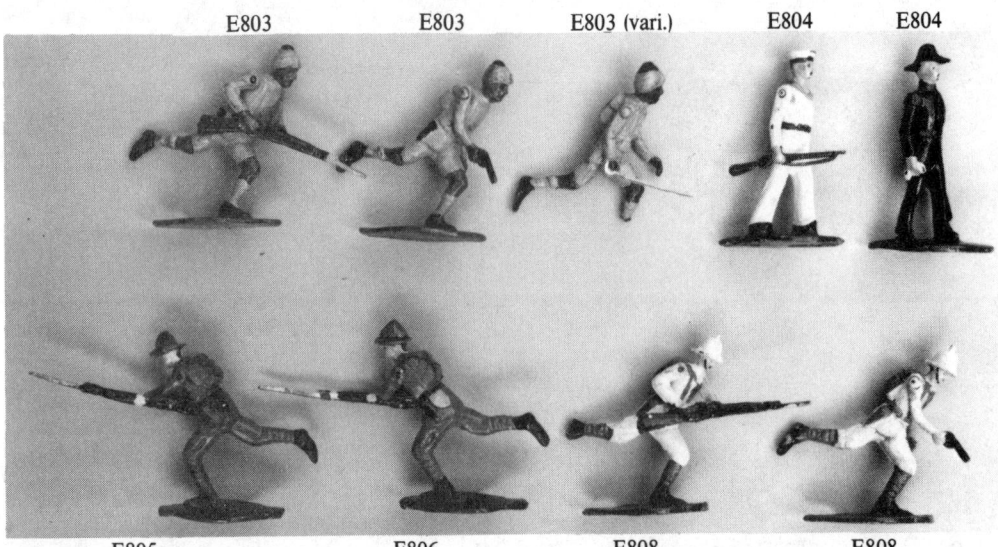

E803   E803   E803 (vari.)   E804   E804

E805   E806   E808   E808
Photo by Bill Nutting

E807
Photo by Vadis Godbey

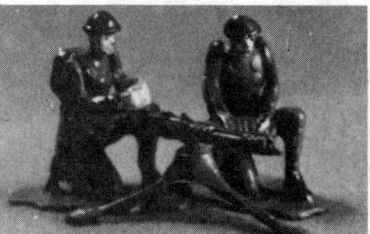

E809
Photo by Mike McAfee

E810
Photo by Mike McAfee

E814
Photo by Mike McAfee

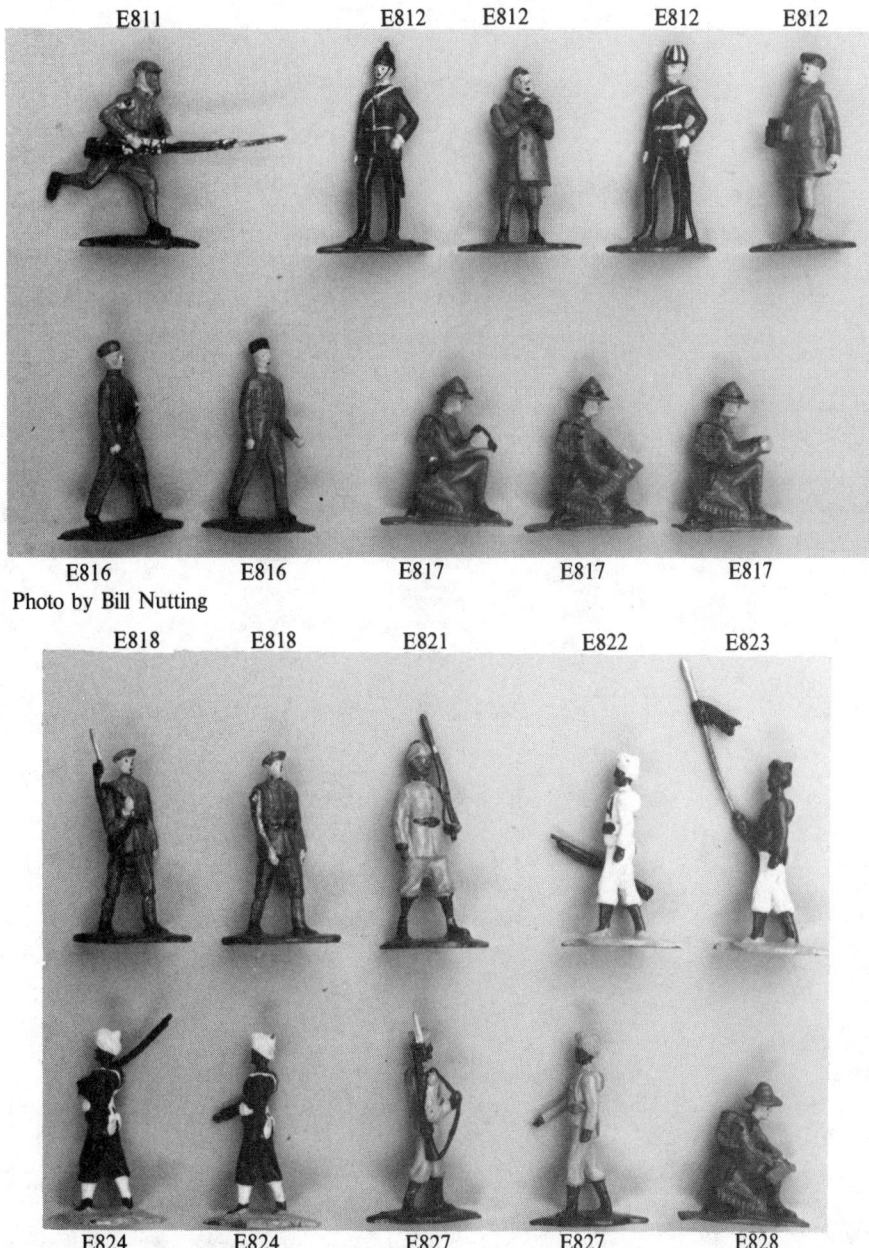

E811   E812   E812   E812   E812

E816   E816   E817   E817   E817

Photo by Bill Nutting

E818   E818   E821   E822   E823

E824   E824   E827   E827   E828

Photo by Bill Nutting

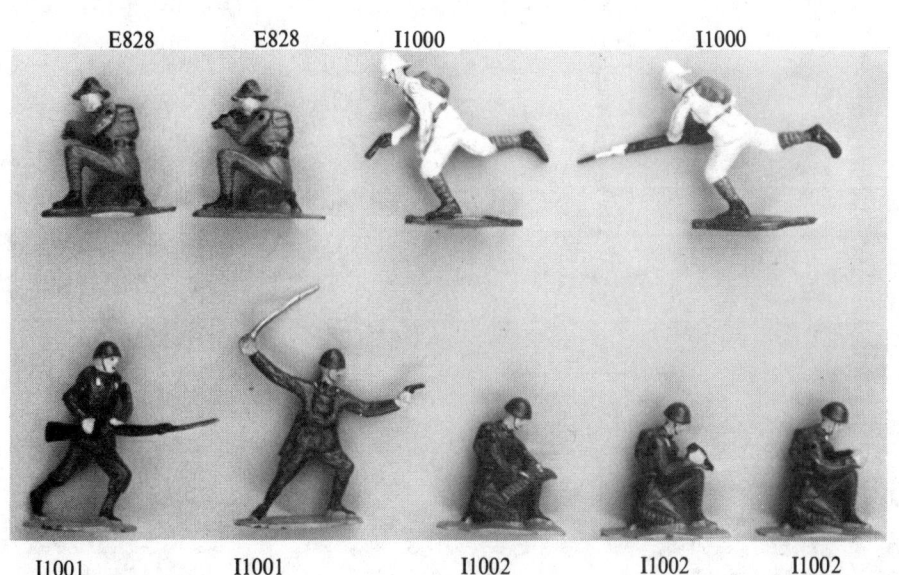

E828   E828   I1000   I1000

I1001   I1001   I1002   I1002   I1002

Photo by Bill Nutting

COMET

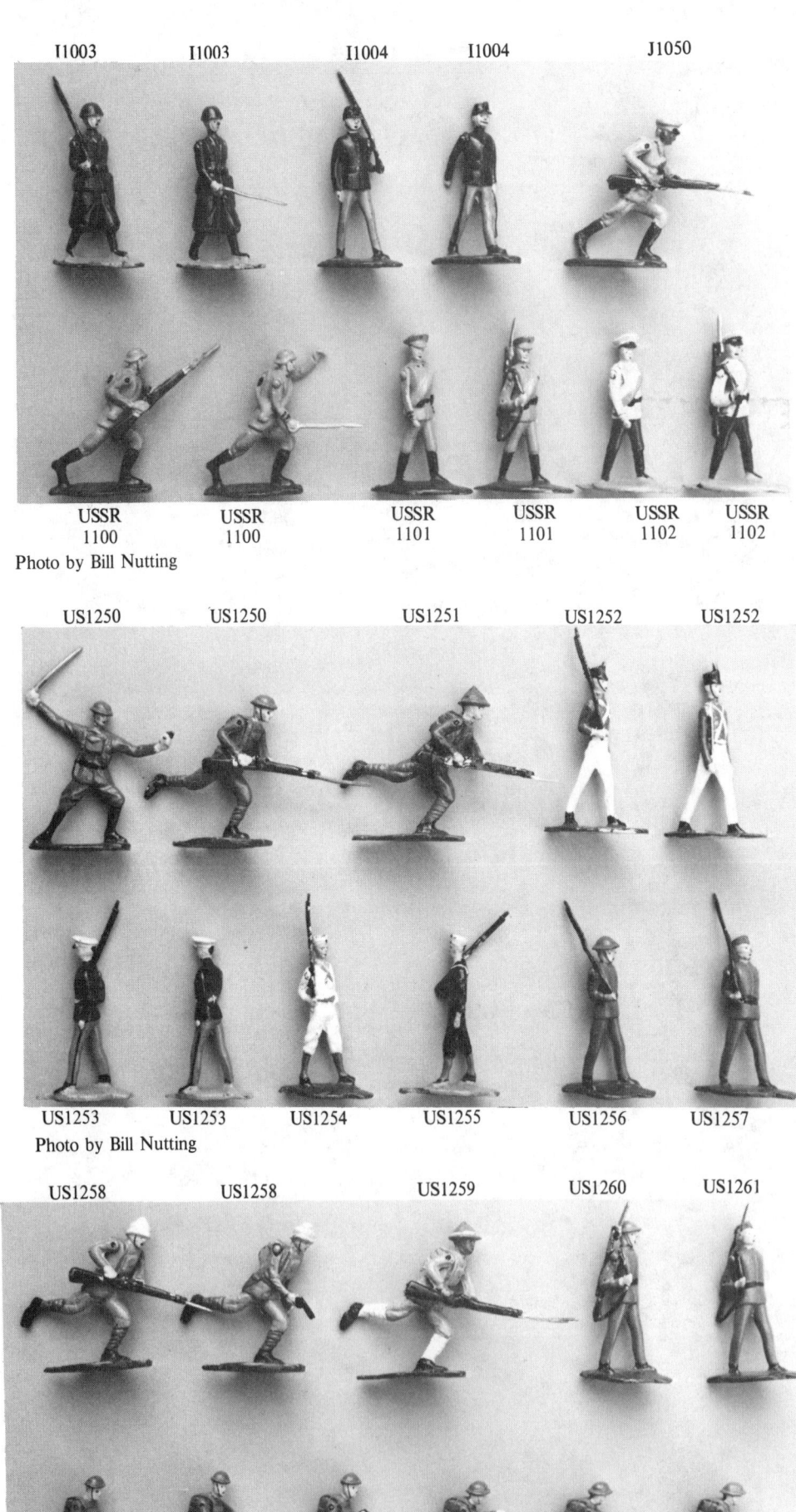

I1003   I1003   I1004   I1004   J1050

USSR   USSR   USSR   USSR   USSR   USSR
1100   1100   1101   1101   1102   1102

Photo by Bill Nutting

US1250   US1250   US1251   US1252   US1252

US1253   US1253   US1254   US1255   US1256   US1257

Photo by Bill Nutting

US1258   US1258   US1259   US1260   US1261

higher head version   US1262   lower head version

Photo by Bill Nutting

343

COMET

US1260 and 1261 Officer
Courtesy Bill Nutting

US1263   US1263   US1263   US1264

US1265 Courtesy Bill Nutting

US1266

US1265
Courtesy Bill Nutting

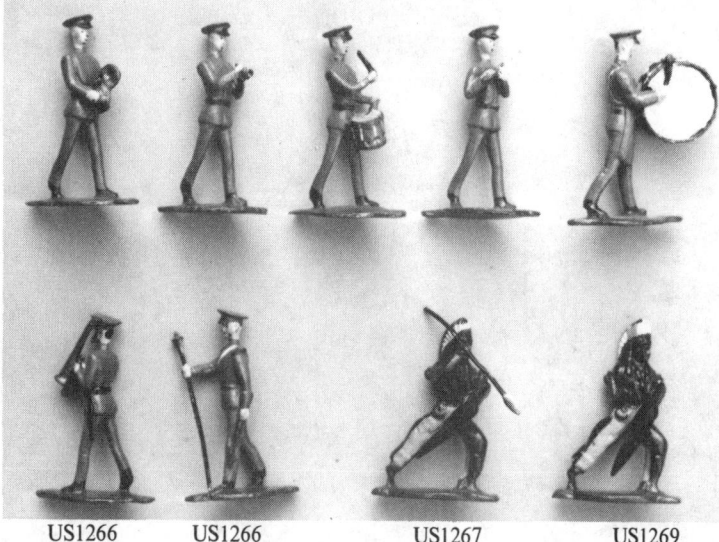

US1266   US1266   US1267   US1269
Photo by Bill Nutting

US1270
Photo by Mike McAfee

US1274   US1274   US1275

US1277
Photo by Vadis Godbey

US1276   US1276   US1278   US1278
Photo by Bill Nutting

344

COMET

US1776   US1776   US1776   US2000   US2001
Photo by Bill Nutting

E2051   E2050
Photo by Mike McAfee

H2150 Courtesy Bill Nutting

H2151 Courtesy Bill Nutting

These may be Lafayette's troops, possibly L2050 or L2051.
Photo by Bill Nutting

Unknown. Perhaps U.S. Infantry Kneeling Steel Helmets.
Photo by Vadis Godbey

Comet **T-1 Farm Animals.** Sold in 1990 in near-mint condition for $112.50
Courtesy K. Warren Mitchell

Unidentified Comets. The bottom three at right are gray helmet variations.
Photo by Bill Nutting

345

US1776   Photo by Mike McAfee

AUTHENTICAST

Authenticast was the name of the company, but as a modern-day ballplayer would put it, it's designer Holger Eriksson who usually gets the ink. Eriksson (1899-1988) began modeling toy soldiers in 1934. In 1936 his 1815 period Scots Grey took second prize in a competition sponsored by the British Model Soldier Society. By 1944 his reputation was such that Comet's owners commissioned him to design 55mm figures and their master molds.

Eriksson's soldiers have a rough-hewn dash that only Manoil's Walter Baetz approached, in his own distinctive way. Their vitality is immediately noticeable, and it is this characteristic, along with the figures' very masculine angularity, that has attracted collectors since 1946, when Authenticasts first appeared on the market.

Authenticast and Authenticast Comet Gaeltacht Industries were the names the soldiers went under. Despite the U.S. location of the firm, Authenticast was a truly international venture. Sweden's Eriksson was brought to the firm's attention by fellow countryman Curt Wennberg, an attache to the U.S. who became associated with Comet during the War, probably because of the firm's work for the Government. Although Comet cast some of its soldiers in America, the majority were turned out in Cladagh, Ireland, where all were also painted, even those cast in the U.S. In addition, Authenticast sold its products abroad through Fred Winkler, a German immigrant with headquarters in England, for whom Wennberg had worked before the War.

Thus there was a United Nations-style approach by Authenticast, and like the United Nations, Authenticast soon found itself mired in disharmony. There were problems at the Irish factory, and often the company was unable to fill all of its orders. Finally, in early 1950 the factory in Eire burned to the ground, and shortly thereafter Wennberg and Winkler emigrated to South Africa in 1951, where they founded the Swedish-African Engineers company, producing "S.A.E." soldiers in 54 and 30mm size, all of the figures sculpted by Eriksson. Authenticast seems to have stopped producing soldiers circa 1950-55.

One reason why Authenticast may have given up the ghost so easily is that the company was already successful in other areas. According to the New York Times, shortly after the brothers Slonim had entered the business, they developed and patented a method of centrifugal casting that enabled them to turn out castings with "an accuracy of detail in microscopically scaled dimensions". According to the article, even the rivets of a battleship could be reproduced in scale, despite being no larger than grains of sand on the model (this news is rather startling to Comet-Authenticast collectors, as their soldiers were hardly outstanding in their detail).

If the Slonims had envisioned a time when WWII would put Britains out of business, they also had the perspicacity to see, in early 1940, that they might have the same problems when the United States entered the war. Accordingly, they sought government contracts to turn out models that could train military personnel to recognize the actual objects. Three days after Pearl Harbor, Comet had a contract from the Navy for 50,000 warships, and that was just the beginning. During World War II the plant operated 24 hours a day (with armed guards patrolling the premises, since much of the company's work was classified), and during that time produced over 10,000,000 models. Thus, because the castings were so authentically detailed, the company took the name Authenticast.

After the War, Comet continued to make models for the government while expanding into models for industry, foreign governments and hobbyists. These included ships, missiles, planes and guns. In 1959 Comet claimed its sales had increased more than 300 percent since 1949, and felt they would rise the same amount by 1969. However, sometime before that the company, which also made parts for washing machines, dryers, cameras, hearing aids, batteries and industrial lead anchors, seems to have gone out of business.

As for Eriksson, he soon became unhappy with the poor quality of the castings produced by S.A.E. and went his own way designing, casting, painting and selling his work by himself (except for a brief association with a Swedish firm which marketed its figures under the name Prins August). Eriksson turned out soldiers on commission in 30mm, 40mm, 54mm, and 85-90mm. Most of the soldiers he designed for Authenticast have the initials "H.E." under the base. Those with "F.R." stand for Frank Rogers, who was a longtime modeler for Comet. Like Comets, Authenticasts were cast in solid metal, but are considerably more sturdy. They were also turned out in other sizes and shapes, but are not considered particularly collectible at this time.

In fact, despite the respect many collectors feel for Eriksson, Authenticasts are not that fervently sought after. In the 1940s, boxed sets of Authenticasts sold for $2.00. Today, despite general inflation and the considerable inflation in the soldiers hobby, foot soldiers average 8 dollars in mint, with a boxed set of them going for 65 dollars or less. Mounted figures go for much more, since Eriksson's horses are almost unequaled in the field. Average price for a single mounted soldier in mint is $30, and a boxed set will sell for about $130.

The following list, using Authenticast's own numbers and descriptions, is from two Authenticast catalogs, circa 1950 and 1955.

AUTHENTICAST

CHINA
50 - Infantry Advancing 1946
51 - Railway Police

ITALY
100 - Grenadiers Fighting 1808
101 - Desert Troops 1942

UNITED STATES
300 - 7 figures - Infantry Lying Firing 1946
301 - 7 figures - Infantry in Action 1946
302 - 7 figures - Marines in Action 1946
303 - 7 figures - Marines Lying Firing 1946
304 - 7 figures - American Revolution Scout 1777
305 - 7 figures - American Revolution 1st Georgia Regiment 1778
306 - 7 figures - Infantry Walking 1946
307 - 7 figures - Marines Walking 1946
308 - 7 figures - Infantry Firing 1946
309 - 7 figures - Marines Firing 1946
310 - 7 figures - Infantry Walking (campaign hat) 1916
311 - 7 figures - Infantry Walking (helmet) 1917
312 - 7 figures - Infantry Automatic Rifle (campaign hat) 1917
313 - 7 figures - Infantry Automatic Rifle (helmet) 1917
314 - American Revolution Maryland Riflemen 1776
315 - American Revolution 3rd No. Carolina Regiment 1776
316 - Northern Infantry Marching 1865
317 - Northern Infantry Charging 1865
318 - Confederate Infantry Marching 1865
319 - Confederate Infantry Charging 1865
320 - Military Police Marching (Marines) 1946
321 - Military Police Infantry 1946
322 - Infantry Marching 1913 (Blue Uniform)
323 - Philippine Troops 1918
324 - Northern Infantry Advancing 1865
325 - Confederate Infantry Advancing 1865
326 - Amer. Indian fighting (spears)
327 - Amer. Indians fighting (tomahawk)
328 - Sailors (blue winter uniform)
329 - Sailors (white summer uniform)
330 - Inf. Dress uniform 1900

FINLAND
400 - 7 figures - Infantry Walking 1944

BRITISH EMPIRE
500 - 4 figures - Musketeers 1600
501 - 4 figures - Pikemen 1600
502 - 7 figures - Infantry 1700
503 - 7 figures - Infantry Walking Guardsmen 1946
504 - 7 figures - Infantry Walking (cap) 1914
505 - 7 figures - Infantry Walking (helmet) 1918
506 - 7 figures - Infantry Near East 1946
507 - 7 figures - Infantry of Line Walking 1946
508 - 7 figures - Infantry Desert Uniform 1946

509 - 7 figures - Infantry of Line Walking 1946 (tam)
510 - 7 figures - Scotch infantry North African Campaign 1942
511 - 7 figures - New Zealand Infantry Walking 1946
512 - 7 figures - Australian Infantry Walking 1946
513 - 7 figures - East Indian Army 1946
514 - 7 figures - West African Troops 1946
515 - 7 figures - Infantry of Line Fighting 1946
516 - 7 figures - Infantry in India Walking 1946
517 - 7 figures - Infantry of Line Firing 1946
518 - 7 figures - Machine Gun Set 1946
519 - 7 figures - Infantry of Line Standing, Firing 1940
520 - 7 figures - Infantry of Line-Dress Uniform

Set 508 British Infantry Desert Uniform 1946. This Authenticast (EIRE) Set consists of one officer and six soldiers and is listed in the Post WW II catalog. It is a poorly painted set with many variations to the base markings. The officer is incised FR; one soldier incised EIRE and F/E; two soldiers incised EIRE and HE; two soldiers incised EIRE and F.H. and one soldier incised only EIRE. Original cost $1.89.
Courtesy Bob Kneale
Photo by Mary Cassavant

Set 528 Scot Infantry Standing 1946 (Kilt and Tam). This Authenticast (EIRE) Set appears in the "New Additions" to the post WW II catalog and consists of one officer and six soldiers. All figures are incised HE and EIRE. Original cost: $1.89.

Set 530 Scot Infantry Standing 1914 (Glen Cap). This Authenticast (EIRE) Set appears in the "New Additions" to the Post WW II catalog and consists of one officer and six soldiers. All figure bases are incised HE and EIRE. Original Cost: $1.89.
Courtesy Bob Kneale
Photo by Mary Cassavant

AUTHENTICAST

521 - 7 figures - Marine Light Infantry-Dress Uniform
522 - 7 figures - Fusiliers-Dress Uniform
523 - 7 figures - Queen's Own Corps of Guides Infantry 1910
524 - 7 figures - Indian Army in Reserve 1910
525 - 7 figures - Indian Army 3rd Sappers and Miners 1910
526 - Scot Infantry Marching 1918
527 - Scot Infantry Marching 1946 (kilt & tam)
528 - Scot Infantry Standing 1946 (kilt & tam)
529 - Scot Infantry Marching 1900 (beaver hat)
530 - Scot Infantry Standing 1914 (glen cap)
531 - Scot Infantry Marching 1914 (glen cap)
532 - Scot Infantry Marching 1900 (sun helmet)
533 - Scot Infantry Marching 1914 (sun helmet)
534 - Infantry Standing 1944 (Winter Uniform)
535 - Infantry Marching 1944 (Winter Uniform)
536 - Coldstream Guards 1946
537 - Welsh Guards Marching 1946
538 - Scot Guards Marching 1946
539 - Grenadier Guards Marching 1946
540 - Scot Infantry Standing 1918 (helmet)
541 - Scot Infantry Standing 1900 (sun helmet)
542 - Scot Infantry Standing 1914 (sun helmet)
543 - Scot Infantry Marching 1944 (helmet)
544 - 15th Ludhiana Sikhs 1900
545 - Scot Infantry Standing 1946 (helmet)
547 - Canadian Mounted Police 1946
548 - Australia Inf. Charging '47
549 - Inf. of Line Dress Unif. Standing '10
550 - Marine Lt. Inf. Dress Unif. Standing '10
551 - Fusilier Dress Unif. Standing 1910
552 - British Drummer 1700
553 - 33rd Punjab Indian Army 1900
554 - Queens Guides Lumsdens 1900

FRANCE

600 - 4 figures - Musketeers 1600
601 - 4 figures - Pikemen 1600
602 - 7 figures - Infantry 1700
603 - 7 figures - Infantry Walking 1871
604 - 7 figures - Chasseur Walking 1871
605 - 7 figures - Turcos Walking 1890
606 - 7 figures - Zouave Loading
607 - 7 figures - Senegalese Aiming 1914
608 - 7 figures - Infantry Walking 1914
609 - 7 figures - Infantry Walking 1915
610 - 7 figures - Infantry Walking 1918
611 - 7 figures - Algerian Troops Walking 1918
612 - 7 figures - Zouave (field uniform) 1945
613 - 7 figures - Senegalese Infantry Walking 1945
614 - 7 figures - Colonial Infantry 1945
615 - 7 figures - Infantry of Line Walking 1946
616 - 7 figures - Fortress Infantry Walking 1946
617 - 7 figures - Desert Troops 1945
618 - Zouaves Marching 1890

619 - Zouaves Charging 1890
620 - Zouaves Aiming 1890
621 - Turcos Charging 1890
622 - Turcos Aiming 1890
623 - Turcos Loading 1890

515 515 864 515
Courtesy K. Warren Mitchell

SAE? 533 533 542
Courtesy K. Warren Mitchell

310 509 527
Courtesy K. Warren Mitchell

349

AUTHENTICAST

705   619   637   644

Courtesy K. Warren Mitchell

535   516   514

Courtesy K. Warren Mitchell

605?   636

Courtesy K. Warren Mitchell

708?   603   515   306   308

Courtesy K. Warren Mitchell

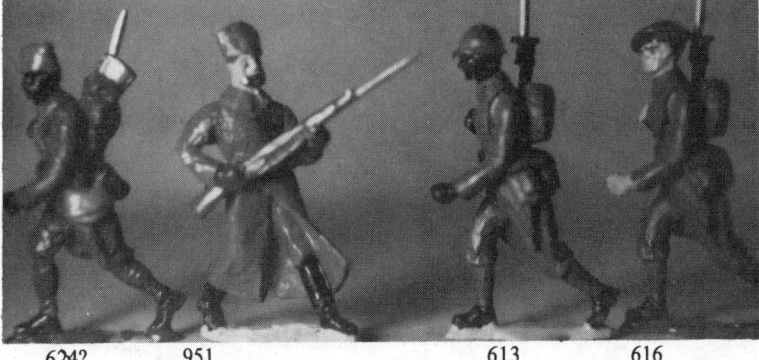

624?   951   613   616

624 - Senegalese Marching 1890
625 - Senegalese Charging 1890
626 - Senegalese Aiming 1890
627 - Senegalese Loading 1890
628 - Senegalese Loading 1914
629 - Senegalese Charging 1914
630 - Senegalese Marching 1914
631 - Zouaves Marching 1914
632 - Zouaves Charging 1914
633 - Zouaves Aiming 1914
634 - Zouaves Loading 1914
635 - Turcos Marching 1914
636 - Turcos Charging 1914
637 - Turcos Aiming 1914
638 - Turcos Loading 1914
*639 - Old Guard of Napoleon March 1806
*640 - Chasseur Marching 1806
*641 - Infantry of Line Marching 1806
*642 - Old Guard of Napoleon Charging 1806
*643 - Chasseur Charging 1806
*644 - Infantry of Line Charging 1808
645 - Infantry on Defense 1871
646 - Chasseur on Defense 1871
647 - Morroccans Charging 1890
648 - North African Infantry 1946
649 - Dragoon Portee Marching 1939
650 - Chasseurs Alpine Marching 1939
652 - Dutch Guards of Napoleon 1808
653 - French Foreign Legion Marching
655 - French Foreign Legion Charging 1914
656 - Moroccans Loading 1890

GERMANY

700 - 7 figures - Prussian Musketeers 1750
701 - 7 figures - Infantry Firing 1890
702 - 7 figures - Jaeger 1890
703 - 7 figures - Walking 1906
704 - 7 figures - Infantry Walking 1915
705 - 7 figures - Infantry Jaeger 1819
706 - 7 figures - Infantry Walking 1945
707 - 7 figures - Afrika Korps 1942
708 - 7 figures - Mountain Troops 1945
709 - 7 figures - Infantry of Line Walking 1945
710 - 7 figures - Frontier Guards Walking 1945
711 - 7 figures - Raiding Party 1945
712 - 7 figures - Hand Grenade Throwers and
    Panzerfaust 1945
713 - 7 figures - Infantry Lying Firing 1945
714 - 7 figures - MG set Lying Firing 1945
715 - 7 figures - Rocket Launchers 1945
716 - 7 figures - Infantry in Action 1945
*717 - Infantry Lying firing 1914
*718 - Saxonian Infantry Marching 1814
*719 - Saxonian Infantry Charging 1814
720 - Infantry Charging 1918

AUTHENTICAST

? ? 616 A 619

Courtesy K. Warren Mitchell

L to R: China 51, French Officer, British Line Infantry, French 642?
Courtesy K. Warren Mitchell

311 617 955 805

Courtesy K. Warren Mitchell

SPAIN

800 - 7 figures - Infantry 1600
*801 - Grenadiers Marching 1815
*802 - Chasseurs Marching 1815
*803 - Grenadiers Charging 1815
*804 - Chasseurs Charging 1815
805 - Carlist Infantry Advancing
806 - Pikemen 1600

IRELAND

1200 - Irish Army 1916
1201 - Irish Free State Infantry
1202 - Irish Infantry 1946

DUTCH BOER

250 - Boer Marching 1900

SWEDEN

850 - 7 figures - Musketeers 1600
851 - 7 figures - Infantry Lying Firing 1700
852 - 7 figures - Guard 1900
853 - 7 figures - Infantry Lying Firing 1900
854 - 7 figures - Infantry Lying Firing 1914
855 - 7 figures - Infantry Lying 1939
*856 - Infantry of Line Marching 1815
*857 - Grenadiers Marching 1815
858 - Infantry Marching 1946
859 - Trench Mortar Sets 1946
860 - Infantry Lying Firing 1946
861 - M.G. Set Lying Firing 1946
862 - Infantry Action Set Crawling 1946
863 - Infantry Kneeling, Firing and Grenade Throw 1946
864 - Infantry in Action 1946
865 - Anti-Tank Gun Riflemen in Action 1946
866 - Anti-Tank Gun Unit and Marching Riflemen 1946
*867 - Infantry of Line Charging 1815

This may be a later Authenticast set as it contains just 6 figures and is numbered 709, though the figures don't match those in the circa 1950 list.
Photo by A.J. (Bob) Mergenthaler

721 - Infantry Marching 1918
722 - Pikemen 1600
723 - Prussian Infantry Marching 1845
724 - Prussian Infantry Advancing 1845
725 - Raiding Party 1918

*868 - Grenadiers Charging 1815
869 - Pikemen 1600
870 - Infantry Marching 1845
871 - Infantry Advancing 1845
872 - Grenadiers Standing 1790
873 - Infantry Standing Firing '46
874 - Drummers 1700

351

AUTHENTICAST

L to R: German 724?, British 529?, British 500?, Russian.
Courtesy K. Warren Mitchell

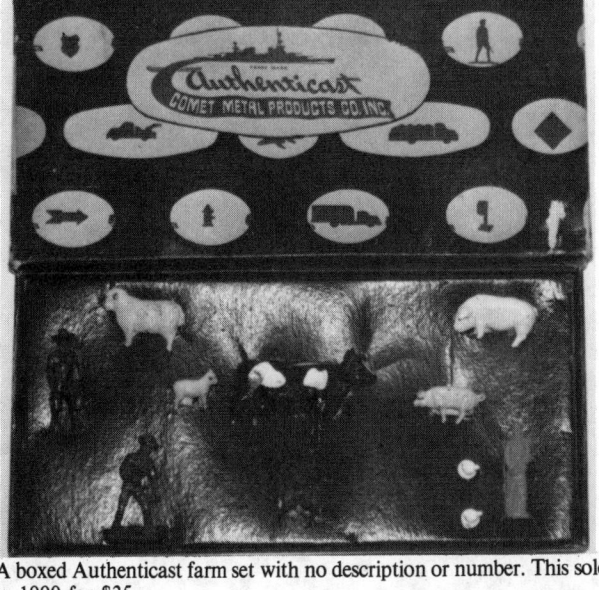

A boxed Authenticast farm set with no description or number. This sold in 1990 for $35.
Photo by Stan Alekna

864   864   864

Courtesy K. Warren Mitchell

HUNGARY

900 - 7 figures - Austro-Hungarian Infantry of Line 1700

901 - 7 figures - Infantry Lying and Firing 1945

902 - 7 figures - Infantry Walking 1945

903 - Infantry Charging '45

?   ?   ?
Courtesy K. Warren Mitchell

RUSSIA

950 - 7 figures - Infantry 1700

951 - 7 figures - Siberian Infantry Charging 1904

952 - 7 figures - Imperial Guard Charging 1904

953 - 7 figures - Infantry of Line Charging 1904

954 - 7 figures - Infantry of Line Charging 1914

955 - 7 figures - Infantry of Line Charging 1935

956 - 7 figures - Infantry of Line Charging 1946

957 - 7 figures - Infantry Winter Uniform 1946

*958 - Infantry of the Line Marching 1812

*959 - Infantry of the Line Charging 1812

Set 956 Russian Infantry of Line Charging 1946. This Authenticast (EIRE) set consists of one officer with sword and six soldiers, all in overcoats. Variations of this set occur only in the heads i.e., Set 953 Russian Inf. of Line Charging 1904 - visorless cap. Set 954 Russian Inf. of Line Charing 1914 - visored cap. Set 955 Russian Inf. of Line Charging 1935 - fur pointed cap. Set 956 Russian Inf. of Line Charging 1946 - modern helmet. All figures are incised HE and EIRE but two figures rubber stamped EIRE in addition. Original price: $1.89.
Courtesy Bob Kneale
Photo by Mary Cassavant

951   952   956   955   955
Courtesy K. Warren Mitchell

Set 711 German Raiding Party. This Authenticast (EIRE) Set consists of seven figures, one of which is the officer at the right. Two variations of this set are known to exist; one being Army (HEER) and the other Africa Corps Dress. The above set is painted in Africa Corps and four figures vary from the Army version. Note the irregular bases and the good example of angular anatomy of the HE designed figures. Original price: $1.98.
Courtesy Bob Kneale
Photo by Mary Cassavant

Set No. 709, German Infantry of Line Walking, 1945. This set marketed under Comet Metal Products Post WW II Brigadiers Line consisted of six figures. The underside of bases are incised with the "HE" monogram and "EIRE". This same set marketed under Authenticast contained seven figures (see Post WW II listing). The rifles were cast separately and affixed to the figures with adhesives. Original price: $1.00 (Comet); $2.00 (Authenticast).
Courtesy Bob Kneale
Photo by Mary Cassavant

Set 711 German Raiding Party. The Authenticast (EIRE) Set above shows the Army (HEER) Dress version of this set. All bases, as with the Africa Corps version, are incised with the HE monogram. Some bases are incised with EIRE, some rubber stamped with EIRE, and some with no indication of EIRE. Original price: $1.98.
Courtesy Bob Kneale
Photo by Mary Cassavant

Set G502, German Infantry Marching. This Pre WW II Comet Metal Products Set consists of eight figures (1 officer and 7 soldiers). Two versions of the officer exist, one with and one without the sword. Note the slotted card and the unique base for the soldiers. Set G507, German Infantry (SS Troops) Marching is identical to the above except for uniform colors. Similarly, Set G500 and G501 differ only in uniform coloring. Original 1940 price: $1.34/set (reduced from $1.39).
Courtesy Bob Kneale
Photo by Mary Cassavant

Set G502 German Infantry Marching. Another view of this pre WW II set showing the soldiers and slotted card within the box. Note that this set is rubber stamped "movable" at the right side of the box cover.
Courtesy Bob Kneale
Photo by Mary Cassavant

AUTHENTICAST
*960 - Infantry Fighting 1808
961 - Infantry Marching 1846
962 - Infantry Advancing 1846
BELGIUM
1000 - 7 figures - Infantry Walking 1946
AUSTRIA
1052 - Infantry Marching 1918
1053 - Bosnian Infantry 1918
POLAND
1150 - Infantry Marching 1939
* Napoleonic Figures

Prussian Officer, 1910 at Present Saber. This figure possibly was part of Set 703, Germany Infantry Walking, 1910 when repainted in England and sold individually. It is not listed in any catalog of Authenticast. The base is inscribed with HE and EIRE. Original 1947 price, individually: $2.50.
Courtesy Bob Kneale
Photo by Mary Cassavant

MISCELLANEOUS
1151 - Infantry Charging 1945 (Poland?)

About 1951 Authenticast came out with a run of special limited edition sets of 250. The sculptor was Frank Rogers, and the prices were quite high for the time, ranging from $7.95 to ten dollars. Because of their rarity, no current prices have emerged. The following numbers and descriptions are Authenticast's own:
BRITISH INDIAN ARMY
No. 1 - Mountain Battery - 4 men, 1 officer, 1 cannon
No. 2 - 16th Cavalry - 1 officer on horse, 3 men
No. 3 - 26th King George's Own Lt. Cavalry - 1 officer on horse, 3 men
No. 4 - 125th Napier Rifles - 1 officer, 3 prone men, 2 kneeling men
No. 5 - 45th Rattray's Sikh The Drums - 1 drum major, 4 drummers
No. 6 - 24th Punjabis - 1 Officer, 6 men
No. 7 - Governor General's Bodyguard - 5 men, 5 lances

Bengal Lancer with Saber, Charging. The title of this figure is conjecture as no mounted figures are listed in the post WW II Authenticast catalogs. It is assumed to be painted in England for the American market. The above figure wears the traditional Indian Army blue tunic, however, another version is known to exist with the figure in a red tunic. The figure does not peg into the horse saddle, but sits into it realistically. The under base is inscribed HE and EIRE. Note medals painted on tunic and the irregular base. Original 1947 price: $3.50.
Courtesy Bob Kneale
Photo by Mary Cassavant

No. 8 - 23rd Cavalry Frontier Force - 1 Officer, 1 Horse, 3 men
No. 9 - 15th Ludhiana Sikhs Drums - 1 Drum Major, 4 Drummers
No. 10 - 95th Russell's Infantry - 1 Officer, 3 Prone Men, 2 Kneeling Men
UNITED STATES ARMY
Set No. 11 - U.S. Spirit of 1776 - 1 Drummer Boy, 1 Drummer, 1 Fife
NAPOLEONIC ARMY
Set No. 12 - Polish Foot Army - 1 Officer, 1 Cannon, 1 Firer, 1 Cleaner

GI JOE

Though there had previously been similar toys, it was Hasbro's GI Joe which truly created the category of the Action Figure.

Don Levine, the Director of Development for Hasbro, conceived the idea of GI Joe while standing outside a Manhattan art supply shop in February, 1963. A licensing agent had suggested a military toy based on a t.v. series, "The Lieutenant." Levine had discarded the idea of a tie-in because the series was for adults, but the thought was in his mind as he looked at an artist's manikin in the shop window. The idea of a boy's soldier with movable parts came to him.

Sam Speers, who worked under Levine, came up with the engineering for GI Joe, both the mechanical and esthetic inventions (for which he received many patents), which included devising a way that enabled the toy to stand on its own (unlike artists' manikins) in various positions and while holding weapons or bearing equipment. Speers also thought of the added touch of the facial scar (the 11½" height was because the Barbie doll was that tall and a great success).

Noted artist Phil Kraczkowski sculpted the head, which was **not** a composite of 23 Medal of Honor winners, despite ad claims to that effect, and though Speers designed the parts and how they should go together, Walter Hansen and Norman Jacques did the sculpting of the body. It wasn't an easy sell to the Hasbro executives for Levine and Speers, but after the first year's enormous success, Levine was upped to Vice President and Speers moved up to Levine's job as Director of Development.

1965 Catalog Illustrations

ADDITIONAL GI JOE INFORMATION
by Barry Goodman

GI Joe first entered the U.S. market in 1964. The 11½" doll would undergo several changes during its eleven-year life span, 1964-75. The first dolls, 1964-69, had painted hair and were based primarily upon military uniforms of World War II. In 1965, Hasbro added six foreigners to the series (Japanese, German, French, Australian, Russian, British). These were distinctly different in appearance. An easy way of knowing if you have a foreigner is that the scar found on the GI is not present.

In 1965, Hasbro introduced a black GI Joe, which today is one of the most sought after.

In 1967, Hasbro introduced its "Vietnam series" outfits, which were pulled off the market very quickly due to the negative response to the Vietnam war raging in southeast Asia. Thus these uniforms (green and tan airborne M.P., Air Security set and Marine Jungle Fighter) are the most sought after and scarcest. This was the year that also produced the extremely scarce nurse doll.

G I JOE

Protests about the war continued, so in 1969 Hasbro dropped the military line and substituted the "adventurer series". GI Joe was transformed from a military doll to an adventure doll. In 1970 GI Joe received flock hair and then a flocked moustache and beard. Furthermore, the "adventurer" line was dropped and the "Adventure Team" line substituted. The theme of this line was that GI Joe would fight nature and the elements, rather than other men.

In 1972, GI Joe was given a "kung-fu" grip. The same year, the oil embargo created havoc because oil-based plastic became prohibitively expensive. Because of this, in 1973 Hasbro changed the basic composition of the plastic, which created a much more fragile doll that by 1975 children had totally lost interest in.

Most collectors concentrate on the 1964-69 dolls. Hasbro consulted military manuals to create the most realistic and authentic boys' doll ever made.

Barry James Goodman is a leading collector and authority on GI Joe dolls and 1960s character figures. As an active toy dealer, he has been able to amass one of the largest collections of GI Joes.

ACTION SOLDIER
(Revised listings by Barry Goodman)

	G	VG	M
7000 - GI JOE 5 Star Jeep, 106mm Rocket Launcher, ¼ ton trailer w/tripod mounted searchlight and four 106mm shells	50.00	100.00	150.00
7100 - "Let's Go Joe" board game	15.00	22.00	40.00
7500 - GI Joe Action Soldier	35.00	50.00	65.00
7501 - Combat Set A -			
Field Jacket	5.00	10.00	15.00
M-1 Rifle	5.00	10.00	15.00
Bayonet	5.00	10.00	15.00
Cartridge Belt	5.00	10.00	15.00
Six hand grenades	5.00	10.00	15.00
Price for 7501 set	35.00	50.00	60.00
7502 - Combat Set B - back pack, canteen and cover, entrenching tool and cover, mess kit, utensils and single pouch cartridge belt, each individually	5.00	10.00	15.00
Price for 7502 set	35.00	50.00	60.00
7503 - Combat Fatigue Shirt	5.00	8.00	12.00
7504 - Combat Fatigue Pants	5.00	8.00	12.00
7505 - Combat Field Jacket	8.00	15.00	20.00
7506 - Combat Field Pack - w/entrenching tool and cover	10.00	20.00	30.00

	G	VG	M
7507 - Combat helmet w/camouflage netting and foliage	10.00	20.00	25.00
7508 - Army Sandbags Set	5.00	10.00	12.50
7509 - Canteen with cover and mess kit w/utensils	5.00	10.00	15.00
7510 - M-1 Rifle with bayonet and cartridge belt with six grenades	20.00	30.00	40.00
7511 - Camouflage netting with poles and foliage	5.00	10.00	15.00
7512 - Bivouac Set A - zippered sleeping bag, M-1 Rifle, bayonet, cartridge belt, canteen with cover, and mess kit with utensils, individually	5.00	10.00	15.00
7513 - Bivouac Set B - tent, stakes, poles, foliage, camouflage netting, entrenching tool with cover	10.00	15.00	25.00
.30 cal. tripod mounted machine gun, ammo box	10.00	15.00	25.00
7514 - 30 cal. tripod mounted machine gun w/ammo box	10.00	15.00	25.00
7515 - Zippered sleeping bag	10.00	15.00	25.00
7517 - Command Post Set - Rain Poncho, .45 pistol w/belt and holster, field radio, field phone, wire roll map and map case, individually	5.00	10.00	15.00
7518 - 45 Pistol, holster, belt	5.00	10.00	15.00
Ammo pouch	5.00	10.00	15.00
Six grenades	5.00	10.00	15.00
Cloth hat	5.00	10.00	15.00
Price for 7518 Set	25.00	45.00	80.00
7519 - Rain Poncho	5.00	10.00	15.00
7520 - Field Phone, Field Radio, Wire Spool, Map Case and map, individually	5.00	10.00	15.00

G I JOE

	G	VG	M
7521 - Military Police Set - "Ike" Jacket, trousers, ascot, white belt, nightstick, .45 pistol, holster, armband and duffel bag, stem gun	35.00	50.00	60.00
7522 - JUNGLE FIGHTER SET - w/belt, entrenching tool, mess kit, utensils, canteen, cover, machete, sheath and Jungle knife . .	35.00	50.00	70.00
7523 - Duffel bag	5.00	10.00	15.00
7524 - MP Uniform	250.00	350.00	500.00
7524 - "IKE" Jacket, ascot and MP armband	15.00	25.00	35.00
7525 - "IKE" Trousers	5.00	10.00	15.00
7526 MP Helmet, black . . .	50.00	100.00	150.00
7526 - MP Helmet, white belt, .45 pistol, holster and nightstick	20.00	30.00	40.00
7527 - Ski patrol helmet, winter white cartridge belt, winter white M-1 rifle and six grenades	20.00	30.00	40.00
7528 - Bazooka and two shells	10.00	20.00	30.00
7529 - Snow shoes, pick axe, climbing rope and sun goggles	15.00	20.00	25.00
7530 - MOUNTAIN TROOPS SET - w/snow shoes, winter white belt, winter white field pack, pick axe, climbing rope, and four grenades	20.00	30.00	40.00
7531 - SKI PATROL SET - w/two-piece white parka, gloves, boots, skis, poles and sun goggles	20.00	40.00	60.00
7532 - SPECIAL FORCES SET - w/uniform, beret, bazooka, two shells and four grenades	25.00	50.00	100.00
7533 - Beret, M-16 rifle and field radio	25.00	50.00	75.00
7536 - GREEN BERET SET - w/G.I. Joe action soldier as dressed in special forces uniform, M-16 rifle, .45 pistol, belt, holster, six grenades and field radio	75.00	150.00	250.00

	G	VG	M
7537 - WEST POINT CADET SET - w/parade uniform, cap, feather, sword, scabbard, M-1 rifle and dress shoes	75.00	150.00	240.00
7538 - HEAVY WEAPONS SET - w/81MM mortar, 3 shells, M-60 machine gun, tripod, ammo belt, bullet proof vest, bullet belt and 2 grenades	40.00	75.00	100.00
7590 - GI JOE talking action soldier	75.00	100.00	125.00
8000 - Official G.I. JOE footlocker	10.00	15.00	30.00
8030 - G.I. JOE desert patrol jeep, w/.50 cal. tripod mounted machine gun, radio antenna and G.I. JOE desert trooper .	200.00	500.00	800.00
ACTION SAILOR			
7600 - G.I. JOE Action Sailor	50.00	75.00	90.00
7601 - Sea Rescue Set A - inflatable raft, oar, sea anchor, tow line, flare gun, knife, scabbard and first aid kit, individually	5.00	10.00	15.00
7602 - FROGMAN SET - w/three pc. black scuba set, swim fins, face mask, oxygen tanks, depth gauge, knife, scabbard, and depth charges	50.00	100.00	150.00
7603 - Black scuba suit jacket and hood	15.00	50.00	100.00
7604 - Black scuba suit pants	7.50	25.00	35.00
7605 - Swim fins, face mask, knife, scabbard, and depth gauge	20.00	30.00	50.00
7606 - Oxygen tanks	5.00	10.00	15.00
7607 - Navy Attack Set - life jacket, semaphore flags, hand held searchlight and binoculars, individually	5.00	10.00	15.00
7610 - Navy attack helmet, hand held searchlight and binoculars	15.00	30.00	40.00
7611 - Life jacket	5.00	10.00	15.00

G.I. JOE

	G	VG	M
7612 - SHORE PATROL SET - w/jumper, neckerchief, trousers, white belt, .45 pistol, holster, nightstick, armband, sailors cap and duffel bag.	35.00	50.00	75.00
7613 Shore Patrol Jumper Set	15.00	30.00	40.00
7614 Shore Patrol Pants	5.00	10.00	15.00
7615 - USN duffel bag	5.00	10.00	15.00
7616 Shore Patrol w/stripe	100.00	150.00	250.00
7616 - Shore patrol helmet, white belt, .45 pistol, holster and nightstick	10.00	25.00	30.00
7618 - .30 cal. tripod mounted machine gun and ammo box	20.00	30.00	45.00
7619 - Dress parade M-1 rifle, bayonet, white cartridge belt and white billyclub	15.00	35.00	50.00
7620 - DEEP SEA DIVER SET - w/divers' suit, gloves, helmet, breastplate, air pump, hoses, weighted belt, weighted shoes, signal float, line, knife, scabbard, and sledge hammer	20.00	40.00	65.00
7621 - LANDING SIGNAL OFFICER SET - w/safety striped jumpsuit, cloth helmet with headphones, goggles, binoculars, signal paddles, clipboard, pad, pencil and flare gun	30.00	50.00	100.00
7622 - SEA RESCUE SET B - same as Sea Rescue Set A set also includes life jackets	10.00	20.00	30.00
7623 - DEEP FREEZE SET -w/fur parka, pants, boots, snow sled, flare gun and ice pick	25.00	50.00	70.00
7624 - ANNAPOLIS CADET SET - w/dress parade jacket, cap, pants, belt, shoes, sword, scabbard and white M-1 rifle	80.00	200.00	275.00
7625 - BREECHES BUOY SET - w/buoy, pulley, slicker jacket, pants, flare gun and hand held searchlight	75.00	135.00	200.00
7626 - LSO helmet w/headphones, signal paddles, flare gun, clipboard, pad and pencil	25.00	50.00	75.00
7627 - USN Life ring	10.00	25.00	30.00
7628 - White sailor's cap, boots, and G.I. Joe dogtags	15.00	25.00	35.00
7690 - G.I. JOE talking action sailor	75.00	150.00	175.00
8050 - OFFICIAL G.I. JOE SEA SLED - w/G.I. Joe frogman	100.00	225.00	300.00

ACTION MARINE

	G	VG	M
7700 - G.I. JOE ACTION MARINE	30.00	55.00	65.00
7701 - COMMUNICATIONS SET - w/M-1 carbine, camouflage poncho, field radio, field phone, wire spool, binoculars, map and map case, individually	5.00	10.00	15.00
7702 - Camouflage poncho.	5.00	10.00	15.00
7703 - Field radio, field phone, wire spool, map and map case	5.00	10.00	15.00
7704 - FLAG SET - w/Old Glory, Army flag, Navy flag, Marine Corps. flag, and Air Force flag	30.00	60.00	100.00
7705 - PARATROOPER SET - w/parachute pack, M-1 carbine, six grenades, knife, scabbard, belt, ammo pouch, canteen and cover, individually	5.00	10.00	15.00
7706 - M-1 carbine, six grenades, knife, scabbard, belt, ammo pouch, canteen and cover, individually	5.00	10.00	15.00
7707 - Camouflage helmet, foliage and helmet cover.	10.00	25.00	30.00
7708 - Camouflage netting, foliage, poles and securing line	5.00	10.00	15.00
7709 - Parachute Pack	12.50	18.75	25.00
7710 - DRESS PARADE SET - w/traditional Marine "dress blues", cap and white M-1 rifle	20.00	40.00	60.00

G.I. JOE

	G	VG	M
7711 - BEACHHEAD SET A - w/flame thrower, camouflage tent, poles, stakes, belt, ammo pouch, mess kit and utensils, individually	5.00	10.00	15.00
7712 - BEACHHEAD SET B - w/M-1 rifle, cartridge belt, six grenades, field pack, bayonet, entrenching tool, cover, canteen and cover, individually .	5.00	10.00	15.00
7713 - Field pack, entrenching tool and cover	10.00	30.00	40.00
7714 - Camouflage fatigue shirt	5.00	8.00	12.00
7715 - Camouflage fatigue pants	5.00	8.00	12.00
7716 - Mess kit, utensils, canteen and cover	5.00	10.00	15.00
7717 - M-1 rifle, bayonet, cartridge belt and six grenades	20.00	30.00	40.00
7718 - Flame thrower	10.00	15.00	20.00
7719 - MEDIC SET - w/stretcher, crutch, satchel, stethoscope, plasma bottle, I. V. tube, splints, bandage rolls, armbands, and hospital flag, cloth bag . .	40.00	75.00	100.00
7720 - crutch, stethoscope, plasma bottle, I.V. tube, splints, and bandage rolls .	10.00	25.00	35.00
7721 - Medic's helmet, satchel and two armbands . .	15.00	30.00	50.00
7722 - Fatigue cap, boots and G.I. Joe dog tags	20.00	25.00	35.00
7723 - G. I. bunk bed	15.00	25.00	35.00
7727 - WEAPONS RACK - with rack, M-1 rifle, M-1 carbine, M-16 rifle and 40 MM grenade launcher . . .	30.00	50.00	60.00
7731 - TANK COMMANDER SET - w/leather jacket, tanker's helmet, belt, .30 cal. M-60 machine gun, tripod, ammo box, radio and tripod .	75.00	100.00	150.00

	G	VG	M
7732 - JUNGLE FIGHTER SET - w/green fatigue shirt, pants, campaign hat, AR-15 rifle, belt, knife, machete, sheath, canteen, cover, flame thrower and field phone	200.00	350.00	500.00
7790 - G.I. JOE talking action Marine			

ACTION PILOT

	G	VG	M
7800 - G.I. JOE action pilot .	30.00	55.00	75.00
7801 - SURVIVAL SET - w/inflatable raft, sea anchor, tow line, oar, knife, scabbard, flare gun, first aid kit and inflatable USAF life vest	50.00	75.00	100.00
7802 - Inflatable raft, sea anchor, tow line, and oar . . .	10.00	25.00	30.00
7803 - DRESS UNIFORM - w/jacket, shirt, tie, pants, garrison cap, wings and captain's bars	20.00	40.00	60.00
7804 - Dress Jacket	10.00	15.00	20.00
7805 - Dress Pants	10.00	15.00	20.00
7806 - Dress Shirt and Cap	10.00	15.00	20.00
7807 - SCRAMBLE SET - w/gray flight suit, inflatable life vest, .45 pistol, holster, belt, clipboard, pad and pencil	25.00	40.00	75.00
7808 - Gray flight suit	5.00	10.00	15.00
7809 - Inflatable life vest, flare gun, knife, scabbard and first aid kit	10.00	20.00	30.00
7810 - Crash helmet w/ oxygen mask	20.00	40.00	50.00
7811 - Parachute pack	10.00	15.00	25.00
7812 - COMMUNICATIONS SET - w/field radio, binoculars, map, map case, clipboard, pad and pencil	20.00	30.00	60.00
7813 Marine Jungle Fighter (Vietnam)	200.00	300.00	450.00
7813 A. P. Helmet Set	10.00	30.00	40.00
7820 - CRASH CREW SET - w/metallic heat suit, hood, gloves, boots, tool belt and CO_2 fire extinguisher	35.00	65.00	90.00
7822 - COLORADO AIR CADET SET - w/uniform, sash, cap, dress shoes, M-1 rifle, sword and scabbard .	75.00	125.00	150.00

G.I. JOE

8200   8201   8202   8203   8204   8205

Courtesy of Sam Speers (the figures in this photo are not those actually sold in foreign uniforms)

	G	VG	M
7823 - FIGHTER PILOT SET - w/G-suit, boots, "Mae West" life jacket, helmet, oxygen mask, flashlight and working parachute	75.00	200.00	375.00
7824 - AIR SEA RESCUE SET - w/three pc. orange scuba suit, mask, swim fins, air tanks, flare gun, first aid kit, rescue life ring and markerbuoy . . .	25.00	60.00	100.00
7890 - G.I. JOE talking action pilot	75.00	200.00	275.00
7900 G.I. JOE ACTION SOLDIER COLORED (sic)	100.00	200.00	300.00
8020 - OFFICIAL G.I. JOE SPACE CAPSULE - w/space suit, boots, gloves, helmet and recording of mercury control communications	80.00	135.00	260.00
8040 - DELUXE CRASH CREW SET - w/fire truck, working water pump, working siren, blinking red light, fire axe, metallic heat suit, boots gloves and hood, white stretcher . . .	200.00	350.00	450.00
GI Jane (1965) Army Nurse	500.00	800.00	1000.00

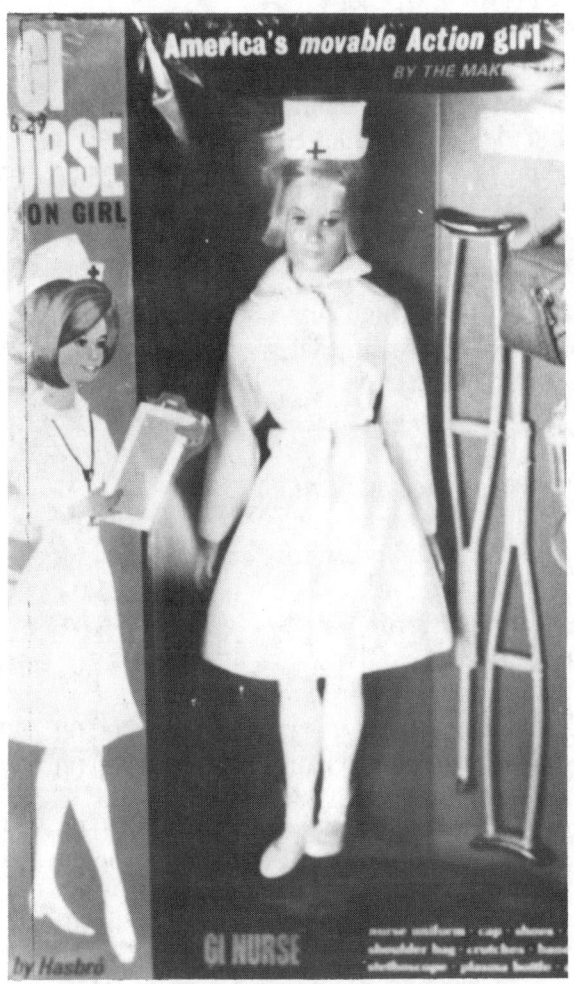

GI Jane
Photo by Barry Goodman

G.I. JOE

"ACTION SOLDIERS OF THE WORLD"

	G	VG	M
8100 - GERMAN STORM TROOPER - w/cartridge belt, luger pistol, holster, field pack, "Potato Masher" grenades, 9mm Schmeisser machine gun and iron cross medal....	140.00	225.00	275.00
8101 - JAPANESE IMPERIAL SOLDIER - w/field pack, Nambu pistol, holster, cartridge belt, Arisaka rifle, bayonet and Order of the Kite medal	150.00	275.00	350.00
8102 - RUSSIAN INFANTRYMAN - w/D.P. light machine gun, bi-pod, field glasses, case, anti-tank grenades, ammo box and order of Lenin medal....	140.00	225.00	300.00
8103 - FRENCH RESISTANCE FIGHTER - w/Lebel revolver, shoulder holster, knife, grenades, radio set, 7.65mm Mas submachine gun and Croix de Guerre medal	140.00	225.00	275.00
8104 - BRITISH COMMANDO - w/gas mask, case, canteen, cover, sten mark 25 submachine gun and Victoria Cross medal.	150.00	240.00	280.00
8105 - AUSTRALIAN JUNGLE FIGHTER - w/grenades, flame thrower, jungle knife, entrenching tool, bush machete, sheath and Victoria Cross medal	140.00	225.00	275.00
8200 - German storm trooper	120.00	175.00	200.00
8201 - Imperial Japanese soldier	140.00	200.00	275.00
8202 - Russian Infantryman	120.00	200.00	225.00
8203 - French Resistance Fighter	120.00	200.00	225.00
8204 - British Commando..	120.00	200.00	225.00
8205 - Australian Jungle fighter	120.00	200.00	225.00

	G	VG	M
8300 - EQUIPMENT FOR GERMAN STORM TROOPER - field pack, Luger pistol, holster, cartridge belt, 9mm Schmeisser machine gun, "Potato Masher" hand grenades and Iron Cross medal	30.00	60.00	100.00
8301 - EQUIPMENT FOR JAPANESE IMPERIAL SOLDIER - cartridge belt, field pack, Arisaka rifle, bayonet, Nambu pistol, holster and order of kite medal	30.00	60.00	100.00
8302 - EQUIPMENT FOR RUSSIAN INFANTRYMAN - field glasses, case, D. P. light machine gun, bi-pod, belt, ammo box, anti-tank grenades and order of Lenin medal.	30.00	60.00	100.00
8303 - EQUIPMENT FOR FRENCH RESISTANCE FIGHTER - shoulder holster, Lebel revolver, 7.65 Mas submachine gun, grenades, radio, knife and Croix de Guerre medal	15.00	20.00	30.00
8304 - BRITISH COMMANDO EQUIPMENT - canteen, case, cartridge belt, gas mask, case, stern mark 2-S submachine gun and Victoria Cross medal.	30.00	60.00	100.00
8305 - AUSTRALIAN JUNGLE FIGHTER EQUIPMENT - flame thrower, jungle knife, grenades, bush machete, sheath, entrenching tool and Victoria Cross medal.	15.00	20.00	30.00

NOTE: The Irwin Company made the following vehicles and planes for GI Joe under license from Hasbro: an Armored Car, a Half Track, two motorcycles, a Duck, three airplanes, a German staff car, a Mine Sweeper and a Racing Car. The

G.I. JOE

boxes are very desirable, and add 70% to the price of each toy. All sell in the following range 200.00 350.00 500.00

Mego also made a crash crew fire truck for GI Joe 100.00 250.00 350.00

Photo Boxes run $400-$500 in Mint.

G.I. JOE ADVENTURERS

Air Adventurer	20.00	35.00	45.00
Land Adventurer	20.00	35.00	45.00
Sea Adventurer	20.00	35.00	45.00
Talking Man of Action	50.00	75.00	100.00
Man of Action, lifelike hair	25.00	30.00	45.00
Talking Adventure Team Commander	35.00	50.00	65.00
Talking Adventure Team Commander, Black	80.00	150.00	225.00
Talking Adventure Team Commander, lifelike hair, beard	35.00	50.00	65.00
Astronaut and Space Capsule Set With Equipment ..	80.00	140.00	200.00
Secret of the Mummy's Tomb Set with figure, vehicle, equipment	40.00	80.00	120.00

Adventure Team Helicopter	20.00	50.00	75.00
Adventure Team Helicopter	20.00	45.00	85.00
Adventure Team Training Tower	20.00	45.00	85.00
Adventure Team Headquarters	25.00	40.00	60.00
Adventure Team Outfit, pants, flare gun	8.00	12.00	16.00
Adventure Team Outfit, trenchcoat, walkie-talkie ...	8.00	12.00	16.00
Adventure Team Outfit, camouflage clothes, gun, holster	8.00	12.00	16.00

END G.I. JOE

MISCELLANEOUS SOLDIERS

These Foreign Legionaires were made by South Africa's SAE. According to collector Cliff Finkelstein, Irving Bechky, a schoolteacher, was the firm's sole U.S. distributor, doing business as HAM Miniatures, Inc., 76-15-85 Drive, Woodhaven, NY. He also had a shop on Hillside Ave. in Jamaica, Queens. Some were special orders made for Bechky. SAE stood for Swedish African Engineers.

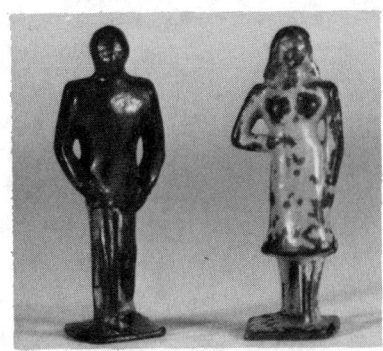

These two very simple 2¼" high solid lead figures of a man and a woman were the first lead "soldiers" to be produced after April 1, 1942. They came out shortly before the War ended, by at least the first week of August, 1945. Price averages $3-5 in mint condition. Company Unknown.

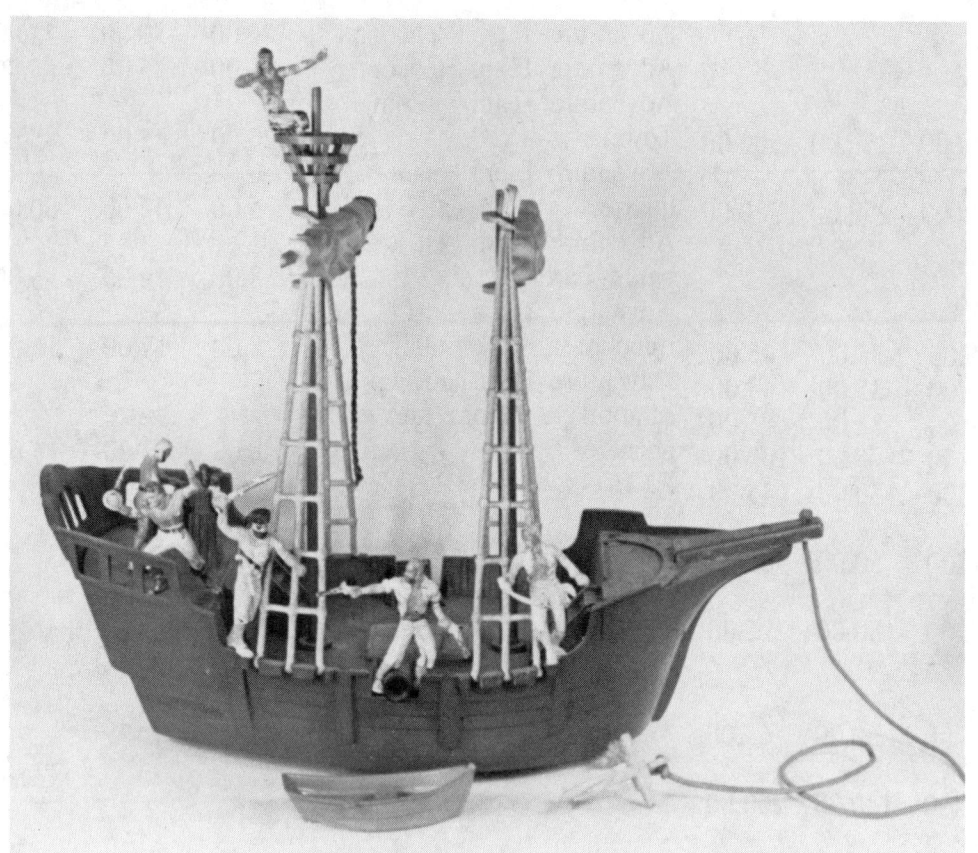

This Ideal pirate ship was first produced in 1953 and featured 6 beautifully designed, very individual-looking pirates. Value for the entire set in mint $200. The ship is made of hard plastic, the figures from soft plastic. Jolly Roger missing.

Four hollow lead figures by unknown companies. The two at the left were discovered by Don Pielin, and the standing rifleman who's just been shot suggests there was a variety of these pieces, at least some of which would have been more standard. The paint on the Indian is of unusually high quality, and the underside of the base is rather like that found on All-Nus. However, the eyes are wrong. Value about $10 in mint. The diver is a crude copy of Manoil's and was probably used as an aerator in fish bowls, as it has a projection on the back to which a hose can be affixed. Value about $8 in mint. No prices found on the two soldiers at left, but they would be of interest to collectors since they're rather well-modeled. Probably made in the late 1930s.

MISCELLANEOUS SOLDIERS

Tru-Craft surrendering Japanese, U.S. Medics, naval personnel, cavalryman and marching soldiers, 38mm high Tru-Craft was a California company in business from before the second world war, continued through it, and is still in business under new owner Jack Scruby. The original owner was Cecil Jackson, and the original sculptor Carl Romanelli. No prices found.
Photo by Ed Poole

NIFTY hollow lead circus figures. No price found.
Courtesy Don Pielin

NIFTY Circus figures. Nifty was a generic compan,
whose toys were distributed by Geo. Borgfeldt & Co.
An original boxed set with a poor box recently sold
for $150.00. Making up the set were a slush lion cage
wagon drawn by 2 horses "Tom and Dick,"
"Samson" weightlifter, "Clarence" clown beating
drum, Ringmaster and "Mae and Maud" woman
riding horse. The cage wagon with horses also sold
separately for $70.
Photo by Don Pielin

NIFTY circus figures.
Courtesy Hank Anton

More NIFTY circus figures. All were slush-cast. No price found.
Courtesy Don Pielin

MISCELLANEOUS SOLDIERS

This circus wagon seems to have been produced by both Nifty and Barclay. The wagon shown was bought in 1990 for $100 **without** the horses. Photo by Stan Alekna

No one knows who made these solid iron nursery rhyme figures. Tentative identification, left to right, is: Chicken Little, Dick Whittington (4" high), elephant, Wee Willie Winkie, White Rabbit. Value about $25 each in mint. Circa 1930s. Photo by John Alliston

Some of the Korean copies of Grey Iron's soldiers that have been sold in recent years, often by flea market dealers as genuine Grey Irons. Generally they can be spotted by inferior paint and large dot eyes. Photo by Roy E. Bonjour

Lead Soldiers
Two Sizes
9 and 18 Piece SETS

The Tur-Boy Company, 3519 Easton Ave., St. Louis, offered these lead soldiers in February, 1921. None is presently known. Tur-Boy made many other very different toys.

This solid lead doctor resembles Barclay's and Jones', but is somewhat different. No price found. Courtesy Charlie Breslow

This solid lead, nearly 1¾" high figure represents John Wayne in the Parker Bros. "Big Trail" game based on the 1930 movie. Value $10 in mint. Photo by Ed Poole

Wheels That Roll
On This Army Truck With Gun Carriage Trailer, No. E-45

A remarkable mould. Makes authentic Cannon with Carriage and set of wheels that roll! Mould includes power truck with set of 4 wheels that also roll. Length, overall 6". Casting can be made either hollow or solid. Price $1.50

U. S. Colonial Cavalry, Horse and Rider

A splendid action figure of these famous soldiers from American History mounted on horseback. Exceptionally large and full rounded. Size 2½"x 3½". Horse stands on own legs without special base. Casting can be made either hollow or solid. Price $1.50.

No. E-47

Unconquered Native African Warriors
No. E-50

An excellent action group with two tribesmen afoot, and one on horseback. Uniforms of both native and colonial type. Sizes 2½" to 2¾". Price $1.50.

UNITED STATES FORT

Be sure to get this mould to go with your soldiers. A substantial fortress with thick walls, gate, observation towers, firing apertures, and American Flag. A very important part of war games and maneuvers. Casting can be made either hollow or solid. Size 3¼"x2¾". Price $1.50

No. E-51

19

Unusual homecasting molds, circa 1936. They were sold by Chicago's Junior Caster (Rapaport Bros.) Photo by Perry R. Eichor

These plastic Jousting Knights were offered as a premium by Kellogg's in 1958. They sold for fifty cents and a Corn Flakes box-top. 3" high. They were operated by a coiled spring. No price found. Photo by Bob Bard

MISCELLANEOUS SOLDIERS

These very interesting, approximately 2½" high hollow lead soldiers bear resemblance to early Barclays, but the mound bases and the charging pose suggest Theodore Hahn. Very rare, with no prices found. The two figures at left are the same piece, with a green uniform, brown helmet and blue plume.
Courtesy Charlie Breslow

Three of these are known to exist. Collector-dealer Bud Born remembers seeing this at Woolworth's in 1939 or 1940 on a counter that sold only Barclay and Manoil soldiers. The piece most resembles Manoil, but puzzles collectors since it is not distinctly so, with none of the crispness of facial features, etc., associated with Manoil's work. Possibly this was a special job for Manoil, and rushed out without the usual chasing of the mold. None of the Manoil relatives remembers it, so for now it remains an "unknown". Because it is both rare and unusual, the price of this would compare to All-Nu's newsreel cameraman, and might even command more.
Courtesy Doug Lambert
Photo by Ron Cadieux

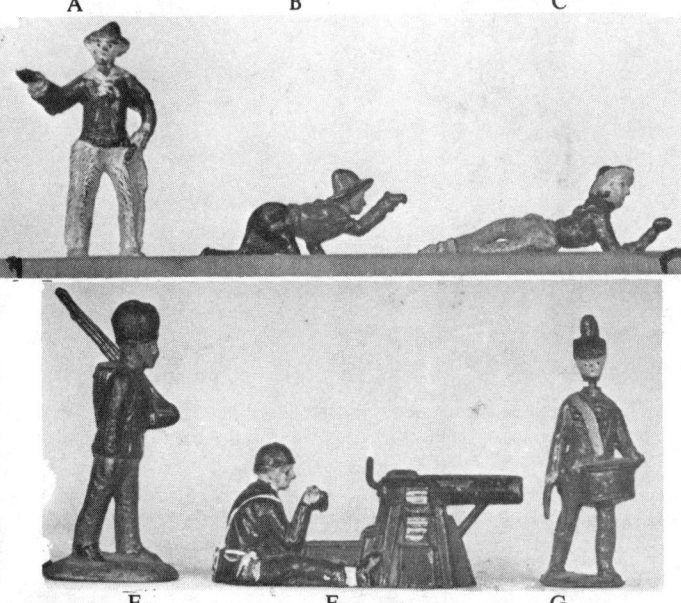

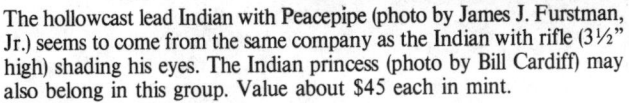

The hollowcast lead Indian with Peacepipe (photo by James J. Furstman, Jr.) seems to come from the same company as the Indian with rifle (3½" high) shading his eyes. The Indian princess (photo by Bill Cardiff) may also belong in this group. Value about $45 each in mint.

Soldiers by unknown makers, probably American
No prices found
Courtesy Charlie Breslow

MISCELLANEOUS SOLDIERS

According to Patrick McCaleb, an expert on German-made toy soldiers, the four 3¼" high hollowcast lead soldiers at left, variously painted as 18th Century American Colonial, French or British soldiers, come from an "obviously German" mold, and were cast by one Milo King at Fort Ticonderoga, where they were sold as souvenirs. Painting was by a woman, Florence Crowninshield. The mounted figure has been found with paint that suggests it too comes from Fort Ticonderoga; probably a Metal Cast mold that had been reworked to turn the figure into a colonial. Foot figure mint value $40.
Photo at right courtesy K. Warren Mitchell

Metal copies of Beton's soldiers occasionally turn up. The maker is unknown; perhaps located in Japan. Prices equivalent to Betons.
Courtesy Charlie Breslow

This officer and marcher are approximately 3⅜" high to the tops of their helmets. The maker is unknown and no price has been established.
Photos by Harold Haseley

This hollow lead soldier is about 3¾" high to the top of his helmet and about 6½" overall. Maker unknown. No price found.
Photo by Harold Haseley

This dimestore motorcyclist resembles those by Barclay and Metal Cast, but seems to be by neither. No price found.
Courtesy Charlie Breslow

Approximately 2¾" high hollow lead soldier. No maker known or price found.
Courtesy Charlie Breslow

This 3¼" high, semi-round iron soldier was auctioned in 1988 for $2▮
Maker unknown   Photo by Phil Savino

367

MISCELLANEOUS SOLDIERS

These fifteen cast iron figures, which range in height from 2½-3", have puzzled collectors. They appear to be Elizabethan types, and with their lack of stands suggest they were arranged in a toy theatre or ship. The figures shown here were found unpainted. No manufacturer known. In 1991, nine of these, in fair condition, were sold for $300. The speculation was that they represented Columbus and his crew.

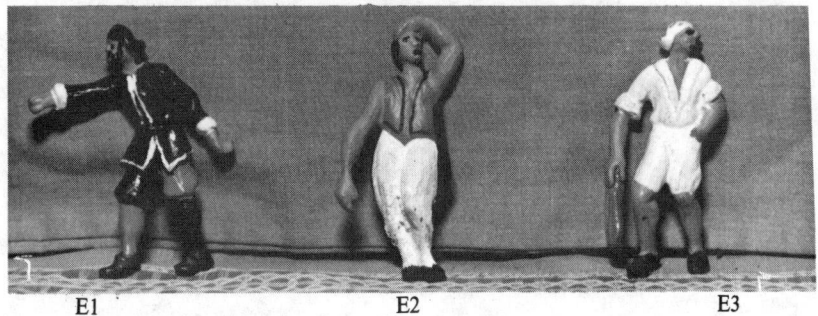

E1   E2   E3

Photo by Bill Cardiff

E4   E5   E6

Photo by Bill Cardiff

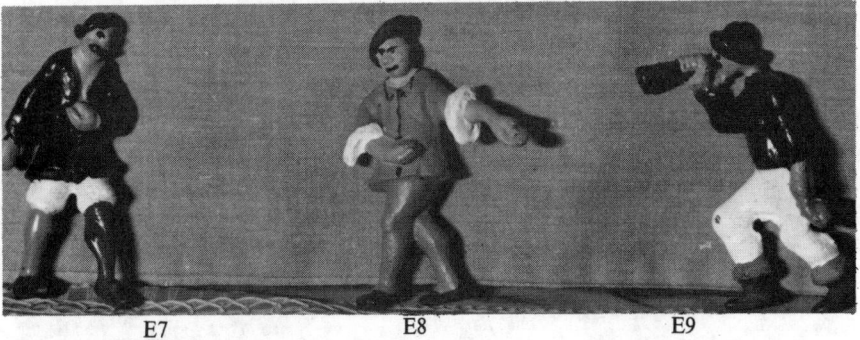

E7   E8   E9

Photo by Bill Cardiff

E10   E11   E12

Photo by Bill Cardiff

MISCELLANEOUS SOLDIERS

E13

E14   E15

Photo by Bill Cardiff

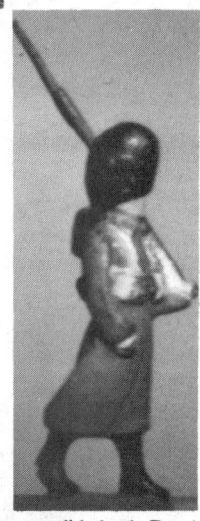

An approximately 3½" high solid cast lead doughboy. Al Lane, who took this photo, thinks there is a resemblance to Manoil, particularly in the rear left foot, which is raised.

Left, an original horseman by an unknown company, about 50mm range. At right a pirate of it by Kast-a-Toy, a homecasting company. No prices found, but about $10 in mint apiece.
Photo by Ed Poole

54mm solid lead Russian which Al Lane, who took th photo, thinks has a Mano look.

Two more variations of this 3¼" diver. The figure at left (knife missing) has no rivets on the breast plate, and the one at right has a face.
Courtesy Charlie Breslow and Roger Johnson

What appears to be a copy of Barclay B127 in a heavier, cruder casting. Value about $12 in mint. Maker unknown.

An unusual solid lead diver. 3¼" high Value about $20 in mint.
Photo by Max Heiss

MISCELLANEOUS SOLDIERS

These hollowcast lead figures are like the ones sold by Theodore Hahn, but are by another, as yet unknown company. These have line-and-dot eyes, flat bases. Prices are equivalent to Hahn's.
Photo by Will Beierwaltes

54mm solid lead Russian officer, which Al Lane, who took this photo, believes bears a design resemblance to Manoil.

A composition flagbearer in a roughly dimestore size. Manufacturer unknown, and no price found.
Courtesy K. Warren Mitchell

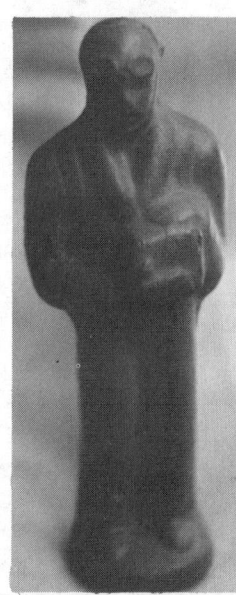

Composition aviator, 3¾" high from the bottom of his shoes to the top of his head. He is holding a square box, possibly meant to be a bomb-sight. Maker unknown and no price found.
Photo by Phil Savino

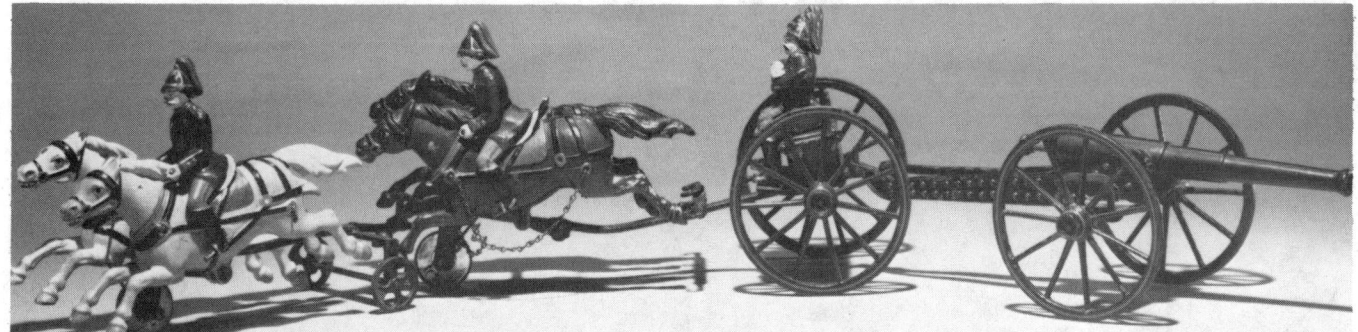

An early American soldier toy. This cast-iron, four-horse-drawn caisson was produced circa 1890 by Pratt & Letchworth, and measures 34" in length. In October, 1990, it was auctioned for $19,250.
Courtesy Christie's East.

MISCELLANEOUS SOLDIERS

This cast iron horse-drawn caisson by Ives, circa 1890, and missing an outrider, was auctioned in December, 1990 for $1760. 21" long. Courtesy Sotheby's New York

A 3½" high iron baseball player. Maker unknown. Auctioned in 1991 for $22. Photo by Leonard H. Schenk

Along with a Marine, these 5½" high ceramic figures were offered in 1943 by Detroit Toy Company, 15439 Mack Avenue, Detroit. Called Paint Pals, they were meant to be painted by the buyer, with paints furnished by Detroit Toy. L to R: Soldier, Sailor, Nurse, Aviator. No price found.
Photo by Bob Hornung

Approximately 2¾" high hollow lead American-made soldier with moving arm. Maker unknown, no price found.
Photo by Will Beierwaltes

According to collector Jerry Combs, this copy of Barclay B262 is not plastic, but hard rubber. Maker unknown, and no price found.
Photo by Jerry Combs

Composition British Grenadiers made for the Kresge five-and-ten chain in 1938 by Elastolin. Value in mint per figure is $12.
Photo by Hank Anton

A plaster Indian, possibly American made. 2⅜" high from bottom of foot to eye level. It resembles Indians made by Japan's Trico. No price found.
Photo by Phil Savino

50 Cowboys & Indians—$1
Packed in a colorful Gift Box, each toy is made of fine quality *Plastic* and stands a full 2" high! This complete Rodeo contains Bucking Broncos, Rodeo Riders, Sheriffs, Cowgirls, Covered Wagons, Warriors, Squaws, etc., etc. Tepee and corral included with each set! Yes, 50 toys for $1. Order from *Cowboys & Indians*, 6612-D Sunset Blvd., Hollywood 28, Calif.

These 2" high plastic cowboys and Indians, apparently semi-round, were offered in 1952.

These two 3" high, solid lead figures look as if they could be prototypes for Metalcast's 34A. The one at right has a tie, the other doesn't. They were found without bases. No price found.
Photo by Hank Anton

MISCELLANEOUS EQUIPMENT

In addition to the pieces shown here, there are a number of accessories that have not been connected to a manufacturer. One possibility for some is the Pulp Reproductions Co. of 3000 W. Clarke St., Milwaukee, Wisconsin, which was listed in the 1944-45 Playthings Directory as making "train tunnels, dugouts, trenches and soldier accessories."

Structo tank No. 48, 11" long. Prices average $200 in good condition, $300 in very good, and $400 in mint. Courtesy Mapes Auctioneers & Appraisers.

Top, l to r: A.C. Williams cast iron tank, 4" long, worth $90 in mint. Kilgore cast iron tank 2½" long, no price found, but presumably worth about $65 in mint. Bottom, L to R: Animate Toys tin litho "U.S. Baby Tank", pat. 6/20/16. However, the first ad ran August, 1918 with the note "taken over a year to perfect". Sold originally for 25 cents, it's now worth $50 in mint. Finally, a diecast Renault tank, manufacturer unknown, 2¾" long (courtesy Roger Johnson), value about $35 in mint.

L to R. Wooden "Ambulance" and "Supply Co. 123rd Field Artillery" truck. These were probably produced by Tillicum (Milton Bradley). Mint price $30 each.

Banner plastic trucks and cannon. Circa WWII. Trucks worth about $25 each in mint, cannon about $10. Banner made no soldiers. Courtesy Charlie Breslow, Roger Johnson

MISCELLANEOUS EQUIPMENT

Marx tin litho bomber, 19" wingspan. Spring wind-up for locomotion and sparkling wing guns. Marx made a number of planes of this type. Their average value is $150 in mint. Photo by Ed Poole

Keystone wooden ships, 8-18" long. Top, torpedo and plane-launching battleship, $260 in mint. Middle: Exploding (break-away) enemy raider, value $150 in mint. Bottom, torpedo-firing submarine, value $100 in mint.
Photo by Ed Poole

Hubley die-cast metal planes, wingspans range 5½-13". Top, L to R: "U.S. Army" pursuit, value $50 in mint, P-38, value $100 mint, "U.S. Army" pursuit, value $40 in mint. Bottom L to R: Bell Airacuda "K801 U.S. Army," value $200 in mint, P40 fighter, value $45 in mint.
Photo by Ed Poole

Buddy L pressed steel LST, 12" long worth $65 in mint.
Photo by Ed Poole

Miscellaneous ships, all slush-cast but the last. Top, L to R: "U.S.S. New Mexico" and "Texas." Bottom, L to R: Ralstoy Battleship 5½" long, celluloid battleship by unknown maker. Prices for the slush-casts would be in the range of Barclay's ships. Celluloid fanciers might pay more than a soldiers collector for the last battleship.
Photo by Ed Poole

Composition ships, almost certainly all produced during WWII. The submarine, both carriers and the smaller destroyer were all produced by New York's Wellmade Doll Co. Presumably the others were too, as the PT boat is very similar to one made by Wellmade, and is presumably a mold variation. The ships range in size from 7¾" long to 11¾" long.
Photo by Ed Poole

MISCELLANEOUS EQUIPMENT

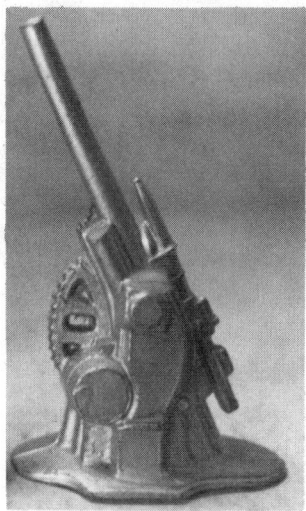

It's not known who made this intricately-designed AA gun. Lead alloy, and hollow. Value in mint $45 (Possibly Jones)
Photo by K. Warren Mitchell

An example of what plastic has done for the hobby. This beautifully done, and relatively inexpensive Viking ship was sold in 1955. The oars move as the ship is pulled or pushed across the floor. And that's a working catapult on the stern. The manufacturer was Renwal, the number **245**, and the length about 17". Value in mint $165.

Renwal plastic planes, wingspans range 4½-9¼", top, L to R: B25 bomber, B17 bomber, C54 transport. Middle, L to R: B17 bomber, P40 fighter, PB2Y flying boat. Bottom, L to R: P47 fighter, P38 fighter. Prices are in the $20-$40 range in mint.
Photo by Ed Poole

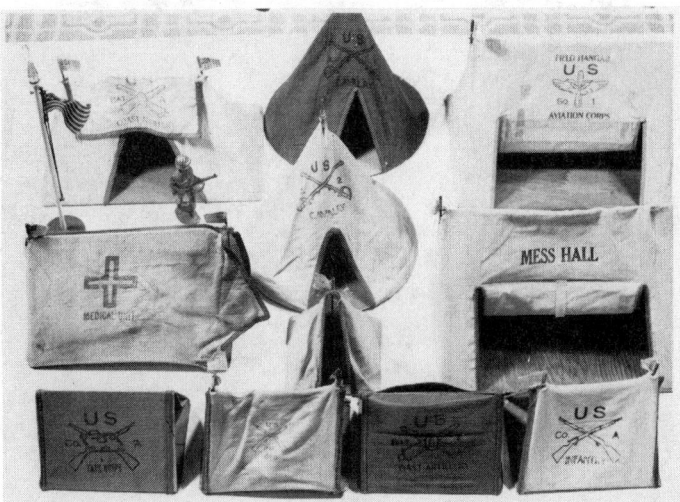

Various tents, sold to go with Dimestore soldiers. Values $15-25 in mint.
Photo by Ed Poole

MISCELLANEOUS EQUIPMENT

The Sail-Me Co. of Chicago probably took its name from an early "Sail-Me" airplane it marketed. It made at least six different paper tents, and the copyright was 1931. The tents appeared in a November 1939 *Parents* magazine article entitled "Playroom in the Air". A boxed set of six in mint is worth $80. Individually they sell for about $3 each.
Photo by Ken Butler

Early WWII all-wood two-engine bomber, 13" wingspan, 9" long. It carries five bombs, which can be dropped. Made by Sessions Clock Co., Forestville, Conn. Value $125 mint.
Courtesy Roger Johnson

A perfect size for dimestore toy soldiers is this cast iron Hubley trimotor America. The wingspan is 17", and the value in mint is $7000.
Photo by Ed Hyers

SUN RUBBER Scout Car, tank, value each $35 in mint. New in 1946.
Photo by Ed Poole

A circa 1890 Fort Sumter wooden game set by Bliss of Rhode Island. 18" wide. Valued at $4000.
Courtesy Lawrence Scripps Wilkinson
Detroit Toy Museum

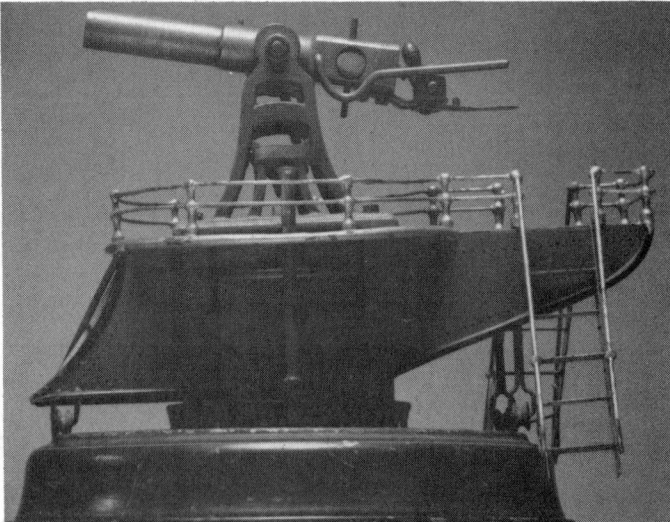

A Marklin (Germany) Coastal Gun, 9" high. It was auctioned in December, 1990 for $990.
Courtesy Sotheby's New York

Chein tin litho Mack truck painted olive drab, 8" long, value in mint $150.
Photo by Ed Poole

MISCELLANEOUS EQUIPMENT

WWII Identification Models 1/36 scale, slush-cast metal, 4-8" long, by H.L. Framberg (Chicago) and Comet Metal (L.I., N.Y.). Britains Ltd. soldier and 1/24 jeep included for comparison.
Prices run $25-65
Photo by Ed Poole

This papier-mache bunker, maker unknown, was sold in the U.S. during WWII. Sold in late 1990 in the above condition (without the shown Barclay soldier) for $27.50
Courtesy K. Warren Mitchell

WWII Identification Models, 1/24 scale, slush-cast metal, 5½-11" long, no manufacturer's marks. Manoil figure included for comparison. Prices run $25-$65.
Photo by Ed Poole

The 7½" long composition jeep is by New York's Wellmade Doll & Toy Co. Presumably the 3½" copy is too. In 1988, the larger was auctioned for $35 in Good.
Photo by Ed Poole

Wood and fibreboard tank, no maker known. 7¾" long, makes "rat-a-tat" noise. Circa WWII. Value about $35 in mint.
Courtesy Roger Johnson

A Holgate wooden "Bucktail Out Post" scaled to 54mm soldiers. Sold circa the 1930s for $8. From the Holgate archives. No price found.
Courtesy Ronald L. Simkoff

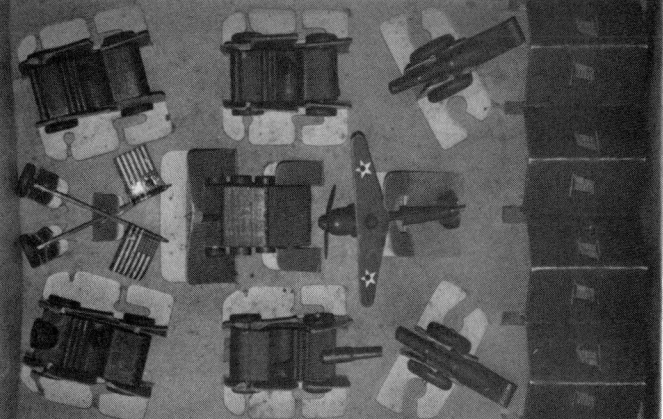

Marx Midgies - Large set, sold in 1990 in excellent plus condition for $75. Wood and cardboard.
Photo by Stan Alekna

MISCELLANEOUS

Marx P35-type two-engine bomber pressed steel, 15⅞" wingspan. Value in mint $140.
Photo by Bob West

Marx P35 fighter, pressed steel, 13½" wingspan (with Barclay podfoot pilot). The plane's value in mint is $120.
Photo by Bob West

Lead alloy planes by C.A.W. (Charles A. Wood) of Clay Center, Kansas. Circa 1930s. Top, L to R: Monoplane, number unknown; No. 29 Sr. Low Wing Monoplane; No. 28 Jr. Low Wing Monoplane. Bottom, L to R; No. 36 Boeing Bomber; No. 37 Army Pursuit Plane "Seversky-Army-37". Wingspans in the 3-4" range. Price in Good $20, in Very Good $40, in Mint $60.

Photo by Perry R. Eichor

Marx Air-Sea Power bombing set. Tin plane and ships. Value mint in box is $750.
Courtesy Jack Matthews

RALSTOY (None imprinted with company name) Top: Transporter with tank, Cannon No. 34, Plane, 9" overall. Middle: "Antiaircraft Unit", 5½" long, Cannon No. 23, 2¾" long. Bottom: Tank 3" long, "U.S. Army", Cannon 3¾" long.
"Antiaircraft Unit", 5½" long - 28.00 good; 42.00 very good; 56.00 mint. Tank, 3" long, "U.S. Army" - 13.00 good; 20.00 very good; 26.00 mint. Transporter with tank, cannon No. 34, plane, 9" overall length - 20.00 good; 45.00 very good; 60.00 mint. Cannon No. 23 - 8.00 good; 12.00 very good; 16.00 mint. Cannon No. 34 - 8.00 good; 12.00 very good; 16.00 mint. Cannon 3¾" long - 8.00 good; 12.00 very good; 16.00 mint.
Photo by Ed Poole

AMERICAN TOY BATTLE PLANE

(PATENTED)

**The Whirlwind Seller of the Year
No Toy Shop Complete Without It
Every Boy and Girl a Customer,
and Old Folks, Too**

Order now for the Holiday trade.

Made of heavy cardboard body, wings and rudder, printed in bright cheerful colors with painted wood wheels. The propeller revolves as the Plane is swung through the air at the end of a string. A duplicate in miniature of the real Aeroplane. Each plane is packed in a strong paper envelope, knocked down.

Easily set up in a few minutes by following printed instructions. **Last call. Don't wait or you will be disappointed.**
Buy the original, others are infringements.

Price: $15.00 Per Gross, in Gross Lots F.O.B. Springfield, Mo.   Shipping Weight: 27 Pounds Per Gross

THE NEW ERA NOVELTY COMPANY, Distributors   212 HOLLAND BUILDING
SPRINGFIELD, MISSOURI

A cardboard Battle Plane, as advertised in the September, 1919 *Playthings*. If color is as striking as the art, it would be worth about $45 in mint. Courtesy *Playthings*.

Marx Anti-Aircraft Gun with box in background. Value in mint, unboxed, $80. Shoots rack of wooden shells.
Photo by Ken Butler.

This delicately-cast lead alloy cannon and limber (a total of 6" in length) was made by C.A.W. (Charles A. Wood) in Clay Center, Kansas. No price found. Circa 1930s.
Courtesy Fred Maxwell and Gary Franson

Marx Turnover Tank No. 3. Value in mint condition $150.
Photo by Max Heiss.

Tin and Glass Cannon Candy Container. Marked "West Bros. Co. Grapeville, Pa." U.S. Serial No. 2862. Auctioned in good to very good condition in late 1990 for $55.
Courtesy James S. Maxwell/Virginia Caputo
Photo by Virginia Caputo

A Holgate wooden Bucktail Garrison Town. It sold for $20 circa the 1930s. Scaled to 54mm soldiers. From the Holgate archives. Courtesy Ronald L. Simkoff.

Two tin clockwork vehicles from Hauser (Germany's Elastolin). The 11" long truck with cannon was auctioned for $605 in June, 1990. The truck at top went for about half that price.
Courtesy Sotheby's New York

Rich fort no.261 (fibreboard). Value in mint condition $100.
Photo by Ron Fink

A Keystone Fort of fibreboard. Value in mint $90.
Photo by Ron Fink

"UNKNOWN" COMPANIES

The following is a listing of pre-World War II American toy soldier companies about which little or nothing is known; there actually seems to be more unknown companies than soldiers who can't be identified by company. Possibly some of these firms employed molds made by Metal Cast or other companies which sold casting kits (both Beton and Ausley are known to have done this at first). This listing is given both to furnish an idea of the many companies that remain to be "discovered", and in the hope that detective work by some readers will result in a few of the mysteries being solved. This list is by no means complete; during my research I didn't always list "unknown" companies, and then there were other companies, such as Tommy Toy and American Alloy, which produced a fair number of soldiers, yet seem never to have been listed in toys publications. Presumably there are more.

Ace Toy Mold Co. of Philadelphia, PA and Toledo, OH advertised its "Kast-A-Toy" sets in the March 1935 Toys and Novelties. Shown was a three-dimensional prone machine-gunner, as well as as its mold and the mold of a mounted officer. The sets were available at least as early as 1934. According to the 1935 ad, "eleven subjects" were then available. Their figures look as if they could have been copies of those manufactured by Lincoln Logs.

American Lead Toy & Novelty Co. was listed in a new business directory August 19, 1939. The officers were Charles Kremm, J. Bracco, Robert Bostwick, Louis Picco and George Miller. This seems to have been the firm that evolved into American Alloy, which was also located in North Bergen, but Picco has no memory of it, although does remember having a company which made "six or seven" soldiers which were sold through Toy Creations, another North Bergen company. These seem not to have been the Tommy Toy copies. There's a possibility the firm used discarded (or purloined) early Barclay molds.

Central Pennsylvania Nov. Works, Milheim, PA, was listed in the March 1933 and July 1934 Toys & Novelties under "Lead Soldiers".

Chambers Mfg. Co.. According to Louis Picco, this firm was owned by three or four brothers named Castelucci (spelling uncertain) at 308 12th Street (formerly Savoye Street) in Union City, NJ. Picco says they made lead cars and soldiers. The firm appeared in the Winter 1934-35 phonebook, and not the previous year.

Conn. Metal Nov. Mfg. Co., 215 Greene St., New Haven, Conn., was listed in the March 1933 and July 1934 Toys and Novelties under "Lead Soldiers", and again in 1941.

Connecticut Toy and Novelty Mfg. Co., This firm was located in Noank, Ct., and owned by J.G. Laffargue. Its soldiers came from homecast molds. It's not known when the company existed.

Deck Mfg. Co., 68 Orchard Street, Newark, NJ, was listed under "Soldiers" in the 1936 Playthings directory.

Donze, Leon, Adolph and John were listed as "Toymakers" at 23 Bline Street in West Hoboken in a 1922-23 business directory. It was shortly after this that Donze formed Barclay Mfg. Co. with Michael Levy. Presumably he brought some of his molds with him to Barclay. Leon and John were father and son. The relationship of Adolph to the others is unknown.

Donze, Leon was located around 1931 or 1932, after leaving Barclay, on 32nd, 33rd or 34th Street near Newark Avenue in West New York. Charles Poretta, chief of maintenance for Barclay, cleaned out Donze's place and returned whatever was salvageable to Barclay. Poretta doesn't remember specifically what Donze made, but thinks it was a "few soldiers and a few cars."

Jones & Co., Inc., Paul, 401 S. Berger St., Mishewaka, Indiana, was listed in the July 1934 Toys & Novelties under "Soldiers".

Jordan Co., Paul A. 2035 E. 19th St., Kansas City, MO was listed under "Lead Soldiers" in the 1941 Toys & Novelties Buyers Guide.

Kansas Metal Nov. Mfg. Co., Salina, Kansas, was listed under "Soldiers" in the 1932 Playthings directory. In March, 1933 and July, 1934, it was listed in Toys & Novelties under "Lead Toys and Animals. Etc." at 218 S. Third Street, Salina.

Kansas Toy & Novelty Co. of Clifton, Kansas, was listed under "Soldiers" in the 1932 Playthings Directory. It was also listed in the March 1933 and July 1934 Toys and Novelties under "Lead Toys and Animals Etc.", at the same location.

Kast-A-Toy - see Ace Toy Mold Co.

Krazifor American Toys, Laurel, Miss., was listed in the 1923-24 Toys & Novelties Buyer's Guide as producing lead soldiers.

Littlefield Mfg. Co. at 702 N. Halstet St., Chicago, Illinois, was listed under "Soldiers" in the 1930 Playthings Directory.

Marbro Mfg. Co., New Orleans, was listed in the 1923 (only) Toys and Novelties Buyers Guide as manufacturing toy soldiers.

Maryland Toy Soldier Mfg., 456 N. Potomac St., Hagerstown, Md., was listed in the March 1933 and July 1934 Toys and Novelties under "Lead Soldiers", and was listed again in 1941, and in a city directory in 1942. The owner was Harry F. Feigley, and he seems to have cast in his home. In 1917-18 he was listed as a blacksmith, and blacksmiths often make molds. In 1922-23 the listing was Maryland Toy Manufacturing Co., in 1929 he and his wife Lela M., were listed as "Doll Hospital and Toy Shop". In 1926-27 the firm made "lead cowboys, Indians, soldiers," etc.

Metal Art Miniature Co., 572 38th Street, San Pedro, California, was listed in the 1935-36 Toys and Novelties Directory as "Mfrs. of lead figures of soldiers and sailors, animals, cannon, cowboys and other objects".

Metal-Craft Nov. Co., 478 Bergenline Ave., West New York, N. J., was listed in the March, 1933 and July, 1934 Toys and Novelties magazine under "Lead Soldiers". No record in the 1934 and 1938 directory of New Jersey Manufacturers, or with the New Jersey Department of State. A "Metal Craft Co.", minus the "Novelty"designation was incorporated in May 1926 at 43 Lincoln Park, Newark, N.J., but whether this was the same company is unknown.

MOB Novelties. Their label suggests 1930s production. Lead hunter, animals and trees known. Probably from homecast molds. Location: Gettysburg, PA.

Montana Toys & Nov. Co., Livingston, Montana, was listed in the 1930 Playthings Directory under "Soldiers". It was listed, at the same address, in the March 1933 and July 1934 Toys and Novelties under "Lead Toys and Animals Etc.".

New Jersey Metal Novelties Mfg. Co., Hawthorne, N. J., was listed in the March 1933 and July 1934 Toys and Novelties under "Lead Soldiers". No record in the 1934 or 1938 directory of New Jersey Manufacturers, or with the New Jersey Department of State. It was listed again in a toys directory in 1941.

N.Y. State Toy & Novelty Co. - Produced lead semi-rounds, from Metal Cast molds. Known figures are a boxer and a mounted cowpoke. Circa 1933-35 (NRA labels on backing cards.) Albany, New York.

Noveltoy - See Lincoln Logs.

Novelty Castings Co., Inc., 1166 Cypress Ave., Brooklyn N.Y., was listed under "Lead Soldiers" in the July, 1934 Toys and Novelties. It was listed again in 1941.

Pitmar Metal Toy Co., 1136 22nd St., San Diego, California, was listed in the 1934 Toys & Novelties under "Lead Soldiers".

Roberts & Co., Dale, 1657 S. Fairfax Ave., Los Angeles, California, was listed in the March, 1933 Toys & Novelties Magazine under "Lead Soldiers".

Russell Mfg. Co. was listed in the 1945-46 Playthings Directory under "Wood Etc. Soldiers". It was located in Leicester, Mass.

Scheuring, J & G. In January, 1927's *Playthings,* Owens-Kreiser, longtime distributor for William Feix, dropped Feix and substituted this firm's "Pewter Soldiers". Nothing else is known.

Selchow & Righter, a game company, manufactured toy soldiers for a number of years (see American Soldier Company).

CANADA

During the World War II era, Breslin Industries of Toronto produced hollow lead toy soldiers that were copies of the Barclays and Manoils no longer available in Canada because of wartime restrictions. A 1950 Breslin catalog shows the firm was still copying those companies, but now just their cowboys and Indians. It also copied the Metal Cast mounted Indian and several of All-Nu's civilian pieces. So far as is known, all their figures were marked to show their Canadian manufacture. Breslin was owned by brothers Sam and Ed Breslin. The value of Breslins is roughly equivalent to those of the pieces they copy. No price has been found on the Mountie, which appears to be a Breslin original.

The soldiers of London Toy, of which there seems to be seven types, are diecast and average a little over 2¾" high. They were produced in London, Ontario, circa 1946-49. They sell for about $50 each in mint condition. London Toy also produced a No. 7 Cannon with red wood wheels similar to Manoil's No. 69, but larger, approximately 4" long. In very good condition, this was auctioned in the fall of 1987 for $35.

LT3   LT4
London Toys
Courtesy K. Warren Mitchell

LT1 LT2
London Toys

LT5   LT6
London Toys

LT7
London Toys
Courtesy K. Warren Mitchell

London Toy (Canada) "Hawker Hurricane", 4½" wingspan. No price found.
Photo by Ed Poole

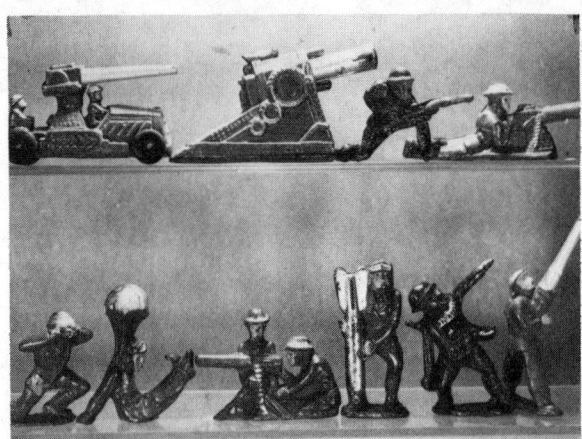

Breslin's soldiers and other toys, all of them copies.
Photo by Don Pielin

Breslin's copy of the Jones motorcyclist. "Canada" is marked on the rear fender.
Photo by Ed Poole

Marked "Made in Canada", this is probably made by Breslin.
Photo by Max Heiss

Breslin (Copy of All-Nu) Barry S. Josephs collection
Courtesy Hank Anton

Breslin
Barry S. Josephs collection
Courtesy Hank Anton

Breslin (Copy of Metal Cast). Barry S. Josephs collection
Courtesy Hank Anton

Breslin
Barry S. Josephs collection
Courtesy Hank Anton

Breslin
Barry S. Josephs collection
Courtesy Hank Anton

Breslin
Barry S. Josephs collection
Courtesy Hank Anton

Figures shown in a 1950 Breslin catalog

#27
INDIAN AND TOMAHAWK
3" high

#26
INDIAN & BOW
2½" high

#21
COWBOY & GUN
3" high

#22
COWBOY & LARIAT
3" high

#85
RUGBY PLAYER
3" high

#37
MOUNTIE
3¾" high

#20 - 3" high
INDIAN ON HORSE

#119 - 3½" High
BUCKAROO & RIDER

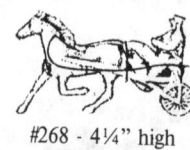

#120 - 3½" high
RACE HORSE & RIDER

#268 - 4¼" high
TROTTER

#69 - 3½" high
INDIAN CHIEF & HORSE

#19 - 3" high
COWBOY ON HORSE

#84
HOCKEY PLAYER
3" high

380

JAPANESE-MADE SOLDIERS

It now appears Trico soldiers were made in Nagoya, to the specifications of New York's Langfelder, Homma & Hayward, Inc. Trico may have stood for Tri Company, with the three in Tri being the owners, Langfelder, Homma and Hayward. Homma suggests a Japanese name; the firm seems to have imported and sold only Japanese goods.

Chinese soldiers have been found in brass. Collector Jim Morris has reported on a group that were bought in China in 1926. In that group of minimally-detailed figures were the following: Lying, firing rifle; walking drummer; standing peering through binoculars; standing firing pistol; advancing with rifle; saluting at attention, marching right shoulder arms; marching, no weapon (officer?); standing with rifle chest-high and outstretched. In 1991 the author saw another group that seems to have come from the same company. It included equipment and perhaps other figures. Unfortunately, he forgot to ask for a photo. At present no price range has been established on these Chinese-made soldiers.

JA 1   JA2   JA3   JA4   JA5

JA6   JA7   JA8   JA9   JA10

These Japanese-made composition figures, about 2¾" high, were sold in the United States prior to World War II. Value in mint about $20 apiece. Courtesy Gene Coffman

JA16   JA17   JA18   JA19   JA20   JA21   JA22

JA23   JA24   JA25   JA26   JA27   JA23

Japanese "Barclays". Most were nearly exact copies, even to the early Barclay "eye," but the sailor flagbearer appears to be a conversion of B49. These were sold circa 1939, and average $35 in mint.

JA36   JA37   JA38

These ceramic soldiers are 2½" high. No price found. Photo by Bob Hornung

JA11   JA12   JA13   JA14   JA15

A boxed set of ceramic soldiers made in Japan and sold in the U.S. prior to World War II. Average $18 in mint. All but the machine gunner were shown in a 1938 N. Shure catalog.   Courtesy Robert D. Worthen

JA28   JA28a   Photo by Ed Poole

Value for Japanese "Barclays" is about $25 in mint.

JA10A
This belongs with the JA1-JA10 grouping.
Photo by Will Beierwaltes

JA31   JA32   JA33

JA34   JA35   JA29   JA30

All of these figures are hollow lead. JA31 and 32 appear to be by the same company. JA33 is unusual in that the bowstring is wire. JA34 is marked "Made in Occupied Japan." JA35 appears to be by the same company, as does a holdup man and Indian with knife (neither shown), all three of them crude copies of Manoils. JA29 and JA30 are Japanese "Barclays" in blue. Value for JA34 and JA35 about $18 in mint. For JA 32-35 $28 in mint.

JA49   JA50   JA51   JA12?   JA52

JA53

More ceramic figures.
Photo by Ron Cadieux

JA48   JA11?

Ceramic figures, 6" high
Photo by Ron Cadieux

JA39   JA40

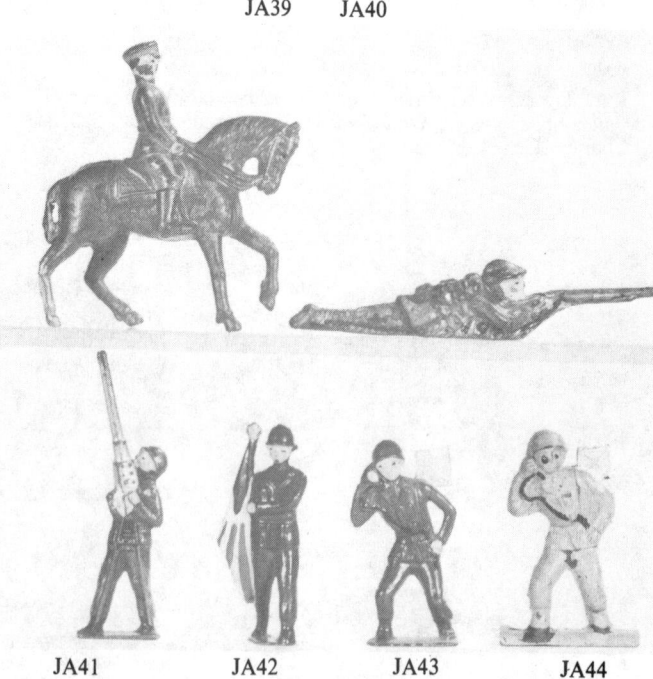

JA41   JA42   JA43   JA44

54mm figures, some of them obviously copies of Barclays. JA44 is plastic. (See photo of boxed set, which contains some of these figures.) All are marked "Japan".
Photo by Ed Poole

382

JAPANESE-MADE

Top, L to R: JA54, JA55, JA56, JA57. Bottom, L to R: JA58, JA59. Composition soldiers with cardboard trench.
Photo by Ron Cadieux

Another shot of the Japanese "Barclays" showing the ensign in blue, and the copies of B18 and B12.
Photo by Ed Poole

JA60

JA61   JA62   JA63 JA64   JA65 JA66 JA67

Courtesy Don Pielin

JA68   JA69   JA70   JA71 JA72   JA73 JA74   JA75

Courtesy Don Pielin

Note the copies of Barclay figures.

JA76   JA77   JA78   JA79 JA80 JA81   JA82   JA83   JA84
Courtesy Don Pielin

383

JA85   JA21

Collector Ed Poole sent this photo showing that even the Japanese copies of Barclays had variations. The previously unknown figure at left has JAPAN written on his back. The other, more common figure, has JAPAN on its base.

AJ85   JA86   JA87   JA88   JA89

The boxtop and the types found in this 9-piece set in an approximately 54mm height. A 1939 Butler Bros. catalog shows some of these pieces in a boxed set that included out-of-scale copies of Barclay's 3¼" soldiers JA19, JA22 and what seems to be an as yet unidentified Barclay copy. These pieces are all hollow-cast lead, and the two figures in gas masks are carrying a stretcher.
Photo by Don Pielin
Courtesy Pielin and *Old Toy Soldier*

JA90

This looks much like JA89, but there are differences, including height, as this is dimestore size; nearly 4" high. Possibly another figure from "Bestmaid" to be sold with the Barclay copies. Value $?? mint
Photo by Ed Poole

JA97   JA98

These are both lead and dimestore size. Value in mint about $?? each.
Photo by Ron Steiner

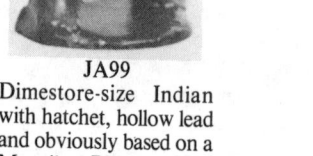

JA99
Dimestore-size Indian with hatchet, hollow lead and obviously based on a Manoil.   Photo by Harold Haseley

JA101
This hollow lead cowboy on bucking broncho is dimestore size. No price found. 4" high to top of hat.
Photo by Robert Worthen

JA102   JA12
Ceramic figures, with JA102 3¾" high. These appear to be the soldiers shown in a 1938 N. Shure catalog.
Value ?? in mint for the horseman, ?? in mint for the other.
Photo by Mike Simes   Courtesy Jerry Combs

384

JAPANESE-MADE

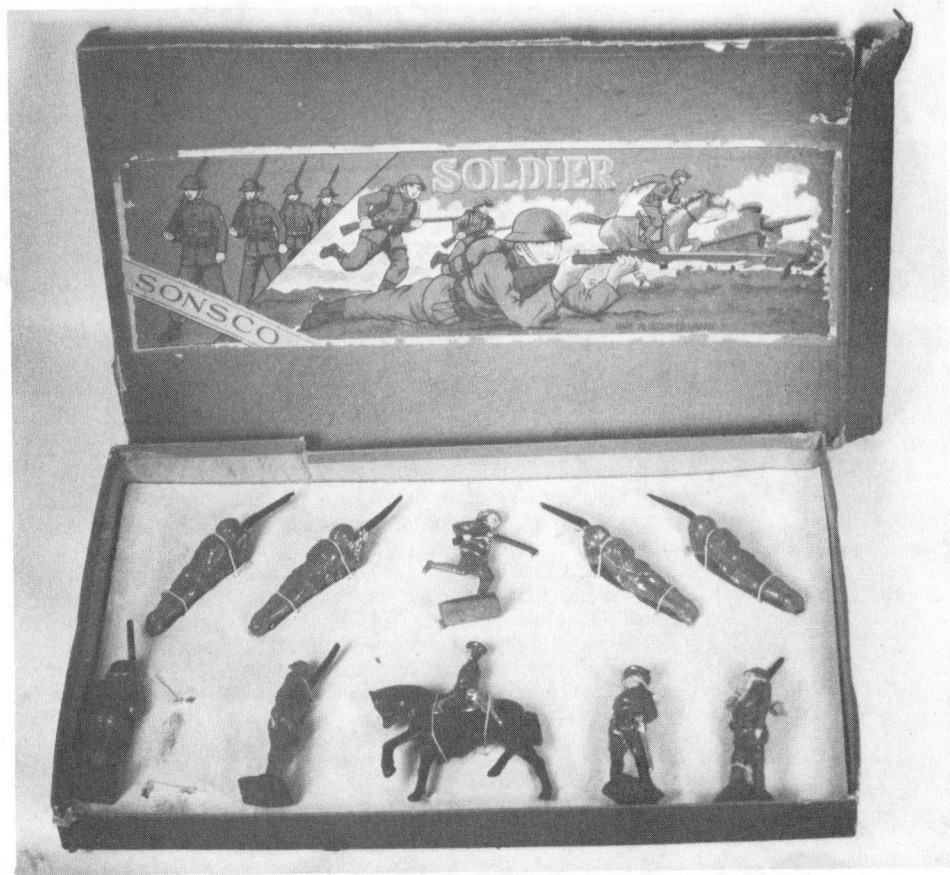

JA103
JA Hollow lead. Value $8 mint
Courtesy Hank Anton

JA104
The paper tag on the flagstaff says "Made in Occupied Japan". Ceramic. Value in mint $??
Photo by Jerry Combs

Soldiers in a box marked "Made in Occupied Japan." Toy soldier collectors might pay $25 for the set. Fanciers of "Made In Occupied Japan" items would pay considerably more.

JA105   JA106   JA107   JA108   JA109
Metal copies of Britains post-WWII U.S. infantry. 54mm. No prices found.
Photo by Will Beierwaltes

JA115
Hollow lead, approx. 3¼" high. No price found (tail missing).
Courtesy Charlie Breslow

JA110   JA111   JA112   JA113   JA114
Metal copies of Britains post-WWII U.S. Infantry. 54mm. No prices found.
Photo by Will Beierwaltes

JA25 (blue) JA116 (ceramic). No prices found.
Courtesy Charlie Breslow

JAPANESE-MADE

JA117

JA117   JA118

The back of JA117 shown to illustrate the rising sun on his back. The 3" high JA118 is by K.I. of Japan. It has been sold attached to a base marked "Rogers Ranger Ft. William Henry, N.Y." Both figures are hollowcast lead. No prices found.

Courtesy Charlie Breslow

Trico soldier, 4⅛" range, value about $30 in mint.
Photo by Jerry Combs

Trico medical figures (all Tricos are composition) in front of a ceramic "Hospital", also made in Japan.
Photo by Ed Poole

These Trico composition figures, 6cm, are copies of Elastolins. Value in mint $20 each.
Photo by Will Beierwaltes

Trico composition U.S. Soldiers, 15cm. These were advertised in 1934. Value per figure in mint, about $30.
Photo by Will Beierwaltes

These soldiers, all marked "Trico", were bought by Larry G. Alkire at a Kresge's five and ten about 1939 or 1940. In the early 1930s Langfelder, Homma & Hayward, importers at 915 Broadway in New York City advertised composition figures "From our Nagoya factory". Several figures marked Trico have been found that match some of the pieces in the ads. In addition to the Tricos shown in this section, other pieces shown in the ads included different cowboys, Indians, U.S. Soldiers in combat and marching figures that were either sailors or marines. Value for foot figures about $30 in mint, horseback about $40 in mint. The foot soldiers in this photo are about 4⅛" high.

Photo by Larry G. Alkire

Trico composition cowboys and Indians, the foot figures about 4¼" high. Value for each foot figure about $15 in mint, $25 in mint for the mounted.
Photo by Jerry Combs

These are rubber, in 7cm range, and copies of Lineols. No price found.
Photo by Will Beierwaltes

Copies of Britains French Sailors, 54mm high, lead alloy. No price found.
Photo by Will Beierwaltes

386

Plastic copies of 7cm plastic Elastolins
Photo by Will Beierwaltes

Copy of Britains cannon, 54mm. No price found.
Photo by Will Beierwaltes

Metal copies of Britains and Charbens Circus figures. No prices found.
Photo by Will Beierwaltes

MINIKIN(S) (made in Japan)
by Will Beierwaltes

"Occupied Japan" is a term synonymous with the generally cheap export goods from the US-controlled post war economy of Japan. It was from this venue that a surprisingly good (though often variable quality) production of toy soldiers named "Minikin" arose. Minikins or Minikin (interchangable) was the name given to a line of figures imported exclusively by International Models, Inc. of New York City by a man named Lou Barnett. G.I.'s returning from Europe after the war brought back some of the fine miniature soldiers from France and England, which largely replaced the toy soldier in popularity until the mid 1980's. It seems that Minikin was aimed at providing figures that would be of high enough quality to fit in with Vertunni and Courtenay figures, but be priced like Britains. While they did not always manage to live up to their expectations, the line has some of the most unusual and beautiful mass-produced

387

single figures available. While all of the figures came boxed, most were in nondescript grey cardboard with the name rubber stamped on the lid. However, the large "sets" of figures had bigger boxes with illustrated labels. These were often printed in 2 or 3 colors. Sets with labeled boxes will be noted in the list, and these when found in their original boxes are more collectible, and increase some 10-20% in value. Minikins figures were made for export and probably never sold in Japan. Most of the early post-war Japanese production seems to have been sold to distributors who packaged or identified them as they saw fit. While Minikin is an exception in its consistency of production, the name and identity are the efforts of Mr. Barnett. The initial group of figures available from Minikin was introduced in 1948 or 1949, and covered catalog enteries from H-1 to H-30. These include obvious copies of Britains 16th Century Knights, Courtenay foot knights and Heyde's ancient Greeks. Figures may carry labels of "made in Occupied Japan", "Made in Japan", "Japan", and "IMP Japan" *(for International Model Products)*. The figures labeled "Occupied" are the earliest production and most collectible as the soldier collector must compete with afficianados of occupied Japan ephemera. Within the catalog were a series of French Colonial figures, a set of Highlanders, and the first of a series of samurai warriors. The catalog was expanded in 1952 to include Minikins' largest and most unique set, H-31; Historic Hannibals Elephant Invasion, additions to the Samurai series, and an American Revolution series. Neither series was sold as a set, each figure being packaged individually. Finally, also in 1952, two small non-military offerings; the "biblical" and "barnyard" series, as well as a less remarkable X-series consisting of American figures were introduced. The entire line seems to have been imported only until 1958, though stock may have been sold well into the early 60's. These later figures do not carry the "occupied Japan" label which was no longer required after 1952 when they appeared in the catalogs. Sales seem to have been localized on the East Coast.

The figures of Minikin(s) were all hand painted, though some more precisely than others. Particularly notable was the Highland series and the Samurai. Interestingly, some of the pieces were also partially painted using a spray technique, then details added by hand. While all of the figures came fully painted, certain of the figures noted were also available finished in brass or in silver (catalog suffix "A"). Additionally, three pieces of the catalog are completely different. These include a large scale Samurai helmet, a large brass cannon, and a 4½" brass-finished armored knight. Most all the other figures are 54-58mm scale, except for the Heyde copies which are approximately smaller.

Because Minikin is the only well-cataloged metal figure of Japanese origin, the name is often used mistakenly to describe all figures imported from Japan. This catalog listing will include the entire documented production of Minikin. Only a set of HO scale train figures which has been attributed to Minikin has been omitted. The reader is directed to the Author's series of Articles in the Old Toy Soldier Newsletter, Volumes 5 & 6, for additional information on MINIKIN.

H1 14th-15th Century Knights *(set of 1 mtd, 4 foot)* 45.00	H7 British dragoon mounted, 1850 .... 35.00
H2 Set like H1 with 2 mtd, 4 foot 60.00	H8 British Coldstream Guard, 1742 .... 18.00
H3 Set like H1 with 4 mtd, 4 foot *(Set boxes illustrated with a castle and knights)* single mounted knight 12.00	*The French Colonial series (H9 thru 15)*
	H9 French Artillery Gunner, 1892 .... 18.00
	H10 French Scout ski trooper, 1936 .... 32.00
H4 Norman Knight *(in red, green, yellow, blue, or black tunics* 24.00	H11 French Algerian tirailleur, 1936 .... 25.00
H4-A same, in brass or silver finish. 20.00	H12 French Chasseur, 1917 28.00
H5 Henry the Fourth, mounted 38.00	H13 French fortress gunner, 1939 .... 20.00
H5-A same, in brass or silver finish 32.00	H14 French senegalian Trailluer, 1914 .... 24.00
H6 Napoleon, mounted crossing the Alps 45.00	H15 French Indochinese soldier, 1925 .... 20.00
H6-A same, in brass or silver finish 36.00	H16 The spirit of 1776, 3 figure set *(box decorated with music of Yankee Doodle)* 45.00
	H17 American Indian mounted 33.00

MINIKINS

H18 Anne, Duc de Montmorency, Constable of France *(4½" tall in brass finish, plastic sword)* 50.00

H19 Miamotono Yoritomo, mounted Samurai 45.00

H19-A same, in brass or silver finish 38.00

H20 Samurai warrior on foot, removable weapon *(came in teal or salmon tunic)* 32.00

H21 Japanese Samurai war helmet 30.00
(3" diameter, cloth cords and tassles)

H22 8 pound field piece, brass, 6" in length 45.00

H23 Roman Crusaders, 1203. Set of 2 mounted, 4 foot 48.00
(40mm figures, hollow bases, unusual foot figure with a torch sometimes found)

H24 Tamerlane (1336-1405) 28.00
The Highland series after Pilkington Jackson figures, H25 thru 30)

H25 Officer, 74th regiment, 1846 .... 32.00

H26 Piper, the Black Watch, 1815 .... 32.00

H27 Drummer, 79th Highlanders, 1914 ...... 28.00

H28 Field Officer, Kings Own Scottish Borders, 1689 .... 25.00

H29 Sgt. Major, Gordon Highlanders, 1914 ...... 30.00

H30 Scotsman boxed set *(all 5 figures, blue box and a descriptive historical insert)* 160.00

H31 Historic Hannibal's Elephant Invasion *(9 pcs., 7 foot w/octagon shields, Elephant and howdah, fully illustrated box showing Elephants on barges)* . 240.00

H32 Benkei, the fighting monk, 1180 .... 25.00

H33 Kato Kiyomn Asa, 1560 .... 23.00

H34 Kinoshita Tokichiro, 1560 .... 23.00

H35 no catalog entry

H36 Anayama Kosuko, 1600 .... 23.00

H37 no catalog entry

H38 no catalog entry

The American Revolution Series (see also H-16).

H39 British 40th Rgt., 1776 20.00

H40 Green Mountain Ranger, 1775 .... 20.00

H41 Green Mountain Ranger, private, 1775 ... 20.00

H42 Pennsylvania Rgt., 1777 .... 20.00

H43 Haslet's Delaware Rgt., 1776 .... 22.00

H44 Gunner, Captain John Lambs NY Artillery 25.00

H45 Warrior of the Kinoshita tribe, 1560 ... 25.00

H46 Archer of the Nitano Shiro Tribe 30.00

The Biblical series

B1 The Nativity Set 60.00
(12 figures; barn animals and holy family)

B2 The Three Wise Men .. 38.00

F1 The "barnyard" "F" series 50.00
(horse, cow, donkey, 2 sheep, rooster, 3 chickens, 2 doves also sold individually

The American "X" series

X1 West Point Kaydet (sic.), 1802 .... 12.00

X1-A West Point Kaydet, 1952 .... 12.00

X2 U.S. Horse Marine, Boxer Rebellion, 1900 .. 15.00

All Minikins photos by Will Beierwaltes

H 1-3

389

MINIKINS

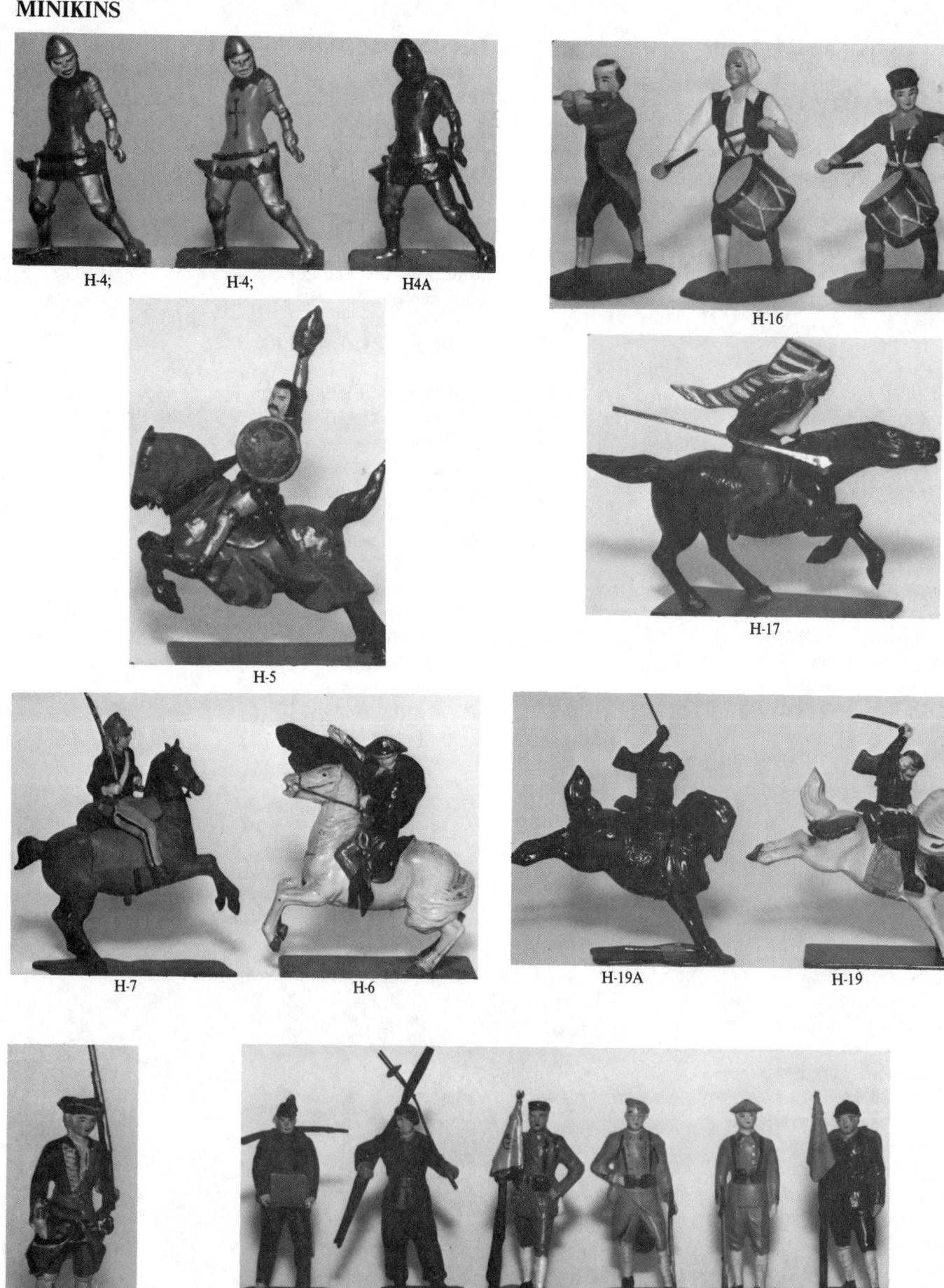

H-4;   H-4;   H4A

H-16

H-5

H-17

H-7   H-6

H-19A   H-19

H-8

H-9   H-10   H-11   H-13   H-15   H-12

H-20   H-32

H-24

H-23

H-29   H-26   H-27   H-28   H-25

H-34   H-33   H-36   H-45   H-46

H-39   H-44   H-40   H-43   H-41   H-42

DANISH MADE TOY SOLDIERS
by Bertel Bruun
(Photos and Captions also by Bertel Bruun)

For its size (5 million inhabitants) and nearness to one of the giants in the toy soldier field, Germany, Denmark has had a quite remarkable number of commercial toy soldier companies, especially in the period immediately following the Second World War. Before that some flats and later solidcast Heydelike figures as well as a number of paper soldiers were made in Denmark, but virtually nothing is written or even known about these. The Danish market was then almost completely dominated by imports from Germany, especially of Heyde and Lineol figures. Other German lead soldier manufacturers as well as Elastolin exported to Denmark, but in lesser quantities.

When WWII ended the German occupation was replaced by a brief period of British occupation. During this brief period the British authorities decreed all German copyrights nul and void in an attempt to strangle any German industrial resurgence in the cradle. The result of this policy was a total failure as is obvious today, but it did result in a freedom for Danish manufacturers to copy anything within sight, especially the previously copyrighted figures by such companies as Lineol and Elastolin. The destruction of Heyde's factory in Dresden at the end of the war effectively knocked that company out of competition. Several Danish companies sprung up to take advantage of this situation.

Of the lead soldier manufacturers Brigader Statuette became outstanding in itself. This company was started in 1946 by Carl Andersen and, until it was closed down in 1977, he designed, cast and, with the help of his wife Ester, painted thousands of lead soldiers to replace Heyde's production. He actually never did that as plastic took over very shortly afterwards and his own production was bought mainly by collectors rather than by children. Andersen produced soldiers of the Danish army in uniforms from the earliest days, but he became most famous for his figures of the Royal Danish Guard in its colorful red and light blue uniform and impressive bearskin hat. Anderson also made foreign troops: English in WWII uniforms, in red and blue uniforms with the tropical pith helmet ably assisted by sepoys in the same uniforms but with turbans and all in action, the Life Guard and the Horse Guard as well as Gordon Highlanders on parade and in action. Germans fought them in their characteristic green WWII uniforms (they were called 'grasshoppers' in Denmark) whereas French troops were depicted in their 'pantaloon rouge' uniforms. More obscure regiments and uniforms were also occasionally made, but these Andersen usually only made to order. Brigader Statuette figures are Heydelike in appearance but recognizable by their very thin armpit area (to better be able to move the arms into the desired position) and their clear and detailed painting. The figures of the Royal Danish Guard now sell for $20-25, other uniforms for somewhat less. Mounted figures cost $30-60 dependent on complexity of painting and rarity. These prices are for mint or close to mint figures of which a surprisingly large number are extant.

Krolyn (ca. 1945 to 1958) made their soldiers in Aluminum obtained initially from broken up German fighter planes sold as scrap immediately after the war. Krolyn mainly copied Lineol and Elastolin figures, Royal Guards, Cowboys and Indians. They did however make some figures of their own design. They had a nice figure of Robin Hood, several knights, mounted and on foot, but are best known for their Vikings (called "Rode Orm" from a novel popular at the time) which are in imaginative and generally ferocious poses. The paint did not fare well on the aluminum surface, but figures with preserved paint are obtainable although very chipped pieces are far more common. The good figures cost $10-20, but prices vary considerably, seemingly with little discernible reason.

Other companies also seem to have made aluminum soldiers at about the same time and of the same format. An attractive little set of Royal Guards by such an unknown company is an example shown here.

Composition figures were also made by several companies, some known, but two with a fairly large production whose figures are readily available.

Danolin (1947-1962) made Danish soldiers in action and Royal Guards on parade as well as a few British WWII soldiers, all based on Lineol's figures, sometimes modified. These soldiers are generally slightly smaller than their Lineol equivalents, but often very well painted. Danolin also made a large variety of animals, some of them virtually indistinguishable from their Lineol counterparts and often as well painted. They cost about 75% of the equivalent Lineol figures - if you can tell the difference!

The other large composition maker was NeoForm (NF) which produced its figures from 1946-1961. The company concentrated on copies of animals, both Lineol and Elastolin. They were made of harder and heavier composition than their German counterparts, probably due to a higher content of Kaolin to make them harder which partially compensated for the lack of metal armaturium. They also made a few original pieces, for instance a Muskox and some, now very rare, Dinosaurus. Their figures are recognizable by the mark "NF" many of them possess, heavy weight and somewhat garish painting. Original NF figures command quite high prices whereas the Lineol and Elastolin copies run at a price 75 - 80% of the original's.

DANISH MADE

Finally, mention should be made of the plastic soldiers (second on the market after Malleable Molds) by Reisler. This company, which was started in 1949 by Kai Reisler and is still in existence, made a large variety of soldiers and animals. They are best known for their Royal Guard figures and the characteristic Danish guardhouse which is particularly attractive. The early painting was very good but has, with time, deteriorated. However, for instance their early camelriders, are quite attractive. These figures are generally very cheap and, if early figures can be found, good bargains at Danish fleamarkets.

Brigader: English Soldier delivering message to officer

Brigader: Danish Dragoon

Krolyn - Ferocious Viking after company's own design

Brigader: Danish Guard - Hussar

Brigader: Royal Danish Guards. Its best known figures

Brigader: Royal Danish Guard presenting arms.

Krolyn - RCMP - here a copy of Elastolin's figure. The horse of Lineol's

Krolyn - Robin Hood. An unique modification of Lineol Indian standing shooting bow.

DANISH MADE

Royal Danish Guard in aluminum by unknown Danish company. Note unusual marching position of musicians.

Danolin: British troops of their own design behind rock copied from Lineol.

Danolin: Danish soldiers in action. All modified copies of Lineol.

Royal Danish Guard. Unmarked but probably Danolin copies of Lineol figures.

JAG (1950-62) produced diecast vehicles, the crew on this one painted as 7th cavalry.

Prairie wagon by JAG. Note metal wire loop under horses allowing vehicle to be moved smoothly without the horses' hooves touching the ground.

Heyde-like Royal Danish Guard figures probably produced by unknown Danish Company post-war.

Reisler: Royal Danish Guard in his characteristic (phallic) Guard house. A continuous best-seller for Reisler.

Reisler: Early camel rider, long out of production.

FRENCH (MISCELLANEOUS)

A fair sprinkling of French-made lead alloy and aluminum soldiers turn up in this country. Particularly notable are the farm figures similar to Manoil's, and the winter figures that suggest Barclay's. The farm figures are about 2⅜" high.

FR1 Farmer with pitchfork	5.00	8.00	11.00	FR39 Man carrying Skis ..	11.00	16.00	22.00
FR2 Farmer cutting grain	5.00	8.00	10.00	FR40 Man Skiing	11.00	16.00	22.00
FR3 Farm woman with				FR41 Walking Skier	11.00	16.00	22.00
pitchfork	5.00	8.00	10.00	FR42 Rider on Bucking			
FR4 Farmer raking	5.00	8.00	10.00	Horse (Frenchal)		No Price Found	
FR5 Farm Woman tying				FR43 Rider on Rearing			
sheaf	4.00	6.00	8.00	Horse (Frenchal)		No Price Found	
FR6 Farm Woman				FR44 Trotter (Frenchal) ...		No Price Found	
gathering	4.00	6.00	8.00	FR45 Jockey on Horseback			
FR7 Farmer walking with				(Frenchal)		No Price Found	
scythe	5.00	8.00	10.00				
FR8 Farmer with axe	5.00	8.00	10.00				
FR9 Farm woman raking? .	5.00	8.00	10.00				
FR10 Farmer sharpening							
Scythe	5.00	8.00	10.00				
FR11 Farmer sowing grain	4.00	6.00	8.00				
FR12 Farm Woman hoeing?							
....	4.00	6.00	8.00				
FR13 Scarecrow	6.00	9.00	12.00				
FR14 Farmer watering	6.00	9.00	12.00				
FR15 Farmer walking with							
staff	6.00	9.00	12.00				
FR16 Farmer walking with							
cane	5.00	8.00	11.00				
FR17 Old Man with staff .	6.00	9.00	12.00				
FR18 Blacksmith	6.00	9.00	12.00				
FR19 Milk Maid	4.00	6.00	9.00				
FR20 Woman with eggs? ..	5.00	8.00	10.00				
FR21 Farmer with cart ...	7.00	11.00	15.00				
FR22 Farmer with							
wheelbarrow	6.00	9.00	12.00				
FR23 Foot Bridge	11.00	16.00	22.00				
FR24 Racetrack Bugler ...		No Price Found					
FR25 Indian Standing							
Firing	15.00	22.00	30.00				
FR26 Farm Horse pulling .	3.00	5.00	7.00				
FR27 Donkey and Cart ...		No Price Found					
FR28 Stack of Sheaves		No Price Found					
FR29 Farmer Sitting	4.00	7.00	9.00				
FR30 Farm Woman Sitting	4.00	7.00	9.00				
FR31 Bench		No Price Found					
FR32 Jockey, smaller size .		No Price Found					
FR33 Indian Kneeling							
Firing	15.00	22.00	30.00				
FR34 Child on Swing	25.00	38.00	50.00				
FR35 Farm Woman with							
basket and umbrella	5.00	8.00	10.00				
FR36 Farmer Drinking ...	5.00	8.00	10.00				
FR37 Woman Sitting On							
Sled	10.00	15.00	20.00				
FR38 Man Lying on Sled .	10.00	15.00	20.00				

FR1   FR2   FR3   FR4   FR5

FR6 FR7 FR8   FR9   FR10   FR11
Courtesy Charlie O'Brien

FR12   FR13   FR14   FR15   FR16   FR17

FR18   FR19 FR20   FR21   FR22
Courtesy Charlie O'Brien

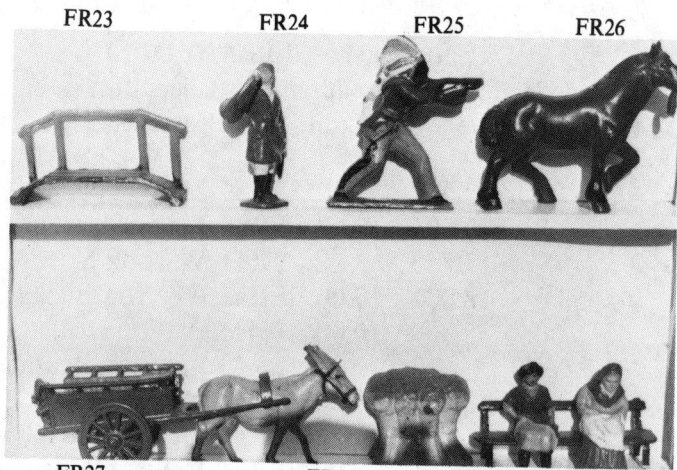

FR23   FR24   FR25   FR26

FR27   FR28   FR29-31
Courtesy Charlie O'Brien

FR33
Courtesy K. Warren Mitchell

FR34   FR35

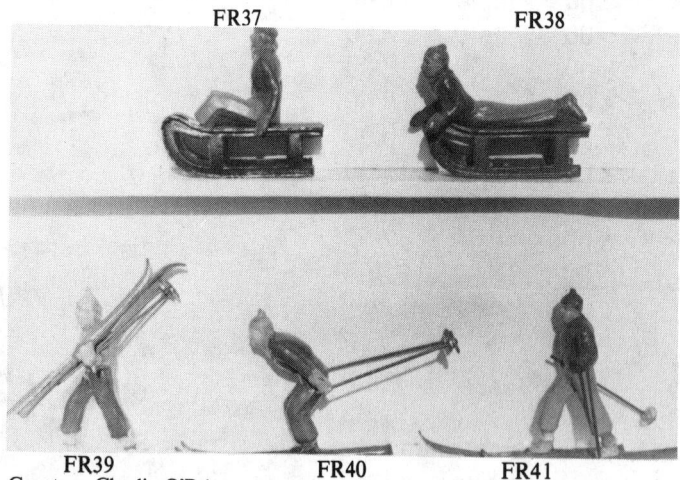

FR37   FR38

FR39   FR40   FR41
Courtesy Charlie O'Brien

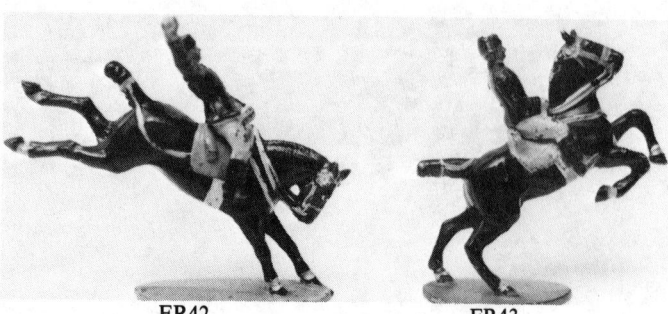

FR42   FR43
These are by Frenchal, and a little larger than Britains.
Photo by Harold Haseley

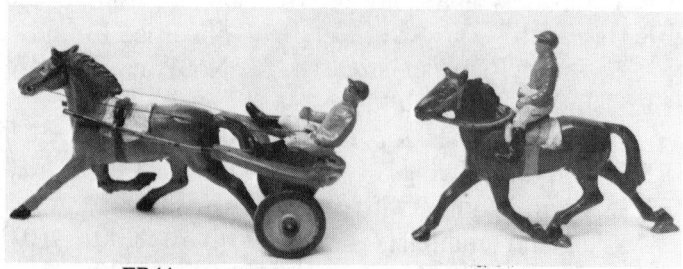

FR44   FR45
These are by Frenchal, and a little larger than Britains.
Photo by Harold Haseley

MIGNOT

The toy soldiers of Mignot fall into the connoisseur category; rarely do they turn up in general collections of toy soldiers.

Although the company has produced in a haphazard, almost cottage-industry fashion from the beginning, it is the longest-surviving of all toy soldier companies, so old that its origins have faded into the mists of time.

Some collectors trace it back to before 1789 when the firm of Lucotte was in business (Mignot took over Lucotte in 1928.) Others suggest 1825 as the date, as CBG (Cuperly, Blondel and Gerbeau) appears to have been founded in that year, becoming Gerbeau and (Henri) Mignot in 1900.

Most of Mignot's soldiers, all of them produced in Paris, are solidcast in a 55mm size. However, the company has also produced flats in 12mm to 30m sizes, semi-flats in 32mm and 40mm, some hollowcast 55mm pieces, and still others in a larger size.

Mignots are not always easy to identify. The heads are usually plugged in, but that fact is often obscured by the paint. The arms, unlike some of the other 54 and 55mm companies', don't move, and the weapons and other equipment are often separate castings which have been soldered to the figure.

Bases are usually square, and generally without markings, except for some which have paper labels marked "Made in France." Some are marked "CBG" and others, the Lucottes (Mignot continued to manufacture them under that name,) marked with an L and a C sandwiching an Imperial Bee.

Another feature of Mignots to watch out for is a certain delicacy of physique (somewhat like Heyde, but considerably more symmetrical); the bodies tend to be more slender than the average toy soldier's, often with very narrow waists. The faces, too, tend to be somewhat thin. Often, unlike most toy soldiers, Mignot's walking figures have the right foot forward.

Since Mignots are still being produced it may be helpful to note that in general the older figures have grey to greyish tan bases, graduating to a dark brown in some of the current sets.

Mignots have always been expensive here, but particularly so after the Second World War. Before the war, a box of 12 infantry sold for about two dollars, approximately double the price of Britains. However, after the war, a box of 12 infantry was priced at $9.25, as compared to $2.00 for a set of Britains. For that reason, Mignots are rare.

The following lists are courtesy of Donald P. Grant, the editor-publisher of the Mignot-Lucotte Historical Review (no longer published). In later years Mignot changed some of its numberings; numbers in parentheses indicate the change. For space reasons, Grant's listings have been condensed, but will perhaps be run in full in a later edition.

Prices given are for full sets, in boxes. Single foot figures average $20 and single mounted $30. Since Mignots tend to turn up in mint condition, that is the price used here. Lesser conditions would average about half mint in Good, with Very Good lying midway between. Prices shown where found.

Get out the magnifying glass for this one! It's Mignot's "War of the Worlds" diorama, which sold at Christie's New York auction in 1985 for $3300. Courtesy Christie's New York

397

55mm Military Figures Produced BY C.B.G.-MIGNOT FROM 1911 TO SPRING 1986
by Donald P. Grant

M

01 Egyptians, 1000 B.C. ...	200.00
02 Assyrians, 600 B.C., marching	200.00
03 Greeks, 400 B.C., marching	200.00
04 Gauls, 100 B.C., in combat	200.00
05 Romans, 100 B.C., marching	200.00
06 Franks, 6th-7th Cent. marching	175.00
07 Crusaders, 11-12th Cent., marching	180.00
08 Saracens, 11-12th Cent.,	200.00
09 Archers, 13-14th Cent., marching	200.00
10 Archers in Combat, 13th & 14th Cents., ...	180.00
10/A English Archers, 13th & 14th Cents., ...	180.00
10/B English Archers in combat, 13th & 14th Cents	175.00
11 Knights on foot marching, 14th Cent., ...	180.00
12 Halberdiers standing, 15th Cent	200.00
13 Infantry Marching, Francis 1st, 16th Cent	200.00
14 Pikesmen Marching, Henry IV, 17th Cent ...	200.00
15 Musketeers Marching, Louis XIII, 17th Cent ..	200.00
16 French Guards, Louis XIV, 1670	200.00
17 Champagne Regiment, Louis XIV, 1670	200.00
18 Swiss Guards, Louis XIV, 1670	280.00
19 French Guards, Louis XV, 1740	325.00
20 Touraine Regiment, Louis XV, 1740	
21 Swiss Guards, Louis XV, 1740	
21/A French Guards, Louis XVI, 1789	
21/B National Guards, Louis XVI, 1789	
21/C Swiss Guards, Louis XVI, 1789	100.00
22 Volunteers Marching, 1793	

22/A Revolutionaries, 1793; assorted civilian dress, severed heads carried on bloody pikes	250.00
22/B Volunteers standing firing 1793	
22/C Volunteers assaulting, 1793	
23 Infantry marching 1794	
24 Chasseurs on foot, 1794	
25 Infantry, Egyptian Campaign, 1799	200.00
26 Grenadiers of the Guard, marching, 1812	200.00
26/A Grenadiers of the Guard, standing firing, 1812	
26/B Grenadiers of the Guard assaulting, 1812 ..	200.00
27 Grenadiers of the Guard at attention, 1812	
28 Grenadiers of the Guard, Sappers and Drummers, 1812	225.00
28/A Grenadiers of the Guard, Sappers, 1812 ...	200.00
28/B Grenadiers of the Guard, Drummers and Drum-Major, 1812	200.00
29 Fusiliers of the Military School of Saint-Cyr marching, 1812	200.00
29/A Fusiliers of the Military School of Saint-Cyr firing, 1812	
29/B Fusiliers of the Military School of Saint-Cyr assaulting, 1812	
30 Voltigeuers (Skirmishers) of the Guard marching at slope, 1812	200
30/A Voltigeurs of the Guard assaulting, 1812 ..	
30/B Voltigeurs of the Guard standing firing, 1812	
31 Marines of the Guard marching, 1812	200.00
31/A Voltigeurs of the 33rd Regiment of the Line, marching, 1812	200.00
31/B Flankers of the Guard, marching, 1812	

MIGNOT

31/H Marines of the Guard at attention, 1812	200.00
31/J Voltigeurs of the 33rd Regiment of the Line, at attention, 1812	200.00
32 Engineers of the Guard, marching, 1812	100.00
32/H Engineers of the Guard at attention, 1812	
33 Dragoons of the Guard, marching (on foot), 1812	100.00
33/A Dragoons of the 17th Regiment of the Line, marching, 1812	200.00
33/B Orphans of the Guard, 5th Battalion, marching, 1812	200.00
33/K Orphans of the Guard, 5th Battalion, at attention, 1812	
34 Voltigeurs of the Light Infantry, marching, 1809	200.00
34/A Voltigeurs of the Light Infantry, standing firing, 1809	
34/B Voltigeurs of the Light Infantry, assaulting, 1809	250.00
34/C Band of the Chasseurs of the 17th Regiment of Light Infantry, 1809	
35 Infantry of the Line marching, 1809	
35/A Infantry of the Line standing firing, 1809	
35/B Infantry of the Line assaulting, 1809	
36 Voltigeurs of the 17th Regiment of the Line, 1809	
36/A Guard of the Department of Paris, 1810	200.00
36/B Voltigeur assaulting, running with one foot on the ground	
36/C Voltigeur standing firing	
36/P Officer wearing fore-and-aft bicorne hat	
36/Q Standard bearer wearing fore-and-aft bicorne hat	
36/S Sapper wearing tall bearskin hat and leather apron	
36/Y Voltigeur, wounded, rifle in right hand, falling with one foot raised and one on ground	
37 Grenadiers of the Line marching, 1809	
37/A Artillery Crew in firing positions, 1809	150.00
38 Italian Grenadiers marching, 1810	200.00
38/A Legion of the Vistula, 1809	
38/F Chasseurs of the Italian Guard assaulting, running on one foot, 1810	200.00
38/J Legion of the Vistula, at attention, 1809	
39 Italian Light Infantry, Regiment of Beauharnais, 1810	200.00
40 Dutch Grenadiers, marching, 1812	200.00
40/A Band of the 3rd Regiment of Grenadiers of the Guard, formerly Dutch Grenadiers, 1809	225.00
40/B Drum Major and Drummers of the 3rd Regiment of Grenadiers, 1812	
41 Dutch Grenadiers at attention, 1812	250.00
41/A 4th Swiss Regiment, 1812, marching	200.00
41/B Imperial Guard of Strasbourg, 1805	
41/C 1st Regiment of Isembourg, 1806	
41/J 4th Swiss Regiment at attention, 1812	
41/K 1st Regiment of Isembourg at attention, 1806 .	
42 Band of the Grenadiers of the Guard, 1805	250.00
42/A Band of the Imperial Guard of Strasbourg, 1805	225.00
43 Austrian Infantry marching, 1800	200.00
43/A Austrian Infantry standing firing, 1800	
43/B Austrian Infantry assaulting, 1800	250.00

43/H Austrian Infantry at attention, 1800 . . . .

44 English Infantry marching, 1812 . . . . 200.00

44/A English Infantry standing firing, 1812 . . . .

44/B English Infantry assaulting, 1812 . . . . 200.00

45 Russian Grenadiers marching, 1812 . . . . 200.00

45/A 8th Bavarian Regiment marching, 1812 . . . . 200.00

45/B Russian Grenadiers standing firing, 1812 . . . .

45/C Russian Grenadiers assaulting, 1812 . . . .

45/E 18th Prussian Regiment of the Line, 1806 . . 200.00

45/H Russian Grenadiers at attention, 1812 . . . .

45/K 8th Bavarian Regiment at attention, 1812 . . . . . .

46 Chasseurs on foot, 2nd Empire period, 1860 . . . .

47 Infantry of the Line, 2nd Empire period, 1860 . . . .

47/A Colonial Infantry marching, 1880 . . . . 200.00

47/B 2nd Regiment of the Foreign Legion in Mexico, 1863 . . . . 200.00

47/M Colonial Infantry assaulting with one foot off the ground, 1880 . . . .

47/N Colonial Infantry standing firing, 1880 . . . .

47/P Colonial Infantry kneeling firing, 1880 . . . .

47/Q Colonial Infantry lying firing, 1880 . . . .

48 Confederates marching in kepis with slung rifles, 1863 . . . .

48/A Confederates marching, kepis, slope arms, 1863 . .

48/B Confederates marching, brim hats, slope arms, 1863 . . . .

48/C Confederates marching with brim hats, slung rifle, 1863 . . . .

49 Confederates standing firing, in kepis, 1863 . . . . . .

49/B Confederates firing, brim hats, 1863 . . . .

50 Confederates assaulting, kepis, 1863 . . . .

50/B Confederate Infantry assaulting, brim hats, 1863 . . . .

51 Confederates kneeling firing, kepis, 1863 . . . .

51/B Confederates kneeling firing, brim hats, 1863 . .

52 U.S. Army marching, kepi, 1863 . . . . 200.00

53 U.S. Army standing firing, kepi, 1863 . . . . 180.00

54 U.S. Army assaulting, kepi, 1863 . . . . 200.00

55 U.S. Army kneeling firing, kepi, 1863 . . . .

56 Confederate Labor Battalion, kepi, 1863 . . . . . .

57 U.S. Army Labor Battalion, kepi, 1863 . . . . . .

57/A Confederate Artillery Crew, kepi, 1863 . . . . 100.00

57/B U.S. Army Artillery Crew, kepi, 1863 . . . . 100.00

57/R Confederate Artillery Crew, red kepi, 1863 . . .

57/S Confederate Artillery Crew, brim hats, 1863 . .

58 Infantry of the Line in tunic, marching, 1914 . . . 150.00

58/A Infantry of the Line in overcoat, marching, 1914 . 150.00

58/B Infantry of the Line assaulting, 1914 . . . . 150.00

58/C Infantry of the Line standing firing, 1914 . . . .

58/D Infantry of the Line kneeling firing, 1914 . . . .

58/E Infantry of the Line lying firing, 1914 . . . .

58/F Infantry of the Line in overcoats running, one foot off ground, 1914 . . .

58/G Motorcyclist, 1914 . . .

58/H Machine Gunner and Machine Gun, 1914 . . . .

58/J Infantry of the Line, 1914, red kepi . . . .

58/X Bicyclists riding 1914 .

58/Y Bicyclists standing next to bicycles, 1914 . . . .

58/W Wounded, 1914 . . . .

59 Labor Battalion or Fatigue Party, 1914, red trousers, red kepi 450.00

59/B Chasseurs on foot, in tunic, marching, 1914 . . .

59/M Labor Battalion, blue trousers, kepis, 1916 . . . .

59/N Labor Battalion, steel helmets, 1916 . . . .

60 Band of the Line, tunic, kepis, 1914 . . . .

60/C Band of the Line, overcoats, kepis, 1914 . . . . . .

61 Zouaves, blue and red uniform, marching, 1914

61/A Band of the Zouaves, blue and red uniform, 1914 . . . .

61/B Zouaves, blue and red uniform, assaulting, 1914

61/C Zouaves, khaki, steel helmets, assaulting, 1915

61/D Zouaves, blue and red uniform, standing firing, 1914 . . . .

61/E Zouaves, blue and red uniform, standing firing, 1914 . . . .

61/F Zouaves, blue and red uniform, lying firing, 1914 . . . .

61/G Zouaves, khaki uniform, steel helmets, standing firing, 1915 . . . .

61/H Zouaves, khaki uniform, steel helmets, kneeling firing, 1915 . . . .

61/J Zouaves, khaki uniform, steel helmets, lying firing, 1915 . . . .

61/K Zouaves, khaki uniform, steel helmets, marching, 1915 . . . .

62 Turcos, blue uniforms, marching, 1914 . . . .

62/A Band of the Turcos, blue uniforms, 1914 . . . .

62/B Turcos, blue uniforms, standing firing, 1914 . . . .

62/C Turcos, blue uniforms, assaulting, 1914 . . . .   200.00

62/D Turcos, blue uniforms, kneeling firing, 1914 . . . .

62/E Turcos, blue uniforms, lying firing, 1914 . . . .

62/F Turcos, khaki uniforms, standing firing, 1915 . . . .

62/G Turcos, khaki uniform, assaulting, 1915 . . . .

62/H Turcos, khaki uniform, kneeling firing, 1915 . . . .

62/J Turcos, khaki uniforms, lying firing, 1915 . . . .

62/K Turcos, khaki uniform, marching, 1915 . . . .

63 Cuirassiers on foot, 1914   150.00

63/H Cuirassiers on foot, horizon blue, 1915 . . . . .

64 Infantry of the Line, blue, marching, overcoat, 1915 . . . .   200.00

64/A Infantry of the Line, blue, assaulting, 1915 . . .

64/B Infantry of the Line, blue, assaulting, 1915 . . .

64/C Infantry of the Line, blue, lying firing, 1915 . .

64/D Infantry of the Line, blue, kneeing firing, 1915

64/E Infantry of the Line, blue, at attention, rifle at present arms, 1915 . . . . .

64/F Infantry of the Line, blue tunic, marching, 1915 . . . .   150.00

64/G Motorcyclists, blue, steel helmet, 1915 . . . . . .   185.00

64/H Machine Gunner and Hotchkiss Machine Gun, 1915 . . . .   170.00

64/J Exercise Uniform, 1915

64/K Line Infantry, khaki uniform, steel helmet, 1935 . . . .

64/L Band of Infantry of the Line, khaki uniform, steel helmets, 1935 . . . .

64/M Band of the Line, blue, steel helmets, 1915 .

64/N Men throwing grenade, blue, steel helmet, 1915 .

64/P Infantry of the Line, running one foot off ground, at slope, blue, 1915 . . . .

64/Q Line Infantry with slung rifles, blue, 1915 . .

64/R Line Infantry at attention, rifle at foot, blue, 1915 . . . .

64/U French Soldier, with wounded Prisoner of War,

blue, steel helmet,
Prussian is 75/Z, khaki,
spiked helmet, 1915 ....

64/W Wounded, blue, 1915

64/X Bicyclists, blue, riding
bicycle, 1915 ....

64/Y Bicyclists, blue, standing by bicycle, 1915 ...

64/Z Medical Unit, blue,
1915 ....

65 Artillery Crew, blue,
1915 .... 120.00

65/B Artillery Crew, dark
blue, 1914 .... 120.00

66 Saint-Cyrians, 1900 .... 150.00

67 Foreign Legion, khaki
uniforms, white kepis,
marching, 1914 .... 225.00

67/A Foreign Legion, khaki,
white kepis, standing firing, 1914 ....

67/B Foreign Legion, khaki,
white kepis, assaulting,
1914 .... 150.00

67/C Foreign Legion, khaki,
white kepis, kneeling firing, 1914 ....

67/D Foreign Legion, khaki,
white kepis, lying firing,
1914 ....

67/E Band of the Foreign
Legion, khaki, white
kepis, 1914 ....

67/H Foreign Legion
Machine Gunner and
Gun, khaki, white kepi,
1914 ....

68 Guards of Paris, 1900 ..

69 Band of the Guards of
Paris, 1900 .... 120.00

70 Alpine Chasseurs, white,
marching with cane, 1914 190.00

70/A Band of the Alpine
Chasseurs, white
uniforms, 1914 ....

70/B Alpine Chasseurs,
white uniform, mule car-
rying mountain cannon
barrel, plus pine tree,
1914 ....

70/C Alpine Chasseurs,
white uniform, mule
carrying mountain cannon

trail, plus pine tree, 1914

70/D Alpine Chasseurs,
white uniform, mule
carrying wheels of moun-
tain cannon, plus pine
tree, 1914 ....

70/E Alpine Chasseurs,
white uniforms, skiers,
plus pine tree, 1914 ....

70/F Alpine Chasseurs,
white uniforms, mule car-
rying ammunition boxes
for mountain cannon,
plus pine tree, 1914 ....

70/H Alpine Chasseurs, blue,
marching, 1914-18 ......

70/J Alpine Chasseurs, blue,
mule carrying mountain
cannon barrel, 1914-18 ..

70/K Alpine Chasseurs, blue,
mule carrying mountain
cannon trail, 1914-18 ...

70/L Alpine Chasseurs, blue,
mule carrying mountain
cannon wheels, 1914-18 .

70/M Alpine Chasseurs,
blue, mule carrying am-
munition boxes for moun-
tain cannon, 1914-18 ...

70/N Alpine Chasseurs, blue,
assaulting, 1914-18 .....

70/P Alpine Chasseurs, blue,
standing firing, 1914-18 .

70/Q Alpine Chasseurs, blue,
kneeling firing, 1914-18 .

70/R Alpine Chasseurs, blue,
lying firing, 1914-18 ....

70/S Alpine Chasseurs, blue,
artillerymen in action,
1914-18 ....

70/Z Alpine infantry skiers,
dark blue tunic, red
trousers, blue beret, 1900

71 Alpine Chasseurs, blue
uniform, marching with
cane, 1914 .... 190.00

71/A Band of the Alpine
Chasseurs, blue uniform,
1914 ....

71/B Alpine Chasseurs, blue
unform, mule carrying
barrel of mountain can-
non, plus pine tree, 1914

MIGNOT

71/C Alpine Chasseurs, blue uniform, mule carrying mountain cannon trail, plus pine tree, 1914 . . . .

71/D Alpine Chasseurs, white uniform, mule carrying wheels of mountain cannon, plus pine tree, 1914 . . . .

71/E Alpine Chasseurs, white uniforms, skiers, plus pine tree, 1914 . . . . .   70.00

71/F Alpine Chasseurs, white uniform, mule carrying ammo boxes for mountain cannon, 1914 .

71/G Alpine Artillerymen, dark blue uniform, red trim, 1914 . . . .   71/N

71/N Alpine Chasseurs, blue overcoat, mule carrying barrel of mountain cannon, plus pine tree, 1914

71/P Alpine Chasseurs, blue overcoat, mule carrying mountain cannon trail, plus pine tree, 1914 . . . .

71/Q Alpine Chasseurs, blue overcoat, mule carrying wheels of mountain cannon, plus pine tree, 1914

71/R Alpine Chasseurs, blue overcoat, mule carrying ammo boxes for mountain cannon, plus pine tree, 1914 . . . .

71/T Alpine Chasseurs, blue uniforms, assaulting, 1914 . . . .

71/U Alpine Chasseurs, blue uniforms, standing firing, 1914 . . . .

71/V Alpine Chasseurs, blue uniforms, kneeling firing, 1914 . . . .

71/W Alpine Chasseurs, blue uniforms, lying firing, 1914 . . . .

71/Z Alpine Chasseurs, dark blue tunic, white trousers, 1900 . . . .

72 Sailors, white uniforms, marching, 1914 . . . .

72/A Sailors, white uniforms, assaulting, 1914   180.00

72/B Sailors, white uniforms, standing firing, 1914 . . . .

72/C Sailors, white uniforms, kneeling firing, 1914 . . . .

72/D Sailors, white uniforms, lying firing, 1914 . . . .

72/M Naval Band, white uniforms, 1914 . . . .

72/N Sailors, white uniforms, labor batallion, 1914 . . . .

73 Sailors, blue uniforms, marching, 1914 . . . .   180.00

73/A Sailors, blue uniforms, assaulting, 1914 . . . .   180.00

73/B Sailors, blue uniforms, standing firing, 1914 . . . .

73/C Sailors, blue uniforms, kneeling firing, 1914 . . . .

73/D Sailors, blue uniforms, lying firing, 1914 . . . .

73/M Naval Band, blue uniforms, 1914 . . . .

73/N Sailors, blue uniforms, labor batallion, 1914 . . . .

74 Marine Fusiliers, marching, 1914 . . . .

74/A Marine Fusiliers, assaulting, 1914 . . . .

74/B Marine Fusiliers, standing firing, 1914 . . . .

74/C Marine Fusiliers, kneeling firing, 1914 . . . .

74/D Marine Fusiliers, lying firing, 1914 . . . .

75 Prussian Infantry, marching, khaki, spiked helmets, 1914 . . . .

75/A Prussian Infantry, assaulting, khaki, spiked helmet, 1914   250.00

75/B Prussian Infantry, standing firing, khaki, spiked helmet, 1914 . . . .   250.00

75/C Prussian Infantry, kneeling firing, khaki, spiked helmet, 1914 . . . .

75/D Prussian Infantry, lying firing, khaki, spiked helmet, 1914 . . . .

75/G Prussian Motorcyclist, khaki, spiked helmet, 1914 . . . .

75/H Prussian Machine Gunner, khaki, spiked helmet, 1914 . . . .

MIGNOT

75/M Prussian Infantry Band, khaki uniforms, spiked helmet, 1914 .... 250.00

75/W Prussian Infantry, wounded, khaki, spiked helmet, 1914 ....

75/V French Aviators, 1914-18 ....

75X Prussian Bicyclist, khaki, spiked helmet, 1914 ....

75Z Prussian Prisoners of War with hands raised, 1914, two with hands raised, one held and assisted by French soldier

76 Highlanders Marching, 1900 ....

76/A Highlanders Assaulting, 1900 ....

76/B Highlanders Standing firing, 1900 ....

76/K Highlanders, khaki, steel helmets, 1914 .....

77 West Point Cadets, winter uniforms, 20th century 125.00

78 West Point Cadets, summer uniforms, 20th century 125.00

79 Prussians, khaki, steel helmets, marching, 1914 .

79/A Prussians, khaki, steel helmets, assaulting, 1914

79/B Prussians, khaki, steel helmets, kneeling firing, 1914 ....

79/C Prussians, khaki, steel helmets, kneeling firing, 1914 ....

79/D Prussians, khaki, steel helmets, lying firing, 1914

79/G Prussians, khaki, steel helmets, motorcyclist, 1914 ....

79/H Prussians, khaki, steel helmets, machine gunner, 1914 ....

79/M Prussians, khaki, steel helmets, Band, 1914 ....

79/W Prussians, khaki, steel helmets, wounded, 1914 .

79/X Prussians, khaki, steel helmets, bicyclist, 1914 ..

80 Firemen Marching, 20th century ....

80/B Firemen in action positions, 20th century ....

81 Prussian Infantry, marching, field gray, steel helmets, 1914 ....

81/A Prussian Infantry, assaulting, field gray, steel helmets, 1914 ....

81/B Prussian Infantry, standing firing, field gray, steel helmets, 1914 .....

81/C Prussian Infantry, kneeling firing, field gray, steel helmets, 1914 .....

81/D Prussian Infantry, lying firing-field gray, steel helmets, 1914 ....

81/G Prussian Motorcyclist, field gray, steel helmets, 1914 ....

81/H Prussian Machine Gunner, field gray, steel helmet, 1914 ....

81/M Prussian Infantry Band, field gray, steel helmets, 1914 ....

81/W Prussian Infantry, wounded, field gray, steel helmets, 1914 ....

81/X Prussian Bicyclist, field gray, steel helmets, 1914

82 Prussian Infantry, marching, blue tunics, spiked helmets, 1914 ....

82/A Prussian Infantry, assaulting, blue tunics, spiked helmets, 1914 ....

82/B Prussian Infantry, standing firing, blue tunics, spiked helmets, 1914 ....

82/C Prussian Infantry, kneeling firing, blue tunics, spiked helmets, 1914 ....

82/D Prussian Infantry, lying firing, blue tunics, spiked helmets, 1914 ....

82/G Prussian Motorcyclist, blue tunics, spiked helmets, 1914 ....

82/H Prussian Machine Gunner, blue tunic, spiked helmets, 1914 ....

82/M Prussian Infantry Band, blue tunic, spiked helmets, 1914 ....

MIGNOT

82/W Prussian Infantry, wounded, blue tunic, spiked helmets, 1914 ....

82/X Prussian Bicyclist, blue tunic, spiked helmets, 1914 ....

83 Goumiers on foot marching, 1900 .... 200.00

84 Touregs marching, 1900 200.00

84/A Touregs standing, firing, 1900 ....

85 Annamites Marching, 1914 ....

86 Senegalese marching, blue, steel helmets, 1915 .

86/A Senegalese Assaulting, blue, steel helmets, 1915 .

86/B Senegalese standing firing, blue, steel helmets, 1915 ....

86/C Senegalese kneeling firing, blue, steel helmets, 1915 ....

86/D Senegalese lying firing, blue, steel helmets, 1915 .

86/P Senegalese Tirailleurs, assaulting, blue tunic, red cap, 1900 ....

86/Q Senegalese Tirailleurs, firing, blue tunic, red fez, 1900 ....

86/R Senegalese Tirailleurs, kneeling firing, blue tunic, red fez, 1900 ....

86/S Senegalese Tirailleurs, lying firing, blue tunic, red fez, 1900 ....

86/T Senegalese Tirailleurs, marching, blue tunic, red fez, 1900 ....

87 Africans firing, 1900 ...

88 Sakalaves standing firing, 1900 .... 200.00

89 Dahomeyans, 1900 ....

90 Siamese Guards, marching, 1900 ....

91 Sudanese marching, 1900 .... 200.00

91/A Sudanese firing, 1900

92 Tonkinese firing, 1900 ..

93 Hindus marching, khaki, 1914 .... 200.00

93/A Hindus assaulting, khaki, 1914 ....

93/B Hindus standing firing, khaki, 1914 ....

94 Boy Scouts, 1900 ......

95 Americans, khaki, marching, montana hats, 1917 ....

95/A Americans, khaki, assaulting, montana hats, 1917 ....

95/B American Band, khaki, montana hats, 1917 .... 225.00

95/C Americans, khaki, standing firing, montana hats, 1917 ....

95/D Americans, khaki, kneeling firing, montana hats, 1917 ....

95/E Americans, khaki, lying firing, montana hats, 1917

95/H American machine gunners, khaki, montana hats, 1917 ....

95/X American bicyclists, khaki, montana hats, 1917 ....

95/Y American bicyclists, khaki, montana hats, 1917 ....

95/Z American stretcher bearers, stretcher and wounded man, 1918 ....

96 Canadians, khaki, marching, 1914 .... 150.00

96/A Canadians, khaki, assaulting, 1914 ....

96/B Canadians, khaki, standing firing, 1914 ......

96/C Canadians, khaki, kneeling firing, 1914 ....

96/D Canadians, khaki, lying firing, 1914 ....

97 Greek Infantry, khaki, marching, 1914 ....

97/A Greek Infantry, khaki, assaulting, 1914 ....

97/B Greek Infantry, khaki, standing firing, 1914 ....

97/C Greek Infantry, khaki, kneeling firing, 1914 ....

97/D Greek Infantry, khaki, lying firing, 1914 ....

97/N Greeks, blue tunics, kepi with white plume, marching, 1900 ....

97/P Greeks, blue tunics, kepi with white plume, assaulting, 1900 ....

97/Q Greeks, blue tunics, kepi with white plume, standing firing, 1900 . . . .

97/R Greeks, blue tunics, kepi with white plume, kneeling firing, 1900 . . . .

97/S Greeks, blue tunics, kepi with white plume, lying firing, 1900 . . . .

98 Japanese Infantry, marching, 1900 . . . .

98/A Japanese assaulting, 1900 . . . .

98/B Japanese standing firing, 1900 . . . .

98/C Japanese kneeling firing, 1900 . . . .

98/D Japanese lying firing, 1900 . . . .

98/W Japanese wounded, two positions, 1900 . . . . .

99 Chinese, marching, 1900   250.00

99/A Chinese assaulting, 1900 . . . .

99/B Chinese standing firing, 1900

100 Americans marching, khaki, helmet, 1917 . . . .

100/A Americans assaulting, khaki, helmet, 1917 . . . .

100/B Americans standing, firing, khaki, helmet, 1917

100/C Americans kneeling firing, khaki, helmet, 1917

100/D Americans lying firing, khaki, helmet, 1917 .

100/X American bicyclists, riding, khaki, steel helmets, 1918 . . . .

100/Y American bicyclists, standing by bikes, khaki, helmet, 1918 . . . .

101 Prussian Chasseurs assaulting, 1914 . . . .

101/B Prussian Chasseurs standing firing, 1914 . . . .

101/C Prussian Chasseurs kneeling firing, 1914 . . . .

101/D Prussian Chasseurs lying firing, 1914 . . . .

101/E Prussian Chasseurs marching, 1914 . . . .

102/A Russian Infantry assaulting, overcoat, peakless cap, 1914 . . . . . .

102/B Russian Infantry standing firing, peakless cap, 1914 . . . .

102/C Russian Infantry kneeling firing, 1914 . . . .

102/D Russian Infantry lying firing, 1914 . . . .

102/E Russian Infantry marching, 1914 . . . .

102/F Russian Infantry assaulting, 1914 . . . .

102/G Russian Infantry standing firing, white cap, 1914 . . . .

102/H Russian Infantry kneeling firing, white cap, 1914 . . . .

102/J Russian Infantry lying firing, white cap, 1914 . .

102/K Russian Infantry marching, white cap, 1914 . .

102/L Russian Infantry assaulting, fur hat, overcoat, 1914 . . . .

102/M Russian Infantry standing firing, fur hat, overcoat, 1914 . . . .

102/N Russian Infantry kneeling firing, fur hat, overcoat, 1914 . . . .

102/P Russians, Pavlowski Regt., 1900 . . . .

102/Q Russians, Grenadiers, 1900 . . . .

102/R Russians lying firing, overcoat, fur hat, 1914 . .

102/S Russians marching, overcoat, fur hat, 1914 (produced?) . . . .

102/T Russians in tunics, marching, 1900 . . . .

102/U Russians marching, tunic, white cap . . . .

102/V Russians marching, tunic, fur hat . . . .

103 Rumanian Infantry marching, 1914 . . . .

103/A Rumanian Infantry assaulting, 1914 . . . .

103/B Rumanian Infantry standing firing, 1914 . . . .

103/C Rumanian Infantry kneeling firing, 1914 . . . .

103/D Rumanian Infantry lying firing, 1914 . . . .

MIGNOT

103/P Rumanian Infantry
marching, 1900 . . . .
103/Q Rumanian Infantry
assaulting, 1900 . . . .
103/R Rumanian Infantry
standing firing, 1900 . . . .
103/S Rumanian Infantry
kneeling firing, 1900 . . . .
103/T Rumanian Infantry
lying firing, 1900 . . . .
104 Serbian Infantry mar-
ching, 1914 . . . .
104/A Serbian Infantry
assaulting, 1914 . . . .
104/B Serbian Infantry standing firing, 1914 . . . .
104/C Serbian Infantry
kneeling firing, 1914 . . . .
104/D Serbian Infantry lying
firing, 1914 . . . .
104/P Serbian Infantry marching, 1900 . . . .
104/Q Serbian Infantry
assaulting, 1900 . . . .
104/R Serbian Infantry standing firing, 1900 . . . .
104/S Serbian Infantry
kneeling firing, 1900 . . . .
104/T Serbian Infantry lying
firing, 1900 . . . .
105 Turkish Infantry mar-
ching, 1914 . . . .
105/A Turkish Infantry
assaulting, 1914 . . . .   200.00
105/B Turkish Infantry stan-
ding firing, 1914 . . . .
105/C Turkish Infantry
kneeling firing, 1914 . . . .
105/D Turkish Infantry lying firing, 1914 . . . .
105/W Turkish Infantry
wounded, 1911 . . . .
106 Italian Infantry mar-
ching, 1914 . . . .
106/A Italian Infantry
assaulting, 1914 . . . .
106/B Italian Infantry standing firing, 1914 . . . .
106/C Italian Infantry kneeling firing, 1914 . . . .
106/D Italian Infantry lying
firing, 1914 . . . .
106/P Italian Infantry marching, 1900 . . . .
106/Q Italian Infantry
assaulting, 1900 . . . .

106/R Italian Infantry standing firing, 1900 . . . .
106/S Italian Infantry kneeling firing, 1900 . . . .
106/T Italian Infantry lying
firing, 1900 . . . .
107 Italian Bersaglieri marching, 1914 . . . .
107/A Italian Bersaglieri
assaulting, 1914 . . . .
107/B Italian Bersaglieri
standing firing, 1914 . . . .
107/C Italian Bersaglieri
kneeling firing, 1914 . . . .
107/D Italian Bersaglieri lying firing, 1914 . . . .
107/P Italian Bersaglieri
marching, 1900 . . . .
107/Q Italian Bersaglieri
assaulting, 1900 . . . .
107/R Italian Bersaglieri
standing firing, 1900 . . . .
107/S Italian Bersaglieri
kneeling firing, 1900 . . . .
107/T Italian Bersaglieri lying firing, 1900 . . . .
107/W Italian Bersaglieri
wounded, 1911 . . . .
107/X Italian Bersaglieri
marching at slope, 1911 .
107/Y Bersaglieri assaulting,
1911 . . . .
107/Z Bersaglieri standing
firing, 1911 . . . .
108 Bulgarian Infantry marching, 1914 . . . .
109 Bulgarian Infantry
assaulting, 1914 . . . .
109/B Bulgarian Infantry
standing firing, 1914 . . . .
109/C Bulgarian Infantry
kneeling firing, 1914 . . . .
109/D Bulgarian Infantry lying firing, 1914 . . . .
109/P Bulgarian Infantry
marching, 1900 . . . .
109/Q Bulgarian Infantry
assaulting, 1900 . . . .
109/R Bulgarian Infantry
standing firing, 1900 . . . .

MIGNOT

109/S Bulgarian Infantry kneeling firing, 1900 ....

109/T Bulgarian Infantry lying firing, 1900 ....

110 Evzones marching, 1914

110/A Evzones assaulting, 1914 ....

110/B Evzones standing firing, 1914 ....

111 Boer Infantry marching, 1914 ....   150.00

111/A Boer Infantry assaulting, 1914 ....

111/B Boer Infantry standing firing, 1914 ....

112 Swiss Infantry marching, 1914 ....

113 Iraeli Infantry marching, winter uniforms, 1948 ....

113/A Israeli Infantry marching, summer uniforms, 1948 ....

113/U Israeli Guerilla fighters in combat, 1948 .

114 Israeli Infantry in combat, summer uniforms, 1948 ....

115 Head of Column, 1st Regt. Gren. of the Guard, 28 figures, 1812 ....

116 Foreign Legion, uniform of 1906, marching 200.00

116/H Foreign Legion machine gun unit, 1906 uniform, gun, operator, feeder, officer with binoculars ....

116/A Band of the Foreign Legion, uniform of 1906

117 Foreign Legion, standing firing, 1906 ....

118 Foreign Legion, uniform of 1906, assaulting 200.00

119 Battalion of Neufchatel, marching, 1808 ....

120 Polish Grenadiers, Legion of the North, marching, 1806 ....

121 Grenadiers of Cleves-Berg, 1812 ....   200.00

122 English Grenadiers, 1st Regiment, marching, 1813   200.00

122/A English Grenadiers, 1st Regiment, standing firing, 1813 ....

122/B English Grenadiers, 1st Regiment, assaulting, 1813 ....   200.00

123 German Infantry in the Austrian Army, marching, 1806 ....   200.00

123/A German Infantry in the Austrian Army, standing firing, 1806 ....

123/B German Infantry in the Austrian Army, assaulting, 1806 ....

124 Royal Deux Ponts Regt., American War of Independence, 1778 ....   200.00

125 English Grenadiers 33rd Regt. American War of Independence, 1776 ....   250.00

126 New England Regiments, American War of Independence, 1776 ..   200.00

127 New York and New Jersey Regiments, American War of Independence, 1776 ......   200.00

128 Elite Gendarmes on foot, 1804, First Empire .

129 Regiment of La Tour d'Auvergne, First Empire, 1806 ....

130 Valaison (Swiss) Battalion, First Empire, 1805

1900-291 Rumanian Chasseurs, 1900 ....

1911-260 Gendarmes (Police), 1900 ....

1911-261 Artillerymen on foot, 1900 ....

1911-262 Engineers, 1900 ..

1911-262/H Engineers, 1900

1911-263 Supply Corps, 1900 ....

1911-265 Transport Cavalry on foot, 1900 ....

1911-265/H Baggage Train, 1916 ....

1911-270 English Infantry, red tunic, spiked helmet, 1900 ....

1911-271 Belgian Infantry marching, 1900 ....

1911-271A Belgian Infantry assaulting, 1900 ....

1911-271B Belgian Infantry standing firing, 1900 ....

MIGNOT

1911-271C Belgian Infantry
kneeling firing, 1900 . . . .

1911-271D Belgian Infantry
lying firing, 1900 . . . .

1911-272 Belgian Infantry
marching, 1914 . . . .

1911-272/A Belgian Infantry
assaulting, 1914 . . . .

1911-272/B Belgian Infantry
standing firing, 1914 . . . .

1911-272/C Belgian Infantry
kneeling firing, 1914 . . . .

1911-272/D Belgian Infantry
lying firing, 1914 . . . .

1911-273 Buffalo Hunters
marching, 1870 . . . .

1911-273/A Buffalo Hunters
assaulting, 1870 . . . .

1911-273/B Buffalo Hunters
standing firing, 1870 . . . .

1911-273/C Buffalo Hunters
kneeling firing, 1870 . . . .

1911-273/D Buffalo Hunters
lying firing, 1870 . . . .

1911-274 Spanish Infantry
in overcoats marching,
1900 . . . .

1911-274/A Spanish Infantry
in overcoats assaulting,
1900 . . . .

1911-274/B Spanish Infantry
in overcoats standing firing, 1900 . . . .

1911-274/C Spanish Infantry
in overcoats kneeling firing, 1900 . . . .

1911-274/D Spanish Infantry
in overcoats lying firing,
1900 . . . .

1911-274/T Spanish Infantry
in tunics marching, 1900

1911-275 English Infantry,
khaki uniform, steel
helmet, marching, 1900 .

1911-275/A English Infan-
try, khaki uniform,
helmet, assaulting, 1900 .

1911-275/B English Infantry,
khaki uniform, helmet,
standing firing, 1900 . . . .

1911-275/C English Infantry,
khaki, helmet, kneeling
firing, 1900 . . . .

1911-275/D English Infan-
try, khaki, helmet, lying
firing, 1900 . . . .

1911-275/G English Infan-
try, khaki, helmet, motorcyclist, 1914 . . . .

1911-275/H English Infan-
try, khaki, helmet,
machine gunner, 1914 . .

1911-275/W English Infan-
try, khaki, helmet, wound-
ed, 1914 . . . .

1911-275/X English Infan-
try, khaki, helmet,
bicyclist, 1914 . . . .

1911-276 Boxers (Chinese
Boxer Rebellion), 1900 . .   200.00

1911-277 American Infan-
try, blue uniforms, kepis,
marching, 1900 . . . .

1911-278 American Infan-
try, blue uniforms, spiked
helmets, marching, 1900 .

1911-278/A American Infantry, blue uniforms, spiked
helmets, assaulting, 1900

1911-278/B American Infantry, blue uniforms, spiked
helmets, standing firing,
1900 . . . .

1916-257 Enemies,
wounded, 1914 . . . .

1916-258 Comrades (soldier
carrying wounded on
back), blue uniforms,
kepis, 1914 . . . .

1916-259 Portugese
Chasseurs marching, 1914

1916-259/A Portugese
Chasseurs assaulting, 1914

1916-259/B Portugese
Chasseurs standing firing,
1914 . . . .

1916-259/C Portugese
Chasseurs kneeling firing,
1914 . . . .

1916-259/D Portugese
Chasseurs lying firing,
1914 . . . .

1929-249 Women of the
Red Cross, 1914 . . . .

1952-31 Prussian
Grenadiers, marching, 1st
Empire Period . . . .

1952-32 Prussian
Grenadiers, firing, 1st Empire Period . . . .

MIGNOT

1952-33 Prussian Grenadiers, assaulting, 1st Empire Period ....

1952-34 Russian Infantry, marching, 1st Empire Period ....

1952-35 Russian Infantry, firing, 1st Empire Period

1952-36 Russian Infantry, assaulting, 1st Empire Period ....

1952-49 Chasseurs on foot, green uniforms, 1st Empire Period ....

1952-205 Siamese Infantry, marching, 1900 (produced?) ....

1952-205/B Siamese Infantry standing firing, 1900 ....

1952-205/C Siamese Infantry, kneeling firing, 1900

1952-206 Egyptian Infantry marching, 1900 ....

1952-206/A Egyptian Infantry assaulting, 1900 .....   200.00

1952-206/B Egyptian Infantry, standing firing, 1900   200.00

1952-206/C Egyptian Infantry, kneeling firing, 1900

1952-206/D Egyptian Infantry, lying firing, 1900 ...

1952-207 Austrian Infantry marching, 1900 ....

1952-207/A Austrian Infantry assaulting, 1900 .....

1952-207/B Austrian Infantry standing firing, 1900 .

1952-207/C Austrian Infantry kneeling firing, 1900 .

1952-207/D Austrian Infantry lying firing, 1900 ....

1952-207/P Austrian Infantry marching, 1914 .....

1952-207/Q Austrian Infantry assaulting, 1914 .....

1952-207/R Austrian Infantry standing firing, 1914 .

1952-207/S Austrian Infantry kneeling firing, 1914 .

1952-207/T Austrian Infantry lying firing, 1914 ....

1952-209 Portugese Infantry, 1914 ....

1952-210 English Grenadiers, 1900 ....

1952-211 English Colonial Infantry, marching, 1880

1952-211/A English Colonial Infantry assaulting, 1880

1952-211/B English Colonial Infantry standing firing, 1880 ....

1952-211/C English Colonial Infantry kneeling firing, 1880 ....

1952-211/D English Colonial Infantry lying firing, 1880

1952-220 Monacans, blue uniforms, 20th Century .   200.00

1952-221 Monacans, white uniforms, 20th Century .   200.00

1952-227 Polytechnicans, 1914 ....

1952-234 Marine Infantry in overcoats marching, 1914

1952-234/A Marine Infantry in overcoats assaulting, 1914 ....

1952-234/B Marine Infantry in overcoats standing firing, 1914 ....

1952-234/C Marine Infantry in overcoats kneeling firing, 1914 ....

1952-234/D Marine Infantry in overcoats lying firing, 1914 ....

1952-234/F Marine Infantry in overcoats running, 1914 ....

1952-234/G Marine Infantry in overcoats standing firing, 1915 ....

1952-234/H Marine Infantry in overcoats kneeling firing, 1915 ....

1952-234/J Marine Infantry in overcoats lying firing, 1915 ....

1952-234/K Marine Infantry in overcoats marching, 1915 ....

1952-234/L Marine Infantry in overcoats assaulting, 1915

1952-234/T Marine Infantry in tunics marching, 1914

1952-239 Moroccans marching, 1914 ....

1952-239/A Moroccans assaulting, 1914 ....

MIGNOT

1952-239/B Moroccans standing firing, 1914 ....

1952-240 North American Indians on foot, 1870 ...

1952-241 Malgaches marching, 1900 .... 200.00

1952-241/A Malgaches assaulting, 1900 ....

1952-241/B Malgaches standing firing, 1900 ....

1952-248 Chasseurs on foot in overcoats marching, 1914 ....

1952-248/A Chasseurs in overcoats assaulting, 1914

1952-248/B Chasseurs in overcoats standing firing, 1914 ....

1952-248/C Chasseurs in overcoats kneeling firing, 1914 ....

1952-248/D Chasseurs in overcoats lying firing, 1914 ....

1952-248/F Chasseurs running, 1914 in overcoats ..

1952-248/G Chasseurs in overcoats standing firing, 1915 ....

1952-248/H Chasseurs in overcoats kneeling firing, 1915 ....

1952-248/J Chasseurs in overcoats lying firing, 1915 ....

1952-248/K Chasseurs in overcoats marching, blue, steel helmets, 1915 .....

1952-248/L Chasseurs in overcoats assaulting, blue, steel helmets, 1915 .....

1952-248/T Chasseurs in tunic marching, 1914 ...

CAVALRY SETS
list by Donald P. Grant

200 Gaul Cavalry at the trot, 100 B.C. 200.00

200/A Roman Cavalry, 100 B.C. 180.00

200/B Greek Cavalry, 400 B.C. 180.00

201 Hun Cavalry, 5th Century 200.00

201/A Frank Cavalry, 5th Century 175.00

202 Mounted Crusaders at the trot, 11/12th century 180.00

203 Mounted Knights of the Middle Ages at the trot, 13th Century 170.00

204 Mounted Knights attacking, 13th century ... 170.00

205 Cavalry of Henry IV at the trot, 1589-1610 ..... 175.00

206 Musketeers of Louis XIII at the trot, 1610-1643 .... 200.00

207 Guards of Richelieu, 1610-1643 .... 200.00

208 Cavalry of Louis XIV, Balthazar Regiment at the trot, 1670, red blue or white ....

209 Cavalry of Louis XV, Anjou Regiment, 1740 ..

210 Dragoons of Louis XV, 1740 ....

211 Grenadiers of the Guard, mounted, 1809 .. 200.00

211/A Dromedary Camel Regiment, Egyptian Campaign, 1799 .... 225.00

211/H Grenadiers of the Guard, mounted, 1809 ..

212 Dragoons of the Guard, 1809 .... 200.00

212/H Dragoons of the Guard, 1809 .... 200.00

213 Guards of Honor, 1813 200.00

213/H Guards of Honor, 1813 ....

214 Cuirassiers, 1809 ..... 200.00

214/H Cuirassiers, 1809 ... 200.00

215 Carabiniers, 1812 ..... 200.00

215/H Carabiniers, 1812 ... 200.00

216 Chasseurs of the Guard, mounted, 1809 .... 200.00

217 Artillerymen, Mounted, 1809 ....

218 Chasseurs of the Line, mounted, 1809 .... 200.00

219 Light Horse Lancers, 1st Regiment, 1812 ..... 200.00

220 Light Horse Lancers, 2nd Regiment, 1812 .... 200.00

221 Light Horse Lancers, 5th Regiment, 1812 ....

222 Elite Gendarmes, 1810

222/H Elite Gendarmes, 1810 . . . .

223 Mamelukes, 1810 . . . . . 200.00

223/H Mamelukes, 1810 . . .

224 Hussars, 1st Regiment, 1808 . . . .

225 Hussars, 2nd Regiment, 1808 . . . . 150.00

226 Hussars, 3rd Regiment, 1808 . . . . 200.00

227 Hussars, 4th Regiment, 1808 . . . .

228 Hussars, 5th Regiment, 1808 . . . .

228/A Imperial Guard of Strasbourg, mounted, 1805 . . . .

229 Polish Lancers, 1812 . . 200.00

229/A Lancers of Berg, 1809

229/H Polish Lancers, 1812 150.00

229/J Lancers of Berg, 1809

230 Lancers of the Vistula, 1808 . . . . 150.00

230/H Lancers of the Vistula, 1808 . . . . 150.00

231 Dutch Lancers, 1812 . . 200.00

231/A Prussian Hussars, 1813 . . . . 200.00

231/B Austrian Hussars, 4th Regiment, 1813 . . . . 200.00

231/H Dutch Lancers, 1812

231/J Prussian Hussars, 1813 . . . . 200.00

231/K Austrian Hussars, 4th Regiment, 1813 . . . . 200.00

232 General Staff, in boxes of 3 or 5 cavaliers, 1st Empire . . . .

233 Confederate Cavalry at the gallop, 1863 . . . . 200.00

234 U.S. Cavalry at the gallop, 1863 . . . .

235 Russian Imperial Guard, 1900 . . . .

235/B Russian Imperial Guard, blue version, 1900

?5/R Russian Imperial ?uard, red version, 1900

?ssacks, red tunics, at ?ack, 1900 . . . . 200.00

?acks, red tunics, ?00 . . . .

?hlans in ? 1900 . . . 150.00

?ans in ?, 1914 . . . 150.00

238 Prussian Hussars, black uniforms, 1900 . . . . 200.00

238/K Prussian Hussars, khaki uniforms, 1914 . . . 150.00

239 African Chasseurs, 1900 200.00

240 Spahis, 1900 . . . . 180.00

241 Goumiers Trotting, 1914 . . . . 200.00

241/A Goumiers on dromedary camels, 1914 .

241/G Goumiers attacking, 1914 . . . .

242 Guards of Paris, 1900 . 200.00

243 Saint Cyrians, 1900 . . .

244 Hussars, 1914 . . . .

244/H Hussars, blue kepis, tunics, 1915 . . . .

245 Dragoons in winter cloaks, 1914 . . . .

245/A Cuirassiers, 1914 . . . 200.00

245/B Dragoons in tunics, 1914 . . . .

245/C Dragoons in blue, steel helmets, 1915 . . . . .

245/D Cuirassiers in blue, 1915 . . . .

246 English Life Guards, full dress, red tunic, 1900 150.00

246/K English Life Guards, khaki, 1916 . . . . 200.00

247 English Horse Guards or "Blues", full dress, 1900 . . . . 200.00

248 USA Cavalry, olive drab uniforms, 1918, montana hats, at trot . . .

248/A USA Cavalry, steel helmets, at trot, 1918 . . .

248/B USA Cavalry, montana hats, at gallop, 1918

248/C USA Cavalry, steel helmets, at gallop, 1918 .

248/H USA Cavalry, montana hats, at halt, 1918 .

249 English 1st Life Guards, 1815 . . . . 200.00

250 Rumanian Hussars, 1900 . . . .

251 Austrian Dragoons, 1914 . . . .

252 Austrian Lancers, 1914

253 Hindu Cavalry, khaki, 1914 . . . .

MIGNOT

254 Kettle Drummers, 1st
  Empire, C.B.G./Mignot
  version, 1st Empire .....
255 Spanish Hussars, 1808 .
256 Hussars, 9th Regiment,
  "Red Hussars", 1812 ....
257 Hussars, 11th Regiment,
  1812 .... 200.00
258 Scouts of the Young
  Guard, 1813 .... 200.00
259 5th Belgian Light
  Dragoons (Waterloo),
  1815 .... 200.00
260 Bengal Lancers, Army
  of India, 1900 .... 200.00
261 Volunteer Hussars of
  Death (French Revolu-
  tion), 1793 .... 200.00
262 7th Hussars (Green
  Hussars), 1st Empire,
  1805-1813 ....
263 Hussars-Lancers of
  Lauzun (American War of
  Independence), 1778-1783 200.00
264 Bavarian Uhlans, 1808 200.00
265 Dragoons of Kleber
  (Egyptian Campaign),
  1799 .... 120.00
266 Foreign Legion in blue
  and white uniforms on
  dromedaries, 1906 ......
1911-322/A English
  Dragoons, full dress
  uniform, 1900 ....
1911-322/K English
  Dragoons, khaki uniforms,
  1916 ....
1911-323/A English Hussars,
  full dress uniform, 1900 .
1911-323/K Engish Hussars,
  khaki uniforms, 1916 ...
1911-324 English Colonial
  Cavalry, 1900 ....
1911-324/K English Colonial
  Cavalry, khaki ....
1911-325/A Italian
  Dragoons, 1900 ....
1911-325/B Italian Lancers,
  1900 ....
1911-325/C Italian Lancers,
  1900 ....
1911-326 Spanish Cavalry,
  1900 ....
1911-328 Japanese Cavalry,
  1900 ....

1911-329 Boer Cavalry,
  1900 ....
1911-335 Cavalry of the
  Transport Corps, 1900 ..
1911-336 Gendarmes, or
  Policemen, 1900 ....
1916-332 Belgian Guides,
  1900 ....
1916-333 Belgian Lancers,
  1900 ....
1929-341 Agent on
  horseback at repose, 1929
1929-342 Engish Cavalry,
  khaki, 1929 ....
1929-350 General Staff,
  1914 uniforms, 1914 ....
1929-351 General Staff, blue
  uniforms, 1915 ....
1933-337 Chinese Cavalry,
  1933 ....
1933-338 Greek Cavalry,
  1933 ....
1933-339 Swiss Cavalry,
  1933 ....
1952-57 Cavalry of Louis
  XIV, red uniforms .....
1952-58 Cavalry of Louis
  XIV, white uniforms ...
1952-301 Russian Dragoons,
  1900 ....
1952-302 Prussian
  Dragoons, 1900 ....
1952-302/K Prussian
  Dragoons, khaki, 1916 ..
1952-303/A Cossacks in blue
  at trot, 1900 ....
1952-303/B Cossacks in blue
  at gallop, 1900 ....
1952-306 Chasseurs a
  cheval, 1914 ....
1952-306/H Chasseurs a
  cheval, blue, 1914 ......
1952-308 Mounted Ar-
  tillerymen, dark blue,
  kepis, 1914 ....
1952-308/H Mounted Ar-
  tillerymen, light blue,
  1915 ....
1952-315 Indians (North
  American), 1870 ....
1952-316 Buffalo Hunters
  (North American), 1870 .
1952-317 Prussian
  Cuirassiers, 1900 ....
1952-317/K Prussian
  Cuirassiers, khaki, spiked
  helmets, 1916 ....

413

MIGNOT

CBG-MIGNOT HISTORIC PERSONAGES ON FOOT
by Donald P. Grant

100 Jeanne d'Arc (415)		
101 Louis XV (433)		
102 Louis XVI (434)		
103 Napleon ler, redingote (443)	40.00	
104 Napoleon ler, Grand tenue		
105 Louis XI (416)		
106 Henri III (426)		
107 Henri IV (428)		
108 St. Louis (Louis IX) (409)		
109 Marechal Joffre (452) .	50.00	
110 Marechal Lyautey (452)		
111 President Poincare (448)		
112 Dames de la Cour de Henri III		
113 Dames de Moyen Age .		
114 Pape (Pope) (441?)		
115 Mme. de Maintenon (432)		
116 Louis XIV (429)		
117 George Washington (440)		
KQ King and Queen (450&451?)		
400 Ramses II, Pharoah, 1300 B.C.	40.00	
401 Nebuchadnezzor, 600 B.C.	40.00	
402 Cleopatra, 1st Century B.C.	40.00	
403 Saint Denis, martyr, 3rd Century A.D.	30.00	
404 Saladin, 12th Century A.D.	40.00	
405 Richard the Lion Hearted	40.00	
406 Simon de Montfort ...	40.00	
407 Raymond de Toulouse	40.00	
408 Blanche de Castille ...		
409 Saint-Louis (Louis IX) .		
410 Duguesclin		
411 Duguesclin, standard ..		
412 Etienne Marcel		
413 John the Fearless		
414 Christopher Columbus, standard	40.00	
415 Joan of Arc	40.00	
416 Louis XI		
417 Charles le Temeraire ..		
418 Tristan l'Hermite		
419 Bayard		

420 Anne de Bretagne	40.00	
421 Diane de Poitiers		
422 Catherine de Medicis ..		
423 Reine Margot		
424 Francois Ier	40.00	
425 Marie Stuart		
426 Henri III	40.00	
427 Charles I of England ..		
428 Henri IV		
429 Louis XIV		
430 Marie-Therese		
431 Madame de Montespan		
432 Madame de Maintenon	40.00	
433 Louis XV	35.00	
434 Louis XVI	35.00	
435 Marie Antoinette		
436 Marie Antoinette at Trianon		
437 Louis XVII, Dauphin .		
438 Princess de Lamballe ..		
439 LaFayette		
440 George Washington ...		
441 Pope Pius VII		
442 Napoleon Ier	40.00	
443 Napoleon Ier, en redingote	40.00	
444 Marie-Louis, Empress .		
445 Josephine, Empress ...		
446 President Lincoln		
447 Queen Victoria		
448 President Poincare		
449 Marshal Joffre		
450 King George of England		
451 Queen Mary of England	50.00	
452 Lyautey, Resident General of Morocco	60.00	
453 General Petain		

CBG-MIGNOT HISTORIC FIGURES ON HORSEBACK
by Donald P. Grant

150 Bonaparte (622 or 623)	60.00	
151 Charlemagne (603)		
152 Joan of Arc (609)		
153 Richelieu (616)		
154 Louis XIV (619)		
155 Napoleon I (624)		
156 Caesar (601)		
157 Vercingetorix (600) ...		
158 St. Louis (608)		
159 Louis XI (610)		
160 Louis XIII (617)		
161 Henry IV (615)		
162 Francois I (613)		
163 Henry III (614)		
164 Napoleon III (633) ...		
165 Marshall Joffre (637) ..	100.00	

MIGNOT

166 Marshall Foch (638) . .	
167 Albert I (636)	50.00
168 Robert E. Lee (635) . . .	45.00
169 Ulysses S. Grant (636) .	
600 Vercingetorix	60.00
601 Julius Caesar	60.00
602 Attila	40.00
602/A Clovis, King of the Franks	
603 Charlemagne	60.00
604 Saladin	60.00
605 Richard the Lion Hearted	60.00
606 Simon de Montfort . . .	50.00
607 Raymond de Toulouse	
608 Saint Louis (Louis IX) .	
609 Joan of Arc	60.00
610 Louis XI	40.00
611 Ane de Bretagne	
612 Bayard	50.00
613 Francois Ier	40.00
614 Henri III	
615 Henri IV	40.00
616 Richelieu	40.00
617 Louis XIII	40.00
618 Charles Ier de Angleterre	50.00

619 Louis XIV	
620 Louis XIV en Empereur romain	
621 Louis XV	
622 Bonaparte, Egyptian campaign	60.00
623 Bonaparte, Ier Consul .	
624 Napoleon Ier	50.00
625 Prince Murat	
626 Marshal Ney	
627 Marshal Berthier	
628 Aide-de-Camp of the Emperor	
629 Officer of the 6th Regiment of the Hussars	
630 Prince Poniatowski . . .	50.00
631 Eugene de Beauharnais	
632 General Lassale	
633 Napoleon III	
634 General Grant	50.00
635 General Lee	50.00
636 Albert the First of Belgium	50.00
637 Marshall Joffre	
638 Marshall Foch	
639 Marshall Lyautey	
640 Queen Elizabeth of England, 20th Century . .	

O1 Egyptians
Courtesy K. Warren Mitchell

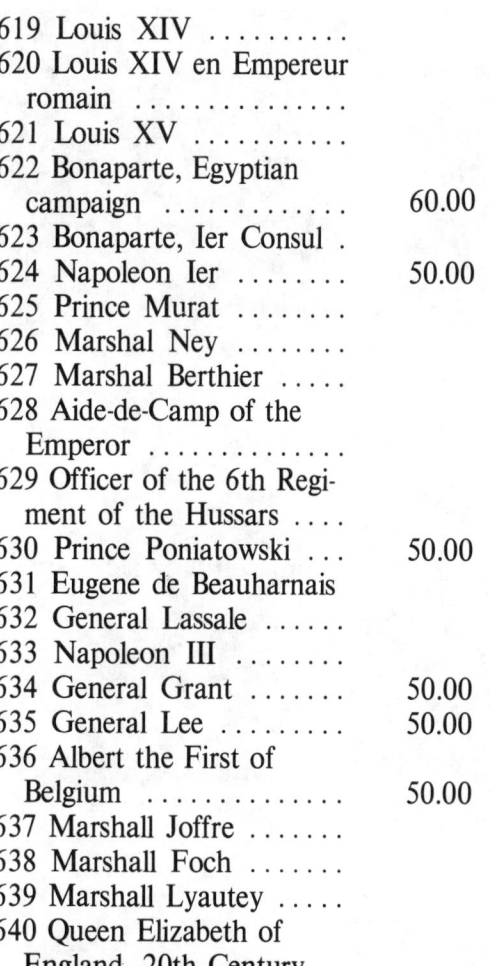

O5 Romans
Courtesy K. Warren Mitchell

O4 Gauls
Courtesy K. Warren Mitchell

33/A Dragoons of the 17th Regt.
Courtesy K. Warren Mitchell

43 Austrian Infantry
Courtesy K. Warren Mitchell

415

57/B U.S. Army Artillery Crew
Courtesy K. Warren Mitchell

67 Foreign Legion
Courtesy K. Warren Mitchell

446 Lincoln, 104 Napoleon
Courtesy K. Warren Mitchell

L to R: 215 Carabiniers, 1812; 218 Chasseurs of the Line.
Courtesy K. Warren Mitchell

GERMAN COMPOSITION
By Jack Matthews

General Description: Method of Manufacture

Composition soldiers and other figures have been manufactured in Germany and other Western European countries since the turn of the century. The method of making such figures derived from materials used in European doll manufacturing since 1850. Pfeiffer of Vienna perfected the soldier technique around 1898.

The process is quite simple. A multi-part accurately machined brass mold is prepared and a cereal-like mixture of wood flour, kaolin and animal glue is hand pressed into both halves. These ingredients, particularly the fine wood flour, were very cheap and readily available. A skeleton is inserted of thin wire having been bent to the proper shape by hand. The molds are then joined, air-dried and then heated for a time, to cure the figures.

After cooling, the figures were removed from the mold, and while still slightly flexible, trimmed by hand and hand painted. There is disagreement among experts as to whether undercoating or fillings were routinely used since the paint usually bonded with the "tacky" surface of the figures. While factory painters were used, most of the figures were painted at home by "kitchen labor" on a piece work basis, according to strict painting instructions and standards laid down by the manufacturer.

Despite their "paper mache" appearance, composition figures are surprisingly tough and resistant to damage. The paint, while subject to some chipping through play and a certain amount of age fading, usually holds up quite well after 50-75 years. Mint or near mint figures made over 75 years ago can still be found. However, if subjected to undue moisture, major damage such as large cracks, rusting and overall deterioration of the composition material will occur. Often in these circumstances the bases will warp. Needless to say, such damage substantially detracts from the value and appearance of the figure. Deterioration in value of such a damaged composition piece is no different than it would be for comparable damage to a Britains or other metal toy soldier.

Elastolin and Lineol

While numerous companies produced composition figures in France, Belgium, Italy, Denmark, Germany, Czechslovakia and Austria during the period 1905-1960 only two achieved prominence in the field: O&M Hausser (Elastolin), founded in 1904 in Ludwigsberg in Southern Germany and Lineol, founded by Oskar Wiederholz in 1905 in Brandenburg/Havel. These firms were major competitors, had the bulk of the composition soldier market and the world-wide sales and marketing networks. For over half a century they produced a vast array of the highest quality soldiers and associated military tinplate toys and trenchworks. Both companies also manufactured a wide range of "civilian" figures, animals, barnyard scenes, castles, forts, zoo scenes, railway sets and Christmas scenes. Both firms were among the major exporters of Christmas creche scenes throughout the world, particularly to the U.S. Lineol also produced a limited line of children's cooking and tea sets and wooden toys while Hausser produced a much larger line of wooden and other toys such as scooters, pull toys, boxed games, and table tennis. Contrary to popular belief, these non-military items constituted the majority of the pieces made. For example, in the 31 page Hausser catalog of 1939-40, at the height of nationalistic, fervor, 20 pages are devoted to "civilian" pieces.

Elastolin

During the early years of the company's existence numerous sizes of figures up to and over 20 cm were made. However, few company records were maintained. During the years 1912-1928 the most popular figures were 10.5 cm in height (approximately 4½"). Few catalogs of this era were published, the most important being the Catalog F of 1920, which had several editions thereafter. These catalogs listed several hundred figures and sets. There were usually not more than two standard sizes in the Elastolin line at any one time, in the 5.0, 6.5 and 10.5 cm sizes, with the emphasis on the latter. From the earliest production known, the basic figures were made without heads. The head would be made separately in appropriate national headress and inserted before painting. This meant that thousands of varieties of figures were possible. The basic body, for almost all figures, was a German one. A marching British figure at slope would have a German torso with German equipment, e.g., bread bag, canteen, handgrenade, etc. The distinguishing features were the head and the way the figure was painted. This company advertised, as did Lineol, that it could manufacture any nation's soldiers, including flags, at no additional cost. Large sale boards with dozens of tinplate flags of different nations were maintained for marketing purposes. Most of the early figures, of any nation, have the distinctive twirling mustaches of the day. Hausser made marvelous boxed scenes of Eskimo hunts, Buffalo Bill's Wild West Show, Tiger Hunting Safaris, complete with large mounted elephants and gunbearers, as well as massive circus sets. Few if any such remain intact in their entirety; although often accumulations of similar figures are attempted to be sold as complete sets.

The 5.0, 5.5, 6.0 and 6.5 cm sizes remain the least popular of Elastolin figures although tens of thousands of these smaller figures were sold in the U.S. painted as WW I doughboys. They are very common, notwithstanding their age, and are not highly sought after by collectors. 10.5 cm figures, while not the most popular size, continue to be an excellent collectible, particularly among European collectors, many of whom tend to shy away from Nazi-era political figures. Again, the common "doughboy" type variety in this size are quite common and not particularly desirable.

During the thirties, around the time the company moved from Ludwigsburg to its new headquarters at Neustadt bei Coburg near the center of the German doll and toy industry, it acquired the assets of some competitors, including Durolin of Czechslovakia. The move coincided with the rise of National Socialism and Hitler. Hausser then emphasized the production of the figures of the German Army and the Nazi era. They are best known for these figures today. During this period the standard size became 7.5 cm (3¼"). It is these figures that are the most highly prized by modern collectors. Advances by the Elastolin technical department resulted in the manufacture of hundreds of different and difficult poses. These include figures firing caps, battery-operated electric fires and searchlights, etc. The thirties period, 1932-1942, can be rightly called the "golden age" of composition figures and related toys, since it was during this period particularly that the marvelous tinplate vehicles, cannon and horse-drawn items made by Hausser, Lineol and Tipp & Co. of Nuremburg were produced. Hundreds of different figures of all the services were produced: Army, Navy, Luftwaffe, Panzer Corps, Flak Corps and all of the various "political" divisions including SA, SS, Labor Corps, Hitler Youth. For collecting purposes, figures of this era may be roughly divided into several categories and subcategories. (a) general army figures consisting of slope, action, leisure, medical, Panzer mounted, artillery, band and communications; (b) navy; (c) luftwaffe; (d) political; (e) civilian; (f) cowboys and Indians and (g) other, including 18th century Frederician Prussians and Knights. Prior to WW II most of these categories, although not all, were made up in the uniforms of numerous foreign countries, the most prominent being France, Italy, Britain, U.S., Belgium, Denmark and Switzerland. In terms of "rarity", a term so often abused, Navy, Luftwaffe, Frederician Prussians and certain political figures are the most difficult to obtain. Immediately after the war, many "political" toys bearing the outlawed swastika were destroyed, and today such figures are still confiscated by German authorities.

In a class by themselves are the Elastolin "personality" figures. These are figures of identifiable personages, such as Hitler, Mussolini, Hindenburg and other national heroes. Prior to the thirties only a few personality figures were manufactured, in 6.0 cm size, including Hindenburg, Von Seekt, George Washington, Frederick the Great and his generals Von Siethen and Seydlitz. Hindenburg, Kaiser Wilhelm II and his Kaiserin were made in the 10.5 size. In the thirties such figures became very popular and over twenty poses in 7.5 cm scale were manufactured, including Generals Von Ludendorf, Von Blomberg, Field Marshall Von Mackensen, President Hindenburg, Admiral Raeder, several versions of Hitler and Goring, party figures Von Schirach (Hitler Youth), Hess and Ernst Roehm (first head of the SA). Foreign dignitaries were included, such as Franco of Spain (two versions, one with porcelain head), Mussolini and General Guisan of Switzerland. In 1936 Elastolin began the manufacture of personality figures with hand painted porcelain heads made by the Hartwig firm of Thuringia. Approximately 10 porcelain-head figures were sold, mostly to adults as "mantle" pieces. Lineol made no figures of this type. Porcelain head personalities are the most difficult Elastolin figures to obtain in good condition and this situation reflects their market price. While comparatively few composition fakes, repaints and restorations abound, fakes of personalities due to their high prices should be watched for.

While accurate records are not available, owner and employee recollections indicate that figure production in the late 20's-early 30's was about one-half million per year but rose to around 3,000,000 by the end of war time production. The percentage of those figures that were exported is unavailable. Apart from the early years, there are numerous pre-war Elastolin catalogs available. Each spans a two-year period. The last war-time catalog is 1939-1940. Reproductions are easily obtainable, at modest cost, from some dealers. Original post-war catalogs, published on an annual basis, may still be found at modest cost.

Hausser figure production ceased in early 1943 as best can be determined. As materials such as paint and good composition materials became more difficult to obtain, the quality of the famous figures commenced a slow but steady deterioration. Paints varied according to availability. These late war or "Kreigs produktion" figures are usually less full bodied than mid-late thirties figures and are often found in one or two colors only, usually all brown or brown and blue-grey. They may corrode more easily. A beginning Elastolin collector should quickly learn to make these quality, time period, and size distinctions since most general toy soldier dealers are not knowledgeable on the subject, and tend to rate all Elastolin figures roughly the same.

Lineol figures
Photo by Ed Poole

Post-War Elastolin

The reconstructed post-war Hausser company continued production of composition figures until the early 1960s. In 1946-47 the American Military Government Control Commission of the occupying forces authorized new production, consistent, of course, with the new strict laws banning any item relating to the Nazi era and its symbols. Thus for twenty post-war years Hausser produced a composition range of Swiss, British, West German and U.S. soldiers, cowboys and Indians, knights and American Revolutionary War figures, together with a very limited range of modified vehicles and cannon painted in khaki, forts, castles and western stockades. No trenchworks were made after WWII. Most of the post-war soldier figures were made from pre-war molds with different heads. And it is reported that much of the remaining pre-war stock of unpainted and even painted figures was utilized when post-war production began. This was achieved by simply removing the old German head, inserting the new non-German head and painting it in the proper uniform colors. The same was true of the limited number of post-war vehicles and cannons marketed. These sell at well less than one-half the price of similar pre-war items. The post-war cowboys and Indians are a significant improvement over their pre-war brethren and in the opinion of many experts, represent the best animation and molding done by the company. While such figures are now becoming more difficult to obtain in excellent condition, until four or five years ago they were perhaps the most common of Elastolin figures, and priced accordingly. Post-war soldiers include a range of over thirty Swiss figures and a lesser number of similar poses representing British and U.S. occupation and West German troops. Again, the usual Elastolin practice of having one basic "German" body with different heads was followed. Special post-war figures clearly identifiable and made to represent a specific, accurate country

ELASTOLIN

Composition figures, mainly Elastolin
Courtesy Christie's New York

Elastolin, top to bottom: S.A. drummers, British infantry, German marching machine gunners.
Courtesy Christie's East

or unit included Scots, British Manchester Regiment, and British Guards. They were made in both mounted and marching poses. These figures are the most difficult to obtain of all post-war figures and are priced higher than a Swiss (the most common), U.S. or British figure.

Hausser gradually moved to its current and extremely attractive range of all plastic figures in the late fifties. A number of transition figures can be obtained, particularly Swiss with plastic insert heads and composition bodies. These have no special additional value. The all-plastic range included an entirely new and broader line of magnificent figures including many more cowboys and Indians, knights, Romans, Huns, Turks, Ottomans, Landsknechts, Tartars, Vikings, Normans, Gauls, American Revolutionary and Civil War troops of both sides and a vast assortment of medieval cannon, siege weapons, castles, stagecoaches, chariots, wagons and domestic animals (including several "personality" figures). Most of these figures are still readily available at retail prices. Many of these figures are now being marketed by the Preiser company following the closing of the Hausser factory in the early 80s.

Lineol

Lineol's production commenced in Brandenburg in 1905. Early soldiers were in a very large 14 cm scale or larger and have a very old toy "heavy" appearance. Old Lineol figures have the trade name embossed on the rectangular base or on the figure itself, if it does not have a base. Like Hausser, Lineol tinplate pieces have the firm's name embossed on the tires, barrels of cannon, etc. Lineol's boxes, like Hausser's, were generally covered by a glazed red paper and often had a colored picture sticker on the top such as a tank climbing an embankment, boys marching in paper hats or the traditional Lineol trademark of three walking geese. Early Lineol sets featured huge parade groupings, some with over 100 figures. Unlike Britains, very few Lineol or Hausser boxed soldier sets or boxed tinplate or horse drawn toys are found today. When they are discovered the boxes are usually in poor condition. Presence of a box however adds a premium to the value of the contents. Like Hausser, Lineol made figures in a number of sizes. Its larger, most popular size in the first 25 years of its existence was 8 to 9.5 cm in height, somewhat smaller than the Elastolin 10.5 cm. The range included, as did Hausser's, a few large horse drawn units. Both companies' items of this type often appear in U.S. or British Army style. Evidently Lineol did not export heavily to the U.S. in these early years, since few 9 cm figures turn up in this country and when they do they are usually in poor condition and of the common U.S. uniform variety. Later Lineol figures were also standardized at 7.5 cm during the 1930's. Except for its excellent horses and animals, Lineol's earlier 9.5 cm figures are not, in the opinion of most experts, as attractive as the large 10.5 cm Elastolin figures. Conversely, Lineol's 7.5 cm figures, which came into vogue as did Hausser's in the 1930's, are generally considered overall to be superior in molding, painting, animation and creativity to those of Elastolin. Thus, most Lineol 7.5 cm figures are priced somewhat higher.

The very large Lineol 1932 Export Catalog, some 125 pages in length, illustrates the large range of figures manufactured prior to that date and is superior in detail to Elastolin catalog F previously described. This catalog was printed in four languages and copies are available with a 20 page English wholesale price list! The large variety of mounted and medieval figures are of particular interest. Like Hausser, Lineol produced catalogs every other year but not as many. Only about eight to ten Lineol catalogs are known to exist and rarely turn up in good original condition. Reproductions of some are easily available, such as the two excellent Lineol Export Catalogs No. 10 of 1937-1938 with text in French/Italian and the other in English/German. Two small catalogs of the post-war East German company "Lineol Plastik Dresden" exist. The quality, lay out and descriptions of the Hausser and Lineol catalogs are comparable.

Apart from foreign troops, which were seldom illustrated, a set of post-1930 catalogs allows a collector to ascertain well over 80% of the "German" production line of both companies. During the late-twenties to early thirties the most common scale, and one greatly exported to the U.S. in common "doughboy" marching groups and associated horse drawn units, was 6.5 cm in height. As in the case of Elastolin, this intermediate size did not prove particularly popular and they are not highly sought after, although antique and general toy dealers often fail to make any distinction, thus substantially overpricing these common figures. 6.5 cm U.S.-Lineol figures in good condition are worth but a few dollars to a regular collector, since they have little trade value and are easily obtainable.

By the end of the decade of the thirties Lineol had produced well over 600 different "German" figures in the 7.5 cm scale.

In 1938, the company introduced a line of marvelously molded and detailed 4 cm figures designed for play on a limited surface. Thus far, they have been discovered painted in German, Danish and Italian uniforms. Several dozen different 4 cm soldiers were produced, including tiny piles of ammunition, flags and Navy and Luftwaffe figures. They are highly sought after but still not too difficult to obtain. They are rarely cracked or chipped, probably due to their size and lack of hard outdoor usage and thus most often are found in very good condition. Only 4 die cast vehicles and cannon were made in this scale and are considered quite rare. Elastolin only produced a few 4 cm figures.

GERMAN COMPOSITION

Since the companies were quite competitive it is not surprising that their lines coincided to a considerable degree. While Lineol did not make the variety of uniforms of German troops and political figures as did Hausser, the number of different poses manufactured during this period was about the same. Lineol's figures, with some exceptions, are clearly superior in all respects and tend to be somewhat hardier. Most of its action figures such as the working gas generator piece, metal pontoon boat, radio troops, motorcycles and its knights and cowboys and Indians cannot be matched by Elastolin. Prices are thus approximately twenty to fifty percent higher. For example, while a common Elastolin marching bandsman can be obtained for from $25-35, a corresponding Lineol piece, depending on condition, would be in the $30-40 range. Foot figures are $15 and $20 respectively.

Lineol's "political" figures also have a clear edge over Elastolin's in quality and particularly robustness. Elastolin's political range, while considerably greater (many different uniform variations on the same figure) tend to be somewhat puny in comparison. Generally, Elastolin SS, SA, Hitler Youth and similar figures tend to be grossly overpriced, perhaps due to the general overall interest in military memorabilia of this era.

Lineol produced over thirty 7.5 cm personality figures during the thirties, few of which were exported, including several different poses and uniforms of Hitler and Goring. Like Hausser, several foreign dignitaries were included. Lineol's rarest figures are those of Emperior Haile Selassie of Ethiopia, Kings Edward VIII and George VI of England, Albert and Leopold of Belgium and General Guisan of Switzerland. The very tall King Christian X of Denmark made in precise scale, was also produced but is comparatively more available, as are the foot and mounted Lineol figures of Mussolini. All Lineol personality figures in good condition are now the highest priced of composition figures, usually selling in the $100 plus range.

Perhaps the most interesting of all Lineol figures are those referred to as "special" figures made to specifically match the foreign soldiers they were intended to represent and not utilizing the cost and time saving device of using the standard German body. Most of these figures are shown on page 23 of the Lineol No. 10 Export Catalog entitled "Assortment of Special English Figures" and page 25, illustrating similar Italian and Abyssinian troops for the Italian-Abyssinian War. Apart from personality figures, these are the most difficult Lineol items to obtain. They include a beautifully sculpted Coldstream Guards Drum Major in State Ceremonial dress, Highlanders, Mounted Life and House Guards, Italian Fascist, Alpine and Bersaglieri troops and the aforementioned Abyssinian war contingent. Unfortunately, paint utilized on the white-uniformed Abyssinian troops and Italian native Askaris tend to flake very badly, thus detracting from the value of such figures. Special figures also included Canadian Mounties, accurate British Line troops, Danish Guards, American Revolutionary War figures and Frederician Prussians. The last two were described only in the 1920's Lineol Export Catalog and are seldom seen.

The last known pre-war Lineol catalog of 1939-40 illustrated about two dozen new figures which are perhaps the best ever produced. A series of nine artillery figures are outstanding. This "set" including men fusing shells, 2 man AA machine gun teams, seated 2 cm integrated composition-metal AA gunner and a map group with a monocled general and staff officer, are unique in their perfection among composition figures. Four tinplate vehicles, mortars and cannon are included in this final company offering. All of these pieces were among the last exported to the United States.

Post-War Lineol

The Lineol factory in Brandenburg/Havel was not destroyed during the war. In 1949 the company was nationalized and moved to Dresden, East Germany. A small late-fifties catalog describes the company as "VEB, Lineol-Plastik Dresden" and illustrates a limited line of new but excellent Indian figures and domestic and wild animals, including mounted camels and elephants. For political reasons, these figures are somewhat difficult to obtain in Germany. A number of post-war Lineol military figures of the German Democratic Republic were also produced. The bases on most (except for band figures) have been changed from the standard rectangular shape to elongated oval (marching) or circular bases (standing). About 15 military figures are known but no "action" poses seem to have been produced. A few flag bearers had linen-type East German cloth flags. These military figures are squat, crude and somewhat poorly painted.

Related Tinplate Items

Both Hausser and Lineol (along with Tipp & Co.) produced a wide range of military vehicles, cannon and horse drawn pieces which modern experts have long since believed to be some of the finest examples of tinplate toys ever made. Most had numerous working parts such as headlights, turn indicators, cap firing AA guns and searchlights and of course complete working key windup motors. The range of vehicles of all three companies included cannon of all sizes, flak and searchlight trucks, ambulances, several staff car versions (Kubelwagons) large lorries, communications vehicles and armored cars and half-tracks ("prime movers"). Horse drawn pieces included several towing cannon, mortars, AA carts, field kitchens and bakeries, covered wagons and ambulances. Most could be ordered with two, four and sometimes six horses. All of these pieces were meticulously modeled after actual items in use by the German Army. So much so that according to the Hausser family all new vehicles produced in the thirties had to receive official clearance and the company had to submit copies of the drawings and photos and an actual working model of the new toy before production could be commenced.

Tipp & Co. produced a broad range of similar pieces but did not make horse drawn pieces. However, unlike Lineol and Hausser, Tipp produced several excellent airplanes, including items which dropped cap firing bombs and dirigibles which today command very high auction prices when complete and in fine condition. Tipp tinplate toys generally sell at much lower prices than do those of Hausser and Lineol and are generally much more common.

The Value and Pricing of Composition Figures

It is impossible to prepare a price list of Elastolin and Lineol figures since literally thousands were produced over the sixty to seventy year history of these companies.

Apart from the English language partial list of German military Elastolin figures contained in Reggie Polaine's 1979 book "The War Toys", no published complete list of Lineol or Elastolin production has ever been compiled and it would probably be impossible to do because of the numerous foreign variations of basic German figures which were never cataloged. Uncataloged figures are constantly turning up, and will continue to do so.

It is possible however to approximate the ranges of prices for the composition figures which today are generally available to the average collector. The ranges given herein will be based on a general knowledge of prices realized for a number of categories of such figures at the major German auction houses over the last several years and of the price lists of composition figures which have appeared in the same time period. Prices in many of these categories, i.e., band, foot, and action pieces, have risen somewhat but remain reasonably stable. The price ranges take into account the "popularity" of certain groups, i.e.; some (eg: SA/SS) are much harder to sell than others. Prices realized at the occasional auctions of composition figures by the major U.S. and British auction houses are of little use since the ranges are so extreme. This situation can perhaps be ascribed to auction fever occurring at such times and the unusually high reserve prices often placed on such pieces by unknowledgeable sources. On a critical note, it is observed that the description and grading of composition condition by the major non-German auction houses continues to with few exceptions be optimistic. This may be ascribed to wishful thinking but more likely on overall lack of expertise in the area.

As is the case with other subject areas of toy soldier collecting, condition cannot be overemphasized. While very minor cracking and fading of compositions can often be expected, major cracks, paint loss and chips significantly detract from an item's value, notwithstanding its apparent rarity. Tinplate vehicles and cannon and horse drawn items bear similar caution. Horse drawn pieces are often found with the tinplate parts in fine shape but with the horse teams in a bad state of deterioration and with the seller making no distinction in price. Such items should be ignored by the beginning collector since he/she will simply have to replace this inferior piece later on.

This listing does not attempt to value the figures produced by the approximately 20 competitors of Lineol and Elastolin such as Durso (Belgium), Durolin, F.F., Schusso, Leyla, N.F. Italy, Armee, Trico (Japan), etc. The quality of the production of these companies varies greatly but generally the figures are clearly inferior to those of the big two. Most collectors either ignore them entirely or collect representative samplings only. Their value is considerably less, in many cases just a few dollars.

The following table of price ranges for types and sizes of Elastolin and Lineol figures assumes Grade II (average, no paint loss, occasional minor cracking at extremities) figures without major corroding, paint fading or any missing or broken parts. It covers figures generally available from collectors, dealers and auction houses, and does not include unusual figures, or hard to obtain personality and special foreign troops (see above narrative). Nor does it attempt to catalog individual prices for the few hundred or so tinplate, horse drawn and trenchwork/fortification pieces manufactured by Lineol, Elastolin and Tipp & Co. While average prices for certain of these pieces, e.g. the Lineol '88 cannon and staff car continue to be reasonably stable, prices for other major tinplate military toys have varied so widely, based it is assumed, on "auction fever", conditions and other elements, as to be deemed meaningless in a general discussion of this sort.

Finally, as is often stated, but often disregarded, a seller of Lineol and Elastolin items in quantity cannot nearly expect to receive a price based on "retail" prices for individual pieces, if it is desired to sell all at one time for personal convenience nor can a dealer pay "retail" prices when buying such items for resale.

GERMAN COMPOSITION

Lineol, top to bottom: French World War II troops, American infantry, American flagbearer and German troops
Courtesy Christie's New York

Lineol

9 cm - marching U.S.	15.00
9 cm - marching foreign . . .	15.00
9 cm - mounted U.S.	25.00
9 cm - mounted foreign . . .	25-35
6.5 cm - marching	6.00
6.5 cm mounted	15.00
6.5 cm action	6-8.00
4 cm single	15-25
4 cm mounted	25-50
7.5 cm (1930-42)	
Luftwaffe - marching	30-40
Luftwaffe - artillery	40-50
Luftwaffe - band	50-60
Luftwaffe - flagbearers	75.00
Navy - marching	60.00
Navy - officer	60.00
Navy - flagbearer	75.00

Knights - foot	50.00
Knights - mounted	80.00
Cowboys/Indians - foot	30.00
Cowboys/Indians - mounted	60.00
Frederick the Great - foot .	40.00

Army

Marching	12-20
Mounted	30-60
Flagbearers	50.00
Band - marching	25-35
Band - standing	50-100
Action/Artillery/communica-tions/hospital/leisure	20-50

Political

Hitler Youth	75.00
Hitler Youth - brown shirt .	60.00

423

GERMAN COMPOSITION

Hitler Youth - band/flag ...	90.00
Hitler Youth - leisure	75.00
Indians/Cowboys - foot/action	35.00
Cowboys/Indians - mounted	65.00
Knights - foot	35.00
Knights - mounted	90.00
SA/SS marching	30-40
SA/SS band	35-70
SA/SS mounted	75-100
SA/SS flagbearers	75.00
SA/SS leisure/communications	75.00

Pre-War Elastolin
10.5 cm (1905-1930)

Slope U.S./British Khaki ...	10-15
Mounted U.S./British Khaki	25-35
Bandsmen/Flagbearers	20-30
Leisure	15.00
Action	15.00
Scots	20.00
Guards	25.00
Foreign Slope	15.00
Foreign Action/Leisure	15.00
Foreign Mounted	25-35

5.5, 6.0 cm (1905-1930)

All Slope/leisure/action	8-9.00
All Mounted	15.00

7.5 cm (1930-1943)

Infantry-average-slope/officers march	12-20
Army - communications ...	20-35
Army - action	15-30
Army - hospital	15-35
Army - leisure	15-35
Army - mounted	40-70
Army - artillery	15-35
Army - pioneers	30.00
Army - flagbearers	30-60
Navy - slope	40.00
Navy - officer	50.00
Navy - band	50.00
Luftwaffe/Flak - slope	40.00
Luftwaffe/Flak - artillery ..	40-60
Luftwaffe/Flak - band	30-60
Luftwaffe/Flak - flagbearer .	60.00

Political

SA/SS - marching	20-25
SA/SS - band	30.00
SA/SS - mounted	40-70
SA/SS - flagbearers	60.00
SA/SS - leisure/communications	25-40
RAD (Labor Corps) - slope .	50.00
RAD (Labor Corps) - band .	60.00
RAD (Labor Corps) - pioneer	60.00

Post-War 7.5 cm

West Point Cadets	25.00
Rev. War - foot	15-20
Rev. War - flagbearer	30.00
Rev. War - George Washington - mounted ..	35.00
Swiss/U.S./British/German Action/leisure/hospital/slope	15.00
Swiss/U.S./British/German mounted	25-35
Swiss Band	20.00
Knights - foot	20.00
Knights - mounted	30.00
Cowboys, foot	15-20
Indians, foot	15-20
Cowboys, mounted	25-40
Indians, mounted	25-40
Scots - marching	30.00
Scots - band	45.00
Guards - marching	35.00
Guards - band	50.00
Coldstream Guards - mounted	70.00
Manchester Guards - foot ..	55.00
Manchester Guards - mounted	70.00

HEYDE

For connoisseurs of the toy soldier, Heyde is one of the three major names, along with Britains and Mignot.

Heyde was in business in Germany at least as early as 1870, under the direction of Gustav Adolf Theodor Heyde, but it was George Heyde who brought the firm to its height. Heyde's soldiers can be appreciated more in the aggregate than singly, as many of them are modeled rather clumsily. Arms can be of unequal length, legs are frequently stumpy, and a general lack of symmetry often prevails. However, when seen in a group, Heydes can arrest, and charm, the eye.

Heydes came in a dizzying variety of positions and themes, often in groups as large as 64. Soldiers on parade and in combat vied with sets depicting a tiger hunt, an Arctic expedition, Hannibal's march on Rome, a buffalo hunt, even a panoramic visit to a cotton plantation, all decorated in bright, eye-catching colors.

Heydes are not easy to identify. They bear no markings, and are similar to figures by other manufacturers (some of whom pirated Heydes). They came in a variety of sizes: infantry were sold in heights of 43, 52 (the most common), 58, 68, 75, 87 and 120 millimeters. Most were solid cast of a soft malleable lead, which enabled Heyde's workers to arrange arms, etc., in different poses before painting. They have plug-in heads, often with carved moustaches, with the necks slightly thinner than those manufactured by other companies. Most Heyde marchers put their right foot forward. Equipment can be detailed, even to allowing bayonets and swords to leave their scabbards. Mounted figures have a peg between the legs which plugs into the horse. Horses are generally semi-flat. Rifles being fired show a blob of flame at the end of the barrel, and weapons, etc. are separate castings soldered onto the figure.

Heyde was thought to have been destroyed in the 1945 bombing of Dresden, but a 1947 phone book shows Heyde still advertising its figures.

Heyde 42-piece French Infantry, Cavalry and Artillery Display.
Courtesy Christie's New York

Heyde advancing WWI British infantry.
Courtesy K. Warren Mitchell

HEYDE

Heyde Roman foot figures. Average price per each in Good condition
$7. Mounted figures average about $10 in Good.
Courtesy K. Warren Mitchell

Heyde Roman Chariot.
Courtesy K. Warren Mitchell

Heyde foot Indians.
Courtesy K. Warren Mitchell

Heyde mounted North American Indians.
Courtesy K. Warren Mitchell

Heyde Cowboys.
Courtesy K. Warren Mitchell

Heyde Sailors.
Courtesy K. Warren Mitchell

Heyde mounted and foot knights.
Courtesy K. Warren Mitchell

426

Heyde had some of the most magnificent sets of all. This is The Sack of Troy, which sold at auction for $1045 in March, 1982 at Christie's New York. Courtesy Christie's New York

Heyde Set 364 U.S. Infantry Band, 12th Regiment.

William Britain

BRITAINS

Britains have long been the most collected of all toy soldiers, and it seems likely they will be for some time to come.

There are a number of reasons for this. Perhaps the foremost is that, due to the superior quality of their painting and their general design, they are almost always pleasing to the eye.

In addition, there is the long continuity of the line, its breadth and depth. Britains soldiers represent virtually every modern army of the past nine decades, and the line of British soldiers alone offers a staggering variety of regiments.

Their initial price has been a help, too, in making them attractive to collectors. Many people collect because they remember having owned a company's products during their childhood; Britains' soldiers have always been reasonably priced, and therefore they were accessible to a large number of children.

Too, this is a company which is still in business, and therefore presumably continues to attract children who will in time become collectors. Finally, it's even possible that the momentum of Britains' explosion onto the scene is still carrying the company along.

Put simply, it was Britains who revolutionized the toy soldier business. In 1893, William Britain Jr. conceived the idea of developing a hollowcast lead soldier. Prior to this time, all lead soldiers had been solid and most had come from Germany.

But by the simple expedient of pouring lead alloy into a mold and then immediately pouring out all but that which adhered to the sides of the mold, Britain came up with a soldier that saved money in lead and shipping.

Britains had been founded around 1850 by William Britain Sr., who from the first designed and manufactured toys. These were of a mechanical variety, and appear to have been successful, but on a small scale.

However, this was the age of the Industrial Revolution and its introduction of mass marketing. Toy Trains were already in vogue, and it was decided to match the figures to the then-popular No. 1 Gauge trains. This worked out to a 54mm high toy soldier. (A simple stroke, but it had its brilliance. Many toy soldier makers have failed, or not been as successful as they might have been, because their figures were manufactured without an eye to fitting any sort of scale.)

Britains' early soldiers were a bit awkward-looking, and may have been designed by an outside hand. However, within a few years William Britain Jr. had mastered the art of sculpting, and until the 1920s his stamp was on all of Britains' soldiers. From that time on, other members of the family and factory also had a hand in the design.

The sale of soldiers got off to a slow start, until the Britains convinced Gamages to present them as a sales promotion in their store. From that point on the company was established, and continued almost without hesitation through World War I, the 1920s and the Depression, until World War II forced a temporary halt. Production resumed in 1946 (or possibly late 1945) and has continued to this day.

The firm was located until 1959 at 28 Lambton Road in Hornsey Rise, on the outskirts of London. During that time it became the largest manufacturer of toy soldiers in the world, with 500 employees in 1937.

Although it is said Britains paid well, and that there was tremendous loyalty to the company by its workers, at least one outside observer saw it another way. Robert H. Greenwell observed in the January, 1938 *Toys and Bicycles* that "an inspection of the factory discloses the fact that most of the work is done by emaciated looking children fourteen years of age and over," which sounds very much like the working conditions of the U.S.' Barclay. Greenwall also described the work and contributed a few figures: "The boys sit at long benches and mould with hand moulds and place the silvery looking, yet hot, toys in large containers to be carried upstairs where girls of the same age and older spray or paint by hand the gay synthetic regalia that makes them so vivid and lifelike. This unique factory (carries) 'in stock' at all times 2,000 types of lead soldiers and novelties."

NOTES ON BRITAINS
by K. Warren Mitchell

PRICING

For most W. Britains collectors, condition is everything. Mismatched sets, damaged pieces, restored or repainted pieces reduce the prices shown, in some cases substantially.

ALL SET prices are based on SET being in the proper box, and the box being in comparable condition to the soldiers themselves. A "set" **without a box** is generally valued at 10-20% less.

GRADING

The grading of W. Britains figures is generally more restrictive. There is no "MINT" price shown, since such a small percentage of sets are found in that condition. Naturally, a truly "MINT" set would command a premium over the price shown --"MINT" being **absolutely** in the condition it was when it left the factory. Normal accepted grading is as follows: "EXCELLENT"- a **minor** chip or two on a figure. "VERY GOOD" - some gloss and at least 95% of the paint remaining. "GOOD" - played with , dullish paint, but still at least 80% of paint remains. Unless extremely rare, a figure or set below "GOOD" loses a great deal of its desirability/collectibility to most collectors.

SET #s & CONTENTS

W. Britains generally used the same set # for a given set since its beginning in 1893. Boxes changed, labels changed, contents changed in number, poses and painting changed, but #1 remained the Life Guards through 73 years. In 1960 most standard 8-piece "foot" sets were reduced by 1 piece. Standard 5-piece mounted sets were reduced to 4 pieces.

In 1961, new cellophane window boxes were used. In 1962, the new numbering system of 9000 series began. **NOTE:** Out of consideration for space and simplicity, the new **9000** number appears next to the original number of the set, if it was continued after 1962. Newly formed sets **after** 1962 are listed at the end of the regular numbers. Keep in mind that in the case of sets carrying 9000 series number, the value shown for the regular numbered set will normally have to be adjusted to take into consideration a change in contents where applicable. Set numbers are in order. Where the sequence skips a number, it indicates that the missing number was a FARM, ZOO, or other non-military item, which in turn can be found under its own special title. Refer to "Order of Appearance".

ORDER OF APPEARANCE

To simplify the finding and identifying of pieces and sets, this section has been set up in the following order: Standard military sets, HALF BOXES, PICTURE PACKS, FARM, RAILWAY, HUNT, ZOO, CIRCUS, GARDEN, 2nd QUALITY PAINT, MISC.

IDENTIFYING

The following is a very basic guide for determining what you have. One of the reasons for W. Britains popularity through the years was their dedication to basic uniform accuracy, compared to their contemporaries. Generally, headgear and "facings" (collar and cuff colors) actually denoted a given regiment. Another reason was the moveable arm existing on the majority of figures made shortly after 1900. In fact, they advertised this feature on many early set labels.

After 1900, the underside of the bases, and horse bellies were marked with a variety of embossed words: "W. BRITAINS LTD.", "PROPERTIES, " "COPYRIGHT," "MADE IN ENGLAND," and often all of these. NOTE: The simple word "England" or abbreviation "COPYRT." appearing on a figure, means it is **not** a W. BRITAINS figure, but rather any one of many competitors. A date under the base or horse belly appeared on many pre-war Britains' figures, **but** it is not really indicative of when the figure was made, but only when the mold was made (and then used until worn out or pose changed). This is also true of those carrying the French word "DEPOSE" (which means EXPORT). W. Britains' had a Paris branch until 1923, when it was closed, and all the molds returned to England. The molds generally continued to be used, and "DEPOSE" has even showed up on a few Post War pieces.

"DATING" OF W. BRITAINS

Determining the age of a Britains' figure is difficult, unless you know what "version" it is, and can compare paint style. There are some simple rules-of-thumb to follow that can aid even the most casual collector.

First, if it's boxed, and the box label reads "Regiments of All Nations," it's post war production of 1949-60. Not all Post War sets carried the "R.O.A.N." label. Some very popular sets continued to carry a Pre War label (i.e: #24, 32, 1711, etc.).

Sets carrying stock # of 1920 or higher were only issued POST WAR (after 1945).

Mustaches appeared on most British regiments until the British Army passed a regulation against "facial hair" in about 1936. W. Britains properly deleted mustaches in painting in late 1936/37.

The earliest versions of artillery pieces and horse drawn wagons were unpainted (gun metal grey).

The swords of earliest mounted figures were very thick from 1893 to about 1920. First bases were round or blunt oval for foot figures, with the transition to rectangular bases starting around 1907. A few sets continued "round" bases

BRITAINS

throughout the Pre War period, such as the officers of the Royal Army Medical Corps (in # 137), Japanese charging of set #134, Serbians charging of set # 173.

The mid-to-late 1930s contained many khaki sets of British and U.S. Army in action. The poses and khaki were the same. When outside their boxes, the only way to tell them apart is that during that period the British had black shoes and boots, green gaiters and packs, while the U.S. had brown shoes and boots, and brown gaiters and packs. U.S. always had grey helmets, while the British varied with grey or khaki.

Motor vehicles started with smooth white rubber tires, then ribbed white tires, then black ribbed tires from late Pre War to Post War until the introduction of plastic tires about 1958.

The following charts were designed to aid in identifying only the standard sets in which a regiment was featured exclusively, or if it appeared differently attired or posed in mixed display set. Also, only those sets are shown which are in the most popular scale of W. BRITAINS in North America -- the 54mm or 2⅛" model.

INFANTRY OF THE LINE - red tunic, dark blue trousers, dark blue spike helmet (except where noted).

	Facings	In Set
THE BUFFS (EAST KENT REGT.)	TAN	#16 STANDING ON GUARD, PLUS A NUMBER OF DISPLAY SETS
EAST YORKSHIRE	WHITE	113 AT ATTENTION
GREEN HOWARDS	GREEN	255 MARCHING
LOYAL NORTH LANCASHIRE	WHITE	1564 AT SLOPE, AND 2125 STANDING AND KNEELING ON GUARD
MIDDLESEX	YELLOW	76 AT SLOPE, PLUS MANY DISPLAY SETS
ROYAL IRISH	BLUE	156 FIRING IN STANDING, KNEELING & PRONE POSITIONS
ROYAL LANCASTER	BLUE (WHITE HELMET)	148 RUNNING AT TRAIL
ROYAL NORFOLK	YELLOW	73 MARCHING
ROYAL WEST SURREY	BLUE	29 (LARGE DISPLAY) MARCHING AND ON GUARD, PLUS MANY OTHER MIXED REGT. DISPLAY SETS. ALSO 2086 IN 3 POSITIONS FIRING
ROYAL WARWICKSHIRE	BLUE	206 AT PRESENT ARMS
ROYAL SUSSEX	BLUE (1st VERSION IN WHITE HELMET THEN BLUE)	36 AT SLOPE
SOMERSET LIGHT INF.	BLUE (DARK GREEN HELMET)	17 STANDING & KNEELING ON GUARD, PLUS 40
YORK & LANCASTER	WHITE	96 RUNNING AT TRAIL

NOTE:
(1) The above regiments, and many others, appear marching in scarce "Parade" series - sets 1556-1602, but are hard to verify without a box present.
(2) Officers sometimes were given gold facings.

FOOT GUARD - REGIMENTS CAN BE IDENTIFIED BY THE COLOR OF PLUME (or lack of) ON THEIR BEARSKIN HATS. All had red tunics and dark blue trousers.

	Plume	In Set
COLDSTREAM GUARDS	RED ON RIGHT	#37 BAND, #90 3 POSITIONS FIRING, 93 DISPLAY - ASSORTED POSES, 120 KNEELING FIRING, 1327 - 3 POSITIONS FIRING (PRE WAR ONLY) AND SEVERAL MIXED DISPLAY SETS
GRENADIER GUARDS	WHITE ON LEFT SIDE	34 STANDING FIRING, 111 AT ATTENTION, 312 MARCHING IN WINTER DRESS, 329 SENTRY & BOX (PRE WAR ONLY) 438 MARCHING, 460 1st VERSION COLOR PARTY, 1283 3 POSITIONS FIRING, 1327 3 POSITIONS FIRING (POST WAR ONLY), 2113 BAND, 2121 3 POSITIONS FIRING, AND MANY MIXED DISPLAY SETS
IRISH GUARDS	LIGHT BLUE ON RIGHT	107 MARCHING, 124 LYING FIRING, 1078 AT PRESENT ARMS, 2096 PIPE BAND, 2123 MARCHING AND SEVERAL MIXED DISPLAYS
SCOTS GUARDS	NO PLUME	69 PIPERS, 70 RUNNING AT TRAIL, 75 MARCHING, 82 PIONEERS WITH AXES, 130 DISPLAY - ASSORTED POSES, 329 SENTRY WITH BOX (POST WAR ONLY), 431 MARCHING, 446 MARCHING, 460 COLOR PARTY WITH FLAGS, 1722 DRUM & PIPE BAND, 2084 COLOR PARTY, 2122 MARCHING WITH FLAG, AND MANY MIXED DISPLAY SETS
WELSH GUARDS	WHITE PLUME WITH GREEN HORIZONTAL LINE, ON LEFT	253 MARCHING, 2083 AT EASE, 2108 DRUM & FIFE BAND

NOTES:
(1) Figures with white plume on **right** are from set 1634 or 1637, and are Governor General's Foot Guards of Canada.
(2) Many of the Irish Guard and Scots Guard sets in marching pose, also included appropriate piper.
(3) All "facings" are dark blue.
(4) Guards are sometimes confused with Fusiliers of sets #7 and #74 because of large headgear. Fusilier headgear is narrower, and red tunic has white cross straps.

HIGHLANDERS - CAN BE IDENTIFIED BY COLOR OF HATCHING ON KILTS, AND TYPE OF HEADGEAR. USUALLY RED TUNICS.

	Tartan	In Set
ARGYLL & SUTHERLAND	GRASS GREEN ON DARK GREEN BACKGROUND	#15 FEATHER BONNET - CHARGING #2063 SUN HELMET - FIRING
BLACK WATCH	DARK GREEN, NO HATCHING	#11 FEATHER BONNET — CHARGING #122 SUN HELMET - STANDING FIRING #449 FEATHER BONNET - MARCHING #480 FEATHER BONNET - MARCHING #2109 PIPE BAND, FEATHER BONNET #2111 COLOR PARTY, FEATHER BONNET #2126 CHARGING, FEATHER BONNET #2179 SMALL PIPE BAND, AND SEVERAL MIXED DISPLAY SETS
CAMERON	RED & YELLOW ON DARK BLUE BACKGROUND	#89 SUN HELMETS, VARIOUS FIRING POSITIONS #114 SUN HELMETS (KHAKI TUNIC) MARCHING #2025 SUN HELMET, VARIOUS FIRING POSITIONS
GORDON	YELLOW ON DARK GREEN BACKGROUND	#77 FEATHER BONNETS, MARCHING #118 SUN HELMETS, LYING FIRING #157 SUN HELMETS, VARIOUS FIRING POSITIONS #437 OFFICERS ON FOOT & MOUNTED, FEATHER BONNETS #441 FEATHER BONNETS, MARCHING #482 FEATHER BONNETS, MARCHING #1325 SUN HELMETS, VARIOUS FIRING POSITIONS AND VARIOUS MIXED DISPLAY SETS
SEAFORTH	RED & WHITE ON DARK GREEN BACKGROUND	#88 FEATHER BONNET, CHARGING #112 FEATHER BONNET, MARCHING #2062 FEATHER BONNET, CHARGING

HIGHLANDERS & LOWLANDER IN TREWS (PLAID TROUSERS)

HIGHLAND LIGHT INFANTRY	RED & WHITE HATCHING ON DARK GREEN	#213 - SHAKO HAT, MARCHING
ROYAL SCOTS	RED & YELLOW HATCHING ON DARK GREEN	#212 - KILMORNOCK BONNET, MARCHING
KING'S OWN SCOTTISH BORDERERS	RED & WHITE HATCHING ON DARK GREEN (OR BLUE)	#1395 - KILMORNOCK BONNET, MARCHING
CAMERONIANS (SCOTTISH RIFLES)	WHITE HATCHING ONLY ON DARK GREEN	#1913 - SHAKO HAT, MARCHING

NOTES:
(1) Sometimes confused with set 114 is similar set 1901, the Cape Town Highlanders, who also had khaki tunics, and sun helmets. Set 1901 has Gordon tartan on kilts and **khaki** sun helmets.
(2) Pipers that accompanied some of the above sets would have proper tartan to match.

HEAVY CAVALRY - BEST IDENTIFIED BY THE HEADGEAR

	Headgear	In Set
HOUSEHOLD CAVALRY:		
1st LIFE GUARDS	SILVER HELMET WITH WHITE PLUME, SILVER BREAST PLATE, RED SLEEVES (WITH SWORDS)	#1 TROTTING HORSE, #4 PAINTED GOLD GILT, #5 PAINTED GOLD GILT, #72 LARGE BLACK PLUME, #400 GRAY WINTER CLOAKS #101 BAND (IN JOCKEY CAPS, WITH GOLD & MAROON STRIPED TUNIC), #430 SUMMER AND WINTER DRESS, #2029 MOUNTED AT HALT & DISMOUNTED, #2085 CARRYING LANCES, #2118 MOUNTED & DISMOUNTED, AND MANY MIXED DISPLAY SETS.
2nd LIFE GUARD	SILVER HELMET WITH WHITE PLUME, SILVER BREAST PLATE, RED SLEEVES. CARRYING CARBINES.	#43 AT GALLOP, IN DISPLAY #129 CARRYING LANCES, PLUS MANY MIXED DISPLAY SETS.
ROYAL HORSE GUARDS	SILVER HELMET WITH RED PLUME, SILVER BREAST PLATE, BLUE SLEEVES, WITH SWORDS	#2 TROTTING HORSE, #103 BAND (JOCKEY CAPS WITH BLUE AND GOLD STRIPE TUNIC), #1343 IN GREY WINTER CLOAKS, #2085 CARRYING LANCES, AND MANY MIXED DISPLAY SETS
DRAGOON GUARDS:		
1st Dragoon Guards	BRASS HELMET WITH RED PLUME, RED CARRYING SWORDS.	IN SET #129 TROTTING HORSES, #2074 ON TROTTING HORSES, CANTERING AND WALKING HORSES.
2nd DRAGOON GUARDS "QUEEN'S BAYS"	BRASS HELMET WITH BLACK PLUME. RED TUNIC. CARRY LANCES	#44 GALLOPING HORSES, PLUS 2 MIXED DISPLAY SETS

BRITAINS

5th DRAGOON GUARDS	BRASS HELMET WITH RED AND WHITE PLUME. RED TUNIC. CARRY SWORDS.	#3 TROTTING HORSES
6th DRAGOON GUARDS	BRASS HELMET WITH WHITE PLUME, BLUE TUNIC. CARRY CARBINES	#106 AT GALLOP
7th DRAGOON GUARDS	BRASS HELMET WITH BLACK & WHITE PLUME, RED TUNIC. LANCE SLUNG BEHIND ARM	#127 TROTTING HORSES

LIGHT CAVALRY - BEST IDENTIFIED BY HEADGEAR

DRAGOONS:

1st ROYAL DRAGOONS	SILVER HELMET WITH BLACK PLUME. RED TUNIC. CARRY SWORDS	#31 TROTTING HORSES
2nd DRAGOONS (ROYAL SCOT GREYS)	BLACK BEARSKIN AS FOOT GUARDS. RED TUNIC. GREY HORSES, CARRY SWORDS	#32 WALKING HORSES, #59 WALKING HORSES, #1720 BAND (KETTLE DRUMMER HAS WHITE BEARSKIN HAT), #1721 LARGER BAND, #2119 MOUNTED AND DISMOUNTED, AND MANY DISPLAY SETS

HUSSARS - BEST IDENTIFIED BY PLUME AND BUSBY BAG (COLOR SWATCH DOWN THE RIGHT SIDE OF CAP)

3rd HUSSARS	LIGHT BLUE BAG, WHITE PLUME. CARRY CARBINES	#13 CANTERING HORSES
4th HUSSARS	YELLOW BUSBY BAG, RED PLUME. CARRY SWORDS	#8 GALLOPING HORSES, PLUS TWO MIXED DISPLAY SETS
7th HUSSARS	RED BUSBY BAG, WHITE PLUME. CARRY SWORDS.	#2075 TROTTING AND CANTERING HORSES.
10th HUSSARS	RED BUSBY BAG, WHITE OVER BLACK PLUME EMPTY HANDED	#315 HORSE AT HALT
11th HUSSARS	RED BUSBY BAG, WHITE OVER RED PLUME. BRIGHT RED BREECHES	#12 CANTERING HORSES, WITH CARBINES, #182 DISMOUNTED WITH HORSES, EMPTY HANDED. #270 MOUNTED AND DISMOUNTED, ALL EMPTY HANDED PLUS MANY MIXED DISPLAY SETS
13th HUSSARS	TAN OR WHITE BUSBY BAG, WHITE PLUME WITH SWORDS	#99 CANTERING HORSES

LANCERS - BEST IDENTIFIED BY PLUME AND PLASTRON (CONTRASTING PANEL ON CHEST OF TUNIC). ALL WITH LANCES.

5th ROYAL IRISH LANCERS	RED PLASTRON GREEN PLUME	**#23** AT HALT, PLUS 2 MIXED DISPLAY SETS.
9th QUEEN'S ROYAL LANCERS	RED PLASTRON, BLACK & WHITE PLUME	#24 AT HALT, PLUS 2 MIXED DISPLAY SETS
12th ROYAL LANCERS	RED PLASTRON, RED PLUME	#128 LANCE SLUNG BEHIND ARM. TROTTING HORSES. #129 LARGE DISPLAY, WITH LANCES ALSO AT CARRY AS WELL AS SLUNG. #2076 TROTTING HORSES, LANCES AT CARRY. PLUS MIXED DISPLAY SET.
16th LANCERS	BLACK PLASTRON BLACK PLUME. RED TUNIC	#33 AT HALT, LANCE AT CARRY. PLUS MIXED DISPLAY SETS
17th LANCERS	WHITE PLASTRON WHITE SUN HELMET	#81 TROTTING AND CANTERING HORSES, LANCES AT CARRY. INCLUDED IN SET 73 WITH NORMAL LANCER CAP AND WHITE PLUME. ALSO IN DISPLAY SET #131.
21st LANCERS	LIGHT BLUE PLASTRON, WHITE PLUME ON LANCER CAP.	#100 ON CANTERING HORSES, LANCE AT CARRY. # 94 IN KHAKI UNIFORM WITH SUN HELMET, AND LATER IN STEEL HELMETS. APPEARED IN #1407 MIXED DISPLAY ALSO IN SUN HELMET, THEN STEEL HELMET, ON GALLOPING HORSES.

NOTE:
Following the combining of the 5th and 16th Lancers in the British Army, W. Britains deleted set # 23 and started in the early 1930's to call set # 33 the 16th/5th Lancers, continuing as such post war, in normal dress of the 16th.

Regiments of the Indian Army

These have always been of great interest to the average Britains' collectors. With the similarity of poses, uniforms, and colors, and the frequent changing of set titles, these same sets have always been a bit confusing. The following should help identify the various regiments.

NOTES: A "turban" is made up of the KULLAH, which is a cone shaped cap, the WRAP turban fabric wound around the cone, and the FLASHES or SLASHES of color appearing on the wrap.

Mounted sets generally came as 4 troopers + trumpeter, but in some cases may appear with native officer instead of trumpeter. Always on galloping horses.

CAVALRY

Set #	Title	Pcs	Carry	Tunic	Turban Wrap/Kullah/Flash
45	3rd Madras renamed in 1937 "7th LIGHT CAVALRY OF INDIA" (Also appear in #61 as 15 pc. set)	5	Swords	Pale Blue	Dark Blue/Yellow/White (KULLAH became Red)
46	10th BENGAL LANCERS renamed in 1927 "HODSON'S HORSES, 4th DUKE OF CAMBRIDGE'S OWN." (Also appear in #63 as 10 pc. set)	5	Lances	Dark Blue Red Plastron	Dark Blue/Red/White
47	1st BENGAL NATIVE CAVALRY renamed 'SKINNERS' HORSE' about 1935 - SEE #271 for change. (Also appear in #62 as 10 pc. set)	5	Swords	Khaki w/Black Plastron	Red/Blue/Yellow
60	1st BOMBAY LANCERS	15	Lances	Lt. green until 1920, then bright green	Black/Red/White
64	2nd MADRAS LANCERS (combined with infantry) renamed "16th LIGHT CAVALRY" in 1938	13	Lances	Lt. Blue	Turban wrap is 1/2 dark blue & 1/2 white, with light blue flashes on white portion.
66	1st BOMBAY LANCERS renamed "13th DUKE OF CONNAUGHTS' OWN"	5	Lances	Dark Green until about 1950, then dark blue	Dark blue/Red/White
271	SKINNER'S HORSE, "1st DUKE OF YORK'S OWN" (NOTE: Britain's duplicated regiments in #47. Short lived from 1928-35, then #271 dropped, and #47 given yellow tunics & lances.	5	Lances	Yellow	Black/Red/Yellow
2013	INDIAN ARMY MOUNTED	12	Sword	Olive Drab	All Khaki

INFANTRY

Set #	Title	Pose	Tunic/Facings	Turban Wrap/Kullah/Flash
64	7th BENGAL INFANTRY (part set with 2nd MADRAS LANCERS) Replaced by 3/7th RAJPUT REGT. at slope of #1342 around 1935	Early at trail, then slope	Red/Yellow Red/Yellow	Blue/Red/White
67	1st MADRAS NATIVE INF. by 1930 renamed "Corps of Madras Pioneers"	At trail then slope At slope	Red/White Red/White	Blue/Red/White Rare White also appears
68	2nd BOMBAY NATIVE INF. Included pioneer with axe prior to 1920. Renamed in 1935 "4th Bombay Grenadiers"	At trail then slope At slope	Blue/Red Blue/Red	Blue/Red/White White/Red
252	1st MADRAS NATIVE INF. (Part set with 3rd MADRAS CAVALRY)	(as in #67)		
1342	3/7th RAJPUT REGT.	At slope	Red/Yellow	Blue/Red/White
1641	3/12th (SIKH) FRONTIER FORCE	At slope	Khaki/Dark Blue	Khaki/Black
1892	INDIAN INFANTRY (with British officer)	At trail	Olive drab	Pale green
1893	INDIAN ARMY SERVICE CORP. (with British officer and mule)	At trail	Olive drab	Pale green

(Special thanks to Lee Schaffer and Bill Miele for their help, as well as Christie's East, Phillips of New York, Joanne and Ron Ruddell, and Hank Anton for some helpful photos).

End Notes by K. Warren Mitchell

BRITAINS

Many Britains soldiers have a number of variations. These are all from early to late Number 28 Mountain Battery sets. At left is the first version and next to him a variation of that first version, and after that a second variation of that first version and then a third variation of that first version. After that, the pre-WWII second version, and finally the post-WWII version.
Courtesy Tom Loback   Photo by Sato Studios

Variations of the mounted officers from the Number 28 Mountain Battery, from left: First version, second version (circa 1924), third version (early postwar) and finally a variation of that figure.
Courtesy Tom Loback   Photo by Sato Studios

Mules from early to late versions of the No. 28 Mountain Battery Set. From left: First version, variation of the first version, second version and finally the post-WWII version.
Courtesy Tom Loback   Photo by Sato Studios.

434

BRITAINS
(set prices include boxes)

#1 - 1st version tin sword

#1 - Last version

#2 - 1st version officer tin sword

#2 - 2nd version trooper tin sword

#2 - 3rd version thick sword

#2 - 4th version trooper & officer

#3 - 1st version trooper & officer

#3 - 3rd version

	G	VG	EXC
1.(9206) The Life Guards, 5 pieces, 1st version	110.00	165.00	220.00
Second version (tin wire sword)	85.00	115.00	150.00
Post-War version	70.00	105.00	140.00
Post-War officer	15.00	22.50	30.00
Post-War trooper	12.00	17.50	25.00
2.(9209) Horse Guards, mounted, 5 pieces, 2nd Version (tin wire sword), 1897	90.00	135.00	170.00
Post-War version	86.00	120.00	160.00
Post-War officer	15.00	22.50	30.00
Post-War trooper	12.00	17.50	25.00

	G	VG	EXC
3. Fifth Dragoon Guards, 5 pieces, produced from 1893-1941 (officer on rearing horse, troopers on trotting horses after 1901), 1st version 1893-02	150.00	225.00	300.00
2nd version, 1897-1902 (tin wire sword, "1902" on horse belly)	90.00	150.00	210.00
Pre-War v. officer	20.00	30.00	40.00
Pre-War v. trooper	15.00	22.50	30.00

435

#6 - 3rd Version (moveable arm)

#6 - 1st Version trooper & officer (fixed arm)

#7 1st version

#7 2nd & 3rd versions
(note back pack)

#7 4th version

#8 - Post War Trooper

	G	VG	EXC
4. Gilt Household Cavalry .	20.00	30.00	45.00
5. Gilt Household Cavalry .	20.00	30.00	45.00
6. Boer Cavalry, set 5 pieces (black hats)	400.00	650.00	950.00
Officer, fixed arm - 1st version	50.00	100.00	150.00
Trooper, fixed arm - 1st version	40.00	80.00	120.00
7. Royal Fusiliers, slope arms, 8 pieces, 1st version	125.00	187.50	250.00
Late 1930s	80.00	105.00	135.00
Late 1930s v. officer	10.50	15.00	20.00
Late 1930s v. troop	8.00	12.00	15.00
8. The Fourth Hussars (Queen's Own) on galloping horses, trumpeter earlier on galloping horse, later on trotting horse, 5 pieces, "1901"	125.00	165.00	220.00
Post-War	85.00	115.50	150.00
Post-War v. trumpeter	12.50	18.75	25.00
Post-War v. trooper	11.00	16.50	22.00
9. Rifle Brigade at the Slope, eight pieces 1897-1918 . .	200.00	300.00	400.00

#9 - 1st, 2nd, 4th, 3rd, (note rifle & base change)

	G	VG	EXC
10. Officer, Band and Colours of the Salvation Army, eight pieces (all male); standard bearer, 2 cornet players 5 officers, early flag is cast, later is tin . .	800.00	1800	2800
Standard Bearer, tin flag . . .	75.00	210.00	250.00
Officer	35.00	52.50	170.00
11. (9135) Black Watch (Royal Highlanders) charging, eight pieces. Post War includes piper. Early versions	55.00	82.50	110.00
1st version, running at trail, plugged-in hand (1893-1903)	150.00	235.00	350.00

#10 - later tin flag version

#11 - Post War, 1st version

#12 - 1st Version Trooper

#12 - 3rd Version Officer

#12 - 3rd Version Trooper

#14 - Late Short Skirt Version

#13 - 3rd Version Short Carbine

#13 1st Version Officer
-horse with throat plume.

	G	VG	EXC
Post-War version 8 pieces ..	50.00	75.00	100.00
Post-War version, 6 pieces .	40.00	60.00	80.00
Early piper	11.00	16.50	22.00
Early troop	5.00	7.50	10.00
Post-War piper	8.00	12.00	16.00
Post-War troop	4.00	6.00	8.00

12. Prince Albert's Own
11th Hussars, 5 pieces, in-

	G	VG	EXC
cludes officer, 1st version	150.00	225.00	300.00
1930s version	115.00	172.50	230.00
1930s v. officer	20.00	30.00	40.00
1930s v. trooper	17.50	26.25	35.00

13. 3rd Hussars, 5 pieces, officer, "1903" (on horse

	G	VG	EXC
belly)	110.00	185.99	250.00
Officer, "1903"	20.00	45.00	65.00
Trooper, "1903"	15.00	30.00	40.00

14. Women Officers, Tim-
brel Band and the War
Cry (Salvation Army),
eight pieces, all women,
four empty-handed, two
with tambourines, one
with collection plate, one
with Society's publication

	G	VG	EXC
"The War Cry", 1906- ...	800.00	1500	2000
Empty-Handed Woman ...	80.00	140.00	200.00

BRITAINS

#16 - 1st version, on guard & bugler

#17 - 1st version

#17 - last version

#18 - 2nd version

#19 - 1st version

#23 - early officer

	G	VG	EXC
15. Argyll & Sutherland Highlanders, running, eight pieces, (round base) early version	90.00	135.00	180.00
1930s	60.00	90.00	120.00
1930s officer	8.00	12.00	16.00
1930s troop	6.00	9.00	12.00
16. East Kent Regiment, on guard, with bugler, drummer, officer, 9 pieces early, 8 pieces later	100.00	185.00	275.00
Officer	10.00	15.00	20.00
Troop	9.00	13.50	18.00
17. (9143) Somerset Light Infantry, standing and kneeling on guard, eight pieces, Pre-War	75.00	125.00	175.00
Post-War	50.00	85.00	120.00
Troop, each	5.00	9.00	13.00
18. Worcestershire Infantry, standing and kneeling on guard, eight pieces (round base), officer, drummer added 1910	120.00	200.00	300.00
Officer	15.00	22.00	28.00
Troop	11.00	16.00	22.00
19. First West India Regiment, early sets have marching fixed arm officer, 9 pieces, 8 pieces later, 1st version (1897)	180.00	270.00	360.00

	G	VG	EXC
2nd version, 1910, with mtd. officer	140.00	210.00	280.00
Pre-War	90.00	135.00	180.00
Pre-War officer	12.50	18.50	25.00
Pre-War troop	10.00	15.00	20.00
20. Display Box, Russian & Japanese infantry and cavalry, 26 pieces.	1000	1800	2600
21. Display Box, 1st Life Guards, 11th Hussars, West India Regiment, East Kent Regiment, 27 Pieces	No Price Found		
22. Display Box, 5th Lancers, Horse Guards Black Watch, Worcestershire Regiment, produced through 1937, 27 pieces	No Price Found		
23. 5th Royal Irish Lancers, mounted at halt, 1894-1932, cross-legged horse pre-1903, 5 pieces	160.00	240.00	320.00

#24 - 1st version fixed arm,
rear horse legs crossed

#24 - 2nd version moveable arm

#24 Post War lance slung behind arm

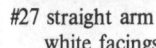

#26 3rd Version

#27 Metal Drum

#25

#27 - 1st Slot arm   #27 3rd

#27 straight arm
white facings

#26 1st Version

	G	VG	EXC
24. (9216) 9th Lancers, mounted at halt, 1894-1941, lances slung on right arm, 5 pieces, Pre-War	110.00	165.00	220.00
Post-War	75.00	125.00	175.00
Post-War officer	16.00	25.00	35.00
Post-War trooper	12.00	18.00	25.00
25. Soldiers to Shoot, 4 pcs. kneeling line infantry, red tunic	400.00	550.00	750.00
spiked helmet, hollow tube rifle, shoots pin via snapping strip of metal (price for one piece)	75.00	130.00	175.00
26. Boer Infantry, circa 1899, 8 pieces	800.00	1200	1800
Boer troop, each	90.00	135.00	180.00
27. Band of the Line, 12 pcs., Pre and Post-War pieces	135.00	200.00	280.00
each	10.00	14.00	18.00
Pre and Post-War drummer	11.00	16.50	22.00

27 early

#30 - 2nd version
Boy Bugler

#30 - 4th version
bent arm, blue
facing

#30
Drummer
Boy

28 early   Courtesy Phillips

No. 30, early

#32 2nd version   3rd   4th
Note: bearskins and tin swords

	G	VG	EXC
Trooper, Royal West Surrey, late	7.00	10.50	14.00
30. (9137) Drums and Bugles of the Line, 1908-1912 8 pcs.	100.00	150.00	200.00
Late 1930s, 1940 (seven pcs)	90.00	125.00	150.00
Postwar (7 and later 6 pcs) .	65.00	87.50	115.00
31. First (Royal) Dragoons, officer on rearing horse, other horses walking, 5 pieces, first version (tin sword)	120.00	220.00	300.00
Second version, "1902" (on horse belly)	110.00	165.00	220.00
1935 officer	22.00	34.50	50.00
1935 trooper	17.00	28.00	35.00
32. (9210) The Royal Scots Greys (2nd Dragoons), 5 pieces with officer "1902", 2nd version	100.00	150.00	200.00
Post-War	60.00	90.00	120.00
Pre-War officer	14.00	22.00	30.00
Pre-War trooper	12.00	18.00	24.00
1960 officer	12.00	20.00	25.00
1960 trooper	10.00	16.00	22.00

	G	VG	EXC
28. (9420) Mountain Gun of the Royal Artillery, 14 pieces, Mounted Officer, 4 mules, 6 marching gunners, 3 pieces of small gun that fit together	225.00	337.50	450.00
Post-War	155.00	225.00	325.00
Officer, 1930s, mounted ...	14.00	22.00	35.00
Gunner, Post-War	9.00	15.00	20.00
Mule	12.00	18.00	24.00
29. Display Box, 1st Life Guards, 3rd Hussars, 9th Lancers, Royal West Surrey Infantrymen, marching and on guard, 1903-1910, 41 pieces	1000	2200	2800
Officer, Royal West Surrey, late	8.00	12.00	16.00

440

#33 - 1st version

#34 - 1st version
Note rifle position

#34 - 3rd version

#36 - 4th version 2nd verison

#35 early

#36 "1910"

#36 - 1st version

#36 3rd & 5th

#35   7th version   6th version   3rd version   2nd version

#37 - 1st version - slot arms

#37 - 1930 version

	G	VG	EXC
33. 16th/5th Lancers, mounted at halt, five pieces, Pre-War	105.00	200.00	300.00
Post-War 5 pcs	80.00	125.00	165.00
1950 Officer	15.00	22.50	30.00
1950 Trooper	12.00	18.00	24.00
34. Grenadier Guards, standing firing, 8 pieces	65.00	97.50	125.00
Trooper	7.00	10.50	13.00
35. (9140) The Royal Marines at slope arms, with officer, 8 pieces, 1920s	90.00	135.00	180.00
Post-War	75.00	105.00	140.00
Officer Post-War	10.00	18.00	23.00
Troop Post-War	7.00	12.00	16.00
36. (9142) Royal Sussex Regiment, slope arms, mounted officer, 1910 version, 7 pieces (white helmets)	115.00	180.00	250.00
Post-War	65.00	97.50	130.00

	G	VG	EXC
Pre-War officer	12.50	18.75	25.00
Pre-War Troop	10.00	15.00	20.00
Post-War officer	10.00	14.00	18.00
Post-War Troop	7.50	11.00	14.00
37. Full Band of Coldstream Guards, 21 pieces, 1st version (round base, plug-in arms)	350.00	550.00	800.00
Pre-War, late 30's	250.00	385.00	600.00
Post-War	225.00	350.00	500.00
Post-War, per standard figure	10.00	16.00	22.00

#38 - 3rd Version

#39 early

#43 - 1st Version

#43 - Last Version

#44 Post War   #44 2nd Version

	G	VG	EXC
38. Dr. Jameson and the South African Mounted Infantry, circa 1896-1908, 5 pieces, fixed arm (see name change of set, following)	400.00	650.00	900.00
1st version trooper	40.00	80.00	120.00
1st version officer with pistol	50.00	100.00	150.00
38. South African Mounted Infantry, moveable arms after 1911 (same as #6 but grey hat)	250.00	500.00	750.00
39. (9419) Royal House Artillery, with gun and limber, 13 pieces, 1895, 6-horse team, large collar on horse's neck, twisted wire traces	450.00	625.00	900.00
Post-War	200.00	350.00	550.00
40. Display Box, 1st Dragoons, Somerset Light Infantry, 14 pieces, Pre-War only	200.00	375.00	600.00
41. (9210) The Royal Scots Greys (2nd Dragoons) and the Grenadier Guards, 14 pieces (13 pieces Post-War)	120.00	200.00	250.00

	G	VG	EXC
42. Display Box, 1st Life Guards, Royal Sussex Regiment, 12 pieces	280.00	420.00	560.00
43. 2nd Life Guards, five pieces, trumpeter, four troopers at gallop, with rifles	125.00	200.00	300.00
Trumpeter	25.00	42.50	60.00
Trooper	20.00	35.00	50.00
44. The Queen's Bay (2nd Dragoon Guards), 5 pieces, galloping bay horses, troopers with lances, officer on trotting horse **or** bugler on trotting horse (the latter more common), 1901 version	100.00	200.00	250.00
Late 1930s	110.00	165.00	220.00
Post-War	110.00	165.00	220.00
Officer, late 1930s	25.00	37.50	50.00
Lancer, late 1930s	20.00	30.00	40.00
Officer, Post-War	20.00	30.00	40.00
Lancer, Post-War	16.00	24.00	32.00

#45 1st Version thick sword

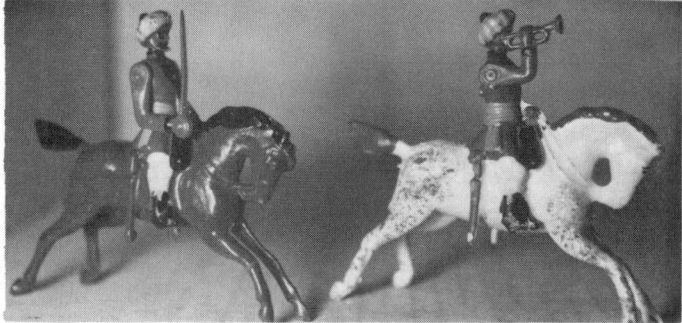

#47 1st Version

#47 (And #271) Last Version

#48 - early - wire tail

#48 - Post War - molded tail

#49 Last Version

	G	VG	EXC
45. 3rd Madras Cavalry, 5 pieces, trumpeter, 4 troopers, with swords early thick sword version ..	200.00	350.00	450.00
Trumpeter, 1930s	24.00	36.00	48.00
Trooper, 1930s	22.00	33.00	44.00
46. Hodson's Horse, 5 pieces, with lances, includes bugler, 1896-1940	125.00	187.50	250.00
Bugler	22.00	33.00	44.00
Lancer	18.00	27.00	36.00
47. 1st Bengal Cavalry, 5 pieces, includes bugler, with lances 1896 to about 1934	105.00	215.99	280.00
Bugler	25.00	37.50	50.00
Trooper	21.00	31.50	42.00
47. (9261) Skinner's Horse (1st Duke of York's Own Lancers), same as above, circa 1934-1966, Pre-War	105.00	200.00	250.00
Post-War, 5 pieces	90.00	125.00	160.00
Post-War bugler	17.50	26.25	35.00
Post-War trooper	15.00	22.50	30.00

	G	VG	EXC
48. (9265) Egyptian Camel Corps, 6 pieces, 6 riders on camels, 1896-1940 ...	270.00	350.00	550.00
Post-War cast tail (3 riders and camels)	80.00	200.00	300.00
Camel and Rider	25.00	47.50	70.00
49. South Austrailian Lancers, 5 pieces, early version has slouch hats, 1896?. Later redone with spiked helmet, through 1941; 1930 version	200.00	450.00	650.00
Late 20s - early 30s officer .	35.00	65.00	85.00
Late 20s - early 30s trooper	25.00	50.00	70.00
50. (9305) The Life Guards and the 4th Hussars, 10 pieces, double box, Pre-War	250.00	375.00	500.00
Post-War	150.00	300.00	400.00
51. Display Box 16th Lancers, 11th Hussars, mounted at halt, 10 pieces, Pre-War only	200.00	450.00	650.00
52. Display Box 5th Lancers, 2nd Life Guards, mounted at halt, produced through 1937, 10 pieces .	250.00	500.00	700.00

#64 Early Version As
"2nd MADRAS LANCERS"

#64 Last Version
7th BENGAL INF

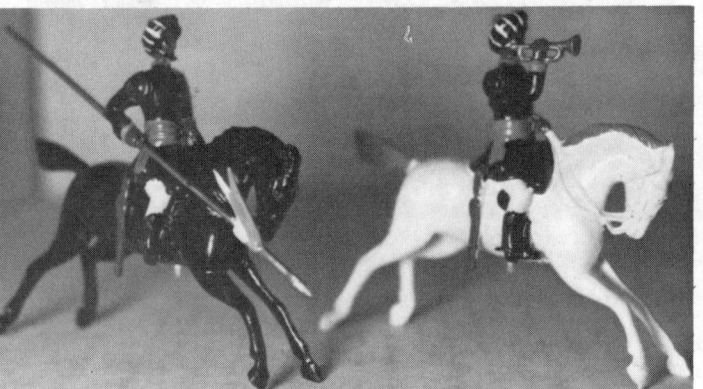

#66 Post War

#67 1st version
at trail

#67 3rd Version at Slope

	G	VG	EXC
53. 4th Hussars with trumpeter, Royal House Guards with officer, Grenadier Guards with Side Drummer and officer, 18 pcs.	250.00	500.00	700.00
54. Display Box, 1st Life Guards, 2nd Dragoon Guards, 9th Lancers, mounted at halt, 15 pcs .	No Price Found		
55. Scots Greys, 3rd Hussars, 16th Lancers at Halt, 15 pieces	No Price Found		
56. Grenadier Guards, East Kent Regiment, 15 pcs.	300.00	550.00	800.00
57. 1st Dragoon Guards (not standard size), 12 pcs	No Price Found		
58. Display Box, Royal Horse Guards, Scots Greys, Mounted Infantry (not standard size), 21 pcs	No Price Found		
59. Scots Greys, 10 pcs	200.00	400.00	600.00
60. 1st Bombay Lancers, 15 pcs., 1896-circa 1935	350.00	650.00	850.00
61. 3rd Madras Cavalry, 15 pcs., 13 troops, bugler, officer, 1896-35	350.00	650.00	850.00
61. 7th Light Cavalry, circa 1936 or 37, same as above	No Price Found		
62. 1st Bengal Cavalry, 10 pcs., 1896 to about 1934	250.00	500.00	650.00
Officer	30.00	45.00	60.00
Trooper	25.00	37.50	50.00
62. Skinner's Horse (1st Duke of York's Own Lancers), same as above, circa 1934-40, 10 pcs	250.00	400.00	500.00
63. 10th Bengal Lancers, 10 pcs., officer, bugler included, 1896-1940	300.00	600.00	850.00
64. 2nd Madras Lancers (5), + 7th Bengal Infantry (8), 1896-circa 1938, 13 pcs	250.00	500.00	700.00
Infantry	12.00	20.00	30.00
Lancer	22.00	35.00	50.00
64. 16th Light Cavalry (5), 7th Bengal Infantry (8), same as above, circa 1938-1940	300.00	500.00	680.00

	G	VG	EXC
65. Display Box, Russian Cavalry and Infantry, 13 pcs	400.00	750.00	1200
66. 1st Bombay Lacers, 5 pcs., 1896-1937	175.00	262.50	350.00
Trumpeter	30.00	45.00	60.00
Trooper	25.00	37.50	50.00
66. (9262) 13th Duke of Connaught's Own Lancers, same as above with blue tunic, 1937-66 .	80.00	120.00	160.00
Trumpeter	17.00	25.00	34.00
Lancer	16.00	24.00	30.00

#68 1st Version - Officer & Pioneer with Axe

#68 Last

#69 1st - 2nd note bases

#69 last

#70 running at trail

#67 Rare White Turban

#71

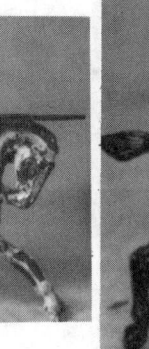

#72 2nd Version

#74

#75 1st Version

#75   1st - 3rd - 4th Note Backpacks

	G	VG	EXC
Later version, 1929 at slope	150.00	250.00	300.00
Officer, 1st version	25.00	37.50	50.00
Troop, 1st version	20.00	30.00	40.00
Officer, later version	20.00	30.00	40.00
Trooper, later version	15.00	22.50	30.00
68. Second Bombay Native Infantry, at the trail, with axes, officer, till 1918 ...	300.00	450.00	600.00
Officer	40.00	60.00	80.00
Troop, later version	30.00	45.00	60.00
68. Second Bombay Native Infantry, at the slope, no other types	150.00	225.00	300.00
Troop	16.00	24.00	32.00
68. 2nd Battalion Fourth Bombay Grenadiers (King Edward's Own), mid 1930s-40s, 8 pcs	100.00	205.00	250.00
69. Pipes of Scots Guards, 6,7,8 pieces	100.00	165.00	225.00
Pre-1930 Piper	12.00	18.00	24.00
Pre-1942 Piper	11.00	16.50	22.00
70. Scots Guards, running, 7 pieces, mounted officer ..	170.00	300.00	400.00
Officer	25.00	47.50	65.00
Troop	20.00	30.00	40.00
71. Turkish Cavalry, 5 pieces, Pre-War	150.00	350.00	450.00
Officer	40.00	60.00	80.00
Trooper	25.00	40.00	55.00

	G	VG	EXC
67. First Madras Native Infantry at trail, officer with sword, 8 pcs., 1896-1918; 1st version, at trail	200.00	350.00	450.00

BRITAINS

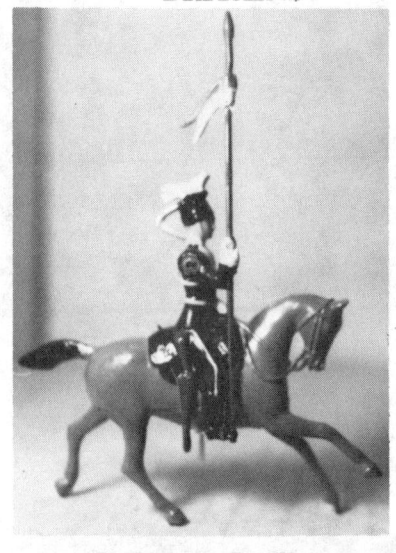

#73 17th Lancer Post-War

#76 1st at trail & last version

#78 2nd version

#77 2nd version with back pack

#77 - last version

#77 - Piper Post-War

#78 Petty Officer

	G	VG	EXC
72. Life Guards at Waterloo & Present fixed arms with tin sword	2200	4500	6000
72. Life Guards at Waterloo, moveable arm, 12 pcs . . .	1400	2800	3500
73. (9407) Royal Artillery, 2nd Life Guards, 17th Lancers, Royal Welsh Fusiliers, Scots Greys, Band of the Line, Gordon Highlanders, General Officer, 73 pcs., Pre-War	650.00	925.00	1500
Post-War, 67 pieces	500.00	850.00	1200
Black Watch at slope	10.00	15.00	20.00
Black Watch Officer	13.00	19.50	26.00
Gordon Highlander	5.00	7.50	10.00
17th Lancers Officer	40.00	60.00	80.00
17th Lancer	35.00	52.50	70.00
74. (9144) Royal Welsh Fusiliers, slope arms, goat mascot, officer, eight pieces, early Pre-War . . .	130.00	195.00	260.00
Post-War	60.00	95.00	115.00

#79 Post War	G	VG	EXC
Pre-War at slope	6.00	11.00	14.00
Post-War at slope	5.00	9.00	12.00
75. (9126) Scots Guards, slope arms, officer, piper, 8 pcs., 1893-1910 (round base)	150.00	225.00	300.00
Post-War, 7 pcs	50.00	70.00	90.00
1st version officer	20.00	30.00	40.00
1st version troop	15.00	22.50	30.00
Pre and Post-War Officer . .	7.00	11.00	14.00
Pre and Post-War troop . . .	6.00	9.00	11.00
76. (9136) Middlesex Regiment, marching at slope, officer, 8 pcs., Pre-War . .	75.00	100.00	130.00
Post-War	55.00	75.00	110.00
Officer	10.00	14.00	18.00
Troop	6.00	9.00	12.00
77. (9131) Gordon Highlanders, with Piper, no officer, slope arms, 8 pcs., Pre-War	90.00	120.00	150.00
Post-War, 8 pcs.	70.00	105.00	130.00
Post-War 6 pcs	40.00	60.00	80.00
Round base piper early Pre-War	12.00	18.00	24.00
Round base troop early Pre-War	10.00	15.00	20.00
Post-War piper	9.00	13.50	18.00
Post-War troop	6.00	9.00	12.00
78. Bluejackets running at trail, 8 pcs., petty officer, 1897-1941; 1930 set	100.00	200.00	300.00
Late 1930s set	100.00	200.00	275.00
Petty officer, very early . . .	11.00	20.00	30.00
Bluejacket, very early	10.00	20.00	25.00
Late 1930s petty officer . . .	15.00	22.50	30.00
Late 1930s bluejacket	11.00	16.50	22.00
79. (9455) Royal Navy Landing Party with Gun, limber, 11 pcs. (9 figures), 1898-41, has officer, semi-oval base till about 1920, caps have blue tops, Pre-War	185.00	325.00	475.00
Post-War set	150.00	250.00	400.00

446

#80 2nd version running at slope

#80 3rd version Running at trail

#81

#81 2nd version - long lance tip

#82 3rd version flag

#82 2nd   3rd   4th
(note pack and bases)

#83 Trooper Green Tunic

#83 Officer

#89 early version

	G	VG	EXC
80. Whitejackets running at slope, 8 pcs., petty officer, after 1920 (approximately), sailors run at trail ...	120.00	220.00	280.00
Running at trail	12.00	22.00	28.00
81. 17th Lancers, trotting and cantering, 5 pcs., 1903	250.00	450.00	650.00
"1903" trooper	40.00	75.00	100.00
Early 30s trooper	30.00	50.00	75.00
82. Scots Guards, Colours and Pioneers with axes, 7 pcs., Pre-War	90.00	165.00	220.00
Post-War	80.00	155.00	190.00
Officer with Flag	20.00	30.00	45.00
Prisoner with Axe	13.00	20.00	25.00
83. Middlesex Yeomanry trotting horse, 5 pcs.	200.00	450.00	650.00
Trooper	35.00	60.00	85.00

	G	VG	EXC
84. Display Box, 2nd Life Guards, 7th Royal Fusiliers, (not standard size), 11 pcs			No Price Found
85. Display Box, 5th Dragoon Guards, Scots Greys, Scots Guards, Northumberland Fusiliers, 22 pcs. (not standard size) ..			No Price Found
86. Lancashire Fusiliers (not standard size), 14 pcs ...			No Price Found
87. 13th Hussars (not standard size, 8 pcs.)			No Price Found
88. Seaforth Highlanders, charging, 16 pcs. (2 pipers)	160.00	220.00	280.00
1st version, plug-in hand and rifle, single figure running	18.00	28.00	40.00
89. Cameron Highlanders standing, lying firing, officer with binoculars, 30 pieces "Black Label" box, 1930	350.00	500.00	850.00

#91 1st version at slope   2nd version on guard   #92 - 1st version officer   #92 - 1st version at trail

#92 2nd version at slope

#90

#94 1st version foreign service helmet

#94 3rd version - steel helmets

#96 1st version   3rd version white facings

	G	VG	EXC
90. The Coldstream Guards standing, kneeling, lying firing, with 2 officers, drummer, bugler, 27 pieces (24 later) Pre-War	200.00	325.00	400.00
27 pcs. - Post-War	200.00	275.00	350.00
24 piece set (Post War)	175.00	225.00	300.00
Officer (Post War)	10.00	14.00	18.00
Troop	8.00	10.50	12.00
Bugler	10.00	15.00	20.00
91. American Blue "Federal Dress" on guard (fixed arm officer early, later has moving arm) "1906" set .	400.00	600.00	800.00
"1906" officer	25.00	37.50	50.00
"1906" troop	22.00	33.00	44.00

	G	VG	EXC
92. Spanish Infantry, slope, 8 pieces, circa 1898 on; 1898 version (round base), officer added 1914	350.00	650.00	900.00
Later version	175.00	280.00	350.00
1898 troop	35.00	52.50	70.00
Later troop	12.50	18.75	25.00
93. Coldstream Guards, Royal Horse Guards galloping with lances, full band, colours, pioneers, 71 pieces	2000	4000	7500
Trooper on full-stretched horse, 1939	30.00	60.00	80.00
Running at trail	15.00	25.00	38.00
94. 21st Lancers, galloping, 5 pcs., has trumpeter ...	300.00	450.00	650.00
Trumpet	40.00	75.00	100.00
Trooper	30.00	65.00	90.00
95. Display Box, Japanese Cavalry and Infantry, 13 pieces	800.00	1400	1800
96. York & Lancaster, infantry, 8 pieces running at trail, Boer War active service dress (khaki)	350.00	650.00	850.00
Whisstock box version (red coat)	200.00	400.00	600.00
Boer War active service dress officer	45.00	67.50	90.00
Boer War active service dress troop	40.00	60.00	80.00
Whisstock Box officer	21.00	31.50	42.00
Whisstock box troop	13.00	19.50	26.00

#97 1st version

97 later

97 early

#97 - 3rd version
blue facings

#98 Post-War #98 early Pre-War

#99 early

#100 Trooper

#101 Pre War Drummer
Arms apart

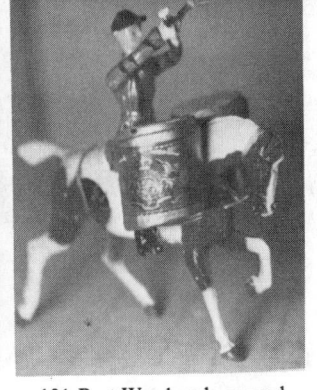

101 Post-War hands crossed

101 Post-War

	G	VG	EXC
97. Royal Marine Light Infantry running at trail, 8 pcs., first version	300.00	650.00	800.00
1910 issue	250.00	450.00	550.00
1930 issue	200.00	375.00	550.00
First version troop	30.00	55.00	75.00
2nd version troop	20.00	42.50	60.00
4th version troop	15.00	25.00	35.00
98. King's Royal Rifle Corps, running at trail, 8 pcs., 1899-1940, 1948-52, has officer, pre-1920s version	150.00	250.00	350.00
Set 1920-40	110.00	175.00	250.00
Set 1948-52	100.00	160.00	220.00
Troop, pre-1920s	15.00	22.50	30.00
Officer, 1920-40	12.50	18.75	25.00
Troop, 1920-40	10.00	15.00	20.00
Post-War officer	15.00	22.50	30.00
Post-War troop	10.00	15.00	20.00

	G	VG	EXC
99. 13th Hussars, pony trot horse, 5 pieces, "1903"	140.00	250.00	350.00
Officer, "1903" (on horse belly)	25.00	45.00	65.00
Trooper, "1903" (on horse belly)	15.00	35.00	45.00
100. 21st Lancers, cantering, 5 pcs	150.00	275.00	375.00
Trumpeter	30.00	45.50	65.00
Trooper	20.00	35.00	55.00
101. (9406) Band of the Life Guards in State Dress, 12 pcs., Pre-War	250.00	450.00	550.00
Post-War	150.00	300.00	400.00
Pre-War instruments	20.00	30.00	40.00
Pre-War music director	25.00	35.00	50.00
Post-War music director	20.00	30.00	40.00
Post-War instruments	18.00	25.00	35.00

#101 1st version - all white horses, slot arms

#104 2nd version

#105 - 2nd version 2-tone uniform   4th version   solid color uniform

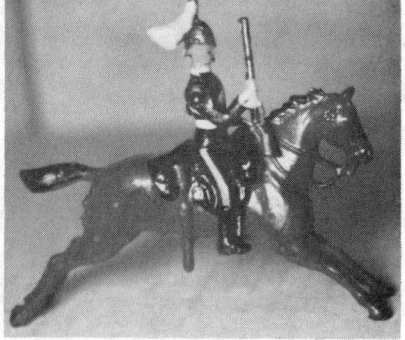

#106 Trooper

#108 3rd version
solid color uniform

#109 1st
smooth helmet

#109 3rd
wolseley helmet

#110 2 variations of 1st version

2nd #110 Last (note helmets)

	G	VG	EXC
102. Display Box, Grenadier, Scots, Irish, and Coldstream Guards, 32 pieces	No Price Found		
Irish Guard, "1901"	17.50	26.50	35.00
Irish Guard, "1905"	16.00	24.00	32.00
103. Band of the Royal Horse Guards, 12 pcs., moveable arm version rarer	1400	3000	4500
104. City Imperial Volunteers, at the ready, 10 pcs. including officer, circa 1900	250.00	425.00	600.00
Later Issue, 8 pieces	200.00	410.00	520.00
Circa 1900 officer	30.00	47.50	70.00
Circa 1900 troop	20.00	35.00	50.00
Later officer	20.00	30.00	40.00
Later troop	16.00	24.00	32.00
105. Imperial Yeomanry, 5 pcs., early versions	250.00	425.00	600.00
106. Sixth Dragoon Guards, holding carbines, mounted, with fixed arm officer, 5 pcs., 1901	220.00	400.00	550.00

	G	VG	EXC
107. Irish Guards, slope, 8 pcs	90.00	145.00	200.00
Troop	9.50	14.00	20.00
108. Sixth Inniskilling Dragoons, 5 pieces, fixed arms	175.00	350.00	450.00
Trooper	30.00	60.00	80.00
109. Dublin Fusiliers, at the trail, 8 pcs., "1901"	175.00	300.00	400.00
Late 1930s	125.00	250.00	300.00
Troop, "1901"	20.00	30.00	40.00
Troop, late 1930s	11.00	20.00	27.00
110. Devonshire Regiment at the trail, 8 pcs	170.00	255.00	340.00
Troop	20.00	30.00	40.00

#111 two types turned head

#111 -
2nd version

#111 -
3rd version

#112, early

#113, 3rd version

#114 - 1st & 3rd   (note helmets)

#114 2nd version

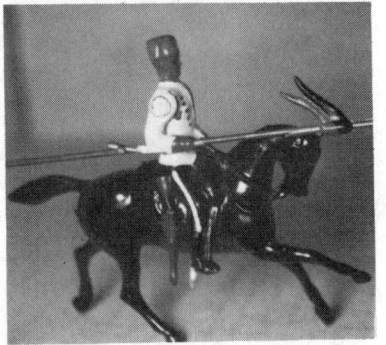
#115 early version long lance tip

#116

#117 Post-War Officer

#118   2 versions

#119 2nd & 3rd version

	G	VG	EXC
111. Grenadier Guards at attention, officer on swayback horse, 7 pieces, "1910"	170.00	285.00	400.00
Late version Pre-War	140.00	255.00	350.00
Officer, "1910"	35.00	52.50	70.00
Troop, "1910"	20.00	30.00	40.00
Late officer	15.00	30.00	45.00
Late troop	10.00	25.00	35.00
112. Seaforth Highlanders, slope, 8 pcs, 1940	85.00	150.00	200.00
Troop	9.00	15.00	20.00
113. East Yorkshire Regiment at attention, 8 pcs.	165.00	300.50	400.00
Troop	15.00	30.00	40.00
114. Cameron Highlanders, at slope, 8 pcs., "1901"	120.00	210.00	300.00
Post-War	100.00	180.00	250.00
Troop, "1901", dated base	17.50	26.25	35.00
Troop, Post-War	11.00	16.50	22.00
115. (9264) Egyptian Cavalry, 4 lancers and officer with sword, 5 pcs, early 1930s	90.00	135.00	200.00
Post-War	80.00	120.00	160.00
Officer, first version	48.00	72.00	96.00
Lancer, first version	27.00	40.50	54.00
Officer, Post-War	15.00	20.00	30.00
Trooper, Post-War	10.00	18.00	24.00

	G	VG	EXC
116. Sudanese Infantry, 8 pcs., walking at trail, 1st version	175.00	300.00	400.00
"1901" troop (round base)	20.00	30.00	45.00
2nd version troop (rectangular base)	17.50	26.50	35.00
117. Egyptian Infantry, at attention, 8 pcs., Post-War	95.00	140.00	200.00
Officer pointing pistol (1957-59 sets only)	22.50	33.75	45.00
Troop	10.00	15.00	20.00
118. Gordon Highlanders, lying, firing, 8 pcs., late 1920s, Whisstock	100.00	150.00	200.00
Troop, feet together or apart	7.00	10.50	14.00
119. Gloucestershire Regiment, standing firing, 9 pcs., (8 later)	120.00	210.00	320.00
Troop, later 30s	10.00	15.00	20.00

BRITAINS

#121 2nd   #121 3rd

#122 1st version

#122 2nd version

(Note Bases)

#123 - 2nd version moulded tail

	G	VG	EXC
120. (9123) Coldstream Guards, kneeling firing, with officer, 8 pcs. Pre-War	75.00	125.00	150.00
Set, Post-War	60.00	95.00	120.00
Officer, kneeling	10.00	18.00	25.00
Trooper firing	7.00	9.00	12.00
121. Royal West Surrey infantrymen, 8 pcs., standing firing, officer with binoculars, early	95.00	140.00	180.00
Late 30s set	80.00	120.00	160.00
Later officer	10.50	17.00	23.00
Later troop	8.00	11.00	16.00
122. Black Watch, 8 pcs., standing, firing, "1901", 1st version	120.00	200.00	300.00
Late 30s	100.00	190.00	270.00
Troop "1901"	12.50	18.75	25.00
Troop, later version	10.00	15.00	20.00
123. Bikanir Camel Corps, 3 pcs., men on camels, 1901-40, early camels have wire tails; 1st version	150.00	250.00	350.00
Second version, moulded tail	120.00	220.00	320.00
Wire tail (1st version)	40.00	65.00	90.00
Moulded tail (2nd version)	30.00	55.00	80.00
124. Irish Guards lying, firing, 8 pcs., with officer	100.00	160.00	200.00
Officer	12.00	17.50	23.00
Troop	9.00	14.00	18.00
125. Royal Horse Artillery (smaller size), 13 pcs., 1901, in blue	195.00	280.00	450.00
1901 Trooper	9.00	13.50	18.00
126. Royal Horse Artillery (smaller size), 13 pcs., in khaki	250.00	350.00	550.00
127. 7th Dragoon Guards galloping with lances, 5 pcs	130.00	250.00	350.00
Officer	23.00	37.50	50.00
Trooper	20.00	33.00	45.00

	G	VG	EXC
128. 12th Lancers, 5 pcs., trotting and cantering, has officer, 1903-1941; "1903"	120.00	200.00	280.00
Officer	20.00	35.00	50.00
Trooper	15.00	30.00	40.00
129. Display Box, First (King's) Dragoon Guards, 12th Lancers, Royal Scots Greys, 11th Hussars, 2nd Life Guards, 70 pcs.	1200	2400	3500
Dragoon (only available in this set)	50.00	75.00	100.00
2nd Life Guard w/lance	30.00	65.00	90.00
12th Lancer	22.00	40.00	55.00
130 Display Set, 118 pcs	3000	7000	11000
Boy Drummer	10.00	15.00	20.00
Troop	9.00	13.50	18.00
Flag bearer	12.00	18.00	24.00

131. Scots Guards, 275 figures, includes extremely rare Guards Camel Corps, sold only in this box. Presentation Box, Royal Horse Artillery, Mountain Battery, British Camel Corps, Scots Greys, 11th Hussars, 5th Dragoon Guards, 17th Lancers, 2nd Life Guards, Royal Horse Guards, Band of Coldstreams, Scots Guards (firing), Gordon Highlanders, and Pipes, Worcestershire Regiment, Bluejackets and Whitejackets with 4.7 naval gun and General Officer (very rare) 5000 9000 15000

#133 - 1st officer   2nd   3rd
At trail   At slope

#133   2nd   3rd At Trail

#134 early lt. blue

#134 late 30s dark blue

#135 3rd version

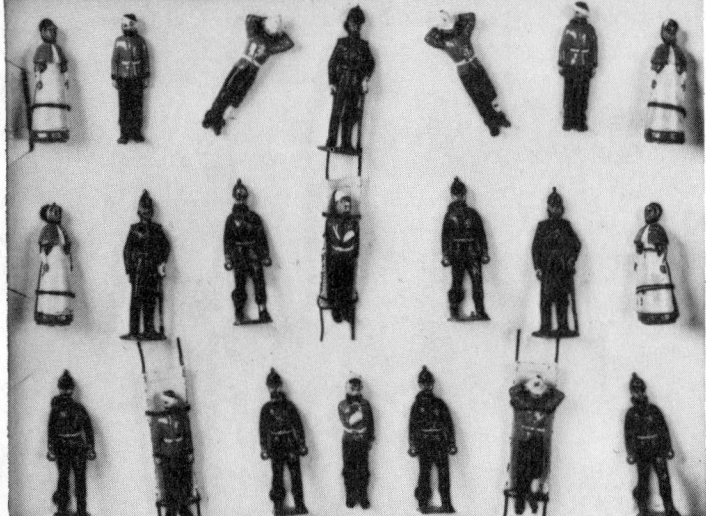

#137 Set - early

#136 Post- War

	G	VG	EXC
134. Japanese Infantry, charging, 8 pcs, "1904" .	160.00	340.00	420.00
1930s set	140.00	280.00	380.00
Troop, "1904"	20.00	30.00	40.00
Troop, 1930s	15.00	25.00	38.00
135. Japanese Cavalry, 5 pcs. 1st version with short carbine, 2nd version with long carbine; 1st version, 1905	400.00	600.00	800.00
Long carbines	250.00	425.00	600.00
Officer, 1st version	40.00	82.50	110.00
Short carbine	30.00	75.00	100.00
Officer, 2nd version	35.00	60.00	80.00
Long carbine	30.00	52.50	70.00
136. (9273) Russian Cavalry, Cossacks, 5 pcs., 1935 issue	105.00	145.00	205.00
Post-War	80.00	135.00	180.00
Officer, Post-War	15.00	25.00	35.00
Trooper, Post-War	13.00	20.00	28.00
137. Royal Army Medical Service, doctors, nurses, wounded, stretcher bearers, 24 pcs	205.00	400.00	500.00
Doctor	11.00	18.50	25.00

	G	VG	EXC
132. Display Box, Royal Horse Artillery, Scots Greys, 11th Hussars, 2nd Life Guards, Horse Guards, 7th Dragoon Guards, Band of the Line, Seaforths with pipes, Welsh Fusiliers, Coldstreams firing, East Kents, Mule Battery, 4.7 Naval Gun, General Officer, 167 pcs		No Price Found	
133. Russian Infantry (Tsarist), officer, 8 pcs., "1904" version, at slope .	140.00	270.00	360.00
At trail	110.00	165.00	220.00
Early officer	25.00	37.50	50.00
Early troop	20.00	30.00	40.00

BRITAINS

#137 2nd version

#138 1st & 2nd versions
Note: small projection on 1st helmet

#139 3rd version

#140

#140 1st version
- rifle plugged in back

#140 2nd version

#141 - 1st   2nd
Lt. blue   dk. blue

#142 Post War

#143 Pre War

	G	VG	EXC
Stretcher Bearer	10.00	15.00	20.00
Stretcher	3.00	5.00	6.00
Wounded	7.00	10.50	14.00
Nurse (1st version, Victorian dress)	7.50	11.25	15.00
138. (9266) French Cuirassiers with officer, 5 pcs., Pre-War	80.00	115.00	150.00
Post-War	70.00	105.00	140.00
Post-War (1960) 4 pcs.	50.00	80.00	115.00
Officer, Post-War	14.00	21.00	28.00
Trooper, Post-War	12.50	18.75	25.00
139. French Chasseurs a Cheval, 5 pcs.	225.00	450.00	550.00
Trooper	40.00	60.00	80.00
140. French Dragoons, 5 pcs.	225.00	450.00	550.00
Officer	45.00	67.50	100.00
Trooper	40.00	60.00	80.00
141. French infantry of the Line, slope, 8 pcs., 1st version	150.00	300.00	400.00
Late 30s	120.00	215.00	270.00
Troop, first version	18.00	27.00	36.00
Troop, late version	12.00	18.00	25.00
142. (9166) Zouaves, charging, 8 pcs., Pre-War	80.00	100.00	130.00
1945-59 set, 7 pcs., with mtd. officer	70.00	95.00	110.00
Troop	5.00	7.50	10.00
Officer, mtd	10.00	15.00	20.00
143. Matelots, running at the trail, 8 pcs., Pre-War	350.00	675.00	900.00
Post-War	300.00	550.00	750.00
Troop, Post-War	30.00	65.00	85.00
144. Royal Field Artillery, 9 pcs., with gun and limber, officer with sword, 6 horses, 3 drivers, limber with 2 seated, cannon with 2 seated	600.00	1000	1400
Officer, "1903"	30.00	55.00	80.00

#145 Pre-War - 2nd version

#145 A Pre-War late

#146 2nd version

¦ #146A

#147 Post War

#150 with 2 versions of "Rifle at Ready".

	G	VG	EXC
145. The Royal Army Medical Corps., horsedrawn ambulance, 7 pcs., one riding "driver" on horse, two seated men	150.00	300.00	400.00
145A. R.A.M.C. Ambulance Wagon, khaki uniforms .	200.00	450.00	550.00
146. Army Service Corps Wagon, 5 pcs., 2-horse team and crew, early issue	120.00	250.00	350.00
Post-War	100.00	200.00	300.00
146A. Army Service Corps Wagon, as above, but uniforms in khaki (available Pre-War only) .	225.00	350.00	500.00
147. (9190) Zulus of Africa, 8 pcs.	80.00	100.00	140.00
Each	7.50	11.25	15.00
148. Royal Lancaster Regiment, 13 pcs., 3 running at slope arms, 4 running at trail, running bugler, running flagbearer, 2 gunners at attention with small cannon, mounted officer on prancing horse, with Beiser's patented display board		No Price Found	
149. American Soldiers, 13 pcs., same variety of pcs. as 148, with Beiser's patented display board . .	400.00	800.00	1200
150. (9189) North American Indians, on foot, with chiefs, 8 pcs., 7 pcs. later	55.00	85.00	120.00
Per figure	4.50	6.50	9.00

BRITAINS

#151

#152

#154 2nd and 3rd versions

#153 last version

#157

#159 1st trooper
(2 tone uniform)

#159 Last trooper & officer

	G	VG	EXC
156. Royal Irish Infantry, standing, kneeling, lying, firing (no officer), 10 pcs. (8 later); early versions	90.00	185.00	250.00
Per figure	9.00	15.00	18.00
157. Gordon Highlanders, 3 positions firing, 8 pcs	80.00	125.00	170.00
Officer	12.00	18.00	25.00
Troop	7.50	12.00	17.00
159. Yeoman, Territorial Army, 5 pcs., mounted with officer	120.00	280.00	350.00
Officer	20.00	42.00	60.00
Per figure	15.00	30.00	40.00
160. Our Territorial Infantry at trail, 8 pcs., 1915 issue	110.00	205.00	270.00
Last version, circa 1930	95.00	190.00	250.00
Per figure, early 30s	11.00	18.00	25.00
161. Boy Scouts, 9 pcs. (8 from 1939), scouts, scoutmaster	120.00	220.00	300.00
162. Boy Scout Encampment, 23 pcs.	270.00	450.00	650.00
Standing with axe	13.00	22.50	30.00
Saluter	14.00	21.00	28.00
Empty-handed	13.00	19.50	26.00
Fallen Tree	8.00	12.00	16.00
163. Boy Scout Signalers, 5 pcs	140.00	280.00	380.00
Per figure	17.50	26.25	35.00

	G	VG	EXC
151. Royal Naval Volunteer Reserve, shoulder arms fixed arm, bearded petty officer, 1907-41, 8 pcs	95.00	170.00	250.00
Petty Officer	11.00	18.50	25.00
Single figure	8.50	13.50	18.00
152. (9289) North American Indians on horses, with rifles and tomahawks, 5 pcs., (4 pcs. later)	65.00	95.00	120.00
Per figure	9.00	14.50	20.00
153. Prussian Hussars, 5 pcs., "1903"	220.00	450.00	550.00
1930	170.00	400.00	450.00
Officer, "1903"	40.00	70.00	90.00
Trooper, "1903"	35.00	52.50	70.00
Officer, 1930	25.00	55.00	75.00
Trooper, 1930	20.00	40.00	60.00
154. Prussian Infantry, marching, 8 pcs	150.00	250.00	350.00
Troop	20.00	30.00	40.00

456

#160 early
Courtesy Phillips

#161-62 Pre-War, blue shorts

Post-War,
matching shorts

#163   Courtesy Phillips

#164

#165 Lancer & Officer

#166   2nd version

#169 Post-War

	G	VG	EXC
166. Italian Infantry, slope,			
8 pcs.	125.00	205.00	300.00
Troop	14.00	21.00	28.00
167. Turkish Infantry, 8 pcs	135.00	275.00	350.00
Troop	13.00	22.00	35.00
169. (9163) The Bersaglieri,			
marching, slung rifles, 8			
pcs., Pre-War	90.00	145.00	190.00
Post-War, with officer	80.00	135.00	180.00
Officer	10.00	15.00	25.00
Troop	8.00	12.00	18.00

	G	VG	EXC
164. (9291) Arabs on			
Horses, 5 pcs.	80.00	105.00	130.00
Per figure	11.50	16.50	24.00
165. Italian Cavalry, 5 pcs.			
with officer	175.00	375.00	500.00
Officer	35.00	72.50	100.00
Trooper	30.00	55.00	80.00

BRITAINS

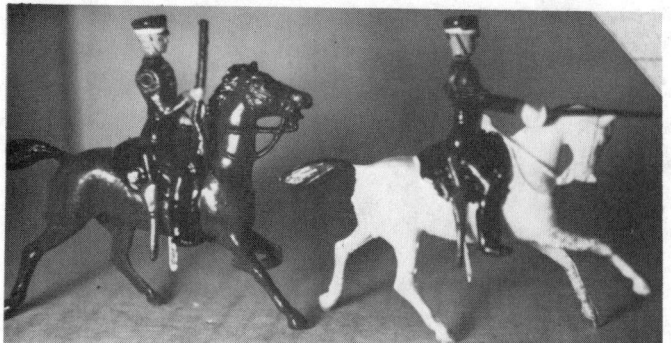

#170 - 2nd version

#171 late 30's

#171

#172 - 1st version
at slope

#174

#179 & 184

#175 These "Lancers" carried swords

#176

#177
3rd version

#178 - 1st & 3rd version

	G	VG	EXC
170. Greek Cavalry, 5 pcs., officer with sword	300.00	575.00	800.00
171. Greek Infantry, 8 pcs., running at trail, with officer	200.00	400.00	550.00
Officer	28.00	47.50	70.00
Troop	22.00	35.00	50.00
172. Bulgarians, 8 pcs., marching at trail, officer with sword	220.00	415.00	620.00
Officer	30.00	60.00	80.00
Troop	22.00	35.00	50.00
173. Serbian Infantry charging, 8 pcs., no officer . . .	140.00	350.00	480.00
Troop	20.00	35.00	45.00
174. Montenegrin Infantry, 8 pcs., marching at slope or walking at trail, officer with sword	200.00	400.00	550.00
Officer	28.00	47.50	70.00
Troop	22.00	35.00	50.00
175. Austro-Hungarian Lancers, 5 pcs.	300.00	600.00	800.00
176. Austro-Hungarian Dragoons, 5 pcs., "1902" version	280.00	525.00	660.00
Trooper	40.00	70.00	95.00
177. Austro-Hungarian Infantry of the Line, 8 pcs	190.00	315.00	420.00
Troop	20.00	33.00	44.00
178. Austro-Hungarian Foot Guards, 8 pcs	110.00	200.00	300.00
Troop	16.00	30.00	40.00
179. (9288) Cowboys, 5 pcs., 4 mounted, 1 on foot, 2 with lassos, 2 with rifles .	60.00	90.00	120.00
Mounted	8.00	12.00	15.00
Foot	5.00	8.00	9.00

458

#181 Post-War, khaki shorts

#182

#183 & #184

#186 1st version

#187

#188 Zulu Kraal

#189

BRITAINS

	G	VG	EXC
180. Boy Scouts Display, 22 pcs., Scoutmaster, Scouts, Signalers, Trek Carts, Trees, Ladder	300.00	450.00	650.00
181. Boy Scouts, 45 pcs., includes Scoutmaster, 6 kneeling and standing scouts with hatchets, 8 hiking, 2 signaling, 2 pulling carts, 3 standing scouts, trees, gate, hurdles, cart	600.00	800.00	1000
Per Scout figure	13.00	19.50	26.00
Cart, Scout pulling	37.50	56.25	75.00
182. (9114) 11th Hussars (Prince Albert's Own), dismounted with horses, 8 pcs., officer	100.00	150.00	200.00
Officer	16.00	24.00	32.00
Trooper	12.00	18.00	24.00
183. (9188) Cowboys on foot, 8 pcs. (7 later), with rifles, pistols, lassos, early version, Pre-War	70.00	100.00	120.00
Post-War	60.00	85.00	105.00
Each	5.00	8.00	10.00
184. Cowboys mounted and on foot, 15 pcs	No Price Found		
185. Wild West Display, Cowboys and North American Indians, 30 pcs	350.00	800.00	1200
186. Mexican Rurales, slung rifles, officer, 1926-40, 8 pcs., early Pre-War	250.00	450.00	650.00
1930s, late	180.00	350.00	450.00
Officer	30.00	45.00	60.00
Troop	27.50	41.25	55.00
187. Arabs on foot, 8 pcs . .	65.00	85.00	110.00
Per figure	7.00	10.00	12.00
188. Zulu Kraals with Warriors, Palm Trees	500.00	1000	1500
189. Belgian Infantry, "on guard", 8 pcs	110.00	215.00	280.00
Per figure	10.00	16.00	21.00

BRITAINS

#190 Trooper & Officer

#191

#192, late Pre-War, in khaki

#193

#194 Pre-War early

#195 early Pre-War,
sand colored helmet

#194 late 30's

#197

#198

#196 Pre-War, red vest
Post-War, black vest

	G	VG	EXC
190. Belgian Cavalry, with officer, 5 pcs., Pre-War ..	110.00	215.00	280.00
Post-War	80.00	120.00	180.00
Officer, Pre-War	25.00	45.00	65.00
Trooper, Pre-War	18.00	30.00	45.00
Officer, Post-War	18.00	30.00	40.00
Trooper, Post-War	14.00	22.00	30.00
191. Turcos, 8 pcs	100.00	200.00	250.00
Troop	11.00	17.00	25.00
192. French Infantry of the Line, 8 pcs., shrapnelproof helmets	100.00	190.00	265.00
Per figure, ...	10.00	17.00	22.00
193. Arabs of the Desert, on Camels, 6 pcs	210.00	350.00	450.00
Each	30.00	50.00	65.00
194. Machine Gun Section, 8 pcs., lying	80.00	100.00	130.00
Black boots late Pre-War ..	6.00	7.50	11.00
Brown boots early Pre-War	7.00	9.00	13.00
195. Infantry of the Line at trail, 8 pcs., with officer, Pre-War	95.00	120.00	160.00
Post-War	70.00	100.00	130.00

	G	VG	EXC
196. (9170) Greek Evzones at slope, no officer, 8 pcs. (7 pcs. 1954-59, six 1960-66); Pre-War, red vest	120.00	165.00	220.00
Post-War, 8 pcs., black vest	85.00	110.00	140.00
Pre-War, per figure	10.00	14.00	20.00
Post-War, per figure	8.00	12.00	17.00
197. Gurkha Rifles, marching at trail, 1916-30s, 1916-30s, 1916-30s, Pre-War	105.00	165.00	220.00
Post-War	90.00	125.00	175.00
Post-War, single	9.00	13.00	16.00
198. British Machine Gunners, 6 pcs., sitting, peak cap	90.00	150.00	200.00
Each, with gun	10.00	14.00	20.00

#199

#200 1st version

#201 Pre-War

#202

#203 2nd version

#204

#205

#206

#207

	G	VG	EXC
199. Motor Cycle Machine Gun Corps, 3 pcs., side car, machine gun, detachable gunner	140.00	250.00	350.00
Each	40.00	75.00	105.00
200. Despatch Riders, 1917-39, 4 pcs., 1st version, fixed wheels	110.00	165.00	225.00
Per piece	20.00	30.00	45.00
201. Officers of the General Staff, mounted, 4 pcs.	100.00	160.00	210.00
Field Marshall, binoculars	22.00	35.00	50.00
General	18.00	30.00	40.00
202. Togoland Warriors, 8 pcs	65.00	105.00	140.00
Each	7.00	11.00	15.00

	G	VG	EXC
203. Pontoon Section Royal Engineers, 4 horses, 2 riders, wagon, pontoon, planking, red tunic, Review Dress	300.00	475.00	700.00
204. Pontoon Section Royal Engineers (as above), Khaki Service Dress	350.00	600.00	850.00
205. Coldstream Guards, present arms, 8 pcs	105.00	165.00	230.00
206. Warwickshire Infantry, present arms, (8 later)	160.00	300.00	400.00
Per figure	12.00	18.50	24.00
207. Officers and Petty officers of the Royal Navy, 8 pcs., 2 midshipmen, 2 admirals, 4 petty officers	120.00	175.00	225.00
Petty officer	9.00	14.00	20.00
Midshipman	9.00	14.00	20.00
208. (9389) North American Indians, 13 pieces, mounted and on foot, chieftain (11 pcs. later)	80.00	120.00	160.00
Per foot figure	5.00	7.00	9.00
Mounted figure	8.00	10.00	14.00
209. (9388) Cowboys, mounted and on foot, 13 pcs., (12 later) with lassos, rifles, pistols			No Price Found

461

BRITAINS

#212

#213

#214 - 1st version
with bayonet

#215

#216

#217 blue/grey uniform

#218 - 1st version
thick sword

#219

	G	VG	EXC
210. North American Indians, 15 pc., mounted on foot, trees	130.00	180.00	230.00
211. 18" Heavy Howitzer No. 2, tractor wheels, 3 shell noses, 10 horse team	600.00	1000	1500
212. (9145) Royal Scots, marching at slope, 8 figures, Pre-War, 4 men plus piper 1948-66; Pre-War	100.00	150.00	220.00
Post-War	75.00	110.00	140.00
Pre-War, per figure	13.00	20.00	25.00
Post-War, per figure	12.00	20.00	25.00
Piper	11.00	16.50	22.00
213. Highland Light Infantry, slope, 8 pcs	165.00	325.00	450.00
Per figure	16.00	28.00	38.00
214. Royal Canadian Mounted Police in Winter Dress, foot, circa 1912-41, 8 pcs	150.00	265.00	350.00
Each	15.00	30.00	40.00
215. French Infantry firing, 14 pcs	120.00	220.00	300.00
Machine gunner	12.00	19.00	25.00
Troop	8.00	13.50	19.00
216. Argentine Infantry, at slope, no officer, 8 pcs. 1912-40, 1946-47, 6 pcs. 1948-49; Pre-War	140.00	270.00	360.00
Post-War	100.00	160.00	210.00
Pre-War troop	18.00	27.00	36.00
Post-War troop	17.50	26.25	35.00
217. Argentine Cavalry, 5 pcs., with officer, 1912-40, 1946-59 (4 pcs. from 1948); Pre-War	150.00	225.00	300.00
Officer, early 30s	28.00	50.00	70.00
Trooper	22.00	40.00	60.00
218. Spanish Cavalry, 5 pcs	275.00	500.00	700.00
Pre-War officer	40.00	75.00	110.00
Pre-War trooper	35.00	60.00	85.00
219. Argentine Military School Cadets at slope, 8 pcs., no officer, 1912-40	200.00	300.00	400.00
Troop	20.00	30.00	40.00
220. Uruguayan Cavalry, 5 pcs. with officer 1912-40, 4 pcs. 1953-59; 4 pc. set	110.00	165.00	260.00
Officer, Pre-War	20.00	35.00	50.00
Trooper, Pre-War	18.00	30.00	40.00

#220 dark blue uniform

#221

#222

#225

#227 Pre-War

#228 Pre & Post

#223 Complete

	G	VG	EXC
221. Uruguayan Military			
School Cadets, at slope,			
no officer, 8 pcs., Pre-War	230.00	345.00	460.00
Post-War version	140.00	230.00	310.00
First version Cadet	24.00	36.00	48.00
Later version Cadet	15.00	22.50	30.00
222. Uruguayan Infantry, no			
officer, 8 pcs	150.00	250.00	350.00
Per figure	17.00	25.50	34.00
223. Arabs, mounted and			
dismounted, 13 pcs.	175.00	350.00	450.00
224. (9491) Arabs of the			
Desert, 2 on camels, 4			
marching at slope, 2 on			
horses, 1 large palm tree,			
2 smaller palm tree			
clusters, 11 pcs	200.00	300.00	400.00
Camel and rider	30.00	45.00	65.00
Large palm	9.00	12.50	18.00
Marching	8.00	12.00	16.00
Mounted on horse	10.00	14.00	18.00
225. (9162) King's African			
Rifles, marching at slope,			
no officer, circa			
1925-1959, 1966, 8 pcs.			
Pre-War	100.00	130.00	165.00

	G	VG	EXC
Post-War, 8 pcs	85.00	110.00	145.00
7 pc. set, Post-War	60.00	90.00	120.00
Troop	8.00	12.50	16.00
226. West Point Cadets,			
Winter Dress, 8 pcs	65.00	102.50	130.00
Cadets	8.50	11.00	14.00
227. U.S. Infantry at slope,			
officer	60.00	90.00	120.00
Officer	8.00	12.00	16.00
Troop	6.50	9.75	13.00
228. (9182) U.S. Marines at			
slope, officer, 8 pcs., Pre-			
War, blue caps, no officer	80.00	120.00	160.00
1940-41 version, white-			
topped cap	90.00	135.00	180.00
Post-War, with officer	65.00	97.50	130.00
Troop, blue cap	8.00	12.00	16.00
Troop, white-topped cap .	9.00	13.50	18.00
229. U.S. Cavalry, 5 pcs., no			
officer	50.00	75.00	100.00
Troop	9.00	13.50	18.00
230. U.S. Sailors, blue-			
jackets, 8 pcs	65.00	105.00	135.00
Each	7.00	10.50	15.00
231. Display Box, U.S. In-			
fantry, West Point Cadets,			
16 pcs.		No Price Found	

BRITAINS

#229

#230

#238

#240

#241

#242

#247

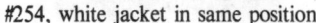
#254, white jacket in same position

#258

NOTE: Few prices turn up between 234 and 500. Following the First World War, there was a general turning away from war toys around the world. Because of this, Britains struggled through the 1920s as it tried to find its market. The company tried all sorts of combinations of troops in sets (most of which were short-lived), and even cut the size of some sets to seven pieces in an effort to lower prices and thus spur buying. Eventually, the firm went into the Farm, Zoo and Civilian figures in a major way, starting with the 500 series. It was the war clouds of the 1930s that triggered the renewal of interest in soldiers. (As it did in the U.S. with dimestore soldiers).

	G	VG	EXC
238. U.S. Girl Scouts, 8 pcs	No Price Found		
Each	36.00	54.00	72.00
240. Royal Air Force, 8 pcs	115.00	162.50	230.00
Pre-War officer	13.00	19.50	26.00
Each	8.00	12.00	16.00
241. Chinese Infantry, 8 pcs	225.00	285.00	375.00
Troop	25.00	35.00	45.00
242. U.S. Infantry, 8 pcs., slope arms, mounted officer	250.00	550.00	800.00
244. North American Indians, 7 pcs., mounted, foot	No Price Found		
245. Cowboys, 7 pcs., mtd., foot	No Price Found		
246. Royal Scots Greys and Scots Guards, 7 pcs.	250.00	550.00	800.00
247. Arabs, mounted and dismounted, 7 pcs	No Price Found		
248. 1st Life guards, and Middlesex Regiment, 7 pcs	No Price Found		
249. British Infantry and Cavalry, service dress, 7 pcs.	200.00	450.00	650.00
250. 2nd Dragoon Guards and Grenadier Guards, 7 pcs	No Price Found		
251. 21st Lancers, Royal Fusiliers, 7 pcs	No Price Found		
252. 3rd Madras Cavalry, 3 pcs., 1st Madras Native Infantry, 4 pcs., circa 1927	No Price Found		
253. Welsh Guards with Mounted Officer, 8 pcs ..	300.00	650.00	1000
254. Bluejackets and White-jackets with Petty Officer, support arms, 9 pcs., circa 1928-41	No Price Found		

	G	VG	EXC
232. (9381) Display Box, U.S. Infantry, Marines and West Point Cadets, 25 pcs	150.00	275.00	350.00
233. Display Box, U.S. Infantry, Cavalry, Marines and West Point Cadets, 29 pieces	No Price Found		

464

#266

#276

#268 & 269

#267 Post War · WW2 Helmets

#271

#272

#272

	G	VG	EXC
256. Cowboys mounted and foot, 17 pcs	No Price Found		
257. North American Indians mtd. and foot, 17 pcs	No Price Found		
258. WWI British Infantry at trail, 8 pcs., gas masks	50.00	75.00	100.00
Each	5.50	8.25	11.00
259. West Point Cadets, 16 pcs	No Price Found		
260. U.S. Infantry Squad, 16 pcs	No Price Found		
261. U.S. Marines, 16 pcs .	No Price Found		
262. U.S. Cavalry, 10 pcs ..	No Price Found		
263. West Point Cadets, 24 pcs	No Price Found		
264. Squad of U.S. Infantry, 24 pcs	No Price Found		
265. U.S. Marines, 24 pcs .	No Price Found		
266. U.S. Cavalry, 15 pcs ..	No Price Found		
267. (9380) U.S. Infantry and Cavalry, various pcs	200.00	450.00	800.00
268. U.S. Sailors, 16 pcs. ..	No Price Found		
269. U.S. Sailors, 24 pcs. ..	250.00	750.00	1100
270. 11th hussars, mounted and dismounted, at halt, 12 pcs	No Price Found		
271. Skinner's Horse, 5 pcs., 1928 to about 1934	125.00	250.00	300.00
Each	21.00	31.50	42.00
272. (9390) North American Indians and Cowboys, mounted and on foot, 13 pcs	150.00	300.00	450.00
273. North American Indians, Cowboys, mounted, foot, 15 pcs	No Price Found		
274. North American Indians, 7 pcs., mounted, foot	90.00	135.00	200.00
275. Cowboys, mounted, foot, 7 pcs	No Price Found		
276. U.S.A. Cavalry in Action, 5 pcs	250.00	500.00	800.00
Each	22.50	33.75	45.00

	G	VG	EXC
255. Green Howards marching, officer, colours, 9 pcs	No Price Found		
Troop	15.00	22.50	30.00

465

BRITAINS

#299 Post-War

#312 Post-War

#313 - 1st version peak caps empty handed

#313 - 2nd version steel helmet contained 2 with ramrods

	G	VG	EXC
277. North American Indians, mounted, foot	No Price Found		
278. Cowboys mounted, foot	No Price Found		
279. Display Box, U.S. Cavalry and Infantry ...	No Price Found		
280. U.S. Infantry and Cavalry, 17 pcs	No Price Found		
281. North American Indians, 8 pcs., mounted, foot, with Bell Tent	No Price Found		
282. Cowboys, 8 pcs., mounted, foot, with tent	No Price Found		
283. U.S. Cavalry and Infantry with Bell Tent, 8 pcs	No Price Found		
284. U.S. Cavalry and Infantry, 21 pcs.	No Price Found		
285. U.S. Cavalry and Infantry, 18 pcs	No Price Found		
286. U.S. Cavalry, 10 pcs., standing and action	No Price Found		
287. U.S. Cavalry and Infantry, 7 pcs	No Price Found		
288. U.S. Marines and Sailors, 16 pcs	No Price Found		
289. Girl and Boy Scouts, 13 pcs., 8 pcs	No Price Found		
290. U.S. Cavalry and Infantry, 13 pcs	No Price Found		
291. U.S. Cavalry and Infantry, 26 pcs	No Price Found		
292. Arabs on horse and foot	No Price Found		
293. Girl and Boy Scouts, 16 pcs.	No Price Found		
294. U.S. Infantry and Marines, 16 pcs.	No Price Found		
295. U.S. Infantry and Cavalry	No Price Found		
296. Arabs on horse and foot	No Price Found		
297. North American Indians, mounted, foot	No Price Found		
298. Cowboys, mounted, foot	No Price Found		
299. (9178) West Point Cadets, summer dress, slope arms, 8 pcs	65.00	92.50	150.00
Each	9.00	13.00	16.00
300. Arabs, mounted and dismounted, 17 pcs	No Price Found		
301. Arabs, mounted and dismounted, with Bell Tent, 8 pcs	No Price Found		

	G	VG	EXC
302. Scots Greys and Scots Guards with Bell Tent, 8 pcs	No Price Found		
303. Life Guards and Middlesex Regiment with Bell Tent, 8 pcs	No Price Found		
304. Territorials, mounted, foot, Bell Tent, 8 pcs. ...	150.00	450.00	600.00
305. North American Indians 10 pcs, mounted, foot	No Price Found		
306. Cowboys, 10 pcs., mounted, foot	No Price Found		
307. Arabs, mounted, foot, 10 pcs	No Price Found		
308. U.S. Cavalry and Infantry, 10 pcs	No Price Found		
309. Scots Greys and Scots Guards, 10 pcs.	No Price Found		
310. Life Guards and Middlesex Regiment, 10 pcs	200.00	500.00	700.00
311. Territorials, 10 pcs., mounted and foot	No Price Found		
312. (9121) Grenadier Guards, winter overcoats, slope arms, officer, 8 pcs	85.00	120.00	150.00
Officer	10.00	15.00	20.00
Troop	7.00	12.00	14.00
313. Team of Gunners, Royal Artillery 8 pcs ...	100.00	175.00	250.00
Officer with binoculars, late 1930s	11.00	18.50	28.00
Troop	9.00	12.00	15.00

466

#315

#318

#329 - Pre-War grenadier guard,
Post-War scots guard

#331 in box

	G	VG	EXC
314. Coldstream Guards at Ease, officer, 8 pcs	95.00	150.00	230.00
Officer	12.00	20.00	28.00
Troop	8.00	16.00	20.00
315. 10th Royal Hussars at halt, 5 pcs	240.00	360.00	500.00
Each	30.00	50.00	75.00
316. Royal Horse Artillery, 9 pcs., review order, horses at halt	1000	1700	2500
317. Royal Field Artillery, review dress, 9 pcs., horses at halt	1000	1700	2500
318. Gun of Royal Artillery (model 1201) with limber and horse team, 17 pcs. .	1200	1900	2700
319. Police, 7 pcs., mounted, foot, traffic	150.00	250.00	400.00
320. Royal Army Medical Corps, 8 pcs	110.00	165.00	240.00
321. Drum and Fife Band of the Line, 17 pcs	450.00	850.00	1200
322. Drum and Fife Band of Coldstream Guards with rank and file, 25 pcs	700.00	1200	1700
Per figure	20.00	30.00	40.00

	G	VG	EXC
323. U.S. Cavalry, Artillery, Marines, Sailors (in action), Infantry of the Line, West Point Cadets, 73 pcs.		No Price Found	
324. U.S. Marines, Sailors, Infantry of the line, West Point Cadets, 81 pcs	1500	3000	4000
325. Cowboys, mounted, 5 pcs		No Price Found	
326. Indians Mounted, 5 pcs.		No Price Found	
327. Cowboys Mounted, 7 pcs		No Price Found	
328. Indians Mounted, 7 pcs		No Price Found	
329. (9426) Sentry Box with Sentry, 2 pcs.	14.00	20.00	28.00
Sentry Box	7.00	10.50	14.00
Sentry	6.00	8.50	12.00
330. U.S. Aviation, 8 pcs., officers, in short coats ..		No Price Found	
Officer	22.50	33.75	45.00
331. U.S. Aviation, officers in overcoats, 8 pcs	250.00	550.00	800.00

BRITAINS

#332 #333

	G	VG	EXC
332. U.S. Aviation, aviators in flying kit, short coats, 8 pcs.	250.00	550.00	800.00
Per figure	22.50	33.75	45.00
333. U.S. Aviation, aviators in flying kit, 8 pcs	250.00	550.00	800.00
334. U.S. Aviation, privates in peak cap, 8 pcs	350.00	650.00	1000
335. U.S.A AirForce, 8 review order, 8 at slope, 16 pcs	No Price Found		
336. U.S.A. AirForce, 8 officers in long coat, and 8 officers in short coat	No Price Found		
337. U.S.A AirForce, 8 privates peaked cap, 8 officers	No Price Found		
338. British Infantry, Service Dress, Gas Masks, 16 pcs	250.00	550.00	800.00
339. U.S. Cavalry Squad, 6 pcs	No Price Found		
340. U.S. Cavalry, service dress	No Price Found		
341. British Army Machine Gun Section, lying, 16 pcs.	No Price Found		
342. Argentine Cavalry and Infantry	No Price Found		
343. Argentine Cavalry and Infantry, 26 pcs	No Price Found		
344. Life Guards and Middlesex Regiment	No Price Found		
345. Scots Greys and Scots Guards	No Price Found		
346. United States Cavalry with Tent, 6 pcs	No Price Found		
347. United States Infantry with Tent, 10 pcs	No Price Found		
348. West Point Cadets with Tent, 10 pcs.	No Price Found		
349. United States Marines with Tent, 10 pcs	No Price Found		

	G	VG	EXC
350. North American Indians with Bell Tent, 10 pcs	No Price Found		
351. U.S.A. AirForce, 2 aviators in flying kit, 2 pilots, 2 privates, 2 officers in overcoat, 1 officer in short coat	No Price Found		
352. U.S.A. Infantry, 1 marching peak cap, 10 privates slouch hat, khaki, marching at slope	No Price Found		
353. West Point Cadets, winter dress, 11 pcs.	No Price Found		
354. West Point Cadets, winter dress, 12 pcs.	No Price Found		
355. Life Guards, Sussex Regiment, 7 pcs	No Price Found		
356. Yeomanry U.S.A. Infantry, 7 pcs	No Price Found		
357. North American Indians, 10 pcs	No Price Found		
358. Cowboys, 10 pcs	120.00	175.00	250.00
359. U.S. Machine Gunners, lying firing, 8 pcs.	No Price Found		
360. Togoland Warriors, in 1931 catalog only	No Price Found		
361. Infantry, Cuirassiers, 1914, 12 pcs.	No Price Found		
362-384. UNKNOWN			
385. Types of the USA Forces, 16 pcs., West Point Cadets in summer dress at slope	No Price Found		
386. Royal Canadian Mounted Police in Winter Dress (same as 214), 1931, 8 pcs	No Price Found		
387. Togoland Warriors, 8 pcs	No Price Found		
388. Types of the French Army	No Price Found		
389. Scots Guards, 10 pcs. .	No Price Found		
390. Middlesex Regiment, 10 pcs	No Price Found		
391. 4th Bombay Grenadiers, 10 pcs	No Price Found		
392. Black Watch, 10 pcs. .	No Price Found		
393. Royal Scots Greys, 6 pcs	No Price Found		
394. Arabs, 6 pcs	No Price Found		
395. 16th Light Cavalry (Indian Army) 6 pcs	No Price Found		
396. 11th Hussars, 6 pcs. . .	300.00	650.00	1000
397. 16th/5th Lancers, 6 pcs	No Price Found		

#399

	G	VG	EXC
398. Life Guards, 6 pcs ...	300.00	650.00	1000
399. United States Marines, 8 pcs. khaki, marching ..	350.00	800.00	1200
400. (9205) The Life Guards, winter dress, 5 pcs., Pre-War	100.00	145.00	185.00
Post-War	90.00	135.00	175.00
Troop	12.00	22.00	25.00
401. Argentine Infantry and Cavalry, 13 pcs	No Price Found		
402. Spanish Cavalry, 10 pcs	No Price Found		
403. Uruguayan Cavalry and Cadets, 13 pcs.	No Price Found		
404. Argentine Cadets, Cavalry and Infantry, 21 pcs.	No Price Found		
405. Uruguayan Infantry, Cavalry and Cadets, 21 pcs.	No Price Found		
406. Spanish and Uruguayan Cavalry, 18 pcs	No Price Found		
407. Display Box, Royal Navy, White-jackets and Blue-jackets at trail, 16 pcs., 2 petty officers, 1931	No Price Found		
408. Royal Navy Blue-jackets at the double, 16 pcs., petty officer, 1931-32	No Price Found		
409. White-jackets at the double, 16 pcs., petty officer, 1931-32	No Price Found		
410. Argentine Cadets and Infantry, 16 pcs	No Price Found		
411. Argentine Infantry, 16 pcs.	No Price Found		
412. Argentine Military School Cadets, 16 piece version of 219, no officers	No Price Found		
413. Uruguayan Cavalry, 10 pcs	No Price Found		

	G	VG	EXC
414. Uruguayan Cavalry, 15 pcs	No Price Found		
415. Argentine Infantry and Uruguayan Cavalry, 12 pcs.	No Price Found		
416. Argentine Infantry and Uruguayan Cavalry, 20 pcs	No Price Found		
417. Admiral with Squad of Blue-jackets, running, 16 pcs., 1931-32, at trail ...	No Price Found		
418. Admiral with Squad of Blue-jackets, running at trail, 24 pcs., 1931-32 ...	No Price Found		
419. Gordon Highlanders, 16 pcs.	No Price Found		
420. Gordon Highlanders, 24 pcs	No Price Found		
421. North American Indians, 10 pcs	No Price Found		
422. North American Indians, 15 pcs	No Price Found		
423. Boy Scouts	No Price Found		
424. West Point Cadets, winter and summer dress, 16 pcs ....;.	No Price Found		
425. Spanish Cavalry and Infantry, double box, 13 pcs	No Price Found		
426. Ideal Flower Support, for real or artificial flowers, one piece	No Price Found		
427. French Cuirassiers and Infantry of the Line, 13 pcs	No Price Found		
428. United States of America Police, 8 pcs ...	No Price Found		
429. (9306) Scots Guards and the Life Guards in Winter Dress, 13 pcs ...	135.00	270.50	350.00
Officer mounted	12.50	18.00	25.00
Troop, on foot	8.50	12.00	14.00
430. Life Guards, summer dress and Life Guards winter dress, 10 pcs	No Price Found		
431. Scots Guards summer dress and Scots Guards winter dress, 16 pcs	No Price Found		

BRITAINS

#432 Pre-War (all grey)

#433 Rare Camouflage version

#433 with pilot

#437

	G	VG	EXC
432. (9169) German Infantry, slope arms, officer, 8 pcs., Pre-War	90.00	115.00	140.00
8 pcs., Post-War	70.00	100.00	125.00
Troop, Post-War	8.50	11.00	15.00
433. Monoplane, 2 pcs., pilot and hangar, square wingtip version	850.00	1300	1800
434. R.A.F. Monoplane with pilot and hangar, 6 aircraftsmen, 8 pcs	1200	3000	4500
435. U.S. Aviation Monoplane with pilot and hangar, 3 pcs	900.00	1500	3000
436. U.S. Monoplane with hangar and 6 aircraftsmen, 8 pcs	1000	2800	4000
437. Gordon Highlanders Officers, walking, 5 pcs., one mounted, circa 1930	150.00	275.00	350.00
438. Grenadier Guards, parade series, 9 pcs	No Price Found		
Officer	7.50	11.25	15.00
Troop	6.00	9.00	12.00
439. Middlesex Regiment, parade series, 9 pcs	No Price Found		
440. 7th Royal Fusiliers, parade series, 9 pcs	No Price Found		

	G	VG	EXC
441. Gordon Highlanders, parade series, 9 pcs	No Price Found		
442. British Infantry, 9 pcs., khaki, parade series	No Price Found		
443. West Point Cadets, 9 pcs., parade series	No Price Found		
444. U.S. Marines, 9 pcs., parade series	No Price Found		
445. U.S. Infantry, 9 pcs., parade series	No Price Found		
446. Scots Guards, 13 pcs., parade series	No Price Found		
447. Royal West Surrey Regiment, 13 pcs., parade series	No Price Found		
448. 7th Royal Fusiliers, 13 pcs., parade series	250.00	500.00	750.00
449. Black Watch, 13 pcs., parade series	No Price Found		
450. British Infantry, 13 pcs., khaki, parade series	No Price Found		
451. West Point Cadets, 13 pcs., winter dress, parade series	No Price Found		
452. U.S. Marines, 13 pcs., parade series	No Price Found		
453. U.S. Infantry, 13 pcs., parade series	No Price Found		
454. West Point Cadets, 9 pcs., summer dress, parade series	No Price Found		
455. West Point Cadets, 13 pcs., summer dress, parade series	No Price Found		
456. U.S. Sailors, 9 pcs., parade series	No Price Found		
457. U.S. Sailors, 13 pcs., parade series	No Price Found		
458. U.S. Infantry and Cavalry, 21 pcs., parade series	No Price Found		
459. U.S. Infantry and Cavalry, 13 pcs., parade series	No Price Found		

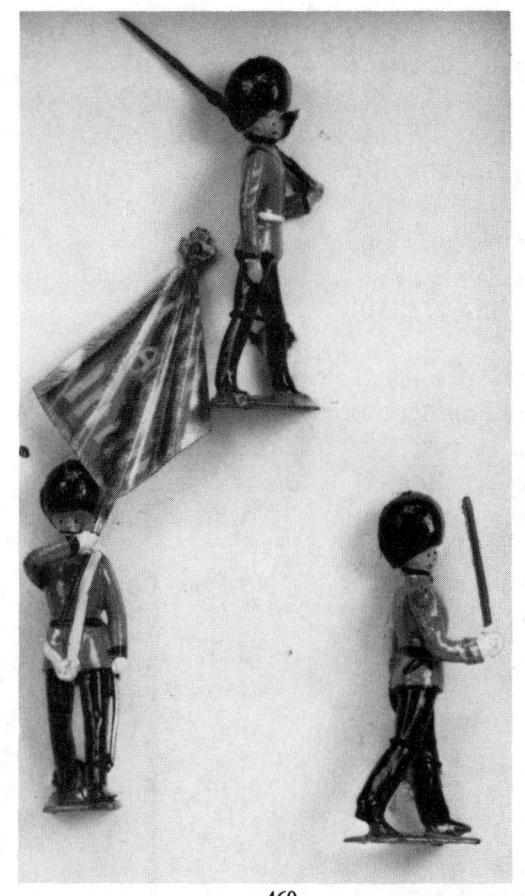

460
Courtesy Phillips

#464

	G	VG	EXC
460. Colour Party and Standard Bearer of Scots Guards (1st version was Grenadier Guards, no price found) 7 pcs.	120.00	250.00	350.00
Officer with flag	22.00	40.00	55.00
Sergeant at slope	15.00	32.00	40.00
461. German Infantry, 16 pcs	No Price Found		
462. Cowboys and North American Indians, 18 pcs	No Price Found		
463. Cowboys, 21 pcs	No Price Found		
464. Cowboys, 26 pcs., 10 mounted, 16 foot	350.00	650.00	850.00
465. U.S.A. Infantry and Cavalry, 26 pcs	No Price Found		
466. U.S.A. West Point Cadets, 32 pcs	No Price Found		
467. U.S.A. Marines, 32 pcs	No Price Found		
468. U.S.A. Bluejackets, 32 pcs	No Price Found		
469. U.S.A. Infantry, 32 pcs	No Price Found		
470. U.S.A. Cavalry, 20 pcs	No Price Found		
471. U.S.A. Infantry and Cavalry, 34 pcs	No Price Found		
472. U.S.A. West Point Cadets, 40 pcs	No Price Found		
473. U.S.A. Marines and Bluejackets, 40 pcs	No Price Found		

	G	VG	EXC
474. U.S.A. Cavalry, 25 pcs	No Price Found		
475. U.S. Cavalry and Machine Gunners, 19 pcs	No Price Found		
476. Arabs, 18 pcs	No Price Found		
477. Lifeguards, Royal Sussex Regiment, 12 pcs	No Price Found		
478. French Cavalry and Infantry, 18 pcs	No Price Found		
479. U.S. Marines and Sailors, parade series	No Price Found		
480. Black Watch with Pipers and Mounted Officer, parade series	No Price Found		
481. Middlesex Regiment Buglers, Drummers and Mounted Officers, parade series	No Price Found		
482. Gordon Highlanders, Pipes and Mounted Officers, parade series	No Price Found		
483. U.S. Infantry, mounted and foot officers, parade series	No Price Found		
484. West Point Cadets, parade series	No Price Found		

	G	VG	EXC
485. U.S. Infantry mounted and foot, parade series ..	No Price Found		
486. U.S. Infantry and Cavalry with foot officer, parade series	No Price Found		
487. U.S. Infantry and Cavalry with foot officer, parade series	No Price Found		
488. U.S. Marines and Sailors, parade series	No Price Found		
489. West Point Cadets ...	No Price Found		
490. Middlesex Regiment with buglers	No Price Found		
491. U.S.A. Infantry and Cavalry, 12 pcs	No Price Found		
492. U.S.A. Infantry and Cavalry, 12 pcs	No Price Found		
493. U.S.A. West Point Cadets, 15 pcs	No Price Found		
494. U.S. Marines and Blue-jackets, 15 pcs	No Price Found		
495. U.S.A. Infantry 15 pcs	No Price Found		
496. Gordon Highlanders, 10 pcs	No Price Found		
497. Royal Scots, 10 pcs ..	No Price Found		
498. U.S.A. Cavalry, 6 pcs .	200.00	350.00	500.00
499. U.S.A. West Point Cadets, 10 pcs	No Price Found		
500. Lifeguards, winter dress	No Price Found		

#1201   Post-War

#1203

	G	VG	EXC
1201. (9715) Gun of Royal Artillery, 5¼" long	15.00	25.00	40.00
1202. Carden-Loyd Tank with Driver	No Price Found		
1203. Carden-Loyd Tank driver, machine-gunner, detachable machine gun, 1932-1940, with rubber tracks, ...	105.00	150.00	220.00
1204. Chinese Infantry, 10 pcs	No Price Found		
1205. French Infantry, 10 pcs	No Price Found		
1206. Kings African Rifles, 10 pcs	No Price Found		
1207. Zulus, 10 pcs	No Price Found		

	G	VG	EXC
1208. West Point Cadets, 10 pcs	300.00	600.00	800.00
1209. Irish Guards, 10 pcs .	No Price Found		
1210. Mexican Infantry, 10 pcs	No Price Found		
1211. Drums and Bugles of the Line, 10 pcs	No Price Found		
1212. German Infantry, 10 pcs	No Price Found		
1213. Turcos, 10 pcs	No Price Found		
1214. Argyll and Sutherland Highlanders, 10 pcs	No Price Found		
1215. Royal Sussex Regiment, 9 pcs	No Price Found		
1216. Royal West Surrey Regiment, 10 pcs	No Price Found		
1217. UNKNOWN			
1218. French Cuirassiers, 10 pcs	No Price Found		
1219. Twenty-First Lancers at the Halt, 5 pcs., circa late 1920s	No Price Found		
1220. Imperial Yeomanry, 6 pcs	No Price Found		
1221. Imperial Yeomanry, 6 pcs	No Price Found		
1222. 6th Dragon Guards, 6 pcs	No Price Found		
1223. North American Indians, 20 pcs	No Price Found		
1224. North American Indians, 16 pcs	No Price Found		
1225. Cowboys, 16 pcs	No Price Found		
1226. UNKNOWN			
1227. U.S.A. Air Force, 10 pcs	No Price Found		
1228. U.S.A. Air Force, 10 pcs	No Price Found		
1229. U.S.A. Air Force, 10 pcs.	No Price Found		
1230. French Mule Battery, 13 pcs	No Price Found		
1231. UNKNOWN			
1232. Nurses	No Price Found		
1233-34. UNKNOWN			
1242-43. UNKNOWN			
1244. 7th Royal Fusiliers, 10 pcs	No Price Found		
1245. York and Lancaster Regiment, 10 pcs	No Price Found		
1246. Italian Infantry, 10 pcs	No Price Found		

#1250

#1251

#1253

#1258

#1257

#1258

#1260

	G	VG	EXC
1247. Argentine Infantry, marching, large set, circa late 1920s		No Price Found	
1248. Argentine Cavalry, 10 pcs		No Price Found	
1249. French Dragoons, 6 pcs		No Price Found	
1250. Royal Tank Corps, marching 8 pcs., Pre-War with moustaches	150.00	375.00	450.00
Late Pre-War, no moustaches	110.00	325.00	400.00
Earlier figure	12.50	19.00	25.00
Later figure	10.00	16.50	22.00
1251. U.S. Infantry, 9 pcs., standing, kneeling, lying, with officer	160.00	300.00	400.00
Troop	15.00	28.00	38.00
1252. Cowboys on foot, 8 pcs., standing, kneeling, firing	125.00	250.00	350.00
1253. (9184) U.S. Sailors, white jackets, with officer, at slope, 8 pcs., (7 in 1960) Pre-War set	80.00	125.00	180.00
Post-War set	65.00	100.00	150.00
Officer, Pre-War	10.00	16.00	20.00
Sailor, Pre-War	8.00	12.00	17.00
Officer, Post-War	8.00	12.00	17.00
Sailor, Post-War	7.00	10.00	15.00
1254. Pontoon Section Royal Engineers, same as 204	500.00	900.00	1450
1255. U.S.A. Bluejackets and Whitejackets, 10 pcs		No Price Found	
1257. (9300) Beefeaters with officer	87.50	131.25	175.00
Officer	12.50	18.75	25.00
Pre-War troop	7.50	11.25	15.00
Post-War troop	5.00	7.50	10.00

	G	VG	EXC
1258. (9497) Knights in Armour, with Squires, Herald and Marshal set .	125.00	225.00	300.00
Mounted	15.00	30.00	40.00
Foot	15.50	25.25	35.00
Marshal	20.00	45.00	60.00
Herald	15.00	25.00	32.00
1259. UNKNOWN			
1260. Infantry with Flat Caps, firing, 9 pcs	125.00	225.00	300.00
Lying firing, first version . .	10.00	18.00	24.00
Kneeling, firing, first version	10.00	18.00	24.00
Lying firing, later version . .	7.00	13.50	18.00
Kneeling firing, later version	7.00	13.50	18.00
1261-62. UKNOWN			

#1263

#1264 with shield

#1265

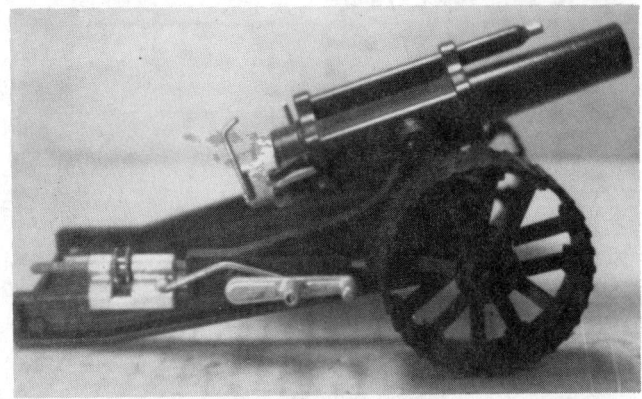

#1266 (Post-War #2107)

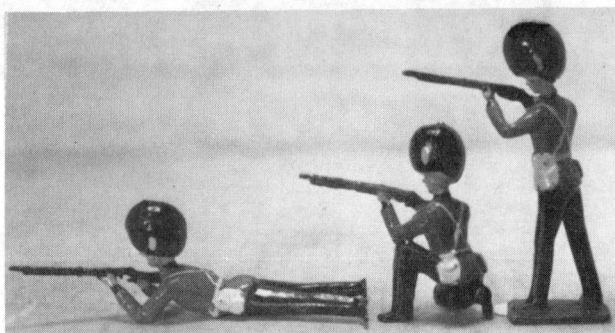

#1283

#1284

#1284

	G	VG	EXC
1263. (9700) Gun of Royal Artillery, 3¾" long	12.00	18.00	25.00
1264. (9730) 4.7 Naval Gun (catalog designation begun 1933, unnumbered previously, shield added sometime before 1930), 7¾" long, 1st version (unpainted)	40.00	75.00	120.00
No shield	35.00	65.00	90.00

	G	VG	EXC
1265. 18" Heavy Howitzer for No. 2 mounted for Garrison work, 1st version (unpainted)	65.00	100.00	140.00
Later version	40.00	70.00	100.00
1266. Heavy Howitzer, 18", 7" long, with wheels	60.00	90.00	130.00
1267. Display Box, Royal Scots, Scots Guards with Pipers, Gordon Highlanders, Scots Greys, Middlesex Regiment, 12th Lancers, Life Guards, 11th Hussars, 83 pcs		No Price Found	
1268. Life Guards, Middlesex Regiment		No Price Found	
1269. Scots Greys and Seaforths		No Price Found	
1270. UNKNOWN			
1271. Territorials, 6 pcs . . .		No Price Found	
1272. North American Indians, 6 pcs		No Price Found	
1273-1275. UNKNOWN			
1276. U.S.A. Bluejackets, 7 pcs		No Price Found	
1277. U.S.A. Infantry, 7 pcs		No Price Found	
1278. U.S.A. Infantry Marines, 41 pcs		No Price Found	
1279. U.S.A. Infantry, Cavalry, West Point Cadets, Machine gunners, 64 pcs		No Price Found	
1280. U.S.A. Infantry, Cavalry, Marines, Bluejackets and Whitejackets, 80 pcs		No Price Found	
1281. U.S.A. Infantry, Cavalry, Marines, West Point Cadets, Sailors, 111 pcs		No Price Found	
1282. U.S.A. Infantry, Cavalry, Marines, West Point Cadets, Machine Gunners, 126 pcs		No Price Found	

#1292

1287
Courtesy Phillips

#1294

#1293
dark khaki

	G	VG	EXC
1283. (9122) Grenadier Guards, standing, kneeling, lying, 8 Pre-War ...	60.00	90.00	120.00
Post-War	50.00	80.00	100.00
Each Post-War	7.00	10.00	13.00
1284. The Royal Marines, 8 marching and 8 running at trail arms, with officers, 16 pcs., Post-War set 175.00	320.00	450.00	
Officer, running at trail ...	14.00	24.00	30.00
Troop, running at trail	10.00	17.00	22.00
1285. Territorials, Yeomanry and Infantry, 13 pcs	No Price Found		
1286. Infantry, Peak Caps, firing, 25 pcs	No Price Found		
1287. British Military Band, 21 pcs	300.00	550.00	700.00
Per figure	16.00	24.00	32.00
1288. Royal Marine Band, blue tunics, 21 pcs	250.00	400.00	550.00
1289. Gun of R.A. (1201) with Team of Gunners and Officers, 8 pcs	200.00	550.00	800.00
1209. Band of the Line, Service Dress (12 pcs)	300.00	450.00	600.00
1291. Royal Marine Band, 11 instrumentalists and drum major, 12 pcs	180.00	370.00	450.00
Per piece	12.00	20.00	28.00
1292. (9710) Gun of Royal Artillery, 4¾" long, Pre-War	12.00	16.00	20.00
Post-War	10.00	14.00	18.00
1293. Durban Light Infantry, 1934-41, slope arms, 8 pcs	500.00	800.00	1200

	G	VG	EXC
1294. British Infantry in Tropical Dress, same as above with lighter shade of khaki, 8 pcs	250.00	500.00	700.00
Each	22.00	45.00	75.00
1295-1298. UNKNOWN			
1299. Zulus and Palm Tree, 9 pcs	No Price Found		
1300. R.A.M.C. Hospital, Marquee and Doctors, 42 pcs	No Price Found		
1301. Military Band (U.S.A.) 11 instrumentalists and Drum Major, 12 pcs	160.00	350.00	450.00
1302. U.S. Military Band (21 pcs)	400.00	900.00	1200
1303. Knights, 17 pcs	No Price Found		
1304. Knights, 8 pcs	No Price Found		
1305. U.S.A. Infantry, Cavalry, 14 pcs	No Price Found		
1306. Landing Party U.S.A. (box 79 painted U.S.A. uniforms)	No Price Found		
1307. (9398) Knights, mounted and on foot, 16th Century, 6 mtd., 3 ft. (11 pcs. 1962-66); 9 pc set	70.00	85.00	125.00
Mounted	7.00	10.50	14.00
Foot	4.00	6.00	8.00
1308. Knights Mounted and on Foot, 16th Century, 11 pcs	150.00	400.00	600.00
1309. UNKNOWN			
1310. Royal Welsh Fusiliers and Scots Guards, marching with officer, circa 1933, 8 pcs	No Price Found		

BRITAINS

#1307 Post-War

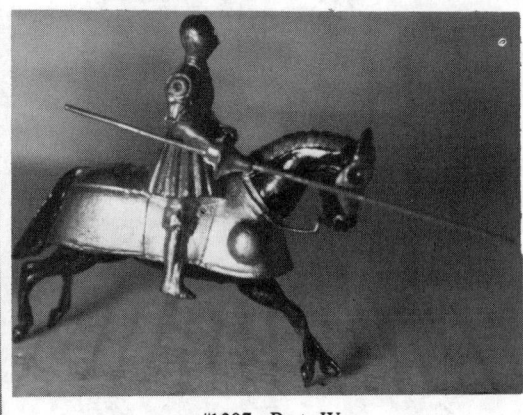

#1307 Post- War

#1313

#1317

#1317

#1320

	G	VG	EXC
1311. Cowboys and North American Indians with Chief, 8 pcs., all foot ...	No Price Found		
1312. North American Indians, mounted and Cowboys, mounted 5 pcs	No Price Found		
1313. Eastern People (Sand Tray Models), 12 pcs ...	500.00	750.00	1200
1314. Eastern People (Sand Tray Models), 20 pcs ...	No Price Found		
1315. Salvation Army Band, 12 pcs., in red, bandmaster, 2 cornets, 2 euphoniums, 1 bass tuba, 2 trombones, 2 side drummer, 1 bass drummer, 1 tenor horn, 1 double bass tuba, 1933-?	No Price Found		
1316. Salvation Army Band, 1933-?, 24 pcs., in blue, bandmaster, 3 cornets, 2 euphoniums, 1 bass tuba, 2 trombones, 1 side drummer, 3 tenor horns, 1 double bass, tuba, standard bearer, 2 officers, 2 men, 2 women, woman with tambourine, woman with "War Cry"	No Price Found		
1317. Salvation Army Band, 25 pcs., red tunic, bandmaster, 7 cornets, 4 euphoniums, 2 bass tubas, 3 trombones, 1 side drummer, 1 bass drummer, 3 tenor horns, 3 double bass tubas, 1 standard bearer 1933-?	1400	2500	3500
1318. (9149) Machine Gun Section. 7 pcs., lying and sitting, Pre-War	65.00	90.00	130.00
1319. Machine Gun Section, lying and sitting, 14 pcs .	No Price Found		
1320. Infantry, Peak Caps, with officers, 9 pcs., lying and firing	125.00	250.00	350.00
Officer, kneeling with field glasses	20.00	40.00	55.00

#1317

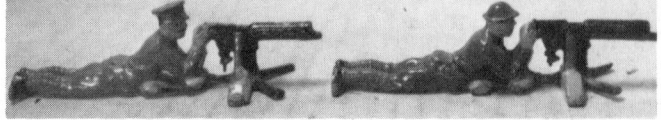

#1318 Pre & Post-War

#1321 - 1st version

#1327 Post-War

#1328

#1330 at walk

#1331 at gallop

#1332

	G	VG	EXC
1321. Armoured Car with Swiveling Gun, 1 piece ..	180.00	350.00	425.00
1322. Carden-Loyd Tank, 7 pcs., squad of Royal Tank Corps walking, 1934-40 .	150.00	250.00	400.00
Officer	11.00	17.00	22.00
Troop	8.50	13.00	17.00
1323. (9345) The Royal Fusiliers, the Seaforth Highlanders, and the Royal Sussex Regiment, with mounted and foot officers, 23 pieces	180.00	260.00	325.00
Fusilier	7.50	10.00	13.00
1324. Scots Guards with Pipers, Middlesex Regiment Officers and Royal Scots, 24 pcs	No Price Found		
1325. Gordon Highlanders firing, lying, standing, kneeling, 16 pcs	125.00	250.00	350.00

	G	VG	EXC
1326. Irish Guards, Gordon Highlanders, with officer and piper, 16 pcs	No Price Found		
1327. Grenadier Guards, 16 pcs. firing, lying, standing, kneeling (14 pcs. 1960-66), Pre-1960	95.00	130.00	170.00
1328. British Infantry Active Service with Peak Caps, firing, 18 pcs	No Price Found		
1329. Royal Army Service Corps, rider, two walking horses, two open wagons (some sets may have galloping horses)	350.00	800.00	1150
1330. Royal Engineers General Service Wagon. Connecting 2-2 wheel wagons, horse drawn. Review dress, red tunic. Horses at gallop	150.00	250.00	350.00
Same, horses at walk	200.00	300.00	450.00
1331. Royal Engineers General Service Wagon. (As Above) Active Service Dress, khaki. Horses at walk	250.00	500.00	700.00
(Note: there also is known to exist a rare steel helmeted version)	No Price Found		
1332. Girl Guides with Guider, 9 pcs	350.00	700.00	1050

BRITAINS

#1335 Pre-War

#1334

#1349

	G	VG	EXC
1333. Army Lorry Caterpillar type with driver, 2 pcs	125.00	200.00	300.00
1334. Lorry, Army, with driver, 2 pcs., 4 wheels, Pre-War	105.00	155.00	200.00
Post-War, early	85.00	125.00	170.00
1335. Lorry, Army, with driver, 2 pcs., 6 wheels, Pre-War	130.00	185.00	250.00
Post-War	115.00	165.00	230.00
1336. UNKNOWN			
1337. Miniature Golf	No Price Found		
1338. Miniature Golf	No Price Found		
1339. Royal Horse Artillery (Active service order), khaki, 13 pcs. at gallop	1000	1700	2500
1340. Miniature Archery	No Price Found		
1341. Royal Irish Regiment, kneeling, review order, circa 1933, 8 pcs	No Price Found		
1342. 7th Rajput Regiment, 8 pcs	250.00	500.00	700.00

	G	VG	EXC
1343. Royal Horse Guards, winter dress, 5 pcs	100.00	150.00	225.00
Trooper	15.00	25.00	35.00
1344. Miniature Archery	No Price Found		
1345. Scots Greys, Scots Guards, 10 pcs	No Price Found		
1346. Scots Greys and Gordon Highlanders, 10 pcs	No Price Found		
1347. Cowboys, 9 pcs	No Price Found		
1348. North American Indians, 9 pcs	No Price Found		
1349. (9256) The Royal Canadian Mounted Police, mounted, summer dress, officer, 5 pcs., 1934-66	70.00	105.00	135.00
Officer	14.00	20.00	25.00
Trooper	10.00	15.00	20.00
1350. Display Box, Gordon Highlanders and Scots Guards, Royal Scots, Life Guards and 11th Hussars, 64 pcs	No Price Found		
1351. U.S.A. Infantry, 20 pcs	No Price Found		
1352. Knights, 10 pcs	No Price Found		
1353. Knights, 6 pcs	No Price Found		
1354. Knights, 11 pcs	No Price Found		
1355. 4th Hussars with officer, Royal Horse Guards with officer, Grenadier Guards with Standard Bearer; Side Drummer and Officer, 18 pcs	No Price Found		
1356. Coldstream Guards standing, kneeling, lying firing, officers, drummer, bugler, standard bearer, 27 or 28 pcs	No Price Found		
1357. French Infantry of the Line, 16 pcs	No Price Found		
1358. Belgian Infantry, review order, 16 pcs	No Price Found		
1359. French Infantry, steel helmets, 16 pcs	No Price Found		
Troop	5.00	7.50	10.00
1360. Zouaves (review order), 16 pcs	No Price Found		
1361. French Infantry, 16 pcs	No Price Found		
1362. Belgian Infantry, review order, 24 pcs	No Price Found		
1363. Zouaves, 24 pcs	No Price Found		

#1383

#1392

	G	VG	EXC
1364. French Infantry, khaki, 24 pcs	No Price Found		
1365. French Cuirassiers and Infantry of the Line (review order), 21 pcs . . .	No Price Found		
1366. French Infantry and Machine Gunners, active service, 7 pcs	175.00	350.00	500.00
Troop	9.00	13.50	18.00
1367. Japanese Infantry and Cavalry, 21 pcs	No Price Found		
1368. Italian Bersaglieri and Cavalry (review order), 13 pcs.	No Price Found		
1369. Highlanders, 8 pcs., assorted positions, infantry officer, circa 1933 . . .	No Price Found		
1370. Gordon Highlanders, 16 pcs. (or Knights at Arms)	No Price Found		
1371. U.S.A.A.S.C. (Box 1460 painted with U.S.A. uniforms)	No Price Found		
1372. U.S. Horsedrawn Ambulance, 7 pcs	No Price Found		
1373. U.S. Army Pontoon System, circa 1935, 7 pcs	1400.00	2700.00	3500.00
1374. U.S.A. 18 pdr. gun, 1 piece	No Price Found		
1375. Gordon Highlanders, 10 pcs	No Price Found		
1376. Gordon Highlanders, 10 pcs	No Price Found		
1377. Coldstream Guards, 10 pcs	No Price Found		
1378. Coldstream Guards, 10 pcs	No Price Found		
1379. Belgian Cavalry, Active Service Order, 5 pcs	No Price Found		
1380. Belgian Cavalry, Serivce Order, 10 pcs . . .	No Price Found		
1381. Belgian Cavalry, Service Order, 15 pcs	No Price Found		

	G	VG	EXC
1382. Belgian Cavalry and Infantry, Service Order, 13 pcs	No Price Found		
1383. Belgian Infantry, 14 pcs., lying, standing, kneeling, with Machine Gunner, steel helmets, 14 pcs	150.00	300.00	450.00
Machine Gunner	10.00	20.00	30.00
Troop	8.00	14.00	20.00
1384. Belgian Infantry firing, with machine gunners, 21 pcs.	260.00	450.00	620.00
1385. French Cavalry, Chasseurs and Dragoons, 10 pcs.	No Price Found		
1386. French Cavalry, Chasseurs, Dragoons and Cuirassiers, 15 pcs.	No Price Found		
1387. French Infantry, firing, with Machine Gunners, 21 pcs	No Price Found		
1388. French Infantry, Turcos and Dragoons, 21 pcs	No Price Found		
1389. Belgian Infantry, 8 pcs., service order, slope arms	125.00	250.00	300.00
Troop	10.00	25.00	30.00
1390. Belgian Infantry and Cavalry, service order, 18 pcs	No Price Found		
1391. Model Fort in stiff cardboard	No Price Found		
1392. Civilian Autogiro with pilot, 1935-1940, 2 pcs . .	1200.00	1800.00	2500.00
1393. Speed Record Car, one piece	No Price Found		
1394. Model Fort with Royal West Surrey Regiment, 7th Fusiliers, 16 pcs	2500.00	6000.00	9000.00

BRITAINS

#1395

#1400

#1413

#1415   (C)   (D)   (E)   (B)   (F)

	G	VG	EXC
1395. The King's Own Scottish Borderers, slope arms, 8 pcs., no officer or piper, circa 1936-40	175.00	350.00	500.00
1396. Marching Board Soldiers, the Grenadier Guards, 8 pcs., circa 1935	No Price Found		
1397. Model Fort with Infantry of the Line, active service, firing, 18 pcs	No Price Found		
1398. Sports Open Tourer Motor Car, one piece	300.00	550.00	850.00
1399. Two-seater Coupe Model Motor Car, one piece	350.00	600.00	900.00
1400. Speed Record Car, one piece, "The Bluebird"	125.00	250.00	350.00
1401. Middlesex, 3rd Hussars, 9 pcs.	No Price Found		
1402. Scots Guards, Life Guards, 9 pcs.	No Price Found		
1403. Gordon Highlanders, 11 pcs	No Price Found		
1404. Territorials and 21st Lancers, 9 pcs	No Price Found		
1405. 7th Fusiliers, 9 pcs	No Price Found		
1406. "Bluebird" (with special painting)	No Price Found		
1407. Display Box, 21st Lancers, galloping, Territorial Yeomanry, Territorial Infantry, 72 pcs	1800.00	4000.00	6000.00
1408. Life Guards, 10 pcs	No Price Found		
1409. Gordon Highlanders, 16 pcs	No Price Found		
1410. Irish and Coldstream Guards, 16 pcs	No Price Found		
1411. Coldstream Guards, 10 pcs	No Price Found		

	G	VG	EXC
1412. Welsh Fusiliers and Middlesex Regiment, 8 pcs	No Price Found		
1413. Police Car with Two Officers	350.00	600.00	900.00
1414. U.S.A. Infantry and Cavalry, 14 pcs	No Price Found		
1415. Buck Rogers, 6 pcs., Buck, Wilma, Killer Kane, Ardala, Dr. Huer, robot (Mekkano Man), sold in stores and as Cream of Wheat premiums, circa 1935-40. Not marked "Britains"	750.00	1400	2000
Buck (A)	150.00	300.00	400.00
Wilma (B)	110.00	250.00	350.00
Killer Kane (C)	110.00	250.00	350.00
Ardala Valmar (D)	110.00	250.00	350.00
Dr. Huer (E)	110.00	250.00	350.00
Robot (F)	110.00	250.00	350.00
1416. Buck Rogers, 10 or 8 pcs., same as above, extra robots	No Price Found		
1417. Royal Irish Regiment, 8 pcs	No Price Found		
1418. Middlesex Regiment, 8 pcs	No Price Found		
1419. U.S.A. Infantry, 8 pcs	No Price Found		
1420 Knights, 5 pcs.	No Price Found		
1421. Line Regiment O. drummers, 8 pcs	No Price Found		
1424. Bodyguard of the Emperor of Ethiopia, at attention, 8 pcs	175.00	375.50	500.00
Pre-War troop	20.00	32.50	40.00
Post-War troop	18.00	30.00	37.00

#1425   #1424

#1426

#1432   #1433 Pre-War

#1433 Post-War · last version

#1435

#1436   #1437

	G	VG	EXC
1431. Military Autogiro, 1935-39, 2 pcs	1500	3000	4000
1432. Army Tender, covered 10 wheel, driver, 2 pcs ..	105.00	135.00	180.00
1433. Army Tender (truck), 2 pcs., with driver, door opens, back drops	95.00	150.00	200.00
1434. Abyssianian Royal Bodyguard and Tribesmen, 16 pcs	200.00	450.00	650.00
1435. Italian Infantry, slope arms, no officer, 8 pcs., Pre-War	100.00	160.00	220.00
Post-War	75.00	125.00	175.00
1436. Italian Infantry, colonial service dress, 8 pcs	140.00	265.00	350.00
Per troop	14.00	26.00	35.00
1437. Italian Carabinieri, 8 pcs. (7 Post-War), Pre-War set, no officer	110.00	195.00	260.00
Post-War set, with officer ..	90.00	135.00	180.00
Pre-War troop	14.00	21.00	28.00
1438. Italian Infantry, colonial service dress, 16 pcs	400.00	800.00	1200
1440. Royal Artillery (late R.H.A.) with gun, active service order, 9 pcs	450.00	875.00	1300

	G	VG	EXC
1425. Ethiopian Tribesmen, slope, 8 pcs	95.00	145.00	185.00
Troop	9.00	14.50	20.00
1426. St. John Ambulance, 8 pcs	500.00	850.00	1200
Nurse (only in this set)	25.00	32.50	100.00
Male Nurse	25.00	32.50	50.00
Stretcher-Bearer	12.50	18.75	25.00
Stretcher	5.00	7.50	10.00

#1448 1st version   2nd version

#1448 3rd version

#1448 4th version

	G	VG	EXC
1448. Staff Car, with officer and driver, 1st version-smooth white tires black fenders	75.00	310.00	385.00
2nd version-white tires, all khaki body	165.00	300.00	375.00
3rd version-1948-50, rectangular windshield, rubber tires	145.00	265.00	325.00
4th version-1951-57, lead tires, painted gray, split windshield	150.00	285.00	350.00
5th version-1958-59, black plastic tires	125.00	225.00	300.00
1449. Scots Guards (Special Painting), 2 pcs	No Price Found		
1450. R.A.M.C. with Ambulance Wagon (Active Service Order), 7 pcs	300.00	650.00	1000
1451. Scots Guards (Special Painting), 1 pc	No Price Found		
1452. Gordon Highlanders (Special Painting), 1 pc . .	No Price Found		
1453. Gordon Highlanders (Special Painting), 1 pc . .	No Price Found		
1454. Scots Guards (Special Painting), 1 pc	No Price Found		

	G	VG	EXC
1455. Argentine Cadets and Cavalry, 21 pcs	No Price Found		
1456. Argentine Cadets and Cavalry, 18 pcs	No Price Found		
1457. 3rd Hussars, 7 Fusiliers, 19 pcs	No Price Found		
1458. Middlesex Regiment Band, lemon yellow facings, 18 pcs	No Price Found		
1459. 10th and 11th Hussars, Grenadier Guards, 16/5th Lancers, Yorkshire Regiment, 59 pcs	No Price Found		
1459. 10th and 11th Hussars, Grenadier Guards, 16/5th Lancers, Yorkshire Regiment, 59 pcs	No Price Found		
1460. Army Service Corps (with wagon), Active Service Order, 5 pcs	250.00	450.00	650.00
1461. 21st Lancers, 5th Dragoon Guards, 23 pcs .	No Price Found		
1462. Covered Lorry, R.A. Gun, drivers, 5 pcs	150.00	350.00	450.00
1464. 4th Hussars, Royal Horse Guards, Grenadier Guards, 16 pcs	No Price Found		
1465. Royal Fusiliers, Royal Sussex Regiment, Seaforth Highlanders, 18 pcs	No Price Found		
1466. Coldstream Guards, 24 pcs.	No Price Found		
1467. Cameron Highlanders, 24 pcs	No Price Found		
1469. Cowboys and North American Indians, 26 pcs	No Price Found		

#1462

#1470

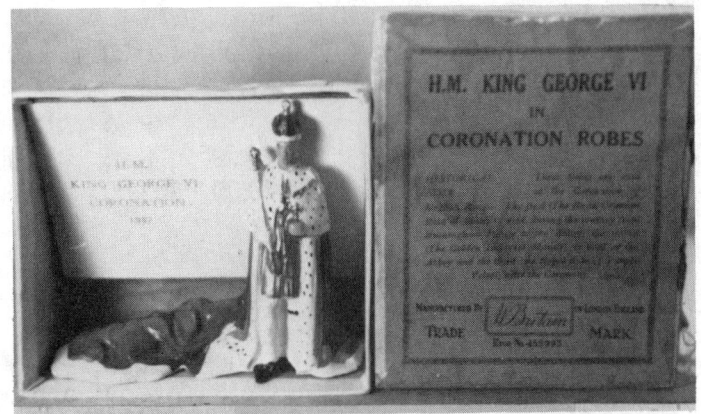

#1473 with box

#1479

#1474

#1475

	G	VG	EXC
1470. (9401) State Coach of England drawn by 8 horses, 11 pieces with riders, Pre-War	135.00	275.00	375.00
Post-War, 11 pieces	100.00	225.00	325.00
1471. Single figure of George VI in copper		No Price Found	
1472. Single figure of George VI, same as above, but in gilt		No Price Found	
1473. Same as above, painted	35.00	70.00	95.00
1474. Coronation Chair, two pcs. (gray stone under seat)	20.00	26.50	35.00
1475. (9404) Display Box, Yeoman of the Guard, Walking Outriders, Footmen, (19 pcs)	150.00	250.00	350.00
Walking outrider	8.00	12.00	17.00
1476. State Coach and Yeomen of the Guard, Outriders, Footmen, 29 pcs	300.00	650.00	850.00
1477. State Coach and Procession, 75 pcs	650.00	1000	1700
1478. Cinderella Coach	350.00	650.00	1000
1479. Royal Artillery Limber (short pole pattern), one piece	55.00	90.00	125.00

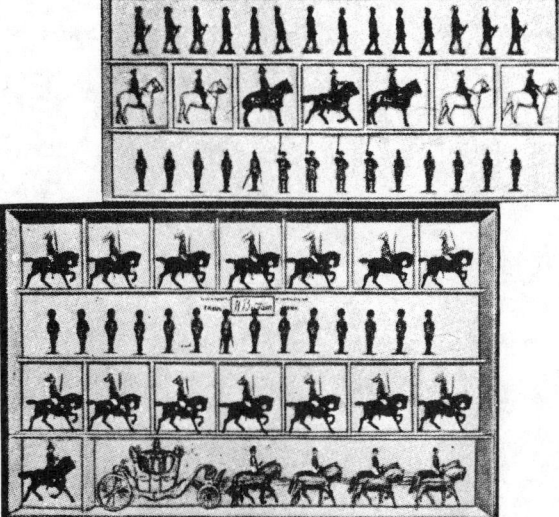

#1477 Box & insert tray

BRITAINS

#1503

#1506

#1510

	G	VG	EXC
1509. Texas Rangers, Cowboys, mounted and on foot, 5 mounted, 8 foot, as above, inspired by movie "The Texas Rangers"	No Price Found		
1510. British Sailors regulation dress, 8 pcs., no weapons or officer, 1937-41, 1946-59; Pre-War	80.00	120.00	160.00
Post-War	62.50	93.75	125.00
Pre-War Sailor	6.50	9.75	13.00
Post-War Sailor	5.50	8.25	11.00
1511. Mounted Police, 5 pcs	270.00	405.00	540.00
1512. Army Ambulance, motor type, 4 pcs., with driver, wounded man, stretcher, 6" long, Pre-War	110.00	165.00	220.00
Post-War	90.00	145.00	200.00
1513. Volunteer Corps Motor Tyre Ambulance, 4 pcs., with wounded man and stretcher, all doors open, 6" long (available unpainted)	350.00	550.00	800.00
1514. Corporation Motor Ambulance, 4 pcs., driver, wounded and stretcher	350.00	600.00	850.00
1515. (9124) Coldstream Guards at the Slope, 8 pcs	70.00	90.00	120.00
Officer	8.00	12.00	16.00
Trooper	7.00	10.50	14.00

#1512 Pre-War

#1512 Post-War

	G	VG	EXC
1493. UNKNOWN			
1494. Army of Argentina; Mounted Grenadiers	No Price Found		
1496-1502. UNKNOWN			
1503. Miniature State Coach	20.00	35.00	50.00
1504. Queen Elizabeth in copper	No Price Found		
1505. Same as above, in gilt	35.00	65.00	100.00
1506. Same as above, painted	35.00	70.00	95.00
1507. UNKNOWN			
1508. Texas Rangers, 5 mounted cowboys (based on 1936 "Texas Rangers" film with Fred MacMurray)	No Price Found		

#1514

#1515

484

#1518 - Post & Pre War

#1519

Britains box lid from set No. 1519, Waterloo Highlanders, w/muskets
Photo by Gary J. Linden

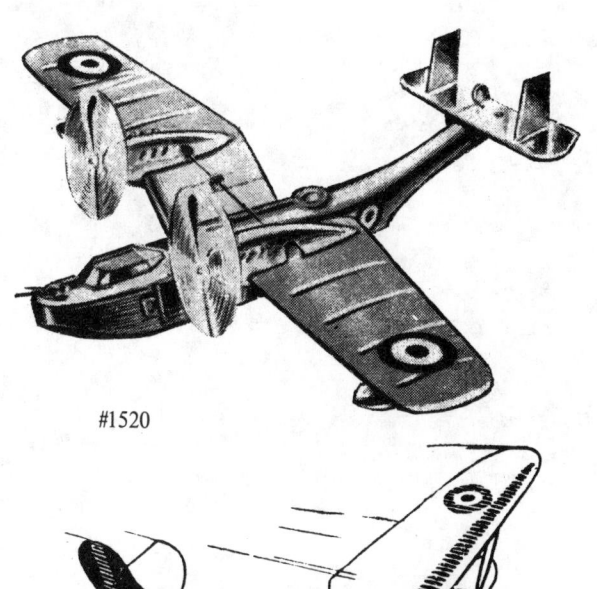

#1520

#1521

#1522

	G	VG	EXC
1516. Line Infantry of 1815, carrying pikes, 8 pcs	135.00	265.00	325.00
1517. Highlanders, 1815, pikes, 8 pcs	155.00	285.00	350.00
1518. Line Infantry, 1815, muskets, 9 pcs	125.00	225.00	300.00
Troop	12.00	20.00	28.00
1519. Highlanders, 1815, muskets, 8 pcs	145.00	245.00	320.00
Officer	20.00	30.00	45.00
Troop	14.00	22.00	30.00
1520. "Short" Monoplane Flying Boat, 1937-39, 1 pc	1000.00	1800.00	2500.00
1521. Model Biplane with Pilot and Hangar, 3 pcs .	1500.00	3000.00	4000.00

	G	VG	EXC
1522. 4½" Anti Aircraft Gun, working model, 1 pc	250.00	450.00	650.00
1523. R.A.F. Band, 11 pcs .	No Price Found		
1525. U.S.A. Biplane with pilot and hangar, 3 pcs ..	No Price Found		
1527. Royal Air Force Band, 12 pcs	250.00	500.00	700.00
1529. U.S.A. Cavalry, Infantry, Artillery, etc., 29 pcs	No Price Found		
1530. Display Set, Mounted Marshal, Knights with plumes, Squires and Heralds, 19 pcs	No Price Found		
1531. U.S.A. Infantry, 16 pcs	No Price Found		
1532. U.S.A. Infantry, 24 pcs	No Price Found		
1533. U.S.A. Infantry and Cavalry, 26 pcs	No Price Found		
1534. U.S.A. Infantry, Cavalry and Artillery, 41 pcs	No Price Found		
1535. U.S.A. Infantry and Cavalry, 80 pcs	No Price Found		
1536. Colonials at Present, 8 pcs	No Price Found		
1537. Territorials (slope, blue uniform), 8 pcs	350.00	650.00	1000
1538. Territorials (slope, green uniform), 8 pcs ...	350.00	650.00	1000
Officer	35.00	70.00	85.00
Troop	25.00	50.00	70.00

BRITAINS

#1540

#1542

#1543

#1544

#1545

#1554

1555
Courtesy Phillips

	G	VG	EXC
1540. Territorials, present arms, 8 pcs., blue uniform	300.00	600.00	900.00
1541. Territorials, present arms, 8 pcs., green uniform	300.00	600.00	900.00
1542. Infantry with Officer (New Zealand) at slope, 8 pcs., Pre-War	120.00	200.00	275.00
Post-War set, 8 pcs	85.00	165.00	220.00
Officer, Pre-War	13.50	20.00	30.00
Troop, Pre-War	10.00	16.00	22.00
Officer, Post-War	12.00	18.50	24.00
Troop, Post-War	9.00	13.00	18.00
1543. New Zealand. Infantry Service Kit, present arms with officer, 8 pcs	300.00	650.00	850.00
1544. Australian Infantry at slope, officer, 8 pcs., Pre-War	150.00	280.00	360.00
Post-War	105.00	225.00	300.00
Troop, Post-War	16.00	24.00	32.00

	G	VG	EXC
1545. Australian Infantry, service kit, present arms with officer, 8 pcs	150.00	350.00	550.00
First version troop	25.00	45.00	70.00
Second version officer (has plume)	30.00	55.00	80.00
1553. UNKNOWN			
1554. (9156) Royal Canadian Mounted Police in summer dress, on foot, 1937-66, 8 pcs set	95.00	135.00	165.00
7 pc. set	70.00	115.00	135.00
Mounted Officer	18.00	27.00	32.00
Pre-War, no gloves version	8.50	11.00	14.00
Post-War, gloves	7.00	9.00	12.00
1555. (9424) The Changing of the Guard at Buckingham Palace, 83 pcs	500.00	1000	1500

1556-1602 ARE THE FAMOUS REGIMENTS OF THE BRITISH ARMY SERIES: Uniform facings (collar and cuffs) are shown in parenthesis. All consist of eight marchers, including officer. Boxes are **especially** important in this series, which is rare.	G	VG	EXC
1556. Lincolnshire Regiment (White)	300.00	650.00	1000
1557. East Yorkshire Regiment (White)	300.00	650.00	1000
1558. Bedfordshire and Hertfordshire Regiment (White)	300.00	650.00	1000
1559. Lancashire Fusiliers (White)	300.00	650.00	1000
1560. East Lancashire Regiment (White)	300.00	650.00	1000
1561. East Surrey Regiment (White)	300.00	650.00	1000.00
1562. South Straffordshire Regiment (White)	300.00	650.00	1000.00
1563. Welsh Regiment (White)	300.00	650.00	1000.00
1564. Loyal North Lancashire Regiment (White)	300.00	650.00	1000.00
1565. Manchester Regiment (White)	300.00	650.00	1000.00
1566. North Staffordshire Regiment (White)	300.00	650.00	1000.00
1567. York and Lancashire Regiment (White)	300.00	650.00	1000.00
1568. Essex Regiment (White)	300.00	650.00	1000.00
1569. Duke of Cornwall's Light Infantry (White) ..	300.00	650.00	1000.00
1570. Oxford and Bucks Light Infantry (White) ..	300.00	650.00	1000.00
1571. Royal West Surrey Regiment (Blue)	300.00	650.00	1000.00
1572. Royal Lancaster Regiment (Blue)	300.00	650.00	1000.00
1573. Royal Warwickshire Regiment (Blue)	300.00	650.00	1000.00
1574. Kings Regiment (Liverpool); (Blue)	300.00	650.00	1000.00
1575. Royal Sussex Regiment (Blue)	300.00	650.00	1000.00
1576. Royal Berkshire Regiment (Blue)	300.00	650.00	1000.00

	G	VG	EXC
1577. Royal West Kents (Blue)	300.00	650.00	1000.00
1578. Somerset Light Infantry (Blue)	300.00	500.00	800.00
1579. Kings Own Yorkshire Light Infantry	300.00	500.00	800.00
1580. King's Shropshire Light Infantry (Blue)	300.00	500.00	800.00
1581. Royal Irish Fusiliers (Blue)	300.00	500.00	800.00
1582. The Buffs (Buff)	300.00	500.00	800.00
1583. West Yorkshire Regiment (Buff)	300.00	500.00	800.00
1584. Cheshire Regiment (Buff)	300.00	500.00	800.00
1585. Prince of Wales Volunteers (South Lancashire Regiment); (White)	300.00	500.00	800.00
1586. Northamptonshire Regiment (White)	300.00	500.00	800.00
1587. Wiltshire Regiment (Buff)	300.00	500.00	800.00
1588. Royal Norfolks (Yellow)	300.00	500.00	800.00
1589. Suffolk Regiment (Yellow)	300.00	500.00	800.00
1590. Border Regiment (Yellow)	300.00	500.00	800.00
1591. Hampshire Regiment (Yellow)	300.00	500.00	800.00
1592. Gloucestershire Regiment (White)	300.00	500.00	800.00
1593. Devonshire Regiment (Lincoln Green)	300.00	500.00	800.00
1594. Sherwood Foresters (Lincoln Green)	300.00	500.00	800.00
1595. Green Howards (Grass Green)	300.00	500.00	800.00
1596. South Wales Borderers (Grass Green)	300.00	500.00	800.00
1597. Dorsetshire Regiment (Grass Green)	300.00	500.00	800.00
1598. Worcesters (White) ..	300.00	500.00	800.00
1599. Royal Northumberland Fusiliers (Gosling Green)	300.00	500.00	800.00
1600. Durham Light Infantry (Dark Green)	300.00	500.00	800.00
1601. Leicestershire Regiment (White)	300.00	500.00	800.00
1602. Duke of Wellington's Regiment (Scarlet)	300.00	500.00	800.00

BRITAINS

#1603   1st version

#1603   Post-War
2nd version

#1610

#1612

#1613

#1613

	G	VG	EXC
1603. Irish Infantry, slope, officer, 8 pc. set, Pre-War	120.00	225.00	300.00
1st version, Post-War, slope	100.00	205.00	280.00
2nd version, Post-War, trail	100.00	170.00	220.00
1604. Argentine Cavalry and Infantry, 34 pcs	No Price Found		
1605. Knights, 6 pcs	No Price Found		
1606. Knights, 10 pcs	No Price Found		
1607. Full Company of the Royal Scots Greys, the Scots Guards, Standard Bearer, Piper, and Officer, Sentry Boxes with Sentries and the Scots Guards' Band (45 pcs)	2500.00	5000.00	8000.00
Fifer	15.00	22.50	30.00
1608. British Infantry and Cavalry, with Dispatch Riders and Machine Gunners (lying, sitting, service dress) 43 pcs	650.00	1200.00	1650.00
1609. State Coach with Escort and Band, 57 pcs	1200.00	2500.00	3500.00
1610. Royal Marines (present arms) 8 pcs	120.00	200.00	280.00
Troop	13.50	20.00	28.00
1611. British Infantry, service dress, gas masks prone, 8 pcs	150.00	275.00	400.00
Troop	6.00	8.50	12.00

	G	VG	EXC
1612. British Infantry, service dress, gas masks, bomb throwers, 8 pcs	55.00	80.00	100.00
Troop	6.50	9.50	12.00
1613. (9146) British Infantry (in action, charging with fixed bayonets) in gas masks, with officer, 7 pcs. (6 pcs. 1960)	50.00	75.00	105.00
6 pc. set	45.00	70.00	95.00
Officer	7.50	11.50	15.00
Troop	6.50	9.50	12.00
1614. (9346) British Infantry, action poses, officer, 24 pcs	135.00	185.00	260.00
Officer	8.00	12.00	16.00
Digging	8.00	12.00	16.00
Troop	5.00	7.50	10.00
1615. British Infantry, charging and prone, throwing grenades, digging, officer, 15 pcs	150.00	250.00	400.00
1616. British Infantry in action, assorted positions, 15 pcs	200.00	400.00	550.00
1617. Line Regiments, Regular and Territorial Army, blue walking out dress, 8 pcs	300.00	500.00	750.00
1618. Rifle Regiments, Regular and Territorial Army, 8 pcs., green walking out dress	300.00	500.00	750.00
1619. Royal Marines at slope, 8 pcs., tropical dress	400.00	850.00	1300.00
Each	25.00	45.00	65.00
1620. Royal Marine Light Infantry, 8 pcs., at the slope	400.00	850.00	1200.00
Officer	30.00	60.00	80.00
Troop	25.00	45.00	60.00
1621. Twelfth Frontier Force Regiment, 3rd Battalion Sikhs, 1937-39, 8 pcs., no officer, at slope	250.00	500.00	700.00
Each	22.50	45.00	65.00
1622. Band of the Royal Marine Light Infantry, 21 pcs	2000.00	3500.00	4500.00
1623. U.S. Infantry, 8 pcs. gas mask, prone	No Price Found		
Each	4.00	6.00	8.00

488

#1631

#1632

#1633

#1634 Red Plume, left side

#1638

#1642

	G	VG	EXC
BRITAINS			
1627. U.S. Infantry in Action, gas masks, 15 pcs ..	No Price Found		
Pre-War troop	7.00	10.00	12.00
1628. U.S. Infantry in Action, gas masks, 15 pcs ..	No Price Found		
1629. Lord Strathcona's Horse 5 pcs., trotting, 1938, officer on rearing horse	500.00	1000.00	1500.00
Officer	70.00	180.00	250.00
Troop	60.00	135.00	200.00
1630. Royal Canadian Dragoons, 5 pcs., at the walk, 1938	500.00	1000.00	1500.00
1631. Governor-General's Horse Guards (Canadian), trotting horses, officer, 5 pcs	70.00	120.00	150.00
Officer	15.00	22.50	30.00
Trooper	11.00	16.00	24.00
1632. Royal Canadian Regiment, 8 pcs slope arms ..	250.00	450.00	700.00
1633. (9157) Princess Patricia's Canadian Light Infantry, officer, slope arms, 8 pcs	80.00	120.00	160.00
Officer	10.00	12.00	16.00
Troop	7.00	10.50	14.00
1634. (9159) Governor-General's Footguards, at slope (Canadian), with officer, 8 pcs	85.00	125.00	170.00
1635. Lord Strathcona's Horse and Royal Canadian Regiment, 13 pcs ..	No Price Found		
1636. Princess Pat's Light Infantry and Royal Canadian Dragoons, 13 pcs ..	No Price Found		
1637. (9356) Governor-General's Horse Guards and Foot Guards, with officers, 13 pcs	120.00	180.00	250.00
1638. Sound Locator, with operator, 2 pcs	20.00	40.00	65.00
1639. Army Range Finder with operator, 2 pcs	15.00	25.00	35.00
1640. (9764) Model Searchlight, uses battery, 1 pc	35.00	75.00	100.00
1641. Lorry, underslung, heavy duty, with driver, 18 wheels, 10½" long, 2 pcs	200.00	350.00	550.00
1642. Heavy Duty Lorry, 5 pcs., underslung, with driver, searchlight, battery and lamp	300.00	500.00	700.00

	G	VG	EXC
1624. U.S. Infantry, 8 pcs., gas masks, bomb throwing	100.00	200.00	300.00
Each	7.00	10.00	12.00
1625. U.S. Infantry, 7 pcs., gas masks, charging	No Price Found		
1626. U.S. Infantry in Action, gas masks, 24 pcs ..	300.00	550.00	800.00

489

BRITAINS

#1643

#1659

#1662

#1663

#1664

#1664

#1664

#1664

#1664

	G	VG	EXC
1643. Heavy Duty Lorry, underslung, with driver, AA Gun, 3 pcs	600.00	900.00	1200.00
1646. Royal Canadian Mounted Police, 13 pcs .	No Price Found		
1647. Naval Display, 56 pcs	No Price Found		
1648. Navy Landing Party Display Set, 51 pcs., circa 1940	1000.00	2000.00	3000.00
1649. Argentine Infantry, 7 pcs	No Price Found		
1650. Line Drums and Bugles, 17 pcs	No Price Found		
1651. Coldstream Guards, 21 pcs	No Price Found		
1652. British Action Infantry, 38 pcs	No Price Found		
1653. British Infantry and Cavalry, 52 pcs	No Price Found		
1655. Coldstream Guards, 10 pcs	No Price Found		
1657. Dublin Fusiliers, 9 pcs	No Price Found		
1659. (9492) Knight with Mace, mounted	30.00	50.00	70.00
1660. (9493) Knight with Sword, mounted	30.00	50.00	70.00
1661. (9494) Knight with Lance, charging and mounted	30.00	50.00	70.00
1662. (9495) Knight with Standard mounted	42.50	70.00	100.00
1663. (9496) Knight with Lance, rearing, mounted .	30.00	50.00	70.00
1664. (9392) Knights on Foot with Lances, Swords, Battleaxes and Mace, 5 pcs	80.00	140.00	185.00
Each	15.00	25.00	35.00
1665. Kings Royal Rifle Corps, 7 pcs	No Price Found		
1666. Yorkshire Regiment, 7 pcs	No Price Found		
1667. Yorkshire and Lancashire Regiment, 7 pcs .	No Price Found		
1668. Warwickshire Regiment, 7 pcs	No Price Found		
1669. Royal Irish Regiment, 8 pcs	No Price Found		
1670. West Surrey Regiment, 8 pcs	No Price Found		
1671. Somerset Light Infantry, 8 pcs	No Price Found		
1672. British Infantry, khaki, 7 pcs	No Price Found		
1673. Scot Guards, 7 pcs ..	No Price Found		

	G	VG	EXC
1674. Grenadier Guards, 7 pcs	No Price Found		
1675. Grenadier Guards, 8 pcs	No Price Found		
1676. Coldstream Guards, 7 pcs	No Price Found		
1677. Coldstream Guards, 7 pcs	No Price Found		
1678. Welsh Fusiliers, 7 pcs	No Price Found		
1679. British Sailors, 7 pcs .	No Price Found		
1680. Royal Marines, 7 pcs	No Price Found		
1681. Royal Marines, 7 pcs	No Price Found		
1682. Action Infantry, 6 pcs	No Price Found		
1683. Action Infantry, 7 pcs	No Price Found		
1684. Zulus, 7 pcs	No Price Found		
1685. Khaki Infantry, 7 pcs	No Price Found		
1686. Royal Canadian Mounted Police, 7 pcs ..	No Price Found		
1687. New Zealand Infantry, 7 pcs	No Price Found		
1688. Cowboys, 7 pcs	No Price Found		
1689. North American Indians, 7 pcs	No Price Found		
1690. Scots Greys, Grenadier Guards, 13 pcs	No Price Found		
1691. 1st Dragoons, Somerset Light Infantry, 13 pcs	No Price Found		
1692. Khaki Infantry, 14 pcs	No Price Found		
1693. Buffs and Grenadier Guards, 15 pcs	No Price Found		
1694. Scots Guards, Grenadier Guards, 14 pcs	No Price Found		
1695. Life Guards, Scots Guards, 12 pcs	No Price Found		
1696. Royal Canadian Dragoons, Canadian Light Infantry, 12 pcs	No Price Found		
1697. Infantry, khaki, firing, 16 pcs	No Price Found		
1698. Cowboys and North American Indians, 12 pcs	No Price Found		
1699. Cowboys, 12 pcs	No Price Found		
1700. Scots Guards, Life Guards, 5 pcs	No Price Found		
1701-1709. UNKNOWN			
1710. Royal Canadian Mounted Police, 5 pcs ..	No Price Found		
1711. (9167) The Foreign Legion at slope with mounted officers, 7 pcs., (6 in 1960)	75.00	102.50	140.00
Officer	13.00	18.50	25.00
Troop	8.00	12.00	16.00

#1711 Officer

#1711

#1717 Pre-War Combines #1715 & #1716

#1719

	G	VG	EXC
1712. French Foreign Legion with Mounted Officer, 15 pcs	350.00	650.00	950.00
1715. (9706) 2-pounder Light Anti-Aircraft Gun, base diameter 2"	12.50	16.50	22.00
1716. Chassis for rigid or mobile mounting for 2 pdr. AA gun and searchlight	90.00	120.00	155.00
1717. (9735) Mobile Unit, 2-pounder light anti-aircraft gun, 4½" long, 2 pcs	30.00	50.00	70.00
1718. (9765) Searchlight, on Screw Jack chassis, uses battery, 2 pcs	30.00	50.00	70.00
1719. Stretcher Party Unit of R.A.M.C., 4 pcs., 2 bearers, stretcher, wounded	65.00	110.00	150.00

BRITAINS

#1720

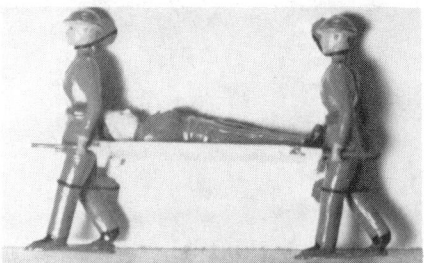

1723 early

1727   Courtesy K. Warren Mitchell

#1730

#1730

	G	VG	EXC
1723. Royal Army Medical Corps Unit, 9 pcs, 2 stretcher, 4 bearers, 2 nurses, 1 wounded, SET	85.00	125.00	180.00
Nurse	7.00	10.00	12.00
Stretcher Bearer	8.00	12.00	16.00
1724. A.A. Units of the British Army, 15 pcs., Searchlight, Sound Locator, Spotting Chairs, Tent and Tenwheel tender	350.00	650.00	1000.00
1725. (9725) 4½" Howitzer, 1939-40s, Pre-War red box	12.50	20.00	30.00
Post-War, thin box	9.50	12.50	18.50
1726. Regulation Type Limber	15.00	22.50	26.00
1727. Complete Mobile Howitzer Unit, 4 pcs., with Limber and Caterpillar Tractor	300.00	550.00	750.00
1728. Predictor, with Operator (AA defense) 2 pcs	14.50	20.00	32.00
1729. Height Finder, 2 pcs., with Operator, Pre-War	18.00	30.00	45.00
Post-War	14.00	20.00	35.00
1730. (9148) Gun Detachment, 7 pcs., 2 kneeling, 2 kneeling with shell, 2 at attention, 1 standing with shell	90.00	125.00	165.00
Post-War, 7 pcs	80.00	115.00	145.00
Officer, Pre-War, late	12.00	18.00	24.00
Officer 1950s	10.00	15.00	20.00
Troop, 1950s	8.00	12.00	16.00
1731. Spotting Chair (Swiveling) with man to lie down, 2 pcs., Pre and Post-War	15.00	25.00	40.00

	G	VG	EXC
1720. (9312) The Band of the Royal Scots Greys (2nd Dragoons), with Kettle Drummer, 7 pcs., all mounted	170.00	300.00	400.00
1721. Band of Royal Scots Greys, mounted, 12 pcs	500.00	800.00	1200.00
Cymbalist	40.00	60.00	80.00
Clarinetist	40.00	60.00	80.00
Cornetist	40.00	60.00	80.00
1722. Drums and Pipes Band of the Scots Guards, 21 pcs.	300.00	500.00	800.00
Piper	12.00	18.00	24.00

No. 1732

	G	VG	EXC
1732. Standard Type Army Hut	500.00	850.00	1200.00

492

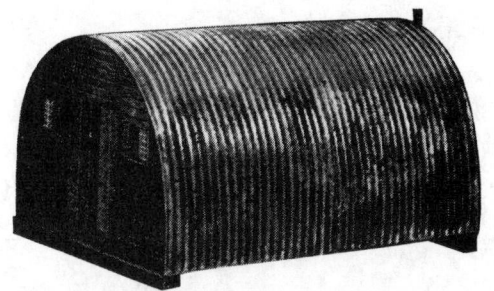

No. 1733

No. 1734

No. 1738

#1757

	G	VG	EXC
1733. Nissen Type Army Hut	500.00	850.00	1200.00
1734. Guard Room	500.00	850.00	1200.00
1735. Gun Shed for housing guns 1643 and 1717	500.00	850.00	1200.00
1736. Gun Shed to house 3 Guns and Limbers	650.00	1000.00	1400.00
1737. Army Transport Shed, to garage 3 vehicles	600.00	900.00	1300.00
1738. Stable to hold 6 horses	500.00	850.00	1200.00
1739. Gunners Quarters	500.00	850.00	1200.00
1740. Flight of Steps	150.00	250.00	400.00
1741. UNKNOWN			
1742. Field Gun Emplacement	200.00	300.00	400.00
1743. Field Gun Emplacement, open type	No Price Found		
1744. Machine Gun Emplacement with Corrugated Roofs and Sandbags	150.00	400.00	600.00

	G	VG	EXC
1745. Machine Gun Emplacement (sandbagged) to take two machine guns	150.00	375.00	480.00
1746. French Type sandbagged (advance position), Gun Emplacement	150.00	300.00	450.00
1747. Barrack Buildings with Parade Ground	No Price Found		
1748. Barrack Buildings with Parade Grounds and two (2) Guard Huts	1600.00	3200.00	5000.00
1749. Balloon with Winch, 2 pcs., 1939	900.00	1500.00	2000.00
Winch	50.00	75.00	100.00
1750. Action Infantry, 9 pcs	No Price Found		
1751. North American Indians, 16 pcs	No Price Found		
1752. 5th Dragoon Guards, 9th Lancers, 12 pcs	No Price Found		
1753. Middlesex Regiment, 7th Fusiliers, 20 pcs	No Price Found		
1754. British Infantry and cavalry, 27 pcs	No Price Found		
1755. British Infantry and cavalry, 38 pcs	No Price Found		
1756. U.S.A. Forces, 31 pcs	No Price Found		
1757. Balloon Barrage Unit (balloon, winch, lorry, 1641), 1939	700.00	1000.00	1600.00

#1758

#1759

BRITAINS

#1791 Post-War

	G	VG	EXC
1758. Fire Fighters of the Royal Air Force, 8 pcs ..	130.00	220.00	300.00
1759. A.R.P. National Service Stretcher Party, 9 pcs	165.00	350.00	450.00
1760. Balloon only (barrage balloon) 1939	350.00	700.00	1000.00
1761. Hiker's or Boy Scout Tent	No Price Found		
1762-63 UNKNOWN			
1764. Cameron Highlanders, 21 pcs	No Price Found		
1765. Arabs, 12 pcs	No Price Found		
1766. Highlanders, 7 pcs ..	No Price Found		
1767. Seaforth Highlanders, 7 pcs	No Price Found		
1768. Black Watch, 7 pcs ..	No Price Found		
1769. Royal Scots, 7 pcs ..	No Price Found		
1770. Governor General Foot Guards, 7 pcs	No Price Found		
1771. Canadian Light Infantry, 7 pcs	No Price Found		
1772. Royal Canadian Regiment, 7 pcs	No Price Found		
1773. Scots Guards, Colours and Pioneers, 6 pcs	No Price Found		
1774. Machine Gunners, 8 pcs	No Price Found		
1775. Gordon Highlanders, 14 pcs	No Price Found		
1776. Seaforth Highlanders, 14 pcs	No Price Found		
1777. Grenadier Guards, and Life Guards, 12 pcs .	No Price Found		
1778. UNKNOWN			
1779. Life Guards and Royal Sussex Regiment, 12 pcs	No Price Found		
1780. Grenadier Guards and Royal Scots Greys, 13 pcs	No Price Found		
1781. Grenadier Guards Buffs, 16 pcs	No Price Found		
1782. Irish Guards, Gordon Highlanders, 14 pcs	No Price Found		
1783. Grenadier Guards 16 pcs	No Price Found		

	G	VG	EXC
1784. Coldstream Guards, 22 pcs	No Price Found		
1785. Scots Guards and Middlesex Regiment, 21 pcs.	No Price Found		
1786. Black Watch, 7 pcs ..	No Price Found		
1787. Grenadier Guards, 6 pcs	No Price Found		
1788. Gordon Highlanders, 7 pcs	No Price Found		
1789. Royal Marines Band, 19 pcs	No Price Found		
1790. Black Watch, Seaforth Highlanders, 21 pcs	No Price Found		
1791. (9153) Royal Corps of Signals, dispatch riders, motorcyclists, 4 pcs	90.00	140.00	180.00
Officer on foot (replaces one piece in 1960 version) ...	10.00	16.50	22.00
Dispatch Rider	15.00	25.00	35.00
1792. Mobile Traffic Police on Motor Cycles, 4 pcs .	No Price Found		
1793. Motor Machine Gun Corps, sidecar with driver and gunner, 2 pcs. Pre-War	80.00	120.00	160.00
2nd version	45.00	67.50	90.00
1794. Detachment of Infantry, 8 pcs., service dress, to operate Searchlight ...	100.00	225.00	300.00
Troop, late 1930s	7.50	11.25	15.00
1795. Life Guards galloping 6 pcs	No Price Found		
1796. 12th Lancers, 6 pcs .	No Price Found		
1797. Cowboys and North American Indians, 6 pcs .	No Price Found		
1798. Prince of Wales Volunteers, at slope, 10 pcs	No Price Found		
1799. Seaforth Highlanders marching, active service order	No Price Found		
1800. Cameron Highlanders, Active Service Order, at slope (10 pcs., no officer) circa 1940	No Price Found		
1801. Grenadier Guards, 10 pcs	No Price Found		
1802. Grenadier Guards, 10 pcs	No Price Found		
1803. East Kent Regiment, 9 pcs., on guard, officer, drummer	No Price Found		
1804. Kings Own Royal Regiment, 10 pcs	No Price Found		

#1832

#1833

#1835

	G	VG	EXC
1819. Gordon Highlanders, Royal Scots Greys, 26 pcs	No Price Found		
1820. U.S.A. Infantry and Cavalry, 27 pcs	No Price Found		
1821. Winch, 1 pc	No Price Found		
1822. Cowboys mounted and on foot, 16 pcs	No Price Found		
1823. British Infantry and A.A. Units, khaki, 31 pcs	No Price Found		
1824. British Service Units, 36 pcs	No Price Found		
1825. Colonial and Empire Troops, 41 pcs	No Price Found		
1826. German, French, Belgian, Russian and Italian troops, 42 pcs ...	No Price Found		
1827. Mechanized Army Troops, 22 pcs	No Price Found		
1828. Infantry of the Battle line, steel helmets, at ease, 8 pcs	150.00	400.00	550.00
1831. R.A. Gun 1201, with Short Pole Pattern Gun Limber, 2 pcs	No Price Found		
1832. 10 Wheel Lorry with 2 pdr. AA Gun on chassis, 4 pcs	350.00	700.00	1000.00
1833. 10 Wheel Lorry with Searchlight on Chassis, 4 pcs	200.00	450.00	675.00
1834. Scots Guards at slope, steel helmets, 8 pcs., circa 1940	1000.00	1750.00	2500.00
1835. Argentine Naval School Cadets, at slope, has officer, 1948-49, 8 pcs	225.00	450.00	650.00
Officer	35.00	60.00	80.00
Cadet	20.00	40.00	60.00
1836. Argentine Military Cadets, at slope, with officer, 1948-49, 8 pcs	450.00	850.00	1200.00
1837. Argentine Infantry, 8 pcs., at slope	300.00	600.00	850.00
1838. Argentine Army, 13 pcs	No Price Found		
1839. Argentine Army, 13 pcs	No Price Found		
1840. Argentine Army, 16 pcs	No Price Found		
1841. Argentine Army, 21 pcs	No Price Found		
1842. Argentine Army, 18 pcs	No Price Found		

	G	VG	EXC
1805. Royal Norfolk Regiment, 10 pcs	No Price Found		
1806. Bluejackets, U.S.A., 10 pcs	No Price Found		
1807. U.S.A. Action firing, 10 pcs	No Price Found		
1808. U.S.A. Action firing, 10 pcs	No Price Found		
1809. Cowboys and North American Indians, 10 pcs	No Price Found		
1810. Life Guards and Grenadier Guards, 16 pcs	No Price Found		
1811. 11th Hussars, S. Lancaster Regiment, 16 pcs .	No Price Found		
1812. 21st Lancers, King's Own Royal Regiment, 16 pcs	No Price Found		
1813. Life Guards, Royal Norfolk Regiment 16 pcs	No Price Found		
1814. Seaforth Highlanders, 12th Lancers, 16 pcs	No Price Found		
1815. Gordon Highlanders, 21st Lancers, 16 pcs	No Price Found		
1816. U.S.A. Cavalry and Infantry, 16 pcs	No Price Found		
1817. Band of the Line, 14 pcs	No Price Found		
1818. Scots Greys, Scots Guards, Welsh Fusiliers, circa 1940	No Price Found		

BRITAINS

#1854

#1856

#1858

No. 1861.

No. 1863.

	G	VG	EXC
1846. Argentine Military Cadets, 16 pcs	No Price Found		
1847. Argentine Naval Cadets, 16 pcs	No Price Found		
1848. Argentine Infantry Khaki, 16 pcs	No Price Found		
1849. Argentine Forces, 36 pcs	No Price Found		
1850. Netherlands Infantry, 8 pcs., slope arms	350.00	950.00	1400.00
1851. Netherlands Infantry, 16 pcs	No Price Found		
1852. Argentine Cavalry, 20 pcs	No Price Found		
1853. Argentine Cavalry, 15 pcs	No Price Found		
1854. Militiamen, 8 pcs., slope arms and slung arms, forage caps	175.00	400.00	600.00
1855. Miniature Balloon Barrage Unit with Lorry, Winch and Balloon (less than half the size of the standard balloon) 1940, 1946	125.00	250.00	350.00
1856. Polish Infantry, 8 pcs., slope arms, has officer (only Post-War), Pre-War	170.00	295.00	380.00
Post-War	140.00	230.00	320.00
Officer	25.00	42.50	60.00
Troop, circa 1939	18.00	30.00	45.00
Trooper, Post-War	16.00	25.00	35.00
1857. Barracks with Soldiers, 41 pcs	No Price Found		
1858. British Infantry (steel helmets), 8 pcs., slung rifles, officer, bren gunner	85.00	115.00	150.00
Officer	10.00	14.00	18.00
Bren Gunner	10.00	12.00	16.00
Troop	7.00	9.00	12.00
1859. Sentry Box with Sentry, active service, 2 pcs .	30.00	55.00	75.00
1860. Sand bags	No Price Found		
1861. Camouflaged Netted Field Emplacement for Heavy Artillery	700.00	1500.00	2200.00
1862. Camouflaged Netted Machine Gun Emplacement	No Price Found		
1863. Concrete Pill Box for Heavy Artillery	No Price Found		
1864. Concrete Pill Box with Detachable Machine Gun Positions	400.00	900.00	1500.00

	G	VG	EXC
1843. Army of Argentina, Mounted Grenadiers and Infantry with Steel Helmets, officer with sword, on horseback, 9 mounted lancers, 8 foot infantry, circa 1939	1400.00	2800.00	4000.00
1844. Argentine Army, 26 pcs	No Price Found		
1845. Argentine Army, 31 pcs	No Price Found		

No. 1866

#1876

#1877 Post-War

	G	VG	EXC
1872. Historical Series sold in 1940 at F.A.O. Schwarz, 16 foot figures from 15, 19, 69, 77, 114, 117, 122, 214, 225, 1293, 1518, 1519, 1542, 1545, 1633	No Price Found		
1873. Historical Series sold in 1940 at F.A.O. Schwarz, 10 mounted figures from 1, 32, 94, 99, 100, 105, 108, 159, 229, 400	600.00	1000.00	1500.00
1874. Historical Series sold in 1940 at F.A.O. Schwarz, 10 mounted figures from 38, 45, 49, 94, 105, 108, 115, 159, 229, 1630	No Price Found		
1875. Historical Series sold in 1940 at F.A.O. Schwarz, 5 mounted figures, eight foot from 1, 32, 99, 100, 400, 160, 338, 1260, 1611, 1612, 1613, 1730 kneeling, 1828	No Price Found		
1876. Bren Gun Carrier with Full Crew, 4 pcs. (3 soldiers, Pre-War	35.00	65.00	80.00
Post-War	30.00	55.00	70.00
1877. Beetle Lorry and Driver, 4 pcs., light troop Transport or General Service Truck, 5" long			
Pre-War	60.00	95.00	135.00
Post-War	50.00	85.00	125.00
1878. UNKNOWN			
1879. Lorry, miniature, pulling trailer loaded with hydrogen gas cylinders for 1855 Barrage Unit, 1940, 1946, 2 pcs	115.00	165.00	210.00
1880-1884 UNKNOWN			
1885. Soldiers in Action, in gas masks crawling, digging, throwing grenades . .	No Price Found		
1886. Historical Series sold in F.A.O. Schwarz, 15 foot figures from 76, 104, 109, 142, 178, 186, 189, 194, 216, 222, 241, 1250, 1568, 1850, 1854	No Price Found		

	G	VG	EXC
1865. Bayonet Practice Frame with 3 hanging sandbags	700.00	1500.00	2200.00
1866. Circular Sandbag Emplacement for AA Gun, searchlight	400.00	900.00	1500.00
1867. Open Field Shelter with Camouflage Roof . .	400.00	900.00	1500.00
1868. A.R.W. Post with Gas Detector Platform	1500.00	3500.00	5000.00
1869. R.A.M.C. Casualty Cleaning Section	900.00	2000.00	2500.00
1870. Historical Series sold in 1940 at F.A.O. Schwarz, 16 foot figures from 91, 134, 141, 192, 196, 219, 226, 227, 228, 299, 399, 432, 1251, 1253, 1435, 1437	600.00	1000.00	1500.00
1871. Historical Series sold in 1940 at F.A.O. Schwarz, 16 foot figures from 16, 34, 36, 74, 75, 78, 80, 97, 111, 206, 207 (all 3 types), 312, 1510, 1619	400.00	800.00	1200.00

BRITAINS

#1893

#1894

#1895 Grey Suit,
dark straps

#1897 Ambulance, Pre-War

	G	VG	EXC
1887. Historical Series sold in 1940 at F.A.O. Schwarz, 15 foot figures from 7, 36, 90 (officer with binoculars), 107, 113, 118, 121 (two firing poses), 124, 137, 157, 1541, 1719 (wounded, khaki stretcher, one stretcher bearer)	No Price Found		
1888. Historical Series sold in 1940 at F.A.O. Schwarz, 16 foot figures from 18 (kneeling), 98, 110, 119, 205, 212, 1515, 1542, 1554, 1597, 1621, 1630, 1633, 1858, 1906 .	No Price Found		
1889. Historical Series sold in 1940 at F.A.O. Schwarz, 16 foot figures from 17 (standing) 74, 82, 88, 120 (officer and man), 157, 172, 182, 314, 1424, 1436, 1617, 1711, 1856 .	No Price Found		
1890. Historical Series sold in 1940 at F.A.O. Schwarz, 10 mounted figures from 24, 31, 46, 106, 128, 164, 220, 315, 1711	No Price Found		
1891. Historical Series, sold in 1940 at F.A.O. Schwarz, 10 mounted figures from 3, 12, 33, 43, 44, 81, 83, 315, 1343, 1631	No Price Found		
1892. Indian Infantry, 8 pcs., at trail, has officer, 1940	300.00	500.00	700.00
1893. Royal Indian Army Service Corps, 7 pcs., officer, 4 infantry, mule and handler, 1940	100.00	190.00	250.00

	G	VG	EXC
Officer	16.00	24.00	30.00
Troop	12.00	20.00	24.00
Mule or handler	13.00	22.00	27.00
1894. Pilots or R.A.F. in Full Flying Kit with Women's Auxiliary Air Force, 6 pilots, 2 WAAFs	250.00	500.00	700.00
Per figure	12.00	25.00	35.00
1895. Pilots of the German Luftwaffe in Full Flying Kit, 8 pcs	350.00	650.00	1000.00
Per figure	30.00	55.00	75.00
1896. R.A.M.C. Stretcher Party, 8 pcs., service order	250.00	550.00	800.00
1897. Motor Ambulance with doctor, wounded, nurses, orderlies, 18 pcs .	175.00	325.00	450.00
Wounded	10.00	15.00	20.00
Nurse	10.00	15.00	20.00
Orderly	10.00	15.00	20.00
1898. (9147) British Infantry (steel helmets) with rifles and tommy guns, officer in battledress, 8 pcs	50.00	75.00	100.00
Officer	5.00	8.00	10.00
Troop	4.00	6.00	8.00
1899. Military Autogiro, with pilot, 2 pcs	1500.00	3000.00	4500.00
1900. Regiment Louw Wepener, 8 pcs., slope, officer, 1939-41, 1948-49 ..	300.00	650.00	900.00
Officer	35.00	65.00	90.00
Troop	30.00	55.00	80.00
1901. Capetown Highlanders, slope, officer, 8 pcs., 1939-41, Pre-War	115.00	165.00	200.00
Post-War	100.00	140.00	175.00
Officer	13.00	20.00	28.00
Troop	8.00	15.00	22.00
1902. Union of South Africa Defense Force, 8 pcs. 1940-41	350.00	700.00	1100.00
Troop	35.00	65.00	90.00

#1900

#1901

#1907

#2002-2004

#1918

#1911

	G	VG	EXC
1907. British Army (Active Service Order), staff officers with dispatch rider, 5 pcs	115.00	165.00	225.00
Officer with swagger stick	13.50	20.00	30.00
Officer with binoculars	13.50	22.00	35.00
1908. Officers of the General Staff, the Guards, Line Infantry, Light Regiments, Fusiliers and Rifle Regiments, number of pieces not known	No Price Found		
1909. R.A.M.C. Doctors, Nurses, Orderlies, Wounded, Stretchers, Hospital Tent, Ambulance, Car and Lorry 28 pcs	No Price Found		
1910. R.A.M.C. Field Hospital Staff with Wounded (Battle Dress), 24 pcs	No Price Found		
1911. Officers and Petty Officers of the Royal Navy, 7 pcs., 1940-, 1946-59	125.00	187.50	250.00
Officer, coat over arm	15.00	32.50	40.00
Officer in shorts	12.00	27.50	35.00
Officer	10.00	17.50	22.00
Petty Officer	10.00	14.50	20.00
1913. Cameronians marching (Scottish Rifles), 7 pcs	No Price Found		
Troop	50.00	100.00	150.00
1914. A.R.P. Wardens, 8 pcs., regulation uniforms	350.00	650.00	1000.00
1915. UNKNOWN			
1916. Reported to be a steel helmeted U.S. Army Band		Sold at	4500.00
1917. UNKNOWN			
1918. The Home Guard, slung rifles, 8 pcs	125.00	250.00	400.00
Troop	12.50	22.00	40.00
1921-2001. UNKNOWN			
2002. Bell Tent, 4½" base	No Price Found		
2003. Bell Tent, 5½" base	No Price Found		
2004. Bell Tent, 6½" base	No Price Found		

	G	VG	EXC
1903. Indian Mountain Battery with Gun, gunners, mules, mounted officer, officer has sword held up, 1940, 12 pcs	650.00	1000.00	1500.00
1904. U.S. Army Air Corps Officer and Men, 8 pcs	No Price Found		
1905. U.S. Army Air Corps Pilots, Officers and Men, 16 pcs	No Price Found		
Pilot	60.00	90.00	120.00
Man	20.00	30.00	40.00
1906. Royal Air Force Pilots, ground staff, and fire fighters, 16 pcs	No Price Found		

BRITAINS

#2009

#2010 & 2011

#2011

#2014

#2015

	G	VG	EXC
2005. Marquee or Hospital Tent, 5½" long base	10.00	18.00	24.00
2006. Marquee or Hospital Tent, 7½" long base	No Price Found		
2007. Marquee or Hospital Tent, 9" long base	No Price Found		
2008. 4½" Howitzer and Limber	100.00	165.00	225.00
2009. Belgian Grenadiers in Greatcoats, 8 pcs	100.00	150.00	200.00
Troop	8.00	12.00	16.00
2010. Parachute Regiment, 8 pcs., 1948-59 (7 in 1960)	90.00	135.00	180.00
7 pc. set	80.00	120.00	160.00
Officer	10.00	18.00	25.00
Slung Rifle	8.00	12.00	18.00
Bren Gun	10.00	16.50	24.00
2011. Display Box, officers, flight sergeant, pilots, WRAF, Dispatch Rider and R.A.F. Regiment officers and men, 23 pcs ..	240.00	360.00	500.00
Fire fighter, asbestos suit ..	10.00	20.00	25.00
WRAF	11.00	18.50	22.50
Bren Gun	11.00	16.50	22.00
Rifle	11.00	16.50	22.00
Officer Swagger Stick	12.00	19.50	26.00
Aircraftsman	9.00	15.00	20.00
2012. Royal Australian Air Force marching, red berets, 8 pcs	No Price Found		
2013. Indian Mounted Army, 12 pcs	No Price Found		
2014. Band of U.S. Marine Corps, 21 pcs	700.00	1300.00	1800.00
2015. Soviet Cavalry and Soviet Guards, 13 pcs ...	No Price Found		
2016. Japanese Imperial Guards, 13 pcs	No Price Found		

	G	VG	EXC
2017. Ski Troops, four, 1948-57	220.00	400.00	600.00
Troop	45.00	65.00	130.00
2018. Danish Army, Guard Hussar Rgt., 8 pcs., with officer and trumpeter ...	280.00	500.00	800.00
Officer and trumpeter	35.00	65.00	100.00
Hussar	25.00	50.00	80.00
2019. Danish LivGarde, 7 pcs	120.00	210.00	275.00
Troop	14.50	22.50	30.00
2020. Portugese Native Infantry, 8 pcs	No Price Found		

#2017

#2018

#2027

#2029

#2019

#2021

#2022

#2028

#2030

#2024

#2025

	G	VG	EXC
2023. Covered Wagon, 6 pcs	No Price Found		
2024. Light Goods Van with Driver, various colors, 2 pcs	250.00	450.00	600.00
2025. (9334) Cameron Highlanders, firing, with pipers, 18 pcs	150.00	225.00	350.00
Officer	12.50	24.00	30.00
Piper	10.00	15.00	20.00
Troop	9.00	13.00	18.00
2026. (9705) 25 pdr. Howitzer	7.00	10.50	14.00
2027. (9172) Red Army Guards in greatcoats, 8 pcs., has officer	75.00	112.50	150.00
Officer	10.00	15.00	20.00
Troop	7.00	10.50	14.00
2028. Red Army Cavalry at parade halt, 5 pcs	100.00	155.00	230.00
Officer	14.00	27.50	35.00
Trooper	12.00	23.50	30.00
2029. (9105) Life Guards, mounted at halt and foot sentries, 6 pcs	65.00	95.00	125.00
Mounted	10.00	15.00	20.00
Foot	8.00	12.00	16.00

	G	VG	EXC
2021. (9183) U.S. Military Police (Snowdrops), 8 pcs., (7 in 1960), no officer	70.00	95.00	125.00
Troop	7.00	9.00	11.00
2022. (9371) Swiss Papal Guards with officer, 9 pcs	120.00	200.00	275.00
Officer	13.50	22.00	30.00
Guard	10.00	18.50	25.00

501

#2032

#2033   #2035

#2031

#2043 Partial

#2044

#2046 Partial

	G	VG	EXC
2030. Australian Infantry in Blue Ceremonial Dress, has officer, 1949-59, 8 pcs	100.00	150.00	200.00
Officer	12.00	18.00	28.00
Troops	10.00	15.00	20.00
2031. Australian Infantry in battledress, at slope, 8 pcs., 1949-59	85.00	125.00	160.00
Officer	10.00	15.00	20.00
Trooper w/slouch hat	8.00	12.00	16.00
2032. Red Army infantry, summer infantry, summer uniforms, marching in review	95.00	130.00	180.00
Troop	8.00	12.00	16.00
2033. (9180) U.S. Infantry marching, steel helmets, w/officer, 8 pcs., (7 in 1960)	55.00	80.00	105.00
Officer	6.50	9.75	13.00
Troop	5.00	7.50	10.00
2034. Covered Wagon, 4 horses, pioneer, wife, 7 pcs	105.00	150.00	200.00
2035. (9175) Svea (Swedish) Lifeguards, 8 pcs., slope w/officer	100.00	160.00	220.00
Officer	12.00	18.00	24.00
Troop	10.00	15.00	20.00
2036. (9311) Scots Greys, Scots Guards, Black Watch, 19 pcs (12 in 1960)	145.00	280.00	350.00
12 pc. set	120.00	200.00	260.00
2037. Ski Trooper, 1 pc	40.00	70.00	125.00
2038. Scots Guards at ease, 8 pcs.	No Price Found		
2039. Colours of the Scots and Coldstream Guards, 8 pcs., 4 color bearers, 4 color sergeants	No Price Found		

	G	VG	EXC
2040. Pipers and Royal Scots, 4 pcs	No Price Found		
2041. Trailer, Universal Clockwork Unit **with key**	35.00	60.00	90.00
2042. Covered Wagon Set and attacking Indians, 13 pcs	400.00	900.00	1300.00
2043. Rodeo Set, 13 pcs	275.00	450.00	700.00
Stockade fence (wood and metal)	25.00	40.00	60.00
Figure Bucking Horse	30.00	65.00	100.00
Seated Cowboys	25.00	30.00	40.00
2044. (9179) U.S. Air Corps, 1949 pattern blue uniform, marching, slung carbines, 8 pcs	65.00	105.00	125.00
Officer	8.50	11.50	15.00
Troop	7.00	10.00	12.50
2045. Clockwork Van, driver, 2 pcs	300.00	650.00	1000.00
2046. (9391) Arab Display, mounted, foot, 12 pcs	175.00	300.00	400.00
Running, foot	12.50	18.75	25.00
Mounted	8.00	12.00	16.00
Marching	5.00	7.50	10.00

#2055

#2057 & 2058

#2059

#2060

	G	VG	EXC
2052. (9448) Anti-Aircraft Unit, 2 predictors, Height Finder, A.A. Gun and Searchlight, 15 pcs	300.00	550.00	800.00
2053. Corral 18" square ...	No Price Found		
2055. (9286) "1862" Confederate Cavalry, officer, 5 pcs	75.00	100.00	125.00
1960, 4 pc. set	50.00	70.00	85.00
Officer	11.00	16.50	22.00
Trooper	10.00	15.00	20.00
2056. (9287) "1862" Union Cavalry, 5 pcs., has bugler, officer	80.00	105.00	130.00
1960, 4 pc. set	55.00	75.00	90.00
Officer	10.00	15.00	20.00
Bugler	10.00	15.00	20.00
Trooper	9.00	13.50	18.00
2057. (9487) "1862" Union Artillery with Gunners, 3 pcs	35.00	65.00	85.00
Gunner	12.50	18.50	25.00
2058. (9486) "1862" Confederate Artillery with Gunners, 3 pcs	35.00	65.00	85.00
2059. (9187) "1862" Union Infantry, 7 pcs	65.00	85.00	115.00
Officer	7.50	10.00	13.00
Troop	6.50	8.50	10.00
2060. (9186) "1862" Confederate Infantry, 7 pcs .	65.00	85.00	115.00
Officer	7.50	10.00	13.00
Flagbearer	5.50	9.50	11.00
Bugler	5.50	9.50	11.00
Troop	6.50	8.50	10.00
2061. Wild West Display, 90 pcs	1000.00	2000.00	2800.00
2062. (9332) Seaforth Highlanders charging, with Pipers, 17 pcs. (15 1960-61, 12 as 9332)	165.00	225.00	300.00
Mounted Officer	22.50	35.00	55.00
Foot	9.00	12.50	16.00
2063. (9133) Argyll & Sutherland Highlanders, firing, 6 pcs. (5 in 1960) .	70.00	115.00	150.00
Troop	8.50	12.75	17.00
2064. (9745) 155mm Gun .	35.00	65.00	100.00
2065. (9400) H.M. Queen on horseback, saluting	20.00	35.00	55.00
2066. Royal Canadian Mounted, one piece, mounted officer	20.00	30.00	45.00

	G	VG	EXC
2047. Knights in Armor, 6 pcs	No Price Found		
2048. Lorry, 25 pdr. and clockwork trailer	140.00	210.00	280.00
2049. Life Guards and Scots Guards in Review Order, 20 pcs	900.00	1500.00	2000.00
2050. Foreign Legion, Zouaves, Cuirassiers, 20 pcs., Legion marching (6) with mtd. officer (8), Zouaves charging (5), Cuirassiers w/officer	700.00	1100.00	1500.00
2051. Uruguayan Military School Cadets, at slope, w/officer, 1953-59, 8 pcs .	180.00	270.00	360.00
Officer	25.00	37.50	50.00
Cadet	20.00	30.00	40.00

#2051

BRITAINS

#2062

#2065

#2065 Canadian Version

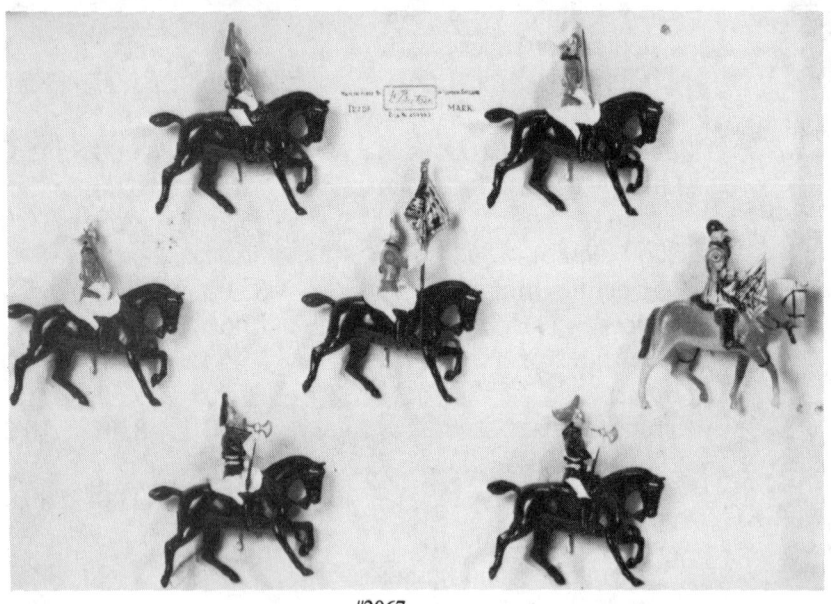

#2067

#2071

#2072

	G	VG	EXC
2067. The Sovereign's Standard of the Life Guards and Escort, 7 pcs. (contents vary)	130.00	250.00	400.00
Farrier	15.00	28.00	40.00
Trumpeter	13.00	25.00	35.00
2068. (9386) "1862" Confederate Cavalry and Infantry, 12 pcs	125.00	200.00	275.00
2069. (9387) "1862" Union Cavalry and Infantry, 12 pcs	125.00	200.00	275.00

	G	VG	EXC
2070. "1862" Display Box, 30 pcs	600.00	1000.00	1500.00
2071. Royal Marines, present arms, 7 pcs., (6 in 1960)	70.00	105.00	140.00
2072. King's Royal Rifle Corps, walking at trail, 1953-59	115.00	200.00	275.00

#2073   #2076   #2078   #2079

#2080   #2082   #2083   #2083   #2084

	G	VG	EXC
2073. Royal Air Force, slope, 8 pcs., officer, 1953-59	115.00	205.00	280.00
2074. (9212) First (King's) Dragoon Guards, walking, cantering and trotting horses, officer, 5 pcs	105.00	150.00	200.00
1960, 4 pc. set	70.00	105.00	150.00
Officer	14.00	22.50	30.00
Trooper	12.00	18.00	24.00
2075. (9214) 7th Queen's Own Hussars, 5 pcs	115.00	165.00	226.00
Officer	15.00	27.00	35.00
Troop	12.00	22.00	28.00
2076. (9217) 12th Lancers, trotting and cantering, 5 pcs	100.00	135.00	195.00
Officer	14.00	24.00	32.00
Trooper	12.00	21.00	28.00
2077. Kings Troop, R.H.A., Gun and Limber, 8 pcs	275.00	400.00	550.00
2078. Irish Guards, present arms, 7 pcs., 1953-59	100.00	130.00	190.00
Troop	10.00	15.00	22.00
2079. (9302) Royal Company of Archers, 13 pcs	250.00	350.00	500.00
Archer	15.00	25.00	32.00

	G	VG	EXC
2080. Sailors Royal Navy, at slope, 1953-61, officer, 8 pcs. (7 in 1960)	95.00	135.00	200.00
Officer	11.50	16.00	25.00
Sailor	9.50	13.00	18.00
2081. The Sovereign's Escort, Coronation of Queen Elizabeth, 211 pcs., which made a display about 15 ft. long	2900.00	4200.00	5500.00
2082. (9125) Coldstream Guards, attention, officer, 8 pcs	70.00	105.00	140.00
Officer	8.00	12.00	16.00
Troop	6.50	9.75	13.00
2083. (9127) Welsh Guards, at ease, with mounted officer, 7 pcs	90.00	135.00	180.00
Officer	11.00	16.50	22.00
Troop	8.00	12.00	16.00
2084. Colour Party of the Scots Guards, 6 pcs	150.00	225.00	300.00
Sergeant	12.00	18.50	25.00

#2085 - 18 with lances

#2093 Dark blue uniforms
trimmed in red.

#2085 - 4 state trumpeters

#2085 - 1 drum horse

#2087

#2089

#2090

#2091
Note: brown gloves

#2092

	G	VG	EXC
2086. (9339) Royal West Surrey Infantry, standing, kneeling, prone firing, 16 pcs	125.00	225.00	280.00
Troop	8.50	11.00	14.00
2087. Dismounted 5th Iniskilling Dragoon Guards, has officer, 1954-59, 8 pcs	135.00	235.00	300.00
Guard	13.00	22.00	32.00
2088. Duke of Cornwall's Light Infantry, 8 pcs., marching at trail, has officer, 1954-59	110.00	205.00	270.00
2089. Gloucestershire Regiment, at left slope, has officer, 1954-59, 8 pcs	135.00	235.00	300.00
Officer	14.00	24.50	35.00
Troop	12.00	22.00	28.00
2090. Royal Irish Fusiliers, at attention, officer, 1954-59, 8 pcs	145.00	260.00	325.00
Officer	18.00	28.00	40.00
Troop	13.50	24.50	32.00
2091. Rifle Brigade, at trail, officer, 8 pcs., 1954-59	135.00	235.00	300.00
Officer	14.00	24.50	35.00
Troop	12.00	22.00	28.00
2092. Parachute Regiment, at left slope, officer, 8 pcs., 1954-59	110.00	215.00	280.00
Officer	12.50	22.50	30.00
Troop	11.00	20.00	26.00
2093. Band of the Royal Berkshire Regiment, 25 pcs., 1954-59, plastic drums after 1955	800.00	1450.00	1800.00
2094. (9402) State Open Landau with team of 6 Windsor Greys, Queen Elizabeth, Prince Phillip, 11 pcs	170.00	250.00	400.00

	G	VG	EXC
2085. (9405) Musical Ride of the Household Cavalry, 23 pcs	700.00	1100.00	1500.00
Single Lancer	25.00	45.00	65.00

#2095

#2096   Tenor drum

#2098

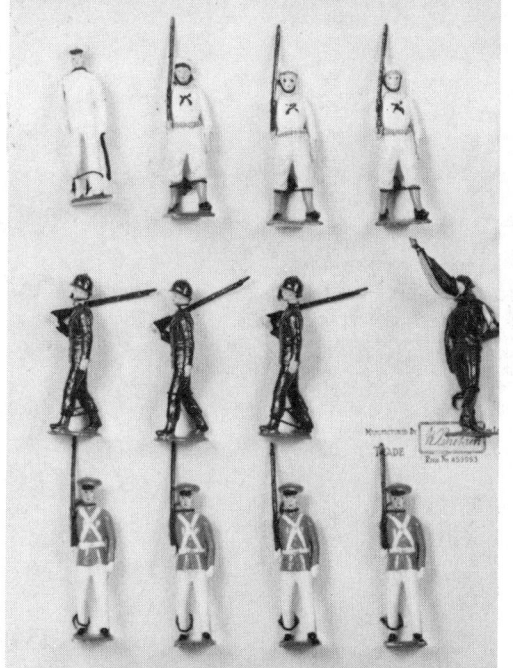

#2100

#2100
Note blue
trim on flap

#2101 Boxed

#2102

	G	VG	EXC
2096. (9428) Drum and Pipe Band of the Irish Guards, 12 pcs	350.00	600.00	900.00
2097. French Foreign Legion and Arabs, 26 pcs	450.00	850.00	1250.00
2098. Venezuelan Military School Cadets, 7 pcs., 6 men, officer with furled flag, 1955-59	125.00	265.00	350.00
Officer	15.00	22.50	40.00
Cadet	12.00	18.00	30.00
2099. Venezuelan Military School Cadets, 15 pcs., 13 men, flagbearer, officer, 1955-59	No Price Found		
2100. (9375) Venezuelan Cadets, Infantry, Sailors, 23 pcs. (sailors in no other set), 1 officer, 7 sailors, 8 cadets, 7 infantry (20 pcs. from 1960 on)	200.00	450.00	700.00
1960 set	150.00	400.00	650.00
2101. (9482) U.S. Marines Color Guard Party, 4 pcs	125.00	165.00	225.00
Flagbearer	20.00	35.00	50.00
Troop	10.00	15.00	20.00
2102. (9760) Austin Champ (jeep-like vehicle)	30.00	50.00	65.00

	G	VG	EXC
2095. (9366) French Foreign Legion in Action, 14 pcs	160.00	265.00	320.00
12 pc. set, 1960-61	125.00	215.00	270.00
13 pc. set, 1962	135.00	245.00	300.00
Mounted Officer	13.00	18.50	24.00
Officer kneeling with binoculars	12.50	22.50	27.50
Machine Gunner	11.50	18.50	24.00
Charging	10.50	17.50	22.00
Standing Firing	8.00	12.00	16.00

BRITAINS

#2106

#2109

#2110

#2112 Boxed

2103. Life Guards, Scots
  Greys, Scots Guards,
  Welsh Fusiliers,
  Coldstream Guards Band,
  32 pcs., SELFRIDGES
  SPECIAL . . . .   No Price Found

	G	VG	EXC
2104. Venezuelan Infantry, 7 pcs., officer with flag, 1955-59	115.00	175.00	250.00
Officer	25.00	37.50	50.00
Troop	12.50	18.75	25.00
2105. Venezuelan Infantry, 15 pcs., officer, officer-flagbearer included, 1955-59	200.00	365.00	450.00
Officer-flagbearer	25.00	37.50	50.00
Officer	15.00	22.50	30.00
Troop	12.50	18.75	25.00
2106. 18" Heavy Howitzer Mounted for Garrison Work	45.00	70.00	100.00
2107. (9740) 18" Heavy Howitzer Mounted on Tractor Wheels	45.00	70.00	100.00
2108. Drums and Fifes of the Welsh Guards, 12 pcs	400.00	750.00	1000.00
2109. (9435) Highland Pipe Band of the Black Watch, 20 pcs	450.00	850.00	1200.00
2110. (9478) U.S. Military Band, full dress, 25 pcs ..	800.00	1400.00	2000.00
2111. Black Watch Colour Party, 6 pcs	225.00	375.00	600.00
2112. U.S. Marine Corps Band, summer dress, 25 pcs	800.00	1600.00	2200.00
Drum Major	45.00	72.50	100.00
Sousaphone	35.00	60.00	80.00
Other	30.00	55.00	75.00

508

#2115

#2117

	G	VG	EXC
2113. Full Band of Grenadier Guards, 25 pcs	1000.00	2400.00	3200.00
Per figure	35.00	75.00	100.00
2114. Band of the Line (plastic drums) 12 pcs	250.00	450.00	700.00
2115. Drums and Bugles of the Royal Marines 12 pcs	250.00	450.00	700.00
2116. Band of the Royal Air Force, 12 pcs	200.00	400.00	550.00
2117. Band of the U.S.A. Army, khaki, 12 pcs	300.00	550.00	850.00
Drum Major	25.00	45.00	65.00
Others	15.00	30.00	40.00

2118 TO 2147 ARE HALF-SETS

	G	VG	EXC
2118. Life Guards, 3 pcs., mounted, dismounted	No Price Found		
2119. The Second Dragoons (Royal Scots Greys), 3 pcs., officer on cantering horse, 2 dismounted troopers at attention with drawn swords	50.00	75.00	100.00
2120. 3rd Kings Own Hussars, 3 pcs	No Price Found		
2121. Grenadier Guards, 4 pcs	No Price Found		
Officer	7.50	11.25	15.00
Troop	4.00	6.00	8.00
2122. Scots Guards, 4 pcs	No Price Found		
2123. Irish Guards, 4 pcs	125.00	300.00	400.00

	G	VG	EXC
2124. Welch Fusiliers, 4 pcs., at attention, 1957-59	No Price Found		
2125. Loyal North Lancanshire, 4 pcs., 2 standing, 1 kneeling, officer standing with binoculars	No Price Found		
Kneeling	11.00	16.50	22.00
2126. Black Watch, 3 pcs	No Price Found		
Mounted Officer	35.00	52.50	70.00
2127. Royal Marines, 4 pcs	No Price Found		
2128. Life Guards and Scots Guards, 3 pcs	No Price Found		
2129. Royal Artillery Gun Detachment, 1957-59, 4 pcs	75.00	112.50	150.00
2130. Infantry in Battledress, 4 pcs., 1957-59	75.00	112.50	150.00
2131. Medium Machine Gunners, 3 pcs	No Price Found		
2132. Royal Army Medical Corps., 5 pcs	No Price Found		
2133. Canadian Governor-General's Horse and Foot Guards, 3 pcs	No Price Found		
2134. Royal Canadian Mounted Police, 3 pcs	No Price Found		
2135. Danish Hussar and Life Guards, 3 pcs	75.00	112.50	150.00
2136. French Foreign Legion, 3 pcs	No Price Found		
2137. French Foreign Legion in Action, 4 pcs	60.00	90.00	120.00
2138. French Tirailieurs, 3 pcs	75.00	200.00	300.00
2139. U.S. Cavalry and Infantry, 3 pcs	No Price Found		
2140. Union Cavalry, 3 pcs	No Price Found		
2141. Confederate Cavalry, 3 pcs	No Price Found		
2142. Union Infantry, 4 pcs	No Price Found		
2143. Confederate Infantry, 4 pcs	No Price Found		
2144. Soviet Russian Infantry and cavalry, 3 pcs	No Price Found		
2145. Cowboys, mounted and on foot, 3 pcs	No Price Found		
2146. North American Indians, 3 pcs	No Price Found		
2147. Arabs, 3 pcs			

END HALF-BOXES

	G	VG	EXC
2148. (9158) Canadian Fort Henry Guards with goat mascot, 7 pcs	65.00	85.00	115.00

509

BRITAINS

#2149

#2150

#2152

#2168

#2155

	G	VG	EXC
2149. Gentleman at Arms, with officer, 9 pcs	350.00	800.00	1200.00
2150. (9770) Centurion Tank	175.00	290.00	400.00
2151. Mounted Kettle Drummer, Life Guards, 1 pc	20.00	40.00	55.00
2152. (9499) Waterloo Gunners with Gun, 3 pcs	50.00	85.00	125.00
2153. Band of the Royal Marines (plastic drums) 12 pcs	200.00	400.00	550.00
2154. Centurion Tank, painted for Desert Warfare	250.00	450.00	600.00
2155. U.N. Infantry, 1957-60, 8 pcs	250.00	600.00	900.00
Officer	15.00	40.00	60.00
Slung Rifle	12.00	22.00	30.00
Bren Gun at Trail	15.00	25.00	45.00
2156. H.M. Queen Elizabeth (Picture Box Souvenir)	No Price Found		
2157. Mounted Kettle Drummer, Life Guards (Picture Box Souvenir), one piece	No Price Found		

	G	VG	EXC
2158. Royal Canadian Mounted Police (Picture Box Souvenir) one piece	No Price Found		
2159. (9460) Fort Henry Guard, Sentry and Box, 2 pc	65.00	100.00	150.00
2160. Fort Henry Guard, 1 pc	No Price Found		
2161. Knights of Agincourt, mounted and foot	175.00	265.00	325.00

2162-2167. ARE SOLID CAST IN NON-LEAD ALLOY FOR EXPORT TO AUSTRALIA, 1954. ONLY MARKED "ENGLAND."

	G	VG	EXC
2162. Cowboys and Indians, 8 pcs	No Price Found		
2163. Cowboys and Indians, 16 pcs	No Price Found		
2164. Infantry in Action, 8 pcs	No Price Found		
2165. Infantry in Action, 16 pcs	No Price Found		
2166. Guards and Infantry of the Line, 8 pcs	No Price Found		
2167. Guards and Infantry of the Line, 16 pcs	No Price Found		

END OF NON-LEAD EXPORTS TO AUSTRALIA

	G	VG	EXC
2168. Gordon Highlanders, Officer Mounted, 1 pc. (Picture Box Souvenir)	30.00	50.00	65.00
2169. 12th Lancers, mounted officer at the halt, 1 pc. (Picture Box Souvenir)	No Price Found		
2170. Mounted Trumpeter of Life Guards Band, 1pc. (Picture Box Souvenir)	No Price Found		
2171. Royal Air Force Colour Party, (extremely rare, semi-unique)	1000.00	2400.00	3000.00

#2172

#2175

#2177

#2182

#2184

BRITAINS

	G	VG	EXC
2173. (9720) Batallion Anti-Tank Gun	9.50	13.50	18.00
2174. (9750) Batallion Anti-Tank Gun with Towing Vehicle	75.00	150.00	200.00
2175. (9748) 155mm Gun, Mounted on Centurion Tank Body	200.00	350.00	500.00
2176. Greek Royal Guards at slope, no officer (circa 1959) 4 pcs	100.00	200.00	300.00
2177. (9154) Band of the Fort Henry Guard, 5 pcs	90.00	150.00	225.00
2178. Fort Henry Guards, Fife and Drums, 10 pcs .	175.00	300.00	450.00
2179. Highland Pipe Band of the Black Watch, plastic drums, 1959-60, 9 pcs	225.00	450.00	650.00
2180. Fort Henry Band Drum Major, 1 pc	No Price Found		
2181. Papal Guards	No Price Found		
2182. Fort Henry Guard Pioneer, one piece. This is the last completely new lead alloy figure made by Britains	15.00	25.00	32.00
2183. Fort Henry Cannon, 1 pc	No Price Found		
2184. Bahamas Police at Attention, 8 pcs., native sergeant, white officer ...	700.00	1200.00	2000.00
Per piece	35.00	57.50	80.00
2185. Bahamas Police Band, 12 or 13 pcs	1200.00	2500.00	3500.00
Per piece	35.00	70.00	100.00
2186. Bahamas Police Band, 26 pcs			
Per piece	35.00	70.00	100.00
2187. (9174) Red Army Guards Infantry in Greatcoats and Summer Uniform, mounted officer, 6 pcs	No Price Found		
2188. Anti-Aircraft Personnel with Predictor, Range Finder and Height Finder, 6 pcs	105.00	175.00	250.00
2189. (9721) 18th Century Cannon plus 6 cannon balls	10.00	20.00	30.00
2190. (9192) Knights of Agincourt, foot, 4 pcs ...	50.00	80.00	105.00

	G	VG	EXC
2172. Algerian Spahi (en grande tenue), Review Order, 5 pcs	300.00	650.00	900.00
Standard Bearer	50.00	100.00	150.00
Trooper	40.00	75.00	120.00

511

BRITAINS

#2186

#9160

9104. Attendants to the State Coach, 6 pcs., (1475)	G	VG	EXC
	70.00	105.00	135.00
9155. Forth Henry Guards, War of 1812, 49th Foot, 7 pcs., (6 later), no officer	60.00	90.00	120.00

	G	VG	EXC
9160. Fort Henry Guards, War of 1812, 89th Foot, 6 pcs., no officer	60.00	90.00	120.00
9302. Attendants to the State Coach, 12 pcs. (1475)	No Price Found		
9345. Ninth Lancers, mounted at halt, with officer, Royal Fusiliers at slope, no officer, 11 pcs .	No Price Found		
9392. Knights of Agincourt, mounted and foot, 9 pcs., (2161)	120.00	185.00	250.00

PICTURE PACKS

Britains military Picture Packs did not follow any logical numbering sequence. When introduced in the 1954 catalog, they were grouped by subjects rather than number. The range was unchanged until discontinued in 1959. Picture Packs listed are shown in the order of their appearance in the catalog. Generally only found in "EXC" or better.

LIFEGUARDS

	Boxed Excellent
37B Trooper, Full Dress ...	30.00
1325B Trumpeter, Regimental Dress	60.00
1270B Farrier, Full Dress ..	55.00
1268B Corporal Major with Standard, Full Dress	60.00
645B Officer, Full Dress ...	30.00
1269B Trumpeter, State Dress	45.00
477B Drummer, State Dress	45.00
116B Trooper, Cloak	35.00
1333B Trumpeter, Cloak ..	60.00

	Boxed Excellent
1333B Farrier, Cloak	60.00
1335B Corporal Major with Standard, Cloak	60.00
844B Officer, Cloak	35.00
1198B Trooper Dismounted	25.00

#1198-B

512

#1344-B

#1339-B

#1345-B

#1342-B

#1341-B

	Boxed Excellent
12th ROYAL LANCERS (Prince of Wales)	
1346B Trooper, Lance at Carry	50.00
1347B Trooper, Lance Slung	50.00
1348B Trumpeter, Full Dress	60.00
1349B Officer, Full Dress	50.00
1st KING'S DRAGOON GUARDS	
1279B Trooper, Full Dress	50.00
1341B Trumpeter, Full Dress	60.00
1342B Standard, Full Dress	60.00
1278B Officer, Full Dress	50.00
1343B Trooper, Dismounted	35.00
ROYAL SCOTS GREYS (2nd Dragoons)	
41B Trooper, Full Dress	40.00
1344B Trumpeter, Full Dress	60.00
668B Officer, Full Dress	45.00
SCOTS GUARDS	
666B Officer, Marching	25.00
915B Officer, Marching, Drawn Sword	25.00
239B Queen's Colour Bearer, (Carry)	35.00
240B Regimental Colour Bearer (Carry)	35.00
340B Queen's Colour Bearer (Slope)	35.00
1006B Officer, Salute	25.00
1350B Officer, Attention	25.00
899B Officer, Greatcoat	25.00
914B Colour-Sergeant, Slope Arms	30.00
339B Pioneer	20.00
28B Guardsman, Marching, Slope Arms	20.00
1005B Guardsman, Present	20.00
778B Guardsman, Attention	30.00
906B Guardsman, At Ease	30.00
898B Guardsman, Greatcoat	20.00
14B Piper	30.00
768B Side Drummer	30.00
1351B Bulger	30.00

	Boxed Excellent
ROYAL HORSE GUARDS	
1336B Trooper, Full Dress	30.00
1337B Trumpeter, Regimental Dress	60.00
1338B Farrier, Full Dress	55.00
1339B Corporal Major with Standard, Full Dress	60.00
281B Officer, full dress	35.00
1340B Trooper, Dismounted	40.00
11th HUSSARS (Prince Albert's Own)	
883B Trooper, Full Dress	50.00
1345B Trumpeter, Full Dress	60.00
647B Officer, Full Dress	50.00
48B Trooper, Dismounted	25.00

BRITAINS

#845-B

#1081-B

#587-B

GORDON HIGHLANDERS

	Boxed Excellent
845B Mounted Officer, Full Dress	65.00
461B Officer, Full Dress	40.00
29B Highlander, Full Dress	30.00
1352B Highlander, Full Dress (Running)	20.00
292B Officer, Field Glasses, (Standing)	35.00
60B Officer, Field Glasses (Kneeling)	35.00
61B Highlander, Standing, Firing	25.00
62B Highlander, Kneeling, Firing	25.00
63B Highlander, Lying, Firing	25.00
327B Piper	25.00

ROYAL MARINES

1353B Officer, Marching	25.00
1354B Officer with Regimental Colour	35.00
1355B Officer, Attention	25.00
1021B Officer, Salute	25.00
67B Marine, Marching	20.00
488B Marine, Present	20.00
1356B Marine, At Ease	30.00
1357B Marine, Attention	30.00

ROYAL NAVY

1290B Officer, Marching	30.00
1289 Bluejacket, Marching, Slope Arms	25.00
429B Bluejacket, Marching	20.00

ROYAL AIR FORCE

	Boxed Excellent
1081B Air Commodore	65.00
1276B Officer, No. 1 Dress	30.00
1277B Airman, Marching	30.00
1054B Pilot, Full Equipment	30.00
66B Pilot, Sidcot Suit	30.00
587B Fire Fighter	40.00
1055B W.R.A.F.	35.00
1149B Officer (Royal Air Force Regiment)	30.00
1151B Bren-gunner (Royal Air Force Regiment)	30.00
1150B Airman (Royal Air Force Regiment)	30.00

YEOMAN OF THE GUARD

219B Officer	35.00
1138B Yeoman	25.00

UNITED STATES OF AMERICA

39B Cavalry, Galloping	60.00
31B Cavalry, Walking	35.00
1205B Infantry Officer	25.00
1206B Infantry Colour Bearer	40.00
1204B Infantry Private	20.00
1157B Officer Marine Corps	25.00
20B Marine	20.00
1226B Air Corps	20.00
107B West Point Cadet	20.00
1190B Military Policeman	20.00

AMERICAN CIVIL WAR, 1862-1865, UNION FORCES CAVALRY

1358B Officer	60.00
1359B Trumpeter	60.00
1360 Trooper	40.00

INFANTRY

1249B Officer	30.00
1361B Officer, Field Glasses	50.00
1250B Standard	30.00
1251B Bugler	25.00
1253B Standing, Firing	20.00
1252B Standing, On Guard	20.00
1255B Kneeling, Firing	20.00
1254B Kneeling on Guard	20.00
1362B Zouave, Charging	30.00

CONFEDERATE FORCES — CAVALRY

1363 Officer	60.00
1364B Trumpeter	60.00
1365B Trooper	40.00

	Boxed Excellent

INFANTRY
1237B Officer	30.00
1366B Officer, Field Glasses	50.00
1238B Standard , ...	30.00
1239B Bugler	25.00
1241B Standing, Firing	20.00
1240B Standing, On Guard	20.00
1243B Kneeling, Firing	20.00
1242B Kneeling, On Guard	20.00

FRENCH FOREIGN LEGION
1329B Officer, Full Dress (Mounted)	35.00
1367B Officer, Full Dress (On Foot)	45.00
1035B Officer, Service Dress (Mounted)	35.00
561B Legionnaire, Marching	20.00
1368B Charging	30.00
1369B Standing, Firing	25.00
1371B Lying, Firing	25.00
1372B Machine Gunner ...	30.00

ARABS (All very rare in Picture Pack)
1232B Mounted, with Spear	40.00
40B Mounted, with Scimitar	40.00
829B Mounted, with Rifle .	40.00
53B Marching	25.00
1229B Running, with Scimitar	35.00
1231B Running, with Rifle	35.00

COWBOYS
34B Mounted, with Pistol .	25.00
1180B Mounted, with Rifle	25.00
35B Mounted, with Lasso .	25.00
1219B Mounted, on Bucking Bronco	95.00
275B Standing, Firing	20.00
274B Crouching, Firing ...	20.00
55B Standing, with Pistol ..	20.00
356B Standing, with Lasso .	20.00
25B Walking, with Rifle ...	20.00

NORTH AMERICAN INDIANS
33B Mounted, with Rifle ..	25.00
32B Mounted, with Tomahawk	25.00
23B Chief, with Tomahawk	20.00
22B Chief, with Knife	20.00
24B Chief, with Tomahawk	20.00
1216B Chief, with Rifle ...	20.00
1217B Brave, with Rifle ...	20.00
74B Brave, with Rifle	20.00
1179B Brave, Crawling with Knife	20.00
143B Brave, with Knife and Tomahawk	20.00

BRITAINS
ROYAL CANADIAN MOUNTED POLICE
1373B Mounted with Lance	85.00
271B Mounted, with Rifle .	30.00
1267B Officer Mounted ...	40.00
591B Regulation Dress, Marching	20.00
1374B Regulation Dress, Attention	40.00
52B Winter Dress, Marching	45.00

#271-B

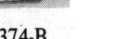

#1374-B   #591-B

BRITAINS

#501   #502   #503   #504   #505

#506   #508

#524   #525

#526

#531   #535   #538   #539

#541   #543

FARM

	G	VG	EXC
501. Farmer	3.75	5.63	7.50
502. Farmer's wife, with basket	4.25	6.38	8.50
503. Farmer's wife, with umbrella	5.00	6.50	8.50
504. Carter, plain arm	4.00	6.00	8.00
505. Carter with whip	4.50	6.75	9.00
506. Shire Horse	4.75	7.13	9.50
507. Shire Colt	3.00	4.50	6.00
508. Cows (assorted colours)	2.00	3.00	4.00
509. Calves (assorted colours) standing	1.50	2.50	4.00
walking	1.50	2.75	4.00
510. Sheep, walking	1.00	2.00	3.00
511. Sheep, feeding	1.00	2.00	3.00
512. Lamb	2.00	3.00	4.00
513. Dogs (assorted colours)	2.00	3.00	4.00
514. Pig (assorted colours)	2.00	3.00	4.00
515. Turkey	2.25	3.38	4.50
516. Fowls, Cocks and Hens (assorted colours)	2.00	3.00	4.00
517. Fowls, Cocks and Hens (white) each	1.50	2.25	3.00
518. Fowls, Cocks and Hens (yellow) each	1.50	2.25	3.00
519. Angry Gander	2.25	3.00	4.50
520. Goose	2.00	3.00	4.00
521. Oak Trees, each	10.00	15.00	20.00
522. Cedar Trees, each	12.50	18.75	25.00
523. Elm Tree	10.00	15.00	20.00
524. Fir Tree	9.00	13.50	18.00
525. Fallen Tree, Pre-War only	8.00	12.00	16.00
526. Shrub	3.50	5.25	7.00
527. Hurdle	1.00	1.50	2.00
528. Large Troughs, each	2.00	3.00	4.00
529. Small Trough	1.50	2.25	3.00
530. Sheep, lying	2.00	3.00	4.00
531. Milkmaid, Pail on Head, circa early 1920s-40s	7.00	9.50	15.00
532. Milkmaid carrying pail	4.50	6.75	9.00
533. Ducks and Drakes (assorted colours), Ducks each	1.75	2.63	3.50
Drakes each	2.00	3.00	4.00
534. Calf, lying	1.75	2.63	3.50
535. Landgirl	6.00	11.00	18.00
536. Sheep and lamb lying together	3.25	4.88	6.50
537. Milkmaid, milking	3.50	5.25	7.00
538. Cow, lying	2.50	3.75	5.00
539. Cow, feeding	3.50	5.25	7.00
540. Goat	2.00	3.00	4.00

	G	VG	EXC
541. Cart Horse	5.00	7.50	10.00
542. Wheatsheaf, stacked . .	2.50	4.00	5.50
543. Horse, feeding	3.00	4.25	6.00
544. Chicks (assorted positions)	1.50	2.25	3.00
545. Hens sitting (assorted colours)	1.50	2.25	3.00
546. Piglets (assorted colours and sizes)	1.25	1.88	2.50
547. Man and Wheelbarrow	6.00	9.00	12.00
548. Hedges and Field Gate	14.00	21.00	28.00
549. Hedges and Garden Gate	11.00	14.50	24.00
550. Cob	2.50	3.75	5.00
551. Scarecrow	5.75	8.50	11.50
552. Donkey	3.50	5.25	7.00
553. Sheaves of Wheat, single bundle (2 types exist)	3.50	5.00	6.50
554. Farmer's son, sitting, circa 1920s-1940	16.00	24.00	32.00
555. Aged Villager, Man, sitting	5.00	8.50	12.00
556. Aged Villager, Woman, sitting	5.00	8.50	12.00
557. Village Girl, walking circa 1920s-40	15.00	22.50	30.00
558. Village Boy, walking, with stick, circa 1920s-40	15.00	22.50	30.00
559. Young Lady, walking .	11.00	16.50	22.00
560. Farm Hand, sitting, for driving farm machine . . .	6.00	9.00	12.00
561. Farmer's Daughter, sitting, circa 1920s-40	8.50	12.50	16.50
562. Golfer, circa 1920s, 1940s	31.00	44.00	60.50
563. Stable Lad, walking . .	6.00	9.00	12.00
564. Man and Swing Water Barrow	8.00	10.00	14.00
565. Goslings, each	2.00	3.00	4.00
566. Field Hayrack	5.00	7.50	10.00
567. Log Seat	2.50	3.75	5.00
568. Garden Seat	4.50	6.75	9.00
569. Dog Kennel	3.50	5.00	6.50
570. Dog Kennel with Baseboard	25.00	35.00	50.00
571. Dog, lying (assorted colours)	3.00	4.00	5.50
572. Dog, for Kennel, sitting (assorted colours)	3.50	5.00	6.50
573. Bull (assorted colours) .	4.75	7.00	9.50
574. Telegraph Pole	5.50	9.00	13.00
575. Dove Cote	5.50	8.00	11.00
576. St. Bernard Dog	3.50	5.25	7.00

#547

#550

#554

#555 & 556 (sitting on #567)

#557

#558

#560 sitting on #568

#561

#562

#563

#564

#569

#571

#572

517

BRITAINS

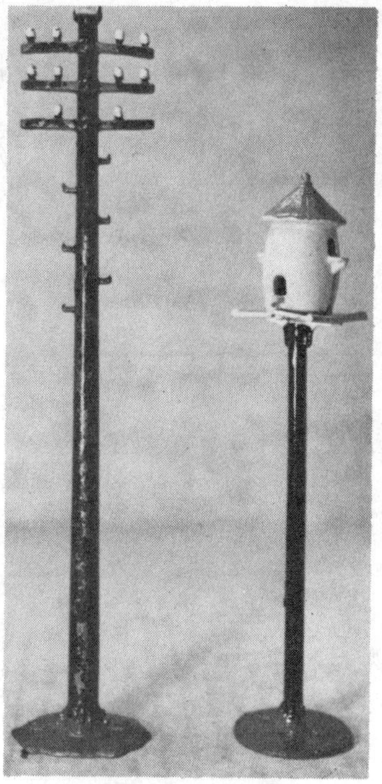

#600

#602

574

575

#577

#578

#587

#589

#591

#592

#593

#595

#596 Sow

#597

#598

#599 Note metal export tag on leg - circa 1930

	G	VG	EXC
577. Shepherd with Crook	6.50	9.50	13.00
578. Automobile Association Scouts, circa 1920s-40, each	25.00	50.00	75.00
579. Automobile Association Sign (destination)	10.00	22.00	30.00
580. Automobile Association Sign (Caution)	10.00	22.00	30.00
581. Rustic Stile	5.50	9.00	11.00
582. Signpost (one direction)	5.50	8.50	11.00
583. Signpost (two directions)	5.50	8.50	11.00
584. Signpost (three directions)	5.50	8.50	11.00
585. UNKNOWN			
586. Fencing, per piece	1.00	2.00	3.00
587. Village Idiot, 1920s-1940	90.00	145.00	190.00
588. Milk Churn	1.00	2.50	4.00
589. Blacksmith with Anvil	9.00	13.00	17.50
590. Pail	1.00	1.50	2.00
591. Dairyman with Yoke and Pails	10.00	15.00	20.00
592. Curate, circa 1920s-40	25.00	55.00	75.00
593. Country Clergyman	6.50	10.00	13.00
594. Shepherd with Lamb	13.00	19.50	26.00
595. Shepherd Boy with Lantern	16.00	24.00	32.00
596. Berkshire Pigs (boars and sows, assorted colours) each	2.50	3.75	5.00
597. Exmoor Horn Sheep (ewes and rams in full fleece) each	2.50	3.75	5.00
598. Gentleman Farmer, mounted	11.00	16.50	21.00
599. Jersey Cow (Champion)	2.25	3.75	4.50
600. Boy on Shetland pony	16.00	24.00	32.00
601. Hampshire Down Ram	2.50	3.75	5.00
602. Foal	1.50	2.25	3.00
603. Rabbit	2.50	3.75	5.00
604. Cat	5.00	8.00	10.50
605. Greyhound, standing	10.00	15.00	20.00
606. Greyhound, running	10.00	15.00	20.00

BRITAINS

#619

#621

#638

#633   #624   #634   #631   #625

#640

#641

#645

#646

#649

#648

	G	VG	EXC
607. Girl Guides and Guider, circa 1920s-40,			
Girl Guide	30.00	50.00	80.00
Guider	35.00	55.00	85.00
617. Folding Table	18.00	27.00	36.00
618. Seesaw, with boy & girl	44.00	66.00	88.00
Girl	12.50	18.75	25.00
Boy	12.50	18.75	25.00
Seesaw	19.00	27.50	38.00
619. Garden Swing, with Boy	27.50	45.00	65.00
620. Hare, running	2.50	3.50	4.50
621. Traffic Policeman	9.00	11.50	16.50
622. Swan and 5 Cygnets, set	6.50	10.00	13.00
624. English Flint Wall straight section	9.00	13.00	17.50
625. English Flint Wall round corner section	9.00	13.00	17.50
626. Stile	14.00	21.00	28.00
627. Flint Wall - gate post section	6.00	10.00	15.00
628. Flint Wall - short cross section	6.00	10.00	15.00
629. Flint Wall - square corner section	7.00	11.00	17.00
630. Five Barred Gate, large	4.50	8.00	12.00
631. Five Barred Gate (small)	2.50	5.50	9.00
632. Tryst Gate Frame (rare)	20.00	33.00	46.00

	G	VG	EXC
633. English Flint Wall-Stone Pier	5.50	8.50	11.00
634. English Flint Wall-Stone Pier for Gate	5.50	8.50	11.00
635. Lithographed Pond (never appeared in catalogs), swan and two cygnets	200.00	300.00	400.00
636. Rabbit, sitting up	5.50	8.50	11.00
637. Dog, begging	22.00	33.00	44.00
638. Spiteful cat	15.00	30.00	40.00
639. Assorted Shrubs (two types)	No Price Found		
640. Tree	3.50	6.75	9.00
641. Motor Cycle with Sidecar, circa 1920s-40	500.00	700.00	1250.00
642. Rhode Island Reds (prize poultry), assorted cocks and hens, each	1.00	2.50	4.00
643. White Leghorns (prize poultry), assorted cocks and hens, each	1.00	2.50	4.00
644. Black Plymouth Rocks (prize poultry), assorted cocks and hens	1.00	3.00	4.50
645. Navvy with Pick Axe	22.50	33.75	45.00
646. Navvy with Shovel	18.00	30.00	40.00
647. Highland Cattle	4.50	7.00	9.50
648. Field Horse	4.00	6.00	8.00
649. Field Horse	4.00	6.00	8.00

519

BRITAINS

#652

#659

#715

#744

#745

#756

#748   #750   #751

	G	VG	EXC
650. Blacksmith (no anvil) .	5.50	8.25	11.00
651. Anvil	2.00	2.50	3.50
652. Milk Roundsman	9.00	13.00	17.50
653. Man on Motor Cycle, circa 1920s-40	200.00	500.00	900.00
654. UNKNOWN			
655. Assortment of Farm Animals (3 dozen)	No Price Found		
656. Assortment of the Larger Farm Animals (1 dozen)	No Price Found		
657. Assortment of Farm People (2 doz)	No Price Found		
658. Assortment of the smaller size Farm Animals (3 dozen)	No Price Found		
659. Policeman, peak cap . .	8.00	11.50	15.50
660. Prize Poultry, assorted cocks and hens, feeding, each	1.00	2.00	4.00
661-662. UNKNOWN			
663. Cafe Table with Sun Shade	No Price Found		
664. Assortment of Farm Animals (3 dozen)	No Price Found		
665. UNKNOWN	No Price Found		
666. Stone Pier for Stone Walling	No Price Found		
667. Garden Roller	1.00	2.50	5.00
668. Crazy Paving, per piece	.25	.50	1.00
669. Sundial	4.00	6.00	10.00

	G	VG	EXC
670. Wheelbarrow	1.00	2.50	5.00
671. Stone Walling	2.00	4.50	6.00
672. Fencing	No Price Found		
673. Lawn Mower	10.00	15.00	20.00
674. Stone Balustrading . . .	4.00	9.00	12.00
675. Cold Frame	15.50	23.00	31.00
676. Hose Reel	15.50	23.00	31.00
677. Pond	38.50	82.50	110.00
678. Man for Wheelbarrow .	3.00	6.00	8.00
679. Man for Mower	5.00	6.50	9.00
680. Man for Roller	5.00	6.50	9.00
681-714. UNKNOWN			
715. Man with Garden Roller	6.50	11.50	15.50
716-743 UNKNOWN			
744. Farmhand Sowing Seed	7.00	12.00	16.00
745. Women's Land Army, single figure, Post-War . .	9.00	16.50	22.00
746. Berkshire Sow, with litter of Piglets	7.00	16.00	30.00
747. Girl, with Feeding Bucket	7.00	9.50	16.00
748. Shell (red pump with red lettering), Motor and Road series	10.50	18.75	25.00
749. Shellmax (red pump with red lettering), Motor and Road Series	10.00	16.50	22.00
750. BP (green pump with black lettering), Motor and Road Series	10.00	16.50	22.00
751. Power (yellow pump with green lettering) Motor and Road series . .	10.00	16.50	22.00
752-755. UNKNOWN			
756. Wild Horse	4.00	6.00	10.00
757. UNKNOWN			
758. Bullock Running	4.00	7.50	10.00
759-768. UNKNOWN			
769. Field Horse (leg down)	5.00	9.00	12.00
770. UNKNOWN			
771. Esso (yellow pump with red lettering), Motor and Road series (very rare) . .	No Price Found		

#775

#776

#780

#782   #783

#786   #785   #784

#7 F (with #532)

	G	VG	EXC
772-774. UNKNOWN			
775. Police Mounted	22.50	37.00	49.50
776. Policeman with Helmet	7.00	13.50	18.00
777-778. UNKNOWN			
779. Ladder	7.50	15.00	25.00
780. Painter carrying Ladder	50.00	75.00	110.00
781. House Painter	50.00	75.00	110.00
782. Suffolk Mare	21.00	31.50	42.00
783. Suffolk Foal	17.50	26.50	35.00
784. Ayrshire Bull	20.00	40.00	70.00
785. Ayrshire Cow	22.00	45.00	75.00
786. Ayrshire Calf	20.00	40.00	70.00
787. Garage Hand	50.00	75.00	100.00
788-799. UNKNOWN			

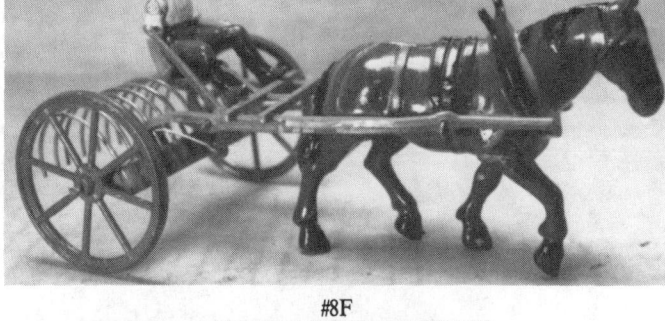
#8F

MODEL HOME FARMS SERIES (Boxed)

#4F

#9F

1F Model Home Farm, 23 pcs 100.00 175.00 250.00

2F Model Home Farm, 19 pcs .... No Price Found

3F Model Home Farm, 73 pcs .... No Price Found

4F Tumbrel Cart, with Farm Hand and Horse, removable Hay Racks and Backboard 25.00 40.00 50.00

	G	VG	EXC
5F Farm Wagon with Farm Hand, 2 horses, removable backboard ...	85.00	125.00	160.00
6F General Purpose Plough with Farm Hand and 2 Horses	50.00	95.00	125.00
7F Tree and Gate	30.00	65.00	95.00
8F Farm Rake, with Driver and Horse, lever	25.00	45.00	70.00
9F Farm Roller with Farm Hand and Horse	25.00	45.00	70.00

BRITAINS

#20F

#40F

#44F

	G	VG	EXC
16F Stable Display, shire horses, colts, cob, stable lad, dog	No Price Found		
17F Farm Display, bull, pigs, piglets, donkey, goat, drover, boy	No Price Found		
18F Farmyard Display, fowls, sheep, lambs, cow and calf, dog, feeding trough, farmer, wife	No Price Found		
19F Tree and Gate with Swing	No Price Found		
20F Farmer's Gig	100.00	150.00	200.00
21F English Flint Wall	200.00	350.00	500.00
22F Flintwall Assortment, 18 pcs	150.00	300.00	450.00
23F-25F UNKNOWN			
26F Farm Cart and Horse .	16.00	24.00	32.00
27F Assortment of pigs, geese, small shrubs and trees, milkmaid carrying pail, Jersey cow	No Price Found		
28F Assortment of pigs, small shrubs and trees, carter, dog, chicken, cob .	No Price Found		
29F Assortment of small shrubs, trees, carter, dog, chicken, cob	No Price Found		
30F Fencing with Gate . . .	100.00	250.00	350.00
31F-35F UNKNOWN			
36F Farmyard Display, stable lad, cow, calf, Bershire pig, collie, cob, sheep	20.00	40.00	60.00
37F Sheep, walking and feeding, farmer, cow, pigs, piglets, lambs, trees, and shrubs	No Price Found		
38F Farmyard Display, 14 pcs	No Price Found		
39F Farmyard Display, sheep walking and feeding, milkmaid, cow feeding, farm hand, cob, geese, fowls, lambs, piglets, small trees and shrubs, 26 pcs	150.00	275.00	375.00
40F Farm Cart and Horse .	15.00	25.00	35.00
41F-42F UKNOWN			
43F A Country Cottage, farmer, farmer's wife, villagers, poultry, pig, trees, seat, flower bed . . .	No Price Found		
44F A Country Cottage in natural colors, with imitation thatched roof	300.00	700.00	1000.00

	G	VG	EXC
10F Shepherds with flock of Sheep and Lambs	No Price Found		
11F Milkmaids with Cows .	No Price Found		
12F Timber Wagon, with Farm Hand and 2 horses, real log	125.00	175.00	250.00
13F Village Group, villagers on garden seat, lady and gentleman riders, boy on pony, dog	No Price Found		
14F Farmyard Display, cows, geese, ducks, turkey, milkmaids	No Price Found		
15F Cattle Display, sheep, cows, pigs, shepherd and boy, man and barrow . . .	No Price Found		

522

#59F (Common driver wears peak cap) Post-War

	G	VG	EXC
45F Milk Float and Horse .	15.00	25.00	35.00
46F-51F UNKNOWN			
52F Large Presentation Box, animals, sheep, pigs, cows, etc., farm people, horse rake with driver, farm wagon with driver	No Price Found		
53F Model Home Farm, Farmer, Farmer's Wife, sheep, horse, lambs and piglets, 9 pcs	35.00	65.00	100.00
54F Model Home Farm, Land Girl Exmoor horn ram and ewe, horse, Jersey cow, pigs, 7 pcs ..	35.00	75.00	120.00
55F Model Home Farm, 10 pcs	55.00	82.50	110.00
56F Model Home Farm, 13 pcs	85.00	150.00	220.00
57F UNKNOWN			
58F Fully modeled tree, 5" high	35.00	65.00	100.00
59F 4-wheeled Lorry with Driver, body tips, 6" long	85.00	150.00	250.00
60F Six-wheeled Lorry with Driver	200.00	300.00	400.00
61F 10-wheeled Lorry with Driver	300.00	550.00	800.00
62F Farmyard Display, 23 pcs	100.00	175.00	250.00
63F Farmyard Display, trees and shrubs, hurdles, cows, prize poultry, sheep feeding, walking, dog, shire horse, stable lad, milkmaid, 23 pcs	No Price Found		
64F-65F UNKNOWN			
66F Farmhouse Scene, cottage and bridge for display of farm animals .	No Price Found		
67F Model Home Farm, stock, farm hands	No Price Found		

	G	VG	EXC
68F UNKNOWN			
69F Farm Assortment, sheep, Rhode Island Red, pig, cow feeding, two trees	No Price Found		
70F Farm Assortment, sheep standing, sheep feeding, sheep lying, Jersey cow, 2 trees	No Price Found		
71F Farm Assortment, horse feeding, calf lying, calf, Rhode Island Red, two trees	No Price Found		
72F Farm Assortment, cow, calf, sheep, pig, 2 trees ..	No Price Found		
73F Farm Assortment, horse, colt, foal, sheep, pig, two trees	No Price Found		
74F Farm Assortment, cow, calf, goose, goat, 2 trees .	No Price Found		
75F-76F UNKNOWN			
77F Farm Assortment, horse, foal, cow, sheep, pig, goose, two trees	No Price Found		
78F-89F UNKNOWN			
90F Builders Lorry with builder's name on sides, driver	No Price Found		
91F Builders Lorry, 6-wheeled, builder's name on sides	No Price Found		
92F Builders Lorry, 10-wheeled, builder's name of sides	No Price Found		
93F UNKNOWN			
94F Farmhouse, natural roof	266.00	399.00	532.00
95F Large Barn and Cart-Shed for farm wagon and tumbrel	No Price Found		
96F Stable with 2-horse box compartments, open section for cart	400.00	800.00	1200.00
97F Country Cottage	No Price Found		
98F Store Shed, corrugated roof	165.00	350.00	500.00
99F Cowshed, for 4 cows ..	No Price Found		
100F Pigsty	35.00	52.50	70.00
101F Rabbit Hutch	250.00	550.00	800.00
102F Chicken House and Run, wire fence	250.00	550.00	800.00
103F Barn, mansard type, large sliding door	No Price Found		
104F-110F UNKNOWN			

BRITAINS

#113F (seated #560)

#128F

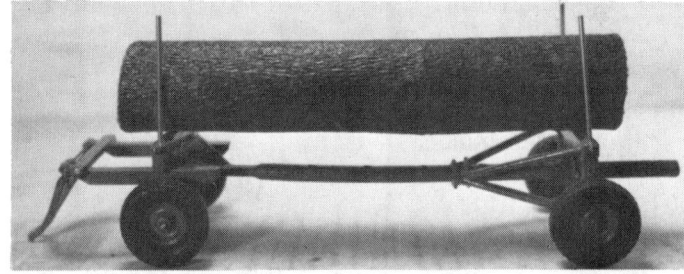

#129F

	G	VG	EXC
124F Farmyard Display, sheep walking, feeding, sheep and lamb lying, dog, lamb, 7 pcs	25.00	45.00	65.00
125F Farmyard Display, cows standing, feeding, calves standing and lying, dog, 7 pcs.	30.00	60.00	85.00
126F Rubber Tyred Farm Cart	12.00	20.00	27.00
127F Fordson Tractor, metal wheels, driver	55.00	85.00	120.00
128F Fordson Major Tractor, with driver, rubber tires	40.00	75.00	100.00

#134F in box

	G	VG	EXC
129F Timber Trailer with real log	25.00	50.00	75.00
130F Farm Trailer, with racks	12.00	20.00	30.00
131F Horse-Drawn Milk Float, milkman, 2 churns	25.00	50.00	75.00
132F Farmyard Display, 23 pcs., includes tumbrel cart, trough	125.00	187.50	250.00
133F Farmyard Display, 7 pcs	35.00	52.50	70.00
134F Tractors and Implements Set, "Fordson Major" tractor, rubber tyres, "Fordson Major" tractor, metal wheels, Timber Trailer, Tipping Trailer, Roller and Disc Harrows	200.00	350.00	500.00
135F Disc Harrow	7.00	10.00	15.00
136F Roller	7.00	10.00	15.00

	G	VG	EXC
111F Farmyard Presentation Box, 50 pcs., includes farmhouse, barn, people, animals, shrubs, fencing .	No Price Found		
112F Greenhouse	125.00	250.00	350.00
113F Garden Shelter	175.00	300.00	400.00
114F-119F UNKNOWN			
120F Farmyard Display, 14 pcs	65.00	100.00	150.00
121F Farmyard Display, 16 pcs	No Price Found		
122F Farmyard Display, 12 pcs	60.00	100.00	150.00
123F Farmyard Display, 7 pcs., pigs, turkey, angry gander, goat, feeding horse, cob	22.00	33.00	44.00

#142F

#172F with attached #174F (#560 driver added)

	G	VG	EXC
137F Clockwork Set, "Fordson Major" tractor with driver, mechanical clockwork trailer, tipping haycart with removable hay racks	180.00	350.00	450.00
138F Four-Farrow Tractor Plough	No Price Found		
139F Clockwork Set "Fordson Major" tractor with driver and mechanical trailer	No Price Found		
140F-141F UNKNOWN			
142F Single Horse General Purpose Plough, with Ploughman	20.00	35.00	50.00
143F UNKNOWN			
144F Haystack, papier mache, 6" x 3½" x 4"	25.00	40.00	60.00
145F Tractor and Implements Set, Muledozer, 3-Furrough Plough and Tipping Trailer, 4 pcs	No Price Found		
146F Tractors and Implements Set, 2 Power Major Tractors, Roller, Muledozer, 3-Furrow Plough, Tipping and Timber Trailers, 7 pcs.	240.00	360.00	480.00
147F Farmyard Display, 5 pcs	25.00	45.00	70.00
148F Farmyard Display, 6 pcs	No Price Found		
149F Farmyard Display, 9 pcs	No Price Found		
150F Farmyard Display, 10 pcs	No Price Found		

BRITAINS

	G	VG	EXC
151F Farmyard Display, 8 pcs	No Price Found		
152F Farmyard Display, 10 pcs	40.00	80.00	120.00
153F Farmyard Display, 11 pcs	No Price Found		
154F Farmyard Display, 12 pcs	No Price Found		
155F Farmyard Display, 13 pcs	No Price Found		
156F Farmyard Display, 21 pcs	No Price Found		
157F Farmyard Display, 21 pcs	No Price Found		
171F "Fordson Power Major" Tractor	No Price Found		
172F "Fordson Power Major" Tractor, no driver	50.00	75.00	100.00
173F Three Furrow Plough	7.00	11.00	16.00
174F Muledozer	No Price Found		
175F Cultivator	No Price Found		
176F Acrobat Rake	No Price Found		
1495 Housepainters, 4 pcs., 2 carrying ladder, 3rd with paintbrush raised, 1954-59	250.00	450.00	600.00

HUNT SERIES

#608

#612   #613

	G	VG	EXC
608. Huntsman, mounted (assorted colours)	10.00	15.00	20.00
609. Huntswoman, mounted, side saddle, at halt	10.00	15.00	20.00
610. Huntsman, mounted, galloping	10.00	15.00	20.00
611. Huntswoman, mounted, galloping	10.00	15.00	20.00
612. Huntsman, standing, dismounted	6.00	9.00	12.00
613. Huntswoman, standing, dismounted	6.00	9.00	12.00

#614   #615   #616

#609   #610

#611

#623

	G	VG	EXC
614. Hounds, standing (assorted positions)	4.00	5.75	8.00
615. Hounds, running	3.00	4.50	6.00
616. Fox	7.50	11.25	15.00
623. Huntswoman, mounted, astride	14.00	20.00	27.50

(Note: Hats may vary from derby to top hat, and jacket colors can be red, black, grey)

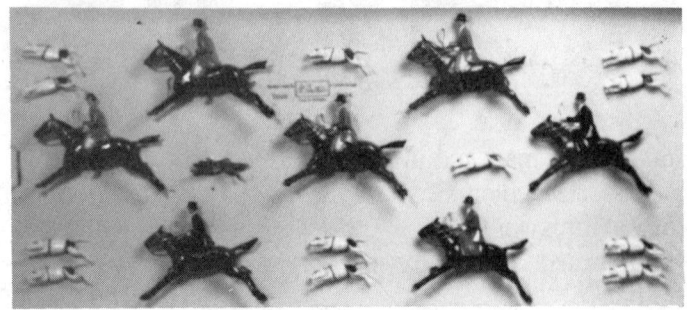

#236 Boxed - Top Tray

	G	VG	EXC
234. (9655) "The Meet," Huntsmen mounted and foot, with hounds, 18 pcs	200.00	350.00	500.00
235. (9656) Huntington Series - "Full Cry," 20 pcs	200.00	350.00	500.00
236. Hunting Series, display box 38 pcs	350.00	600.00	850.00

	G	VG	EXC
243. Huntsmen and Huntswomen, with Hounds, in 1934 catalog	No Price Found		
1235. Huntsman, mounted, hounds, 3 pcs	No Price Found		
1236. Huntswoman mounted sidesaddle, hounds, 3 pcs	No Price Found		
1237. Huntsman mtd. galloping, hounds, 3 pcs .	No Price Found		
1238. Huntswoman mtd. galloping, hounds, 3 pcs .	No Price Found		
1239. Huntswoman astride, hounds, 3 pcs	No Price Found		
1240. Huntsman mounted walking, hounds, 3 pcs ..	No Price Found		
1241. Gentleman Farmer, standing hounds, 3 pcs ..	No Price Found		
1445. Huntsmen, Mounted and Dismounted, 11 pcs .	No Price Found		
1446. (9650) "The Meet," 11 pcs., huntsmen, mounted and dismounted, 11 pcs .	No Price Found		
1447. (9651) "Full Cry," 10 pcs., huntsmen mounted with hounds and fox	55.00	90.00	120.00

#901 1st version, rare rubber trunk

#915   #916   #918

#902   #903   #904

#921 many colors   #922   #923

#906   #907   #909

#910   #911   #913

#931 short   #933

ZOO SERIES	G	VG	EXC
901. Indian Elephant (boxed)	30.00	55.00	100.00
902. Kangaroo	3.50	5.75	8.00
903. Penguin	2.50	3.75	5.00
904. Monkey	2.50	4.75	8.00
905. Adult Hippopotamus .	6.00	12.00	18.50
906. Gorilla	6.00	9.00	13.00
907. Zebra	4.00	7.50	10.00
908. Adult Rhinoceros	8.00	15.50	20.00
909. Pelican (open beak) ...	3.50	6.75	9.00
910. Lion	4.00	7.50	10.00
911. Lioness	3.00	5.75	8.00
912. Giraffe (adult) Pre-War only	66.00	110.50	165.00
913. Pelican (spread wings) .	2.50	5.25	7.00
914. Polar Bear (sitting) ...	7.00	11.50	15.00
915. Chimpanzee	4.00	7.50	10.00
916. King Penguin	2.00	4.50	6.00

	G	VG	EXC
917. Adult Nile Crocodile .	10.00	21.00	28.00
918. Bactrian Camel	10.00	20.00	30.00
919. Coconut Palm	10.50	18.75	25.00
920. Date Palm	7.00	13.50	18.00
921. Guinon Monkey (walking)	3.50	6.00	9.00
922. Ostrich	3.00	7.00	10.00
923. Llama	3.50	6.50	8.50
924. Gate with Posts	10.00	16.50	22.00
925. Railing (straight section)	2.50	5.25	7.00
926. Railing (curved section)	2.50	5.25	7.00
927. Standard Post, two way (straight)	6.00	9.00	12.00
928. Straight Post, two way (right angle)	6.00	9.00	12.00
929. Standard Post, three way	6.00	9.00	12.00
930. Standard Post, four way	5.00	7.50	10.00
931. Zoo Keeper, tall version	9.00	16.50	22.00
Short version	9.00	16.50	22.00
932. Zoo Keeper (for seating astride elephant)	50.00	85.00	140.00
933. Eland Bull	4.25	6.38	8.50

BRITAINS

#936   #940   #941

#959

#942   #943

#960   #961

#945   #946   #947

#962   #963   #964

#952

#953

#954   #955   #956

#958

	G	VG	EXC
936. Cub bears, sitting, walking	3.50	5.25	7.00
937. Giant Tortoise	6.00	9.00	12.00
938. Howdah for Elephant	15.00	25.00	40.00
939. Boy or Girl for Howdah	11.00	16.50	24.00
940. Baby Hippoptamus	3.00	5.50	7.00
941. Tiger (walking)	4.50	6.50	12.00
942. Wild Boar	3.00	5.75	8.00
943. Baby Camel	3.00	5.75	8.00
944. Baby Elephant	2.50	5.50	7.00
945. Sable Antelope	4.00	7.50	10.00
946. Stork	2.00	4.50	6.00
947. Flamingo	2.50	5.25	7.00
948. Wart Hog	2.50	4.00	5.50
949. Malay Tapir	2.75	5.00	6.50
950. Baby Kangaroo (Wallaby)	2.00	4.00	5.50
951. Baby Rhinoceros	3.00	6.00	8.00
952. Young Indian Elephant	9.00	14.50	20.00
953. Bactrian Camel with Boy Rider	65.00	105.00	155.00
954. Gorilla with Pole	6.50	9.50	12.50
955. Wolf	7.00	10.00	14.00
956. Walrus	3.00	4.50	7.00
957. Red Deer	6.50	12.00	16.00
958. Young Crocodile	8.00	13.00	17.50
959. Young Hippopotamos	4.25	7.50	10.50
960. Young Rhinoceros	4.00	7.25	10.00
961. Young Giraffe	9.00	16.00	21.00
962. Lion Cub	2.50	4.75	7.00
963. Gazelle	3.50	5.75	8.00
964. Sea Lion	3.50	5.75	8.00

	G	VG	EXC
934. Brown Bear	4.50	6.50	9.00
935. American Bison	14.00	22.00	30.00

#968

#969

#965   #967

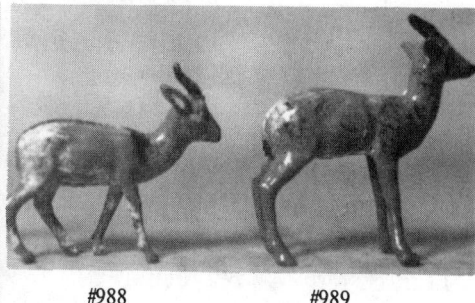

#988   #989

	G	VG	EXC
965. Himalayan Bear (sitting)	4.00	7.00	10.00
966. Polar Bear (walking)	4.00	7.50	10.00
967. Polar Bear (standing)	3.50	6.50	9.00
968. Indian or Water Buffalo	5.00	9.75	14.00
969. Giant Panda	4.00	7.50	10.00
970. Baby Panda (two positions) sitting, on all fours, each	2.50	4.00	6.00
971. The Panda Family (969-970) boxed	60.00	145.00	200.00
972. Assortment of Zoo animals, 37 pcs	No Price Found		
973. Assortment of Zoo animals, 24 pcs	No Price Found		
974. Assortment of Zoo animals, 12 pcs	No Price Found		
975. UNKNOWN			
976. Boy Rider for Camel or Elephant	15.00	25.00	40.00
977. UNKNOWN			
978. Baby Chimpanzee	6.50	12.50	16.50
979-985. UNKNOWN			
986. Panther, Post-War only	15.00	30.00	50.00
987. Baboon, Post-War only	10.00	20.00	30.00
988. Springbuck, Post-War only	13.00	25.00	33.00
989. Bushbuck, Post-War only	16.50	30.00	37.50
990. Vulture, Post-War only	11.00	20.00	27.50
991. King Cobra	6.50	12.50	16.50
992. Tiger (sitting)	8.00	13.00	17.50
993. Curved railing section	4.00	7.50	10.00
994. Straight railing section	6.00	10.00	14.00
995-999. UNKNOWN			

BRITAINS ZOO SETS

	G	VG	EXC
1Z. Boxed Zoo Set, lion, lioness, zebra, gorilla, 2 monkeys, 2 pelicans, 2 penguins, 10 pcs	65.00	100.00	150.00
2Z. Boxed Zoo Set, lion, lioness, camel, zebra, polar bear, kangaroo, 2 monkeys, 2 pelicans, 4 penguins, 15 pcs	No Price Found		
3Z. Boxed Zoo Set, camel, polar bear, lion, lioness, zebra, kangaroo, chimpanzee, gorilla, monkey, 2 pelicans, 2 penguins, 2 date palms and 1 coconut palm, 16 pcs	125.00	225.00	325.00
4Z. Boxed Zoo Set, elephant, rhinoceros, hippo, giraffe, crocodile, camel, lion, lioness, polar bear, llama, kangaroo, zebra, gorilla, ostrich, chimpanzee, monkeys, 2 penguins, 2 pelicans, 2 date palms and 2 coconut palm, 24 pcs	No Price Found		
5Z. Boxed Zoo Set, camel, crocodile, eland bull, polar bear, ostrich, llama, bison, brown bear, lioness, lion, kangaroo, giraffe, zebra, hippo, rhinoceros, 2 date palms, 2 coconut palms, 19 pcs	No Price Found		
6Z. Boxed Zoo Set, brown bear, 2 monkeys, chimpanzee, eland bull, ostrich, 2 bear cubs, bison, llama, 10 pcs	No Price Found		

BRITAINS

	G	VG	EXC

11Z. Boxed Zoo Set, eland bull, crocodile, sable, antelope, monkey, zebra, walrus, llama, ostrich, rhinoceros, hippopotamus, giraffe, elephant, 11 pcs . **100.00 180.00 250.00**

17Z. Boxed Zoo Set, eland bull, crocodile, ostrich, boar, pelican, gorilla, 9 pcs . . . . **No Price Found**

18Z. Mammal House, rhino, water buffalo, eland bull, 2 zebras . . . . **No Price Found**

19Z. Polar Bear Pool, cave, sitting, standing and walking Polar Bears **250.00 450.00 650.00**

20Z. Large Pool enclosure, rock formation sides, penguins, tortoise, walrus, sea lions . . . . **No Price Found**

21Z. Monkey Hill, a natural layout with variety of monkeys including chimpanzees and gorilla . . . . . **No Price Found**

22Z. Animal Houses, with enclosure, assorted animals (wart hogs, Malay tapirs, wild boars) . . . . . . **No Price Found**

23Z. Rock Pool with trees, pelican, storks and flamingos . . . . **No Price Found**

24Z. Box Zoo Set, Elephant with keeper, Howdah and children, camel with boy and baby camel, llama, zebra, eland bull, tiger, wart hog, wild boar, giant tortoise, panda and 2 cubs, date palm, fencing, 55 pcs **350.00 650.00 1000.00**

25Z. Elephant with Keeper, Howdah, Boy, Girl **100.00 150.00 200.00**

26Z. Display Box, contains Hippo, Rhinoceros, Elephant, Giraffe, Lioness, Zebra, Leopard, Gorilla and Eland Bull . . **No Price Found**

#25Z

	G	VG	EXC

27Z. Display Box, contains Elephant, Hippo, Zebra, Crocodile, Leopard, Baby Elephant, Chimpanzee, Gazelle, Giraffe, Sable Antelope, Gorilla, Guenon Monkey, Ostrich, Lion, Lioness, Rhinoceros, Bush Buck . . . . **No Price Found**

28Z. Display Box, contains Elephant, Hippo, Zebra, Crocodile, Leopard, Baby Elephant, others, 17 pcs. (1960 catalog) . . . . **No Price Found**

32Z. Box Zoo Set, 2 Date Palms, Camel, Kangaroo, Gorilla, Zebra, Lion, Lioness, Monkey, Chimpanzee, Penguin, Polar Bear, Coconut Palm **125.00 225.00 300.00**

MAMMOTH CIRCUS (Individual Pieces)

	G	VG	EXC
351B Prancing Circus Horse	18.00	30.00	36.00
352B Trotting Circus Horse	18.00	30.00	36.00
353B Circus performer on stilts	16.00	27.00	34.00
354B Clown with Hoop	18.00	25.00	35.00
355B Circus Equestrienne	18.00	28.00	35.00
356B Circus Cowboy Performer with Lasso (probably Pre-War only)	No Price Found		
357B Circus Ringmaster	16.00	27.00	32.00
358B Clown, Standing	14.00	25.00	30.00
359B Circus Elephant with blanket on back and hole in head to fit equestrienne or clown with hoop	18.00	28.00	40.00
446B Tub	6.50	9.00	12.00
447B Boxing Clown	15.00	25.00	35.00
448B Lion Tamer	16.00	27.00	32.00
449B Performing Tiger	8.00	12.50	16.00
450B Performing Elephant (without tub)	20.00	37.50	50.00
451B Boxing Kangaroo	15.00	25.00	35.00
? Circus Ring, red, pressed wood, 7" diameter	20.00	30.00	40.00

#451B   #447B

#449B   #448B

#1539

BRITAINS

	G	VG	EXC
1439. Circus Roundabout ..	No Price Found		
1441. Circus - The Flying Trapeze, a high wire act, 3 pcs	600.00	1000.00	1500.00
1442. Mammoth Circus, 6 pcs., 1936-40	No Price Found		
1443. Mammoth Circus, 10 pcs., 1936-40	No Price Found		
1444. Mammoth Circus, 14 pcs., 1936-40	350.00	750.00	1200.00
1539. Mammoth Circus, 23 pcs., 1937-41; 1948-61 ..	375.00	750.00	1000.00
2054. Mammoth Circus, 1951-61, 12 pcs	200.00	400.00	600.00

#1439 Roundabout, with six Riders which swings round with a spin of the fingers. No mechanism to get out of order. Beautifully finished (assorted colourings). Measures 5½" diam., by 5" high.

#1441 The Flying Trapeze. A working model, comprising Clown with Umbrella and Fairy. The model is so constructed that as the performers travel along a stretched wire the umbrella twirls. The effect is very realistic. Sufficient wire is supplied to stretch across a normal room. Measures 8" high.

RAILWAY

	G	VG	EXC
800. Porter to push trolley .	7.00	13.50	18.00
801. Porter to carry luggage	10.00	18.00	24.00
802. Station Master	8.00	15.00	20.00
803. Guard with Flag	12.00	27.50	50.00
804. Guard with Lamp	12.00	20.00	28.00
805. Ticket Collector	8.00	15.00	20.00
806. Lady Passenger, Pre-War - 1st	20.00	30.00	40.00
807. Gentleman Passenger, Pre-War	20.00	30.00	40.00
808. Policeman	9.00	14.00	18.00
809. Engine Driver	12.00	22.50	30.00
810. Stoker with separate shovel	30.00	45.00	66.00
811. Trolley	5.00	8.00	12.00
812. Trunk	3.50	6.00	9.00
813. Dress Basket	3.50	6.00	9.00
814. Portmanteau	4.50	7.25	13.00
815. Golf Sticks	5.00	8.00	14.00
816. Rugs and Sticks	4.50	7.00	12.50
817. Yachtsman	20.00	45.00	65.00

STATION STAFF AND SUNDRIES NO. "0" GAUGE

	G	VG	EXC
818. Platelayers (assorted), each	No Price Found		
819. Golfer	20.00	30.00	40.00
820. Guard with Flag	No Price Found		

"Lady Passengers"

1st vers.　　　　2nd vers.　　　Post-War Set #1R

"Gentleman Passenger"

1st vers.　　Post-War Set #1R　　#Set #168　　#817
(Both with pipe)

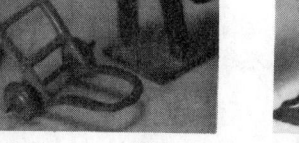   

#800 (811)　　#801　　#802　　#803

#804　#805
Empty handed　　#808
Red & white
Wristband　　　#810

#155 (Circa 1920-25)

	G	VG	EXC
155. Railway Staff, 12 pcs., "1908"	150.00	300.00	400.00
158. Railway Station Staff, 25 pcs	400.00	600.00	800.00
168. Civilians, 8 pcs	200.00	300.00	400.00
1256. Station Figures (17 pcs.)	250.00	500.00	850.00

	G	VG	EXC
1422. "0" Gauge Railway, 9 pcs.	No Price Found		
1423. Station Staff, 9 pcs ..	200.00	350.00	600.00
1-R. Station Set, 20 pieces (1954-59 only)	No Price Found		

MINIATURE GARDENING

The Miniature Gardening Series was available in the 1930's. The flowers were made with a special alloy of almost pure lead. This allowed bending of the stems and flowers to give a three-dimensional effect. The series was dropped from the 1940 catalog due, in part, to critical shortages of lead during the early years of WW II, but some pieces were added to the Farm section in that year and are noted with an asterisk and the "New" Farm number. No prices found except where noted.

	G	VG	EXC
01 Flower Bed with grass border, straight section	4.00	6.00	8.00
02 Flower Bed with grass border, finishing circular section	4.00	6.00	8.00
03 Flower Bed with grass border, return square section	4.00	6.00	8.00
04 Flower Bed with grass border, return circular section	4.00	6.00	8.00
05 Flower Bed with grass border, half straight section	3.00	5.00	7.00
06 Flower Bed with grass border, finishing corner section	3.00	5.00	7.00
*07-666 Post for Stone Wall	5.00	8.00	11.00
*08-667 Garden Roller			

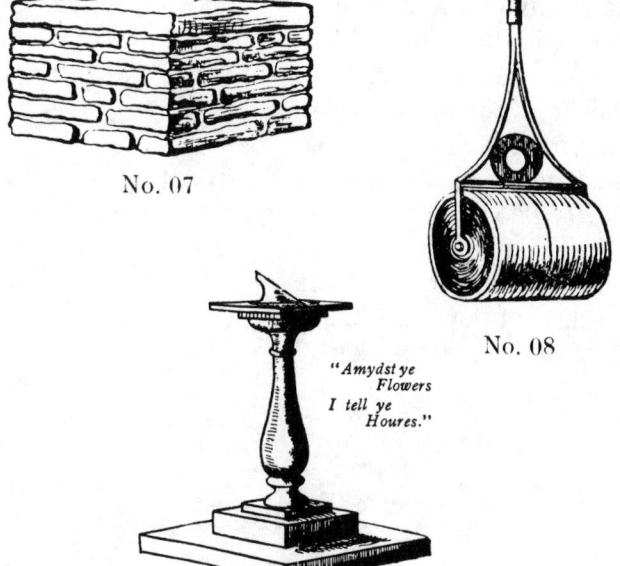

No. 07

No. 08

No. 010

"Amydst ye
Flowers
I tell ye
Houres."

	G	VG	EXC
*09-668 Crazy Paving, per 10 pieces	3.50	5.25	7.00
*010-669 Sundial on pedestal	5.00	8.00	10.00
*011-670 Garden wheelbarrow	3.00	5.00	7.00

BRITAINS

	G	VG	EXC
*012-671 Stone wall	6.00	9.00	13.00
013 Pergola Section, used with rambler roses or similar plants	12.00	18.00	24.00
014 Rustic arch	12.00	18.00	24.00
015 Mound, for mounting single plants, rose bushes, rustic arch or pergola	2.50	3.75	5.00
016 Coloured vase, holds conifer or any single plant .	2.50	3.75	5.00
017 Garden seat, white			
*018-672 Interlaced board fence with trellis	8.00	12.00	16.00
019 Rambler Rose, varied colors	5.00	7.50	10.00
020 Lobelia (L. Gacilis, L. Erinus) a beautiful blue border flower	.10	.20	.30
021 Geranium, reds, whites, pinks, packet of 10 pieces ..	2.00	3.00	4.00
022 Torch Lily, (Knipholia), red hot poker, packet of 5 pieces	2.00	3.00	4.00
023 Conifer, dwarf trees, used in pots and tubs	2.00	3.00	4.00
024 Sunflower (Helianthus) .	4.50	6.00	9.00
025 Poppy (Papaver) large range of colors, packet of 6 pcs.	2.50	3.75	5.00
026 Lupin (Lupinus), beautiful colored spikes of flowers, per 5 pcs.	2.50	3.75	5.00
027 Half Standard Rose, a variety in which the branches are only allowed to grow from a single stem some height above the ground			
028 Rose Bush, various colors	2.50	3.75	5.00
029 Aster, excellent for borders	2.00	3.00	4.00
030 Hollyhock, double (Althaea rosea), pinks, yellows, whites, good for background	2.50	3.75	5.00
031 Antirrhinum (Snapdragon), various colors, packet of 10 pcs.	2.00	3.00	4.00
032 Dahlia, double, packet of 4 pieces	2.00	3.00	4.00
033 Dahlia, single	2.00	3.00	5.00
034 Gladioli, lily-like flowers, packet of 10 pieces	2.00	3.00	4.00

BRITAINS

	G	VG	EXC
035 Wallflower (Cheiranthus), suitable for beds or borders			
036 Foxglove (Digitalis), packet of 10 pcs.	2.00	3.00	4.00
037 Chrysanthemum, packet of 5 pieces	2.50	3.75	5.00
038 Full Standard rose			
039 Delphinium, packet of 5 pieces	2.00	3.00	4.00
040 Hyacinth (Hyacinthus), various colors	2.00	3.00	4.00
041 Tulip, various colors, packet of 8 pieces	2.00	3.00	4.00
042 Crocus, various colors, packet of 13 pcs.	4.00	6.00	8.00
043 Snowdrop (Galanthus), packet of 11 pcs.	2.00	3.00	4.00
044 Daffodil, of the Narcissus family, yellow			
045 Narcissus, border plant, white with yellow/orange centers	2.00	3.00	4.00
046 Sweet Alyssum (A. Maritimum), white border, packet of 10 pcs.	2.00	3.00	4.00
047 Square Tub, holds conifer or any single plant	2.00	3.00	4.00
048 Small flower bed, holds 7 plants	3.00	4.50	6.00
049 Lawn Section, 1¾"x1¾" colored green, representing well kept lawn	1.00	2.00	3.00
*050-673 Lawn Mower with removable grass box	37.00	56.00	75.00

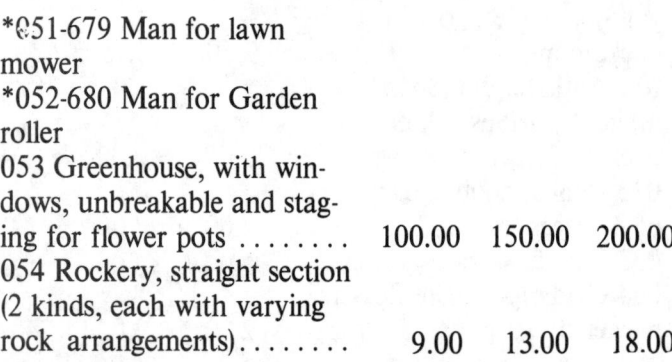

No. 050

*051-679 Man for lawn mower
*052-680 Man for Garden roller

	G	VG	EXC
053 Greenhouse, with windows, unbreakable and staging for flower pots	100.00	150.00	200.00
054 Rockery, straight section (2 kinds, each with varying rock arrangements)........	9.00	13.00	18.00

	G	VG	EXC
055 Rockery, inner return corner	9.00	13.00	18.00
056 Rockery, outer corner .	9.00	13.00	18.00
057 Rockery, upper steps ..	9.00	13.00	18.00
058 Rockery, lower steps ..	9.00	13.00	18.00
059 Flower Pots, large, medium and small for greenhouse, etc.	2.00	3.00	4.00
060 Blocks (wooden, 1¾"x1¾"x⅞", for varying levels or terracing, per each	4.00	6.00	8.00
*061-674 Balustrading, long section	12.00	18.00	24.00

No. 062

	G	VG	EXC
062 Balustrading, short section	7.00	11.00	14.00
063 Post for balustrading ..	2.00	3.00	5.00
*064-675 Cold Frame, to open	27.00	41.00	55.00
065 Round bed, without grass verge	6.00	9.00	13.00
066 Square Bed, without grass verge	6.00	9.00	12.00
*067-677 Lily Pond, very brightly painted in natural colors, and may be filled with water if desired	55.00	82.00	110.00
*068-676 Hose on reel	30.00	45.00	60.00
069 Seed Boxes, for use in cold frame and/or greenhouse	6.00	9.00	12.00

*070-678 Man for Wheelbarrow
071 Assortment of 2 dozen packets of flowers. Appeared first in the 1938 catalog

No. 068

536

Miniature Gardening Display Sets

Each set is complete in itself and will make up into various designs, the larger ones being more variable than the smaller.

1 MG A collection of flower beds and flowers to form a complete circular bed

2 MG A similar layout as 1 MG but with different flowers

3 MG A collection of flower beds and flowers to form a completed square bed

4 MG A collection of various flower beds and other accessories with flowers

5 MG A collection of flower beds and flowers forming a large oval or circular bed, etc.

6 MG A similar collection as 5 MG with different flowers to form square, oblong or other beds

7 MG A Collection of various flower beds, accessories and flowers making a nice display

8 MG A larger collection as 7 MG including crazy paving, capable of a number of variations

9 MG A collection of pieces with flower beds, crazy paving, stone walling, rustic arch, etc. and flowers, permitting many pleasing variations of design.

10 MG A collection of flower beds, flowers, crazy paving, stone walling, fencing and with Rambler Roses, makes a number of designs

11 MG A collection of flower beds, crazy paving with lawn and sundial and variety of flowers making a large layout with many variations.

12 MG A collection of flower beds and accessories, including fencing and stone walling and varieties of flowers, giving extremely pleasing layouts.

13 MG A large collection of pieces and flowers permitting many ideal layouts.

14 MG A collection of flower beds and bulbs making a well-filled circular section

15 MG A similar collection as 14 MG, but to form a square bed.

16 MG A variety of flower beds and bulbs, making some very attractive layouts.

Nos. 17 MG through 22 MG are small beds well filled with flowers and suitable as beginners sets, or for placing on Miniature Garden Lawns to form Center beds. Each in an attractive box.

17 MG Round bed filled with Hyacinths and Crocuses.

18 MG Round bed filled with Tulips and Crocuses

19 MG Round bed filled with geraniums, gladioli, foxglove, and red hot poker

20 MG Round bed filled with geraniums, aster and delphiniums

21 MG Square bed filled with lobelia, sweet alyssum and chrysanthemums

22 MG Square bed filled with lobelia, gladioli and bush rose

23 MG A large collection of rockery with blocks for terracing, flowers and flower beds, crazy paving, lawn, balustrading, etc.

24 MG A collection on similar lines to 23 MG, but not as large

25 MG A collection rockery pieces and accessories

26 MG A varied assortment of rockery with flower beds and a good range of flowers

BRITAINS

27 MG A collection on similar lines to 26 MG but with variation of pieces and flowers

28 MG Garden shelter, measures 4¼" long

29 MG A large well-fitted presentation box, containing cottage and varied collection of miniature gardening pieces, flowers, etc.

30 MG A larger collection than the preceding, containing cottage, rockery, greenhouse, garden shelter, cold frames, lily pond, flowers, lawn, crazy paving, etc.

31 MG A fully modeled tree, in which the foliage fits on to a central trunk. Perfectly natural from all angles of view, measures 5" high.

"1938" - Display Sets listed below are in cellophane wrapped boxes and attractively displayed with brightly colored labels.

32 MG Containing a selection of plants, flower beds, crazy paving, lawn, conifers in pots, stone walling and posts.

33 MG Containing a selection of plants, flower beds, crazy paving, lawn, rustic arch, stone walling and posts, similar to 32 MG but a larger selection.

34 MG Containing a selection of plants, flower beds, crazy paving, lawn, stone walling, balustrading, sundial, arch and colored vases.

35 MG Containing a larger selection of plants, flower beds, rockery, balustrading and posts, crazy paving, lawn, wooden terracing blocks, sundial, man, garden roller, lawn mower, wheelbarrow, garden seat, rustic arch, pergolas, stone walling, cold frame and seed boxes.

	G	VG	EXC

"B" SERIES

1896-1907 Round Base, 1907-1914 Square Base, 44 mm high, sold in sets. Price is per piece.

	G	VG	EXC
1b 1st Life Guards	10.00	15.00	20.00
2b Royal Horse Guards . . .	No Price Found		
3b 5th Dragoon Guards . . .	No Price Found		
4b Scots Guards	No Price Found		
5b 1st Dragoon Guards	No Price Found		
6b Royal Scots Greys	6.00	9.00	12.00
7b 2nd Life Guards	10.00	15.00	20.00
8b 7th Royal Fusiliers	No Price Found		
9b 13th Hussars	No Price Found		
10b 11th Hussars	9.00	13.50	18.00
11b Japanese Cavalry	No Price Found		
12b 16th Lancers (active service)	7.50	11.25	15.00
13b 17th Lancers	No Price Found		
14b Russian Cavalry (Cossacks)	15.00	22.50	30.00
15b Mounted Infantry	15.00	22.50	30.00
16b Coldstream Guards . . .	No Price Found		
17b Lancashire Fusiliers . . .	No Price Found		
18b Grenadier Guards	11.00	16.50	22.00
19b Dublin Fusiliers	9.00	13.50	18.00
20b Manchester Regiment .	4.50	6.75	9.00
21b Northumberland Fusiliers	3.50	5.25	7.00
22b Bluejackets, R.N.	4.00	6.00	8.00
23b Cameron Highlanders (active service)	10.00	15.00	20.00
24b Whitejackets, R.N.	7.00	11.00	15.00
25b Japanese Infantry	15.00	22.00	30.00
26b Russian Infantry	No Price Found		
125 Royal Horse Artillery (review order with outriders)	No Price Found		
126 Royal Horse Artillery (active service order with outriders)	No Price Found		

"W" SERIES

1912-1940 45mm, sold in sets by F.W. Woolworth chain only at first, 2nd grade painting. 5 pieces mtd, 8 pcs. foot. Average price $8 in very good for mounted, $6 for foot, boxed sets average $50.00 in very good.

British Army and Navy

11w Grenadier Guards
12w Highlanders
28w Highlanders
8w Hussars
30w Hussars
14w Hussars (gilt)
10w Infantry of the Line

538

9w Lancers
15w Lancers (gilt)
7w Life Guards, the
13w Life Guards (gilt)
29w Life Guards, the
19w Sailors (bluejackets),
   R.N.
26w Sailors (bluejackets),
   R.N.
20w Sailors (whitejackets),
   R.N.
25w Sailors (whitejackets),
   R.N.
18w Scots Greys, The
27w Scots Greys, The

Displays and Types of the British Army

39w Infantry of the Line
   and The Life Guards
40w Grenadier Guards and
   Hussars
41w Highlanders and Scots
   Greys
21w British Army Encamp-
   ment with Tent
32w Infantry of the Line
   and The Life Guards
33w Hussars and Grenadier
   Guards
34w Scots Greys and
   Highlanders
35w Lancers and Infantry of
   the Line
22w British Army Encamp-
   ment with tent, trees and
   shrubs
23w British Army Encamp-
   ment with tent, trees,
   shrubs and gun
24w British Army Encamp-
   ment with trees, shrubs,
   tents and guns

United States of America Army

54w Cavalry (service dress)
47w Cavalry (service dress)
64w Cavalry (service dress)
55w Infantry (service dress)
46w Infantry (service dress)
65w Infantry (service dress)

Displays and Types of the U.S.A. Army

36w Cavalry and Infantry
   (service dress) with tent

37w Cavalry and Infantry
   (service dress) with trees,
   shrubs and tent

Miscellaneous

59w Cowboys (on foot)
51w Cowboys (on foot)
61w Cowboys (on foot)
58w Cowboys (mounted)
50w Cowboys (mounted)
60w Cowboys (mounted)
57w North American
   Indians (on foot)
53w North American
   Indians (on foot)
63w North American
   Indians (on foot)
56w North American
   Indians (mounted)
52w North American
   Indians (mounted)
62w North American
   Indians (mounted)
145w The Life Guards,
   review order, (4 pcs.)
146w The Scots Greys,
   review order, (4 pcs.)
147w British Cavalry, khaki,
   peak caps, (4 pcs.)
148w The Hussars, review
   order, (4 pcs.)
149w North American
   Indians, mounted and on
   foot, (5 pcs.)
150w Cowboys, mounted
   and on foot, (5 pcs.)
151w Infantry of the Line,
   review order, marching, (6
   pcs.)
152w Grenadier Guards,
   review order, running, (6
   pcs.)
153w Highlanders, review
   order, marching, (6 pcs.)
154w North American
   Indians, on foot (6 pcs.)
155w Cowboys, on foot,
   standing position, (6 pcs.)
156w Bluejackets and Whitejackets, marching, (6 pcs.)
157w U.S.A. Cavalry, peak
   caps, (4 pcs.)
158w U.S.A. Infantry, marching (6 pcs.)

BRITAINS

159w Infantry of the Line, review order, marching, (10 pcs.)

160w Highlanders, review order, marching, (10 pcs.)

161w Grenadier Guards, review order, running (10 pcs.)

162w Bluejackets and White-jackets, marching (10 pcs.)

163w North American Indians, on foot (10 pcs.)

164w Cowboys, on foot, standing position (10 pcs.)

165w Life Guards and Infantry of the Line, review order (9 pcs.)

166w Scots Greys and Highlanders, review order (9 pcs.)

167w Hussars and Grenadier Guards, review order (9 pcs.)

168w Lancers and Infantry of the Line, review order (9 pcs.)

169w Cowboys and Indians, mounted and on foot (10 pcs.)

170w North American Indians, mounted and on foot (9 pcs.)

171w Cowboys, mounted and on foot, (9 pcs.)

172w North American Indians and Cowboys, mounted and on foot (9 pcs.)

173w U.S.A. Infantry, marching (10 pcs.)

174w U.S.A. Cavalry and Infantry (9 pcs.)

Added in 1940

200w Royal Horse Artillery, gun, limber and team, galloping, khaki, (8 pcs.)

201w Royal Horse Artillery, gun, limber and team, galloping, review order (8 pcs.)

"A" SERIES
(circa 1911-1941)
Average prices for foot $9 in excellent condition, $12 for mounted.

British
Cavalry

4A Cavalry (khaki)
16A Cavalry (khaki)
5A Cavalry (service dress)
10A Cavalry (service dress)
8A 1st Dragoons
9A 1st Dragoons
122A 1st Dragoons
6A 3rd Hussars
13A 3rd Hussars
1A 12th Lancers
14A 12th Lancers
3A Life Guards, The
12A Life Guards, The
116A Life Guards, The
2A Royal Horse Guards
11A Royal Horse Guards
7A Scots Greys
15A Scots Greys

Infantry

19A Black Watch, The
29A Black Watch, The
25A Buffs, The (East Kent Regiment)
36A Buffs, The (East Kent Regiment)
326A Buffs, The (East Kent Regiment), khaki
23A Highlanders (charging, khaki)
32A Highlanders (charging, khaki)
121A Highlanders (marching)
17A Infantry of the Line (khaki)
30A Infantry of the Line (khaki)
20A Royal West Surrey Regiment
28A Royal West Surrey Regiment
26A Rifle Brigade, The
33A Rifle Brigade, The
18A Sailors
31A Sailors
327A Sailors
42A Sussex Regiment, with mounted officer

540

44A Sussex Regiment with
Mounted Officer

325A Sussex Regiment

"A" SERIES
Displays and Types of the British Army

140A Sussex Regiment and
Life Guards

124A Sussex Regiment and
1st Dragoons

123A Scots Greys and
Highlanders (marching)

91A Hussars and Sussex
Regiment

92A Highlanders and Sussex
Regiment

247A The Life Guards and
1st Dragoons

249A The Life Guards and
Highlanders

309A Scots Greys and
Highlanders (marching)

310A Cavalry (service dress)
and Highlanders
(charging)

311A Cavalry (shrapnel
helmet) and The Buffs
(khaki)

312A The Life Guards,
Sussex Regiment, The
Buffs, The West Surrey
Regiment (kneeling) and
The West Surrey Regi-
ment (lying)

301A Scots Greys and
Highlanders (marching)

302A The 1st Dragoons and
The Sussex Regiment

308A The West Surrey Regiment, Highlanders (mar-
ching) and The East Kent
Regiment

303A The Life Guards,
Sussex Regiment, West
Surrey Regiment, (stand-
ing, kneeling and lying)
and The Buffs

267A Scots Greys and
Highlanders (marching)

268A The Life Guards, East
Kent Regiment (review
order), The Sussex
Regiment

298A Cavalry (active service
dress and shrapnel-proof
helmets), The Buffs
(khaki) and Highlanders
(charging)

299A The Life Guards,
Lancers, Sussex Regiment,
The Buffs (review order)
Machine Gunners and
West Surrey Regiment
(kneeling)

300A The Scots Greys, The
1st Dragoons, Sussex
Regiment, and
Highlanders (marching)

291A Cavalry (active service
dress and shrapnel-proof
helmet), Highlanders
(charging), The Buffs
(khaki) and Machine
Gunners

292A Highlanders (mar-
ching), Sussex Infantry,
Scots Greys and Hussars

293A The Life Guards, 1st
Dragoons, Sussex Regi-
ment, The Buffs (review
order), West Surrey Regi-
ment (kneeling and lying)

United States of America
Army and Navy

54A Cavalry (active service
dress)

59A Cavalry (active service
dress)

117A Cavalry (active service
dress)

41A Infantry, with Mounted
Officer

55A Infantry (active service
dress)

60A Infantry (active service
dress)

67A Infantry (active service
dress)

71A Infantry (active service
dress)

119A Infantry (active service
dress)

57A Marines (marching)

61A Marines (marching)

83A Marines (marching)

323A Marines (marching)

BRITAINS

58A Sailors
63A Sailors
82A Sailors
324A Sailors
56A West Point Cadets
(winter dress)
62A West Point Cadets
(winter dress)
68A West Point Cadets
(winter dress)
194A West Point Cadets
(summer dress)
195A West Point Cadets
(summer dress)

Displays and Types of the U.S.A. Army and Navy

141A Infantry and Cavalry
(service dress)
127A Infantry and Cavalry
(service dress)
48A Infantry and Cavalry
(service dress)
73A Sailors and Marines
319A Infantry and Cavalry
(marching) and Infantry
(kneeling, lying and
charging)
306A Marines, West Point
Cadets (winter and sum-
mer dress), Sailors,
Marines (service dress)
and Whitejackets (sailors)
307A Infantry and Cavalry
(service dress), Machine
Gunners (lying) and Infantry (lying, kneeling and
charging)
294A Infantry (marching, lying, kneeling and charg-
ing) and Machine Gun-
ners (lying)
295A Cavalry and Infantry
(service dress), Machine
Gunners (lying), and In-
fantry (lying, kneeling and
charging)
290A Cavalry and Infantry
(service dress), Machine
Gunners (lying), and In-
fantry (lying, kneeling and
charging)
330A Marines (service dress)
and Marines (review
dress), Sailors (white-

jackets) and Sailors
(review dress), West Point
Cadets (summer and
winter dress) and Infantry
Officer

Native Warriors and Types of the Wild West

37A Cowboys on Foot
138A Cowboys (mounted
and dismounted)
143A Cowboys (mounted
and dismounted)
120A Cowboys on Foot
328A Cowboys (standing, firing and kneeling)
38A Cowboys on Foot
65A Cowboys on Foot
69A Cowboys on Foot with
tent
254A Cowboys (mounted
and dismounted)
320A Cowboys on foot
(kneeling and standing)
and mounted
304A Cowboys (kneeling,
standing and mounted)
296A Cowboys (kneeling,
standing and mounted)
27A North American
Indians (crawling)
35A North American
Indians on Foot
139A North American
Indians (mounted and
dismounted)
142A North American
Indians (mounted and
dismounted)
118A North American
Indians on Foot
329A North American
Indians (mounted and
dismounted)
21A North American
Indians (crawling)
24A North American
Indians on Foot
64A North American
Indians on Foot
70A North American
Indians on Foot, with
Tent
255A North American
Indians (mounted and
dismounted)

321A North American Indians (mounted and dismounted and crawling)

305A North American Indians (mounted, dismounted and crawling)

297A North American Indians (mounted, dismounted and crawling)

34A Zulus (African)

22A Zulus (African)

Displays

50A Cowboys and North American Indians on foot with Chief

248A Cowboys and North American Indians (mounted and on foot)

270A Cowboys and North American Indians (mounted and dismounted)

271A North American Indians (mounted and on foot)

288A North American Indians with Chief (mounted, dismounted and crawling), Cowboys (mounted, dismounted and kneeling)

Sets Renumbered or Added Circa 1935

694A Life Guards (review order) and Foot Guards (review order, slope arms) (6 pcs.)

695A Scots Greys (review order), and Highlanders (review order, marching) (6 pcs.)

696A 1st Dragoons (The Royals) (review order), and Royal Sussex Regiment (review order) (6 pcs.)

697A British Cavalry, shrapnel helmet, khaki and Highlanders (charging), khaki (6 pcs.)

698A Lancers (review order) and East Kent Regiment (The Buffs) (review order) (6 pcs.)

	G	VG	EXC

699A British Cavalry, service dress, and East Kent Regiment (The Buffs), khaki (6 pcs.)

700A Royal West Surrey Regiment (lying, kneeling and standing, firing) (8 pcs.)

701A Foot Guards (review order, marching, slope arms) (8 pcs.)

702A Highlanders (marching, review order, 8 pcs.)

703A North American Indians (crawling, 8 pcs.)

704A Zulus (standing), with Shield and Knobkerrie (8 pcs.)

705A East Kent Regiment (The Buffs) (review order, marching, 8 pcs.)

706A British Infantry, service dress (lying, kneeling and standing, firing, 8 pcs.) per piece 4.50 6.75 9.00

707A Cowboys (kneeling, firing, standing with pistol and standing firing, 8 pcs.)

708A Foot Guards (standing, kneeling and lying, firing, review order, 8 pcs.)

709A Royal Navy, bluejackets (marching, 8 pcs.)

710A Highlanders, khaki (charging with bayonet, 8 pcs.)

711A North American Indians (standing), with knife and hatchet and Indian Chief, (8 pcs.)

712A U.S.A. West Point Cadets, winter dress (slope arms, marching, 8 pcs.)

713A U.S.A. West Point Cadets, summer dress (slope arms, marching), 8 pcs.

714A U.S.A. Sailors (slope arms, marching, 8 pcs.)

715A U.S.A. Marines (slope arms, marching, 8 pcs.)

716A U.S.A. Sailors, whitejackets (slope arms, marching, 8 pcs.)

BRITAINS

717A U.S.A. Marines, service dress (slope arms, marching, 8 pcs.)

718A U.S.A. Infantry, slouch hat, (standing, kneeling and lying, firing, 8 pcs.)

719A U.S.A. Infantry and officer (marching, 8 pcs.)

720A U.S.A. Cavalry and Infantry (marching), slouch hats, 6 pcs.

721A Royal Sussex Regiment (review order, marching, slope arms, 12 pcs.)

722A Foot Guards (review order, marching, slope arms, 12 pcs.)

723A Highlanders (review order, marching, slope arms, 12 pcs.)

724A North American Indians (crawling and standing) with knife and hatchet, and Indian Chief, 12 pcs.

725A Zulus of Africa (standing), with Shield and Knobkerrie, 12 pcs.

726A Royal West Surrey Regiment (review order, lying, kneeling and standing firing, 12 pcs.

727A East Kent Regiment (The Buffs) (review order, slope arms, 12 pcs.)

728A British Infantry, khaki (lying, kneeling and standing, firing, 12 pcs.)

729A Cowboys (kneeling and standing firing, and standing with Pistol, 12 pcs.)

730A Foot Guards (review order, lying, kneeling and standing, firing, 12 pcs.)

731A Royal Navy Bluejackets (marching, 12 pcs.)

732A Highlanders, khaki (charging with bayonet, 12 pcs.)

733A Life Guards and Foot Guards (slope arms, review order, 10 pcs.)

734A Scots Greys and Highlanders (marching, review order, 10 pcs.)

735A 1st Royal Dragoons and Royal Sussex Regiment (review order, 10 pcs.)

736A Hussars and East Kent Regiment (The Buffs, review order, 10 pcs.)

737A British Cavalry and Infantry, service dress (lying, kneeling and standing firing, 10 pcs.)

738A British Cavalry, shrapnel helmet, khaki and Highlanders, khaki (charging with bayonet, 10 pcs.)

739A Cowboys (mounted and dismounted, various positions, 9 pcs.)

740A North American Indians and Chief (mounted, crawling and standing), with Knives and Hatchets, 9 pcs.

741A U.S.A. Infantry and Officer, slouch hats (lying, kneeling and standing, firing, 12 pcs.)

742A U.S.A. Bluejackets and Marines (marching, slope arms, 12 pcs.)

743A U.S.A. West Point Cadets, winter and summer dress (12 pcs.)

744A U.S.A. Bluejackets and Whitejackets (slope arms, 12 pcs.)

745A U.S.A. Marines (blue uniforms and service dress, 12 pcs.)

746A U.S.A. Infantry, slouch hat (marching) with Officer, peak cap (marching), 12 pcs.

747A U.S.A. Cavalry and Infantry (marching), slouch hats, 10 pcs.

748A Scots Greys and Highlanders (marching, review order, 13 pcs.)

749A Life Guards and Foot Guards (marching, review order, 13 pcs.)

544

750A 1st Royal Dragoons and Royal Sussex Regiment (review order, 13 pcs.)

751A Lancers and East Kent Regiment, the Buffs (review order, 13 pcs.)

752A British Cavalry, shrapnel helmet, khaki and Highlanders, khaki, charging with bayonet (13 pcs.)

753A British Cavalry, service dress and infantry, khaki (lying, kneeling and standing, firing, 13 pcs.)

754A Life Guards and 1st Royal Dragoons (review order, 9 pcs.)

755A Foot Guards and Highlanders (marching, slope arms, review order, 16 pcs.)

756A British Infantry, khaki, peak caps (lying, kneeling and standing, firing, 16 pcs.)

757A Foot Guards (review order, lying, kneeling and standing, firing, 16 pcs.)

758A North American Indians and Cowboys (mounted and on foot, various positions) with Indian Chief (12 pcs.)

759A Cowboys (mounted and on foot, various positions, 12 pcs.)

760A North American Indians (mounted, crawling and standing) with Indian Chief, 12 pcs.

761A U.S.A. Cavalry, slouch hats, 9 pcs.

762A U.S.A. Infantry, slouch hats (lying, kneeling and standing, firing, 16 pcs.)

763A U.S.A. Cavalry, slouch hats, and infantry (lying and kneeling, firing and marching, 13 pcs.)

764A Life Guards (review order) and Foot Guards (review order, lying, kneeling and standing, firing, 16 pcs.)

765A British Cavalry, service dress and infantry, khaki (lying, kneeling and standing, firing, 16 pcs.)

766A 1st Royal Dragoons (review order) and Royal West Surrey Regiment (review order, lying, kneeling and standing, firing, 16 pcs.)

767A Scots Greys (review order) and Highlanders (review order, marching, slope arms, 16 pcs.)

768A Life Guards (review order) and Foot Guards (review order, marching, slope arms, 16 pcs.)

769A Hussars (review order) and Royal Sussex Regiment (review order, marching, slope arms, 16 pcs.)

770A North American Indians and Cowboys (mounted and dismounted, various positions, 16 pcs.)

771A North American Indians (mounted and dismounted, various positions) with Indian Chief, 16 pcs.

772A Cowboys (mounted and dismounted, various positions, 16 pcs.)

773A U.S.A. Cavalry and Infantry (marching, slope arms) slouch hats, with Officer, peak cap, 16 pcs.

774A U.S.A. Cavalry and Infantry (lying, kneeling and standing, firing) slouch hats, with officer, peak cap, 16 pcs.

775A Scots Greys and Highlanders (marching, slope arms, review order, 19 pcs.)

776A British Cavalry and Infantry (lying, kneeling and standing, firing) service dress, 19 pcs.

BRITAINS

777A 1st Royal Dragoons, Foot Guards and Royal Sussex Regiment (marching, slope arms, review order, 19 pcs.)

778A Cowboys (mounted and dismounted, various positions, 20 pcs.)

779A North American Indians (mounted and dismounted, various positions) with Indian Chief, 20 pcs.

780A North American Indians and Cowboys (mounted and dismounted, various positions, 20 pcs.)

781A U.S.A. Cavalry, slouch hats, and Infantry (lying and kneeling, firing and marching), with Officer, peak cap, 19 pcs.

782A Life Guards, Scots Greys, Foot Guards and Highlanders (marching, slope arms, all review order) with Marquee, 25 pcs.

783A Royal Horse Guards, East Kent Regiment (The Buffs) (marching, slope arms) and Royal West Surrey Regiment (lying, kneeling and standing, firing, all review order) with Marquee, 25 pcs.

784A British Cavalry (service dress) and Infantry (khaki with peak caps, lying, kneeling and standing, firing and running), with Marquee, 25 pcs.

785A Cowboys (mounted and dismounted, in various positions) with Indian Chief and Wigwam, 25 pcs.

786A North American Indians (mounted and dismounted, in various positions) with Indian Chief and Wigwam, 25 pcs.

787A North American Indians and Cowboys (mounted and dismounted, in various positions) with Indian Chief, 25 pcs.

788A U.S.A. Cavalry and Infantry (various positions), slouch hats, with officer, peak cap, and Marquee, 24 pcs.

789A British Cavalry (service dress with peak caps and shrapnel helmets), Infantry khaki (lying, kneeling, standing, firing, running) Officer, peak cap, and Highlanders, khaki, charging with bayonet, with Marquee, 32 pcs.

790A Life Guards, Scots Greys, Foot Guards (lying, kneeling and standing, firing) and Highlanders (marching, slope arms) All review order with Marquee, 32 pcs.

791A Royal Horse Guards, 1st Royal Dragoons, Royal West Surrey Regiment (lying, kneeling and standing, firing), East Kent Regiment (The Buffs) and Royal Sussex Regiment (marching, slope arms). All review order with Marquee, 32 pcs.

792A Cowboys (mounted and dismounted, in various positions) with large Bell Tent, 32 pcs.

793A North American Indians (mounted and dismounted, in various positions) with Wigwam and Indian Chief, 32 pcs.

794A Cowboys and North American Indians, with Chief (mounted and dismounted in various positions) 34 pcs.

795A U.S.A. Cavalry and Infantry (various positions), slouch hats with officer, peak cap and Marquee, 31 pcs.

796A-809A Probably Vacant
810A U.S.A. Infantry (in various positions) and West Point Cadets, summer dress, 24 pcs.
811A U.S.A. Cavalry, 13 pcs.
812A North American Indians (on foot, various positions) with Chiefs, 24 pcs.
(There are probably more in this series)

The following sets were added in 1940 and issued only for one year.
1081A Bluejackets, 8 pcs.
1082A British Infantry (standing, kneeling, firing) in Battledress, 8 pcs.
1083A British Infantry, with rifles and Tommy guns, 8 pcs.
1084A British Infantry, charging, 8 pcs.
1085A British Infantry, battledress, in various positions (kneeling, standing, firing) with rifles and Tommy guns, 16 pcs.
1086A British Infantry, battledress, in various positions (kneeling, standing, firing) with Rifles and Tommy Guns, and Machine Gunners, 19 pcs.
1087A British Infantry, khaki, peak caps (lying, kneeling and standing, firing) with Folding Fort, 17 pcs.
1088A Foot Guards, review order (lying, kneeling and standing, firing) with Folding Fort, 17 pcs.

THE "A" PARADE SERIES
Like the regular Parade Series, the "A" Series parade figures were introduced during the 1920's and discontinued in 1934. A slotted baseboard was included in each set. Numbers are listed in the order of their appearance in the catalogs.
228a Black Watch, The
279a Highlanders, marching
243a Highlanders, marching, with Mounted Officers

BRITAINS

244a Highlanders, marching, with Mounted Officers
226a Royal West Surrey Regiment, with Mounted Officer
227a Royal West Surrey Regiment
241a Sussex Regiment with Mounted Officers
242a Sussex Regiment with Mounted Officers

United States of America
201a Infantry, service dress
205a Infantry, service dress
206a Infantry, service dress, with Mounted and Foot Officers
207a Infantry, service dress, with Mounted Officer
222a Infantry, service dress, with Mounted Officer
198a Marines
203a Marines
200a Sailors
204a Sailors
199a West Point Cadets, winter dress
202a West Point Cadets, winter dress
229a West Point Cadets, summer dress
230a West Point Cadets, summer dress
237a West Point Cadets, winter and summer dress
238a West Point Cadets, winter and summer dress
225a Cavalry and Infantry, service dress
239a Marines and Sailors
233a Cavalry and Infantry, service dress
236a Cavalry and Infantry, service dress, with Foot Officer
240a Marines and Sailors
234a Cavalry and Infantry, service dress, with Foot Officer
235a Cavalry and Infantry, service dress, with Foot Officer
231a Cowboys, on foot
232a Cowboys, on foot

BRITAINS

<table>
<tr><td></td><td>G</td><td>VG</td><td>EXC</td></tr>
</table>

245a Cowboys, mounted and
dismounted
246a Cowboys, mounted and
dismounted
281a North American
Indians, on foot
331a North American
Indians, on foot, with
Mounted Brave
282a North American
Indians, on foot
332a North American
Indians, on foot, with
Mounted Brave
283a North American
Indians, on foot, with
Mounted Braves
284a North American
Indians, on foot, with
Mounted Braves
333a Cowboys and North
American Indians, on foot
334a Cowboys and North
American Indians on foot
and horse

"H H"   Standard

"HH" SERIES
Circa 1936 - 1940

Extra large size, 83mm (3¼"), bulk series, sold by the
dozen for retailing singly.

	G	VG	EXC
1hh Infantry of the Line ...	No Price Found		
2hh Foot Guards, each	37.00	56.00	75.00
3hh Highlanders	No Price Found		
4hh Assorted Box (1 dozen each of 1hh, 2hh, 3hh). Changed in 1939 to 4 each of 1hh, 2hh, 3hh...	No Price Found		

"C" SERIES

1920's to circa 1935. Best quality, 54mm. Sold in bulk
by the dozen for retailing singly. Mostly British Army.
Numbers listed as they appear in the catalog. No prices
found except where indicated. Price per figure

British Army - Cavalry

13c Cavalry, shrapnel helmet
11c Cavalry, service dress
14c 1st Dragoons
12c Lancers
8c Lancers, with lance
9c Lancers, with sword
7c Life Guards, The
15c Horse Guards, The
16c Hussars
10c Scots Greys

<table>
<tr><td></td><td>G</td><td>VG</td><td>EXC</td></tr>
</table>

British Army - Infantry

	G	VG	EXC
21c Buffs, khaki			
23c Buffs, review order			
19c Highlanders			
20c Highlanders, charging			
24c Highlanders, running, khaki	3.00	5.00	7.00
18c Infantry	3.00	5.00	7.00
22c Rifles, The			
26c Sailors, R.N.			

United States of America - Army and Navy

	G	VG	EXC
17c Cavalry, service dress			
51c Cavalry, slouch hat			
32c Infantry, service dress			
43c Infantry, charging	5.00	8.00	10.00
41c Infantry, kneeling, firing	5.00	8.00	10.00
42c Infantry, lying, firing			
31c Marines, review order			
38c Marines, service dress			
40c Machine Gunners, lying with Gun			
33c Sailors			
39c Sailors, whitejackets	4.00	6.00	9.00
34c West Point Cadets, winter dress	4.00	6.00	8.00
37c West Point Cadets, summer dress			

Miscellaneous

	G	VG	EXC
29c Boy Scouts			
30c Cowboys, on foot			
36c Cowboys, mounted with Revolvers			
27c North American Indians, crawling	2.00	3.00	5.00
25c North American Indians, on foot, with Rifle			
35c North American Indians, mounted, with Hatchet			
28c Zulus	2.00	3.00	4.00

(There are probably more in this series)

"P" SERIES   (Changed to "N"
Circa 1932 - 1935   series in 1936)

Standard size, 54 mm, bulk series, sold by the dozen to
retail singly. Second grade painting. No prices found,
except where noted.

1p Boy Scouts
2p Buffs, khaki
3p Buffs, review order
4p Cowboys, kneeling
5p Cowboys, on foot, with
Pistol
6p Cowboys, on foot, standing, firing

	G	VG	EXC
7p Highlanders, charging ..	12.50	18.75	25.00
8p Highlanders, marching ..	15.00	22.50	30.00

9p Infantry, British, kneeling, firing
10p Infantry, British, lying,
firing
11p Infantry, British, standing, firing
12p Machine Gunner, lying,
with Gun
13p Machine Gunner, sit-
ting, with Gun
14p North American Indian,
Chief
15p North American Indian,
crawling
16p North American Indian,
with Knife and Hatchet
17p North American Indian,
standing
18p Rifles, The
19p Sailors, British
20p Sussex Regiment
21p Zulus

2p

21P

"D" SERIES - 1¾"

The "D" Series contained smaller size pieces used for games and novelties. 29d-31d were added during the 1930's and available in six different colors. They were flat models, able to stand erect, and were suitable for board games. All were discontinued in 1940. 44d and 86d were gold-painted souvenir items added to commemorate the 1953 coronation. No prices found, except where noted.

1d Life Guards, The
2d Hussars
3d Lancers
26d Gun, mounted on
wheels
27d Armoured Car
29d Racing Motor
30d Yacht
31d Cyclist

86d Coronation Chair	10.00	15.00	20.00
44d Her Majesty's State Coach	40.00	60.00	80.00

27d   26d

BRITAINS
"N" SERIES

Standard size, 54mm. Sold in bulk for retailing singly. The painting was 2nd grade. This series was available just before World War II, and contained many distinctive action poses not found in the main range. It replaced the "C" and "P" series which had been phased out earlier. No price found except where noted.

1N Boy Scouts

2N East Kent Regiment, The Buffs, khaki. On Guard position	6.00	9.00	13.00

3N East Kent Regiment,
The Buffs, review order.
On Guard position.
4N Cowboys, crouching, firing Pistol

5N Cowboys, on foot, with Pistol	5.00	7.00	10.00

6N Cowboys, standing, firing Pistol

7N Highlanders, khaki, charging with Bayonet. shrapnel proof helmet .	3.00	4.50	6.00

8N Highlanders, review
order, marching, slope
arms

13N

9N British Infantry, khaki,
with peak caps, kneeling,
firing
10N British Infantry, khaki,
with peak caps, lying,
firing

14N

11N British Infantry, khaki,
with peak caps, standing,
firing
12N British Infantry,
machine gunner, khaki, lying position, with Gun
13N British Infantry,
machine gunner, khaki,
sitting position, with Gun
14N North American Indian
Chief

15N North American Indian, crawling, with Hatchet	5.00	8.00	11.00

16N North American
Indian, standing, with
Knife and Hatchet

17N

17N North American
Indian, standing, with
Rifle

18N The King's Royal Rifle Corps, running position, with Rifle	8.00	12.00	16.00

BRITAINS

	G	VG	EXC
19N British Sailor	6.00	9.00	12.00

20N The Royal Sussex Regiment, review order, marching, slope arms

21N Zulus with Shield and Knobkerri

	G	VG	EXC
22N U.S.A. Army, Infantry, slouch hat, marching, slope arms	2.50	3.75	5.00

23N U.S.A. Army, Infantry, slouch hat, standing, firing position

24N U.S.A. Army, Infantry, slouch hat, charging with Bayonet

25N U.S.A. Army, Infantry, slouch hat, kneeling, firing position

26N U.S.A. Army, Infantry, slouch hat, lying firing position

27N U.S.A. Army, Infantry Officer, peak cap

28N British Foot Guards, review order, marching, slope arms

29N British Infantry, khaki with peak cap, running position

30N British Foot Guards, review order, lying firing position

31N British Foot Guards, review order, kneeling firing position

	G	VG	EXC
32N Highlander, khaki, lying firing position	4.00	7.00	9.00

33N Highlander, khaki, kneeling firing position

34N Highlander, khaki, standing firing position

	G	VG	EXC
35N U.S.A. Army Infantry, peak caps, running position	4.50	6.75	9.00

36N U.S.A. West Point Cadet, winter dress

37N U.S.A. West Point Cadet, summer dress

38N U.S.A. Navy, bluejacket

39N U.S.A. Navy, Marine, blue uniform

	G	VG	EXC
40N British Infantry Officer, khaki, peak cap	5.00	8.00	10.00

41N The Queen's Royal Regiment, West Surrey, review order, kneeling, firing

42N The Queen's Royal Regiment, West Surrey, review order, lying firing

43N The Queen's Royal Regiment, West Surrey, review order, standing firing

44N British Foot Guards, review order, standing firing position

45N U.S.A. Navy, whitejacket

46N U.S.A. Navy, Marine, service dress

47N U.S.A. Army, Machine Gunner, sitting position, with Gun

48N U.S.A. Army Machine Gunner, lying position, with Gun

49N Royal Navy, Bluejacket, shoulder arms

50N Royal Navy, Whitejacket, shoulder arms

51N Royal Navy, Midshipman

52N British Cavalry, The Life Guards, review order

53N British Cavalry, The Lancers, review order, with Lance, movable arm

54N British Cavalry, The Lancers, review order, with Sword, movable arm

55N British Cavalry, The Royal Scots Greys, 2nd Dragoons, review order

56N British Cavalry, khaki, service dress

57N British Cavalry, The Lancers

58N British Cavalry, khaki with shrapnel helmet

	G	VG	EXC
59N British Cavalry, 1st Royal Dragoons, review order	6.00	9.00	12.00

60N British Cavalry, Royal Horse Guards, review order

61N British Cavalry, The Hussars, review order

19N

20N

28N

29N

33N

55N

58N

61N

63N

BRITAINS

62N U.S.A. Army, cavalry, with peak cap

63N North American Indian on Horseback, with Hatchet

64N Cowboy on Horseback, with Pistol

65N U.S.A. Army, Cavalry, with slouch hat

66N North American Indian, galloping, on grey horse

64N

	G	VG	EXC

67N Arab on Horseback, with Scimitar

68N Egyptian Camel Corps

	G	VG	EXC
71N Highlanders, running, khaki	5.00	7.50	10.00
72N British Infantry, marching, slope arms, khaki	3.00	4.50	6.00

73N British Army Drummer Boy, with peak hat

74N British Army Bugler Boy, with peak hat

87N Battledress officer

71 N

	G	VG	EXC
88N Battledress man, charging	4.00	6.00	8.00
89N Battledress man, on guard	5.00	7.50	10.00

90N Battledress man, standing, firing

91N Battledress man, kneeling, firing

92N Bluejacket, new regulation

93N Tommy-gunner

69N Assorted Box, containing, three dozen well assorted (12 different kinds) "N" Infantry

70N Assorted Box containing one dozen (12 different kinds), "N" Cavalry

There may be more in this series

88N   93N

"H" SERIES

Circa 1930(?) - 1940. Large size 70mm. bulk series for retailing singly. Painting grade usually was between "Best Quality" and Second Grade.

	G	VG	EXC
4h Infantry of the Line	No Price Found		
5h Foot Guards	7.00	11.00	15.00
6h Highlanders	7.00	11.00	15.00

BRITAINS

In addition to the military pieces, certain novelty items were designated "H" Series. These are all from the period 1930-1940. Numbers 16h through 21h were manufactured through special license from Walt Disney - Mickey Mouse LTD. Numbers 12h and 22h were for Garden Ornament use.

	G	VG	EXC
7h Terrier Dog, 4½" long	80.00	120.00	160.00
9h Pug Dog, 2¾" long			
10h Stag, 4" long	45.00	67.50	90.00
11h Doe, companion model to 10h			
12h A large scale model of a Seagull with wings outstretched, 4¼" across the wing tips	10.00	15.00	20.00
16h Mickey Mouse			
17h Minnie Mouse			
18h Pluto			
19h Donald Duck			
20h Clarabelle the Cow			
21h Goofy			
22h Large scale model of a Seagull with wings folded, 2¼" tall to beak	14.00	21.00	28.00

"E" SERIES
The "Scenic" Range

Only issued for several years during the 1930's, this range utilized an illustrated box that could be opened to form a colored back drop 20" long. Numbers listed as they appear in the 1936 catalog. No prices found.

44E The Grenadier Guards, with Bell Tent, trees and hedges, 13 pcs.

45E Highlanders in lying, kneeling and standing positions, with Bell Tents and trees, 10 pcs.

46E North American Indians, assorted positions, with Bell Tents and trees, 11 pcs.

47E Cowboys of the Wild West, assorted positions, with Bell Tents and trees, 10 pcs.

48E The Farm Display, with farmer, animals; trees and hedges, 14 pcs.

49E The Hunting Display, with Huntsmen, mounted and dismounted, hounds and trees, 10 pcs.

BRITAINS

	G	VG	EXC
50E The Park Showpiece, containing Nurse and Child, young lady, dog, flower beds and flowers, trees and conifer in pot, 13 pcs.			
54E Zoological Set, lioness and cubs, bear and cubs, tiger and trees, 10 pcs.			
There may be more in this series			

FORT RANGE - S AND P

These were Britain's Post-war second grade figures (simplified painting with no details). All were in 54mm. They were first introduced in the 1950 "New Lines" section of the catalog. Later in 1956, the series was upgraded and became the "New Crown Range." The "P" Series was designed to offer individual pieces from counter displays. All second grade ranges were discontinued in 1959. No prices found except where noted. There may be more in this series. Price per figure

"Fort Range"
(single row boxes)

	G	VG	EXC
94S British Foot Guards, marching at slope arms, review order, 6 pcs., per troop	5.00	7.50	10.00
95S British Line Regiments, marching at slope arms, review order, 6 pcs., per troop	5.00	7.50	10.00
96S Highlanders, marching at slope arms, review order, 6 pcs.			
97S British Foot Guards, standing, kneeling, lying firing, review order, 6 pcs.			
98S Highlanders, standing, kneeling and lying firing, active service, khaki, 6 pcs.			
100S Cowboys, mounted and on foot, assorted positions, 5 pcs.			
101S North American Indians on foot, assorted positions, 5 pcs.			
103S Sailors, Royal Navy, 6 pcs.			
104S North American Indians, mounted and on foot, assorted positions, 5 pcs.	3.00	5.00	7.00

	G	VG	EXC
105S Cowboys, on foot, assorted positions, 6 pcs.	3.00	5.00	7.00
119S Infantry, battledress, assorted positions: at the ready, standing and kneeling, firing and with Tommy Guns, 6 pcs.	5.00	7.50	10.00
123S Infantry of the Line, on guard, review order, 6 pcs., per troop	5.00	7.50	10.00
144S French Infantry of the Line, on guard, review order, 6 pcs.			
145S Belgian Infantry of the Line, on guard, review order, 6 pcs.			
149S Footguards and Lifeguards, marching, review order, 5 pcs.			
150S French Infantry with mounted officer, review order, 5 pcs.			
201S Footguards, standing firing, kneeling firing, lying firing, 5 pcs.			
202S Lifeguard and Footguards, 4 pcs.			
203S Highlanders, 5 pcs.			
204S Cowboys, 4 pcs.			
205S North American Indians, 4 pcs.			
206S Scots Grey and Highlanders, 4 pcs.			
207S Infantry of the Line, 5 pcs.			
208S Infantry in Battledress, 5 pcs.			
209S French Infantry and Zouave, 4 pcs.			
210S Union Infantry, 1862, 4 pcs.	3.00	5.00	7.00
211S Confederate Infantry, 1862, 4 pcs.	3.00	5.00	7.00

"Duofort" Range
(double row boxes)

106S Infantry and Cavalry, Line Regiments and Highlanders, assorted positions, khaki, 10 pcs.

108S North American Indians and Cowboys, mounted and on foot, assorted, 10 pcs.

109S British Life Guards, Foot Guards and Highlanders, review order, 9 pcs.

110S British Foot Guards and Line Regiments in assorted positions, review order, 12 pcs.

111S Scots Greys and Foot Guards, in assorted positions, review order, 9 pcs.

120S Infantry in Battle Dress, assorted positions, with Officer, 12 pcs.

146S Belgian Grenadiers and Chasseurs a' Pied, review order, 12 pcs.

147S French Zouaves and Infantry of the Line, with mounted officer, review order, 11 pcs.

212S Cowboys and Indians, 7 pcs.

213S U.S. Sailors and West Point Cadets, 9 pcs.

214S Hussars and Infantry of the Line, 7 pcs.

215S Footguards, 8 pcs.

216S Scots Greys and Highlanders, 7 pcs.

217S Infantry in Battledress, 9 pcs.

218S French Infantry and Zouaves, 8 pcs.

219S Confederate Cavalry and Infantry, 1862, 7 pcs.

220S Union Cavalry and Infantry, 1862, 7 pcs.

221S Cowboys, 7 pcs.

222S North American Indians, 7 pcs.

237S Footguards, 9 pcs.

"Trifort" Range
(treble row boxes)

112S Highlanders and Scots Greys, various positions, assorted, khaki and review order, 15 pcs.

114S North American Indians and Cowboys, mounted and on foot, in various positions, 14 pcs.

115S British Foot Guards, standing, kneeling and lying, firing and marching slope arms, review order, 18 pcs.

116S Infantry of the Line and Hussars, assorted positions, review order, 15 pcs.

117S Life Guards, Highlanders and Foot Guards, various positions, review order, 14 pcs.

148S Belgian Horse Gendarmes, Chasseurs a' Pied and Infantry of the Line, review order, 15 pcs.

223S Scots Greys and Highlanders, 10 pcs.

224S Cowboys and Indians, 10 pcs.

225S Footguards, 12 pcs.

226S Hussars and Infantry of the Line, 10 pcs.

	G	VG	EXC
227S French Cavalry, Infantry and Zouaves, 10 pcs, set	37.50	56.25	75.00
228S Confederate Cavalry and Infantry, 1862, 10 pcs., price for cavalry	5.00	8.00	10.00
229S Union Cavalry and Infantry, 1862, 10 pcs., prices for cavalry	5.00	8.00	10.00
230S Infantry in Battledress, 14 pcs.	5.00	8.00	10.00

BRITAINS
"Super-Fort" Range

No. 41P   No. 42P.   No. 45P. & No. 123P.   No. 96P

	G	VG	EXC
231S Lifeguards and Footguards, 12 pcs.			
232S Scots Greys and Highlanders, 13 pcs.			
233S Hussars and Infantry of the Line, 13 pcs.			
234S Cowboys and Indians, 14 pcs.			
235S Infantry in Battledress, 16 pcs.	80.00	120.00	160.00
236S Union and Confederate Cavalry and Infantry, 1862, 14 pcs.			

No. 111P

122P   123P

"New Crown" Range
"P" SERIES

Soldiers, Cowboys and Indians, packed in bulk for retailing singly. 2nd quality painting, issued in 1956. 54mm high.

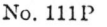

No. 125P

	G	VG	EXC
41P Footguard, marching, slope arms, review order .	4.00	6.00	9.00
42P Infantry of the Line, on guard, spike helmet, review order	5.00	8.00	10.00
43P Infantry of the Line, marching, slope arms, review order	6.00	9.00	12.00
45P Highlander, standing, firing, khaki	No Price Found		
46P Infantry of the Line, on guard, shrapnel helmet, khaki	No Price Found		
51P North American Indian, on foot, with Rifle	5.00	7.50	10.00
52P North American Indian, on foot, with knife and hatchet	5.00	7.50	10.00
56P Highlander, lying, firing, khaki	No Price Found		
57P Highlander, kneeling, firing, khaki	5.00	7.50	10.00
58P British Footguard, firing, standing, review order	4.00	6.00	8.00
59P British Footguard, kneeling, firing, review order	5.00	7.50	10.00
60P British Footguard, lying, firing, review order	4.00	6.00	8.00
80P Cowboy, crouching, firing pistol	No Price Found		
83P Cowboy on foot with pistol	3.00	5.00	7.00

	G	VG	EXC
92P U.S.A. Bluejacket	6.00	9.00	12.00
93P U.S. West Point Cadets, in grey uniforms, winter dress	No Price Found		
96P Cowboy on foot, firing pistol	No Price Found		
98P Highlander, marching, slope arms, review order .	4.00	6.00	8.00
99P North American Indian Chief	5.00	7.50	10.00
110P Infantry Officer, battle-dress	4.50	7.00	9.00
111P Infantry, charging, battledress	4.50	7.00	9.00
112P Infantry, on guard, battledress	No Price Found		
113P Infantry, standing, firing, battledress	4.50	7.00	9.00
114P Infantry, kneeling, firing, battledress	4.50	7.00	9.00
115P Infantry, with Tommy-guns, battledress	4.50	7.00	9.00
116P British Bluejacket	3.50	5.00	7.00
122P Nurse, R.A.M.C.	5.00	7.50	10.00
123P Highlander, standing, firing, review order	4.00	6.00	8.00
124P Highlander, kneeling, firing, review order	No Price Found		
125P Highlander, lying, firing, review order	No Price Found		

126P

127P

No. 136P.

152P

No. 154P

No price found except where noted . Price per each

	G	VG	EXC
64P Life Guard, review order			
65P Scots Grey, review order			
66P Horse Guard, review order			
68P Hussar, review order	7.00	11.00	14.00
70P British Cavalry, shrapnel helmet, khaki			
72P U.S.A. Cavalry, slouch hat, khaki	7.00	11.00	14.00
117P North American Indian, mounted with hatchet			
118P Cowboy, mounted with pistol			
121P Royal Canadian Mounted Police	7.00	10.00	14.00
135P Belgian Horse Gendarme	10.00	15.00	20.00
151P Red Army Cossack			
156P Highland Officer, mounted with white tropical helmet			
120MP Assorted Infantry Pack of 48 pcs. (8 different kinds)			
121MP Assorted Pack of 24 Cavalry Models (8 different per box)	7.00	11.00	14.00
123MP Assorted Pack of 30 pcs., consisting of 6 Cavalry & 24 Infantry			
124MP Assorted Pack of 3 dozen			
148P Motor Cycle Dispatch Rider	4.50	6.75	9.00
149P Speed Cop			

	G	VG	EXC
126P Zouave (French Army), charging	5.00	7.50	10.00
127P French Infantry, on guard, review order	5.00	7.50	10.00
128P French Infantry, standing, firing	5.00	7.50	10.00
129P French Infantry, kneeling, firing	5.00	7.50	10.00
130P French Infantry, lying, firing	5.00	7.50	10.00
132P Belgian Grenadier marching, review order . .	No Price Found		
133P Belgian Chassueur a'Pied, running	3.50	5.00	7.00
134P Belgian Line Infantry, on guard, review order . .	No Price Found		
136P North American Indian Chief , carrying rifle	6.00	9.00	12.00
137P North American Indian, crouching with rifle	5.00	7.50	10.00
150P Pilot in full flying kit .	7.00	11.00	14.00
152P Red Army Infantry, charging	10.00	15.00	20.00
153P Royal Canadian Mounted Police on foot, slope arms	No Price Found		
154P Cowboy on foot, firing pistol	5.00	8.00	10.00
155P North American Indian, on foot, swinging club	No Price Found		

No. 148P

No. 64P.

No. 118P

BRITAINS

51S Highland Infantry, mounted officer, review order, 6 pcs.

52S Hussars, mounted with Infantry of the Line, review order, 5 pcs.

53S The Scots Greys, with Highland Infantry, review order, 5 pcs.

54S British Foot Guards, firing, review order, 7 pcs.

55S The Life Guards, mounted, and Foot Guards, review order, 5 pcs.

56S Infantry in battle dress, with officer, 7 pcs.

57S Royal Canadian Mounted Police, mtd. and foot, full dress, 5 pcs.

58S North American Indians, mtd. and foot, 6 pcs.

59S Cowboys, mtd. and foot, 5 pcs.

60S French Infanterie, with mounted officers, review order, 5 pcs.

61S The Scots Greys, with British Foot Guards, review order, 11 pcs.

62S Infantry in battle dress with officer, 14 pcs.

63S The Scots Greys, with Highland Infantry, review order, 10 pcs.

64S North American Indians, mtd and foot, 10 pcs.

65S Cowboys, mounted and foot, 10 pcs.

66S Cowboys and North American Indians, mtd. and foot, 10 pcs.

67S Scots Greys with British Foot Guards, review order, 17 pcs.

68S British Inf. in battle dress, with officer and machine gunner, 20 pcs.

69S Scots Greys, mounted with Highlanders on foot, review order, 17 pcs.

70S Cowboys and North American Indians, mtd. and foot, 17 pcs.

71S A modern type gun (with 6 shells to fire) and ass't of British Inf. in battle dress, 6 pcs.

Britains box cover and contents from No. 57s Royal Canadian Mounted Police
Photo by Gary J. Linden

Football Teams

The Football Teams first appeared in the 1905 catalog. Numbers were not assigned at that time. These round based models were made in positions representing Forwards, Half-Backs and Full Backs. Special Teams and color combinations could be ordered upon request - all utilizing the same figures. The line was discontinued in 1941. No prices found except where noted. These are seldom found in mint condition.

258b Football
257b Corner flag on post
254b Referee
255b Linesman with flag
256b Goalposts
189b Goalkeeper
   (green/white)

ARSENAL
ASTON VILLA
BIRMINGHAM
BLACKBURN ROVERS
BOLTON WANDERERS
BRADFORD CITY
BURNLEY
BURY
CARDIFF CITY
CHELSEA
CORINTHIANS
DERBY COUNTY
EVERTON
HUDDERSFIELD TOWN
LIVERPOOL
MANCHESTER CITY
MANCHESTER UNITED
MIDDLESBOROUGH
NEWCASTLE UNITED
NOTTS COUNTY
OLDHAM ATHLETIC
PRESTON NORTH END
PLYMOUTH ARGYLE
SHEFFIELD WEDNESDAY
STOKE
SUNDERLAND
TOTTENHAM HOTSPUR
WEST BROMWICH ALBION
WOLVERHAMPTON
   WANDERERS
WOOLRICH ARSENAL

	G	VG	EXC
172b Red and white striped shirts, black knickers, black stockings			
173b Red and white striped shirts, white knickers, black stockings			
174b Red and white striped shirts, blue knickers, black stockings			
175b Blue and white striped shirts, white knickers, black stockings			
176b Blue and white striped shirts, blue knickers, black stockings	11.00	16.50	22.00
177b Black and white striped shirts, black knickers, black stockings	11.00	16.50	22.00
178b Black and white striped shirts, white knickers, black stockings			
179b Blue and white quartered shirts, white knickers, black stockings			

BRITAINS

	G	VG	EXC
180b White shirts, blue knickers, black stockings			
181b White shirts, black knickers, black stockings			
182b Dark blue shirts, white knickers, black stockings .	11.00	16.50	22.00
183b Red shirts, white knickers, black stockings			
184b Tangerine shirts, white knickers, black stockings			
185b Sky blue shirts, white knickers, black stockings .	11.00	16.50	22.00
186b Old gold shirts, black knickers, black stockings			
187b Claret and light blue shirts, white knickers, black stockings	11.00	16.50	22.00
188b Claret and amber shirts, white knickers, black stockings	21.00	31.50	42.00
189b Green (goalkeeper) shirts, white knickers, black stockings	20.00	30.00	40.00
189b Goalkeeper, bareheaded, 2nd version .	35.00	52.50	70.00
190b Red, white collar shirts, white knickers, black stockings			
191b Red, white collars and sleeves shirts, white knickers, black stockings			
209b White and green banded shirts, white knickers, black stockings			
210b Royal blue shirts, white knickers, red topped stockings			
211b White with black horizontal shirts, white knickers, black, white topped stockings			
255b Linesman with flag ..	22.00	33.00	45.00
270b Green, black collars and cuff shirts, white knickers, black stockings			

"FOOTBALL" (Soccer)

1524. Right Angle Football Game, 16 pcs., board, football, 2 dice, 12 players (forwards, running) in 1937 catalog		No Price Found	
1528. Right Angle Football Game, 16 pcs., board, football, 2 dice, 12 players (forwards, running) in 1937 catalog		No Price Found	

BRITAINS MISC.

	G	VG	EXC
Un-numbered "Famous Football Teams", 18 pcs., includes goal, 3 flag markers, and ball	No Price Found		
Singles	12.00	22.00	32.00

Various Teams

RACING COLORS

Typical "Racing colours"
(detachable rider)

	G	VG	EXC
average/boxed ...	35.00	70.00	125.00

	G	VG	EXC
237. Racing Colours, horse and removable rider, 6 pcs	No Price Found		
1463. Racing Colours of famous owners, 6 pcs ...	No Price Found		
1480-92. Racing Series - Jockeys with horses	30.00	50.00	75.00
1713. Racing Colors - F.D. Buhl	No Price Found		
1714. Racing Colors - A.G. Vanderbilt	No Price Found		
1829. Racing Colours of Famous American Owners, 6 pcs	No Price Found		
1830. Racing Colours of Famous American Owners, 6 pcs	No Price Found		

TRAFFIC SIGNS

Typical Traffic Signs

	G	VG	EXC
239. Motor patrol and Road signs	200.00	400.00	600.00
1427. Traffic Signs, 8 pcs ..	200.00	500.00	750.00
1428. Traffic Signs, with policeman, 16 pcs	No Price Found		
1429. Traffic Signs, with policeman, 24 pcs	No Price Found		
1430. Traffic Signs, traffic display, 22 pcs	No Price Found		
1468. Traffic Signs, 5 pcs ..	No Price Found		

1546-49. UNKNOWN	**G**	**VG**	**EXC**
1550. Noah's Ark (25 pcs.) .	1500	2500	3500

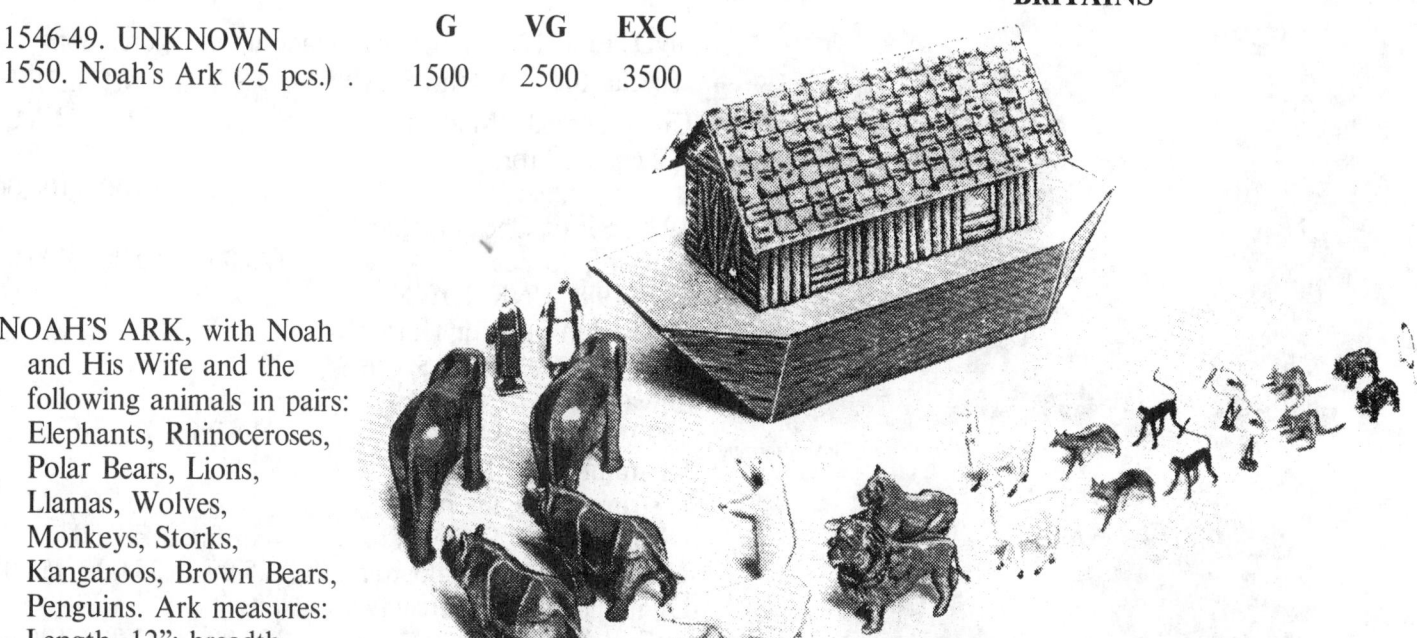

NOAH'S ARK, with Noah and His Wife and the following animals in pairs: Elephants, Rhinoceroses, Polar Bears, Lions, Llamas, Wolves, Monkeys, Storks, Kangaroos, Brown Bears, Penguins. Ark measures: Length, 12"; breadth, 5¾"; height, 6" 25 pieces

BRITAINS LTD presents
MICKEY MOUSE MODEL SERIES

WITH MOVABLE HEADS
BY PERMISSION WALT DISNEY-MICKEY MOUSE LTD.

Measures 12" x 8¾"

No. 1644 MICKEY MOUSE AT THE CINEMA
This is an ingenious display box, containing: Mickey Mouse, Minnie Mouse, Pluto, Donald Duck, Clarabelle and Goofy, and so designed to represent a cinema show. The characters are arranged behind the title screen which can then be drawn up, so that the figures then appear as seen at the Cinema. Provides lots of fun.

1644. Mickey Mouse at the
cinema . . . .   No Price Found
1645. Mickey Mouse set (6
pcs.) . . . .   No Price Found

1654. Snow White and	**G**	**VG**	**EXC**
Seven Dwarfs, 8 pcs	200.00	525.00	750.00
Each	20.00	60.00	80.00

#1552

1526. All Metal Flower
Holder, 5¼" wide, 1 pc .   No Price Found
1552. Royal Mail Van, 2
pcs. with driver . . . .   No Price Found
1656. John Cobb's Railton
Wonder Car 200.00   350.00   500.00
1658. John Cobb's Railton
Wonder Car (Chromium
Plated Body) . . . .   No Price Found
1912. Historical Figures -
(issued November 1940)
includes . . . .   No Price Found

T-1   T-4   T-5 Broom missing

Madame Tussaud

T3

Mikado (fan missing)

Life Boatman   Sir Kreemy Knut

(NOTE: 1912 & 1919 were made up of figures done special for MADAME TUSSAUD'S WAX MUSEUM)

	G	VG	EXC
Un-numbered - Madame Tussaud, bronze painted bust	35.00	70.00	100.00
1920. Set of Chessmen, with board, 25 pcs	120.00	250.00	400.00
1921-1989 UNKNOWN (Used in part for Horton's Toys. See "Reno" Sports Games)			
1990. Chess Set	No Price Found		
Un-numbered - Mikado string pull spins parsal, circa 1900	No Price Found		
Un-numbered, Life Boatman	25.00	35.00	55.00
Un-numbered, Sir Kreemy Knut	50.00	75.00	100.00

RACING GAME MODELS

It is believed these models date from 1905. Sometime during the 1920's, they were assigned catalog numbers. After being out of production from 1946 through 1953, they were reintroduced in 1954. The Milton Bradley Company issued a horse racing board game that included these figures. They were discontinued in 1959.

	G	VG	EXC
19D Jockey on horse, assorted colors, 2¼" long,	14.00	21.00	28.00
123b Jockey for Race Games, assorted colors, 3¾" long, reassigned number 96D in 1954	No Price Found		

#96D $20-35-55

	G	VG	EXC
T-1 King Henry VIII	35.00	60.00	90.00
T-3 Little Red Riding Hood	No Price Found		
T-4 Queen Elizabeth	35.00	60.00	90.00
T-5 Cinderella	35.00	60.00	90.00
1919. Historical Figures, (issued December 1940) includes #86D Chair	No Price Found		
T-1 King Henry VIII	35.00	60.00	90.00
T-4 Queen Elizabeth	35.00	60.00	90.00

CADBURY COCOCUBS

These delightful and colorful characters were given as a sales promotion with Cadbury Cocoa during the mid 1930's. In addition to the figures, club members were sent Cococub Newsletters and issued badges in the shape of a star. Only pieces with bases are stamped "Cpryt Britains Cadbury." The smaller figures averaged 40mm tall, while the larger were almost 80mm. The numbering system included here has been designed by V.J. Medcalf for ease of identification. S = small, L = large.

	G	VG	EXC
S1a Dumpty Doo Duck, open beak, large hat	No Price Found		
S1b Dumpty Doo Duck, half open beak, bowler hat ...	No Price Found		
S1c Dumpty Doo Duck, half open beak, cap	No Price Found		
S1d Dumpty Doo Duck, closed beak, very small hat.................	14.00	21.00	28.00
S2 Dan Crow	12.00	18.00	25.00
S3 Silas Slink (fox)	12.00	18.00	25.00
S4 Freddie Frog	14.00	21.00	28.00
S5 Monty Monkey	14.00	21.00	28.00
S6 Gussie Robin	10.00	15.00	20.00

Cadbury Cococubs, L to R: S1b, S15

S7 Tom Kitten	11.00	16.00	22.00
S8 Timothy Tortoise	No Price Found		
S9 Tubby Bear	11.00	16.00	23.00
S10 Pat Pelican	No Price Found		
S11 Mrs. Cacklegoose	12.00	18.00	25.00
S12 Captain Kangaroo	13.00	19.00	26.00
S13 Will Mouse	11.00	16.00	22.00
S14 Percy Parrot	11.00	16.00	22.00
S15 Granny Owl	12.00	18.00	24.00
S16 Bill Badger	No Price Found		
S17 Mrs. Henrietta Fussy Feathers	12.00	18.00	25.00
S18 Nutty Squirrel	12.00	18.00	25.00
S19 Piglet	11.00	16.00	22.00
S20 Brother Rabbit	11.00	16.00	22.00
S21 Percy Penguin	13.00	19.00	26.00
L1 Jonathan (boy)	75.00	112.00	150.00
L2 Peter Pum (poodle)	17.00	25.00	34.00
L3 Whiskers Rabbit	No Price Found		
L4 Mr. Pie Porker	11.00	16.00	22.00
L5 Mrs. Pie Porker	No Price Found		

BRITAINS

	G	VG	EXC
L6 Tiny Tusks (elephant) ..	No Price Found		
L7 Squire Rooster	20.00	30.00	40.00
L8 "Name Unknown", boy eating chocolate, wearing blue Edwardian sailor suit	No Price Found		

LILLIPUT

Lilliput figures were first issued in the 1950 catalog supplement and finally entered into the main catalog in 1954. They were manufactured by W. Horton LTD (established in 1832), under license from Britains LTD. They were distributed in the United Kingdom by Horton, while Britains handled all export orders. A foot figure in this series is 13/16" or 21mm in height. This was compatible with "00" and "HO" scales. No prices found except where noted.

"Farm"

LB/513 Tree			
LB/514 Shire horse			
LB/515 Farmer...........	3.50	5.00	7.00
LB/516 Farmer's Wife.....	3.50	5.00	7.00
LB/517 Nurse and Child ...	10.00	15.00	20.00
LB/518 Foal.............	3.00	4.50	6.00
LB/519 Cob..............	3.00	4.50	6.00
LB/520 Standing Cow.....	3.00	4.50	6.00
LB/521 Feeding Cow	3.00	4.50	6.00
LB/522 Calf, lying	2.00	3.00	4.00
LB/523 Collie Dog........	1.00	2.00	3.00
LB/524 Goose...........	2.50	3.75	5.00
LB/525 Sheep, standing....	2.00	3.00	4.00
LB/526 Sheep, feeding.....	3.00	4.50	6.00
LB/527 Pig.............	2.00	3.00	4.00
LB/528 Lamb...........	3.00	4.50	6.00
LB/529 Ducks and Drakes..	2.00	3.00	4.00
LB/530 Hurdle...........	.50	1.00	2.00
LB/531 Stable Lad........	3.50	5.25	7.00
LB/532 Land Girl........	3.50	5.25	7.00

"Railway"

LB/533 Porter with Barrow	7.00	10.50	14.00
LB/534 Guard	4.00	6.00	8.00
LB/535 Station Master	4.00	6.00	8.00
LB/536 Civilian			
LB/537 Porter with luggage	5.00	7.50	10.00
LB/538 Newsvendor	1.50	3.00	4.00
LB/539 Lady with case.....	5.00	7.50	10.00
LB/540 Man with book....	5.00	7.50	10.00
LB/541 Man with umbrella.	5.00	7.50	10.00
LB/542 Lady with hatbox ..	5.00	7.50	10.00
LB/543 Golfer	2.00	4.00	5.50
LB/544 Barrel			
LB/545 Hamper			

LILLIPUT "OO & HO" SCALE MODELS
(METAL)
HIGH QUALITY MODELLING AND FINISH

Measures 2¼-in. long
No. LV/601   Open Sports Car

Measures 2¼-in. long
No. LV/602   Saloon Car

Measures 4-in. long
No. LV/603   Articulated Lorry, Farm
or Civilian

Measures 1½-in. long
No. LV/604   "Fordson"
Tractor with Driver

Measures 2¼-in · long
No. LV/605   Milk Float
and Horse

Measures 2¾-in. long
No. LV/606   Tumbrel Cart and
Horse with Hay Racks

Measures 3¼-in. long
No. LV/607   3-Ton
Army Covered Truck

Measures 3¼-in. long
No. LV/608   3-Ton
Farm or Civilian Lorry

Measures 1½-in. long
No. LV/609   The Austin
Champ

Measures 3¼-in. long
No. LV/611   The Sexton
Self Propelled Gun

Measures 2⅛-in. long
No. LV/612   1½-Ton
Army Truck

Measures 3-in. long
No. LV/613   1½-Ton
Covered Army Truck

Measures 4⅝-in. long
No. LV/614   Articulated
Truck, Farm or Civilian

Measures 2⅜-in. long
No. LV/615   Saracen
Armoured
Personel Carrier

Measures 2⅛-in. long
No. LV/616   1½-Ton
Farm or Civilian
Truck

Measures 3-in. long
No. LV/617   Local
Authority Ambulance

Measures 3-in. long
No. LV/618   Army
Ambulance

Measures 3-in. long
No. LV/619   Post
Office Royal Mail Van

Measures 3¼-in. long
No. LV/620   3-Ton
Open Army Truck

ALL MODELS ARE TO SCALE WITH EACH OTHER

BRITAINS

"Railway"

	G	VG	EXC
LB/546 Large packing case .	3.50	5.25	7.00
LB/547 Small packing case .	3.00	4.50	6.00
LB/548 Telegraph Boy			
LB/549 Electric Trolley	4.00	6.00	8.00
LB/550 Speed Cop			

"Hunting Series"

LB/559 Huntsman, mounted, galloping, top hat

LB/560 Huntswomen, mounted, galloping, top hat

LB/561 Hounds, running, legs outstretched

LB/562 Hounds, running, legs closed

LB/563 Fox, running

LB/564 Huntswoman, mounted, galloping, bowler hat

LB/565 Huntsman, mounted, galloping, cap

"LILLIPUT WORLD"
(Picture Packs)
"Farm"

LP 501 4 standing sheep, 4 feeding sheep, 3 lambs

LP 502 3 standing cows, 3 feeding cows

LP 503 12 Hurdles	7.50	11.25	15.00
LP 504 5 cobs, 2 foals	20.00	30.00	40.00
LP 505 4 geese, 6 ducks, 1 land girl	32.00	48.00	65.00

LP 506 4 shire horses, 1 stable lad, 1 collie dog

LP 507 2 feeding cows, 3 standing cows, 2 lying calves

LP 508 8 pigs, 1 farmer, 1 collie dog

LP 509 1 farmer, 1 farmer's wife; 2 land girls, 2 stable lads, 1 collie dog	21.00	31.50	42.00

"Railway"

LP 510 Guard, station master, porter for trolley, porter with luggage, newsvendor, two-wheeled trolley, 6 pcs.

	G	VG	EXC

LP 511 Lady with attache case, man with book, man with umbrella, lady with hat box, golfer, nurse with child, 6 pcs.

LP 512 Electric trolley, two-wheeled trolley, 2 barrels, 2 hampers, 2 large packing cases, 2 small packing cases, 10 pcs.

LP 513 18 trees (this later changed to the Hunt Picture Pack in 1958 which contained huntsman, huntswomen, 3 dogs (assorted positions), 1 fox

"Lilliput Vehicles"

LV/601 Open Sports Car	20.00	30.00	40.00
LV/602 Saloon Car	20.00	30.00	40.00
LV/603 Articulated Lorry	20.00	30.00	40.00
LV/604 Fordson Tractor with driver	20.00	30.00	40.00
LV/605 Milk Float and horse with milkman	22.00	33.00	45.00
LV/606 Tumbrel Cart and horse with hay racks and carter	20.00	30.00	40.00

LV/607 Army covered 3 ton truck with removable plastic top, khaki

LV/608 3 Ton farm lorry. Spare wheel fitted, ass't colors, measures 3¼" long

LV/609 The Austin "Champ," all purpose vehicle with removable hood

LV/610 Centurion tank	25.00	38.00	50.00

LV/611 The Sexton. A fine model of the most modern self propelled gun. Not fitted to fire, measures 3¼" long	27.00	41.00	55.00

LV/612 1½ Ton Army truck, with spare wheel, measures 2 $^{13}/_{16}$" long

LV/613 1½ Ton covered Army truck with spare wheel, measures 3" long

	G	VG	EXC

LV/614 Articulated truck with spare wheel, measures 4⅝" long

LV/615 "Saracen" Armoured personnel carrier, measures 2⅝" long

LV/616 1½ Ton Farm or Civilian truck with spare wheel, measures 2 ¹³⁄₁₆" long

LV/617 Local authority ambulance, cream, measures 3" long 8.00 15.00 20.00

LV/618 Army ambulance, measures 3" long

LV/619 Post Office Royal Mail Van, measures 3" long

LV/620 3 Ton open Army truck with spare wheel, measures 3¼" long

LV/SA Boxed set containing: 1 LV/601, 1 LV/602, 1 LV/603, 1 LV/604 with driver, 1 LV/605 with Milkman, 1 LV/606, with accessories and Carter as listed in the 1951 Catalog Supplement 65.00 125.00 200.00

LV/SA

	G	VG	EXC
L1 1 Shire horse; 1 land girl; 1 standing cow; 1 standing sheep; 1 feeding sheep; 2 ducks	5.00	10.00	15.00
L2 1 Cob; 1 farmer; 1 goose; 1 pig; 1 farmer's wife; 1 feeding cow	5.00	10.00	15.00
L3 1 Duck; 1 pig; 1 land girl; 1 standing cow; 1 stable lad, 1 goose; 1 lying calf	5.00	10.00	15.00
L4 1 farmer; 1 foal; 1 shire horse; 1 collie dog; 1 feeding sheep; 1 stable lad; 1 standing sheep			
L5 1 feeding cow; 1 farmer's wife; 2 lying calves; 1 land girl; 1 standing cow	12.00	18.00	25.00
L6 1 standing cow; 1 goose; 1 pig; 1 lamb; 1 collie dog; 1 duck; 1 cob; 1 standing sheep	5.00	10.00	15.00

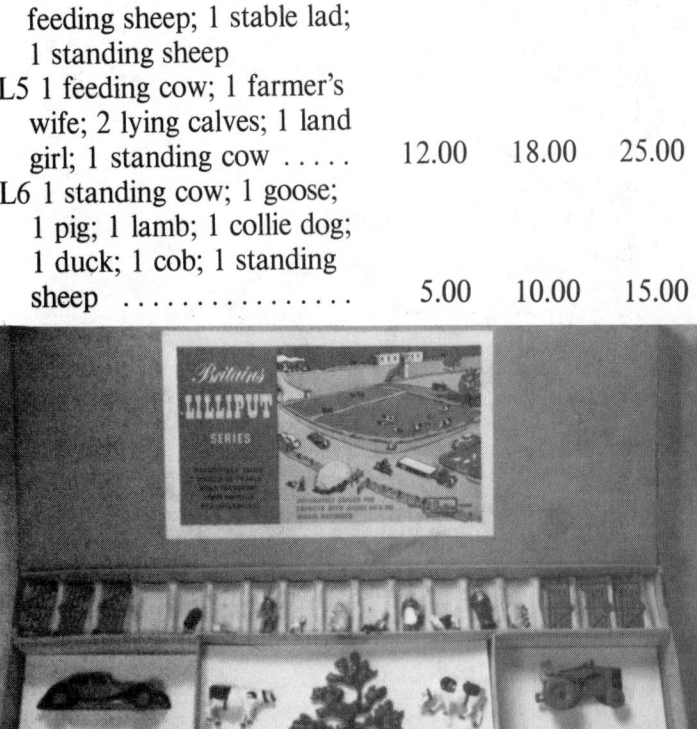

L-7

L7 Lilliput Display Box containing Saloon Car, tractor, tumbrel cart and milk float, farmer, farmer's wife, stable lad, farm girl and dog, horses, cows and calf, sheep and lamb, pig geese, hurdles and tree, 28 pcs .... 75 .00 150.00 250.00

L8 Roadside Inn or Country House

L9 Two country cottages, back and front elevations are different

BRITAINS

L10 Typical Barn and cart stable

L11 Lilliput Railway Personnel & Vehicles: saloon car, lorry, sports car, articulated lorries, Austin "Champ," motor cyclists, station trollies, packing cases, barrels, hampers, porters w/trollies, guards, station master, porters with luggage, newsvendor, general public asst., 43 pcs.

L12 Scenic Display containing 8 battledress soldiers in various attitudes

LL14 Wallet Pack; 8 battledress soldiers; khaki color only

L51 Land Girl, stable lad and 11 assorted animals, 13 pcs.

L52 Hurdles, 2 standing sheep; 2 feeding sheep; 1 collie dog, 1 farmer, 1 standing cow, 1 shire horse, 2 lying calves

L53 2 feeding sheep; 2 standing sheep, 2 lambs, 1 collie dog, 2 foals, 1 standing cow, 1 feeding cow, 2 lying calves, 2 geese

L101 2 geese; 2 lambs; 1 standing sheep; 1 farmer; 1 feeding sheep; 2 standing cows, 2 ducks, 2 lying calves, 1 farmer's wife, 1 foal, 1 shire horse, 2 feeding cows, 1 land girl, 1 stable lad, 2 pigs

L102 2 pigs; 2 standing sheep, 2 feeding sheep, 2 cobs; 4 lambs; 2 geese, 2 shire horses, 2 foals, 1 farmer, 1 land girl, 1 stable lad

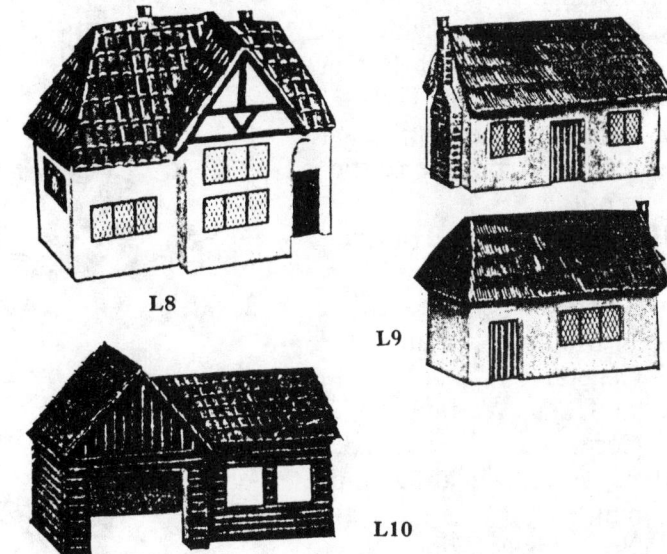

L8

L9

L10

565

BRITAINS PLASTICS

HERALD: These highly-regarded plastic figures were made in both Britain and Hong Kong. The former are more arrestingly colored, but the plastic is brittle.

Herald Romans & Trojans

4590 Roman Chariot (driver, 2 horses)	25.00
4594 Mounted Trojan General	8.00
4595 Trojan Warriors, 6 pieces	35.00
Price per individual figure in mint	5.00
7599 Trojan Warriors, 25 pieces, made in Britain . .	175.00
7599 Trojan Warriors, 25 pieces, made in Hong Kong	100.00
594 Mounted Trojan General	8.00
595 Warrior with Spear . . .	5.00
596 Warrior Defending with Shield	5.00
597 Warrior attacking with Sword	5.00
598. Archer	5.00
599. Warrior standing	5.00

Herald Knights (all made in Hong Kong)

4406. Knights, 6 pieces	18.00
4415 Standing Knights, 6 different	5.00
4420 Mounted Knights, 4 different	70.00
7404 Knights, 11 pieces . . .	70.00
7406 Knights, 14 pieces . . .	85.00
7409 Knights, 26 pieces . . .	150.00
Foot knights, per figure, mint	5.00
Mounted knights, per figure, mint	15.00

Herald Civil War & 7th Cavalry

H431 Confederate Officer, advancing	5.00
H432 Confederate Bugler . .	5.00
H433 Confederate Infantryman, advancing	5.00
H434 Confederate Infantryman, standing firing . .	5.00
H461 Federal Officer, advancing	5.00
H462 Federal Bugler	5.00
H463 Federal Infantryman, advancing	5.00

H594

H595

H596

H597

H598

Herald Trojans
Courtesy Bob Bard

H433 H433 H431

H434 H434 H432
Herald Civil War Photo by Gary J. Linden

H463 H463 H461

Herald Civil War Photo by Gary J. Linden

H464 Federal Infantryman, standing firing	5.00
7th Cavalry (made in Hong Kong) mounted, per mint figure	5.00
7th Cavalry foot figures, mint each	5.00

Herald Cowboys and Indians

H602 Cowboy, lassoing, foot, made in Britain, mint	4.00
H602 Cowboy, made in Hong Kong, mint	3.00
H603 Cowboy, kneeling firing, made in Britain, mint	4.00
H603 Cowboy, made in Hong Kong	3.00
H604 Cowboy, clubbing with rifle, foot, made in Britain, mint	4.00
H604 Cowboy, made in Hong Kong	3.00
H605 Cowboy, firing twin guns, made in Britain, mint	4.00
H605 Cowboy, made in Hong Kong	3.00

H602

H603

H604

H605

566

H620 Cowboy, throwing lasso, mounted, made in Britain, mint 6.00

H620 Cowboy, made in Hong Kong 5.00

H621 Cowboy, masked bandit, firing six-shooter, mounted, mint, made Britain 6.00

H621 Cowboy, made in Hong Kong 5.00

H502 Indian, with tomahawk, foot, made in Hong Kong 4.00

H503 Indian, firing rifle, foot, made in Hong Kong 4.00

H504 Indian, with bow and arrow, foot, made in Hong Kong 4.00

H505 Indian Chief, pointing, foot, made in Hong Kong 4.00

H506 Indian Chief, sitting . No Price Found

H507 Squaw, nursing Papoose 4.00

H508 Indian Chief, standing No Price Found

H509 Camp Fire . . . . No Price Found

H510 Totem Pole . . . . No Price Found

H511 Tepee (Wigwam) . . . . No Price Found

H520 Indian Chief with spear and shield, mounted, made in Hong Kong 6.00

H521 Indian Brave with bow and arrow, mounted, made in Hong Kong 6.00

Herald Gordon Highlanders

H100 Highlander officer, mtd. . . . .

H101 Highlander, at attention, made in Britain, mint 3.00

H101 Highlander made in Hong Kong 2.00

H102 Highlander, marching at the slope, made in Britain, mint 3.00

H102 Highlander, made in Hong Kong 2.00

H103 Officer with sword, marching, made in Britain, mint 3.00

H103 Officer, made in Hong Kong, mint 2.00

H104 Piper, marching, made in Britain, mint 3.00

H104 Piper, made in Hong Kong, mint 2.00

H502

H503

H504

H505

H520

H521

567

BRITAINS PLASTIC

H621

H620

Herald Cowboys & Indians
Courtesy Bob Bard

H105 Drummer with side drum, marching, made in Britain, mint 3.00

H105 Drummer, made in Hong Kong, mint 2.00

H106 Drummer with bass drum, marching, made in Britain, mint 3.00

H106 Drummer, made in Hong Kong, mint 2.00

H107 Drum Major, marching, made in Britain, mint 3.00

H107 Drum Major, made in Hong Kong, mint 2.00

Herald Black Watch

H120 Highlander officer, mounted 4.00

H122 Highlander, marching at the slope, made in Britain, mint 3.00

H122 Highlander, made in Hong Kong, mint 2.00

H123 Officer with sword, marching, made in Britain, mint 3.00

H123 Officer, made in Hong Kong, mint 2.00

H124 Piper, marching, made in Britain, mint 3.00

H124 Piper, made in Hong Kong, mint 2.00

H125 Drummer with side drum, marching, made in Britain, mint 3.00

H125 Drummer, made in Hong Kong, mint 3.00

H126 Drummer with bass drum, marching, made in Britain, mint 3.00

H126 Drummer, made in Hong Kong, mint 2.00

H127 Drum Major, marching, made in Britain, mint 3.00

H127 Drum Major, made in Hong Kong, mint 2.00

H101

H102
H122

H103
H123

H104
H124

H105
H125

H106
H126

H107
H127

BRITAINS PLASTIC

Herald British
Courtesy Bob Bard

H100
H120

H200

407 Pikeman

402

Herald Guards
H200 Officer, mtd.	4.00
H201 Guardsman, at attention at the slope, made in Britain, mint	3.00
H201 Guardsman, made in Hong Kong, mint	2.00
H202 Guardsman, marching at the slope, made in Britain, mint	3.00
H202 Guardsman, made in Hong Kong, mint	2.00
H203 Officer with sword, marching, made in Britain, mint	3.00
H203 Officer, made in Hong Kong, mint	2.00
H204 Guardsman, at ease, made in Britain, mint . . .	3.00
H204 Guardsman, made in Hong Kong, mint	2.00
H205 Guardsman, presenting arms, made in Britain, mint	3.00
H205 Guardsman, made in Hong Kong, mint	2.00
H206 Queen's Colour Bearer (Red Standard) marching, made in Britain, mint . . .	4.00
H206 Queen's Colour Bearer, made in Hong Kong, mint	3.00
H207 Regimental Colour Bearer (Blue Standard), marching, made in Britain, mint	4.00
H207 Regimental Colour Bearer, made in Hong Kong, mint	3.00

H201

H203

H206

H204   H205

Herald Roundheads
402 Mounted Officer, mint	35.00
407 Pikeman, foot, mint . . .	20.00
408 Trooper, foot, mint . . .	20.00

417 Trooper

418 Musketeer

Herald Roundheads and Cavaliers
Courtesy Bob Bard

412 Mounted Officer

Herald Cavaliers
412 Mounted Officer, mint	35.00
417 Trooper, foot, mint . . .	20.00
418 Musketeer, foot, mint .	20.00

Herald Farm Figures
2045 Shepherd, mint	4.00
2046 Labourer with rake, mint	4.00
2047 Labourer with hoe, mint	4.00
2048 Labourer with broom, mint	4.00
2049 Labourer with pitch fork, mint	4.00
2050 Farmer	4.00
2051 Farmer's Daughter . . .	4.00
2052 Landgirl	4.00
2053 Girl Milking	4.00
2054 Man with sack	4.00
2055 Rider for horse or tractor	4.00

2045 Shepherd

2046

2053 Girl milking

408 Trooper

2050 Farmer

2051 Farmer's Daughter

Herald Farm Figures
Courtesy Bob Bard

2052 Landgirl

H306   H307   H303

H305   H304
Herald Khaki Infantry   Photo by Gary J. Linden

Herald Khaki Infantry (in Battledress)

H301 Infantryman, at attention, made in Britain,
mint 6.00

H301 Infantryman, made in
Hong Kong, mint 4.00

H302 Infantryman, charg-
ing, made in Britain, mint   6.00

H302 Infantryman, made in
Hong Kong, mint 4.00

H303 Infantryman, kneeling
firing, made in Britain,
mint 6.00

H303 Infantryman, made in
Hong Kong, mint 4.00

H304 Infantryman, standing
firing, made in Britain,
mint 6.00

H304 Infantryman, made in
Hong Kong, mint 4.00

H305 Infantryman, throwing
grenade, made in Britain,
mint 6.00

H305 Infantryman, made in
Hong Kong, mint 4.00

H306 Officer with pistol, advancing, made in Britain,
mint 6.00

H306 Officer, made in Hong
Kong, mint 4.00

H307 Radio Operator
(Walkie Talkie), kneeling,
made in Britain, mint . . .   6.00

H307 Radio Operator, made
in Hong Kong, mint 4.00

H308 Infantryman with
fixed bayonet, attacking,
made in Britain, mint . . .   6.00

H301

H308

Herald Khaki Infantry
Courtesy Bob Bard

H308 Infantryman, made in
Hong Kong, mint 4.00

H309 Infantryman, falling
wounded, made in Britain,
mint 6.00

H309 Infantryman, made in
Hong Kong, mint 4.00

4307 Khaki Infantry,
howitzer, 5 men 35.00

4312 British Assault Craft,
boat, 2 figures 12.00

4315 Khaki Infantry, 6 dif-
ferent 40.00

4316 Khaki Infantry, 6 different, Hong Kong 25.00

7309 Khaki Infantry,
howitzer, 24 infantry, 2
sentry boxes 90.00

H309

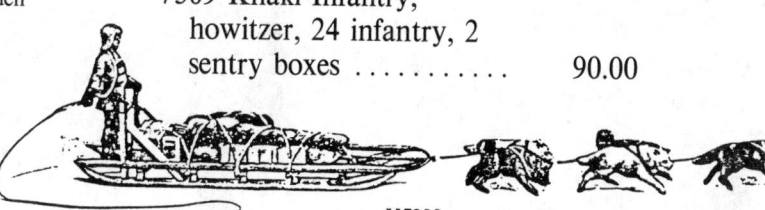

H5299

Herald Antarctic
Courtesy Bob Bard

Herald Antarctic

H5299 Sledging Team, mint   200.00

H1299 Polar Skier . . . .   No Price Found

H1299

Herald Sikh Infantry

401 Indian Infantryman
(Sikh) in Parade Uniform,
at attention . . . .   No Price Found

Herald British Life, Horse and Scots Guards

801 Life Guard Standard
Bearer, mounted, made in
Britain, mint 10.00

801 Life Guard made in
Hong Kong, mint 6.00

802 Life Guard Trumpeter,
mounted, made in Britain,
mint 10.00

802 Life Guard made in
Hong Kong, mint 6.00

803 Life Guard Trooper
with sword, mounted,
made in Britain, mint . . .   10.00

803 Life Guard made in
Hong Kong, mint 6.00

BRITAINS PLASTIC

H802–H902

H801–H901

H803–H903

804 Life Guard Standard
Bearer, dismounted, made
in Britain, mint 5.00
804 Life Guard, made in
Hong Kong, mint 3.00
805 Life Guard, Trumpeter,
dismounted, made in Bri-
tain, mint 5.00
805 Life Guard made in
Hong Kong, mint 3.00
806 Life Guard Trooper
with sword, dismounted,
made in Britain, mint . . .   5.00
806 Life Guard made in
Hong Kong, mint 3.00
901 Horse Guard Standard
Bearer, mounted, made in
Britain, mint 10.00
901 Horse Guard made in
Hong Kong, mint 6.00
902 Horse Guard
Trumpeter, mounted,
made in Britain, mint . . .   10.00
902 Horse Guard made in
Hong Kong, mint 6.00
903 Horse Guard Trooper
with sword, mounted,
made in Britain, mint . . .   10.00
903 Horse Guard made in
Hong Kong, mint 6.00
904 Horse Guard Standard
Bearer, dismounted, made
in Britain, mint 5.00
904 Horse Guard made in
Hong Kong, mint 3.00
905 Horse Guard
Trumpeter, dismounted,
made in Britain, mint . . .   5.00
905 Horse Guard made in
Hong Kong, mint 3.00

H804
H904

H805
H905

H806
H906

906 Horse Guard Trooper
with sword, dismounted,
made in Britain, mint . . .   5.00
906 Horse Guard made in
Hong Kong, mint 3.00
H903 Horse Guard Trooper
Mounted 20.00
4120 Mounted Scots Guard
Officer 15.00
4206 Scots Guards, 5 foot,
sentry box 50.00
4215 Scots Guards, 5 figures   42.00
Price per individual figure,
in mint 8.00
4806 Life Guards, 6 pieces .   35.00
Price per figure, mint, Bri-
tain 5.00
Price per figure, mint,
Hong Kong 3.00
4906 Horse Guards, 6 pieces   35.00
Price per figure, mint, Bri-
tain 5.00
Price per figure, mint,
Hong Kong 3.00
4815 Regimental Soldiers, 8
figures 45.00
Price per mint standing
figure, Britain 5.00
Price per mint standing
figure, Hong Kong 3.00

4820 Mounted Life Guards,
6 pieces, Britain 65.00
4820 Mounted Life Guards,
6 pieces, Hong Kong . . .   30.00
4920 Mounted Horse
Guards, 6 pieces, Britain   65.00
4920 Mounted Horse
Guards, 6 pieces, Hong
Kong 30.00
7209 Guards Set, 28 pieces,
24 foot, 1 mounted, 2
sentry boxes 120.00
7804 Horse and Life
Guards, 11 pieces 70.00
7806 Horse and Life
Guards, 14 pieces 14.00
7809 Horse and Life
Guards, 22 pieces 150.00

Herald Life and Horse Guards
Courtesy Bob Bard

SWOPPETS: These figures, with pieces that interlocked and could be interchanged with others in the series, were introduced by Herald in 1958.

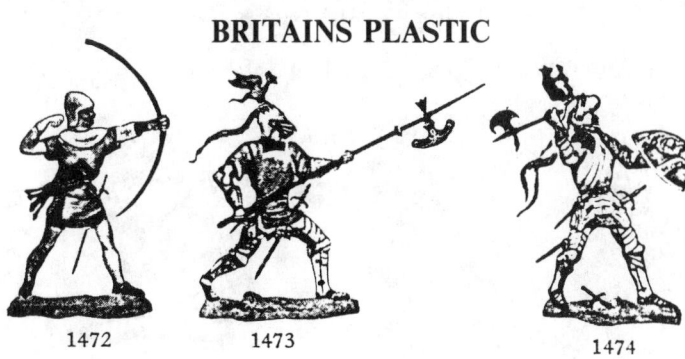

BRITAINS PLASTIC

1472   1473   1474

1450

1451

1452

1453

Swoppet Knights

1450 Mounted with Standard	35.00
1451 Mounted Charging with Lance	35.00
1452 Mounted Attacking with Sword	35.00
1453 Mounted Defending with Lance	35.00
1470 Foot Standing with Lance	15.00
1471 Foot Attacking with Sword	15.00
1472 Foot Standing Firing Longbow	15.00
1473 Foot Attacking with Pike	15.00
1474 Foot Attacking with Axe	15.00
1475 Foot Kneeling Firing Crossbow	15.00
7479 Set of all 6 foot	90.00
7481 3 mounted, 5 foot ...	180.00

Revolutionary War

7364 1776 British Infantry, per figure	No Price Found
7384 1776 Colonial Infantry, per figure	No Price Found

1470

1471

Civil War

420 Mounted Confederate Officer	40.00
421 Mounted Confederate Standard Bearer	40.00
422 Mounted Confederate Bugler	40.00
423 Mounted Confederate Trooper	40.00
425 Confederate Infantry Officer, foot	15.00
426 Confederate Infantry Standard Bearer	17.00
427 Confederate Infantryman Advancing	15.00
428 Confederate Standing Firing	15.00
429 Confederate Kneeling Firing	15.00
430 Confederate Prone Firing	15.00
450 Mounted Union Officer	40.00
451 Mounted Union Standard Bearer	40.00
452 Union Mounted Bugler	40.00
453 Mounted Union Trooper	40.00
455 Union Officer, foot ...	15.00
456 Union Standard Bearer, Infantry	16.00
457 Union Infantry Advancing	15.00
458 Union Infantry Standing Firing	15.00
459 Union Infantry Kneeling Firing	15.00
460 Union Infantry Prone Firing	15.00
4435 Confederate Gun Crew and Gun, 5 pieces	100.00
4465 Union Gun Crew and Gun, 5 pieces	100.00

Swoppet Knights
Courtesy Bob Bard

BRITAINS PLASTIC
Swoppet World War II British Infantry

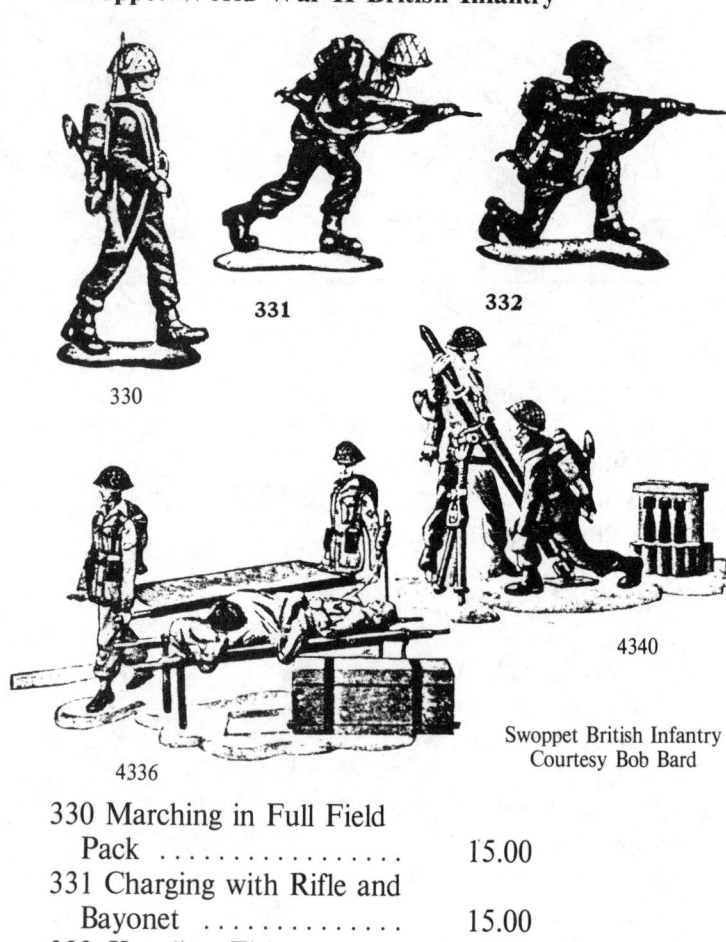

331

332

330

4336

4340

Swoppet British Infantry
Courtesy Bob Bard

330 Marching in Full Field
Pack 15.00
331 Charging with Rifle and
Bayonet 15.00
332 Kneeling Firing 8.00

4336 Stretcher Party, 6
pieces 175.00
4340 Mortar Team, 4 pieces 150.00

Swoppet Cowboys and Indians

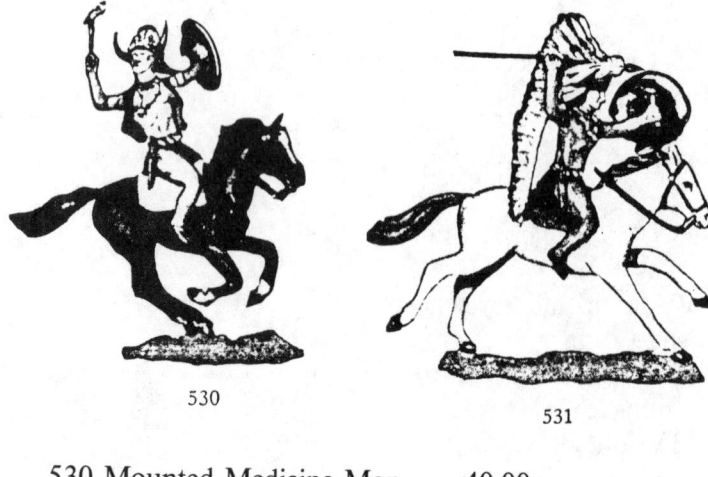

530

531

530 Mounted Medicine Man 40.00
531 Mounted Chief with
Spear 40.00
532 Mounted Brave with
Bow 40.00

534

535

533 Mounted Chief with
Dagger 40.00
534 Mounted Brave with
Bow and Arrow 40.00
535 Mounted Brave with
Tomahawk 40.00
550 Foot Medicine Man ... 15.00
551 Foot Chief with Spear . 15.00
552 Foot Brave Standing
Firing Bow 15.00
553 Foot Chief with Dagger . 15.00
554 Foot Brave Kneeling
Firing Bow 15.00
555 Foot Brave with
Tomahawk 15.00
630 Mounted Sheriff 40.00
631 Mounted Bank Robber . 40.00
632 Mounted Cowboy
Throwing Lasso 40.00
633 Mounted 2-Gun
Cowboy 40.00
634 Mounted Cowboy Fir-
ing Rifle 40.00
635 Mounted Wounded
Cowboy 40.00
636 Mounted Cowboy
Holding Lasso 40.00
637 Mounted Mexican on
Guard 40.00
638 Mounted Mexican
Resting 40.00
639 Mounted Cowboy
Knifefighter 40.00
640 Mounted Cowboy
Prisoner 40.00
641 Mounted Cowboy Fir-
ing Pistol 40.00
650 Foot Sheriff 15.00
651 Foot Bank Robber 15.00
652 Foot Cowboy Throwing
Lasso 15.00
653 Foot 2-Gun Cowboy .. 15.00

550

551

553

554

Swoppet Indians
Courtesy Bob Bard

572

630   631

634   635

650   651   652

Swoppet Cowboys
Courtesy Bob Bard

654 Foot Cowboy Firing Rifle	15.00
655 Foot Wounded Cowboy	15.00
656 Foot Cowboy Gunslinger	15.00
657 Foot Mexican on Guard	15.00
658 Foot Cowboy Resting .	15.00
659 Foot Cowboy Knifefighter	30.00
660 Foot Cowboy Tied to Tree	
661 Foot Cowboy Firing from behind keg	30.00

BRITAINS PLASTIC

DEETAIL: Introduced in 1971, Deetails were plastic, mounted on a metal base. Prices are for mint in the box or on the card. Individual prices for mint.

Contemporary British Troops

7250 Scots Guards, 6 different	25.00
Individual figures $4.00 each	
7256 Scots Guards, 6 different	25.00
Individual figures $4.00 each	

Civil War-7th Cavalry

7422 Confederate Forces, 3 mounted, 9 foot, accessory	50.00
7423 Confederate Patrol, Gatling Gun, 5 foot	50.00
7426 Confederate, foot, 7 figures	25.00
7427 Confederate, 6 foot, 2 accessories	35.00
7428 Confederate, 2 mounted, 3 foot	25.00
7439 Confederate Cavalry, 6 different	40.00
Individual figures $6.00 each	
7440 Confederates, foot, 6 different	26.00
Individual figures $4.00 each	
7449 Federal (Union) Cavalry, 6 different	40.00
Individual figures, $6.00 each	
7450 Federal (Union) foot, 6 different	26.00
Individual figures, $4.00 each	
7452 Federal (Union) Forces, 2 mounted, 3 foot, accessory	40.00
7456 Federal (Union), 3 mounted, 9 foot, 2 accessories	80.00
7457 Federal (Union), 6 foot, accessory	35.00
7462 Confederate and Federal Forces, 6 mounted, 12 foot, 2 accessories	135.00
7470 Confederate Gatling Gun	15.00

BRITAINS PLASTIC

7489 7th Cavalry mounted,
6 different 45.00
Individual figures $7.00 each
7490 7th Cavalry foot, six
different 35.00
Individual figures $5.00
each

Cowboys, Indians, Mexicans, Apaches
7519 Mounted Mexicans, 6
different 75.00
Individual figures, $12.00
each
7520 Mexicans, foot, 6 dif-
ferent 35.00
Individual figures $5.00 each
7539 Mounted Indians, 6
different 20.00
Individual figures, $3.00
each
7540 Foot Indians, 6 dif-
ferent 26.00
Individual figures $4.00 each
7547 Indians, 12 figures, 2
accessories 75.00
7549 Mounted Apaches, 6
different 70.00
Individual figures $10.00
each
7550 Foot Apaches, 6 dif-
ferent 65.00
Individual figures $10.00
each
7557 Apaches and Mex-
icans, 12 figures, 2 ac-
cessories 75.00
7639 Mounted Cowboys, 6
different 20.00
Individual figures $3.00 each
7640 Foot cowboys, 6
figures 70.00
7647 Cowboys, 12 figures, 2
accessories 85.00
7650 Foot Cowboys, 6 dif-
ferent 15.00
Individual figures $2.00 each
7660 Foot cowboys, 6
figures 70.00
7670 Foot cowboys, 6 dif-
ferent 55.00
Individual figures $8.00 each

Knights and Turks
7720 Knights, foot, Swoppet
type, 6 different 100.00
Individual figures $15.00 each

7729 Knights, mounted,
Swoppet type, 6 different 80.00
Individual figures $12.00
each
7730 Knights, foot, 6 dif-
ferent 35.00
Individual figures $5.00 each
7739 Knights mounted, 6
different 45.00
Individual figures $7.00 each
7740 Knights, foot, 6 dif-
ferent 35.00
Individual figures $5.00 each
7749 Turks mounted, 6 dif-
ferent 35.00
Individual figures $5.00 each
7750 Turks foot, 6 different 35.00
Individual figures $5.00 each
7760 Black Knights, foot, 6
different 35.00
Individual figures $5.00 each
7669 Black Knights,
mounted, 6 different 45.00
Individual figures $7.00 each

Foreign Legion and Arabs
7770 Foreign Legion Gatling
Gun, 2 figures, gun 24.00
Individual figures $8.00 each
7775 Foreign Legion and
Arabs, 2 mounted, 4 foot,
accessory 85.00
7779 Foreign Legion
Cavalry, 6 different 85.00
Individual figures $13.00
each
7780 Foreign Legion Infan-
try, 6 different 55.00
Individual figures, $8.00
each
7783 Foreign Legion Patrol,
5 figures, Gatling 70.00
7784 Foreign Legion, 6 foot,
all different, 2 accessories 70.00
7789 Mounted Arabs, 6 dif-
ferent 85.00
Individual figures $13 each
7790 Arabs, foot, 6 different 55.00
Individual figures $8.00 each
7794 Arabs, 6 pieces, 2 accessories 65.00
7797 Arabs, 3 mounted, 9
foot, 2 accessories 150.00
7799 Foreign Legion and
Arabs, 12 figures, 2 ac-
cessories 175.00

BRITAINS PLASTIC

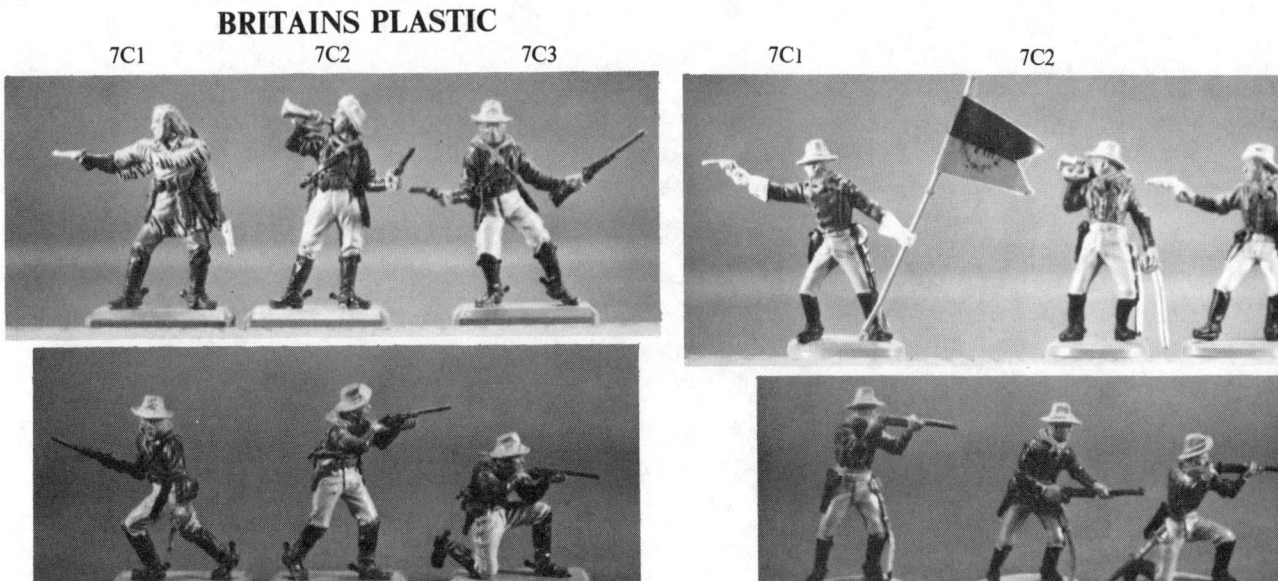

7C1   7C2   7C3

7C1   7C2   7C3

7C4   7C5   7C6

Britains Deetail 7th Cavalry
Photo by Gary J. Linden

7C4   7C5   7C6

Britains Herald 7th Cavalry figures
Photo by Gary J. Linden

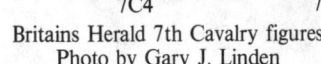

FL1   FL2   FL3   FL4-6

FL7   FL8   FL9   FL10

Britains **Deetail** Foreign Legionaires. There are several variations of FL7,
with the one shown probably the most striking.

AR7   AR8   AR9   AR10   AR11   AR12

Britains **Deetail** Arabs

575

AR1   AR2   AR3

AR4   AR5   AR6

Britains Deetail Arabs.

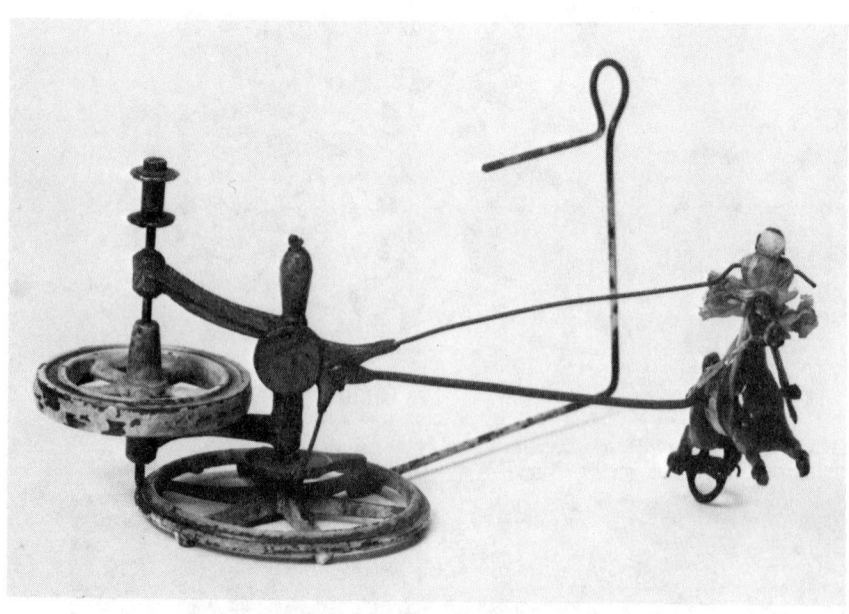

Early Britains Mechanical Equestrienne
Courtesy Christie's East

Unnumbered: Mandarin
Courtesy Phillips

Waterloo

7944 British Infantry, foot,
6 pieces, 5 different 75.00
Individual figures $12.00
each

7945 British Forces, 2
mounted, 4 foot, ac-
cessory 80.00
7947 British Forces, 3
mounted, 9 foot, 2 ac-
cessories 110.00
7949 British Cavalry, 6 different 100.00
Individual figures $15 each
7950 French Infantry, foot,
6 different 80.00
Individual figures, $12 each
7954 French Infantry, 6
foot, 2 accessories 70.00
7955 French, 2 mounted, 4
foot, accessory 75.00
7957 French, 3 mounted, 9
foot, 2 accessories 120.00
7959 French Cavalry, 6 different 100.00
Individual figures, $15 each
7960 British and French, 3
mounted, 9 foot, 2 ac-
cessories 110.00
7965 British and French, 6
pieces, accessory 45.00

World War II, American, British, German, Japanese

7333 German Mortar, 3
pieces 30.00
Individual figures, $9.00
each
7334 U.S. Recoilless Rifle, 3
pieces 25.00
Individual figures $6.00 each
7337 Japanese Recoilless Rifle, 3 pieces 50.00
Individual figures $15 each
7338 British Mortar, 3
pieces 50.00
Individual figures $15 each
7339 8th Army Vickers
Machine Gun, 3 figures . 60.00
Individual figures $17 each
7340 U.S. Infantry, 6 different pieces 25.00
Individual figures $3.00 each
7342 British Infantry, 6 different pieces 25.00
Individual figures $3.00 each

7346 British Infantry, 18
figures, 4 accessories 150.00
7347 U.S. Infantry, 18
figures, 4 accessories 50.00
7350 German Infantry, 6
different pieces 40.00
Individual figures $3.00 each
7356 Japanese Infantry, 18
figures, 4 trees 150.00
7380 German Infantry, 6
different pieces 40.00
Individual figures, $3.00
each
7386 German Infantry, 7
figures 45.00
7390 British 8th Army, 6
figures 40.00
Individual figures 8.00

Superdeetail:

6016 Ballet, 4 different 40.00
7850 Hospital, 6 different .. 75.00
7851 Doctor and Patient .. 20.00
7852 Nurse and Patient ... 20.00
7853 Nurse, Mother, Baby . 20.00
7854 Nursing Sister, Patient 20.00
7857 Hospital Ward 150.00
7858 Hospital X-Ray
Department 150.00
7859 Hospital Maternity
Unit 150.00

JOHILLCO

Johillcos are the equivalent of America's dimestore toy soldiers. Since John Hill & Co. seems not to have given a hoot about aesthetics or authenticity, anyone who collects its figures can relax and simply enjoy them for what they are; toy soldiers, plain and simple. There's much to be said for that.

Despite the official name of the company, its owner was not John Hill, but George Wood. A defector from Britains, Wood set up operations about 1900. In time his firm became Britains' greatest competitor.

Almost all of Johillco's soldiers were hollow-cast in a 54mm size (plastics began in 1956, according to John Garratt) and had a fairly diverse range, from ancient Romans, Ethiopians, Boers, Arabs and mahouts to the usual mix of British and American troops and American Indians and cowboys. Of greater interest to collectors is the fact that Johillcos were issued in far more positions than Britains, and though quality of design varied greatly, a large number had a dynamism and zest that compare to the U.S.'s Manoil. The fact that most were sold separately, rather than in sets, probably accounts in large part for their individuality.

Most Johillcos are marked. The earliest bear the imprint "J. Hill & Co.," the majority are inscribed "Johillco" and some can be found that read "J. Hill" or "Jo Hill" (the plastic figures, not listed here, were marked "Hillco/Made in England").

According to Shamus O.D. Wade, only about 80% of Johillco's output is known. New figures continually turn up, to the delight of those who find them and to considerably more mixed reactions from those who don't. Although the company was in business until 1960, the destruction of its Tottenham factory during the Second World War seems to have been a blow from which it never quite recovered. The following listing is, of course, incomplete, but is a representative sampling of the company's output and the prices its figures bring today. For space reasons, and the fact that they turn up rarely in sales lists, only a few sets have been listed. **Numbers in parentheses are Johillco's mold numbers.**

	G	VG	M		G	VG	M
(J1) 581 Roman Chariot, painted, and Charioteer, .	50.00	75.00	100.00	(J12) 688 Policeman, small .	No Price Found		
(J2) 755 Wild West Stage Coach, with driver and armed guard	50.00	75.00	100.00	(J13) 156 Policeman	11.00	16.00	22.00
				(J14) 591 Speed Cop, solo .	No Price Found		
				(J15) 592 Speed Cop, combination, sidecar	32.00	48.00	65.00
(J3) 681 Nurse, standing ...	6.00	9.00	12.00	(J16) 932 Mounted Policeman	6.00	9.00	12.00
(J4) 681 Nurse, kneeling ...	7.00	11.00	14.00	(J17) 934 Police Van	No Price Found		
(J4A) 686 Doctor in service dress	12.00	18.00	25.00	(J18) 935 Police Box	No Price Found		
(J5) 913 Stretcher with wounded soldier, two pieces	7.00	11.00	15.00	(J19) 4P Cavalry (Lifeguard)	8.00	12.00	16.00
				(J20) 4½" Khaki Cavalry ..	No Price Found		
				(J21) 5P Infantry	5.00	8.00	11.00
(J6) 914 Stretcher, wounded soldier, two stretcher bearers	20.00	30.00	40.00	(J22) 9A Charging Infantry, khaki	5.00	8.00	11.00
(J7) 920 Wounded soldier, red coat, on stretcher, stretcher bearers	No Price Found			(J23) 10A Firing Infantry, khaki	5.00	8.00	11.00
				(J24) 11AC Kneeling Highlanders	4.00	6.00	8.00
(J8) 922 Senior Medical Officer, Red Cross, full dress	8.00	12.00	16.00	(J25) 12AC Prone Highlanders	4.00	6.00	8.00
(J9) 923 Junior Medical Officer, Red Cross, full dress	9.00	13.00	18.00	(J26) 13B Bugler, khaki ...	5.00	8.00	10.00
(J10) 905 Policewoman	No Price Found			(J27) 13D Drummer, khaki .	4.00	6.00	8.00
(J11) 906 Policeman, running	No Price Found			(J28) 451C Officer, khaki ..	7.00	10.00	14.00
				(J29) 523C Firing Fusiliers .	No Price Found		

	G	VG	M		G	VG	M
(J30) 524C Firing Lincolnshire Regt	No Price Found			(J59) 267MC R.A.F. mechanic	6.00	9.00	12.00
(J31) 593AC Marching Infantry, khaki	4.00	6.00	8.00	(J60) 191A Small submarine	No Price Found		
(J32) 594C Marching Infantry, khaki	7.00	10.00	14.00	(J61) 644A Racehorse and jockey	No Price Found		
(J33) 611 Colour bearer, khaki	No Price Found			(J62) 11A Gordon Highlander, kneeling	No Price Found		
(J34) 614A Kneeling machine gunner, plain ..	7.00	11.00	14.00	(J63) 12A Argyle and Sutherland Highlander, prone	No Price Found		
(J35) 615A Prone machine gunner, plain	No Price Found			(J64) 16AP Black Watch ..	No Price Found		
(J36) 689C Marching Fusiliers	4.00	6.00	9.00	(J65) 523A Firing Fusilier .	No Price Found		
(J37) 933 Infantry, prone, khaki	5.00	8.00	11.00	(J66) 524A Firing Lincolnshire Regt.	No Price Found		
(J38) 909C Fusilier (Attention!)	No Price Found			(J67) 614P Kneeling machine gunner	No Price Found		
(J39) 912 Manchester Regt. kneeling	No Price Found			(J68) 615P Prone machine gunner	No Price Found		
(J40) 915C Liverpool Regt., slope arms	5.00	8.00	10.00	(J69) 689 Inniskilling Fusiliers, marching	No Price Found		
(J41) 20A Indian brave	4.00	6.00	8.00	(J70) 19A Cowboy with rifle	4.00	6.00	8.00
(J42) 20S Creeping Indian .	No Price Found			(J71) 10AC Indian, foot, creeping	5.00	8.00	10.00
(J43) 20T Indian Chief	No Price Found			(J72) 27A North American Brave	5.00	8.00	10.00
(J44) 27C North American Indian	No Price Found			(J73) 265A Crawling Indian	5.00	8.00	10.00
(J45) 265C Crawling Indian	No Price Found			(J74) 21A Kneeling sailor ..	No Price Found		
(J46) 590A Mounted Indian	10.00	15.00	20.00	(J75) 106A Zulu, charging .	4.00	6.00	8.00
(J47) 917 Indian firing rifle	4.00	6.00	8.00	(J76) 171L Knight in armour, foot	4.00	6.00	8.00
(J48) 917A Kneeling Indian firing bow and arrow ...	4.00	6.00	9.00	(J77) 6P Lifeguards	7.00	10.00	14.00
(J49) 19C Foot Cowboy with rifle	3.00	5.00	7.00	(J78) 33P Scots Greys	7.00	11.00	15.00
(J50) 530C Foot cowboy, with revolver	3.00	5.00	7.00	(J79) 215A Scots Guards, marching	4.00	6.00	8.00
(J51) 589A Mounted cowboy	10.00	15.00	20.00	(J80) 215P Piper	5.00	8.00	11.00
(J52) 916 Cowboy firing rifle	3.00	5.00	7.00	(J81) 243A Grenadier Guards, running	4.00	6.00	8.00
(J53) 916A Kneeling cowboy firing revolvers	3.00	4.00	6.00	(J82) 244A Black Watch, marching	3.00	5.00	7.00
(J54) 21C Kneeling sailor ..	3.00	5.00	7.00	(J83) 245A Manchester Regt., running	No Price Found		
(J55) 47C Standing Sailor ..	5.00	8.00	10.00	(J84) 535A Cavalry, service dress	8.00	12.00	16.00
(J56) 106C Charging Zulu .	4.00	6.00	8.00	(J85) 535B Cavalry, service dress with steel helmet ..	No Price Found		
(J57) 267PC R.A.F. pilot ..	6.00	9.00	12.00				
(J58) 267RC R.A.F. rigger .	6.00	9.00	12.00				

(J1) 581

(J2) 755

(J3-J6) 681, 682, 913, 914

(J7-J9)
923 920 921 922

905 (J10)

(J11) 906

(J13) 156

(J15) 592

(J17) 394

(J18) 935

(J14) 591

(J19) 4P

(J20) 4½

(J30) 524C

(J32) 594C

(J27) 13D

(J28) 451C

(J21) 5P

(J22) 9A

(J37) 933

(J34) 614A

(J38) 909C

(J39) 912

(J40) 915C

(J36) 689C

(J33) 611

(J26) 13B

(J35) 615A

(J47) 917

(J48) 917A

(J51) 589A

(J52) 916

(J41) 20A

(J46) 590A

(J53) 916A

(J61) 644

(J62) 11A

12A (J63)

(J70) 19A

(J71) 20AC

(J72) 27A

(J74) 21A

(J73) 265A

(J77) 6P

(J78) 33P

JOHILLCO

(J76) 171L   (J79) 215A   (J80) 215P   (J81) 243A   (J82) 244A   (J83) 245A   (J84) 535A   (J90) 908

(J91) 910   (J92) 911   (J93) 924   (J94) 925   (J95) 936   (J96) 937   (J97) 938   (J98) 939   (J99) 940

(J100) 941   (J101) 942   (J102) 943   (J103) 260P   (J104) 303L   (J105) 304L   (J106) 530A   (J107) 903C

(J108) 20C   (J109) 918   (J110) 904C   (J111) 931   (J112) 902C   (J113) 501A

(J114) 172L   (J115) 105A   (J116) 176P   (J117) 944   (J118) 945   (J119) 569A   (J120) 177P

(J121) 251L   (J122) 249L   (J123) 691   (J124) 677

(J125) 591D   (J126) 691   (J127) 40P   (J128) 692

J136

L to R: J94, J120, J116 Courtesy Wilbur Bittenbender

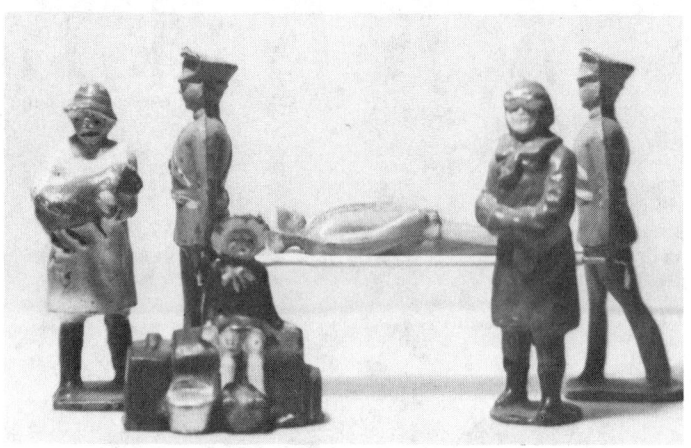

Front, L to R: 364, 239, J57. Rear, J6.

Courtesy Paul Stadinger

L to R: 68/1 Scots Grey, 907 Field Marshal, 691 Scots Greys Trumpeter, 6P Life Guard.
Courtesy Wilbur Bittenbender

Second from left, 403 Tramp, middle is 315 Miller
Courtesy Wilbur Bittenbender

At right is ¹J119 Roman Gladiator.
Courtesy Stad's

J177
Courtesy Stad's

J54   J55
J56   J75
J58   J57   J59
J141
J142
J143
J145B   J145   J145A
J154A   J154B
J155

	G	VG	M		G	VG	M
(J86) 614 Machine gunner, kneeling, service dress ...	No Price Found			(J99) 940 Infantry, marching, service uniform ..	4.00	6.00	8.00
(J87) 615 Machine gunner, prone, service dress	No Price Found			(J100) 941 Infantry, captain, service uniform	4.00	6.00	9.00
(J88) 691G Gilt trumpeter, mounted	No Price Found			(J101) 942 Infantry, gun crew, kneeling with gas mask, service uniform ...	7.00	11.00	14.00
(J89) 692G Gilt standard bearer, mounted	No Price Found			(J102) 943 Infantry, gun crew, standing with gas mask, service uniform ...	7.00	11.00	14.00
(J90) 908 Black Watch, charging	5.00	8.00	11.00	(J103) 260P Mounted Cowboy firing rifle	No Price Found		
(J91) 910 Middlesex Regt., present arms	No Price Found			(J104) 303L Cowboy walking with lasso	4.00	6.00	8.00
(J92) 911 Scots Guards, standard bearer	No Price Found			(J105) 304L Cowgirl with whip	4.00	6.00	8.00
(J93) 924 Hussar, mounted .	6.00	9.00	12.00	(J106) 530A Cowboy on foot firing pistol	5.00	8.00	11.00
(J94) 925 12th Lancers, Prince of Wales' Royal ..	7.00	11.00	14.00	(J107) 903C Mounted Cowboy, firing pistol ...	10.00	15.00	20.00
(J95) 936 Officer (Sussex Light Infantry) with field glasses	No Price Found			(J108) 20C Indian Chief with hatchet	4.00	6.00	8.00
(J96) 937 Royal Marines, captain	No Price Found			(J109) 918 Mountie with rifle	No Price Found		
(J97) 938 Royal Marines, marching	No Price Found			(J110) 904C Cowboy firing from behind horse	12.00	18.00	24.00
(J98) 939 Royal Marines, bugler	No Price Found						

	G	VG	M		G	VG	M
(J111) 931 Cowgirl on horse	6.00	9.00	12.00	(J135) 562A Cowboy on foot, firing rifle	No Price Found		
(J112) 902C Mounted Indian firing rifle	10.00	15.00	20.00	(J136) 565A Indian on foot, with tomahawk	5.00	8.00	10.00
(J113) 501A Mounted Indian with rifle	10.00	15.00	20.00	(J137) 575A Officers marching, khaki	No Price Found		
(J114) 172L Mounted knight w/lance	10.00	15.00	20.00	(J138) 575B Infantry marching, khaki	No Price Found		
(J115) 105A Jockey on galloping horse	No Price Found			(J139) 577A Crusaders	4.00	6.00	8.00
(J116) 176P Camel with rider	10.00	15.00	20.00	(J140) 26A Mounted cowboy, large, with revolver	No Price Found		
(J117) 944 Civil Air Guard, instructor	No Price Found			(J141) 695 Range rider with rifle and horse	7.00	11.00	15.00
(J118) 945 Civil Air Guard, pupil	No Price Found			(J142) 773 Royal Canadian Mounted policeman	11.00	16.00	22.00
(J119) 569A Roman Gladiator	4.00	6.00	9.00	(J143) 946 Texas Ranger ..	7.00	11.00	15.00
(J120) 177P Elephant with rider	9.00	13.00	18.00	(J144) 678 Bedouin Arab on camel	14.00	21.00	28.00
(J121) 251L Mounted Cowboy with lasso, large	8.00	12.00	16.00	(J145) 673 Mule carrying light mountain gun	11.00	16.00	22.00
(J122) 249L Cowboy riding backing broncho	12.00	18.00	24.00	(J145A) Mule carrying gun wheels	11.00	16.00	22.00
(J123) 691 Range Rider with revolver and horse	7.00	11.00	15.00	(J145B) Mule carrying ammo boxes	11.00	16.00	22.00
(J124) 677 Sudanese Camel Corps	17.00	26.00	35.00	**Regimental Bandsmen: Grenadier Guards**			
(J125) 591D Dispatch Rider, on motorcycle	18.00	27.00	36.00	(J146) 50/1 Drum Major ...	No Price Found		
(J126) 691 Scots Greys trumpeter	11.00	16.00	22.00	(J147) 50/2 Bass Drum	No Price Found		
(J127) 40P Mounted Arab .	11.00	16.00	22.00	(J148) 50/3 Side Drum	No Price Found		
(J128) 692 Scots Greys standard bearer	No Price Found			(J149) 50/4 Saxhorn	No Price Found		
(J129) 191A Large submarine	No Price Found			(J150) 50/5 Trumpet	No Price Found		
(J130) 261 Mounted Arab .	No Price Found			(J151) 50/6 Trombone	No Price Found		
(J131) 267B Airship	No Price Found			(J152) 50/7 Clarionet	No Price Found		
(J132) 31A Lancers, khaki, large	No Price Found			(J153) 50/8 Fife	No Price Found		
(J133) 213A Mounted Hussars, large	7.00	11.0	14.00	(J154) 50/9 Cymbals	No Price Found		
(J134) 907 Field Marshal, mounted	6.00	9.00	12.00	End Regimental Bandsmen			
The following five lines are larger than the ordinary lines being approximately 3½" in height.				(J154A) Ethiopian, slung rifle	6.00	9.00	12.00
				(J154B) Italian Colonial, slope arms	18.00	27.00	36.00
				(J155) Ethiopian Tribesman, standing at ready	5.00	8.00	10.00
				(J156-7) Ethiopian Regular Army stretcher bearers, stretcher and wounded man (Ethiopians in khaki uniform, bare-footed) ...	20.00	30.00	40.00

JOHILLCO

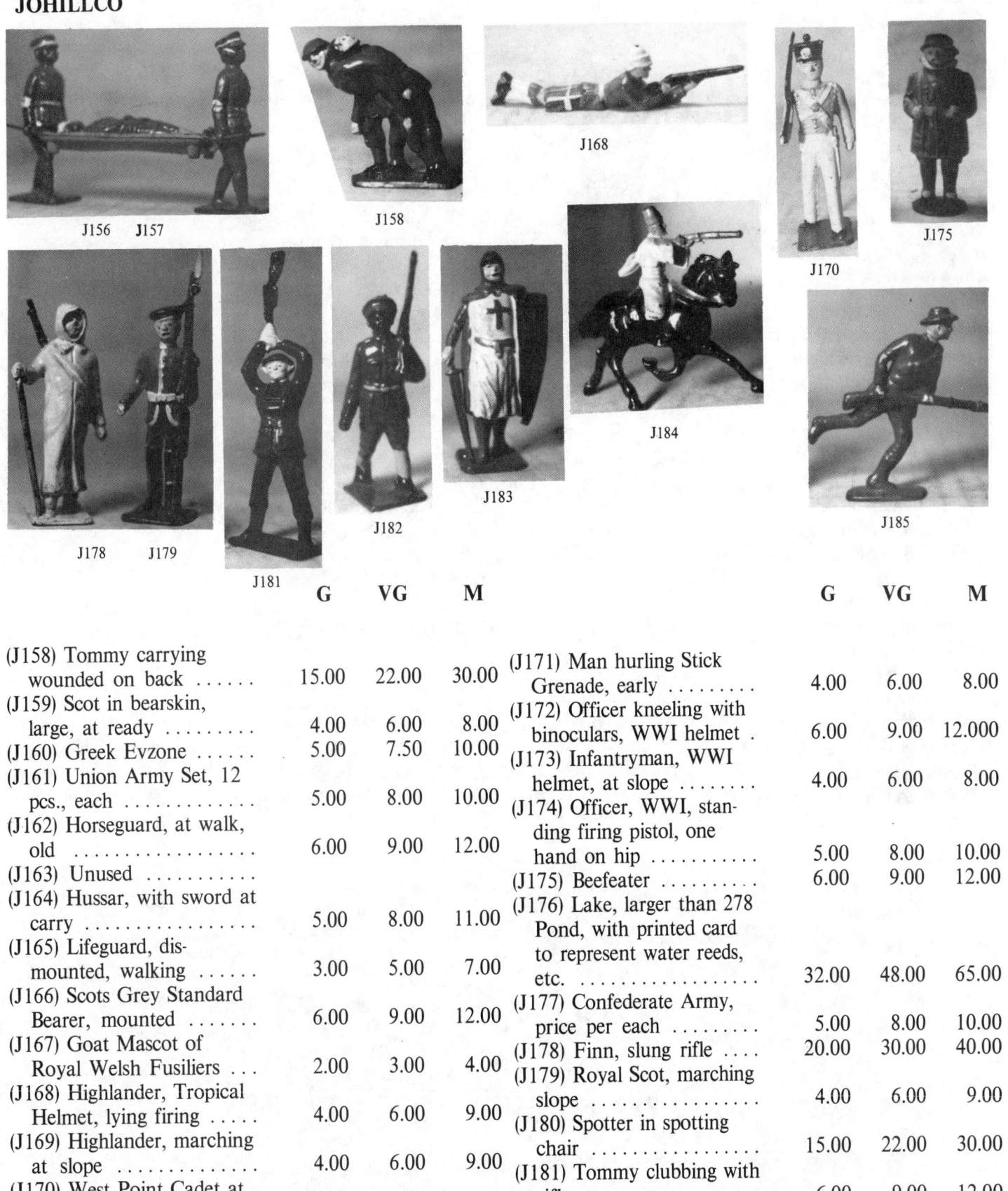

J156 J157

J158

J168

J170

J175

J178 J179

J181

J182

J183

J184

J185

	G	VG	M
(J158) Tommy carrying wounded on back	15.00	22.00	30.00
(J159) Scot in bearskin, large, at ready	4.00	6.00	8.00
(J160) Greek Evzone	5.00	7.50	10.00
(J161) Union Army Set, 12 pcs., each	5.00	8.00	10.00
(J162) Horseguard, at walk, old	6.00	9.00	12.00
(J163) Unused			
(J164) Hussar, with sword at carry	5.00	8.00	11.00
(J165) Lifeguard, dismounted, walking	3.00	5.00	7.00
(J166) Scots Grey Standard Bearer, mounted	6.00	9.00	12.00
(J167) Goat Mascot of Royal Welsh Fusiliers ...	2.00	3.00	4.00
(J168) Highlander, Tropical Helmet, lying firing	4.00	6.00	9.00
(J169) Highlander, marching at slope	4.00	6.00	9.00
(J170) West Point Cadet at slope	4.00	6.00	8.00

	G	VG	M
(J171) Man hurling Stick Grenade, early	4.00	6.00	8.00
(J172) Officer kneeling with binoculars, WWI helmet .	6.00	9.00	12.000
(J173) Infantryman, WWI helmet, at slope	4.00	6.00	8.00
(J174) Officer, WWI, standing firing pistol, one hand on hip	5.00	8.00	10.00
(J175) Beefeater	6.00	9.00	12.00
(J176) Lake, larger than 278 Pond, with printed card to represent water reeds, etc.	32.00	48.00	65.00
(J177) Confederate Army, price per each	5.00	8.00	10.00
(J178) Finn, slung rifle	20.00	30.00	40.00
(J179) Royal Scot, marching slope	4.00	6.00	9.00
(J180) Spotter in spotting chair	15.00	22.00	30.00
(J181) Tommy clubbing with rifle	6.00	9.00	12.00

JOHILLCO

J186

J188

J189   J190

	G	VG	M
(J182) Marching Ethiopian .	16.00	24.00	32.00
(J183) Crusader knight	4.00	6.00	8.00
(J184) Mounted Turk firing rifle	15.00	22.00	30.00
(J185) Australian charging slouch hat	11.00	16.00	22.00
(J186) Gordon Piper	5.00	8.00	11.00
(J187) Highlander kneeling firing, Glengarry cap	4.00	6.00	9.00
(J188) Guard winter dress . .	4.00	6.00	9.00
(J189) 12 Chief with peace pipe, movable arm	6.00	9.00	12.00
(J190) 9 Indian doing war dance, long headdress . . .	4.00	6.00	9.00
(J191) Totem Pole	6.00	9.00	12.00
(J192) Indian Kneeling firing	4.00	6.00	9.00
(J193) Highlander, tropical helmet, kneeling firing . .	4.00	6.00	9.00
(J194) Marching, Gas Mask bag (15)	5.00	8.00	10.00

	G	VG	M
(J195) Firing Bren Gun (S15)	5.00	8.00	10.00
(J196) Gun Crew Kneeling, no gas mask (S30)	5.00	8.00	10.00
(J197) At Ease (S36)			
(J198) Marching, ring hand (to hold weapon) (S39) . .	5.00	8.00	10.00
(J199) Kneeling Firing (S42)	5.00	8.00	10.00
(J200) Kneeling Infantry (S45)	5.00	8.00	10.00
(J201) Kneeling w/binoculars (S54)	5.00	8.00	10.00
(J202) Charging (56)	5.00	8.00	10.00
(J203) Standing Firing (57) .	5.00	8.00	10.00
(J204) U.S.A. Standing Firing (S554)	5.00	8.00	10.00
(J205) U.S.A. Advancing (S555)	5.00	8.00	10.00
(J206) U.S.A. Lying Firing .	5.00	8.00	10.00
(J207) U.S.A. Officer (S557)	5.00	8.00	10.00
(J208) U.S.A. Flagbearer (S558)	5.00	8.00	10.00
(J209) U.S.A. Marching (S560)	5.00	8.00	10.00
(J210) U.S.A. Standing Firing (S565)	5.00	8.00	10.00
(J211) U.S.A. Advancing (S566)	5.00	8.00	10.00
(J212) U.S.A. Flag Bearer (S569)	5.00	8.00	10.00
(J213) 7th Cavalry (S572) . .	5.00	8.00	10.00
(J214) U.S. Sailor Marching	5.00	8.00	10.00
(J215) U.S. Marine (S199) . .	5.00	8.00	10.00
(J216) Large Indian w/Lance	6.00	9.00	12.00

J194   J195   J33   J196   J102   J197   J198

J199   J200   J181   J158   J201   J202   J203

Unpainted castings courtesy Ken Wittenrich, West Falls Toy Co.

586

JOHILLCO

J204 J205 J206 J207 J208 J209

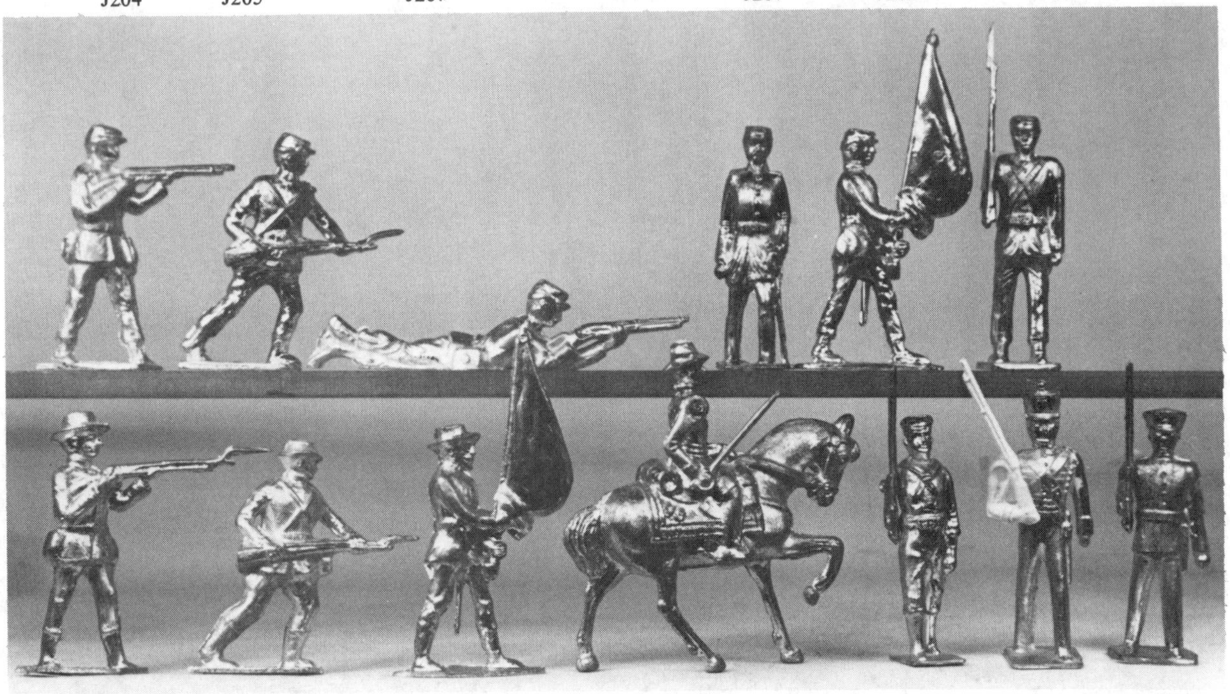

J210 J211 J212 J213 J214 J170 J215

Unpainted castings courtesy Ken Wittenrich, West Falls Toy Co.

J216 J136 J217 J218 J108

J189 J71 J43 J219 J220 J47 J192

Unpainted castings courtesy Ken Wittenrich, West Falls Toy Co.

	G	VG	M		G	VG	M
(J217) Indian - mounted ...	5.00	8.00	10.00	(J222) Cowboy to Ride			
(J218) Indian with Spear ...	4.00	6.00	9.00	Horse	3.00	4.00	5.00
(J219) Indian with scalp ...	6.00	9.00	12.00	(J223) Marshal (S304)	4.00	6.00	9.00
(J220) Chief with Blanket ..	4.00	6.00	9.00	(J224) Cowboy with Lasso .	5.00	8.00	10.00
(J221) Large Cowboy Firing				(J225) Loading Mortar -			
(S296)	6.00	9.00	12.00	WWII	5.00	8.00	10.00

587

J109   J221   J222   J223   J224

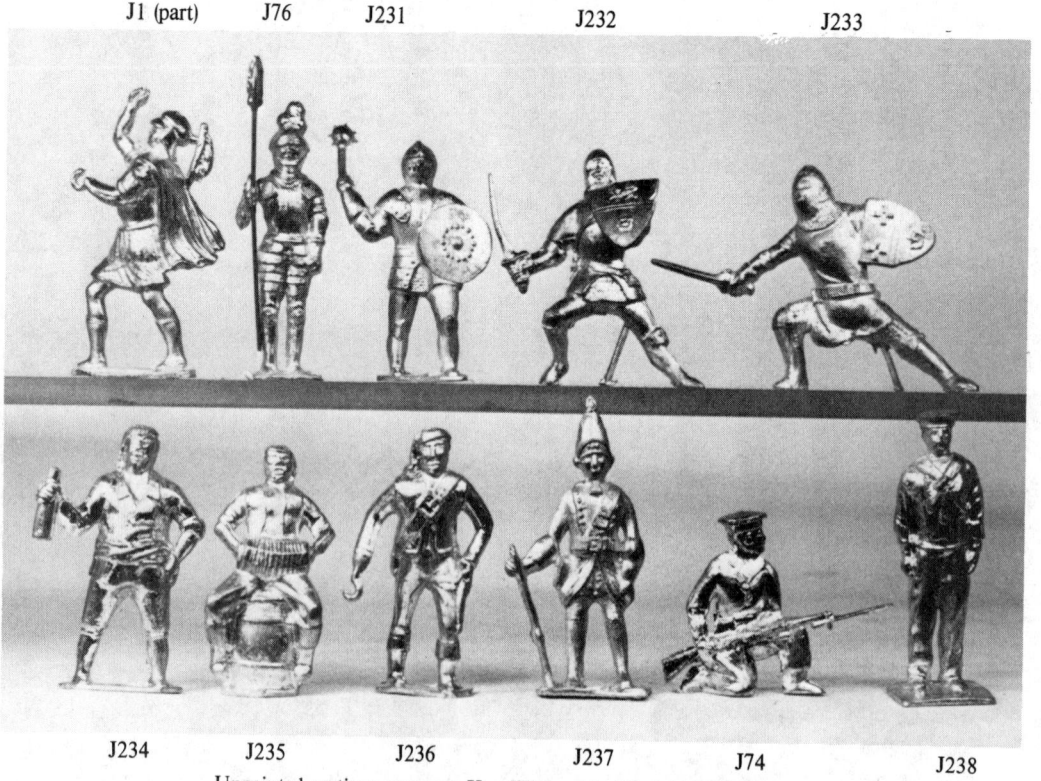

J225   J226   J227   J228   J229   J230

Unpainted castings courtesy Ken Wittenrich, West Falls Toy Co.

J1 (part)   J76   J231   J232   J233

J234   J235   J236   J237   J74   J238

Unpainted castings courtesy Ken Wittenrich, West Falls Toy Co.

JOHILLCO

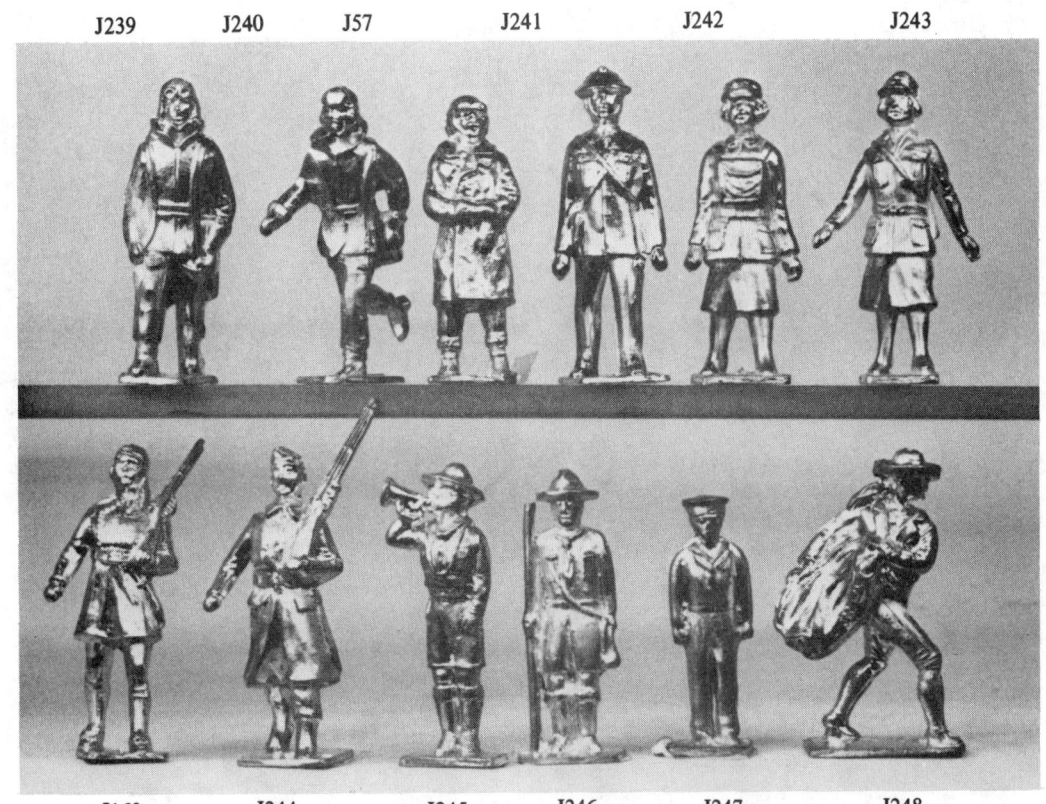

J239 J240 J57 J241 J242 J243

J160 J244 J245 J246 J247 J248

Unpainted castings courtesy Ken Wittenrich, West Falls Toy Co.

	G	VG	M		G	VG	M
(J226) Mine Sweeper - WWII	5.00	8.00	10.00	(J245) Boy Scout Blowing Bugle (S393)	4.00	6.00	8.00
(J227) Flamethrower - WWII	5.00	8.00	10.00	(J246) Boy Scout with Staff (S394)	4.00	6.00	8.00
(J228) Charging WWII	4.00	6.00	9.00	(J247) Sea Scout? (S394)	4.00	6.00	8.00
(J229) Kneeling Firing - WWII	4.00	6.00	9.00	(J248) Bullfighter (S372)	5.00	8.00	10.00
(J230) Crawling - WWII	4.00	6.00	9.00	(J249) Large Officer (S13)	6.00	9.00	12.00
(J231) Knight with Mace	4.00	6.00	9.00	(J250) Present Arms (S49)	5.00	8.00	10.00
(J232) Knight with Sword, no visor	5.00	8.00	10.00	(J251) Marching (S191)	5.00	8.00	10.00
(J233) Knight with Sword, visor	5.00	8.00	10.00	(J252) At Ready (S19)	5.00	8.00	10.00
(J234) Pirate with a Bottle	4.00	6.00	9.00	(J253) At Ready, larger (S20)	5.00	8.00	10.00
(J235) Pirate Playing Concertina	5.00	8.00	10.00	(J254) Guard Officer	5.00	8.00	10.00
(J236) Pirate with Hook	4.00	6.00	9.00	(J255) Guard Kneeling, Firing (S4)	5.00	8.00	10.00
(J237) Grenadier - 1750?	5.00	8.00	10.00	(J256) Guard Lying Firing	5.00	8.00	10.00
(J238) Sailor Standing (S196)	5.00	8.00	10.00	(J257) Boy Guard Side Drummer (S124)	5.00	8.00	10.00
(J239) Pilot Walking (S172)	5.00	8.00	10.00	(J258) Guard Bandsman, tuba (S128)	5.00	8.00	10.00
(J240) Pilot Running (S173)	5.00	8.00	10.00	(J259) Guard Side Drummer (S132)	5.00	8.00	10.00
(J241) Air Raid Warden (S237)	5.00	8.00	10.00	(J260) Guard Marching, Great Coat (S133)	5.00	8.00	10.00
(J242) W.A.A.F., arms straight down (S262)	5.00	8.00	10.00	(J261) Guard Officer in Great Coat (S135)	5.00	8.00	10.00
(J243) W.A.A.F., arms down at angle	5.00	8.00	10.00	(J262) Guard Marching (S147)	5.00	8.00	10.00
(J244) Marching in Greatcoat, cap (S359)	5.00	8.00	10.00	(J263) Royal Welch Fusiliers Goat Handler (S163)	6.00	9.00	12.00

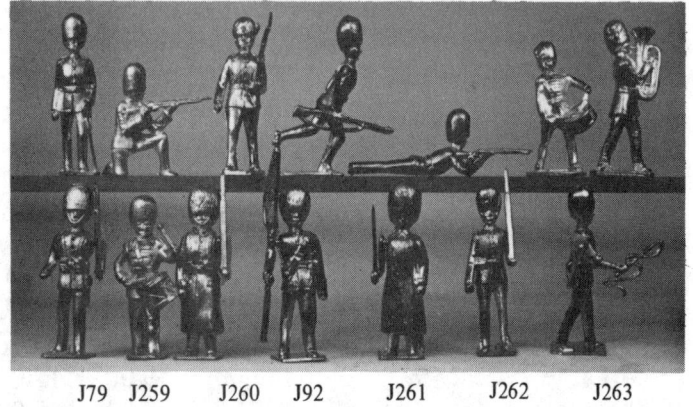

J249   J34   J250 J28 J251

J252   J253   J40   J30

Unpainted castings courtesy Ken Wittenrich, West Falls Toy Co.

J254 J255   J36 J81   J256   J257 J258

J79   J259   J260   J92   J261   J262   J263

Unpainted castings courtesy Ken Wittenrich, West Falls Toy Co.

J264   J265   J266   J267

J82   J268   J269   J270   J98   J271 J179 J193

Unpainted castings courtesy Ken Wittenrich, West Falls Toy Co.

J6 (part)   J7 (part)   J156-J157   J154B

J13   403   135G   135Q   760 (part)

Unpainted castings courtesy Ken Wittenrich, West Falls Toy Co.

	G	VG	M
(J264) Horse Guard	5.00	8.00	10.00
(J265) Large Life Guard (S76)	6.00	9.00	12.00
(J266) Life Guard (S70) . . .	5.00	8.00	10.00
(J267) Hussar (S83)	5.00	8.00	10.00
(J268) Black Watch Officer (S136)	5.00	8.00	10.00
(J269) Highland Officer (S137)	5.00	8.00	10.00
(J270) Highland Light Infantry	5.00	8.00	10.00
(J271) Royal Scots Officer .	5.00	8.00	10.00

Railway Staff, etc.	G	VG	M
134 Stollworks Machine . . .	7.00	11.00	15.00
135A Guard	5.00	8.00	10.00
135B Trolley Porter (for 135D)	3.00	5.00	7.00
135C Station Master	6.00	9.00	12.00
135D Small Luggage Trolley	3.00	5.00	7.00
135E Old Lady Passenger .	5.00	8.00	11.00
135F Old Gentleman Passenger	5.00	8.00	11.00
135G Lady with Bag	5.00	8.00	11.00
135H Young Man Passenger	5.00	8.00	11.00
135I Sitting Lady Passenger	5.00	8.00	11.00
135J Sitting Gentleman Passenger	6.00	9.00	12.00
135K Girl with Basket	6.00	9.00	12.00
135L Schoolboy Passenger .	6.00	9.00	12.00
135M Station Master's Dog	No Price Found		
135N Station Cat	No Price Found		

135A   135O   135P   135Q

134

135B 135D   135C 135E 135F 135G 135H

135I 135J
229 Seat.   220   221   228

232

	G	VG	M
157 Hedge	4.00	6.00	8.00
157A Small Oak Tree	6.00	9.00	12.00
157B Pine Tree.	6.00	9.00	13.00
223 Milk Churn	No Price Found		
246 Sign Post	6.00	9.00	12.00
246A Walnut Tree	7.00	11.00	14.00
246B Large Oak Tree	6.00	9.00	12.00
246C Fir Tree	7.00	11.00	14.00
246D Bulrushes	2.50	3.75	5.00
246E Flags or Iris	2.50	3.75	5.00
246F Foot-bridge	7.00	11.00	14.00
246G Gate and Gate Post .	7.00	11.00	14.00
246H Hurdle	2.00	3.00	4.00
246I Stile	7.00	11.00	14.00
246J Dove Cote	5.00	8.00	10.00
246K Pigeons or Doves, each	1.00	2.00	3.00
246L River Bridge	12.00	18.00	25.00
246M Farm Ladder	4.00	6.00	8.00
246MS Haystack Ladder . .	4.00	6.00	8.00
246N Pig Sty	8.00	12.00	16.00
246OW Sow Pig, white	2.00	3.00	4.00
246OB Sow Pig, black	2.00	3.00	4.00
246PW Piglets, white, assorted positions, each . .	2.00	3.00	4.00
246PB Piglets, black, assorted positions	2.00	3.00	4.00
246Q Pig Trough	2.00	3.00	4.00
246R Beehive	5.00	8.00	10.00
246T Fencing	4.00	6.00	8.00
254 Kennel and Bull-dog . . .	14.00	21.00	28.00
254D Bull-dog	5.00	8.00	10.00
258 Farmer	4.00	6.00	8.00
259 Huntsman	5.00	8.00	10.00
264 Steer	2.00	3.00	4.00
275 Rabbit Hutch	4.00	6.00	9.00
276 Large Rabbit	2.00	3.00	5.00
277 Small Rabbit	2.00	3.00	4.00
278 Pond, each in box	25.00	38.00	50.00
279 Swimming Duck	2.00	3.00	4.00
280 Walking Duck	2.00	3.00	4.00
281 Duckling	No Price Found		
282 Fowls, Cock	1.00	2.00	3.00
283 Fowls, Hen, feeding . . .	2.00	3.00	4.00
284 Chicks, walking	2.00	3.00	4.00
285 Chicks, running	No Price Found		
286 Fowls, Hen, sitting	2.00	3.00	4.00
287 Nest Box	4.00	6.00	8.00
288 Hen Coop	4.00	6.00	8.00
289 Corn Stack	12.00	18.00	24.00
290 Walking Sheep	1.00	2.00	3.00
291 Farm Labourer	4.00	6.00	8.00
292 Farm Barrow	4.00	6.00	8.00

	G	VG	M
135O Engine Driver	20.00	30.00	40.00
135P Stoker	6.00	9.00	12.00
135Q Milk Truck Porter . .	No Price Found		
135R Air Mail Pillar Box . .	No Price Found		
135S Tourist	No Price Found		
137 Fire Alarm	4.00	6.00	8.00
138 Electric Light Standard	7.00	11.00	14.00
139 Nestle's Chocolate Machine	7.00	11.00	14.00
140 Station Board	8.00	12.00	16.00
141 Weighing Machine	7.00	11.00	15.00
142 Ticket Machine	7.00	11.00	15.00
220 Lady Passenger	5.00	8.00	10.00
221 Gentleman Passenger . .	6.00	9.00	12.00
222 Milk Truck	5.00	7.50	10.00
223 Milk Churn with Lid, large	3.00	4.50	6.00
224 Brief Bag	5.00	7.50	10.00
225 Oval Trunk	4.00	6.00	8.00
226 Cabin Trunk	4.00	6.00	8.00
227 Rug and Umbrella	5.00	7.50	10.00
228 Porter carrying Suitcase	5.00	8.00	11.00
229 Station Seat	6.00	9.00	12.00
232 Pillar Box	No Price Found		
239 Child sitting on Luggage	12.00	18.00	25.00

JOHILLCO	G	VG	M
294 Weeping Willow	4.00	6.00	8.00
295 Small Bush	3.00	4.50	6.00
296 Medium Bush	4.00	6.00	9.00
297 Large Bush	9.00	13.00	18.00
298 Fern	3.00	4.50	6.00
299 Haystack	8.00	12.00	16.00
306 Milkmaid, sitting	4.00	6.00	9.00
307 Milking Cow	3.00	4.00	5.00
308 Feeding Cow	3.00	4.00	6.00
309 Feeding Horse	3.00	4.00	6.00
310 Cart-horse	3.00	4.00	6.00
311 Colt	2.00	3.00	5.00
312 Lamb	1.00	2.00	3.00
313 Calf	2.00	3.00	4.00
314 Windmill, each inbox ..	20.00	30.00	40.00
315 Miller	3.50	5.25	7.00
316 Miller's labourer carry- ing flour sack	6.00	9.00	12.00
317 Cornshucks	5.00	8.00	10.00
318 Milkmaid and Yoke with two pails	4.00	6.00	9.00
328 Village Blacksmith	3.00	4.50	6.00
329 Cornbin	8.00	12.00	16.00
330 Flour Sack, full	3.00	4.50	6.00
331 Flour Sack, partly filled	4.00	6.00	8.00
332 Sleeping Pig	No Price Found		
338 Forge	20.00	30.00	40.00
339 Anvil	2.00	3.00	4.00
340 Anvil Blacksmith......	6.00	9.00	12.00
341 Blacksmith Shoeing ...	10.00	15.00	20.00
342 Horse for shoeing	10.00	15.00	20.00
343 Owl	No Price Found		
344 Crow	2.00	3.00	4.00
345 Greenhouse, each in box	60.00	90.00	120.00
346 Lying Horse	3.00	4.50	6.00
347 Lying Colt	4.00	6.00	8.00
348 Traffic Sign, assorted directions	6.00	9.00	12.00
350 Signpost, two arms	5.00	8.00	10.00
351 Signpost, three arms ...	No Price Found		
352 Signpost, four arms ...	15.00	22.00	30.00
353 Well, with bucket	11.00	16.00	22.00
354 Pump	7.00	11.00	15.00
355 Cattle Drinking Rack ..	3.00	4.50	6.00
356 Gardener (for 357)	4.00	6.00	8.00
357 Gardener's Barrow	6.00	9.00	12.00
358 Flowerpots with plants	No Price Found		
359 Open Dovecote	6.00	9.00	12.00
360 Miller's Labourer (for 361	No Price Found		
361 Miller's Barrow ·······	No Price Found		
364 Shepherd and Lamb ...	5.00	8.00	11.00
365 Milking Stool	2.00	3.00	5.00
366 Village Bride	4.00	6.00	9.00

592

JOHILLCO

600A

600B

600

601D

600D

600Q

600O

600X

601K

601H

601O

	G	VG	M
389 Cattle Float, Horse and Show Cow, each in box ...	No Price Found		
390 Golden Eagle	No Price Found		
391 Farmer's Collie Dog ...	4.00	6.00	8.00
392 Farm Sack Trolley	No Price Found		
393 Corn Truck	7.00	11.00	14.00
394 Birds - Robin, Green-finch, Chaffinch, etc.	2.50	3.75	5.00
395 Fox Terrier	No Price Found		
396 Farm Cat	4.00	6.00	9.00
397 Fox and Duck	No Price Found		
398 Garden Seat	4.00	6.00	9.00
399 Farmer's Daughter	No Price Found		
400 "Near London" Milestone	7.00	11.00	15.00
401 Country Milestone	6.00	9.00	12.00
402 Lying Sheep	2.00	3.00	4.00
403 Tramp	6.00	9.00	12.00
404 Horse Float and Horse, each in box	No Price Found		
405 Horse Float, Horse and Show Horse, each in box ..	No Price Found		
407 Running Fox	4.50	6.75	9.00
410 Milk Churn and Lid ...	3.00	4.50	6.00
411 Field Hurdle	2.00	3.00	4.00
412 Level Crossing Sign ...	No Price Found		
413 Covered Country Seat .	11.00	16.00	22.00
414 Punt and Child	15.00	22.00	30.00
415 Sitting Child	6.00	9.00	12.00
416 Cattle Drover	4.50	6.75	9.00
417 Tennis Players (male and female), assorted positions	No Price Found		
425 Hare	No Price Found		
500A Shire Horse	6.00	9.00	12.00
500B Lying Cow	2.00	3.00	5.00
500C Lying Calf	2.00	3.00	5.00
500D Standing Calf	2.00	3.00	5.00
500E Feeding Sheep	2.00	3.00	4.00
500F English Bull	2.00	3.00	4.00
500G Swan.............	3.00	4.50	6.00
500H Frog	4.00	6.00	9.00
500J Witch	No Price Found		
500K Witch's Fire	No Price Found		
500L Witch's Cauldron....	12.00	18.00	25.00
500M Log	6.00	9.00	12.00
500N Goat	2.00	3.00	4.00
500O Turkey............	3.00	4.00	5.00
500P Sitting Pig	No Price Found		
500Q Donkey	2.00	3.00	4.00

	G	VG	M
367 Village Bridegroom ...	No Price Found		
368 Village Parson	6.00	9.00	13.00
369 Village Curate	6.00	9.00	13.00
370 Village Bridesmaid	5.00	8.00	10.00
3715 Dairymaid, sitting on stool	5.00	8.00	10.00
372 Shepherd's Dog, lying .	3.00	4.00	6.00
373 Squirrel, sitting	No Price Found		
3745 Farmer's Wife, sitting on stool	6.00	9.00	12.00
3755 Aged Villager, sitting on stool	6.00	9.00	12.00
376 Farmhouse steps	5.00	8.00	10.00
377 Punt	6.00	9.00	12.00
379 Summerhouse, large ...	60.00	90.00	120.00
380 Summerhouse, small ...	45.00	68.00	90.00
381 Summerhouse table ...	6.00	9.00	12.00
383 Golfer	12.00	18.00	25.00
384 Tennis Player, male or female, each	12.00	18.00	24.00
385 Innkeeper	10.00	15.00	20.00
386 Child to ride Carthorse	10.00	15.00	20.00
387 Running Pig	3.00	4.00	5.00
388 Cattle Float and Horse, each in box	No Price Found		

JOHILLCO

	G	VG	M		G	VG	M
500R Mule	3.00	4.00	6.00	600U Hippotamus	No Price Found		
500S Standing Horse	3.00	4.50	6.00	600VG Bear Cub, Grizzly	6.00	9.00	12.00
500T Gander	2.00	3.00	4.00	600VP Bear Cub, Polar	No Price Found		
500U Goose	2.00	3.00	4.00	600W Penguin	2.00	3.00	4.00
500V Black Swan	No Price Found			600X Rhinoceros	No Price Found		
919 Thatched Cottage	No Price Found			600Y Pelican	3.00	4.50	6.00
600 Ostrich	6.00	9.00	12.00	600Z Kneeling Camel	No Price Found		
600A Lion	8.00	12.00	16.00	601A Giant Tortoise	No Price Found		
600B Tiger	8.00	12.00	16.00	601BG Bear Sitting, Grizzly	3.00	5.00	7.00
600C Chimpanzee	5.00	7.50	10.00	601BP Bear Sitting, Polar	No Price Found		
600D Bison	No Price Found			601C Stag	4.00	6.00	8.00
600E Seal	No Price Found			601D Kangaroo	8.00	12.00	16.00
600F Small Frog	No Price Found			601E Baby Kangaroo	No Price Found		
600G Large Frog	5.00	8.00	10.00	601F Gander	No Price Found		
600H Tortoise	6.00	9.00	12.00	601G Goose	No Price Found		
600I Squirrel	No Price Found			601H Otter	No Price Found		
600J Lying Rat	No Price Found			601J Walrus	No Price Found		
600K Sitting Rat	No Price Found			601K Flamingo	No Price Found		
600L Sitting Rabbit	No Price Found			601L Lizard	No Price Found		
600M Eagle	No Price Found			601M Stork	No Price Found		
600N Polar Bear	6.00	9.00	12.00	601N Black Swan	No Price Found		
600O Giraffe	No Price Found			601P Panda, Sitting	No Price Found		
600P Grizzly Bear	4.00	6.00	8.00	601Q Panda, lying	No Price Found		
600Q Elephant	No Price Found			601R Panda, sitting and Chair	No Price Found		
600R Camel	6.00	9.00	12.00				
600S Alligator	7.00	11.00	15.00	760 (set) Lamp post with ladder & cleaning man	50.00	75.00	100.00
600T Leopard	5.00	8.00	10.00				

TIMPO   (TOY IMPORTERS CO.)

Timpo, also known as Model Toys Ltd., is an English company that emerged after World War II, and is probably the best of the post-War British companies. Its World War II G.I.'s are widely respected, and the company is also given high marks for its "age of chivalry" figures and cowboys and Indians. John Garratt's *The World Encyclopaedia of Model Soldiers* states that the company turned from hollowcast alloy to plastic in 1956. Timpo's plastic pieces have been variable, some quite well-modeled, others not so. Additionally, some of its plastic figures sold about 1958 are prone to fatigue; they tend to break as age catches up with them. In 1991, Toyway of Letchworth, Hertfordshire, England, began producing unpainted Timpo plastic figures from the original molds.

The following list of lead soldiers is not complete, but includes most of the salient pieces and samples of the others.

Timpo G.I.'s in action.
Photo and diorama by Terry Sells.

U.S. INFANTRY (G.I.'s)

	G	VG	M		G	VG	M
914 Boxed set. Officer with field glasses, 2 machine gunners, 3-piece mortar team	35.00	52.00	75.00	9009 Officer, crouching with pistol	8.00	12.00	16.00
9000 At ease	8.00	12.00	16.00	9010 On Guard, rifle across waist	9.00	13.00	18.00
9000B. As above, black soldier	16.00	24.00	32.00	9010B As above, painted as black soldier	17.00	25.00	34.00
9001 Marching, carrying satchel	8.00	12.00	16.00	9011 Standing Firing	8.00	12.00	16.00
9001B as above, black soldier	16.00	24.00	32.00	9011B As above, painted as black soldier	16.00	24.00	32.00
9002 Observer, with binoculars	8.00	12.00	16.00	9012 Mortar Unit, 3 pcs.	15.00	22.00	30.00
9003 Mine Detector	8.00	12.00	16.00	9013 G.I. Charging, leaning forward	9.00	13.00	18.00
9004 Crawling with Rifle	8.00	12.00	16.00	9014 Grenade Thrower	9.00	13.00	18.00
9005 Officer with Map	6.00	9.00	13.00	9015 Tommy Gunner	9.00	13.00	18.00
9006 Officer kneeling with Field Phone	7.00	11.00	14.00	9016 Bazooka	9.00	13.00	18.00
9007 Dispatch Rider, removable rider on motorcycle	20.00	30.00	40.00	9017 Seated Machine Gunner	9.00	13.00	18.00
				9018 Kneeling Firing	9.00	13.00	18.00
				9019 Lying Firing	7.00	11.00	14.00
				9020 Ceremonial Marching	8.00	12.00	17.00
				9021 Ceremonial Flagbearer	12.00	18.00	24.00
9008 Walkie Talkie, with wire antenna	8.00	12.00	16.00	9022 Ceremonial Officer	9.00	13.00	18.00
				9023 G.I. washing clothes in bucket	9.00	13.00	18.00

595

9001   9001   9001   9001   9011   9002

Photo by Terry Sells   9007   9006   9005   9012
                                                        Photo by Terry Sells

9025   9001B   9010B   9000B
                        Courtesy K. Warren Mitchell

9026   9025   9023   9008
Photo by Terry Sells

	G	VG	M
9024 Set. Stretcher Unit; 2 bearers and stretcher with wounded man	20.00	30.00	40.00
9025 Wounded Walking ...	9.00	13.00	18.00
9026 Eating, kneeling with sandwich and cup	9.00	13.00	18.00
9027 Sailor, walking	5.00	8.00	10.00
9028 Sailor with Telescope .	6.00	9.00	12.00
9029 Sailor on Guard	5.00	8.00	10.00
9030 Naval Officer	9.00	13.00	18.00
9032 Military Police	6.00	9.00	12.00
No Number. Doctor in cap from CU 74 Casualty Station	No Price Found		
No Number. Bareheaded doctor from CU 72 First Aid Post	No Price Found		

WEST POINT CADETS

	G	VG	M
7000 Drum Major	9.00	13.00	18.00
7001 Fifer	9.00	13.00	18.00
7002 Side Drummer	9.00	13.00	18.00
7003 Cymbal player	9.00	13.00	18.00
7004 Bugler	9.00	13.00	18.00
7005 Trumpeter	9.00	13.00	18.00
7006 Trombonist	9.00	13.00	18.00
7007 Tuba Player	9.00	13.00	18.00
7008 Bass Drummer	9.00	13.00	18.00
7009 Flag Bearer	No Price Found		
7010 Officer marching with sword	9.00	13.00	18.00
7011 Present Arms	9.00	13.00	18.00
7012 Marching, at slope ...	9.00	13.00	18.00

7017   7004   7013
Courtesy Stad's

	G	VG	M
7013 At ease	9.00	13.00	18.00
7014 Standing Firing	9.00	13.00	18.00
7015 Firing Kneeling......	9.00	13.00	18.00
7016 Officer Mounted	15.00	22.00	30.00
7017 Officer Walking	9.00	13.00	18.00
7018 Cadet Saluting	9.00	13.00	18.00
7019 Officer at ease, hands behind back	9.00	13.00	18.00

HOPALONG CASSIDY

	G	VG	M
2100 Hopalong, standing ..	No Price Found		
2101 Hopalong, Fighting (bareheaded)	10.00	15.00	20.00
2102 Lucky, Standing	6.00	9.00	13.00
2103 California, Standing ..	No Price Found		
2104 Hopalong, Mounted ..	No Price Found		
2105 Lucky, Mounted	7.00	11.00	15.00
2106 California, Mounted ..	No Price Found		

COWBOYS AND INDIANS

	G	VG	M
WW 2000 Mounted Cowboy, bandit with 2 drawn guns	8.00	12.00	16.00

Timpo knight, skindiver, Indian maiden, cowboy bandit, clown. Courtesy Wilbur Bittenbender

	G	VG	M
WW 2001 Mounted Cowboy, rifle on back ...	8.00	12.00	16.00
WW 2002 Buffalo Bill on horse	12.00	18.00	25.00
WW 2003 Mounted Sheriff (with whip)	8.00	12.00	16.00
WW 2004 Cowboy on Galloping Horse with lasso (string)..........	9.00	13.00	18.00
WW 2005 Mounted Cowboy, hands bound and gagged	8.00	12.00	16.00
WW 2006 Mounted Cowboy, hat in hand, wiping brow	8.00	12.00	16.00
WW 2007 Mounted Cowboy with Lasso, rearing horse, plus wild horse to lasso ..	15.00	22.00	30.00
WW 2008 Mounted Cowboy Surrendering	8.00	12.00	16.00
WW 2009 Cowboy, Mounted, Wounded, clubbing with rifle	8.00	12.00	16.00
WW 2010 Mounted Indian with Shield, pointing	8.00	12.00	16.00
WW 2011 Mounted Cowboy firing rifle down and to side	8.00	12.00	16.00

TIMPO

	G	VG	M
WW 2012 Cowboy tied to tree (two pieces)	12.00	18.00	24.00
WW 2013 Mounted Indian with Bow	8.00	12.00	16.00
WW 2014 Mounted Indian with Spear	9.00	13.00	18.00
WW 2015 Indian with Bow, standing	4.00	6.00	8.00
WW 2016 Indian with Bow, kneeling	4.00	6.00	8.00
WW 2017 Campfire Scene, cowboys with instruments, etc	17.00	25.00	35.00
WW 2017 Cowboy sitting with accordion	4.00	6.00	9.00
WW 2017 Cowboy with guitar	4.00	6.00	9.00
WW 2018 Indian crawling, hand shielding eyes	4.00	6.00	8.00
WW 2019 Indian running with tomahawk	4.00	6.00	9.00
WW 2019 Indian running with War Club (only came in sets)	5.00	8.00	11.00
WW 2020 Canadian Mounted Police	No Price Found		
2021 Indian large Tom Tom	5.00	8.00	10.00

	G	VG	M
2022 Indian small Tom Tom	5.00	8.00	10.00
2023 Indian Walking with upraised tomahawk	5.00	8.00	10.00
2024 Indian with Rifle	No Price Found		
2025 Chief Standing	No Price Found		
2026 Chief Sitting	5.00	8.00	11.00
2027 Sheriff Standing	5.00	8.00	11.00
2028 Timpo Tim	4.00	6.00	9.00
2029 Slim	4.00	6.00	9.00
2030 Bandit Right (pistol in right hand)	5.00	8.00	10.00
2031 Bandit Left (pistol in left hand)	4.00	6.00	8.00
2032 U.S. Mail (bandit with satchel)	7.00	11.00	14.00
2033 Squaw, standing	5.00	8.00	11.00
2034 Cowboy tied to Tree Trunk	No Price Found		

2027   2032   2028
Photo by Gary J. Linden

Timpo Foreign Legionaires and Arabs. All but the mounted Arab at bottom right were made circa 1958 in a plastic that becomes fragile with time (note the nearly broken-off rifle and sword at top left). The bottom figure at right, sold in the 1970s, is of a better grade of plastic, but isn't as well sculpted. Arabs on camels worth $20 mint - Foot figures $9 in mint.

TIMPO	G	VG	M
"IVANHOE" SERIES			
KN55 Ivanhoe, mounted ..	37.00	56.00	75.00
KN56 Brian de Bois			
Guilbert, mounted	17.00	25.00	35.00
KN57 Hugh de Bracy,			
mounted	17.00	25.00	35.00
KN58 Front de Boeuf,			
mounted	17.00	25.00	35.00
KN59 Philip de Malvoisin,			
mounted	17.00	25.00	35.00
KN60 Ralph de Vipont,			
mounted	17.00	25.00	35.00
KN61 Crusader, mounted ..	20.00	30.00	40.00
MEDIEVAL (MGM's "Quentin Durward")			
HF501 Quentin Durward,			
mounted, bareheaded ...	22.00	33.00	45.00
HF502 Duke's Guard,			
mounted	22.00	33.00	45.00
HF503 Duke's Guard stand-			
ing	15.00	22.00	30.00
HF504 Philip de Creville,			
mtd.	22.00	33.00	45.00
HF508 Lanzknecht with			
Crossbow, real plume,			
standing	15.00	22.00	30.00
HF510 Royal Guard, stand-			
ing	15.00	22.00	30.00
MEDIEVAL ("Knights of the Round Table")			
1 Sir Lancelot, mtd.	15.00	22.00	30.00
2 Sir Percival, mtd.	15.00	22.00	30.00
3 Sir Gawaine	15.00	22.00	30.00
Timpo Miscellaneous			
Arctic Set, boxed 15 pcs. ..	50.00	75.00	100.00

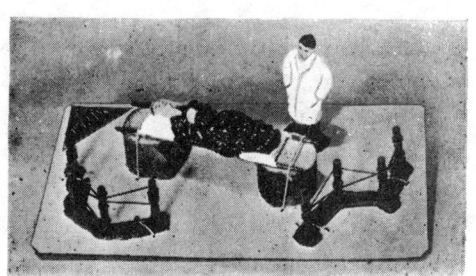

CU72 First Aid Post

CU 74 Casualty Station

Timpo Arctic Set
Courtesy K. Warren Mitchell

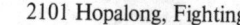

2100 Hopalong, Standing   2101 Hopalong, Fighting   2102 Lucky, Standing   2103 California, Standing

2104 Hopalong, Mounted   2105 Lucky, Mounted   2106 California, Mounted

TA1   TA2   TA3   TA4   TA5   TA6

Timpo plastic swoppet Arabs. Value $10 each foot, $15 mounted.
Photo by Gary J. Linden

N1   N2   N3

Timpo 54mm soft plastic Napoleonic figures. Value $6 each in mint.
Photo by Gary J. Linden

C1   C2

Timpo 54mm soft plastic Cossacks. Value $10 each in mint.
Photo by Gary J. Linden

CRESCENT

According to Garratt's "Encyclopaedia," Crescent began in 1921 with its cut-off date not known. It made both hollowcast lead soldiers and plastic figures. Again according to Garratt, the company began producing military figures in 1930 and moved into plastics in 1956. They were in business through at least 1975. Following are some representative prices in today's market. According to Andrew Rose's "Toy Soldiers", Crescent was located in Tottenham in North London, and was "operating on the fringes of the toy and novelty market since 1925". Crescent bought most of Reka's molds in 1930, and seems to have bought many or all of its other molds from other companies.

	G	VG	M		G	VG	M
(CR1) Knight with halberd, standing	4.00	6.00	8.00	(CR26A) Milkmaid carrying buckets	3.00	5.00	7.00
(CR2) Knight swinging sword overhead	4.50	6.75	9.00	(CR27) Milkmaid seated on separate stool	5.00	7.50	10.00
(CR3) Knight, sword overhead, no shield	4.50	6.75	9.00	(CR28) Farmer with pitchfork	3.00	5.00	7.00
(CR4) Mounted knight on charging horse	8.00	12.00	16.00	(CR29) Farmer shoveling	4.50	6.75	9.00
(CR5) Mounted knight with lance	6.00	9.00	12.00	(CR30) Farmer dumping bucket	4.50	6.75	9.00
(CR6) Mounted Crusader	6.00	9.00	13.00	(CR31) Farmer in derby, with cane	4.00	6.00	8.00
(CR7) Masked Bandit with gun	3.00	5.00	7.00	(CR32) Butcher in straw hat, cleaver raised	12.00	18.00	24.00
(CR8) Masked Bandit drawing gun	3.00	5.00	7.00	(CR33) Butcher's assistant, plate in one hand, tray in other	10.00	15.00	20.00
(CR9) Mounted Cowboy firing pistol	4.50	6.75	9.00	(CR34) Grenadier Guard standing firing	3.00	5.00	7.00
(CR10) Infantry kneeling firing, WWII	3.00	4.50	6.00	(CR35) Grenadier Guard kneeling firing	3.00	5.00	7.00
(CR11) Infantry prone with bren gun, WWII	3.00	5.00	7.00	(CR36) Grenadier Guard lying firing	3.00	5.00	7.00
(CR12) Infantry standing with tommy gun, WWII	3.00	4.50	6.00	(CR37) Life Guard at attention with sword, foot	4.00	6.00	8.00
(CR13) Officer firing pistol, helmet	4.00	6.00	8.00	(CR38) Sailor at slope	4.00	6.00	8.00
(CR14) Infantry lying with wire cutters	10.00	15.00	20.00	(CR39) Mountie kneeling	7.00	11.00	15.00
(CR15) Artillery piece	10.00	15.00	20.00	(CR40) Mountie, rifle at foot	7.00	11.00	15.00
(CR16) U.S. Marine, saluting	5.00	7.50	10.00	(CR41) Mountie, marching at slope	4.00	6.00	8.00
(CR17) U.S. Marine, parade rest	5.00	7.50	10.00	(CR42) Buffalo Bill, mounted, arm in air	15.00	22.00	30.00
(CR18) U.S. Marine, marching at slope	5.00	7.50	10.00	(CR43) Annie Oakley with shotgun, standing	6.00	9.00	13.00
(CR19) U.S. Marine empty-handed	5.00	7.50	10.00	(CR44) Egyptian tourist, riding camel	6.00	9.00	12.00
(CR20) Indian firing rifle, long headdress	3.00	5.00	7.00	(CR45) Civilian stretcher party, 2 bearers, stretcher, injured	15.00	22.00	30.00
(CR21) Indian crawling with tomahawk	3.00	4.50	6.00	(CR46) Doctor with stethoscope	5.00	7.50	10.00
(CR22) Indian kneeling with bow	3.00	5.00	7.00	(CR47) Nurse holding towel	5.00	7.50	10.00
(CR23) Mounted Indian, shielding eyes	5.00	8.00	10.00	(CR48) Nurse, hands in front	5.00	7.50	10.00
(CR24) Indian walking with rifle, headdress	3.00	4.50	6.00	(CR49) Coronation Coach, 8 horses, 4 outriders	37.00	55.00	75.00
(CR25) Indian walking with tomahawk	3.00	4.50	6.00	(CR50) G.I. mortar shell loader, bronze body	3.00	4.50	6.00
(CR26) Crescent stagecoach	30.00	45.00	60.00				

CRESCENT

	G	VG	M
(CR51) G.I. standing with mortar shell, bronze body	3.00	4.50	6.00
(CR52) G.I. throwing grenade	3.00	4.50	6.00
(CR53) G.I. walking at trail	3.00	4.50	6.00
(CR54) G.I. with flame thrower	3.00	4.50	6.00
(CR55) G.I. standing with tommy gun	3.00	4.50	6.00
(CR56) G.I. lying firing ...	3.00	4.50	6.00
(CR57) G.I. charging with pistol	3.00	4.50	6.00
(CR58) Bandsman trombone player	4.00	6.00	8.00
(CR59) Bandsman tuba player	4.00	6.00	8.00
(CR60) Bandsman bassoon player	4.00	6.00	8.00
(CR61) Bandsman cymbals player	4.00	6.00	8.00
(CR62) Bandsman drummer	4.00	6.00	8.00
(CR63) Bandsman, cornetist	4.00	6.00	8.00

	G	VG	M
(CR64) Dan Dare set	No Price Found		
(CR65) Treen (space alien from Dan Dare set) standing firing	14.00	21.00	28.00
(CR66) Senegalese officer carrying flag	6.00	9.00	12.00
(CR67) Senegalese bugler in white bearskin	6.00	9.00	12.00
(CR68) Senegalese marching at slope	5.00	7.50	10.00
(CR69) French Foreign Legion marching at slope	5.00	7.50	10.00
(CR70) 700 Royal Engineers, field telephone, 2 soldiers, one has detachable reel of wire, telegraph pole, boxed ...	22.00	33.00	45.00
(CR71) 2537 Knight set, 13 pieces	62.00	93.00	125.00
(CR72) Policemen and horse, set	No Price Found		

CR6   CR5   CR1
Courtesy K. Warren Mitchell

CR4
Courtesy K. Warren Mitchell

CR9

CR15   CR8   CR7   CR22
Courtesy K. Warren Mitchell

CR12    CR13

CR20

CR23

CR24

CR17   CR18   CR19

Photo by
Roger W. Hocking

CR25

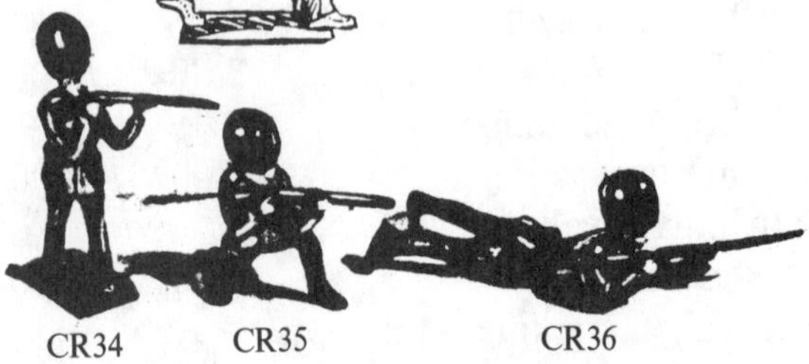

CR34   CR35   CR36

602

CRESCENT

CR29   CR26A   CR28
Courtesy K. Warren Mitchell

CR43   CR42   CR10
Courtesy K. Warren Mitchell

CR37

CR45

CR47

CR48

CR58   CR59   CR60   CR61   CR62   CR63

CR64 boxtop.
Courtesy Paul Stadinger

CR64
Courtesy Paul Stadinger

CR69

CR68   CR66   CR67

Crescent Policeman and horse - (CR72)
Photo by Gary J. Linden

CHERILEA

England's Cherilea began in 1948, according to Garratt's "Encyclopaedia." Its figures were hollowcast in lead alloy at first, in 54mm and a slightly smaller size. Later the company turned to plastic, and in 1973 was bought by Sharna Ware Mfg. Co. Ltd. The following are representative prices the figures sold for in recent years.

Figures by Cherilea, piper, native, archer, knights.
Courtesy Wilbur Bittenbender

	G	VG	M		G	VG	M
(CH1) Crusader swinging sword	4.00	6.00	8.00	(CH7) Highlander at slope .	3.00	4.50	6.00
(CH2) Knight in Armor, sword on ground	3.00	5.00	7.00	(CH8) Highlander Piper ...	4.50	6.75	9.00
(CH3) Mounted knight, holding hilt of sword up .	6.00	9.00	13.00	(CH9) Grenadier Guard at slope, 50mm	3.00	4.50	6.00
(CH4) Medieval Bowman ..	6.00	9.00	12.00	(CH10) Line Infantry at slope	3.00	4.50	6.00
(CH5) Crusader standing with shield at side	4.00	6.00	8.00	(CH11) Spaceman, arms in air	8.00	12.00	16.00
(CH6) Indian kneeling with tomahawk	3.00	5.00	7.00	(CH12) No. 1001 Journey Into Space (Spacemen), 7-piece set	80.00	120.00	160.00
(CH6A) Indian in headdress holding rifle	3.00	5.00	7.00	(CH12A) No. 51 Spaceman with Atom Gun	8.00	12.00	16.00
(CH7A) Guardsman at ease	4.00	6.00	8.00	(CH13) Royal Scots Greys at the halt	5.00	8.00	11.00

CHERILEA

	G	VG	M
(CH14) Dragoon Guard, full gallop, lance	9.00	13.00	18.00
(CH15) Life Guard, marching with drawn sword .	5.00	7.00	9.00
(CH16) Lancer at the gallop	10.00	15.00	20.00
(CH17) 5114 Middlesex Regiment, at slope with rifle	4.00	6.00	8.00
(CH18) GI Advancing with rifle across waist	4.50	6.75	9.00
(CH19) GI At ease	4.50	6.75	9.00
(CH20) GI Throwing Grenade	4.50	6.75	9.00
(CH21) GI Flame thrower	4.50	6.75	9.00

	G	VG	M
(CH22) GI Marching with slung rifle	4.50	6.75	9.00
(CH23) GI Marching at slope	4.50	6.75	9.00
(CH24) Woman's Army figure, marching eyes left	10.00	15.00	20.00
(CH25) Woman's Army figure, eyes forward	5.00	8.00	10.00
(CH26) U.S. Marine Bugler	4.50	6.75	9.00
(CH27) U.S. Marine marching at slope	4.50	6.75	9.00
(CH28) U.S. Marine saluting	4.50	6.75	9.00
(CH29) Mounted Cowboy, holding pistol	5.00	8.00	10.00
(CH30) Bareheaded cowboy, foot, firing pistol	No Price Found		

CH30

CH26   CH27   CH28
Photo by Roger W. Hocking

CH12
Courtesy K. Warren Mitchell

BMC-SOLDARMA

According to Andrew Rose's book *Toy Soldiers,* BMC began as the Britannia Model Company during World War I. When Johillco, which had registered Britannia as a trademark, sued, the name was changed to Soldarma. The company went out of business in 1933, defeated by the Depression. Its hollow-cast lead figures were generally in a 60mm range, though at times as small as 45mm and as large as 70mm. They are well-regarded by collectors, as evidenced by the prices realized on the two sets shown here.

This set of BMC French Line Infantry 1914, made circa 1920, was auctioned in December, 1989 for $500.
Courtesy Phillips New York

This set of BMC No. 121 American Cowboys (with Lasso), circa 1920s, was auctioned in December, 1989 for $275. There was some paint chipping, and a portion of one of the horses' legs was missing.
Courtesy Phillips New York·

COURTENAY
by Bob Hornung

Richard Courtenay, born in England in 1892, began making toy soldiers in 1918. However, the figures commonly associated with him weren't produced until 1928.

Although his medieval fighting knights are what he's known for, Courtenay also produced a series of ancient warriors, many historical personalities and mounted jockeys. In all, he created a total of nearly 150 different figures. Variations were possible via changing arms, heads or weapons.

Courtenay figures are known for their superb animation and exquisite painting. From the start they were painted with the heraldry of actual knights of the "Hundred Years War" period. Courtenay's painting continued to improve, so that by the late 1940s and the 1950s he was producing true works of art. Both heraldry and faces were executed with exceptional detail.

Richard Courtenay died in 1963, ending a long and rewarding career. His molds were first passed to miniaturist Freddy Ping. His versions of Courtenay figures continued till his death in 1977. In 1978 Peter Greenhill (see Newer Makers), acquired the molds. His Courtenay-Greenhill figures are of the same outstanding quality as the finest Courtenays.

Early Courtenay figures were often unsigned. Later they normally had the name of the knight signed in gold on the base. The bottom was usually signed "Made in England" or "Made in England by R. Courtenay". The position number was often added as well. There are many copies of Courtenays. In fact, a company in New York copied nearly all of his work in the 1950s. Quality is generally very poor on these.

Prices vary widely as most Courtenays are sold at auction. Generally, foot range from $100-$300 in mint and mounted $200-$500 in mint. Special figures with unusual heraldry or converted pieces often command much more. Pings tend to go for $50-$150 in mint. Copies generally have little value.

1   2   3   4   5

6   7   8   8A   9   Photo by Bob Hornung

10   11   12   13A   14

15   16   17   18   19

Photo by Bob Hornung

20   21   22   Z1   Z2

Z3   Z5   Z6   Z8   Z11

Photo by Bob Hornung

Top row, L to R: Z15; 13th Century knight; Archer; Order of Garter; Order of Golden Fleece, Edward I with the Baby Prince of Wales. Bottom, L to R: Crusader, Henry VIII; Queen of Henry; Cardinal Wolseley; 15th Century Gentleman; Executioner.
Photo by Bob Hornung

H1   H2   H3   H11   H12   H13

H4   H6   H8A

Left to right: Tournament Knight; Henry V; M2; Cruciform.
Photo by Bob Hornung

Photo by Bob Hornung

NEWER MAKERS

A number of small companies have made and are currently making soldiers in dimestore and 54mm sizes, geared to the collector. Following is a necessary abbreviated list.

DIMESTORE SIZE

Holt's Hobbies figures

HOLT'S HOBBIES began producing original Hollowcast WW I dimestore size lead soldiers and accessories as a family business in June of 1984. Collector Lynton "Bill" Holt designs, sculpts and makes the slush casting moulds. His wife, Sharon, does the marketing and shipping.

Holt's objective is to continue where the old dimestore manufacturers left off. For current catalog send $5 to: Holt's Hobbies, 19800 SW 180th Ave., Box 40, Miami, Florida 33187.

New Era Metal Models

NEW ERA METAL MODELS had its beginnings in 1982 when owner-designer Phil Richards was selling and repairing toy trains and decided to cast some WW II-style enemy helmets for a large group of paintless or damaged Barclay and Manoil castings. His first efforts turned out well and he experimented with converting figures for other collectors and selling figures he'd converted at shows. Near the close of 1982, he developed the idea of having castings produced from his master patterns, and assembling these castings into toy soldiers. This was the beginning of New Era Metal Models, first appearing in a 1983 catalog. For current update on figures send SASE to New Era Models, 1403 N. W. 53rd Avenue, Gainesville, Florida 32606.

NEWERMAKERS

VINTAGE CASTINGS (Bill Lango) casts from original Barclay and Metal Cast molds (hollow castings). It also sells previously unproduced Barclays (making molds from the original plaster models), original designs and vehicles. Free brochure. 127-74th Street, North Bergen, NJ 07047.

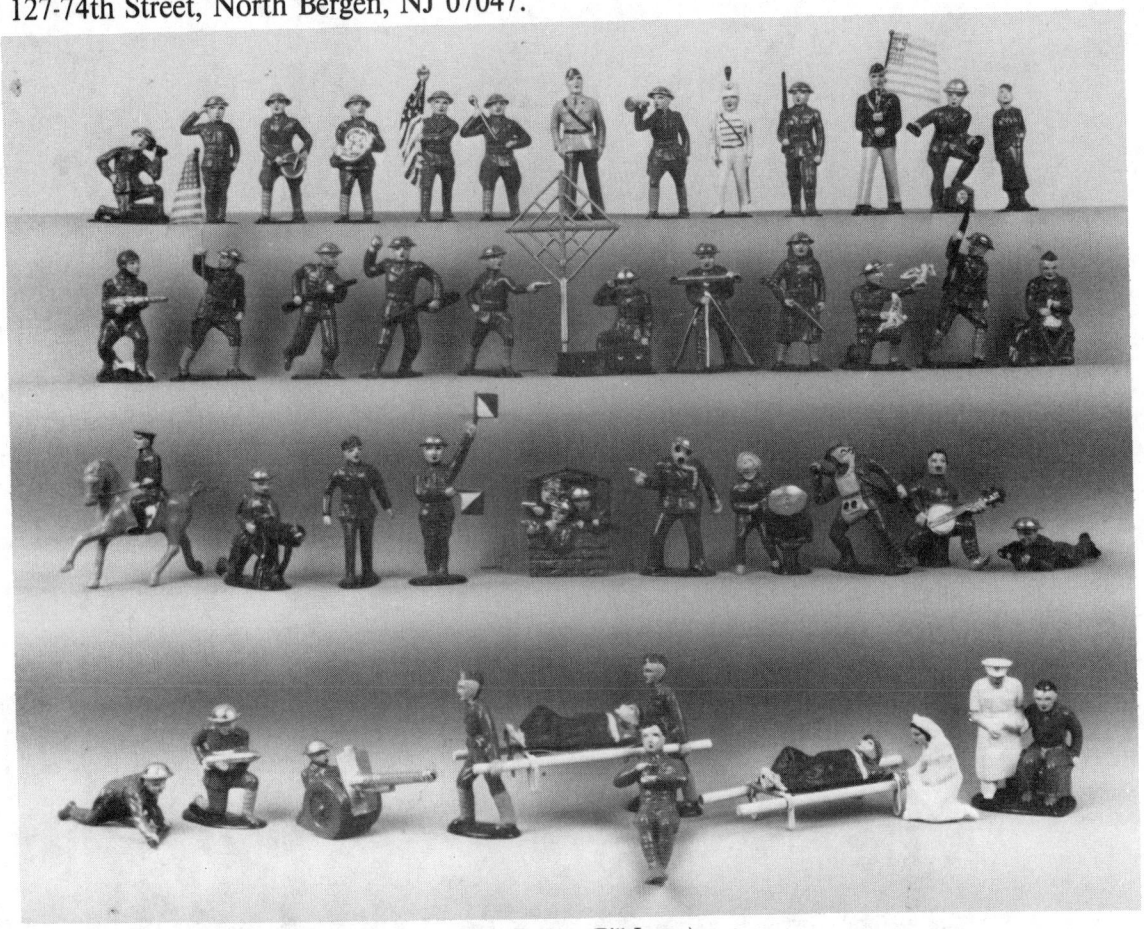

Vintage Castings (Bill Lango)

ECCLES BROTHERS (Ron Eccles) casts from original Barclay, Manoil and other molds; soldiers, airplanes, vehicles, etc. Catalog $3.00. R.R. No. 1, Box 253-D, Burlington, IA 52601.

Postwar Manoils currently being cast from the original molds by Ron Eccles.

611

G.M.G. (German Modeling Group) began producing limited editions, in white metal, of 70mm Lineol figures. Production seems to have begun in 1987. P.O. Box 152, Fryeburg, ME 04037.

G.M.G.

COMBAT READY COLLECTIBLES, owned by Wayne and Mary Hill, is Wayne Hill's attempt to carry on the podfoot line begun by Barclay. In fact, his figures and painting are an improvement on Barclay's. For free listing, write to Combat Ready Collectibles, 5 Starwood Drive, Hampstead, NH 03841.

Combat Ready Collectibles

RIFLE & SABER MINIATURES, about 1987 began production of solid cast metal personality figures, among them Mussolini, Sgt. York and Rommel. The sculptor hired by owners Ed and LaVerne Miller was exceptional, but with one exception, all the pieces were a bit too big for the dimestore scale. The exception is Perishing (foot), which is not only the right size, but superbly done. 1604 Lauckson Place, Point Pleasant, NJ 08742. The Millers now specialize in Civil War figures, 54mm.

Rifle & Saber Miniatures

NEWERMAKERS

FRANK POETH of the Netherlands sculpts his own dimestore-sized solid cast metal soldiers. Production began about 1989. He also produces 54mm figures, some based on Dorset, but with Dutch heads and equipment. For information, write: Frank Poeth, Nachtegaalstr:63, 5932 CB Tegelen, Netherlands

Frank Poeth

STANLEIGH'S BUNKERS are the handiwork of Stan Cann. Production began about 1990, with the size designed for Lineol and Elastolin, but also a good size for dimestore soldiers. Others are made to a 54mm scale. For a catalog, send a SASE to Stan Cann, 543 NE 72nd St., Miami, FL 33138.

Stanleigh's Bunkers

54 MM SIZE

Figures by Martin Ritchie

MARTIN RITCHIE, manufacturer of 54mm, solid cast, hand painted original model soldiers, has been in business since October, 1979. It began under the trade name of Marcat Miniatures. It is solely owned and operated by Martin Ritchie who does the research, design and sculpting. Currently there are four assistants. All of the 35 sets now being produced follow the theme of the American Armed Forces on parade. Each branch of the Armed Forces is represented as well as the Service Academies and elite units of the various branches. The one exception is the full band of the Pipes and Drums of the Black Watch Highland Regiment. Each unit of the Americans will have variations such as Guidons, Mascots, bands and color guards. The business is now operated using his own name as a trademark. Martin Ritchie, RD3, Box 343-B, Hickory Lane, Kunkletown, PA, 18058 (215) 681-5324.

LeMAN'S COLLECTION began about 1985. Owner-sculptor James Man features a wide-ranging line, from American Revolution to Civil War to French Imperial Guards to Hunters-Jumpers to Carousel horses. 3401 Brennan D-22, Amarillo, Texas 79121 (806) 355-3683.

Union Gatling Gun and Crew

LeMan's

Union and Confederate Cavalry

GREENHILL MINIATURES were begun in 1975 by Peter Greenhill. Greenhill's designs met with early commercial success and prompted the late miniaturist Freddy Ping to suggest to Hummels of Burlington Arcade that they might consider entrusting the molds of the late Richard Courtenay to his care. In February 1978 Greenhill and his wife, the actress Gillian Barclay (who does some of the painting) bought the complete collection of 180 Courtenay molds from Hummels. These molds produce 118 basic figures. The firm has been so successful that it's often booked a year in advance. Peter Greenhill, 5 Westbourne Park Road, Bournemouth, Dorset, BH4 8HG England.

Greenhill-Courtenay miniature

NEWERMAKERS

ALYMER of Spain has been in business since about 1928. Its current line is wide and varied, basically in a roughly 54mm size. Its extensive range of 54mm knights were designed by American dealer K. Warren Mitchell, sculpted by A. Comes, with heraldry by Peter Greenhill.

Alymer

MINIFIGURE of Tucson, Arizona, was in business in the 1950s and perhaps later, with many of its figures sold through mail order via Bob Bard. Early U.S. troops, French Foreign Legion and British troops of the 1880s were part of its line.

Minifigures

AMERICAN METAL TOY COMPANY was owned by Bill Long and located in Bay City, Michigan. It cast the post-WWII Lincoln Logs figures. About 1955 it seems to have begun production of its only original figures, in a "hard metal". They consisted of Spaniards of 1520 and ancient Romans.

American Metal Spaniards

615

NEWERMAKERS

BOB HORNUNG: After creating a series of dimestore-sized doughboys, their design based on previously manufactured plastic GIs, Hornung turned to a series of originals called "Tournament Knights". A highlight of this series is the exquisite detail in the painting. Bob Hornung, 32 E. Charlotte, Cincinnati, Ohio 45215.

Bob Hornung Tournament Knights

DJ's Originals, set #2

DJ'S ORIGINALS began as an offshoot of DJ's Miniatures catalog of old and new toy soldiers. Don and Jean Porter had begun selling toy soldiers in 1976. Don had collected WW I items since childhood, and they felt this important part of history was not well represented by toy soldiers. Thus DJ's Originals was launched as a continuous line of 54mm WWI troops. DJ's provides exceptional variety. By ordering different arms and heads, hundreds of unique figures are available. All figures are original, not recasts or conversions. DJ's Miniatures, 4562 Everett Court, Wheat Ridge, Colorado 80033.

BRIGADIER began in 1979, owned by John Harvey and Marshall Clark, both of whom apparently do the designing, mold-making and casting. Brigadier makes soldiers of several countries but understandably specializes in Australian troops. Brigadier, P.O. Box 131, Kooringal, N.S.W., 2650, Australia.

Brigader

616

Ron Wall Civil War set with U.S. Grant, a Union Artillery Crew and a 6 pound Napoleon Bronze.

RON WALL MINIATURES. Ron Wall fell in love with toy soldiers at the age of three and has been sculpting, casting and selling them since 1975. Most of his figures are American, basically modern and Civil War, and all of them are signed and dated by year. The figures are made of solid tin and lead. Ron Wall, 7311 Christopher Dr. St. Louis, MO 63129.

TIFFANY SOLDIERS was named by owner-sculptor Jacques Cuypers for his daughter. His figures mainly deal with 14th and 15th century knights from Burgundy, Belgium and the low countries, both mounted and foot, plus everyday castle life. Most of the figures have movable arms and visors and come with detachable swords and helmets. 5075 West 4700 South No. 153, Kearns, UT 84118 (801) 969-8302.

Tiffany

THOMAS' TIN SOLDIERS (PANACHE FIGURINES) is owned by Tom Loback, who is also the sculptor. Concentration at present is on Civil War, with some accent on the 54th Massachusetts. There is also a good line of French Foreign Legion. 152 West 26th Street, No. 36, New York, NY 10001. The figures are made from pure tin.

Thomas' Tin Soldiers 54th Massachusetts Monument Series
Photo by Sato Studios

BLENHEIM began production of prototypes in London by Frank and Jan Scroby in December, 1973. However, boxed sets didn't appear on the market until November, 1975. Production ceased April, 1982. The majority of the figures were of British troops of the 1800s.

Sets B28, B29, B30 and B31 Royal Welsh Fussiliers 1890 by Blenheim Military Models.
Courtesy Hank Anton

NEWERMAKERS

WAGONS OF WOOD, 39 Seneca Trail, Wayne, NJ 07470, first began producing 54mm wagons in 1983. The firm, owned by Don Paulussen, is the foremost wagon supplier to those who collect 54mm toy soldiers. All wagons are made of hard wood - bass and spruce, with wheels, horses and crews in metal. Eighteen wagons (the first was the British Mobile Pigeon Loft), plus a Nile River Boat and a 19th Century Balloon and wagon complete the line.

Wagons of Wood.
Photo by Michael Reiners Studio, Union, NJ

MARKTIME TOY SOLDIERS were first produced in September of 1976 by a two husband and wife partnership in England. Peter and Chris Cowan and Jim and Margaret Borrowman made up the original partnership. The firm made 54mm toy soldiers compatible with Britains and took over Steadfast Soldiers from Andrew Rose in July of 1979. Marktime was discontinued as of March 1980. The Borrowmans continued to operate as Borbur Enterprises, Ltd. and make and sell the Steadfast Range of toy soldiers. Marktime are not marked but are very similar in paint to pre-war Britains.

Marktime Toy Soldiers made in England for a short period of time.

BRITISH BULLDOG. August of 1975 was the approximate date of new toy soldiers called "British Bulldog". Located in Swansea, England the firm was owned by Mr. Mike Drewson and Mr. Peter Jones who did all the designs, molds, casting and painting. Their range covered British Regiments of the Victorian period. Individual pieces were available and painted to regimental specifications of your choice in some cases. In July of 1981 limited edition boxed sets were issued. The firm is no longer in business.

619

NEWERMAKERS

CHARLES HALL of Edinburgh, Scotland issued a series of figures in a wide range. Originally starting in 1977 his first figures were designed by the late John Niblett. Further designs were done by Tommy Park of Glasgow, Scotland and Charles Hall. Most Charles Hall toy soldier figures were issued as single individual pieces and sets were left to the collector's fancy. The original issue was concentrated on Scottish Highland Regiments but the "sky is the limit" from there. About 300 different items have been produced so far. All the painting, which is the distinguishing characteristic of Hall's toy soldiers, is done by Charles and his brother William Hall. Photo shown was taken by Steve MacAvoy. Production is very limited and demand for this top quality collectible toy soldier far exceeds the supply. (Now out of business with molds sold).

Charles Hall

FIFE & DRUM MINIATURES Toy soldiers for collectors were produced by Fife & Drum Miniatures, Havertown, PA, by Mr. John Gross. The first sets were put into production on about August of 1979. The sets were issued in limited editions of approximately 350 boxed sets of 6 pieces. Sculpting was done by Mr. Bill Greer from design ideas by John Gross and casting was done by Mr. Jim McCaron of Stone Mountain Miniatures. The range was to be concentrated on "American History Themes". Up to twelve "proof" sets were issued on each production run. Unfortunately, due to a myriad of technical and other problems the range was discontinued in the early 1980s.

Fife & Drum 7th Cavalry, Set #2
Photo by Gary J. Linden

SOLDIER CENTRE SOLDIERS Mr. Ed Carrigg, the Soldier Centre, P.O. Box 38, West Roxbury, MA 02132 is issuing a range of collector's toy soldiers in the 54mm (standard Britains compatible scale). The sets were first issued in May of 1980 and have continued currently. The sculpting, casting and painting is done by Ed and his son, Robert Carrigg. He is also fortunate in getting full support in his efforts from his wife. The range is British army around the turn of the century.

Soldier Centre Soldiers
Set 4 Royal Army Medical Corp. Ambulance Wagon
Courtesy Hank Anton

BRITANNIA, LTD. (San Francisco, California).
Owner Mr. John Sandy, who along with R.D. Bielby did design. Castings were done by Joe Shimek. The range, very similar to British Bulldog, was British Regiments of the Victorian period. This firm was to be affirmed with British Bulldog but after a false start, went on their own. Production started about September of 1978. Sculpture of their 25th Foot - Scottish Borderers, was by Les Saulsbury.

NOSTALGIA was begun in 1974 by dealer Shamus O.D. Wade. The idea was to revive the traditional British toy soldier. Sculptors, casters and painters were Frank and Janet Scroby. London-based.

Nostalgia

SOLDAT by Jose M. Alarcon Ricart 16-18 Barcelona, Spain. Range: 65mm figures on wooden bases. Includes German Army WWII, Napoleonics, U.S. Army and U.S. Marines. Extensive selection availble through local dealers.

TRADITION 5A & 5B Shepherd Street Mayfair, London W1 England. Ed and Miriam Studer, Representatives in U.S.A. 12924 Viking Drive, Burnsville, MN 55337 Design: David Scheiman. Extensive range of 54mm.

NEWERMAKERS

SOLDIERS by John Tunstill 44/46 Kennington Road, London S E 1 7 B L England. Owner: John Tunstill did most design, casting, etc. Started 1977. Extensive range of British Victorian period Regiments in 54mm. An entirely customized army could be ordered from Soldiers. Out of business.

M.J. MODE 1 Southfields Avenue, Oadby, Leicester, England. Owner: Jim Johnston started in late 1978. Range: 54mm Indian Army, German Army, Ceremonial Regiments, WWII Armies. There is a new owner and new address.

HERRINGS SOLDIERS P.O. Box 1195, Greenwich, CT 06830. Daniel W. Keefe, Jr., President.

DUCAL MODEL SOLDIERS 5 Weavills Road Bishopstoke, Eastleigh Hants; SO5 6 H Q England. Owner: Jack Duke who does design, castings and molds. Started: early 1979. Extensive line of turn of the century British Empire troops.

Ducal Colour Party

DORSET (METAL MODEL) SOLDIERS 19 Salisbury Street, Shaftesbury, Dorset, England. Owner: G.S. Brown. Started in 1975. Original models were copies of Hollowcast. Range: 54mm British, Colonial and Foreign Armies 1880 to 1940.

Dorset soldiers

NEWERMAKERS

A W MILITARY FIGURES 12 Addison Road Brockenhurst, Hampshire, England. Owner: Unknown. Started: early 1979. Range: 54mm British Empire vehicles and figures.

ALBION FIGURES 29 Woodlands Ave., Wanstead, E 11 3 R A, London, England. Owner: Peter Cowan (one of the former owners of Marktime). Range: was to issue new (Marktime) sets never issued before but evidently went in another direction casting the Andrew Rose designed Nostalgia Series. Now known as Kingcast .

BRITISH SOLDIERS 9340 Northeast 176th St., Bothell, WA 98011. Started: Early 1980. Reproductions of 54mm scale Hollowcasts.

AMERICAN IN MINIATURE P.O. Box 55, Ryegate Corner, VT 05042. Owner: Mr. Arnold Mead, who does design, casting and hires painters. Started in April of 1977. Range: U.S. Military units throughout history. Extensive selection of 54mm figures are available.

AMHERST MINIATURE 917 H. Terrace Lane, Ypsilanti, MI 48197. Owner: Mr. W.J. Marshall started in 1982. Range: 54mm Canadian units and British Colonials.

IMPERIAL PRODUCTIONS produces figures from the British wars of the 1880s, Civil War and turn-of-the-century civilians. P.O. Box 94, Greytown, New Zealand.

Imperial civilians

SCHULMAN & TOFANO ENTERPRISES LTD. produces pewter figurines. Address for the East Coast office is Stephen M. Tofano, 4 Sharon Lane, Rye, New York 10580.

HM of GREAT BRITAIN was launched in 1989, went into liquidation, then reorganized. It specializes in British troops of the past and present. Unit 8, 22 Leyburn Road, Sheffield S80XA, England.

QUARTERMASTER CORPS produces a wide range of soldiers of the 19th and 20th centuries. Owners are Carl and Adele Hoegermeyer, with sculpting by Mister Hoegermeyer and his son. P.O. Box 908, Buckingham, PA 18912. (215) 794-5606.

Quartermaster Corps set No. 38

IRON BRIGADE MINIATURES is owned by Terry Cannarsa. Its pewter figures seem to deal exclusively with the Civil War. 2121 W. Shawnee, P.O. Box 1705, Muskogee, OK 74402.

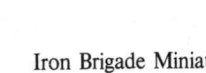

Iron Brigade Miniatures

GARIBALDI & CO. TOY SOLDIERS. Made in Italy, they feature Romans, Garibaldini, Crimea, Independence Wars, European Armies, Seven Years War in Canada, Peking. U.S. agent: Thomas Shydler 724 Chabot Drive, Las Vegas, NV 89107. SASE for information.

RECOMMENDED PUBLICATIONS

Old Toy Soldier - Bimonthly publication. Articles, many ads. Subscriptions $18 bulk rate, $28 first class, $33 overseas airmail. 209 North Lombard, Oak Park, IL 60302.

Toy Soldier Review - Quarterly publication. Articles, many ads. Subscriptions $12 bulk rate, $18 first class, $24 U.K. & Europe air mail, $28 Africa, Australia and Far East airmail. 127-74th St. North Bergen, NJ 07047.

Plastic Figure & Playset Collector - Marx and other plastic. Bimonthly, articles, ads. Subscriptions $18 bulk rate, $26 first class, $27 foreign surface rate, $33 foreign air mail rate. P.O. Box 1355 LaCrosse, WI 54602-1355.

The Art of the Toy Soldier by Henry I. Kurtz & Burtt R. Ehrlich. Beautifully done coffee-table book. Abbeville Press, NY., 1987. (New Cavendish in England).

Toy Soldiers by Andrew Rose. All color, beautifully done. Even veteran collectors find new things here. 1985, Salamander Books, Ltd., London.

Britains Toy Soldiers 1893-1932 by James Opie. The best book on this subject. 1985, Harper & Row, New York.

Holger Eriksson Collector Society - Newsletter on the subject. $15 annual dues. c/o Lou Sandbote, 5307 East Mockingbird, Capital Bank Building Suite 802, Dallas, Texas 75206-5109.

Toy Armies by Peter Johnson. Wonderfully readable. Doubleday & Co., New York

Making & Collecting Military Miniatures by Bob Bard. Detailed approach to the subject. 1957, Robert McBride Co. Inc., NY.

The World Encyclopedia of Model Soldiers by John G. Garratt, Not scrupulously accurate, but there's nothing else like it. Monumental. 1981, Frederick Muller Limited, London.

Old British Model Soldiers by L.W. Richards. Highly respected.

Regiments of All Nations (Postwar Britains) by Joe Wallis. A miracle of detail and painstaking accuracy. Joe Wallis, P.O. Box 7422, Silver Spring, MD 20910-7422. $25.

The Barclay Catalog Book. Early Barclay catalogs, photos, sketches. $15 from Richard O'Brien, 135 Stephensburg Rd. RD2, Port Murray, NJ 07865

Guide for Non-Metallic Toy Soldiers of the U.S. by Timothy J. Geppert. Well over 1000 plastic soldiers illustrated and coded. Self-published. 1986. Timothy J. Geppert, 2416 Purdue Rd., Ft. Collins, CO 80525.

Plastic Warrior. European plastics. Bimonthly, $25 a year. Paul Stadinger, 905 Harrison Street, Allentown, PA 18103.

LEADING COLLECTORS AND DEALERS

It's suggested you enclose a stamped, self-addressed envelope, known as SSAE or SASE to collectors, when writing to any of the following.

ED POOLE - Toy Soldiers, 1/36 scale ID vehicles, old wooden military vehicle kits. 54mm Hundred Years War Figures for sale. 926 Terrace Mountain Drive, Austin, Texas 78746.

K. WARREN MITCHELL - Dealer in all old metal toy soldiers (W. Britains, Barclay, Manoil, etc.). Regular Lists. P.O. Box 1123, Pataskala, Ohio, 43062.

LONDON BRIDGE COLLECTOR'S TOYS - (Ron Ruddell). Dealers in Britains, etc., also Britains replacement parts. East Penn Plaza, 1325 Chestnut St., Emmaus, PA 18049 (215) 967-6887.

HANK ANTON - Monthly dimestore auctions, Toy Soldier information service, 92 Swain Ave., Meriden, Connecticut 06450, (203) 237-5356.

DON PIELIN - Toy soldiers, especially Dimestore. 1009 Kenilworth, Wheeling, Illinois 60090.

BARBARA and JONATHAN NEWMAN - Dealers in paper and cardboard soldiers, etc. The Paper Soldier, 8 McIntosh Lane, Clifton, NY 12065.

JOE WALLIS - Britains soldiers. P.O. Box 2294, Washington, DC 20013.

BILL LANGO - Dimestore soldiers, animals, vehicles from original and new molds. Vintage Castings, 127-74th Street, North Bergen NJ 07047. Free color brochure.

RON ECCLES - Barclay and Manoil soldiers, civilians, Happy Farm from original molds, plus accessories. Eccles Brothers, R.R. No. 1, Box 253-D, Burlington, Iowa 52601. Catalog $3.00.

ROGER JOHNSON - Dimestore collector, converter, restorer (for trade only). 31 Rolfe Place, Metuchen, NJ 08840.

RICHARD MACNARY - Soldiers, Marx military trains, Built-Rite. 4727 Alpine Drive, Lilburn, GA 30247.

STEVE BALKIN - Dealer in toy soldiers. Burlington Toys, 1082 Madison Avenue, New York, NY 10028.

MEMORABLE THINGS - Regular lists of old American and imported soldiers. P.O. Box 10505, Towson, Maryland 21204. (Shop address: 31 W. Allegheny Avenue, Towson, MD, 2nd floor).

JENNY BURLEY - Dealer in Britains, Mignot, Heyde, Charbens, Timpo, etc. 34D Upper Montagu St., London, W.I., England.

SECOND CHILDHOOD - Old Soldiers (shop only). 283 Bleecker Street, New York, NY.

THE SOLDIER SHOP - Britains, other soldiers. 1222 Madison Ave., New York, NY 10128 (212) 535-6788.

CLASSIC TOYS - 69 Thompson St., New York, NY 10012 (212) 941-9129. Plastic soldiers, Britains, Mignot, etc.

PHIL SAVINO - Bimonthly auctions, Dimestore and European, SASE for lists. Rt. 2, Box 76, Micanopy, FL 32667.

STAD'S - Plastic soldiers, Marx, Airfix, etc. $4 for six months of lists. 905 Harrison St. Suite 122, Allentown, PA 18103. (215) 770-1140.

BOB WALES - Molds for metal casting, solid repros of Britains, etc. Toy Soldier Factory, P.O. Box 3234, Apollo Beach, FL 33570.

A. (GUS) HANSEN - Mignot, Dimestore, Britains, etc. 4645 Lilac Ave., Glenview, IL 60025.

HOWARD WEHNER - Sells molds, casting supplies, soldier sets and cast soldiers. Coastal Enterprises, P.O. Box 1053, Brick, NJ 08723.

RUSTY HALLER - G.I. Joes, Captain Actions, Irwin Co., G.I. Joe vehicles. 314 Hillfield Rd., Mt. Carmel, CT 06518.

JOHN D. (JACK) MATTHEWS - German Composition and Tinplate, World War II paper, Dimestores, etc. 13 Bufflehead Drive, Kiawah Island, SC 29455.

CHARLIE BRESLOW - Figures of all types, paper, buy, sell, trade. 971 Canton Drive, Toms River, NJ 08753 (908) 286-7618.

TONY AND JACKI GRECCO - Toy soldiers and related items. P.O. Box 3490, Poughkeepsie, NY 12603 (914) 462-8829.

TONY DIKSA - Dimestore soldiers and accessories. 614 E. Grove St., Nanticoke, PA 18634.

BILL HANLON - Plastic figures. 5063 Camino Alta Mira, Castro Valley, California. (415) 886-0976.

JAMES DELSON - Lists of plastic and metal soldiers for sale. The Toy Soldier Company, 100 Riverside Drive, New York, NY 10024.

PHILLIPS - Auctions of soldiers. 406 East 79th Street, New York, NY 10021.

CHRISTIE'S EAST - Auctions of soldiers. 219 East 67th St., New York, NY 10021.

TOYS AND SOLDIER'S MUSEUM - 1100 Cherry St., Vicksburg, Mississippi

EDWARD H. BURLEY - Molds and castings. 5620 Bayshore Rd., Palmetto, Florida 33561

AL SMITH - Dimestores, etc. for sale 102 N. Cherry St. Falls Church, VA 22046.

VINCE PUGLIESE - Manoil, Barclay, Britains, etc., buy and sell. P.O. Box 309, Albertson, NY 11507 (516) 484-9514.

JERRY COMBS - Buy and trade toy soldiers. 1115 Riggle Drive, Zanesville, Ohio 43701 (614) 454-0470.

ROSCHA (Walter Schramm - Rosalie Green), dealers in toy soldiers of all types. 22 Leroy St., New York, NY 10014 (212) 242-4353.

ROBERT A. HELM - American and foreign, mail and shows. 349 Sound Beach Ave., Old Greenwich, CT 06870 (203) 637-3532.

THE TOY SOLDIER (James H. Hillestad) - Soldiers of all types, also museum (by appointment only). Paradise Falls, RR1, Box 379, Cresco, PA 18326 (717) 629-7227.

EVELYN ALEXANDER - Toy Soldiers and Militaria. Route 1, Box 32A, Collins, MS 39428 (601) 765-8708.

TOM GLASSIC - Soldiers of all types. 1030 S. Pine Drive, Bailey, Co. 80421.

BRUTON'S BARRACKS (Pam and Bill Brunton) - Buy, sell, trade, old and new. Mail order, repairs, appraisals. 415 S. Montezuma, Prescott, AZ 86303-4223 (602) 778-1915.

STAN ALEKNA - Dimestore collector and dealer. 724 Oceanfront Drive, Neptune Beach, FL 32233.

BRIGADOON SHOPPE (Bill Coakley & Tony Robinson) - Toy Soldiers, Military Miniatures. P.O. Box 1006 W. Newbury, MA 01985 (508) 692-3122, evenings (Coakley), (508) 363-2410, evenings (Robinson).

N. ROY EASTON, JR. - Military Miniatures, shop and mail, SASE for list. 4540 Merrill Street, Torrance, CA 90503 (213) 543-5015.

JOHN P. RICHARDSON - Buy, sell, trade. 7 Sturbridge Dr. Chelmsford, MA 01824 (508) 256-0436.

EXCALIBUR HOBBIES LTD. - Toy soldiers, all types. 63 Exchange Street, Malden, MA 02148-5523 (617) 322-2959.

G.M. HALEY - Britains and other soldiers. "Hippins" Blackshaw Head, Hebden Bridge, W. Yorks, England.

BARRY GOODMAN - G.I. Joes, Robots, Barbies, etc. P.O. Box 218 Woodbury, NY 11797 (516) 338-2701.

GARY J. LINDEN - Marx and other plastic soldiers and toys. P.O. Box 5243, River Forest, IL 60305.

R. DON PATMAN - Dimestore Collector, particularly All-Nu, Tommy Toy. 3600 Gaston Ave., Wadley, Dallas, Texas 75246 (214) 827-7500.

BERTEL BRUUN - Dealer-Collector, specializing in composition. March of Time, P.O. Box 400, Westhampton, NY 11977 (Shop at Antique Center at the Mall, 164 Montauk Highway, Remsenberg, LI, NY 11960).

KEN WITTENRICH - WEST FALLS TOY COMPANY. Solid castings from original Johillco molds. SSAE for list. P.O. Box 3, West Falls, NY 14170

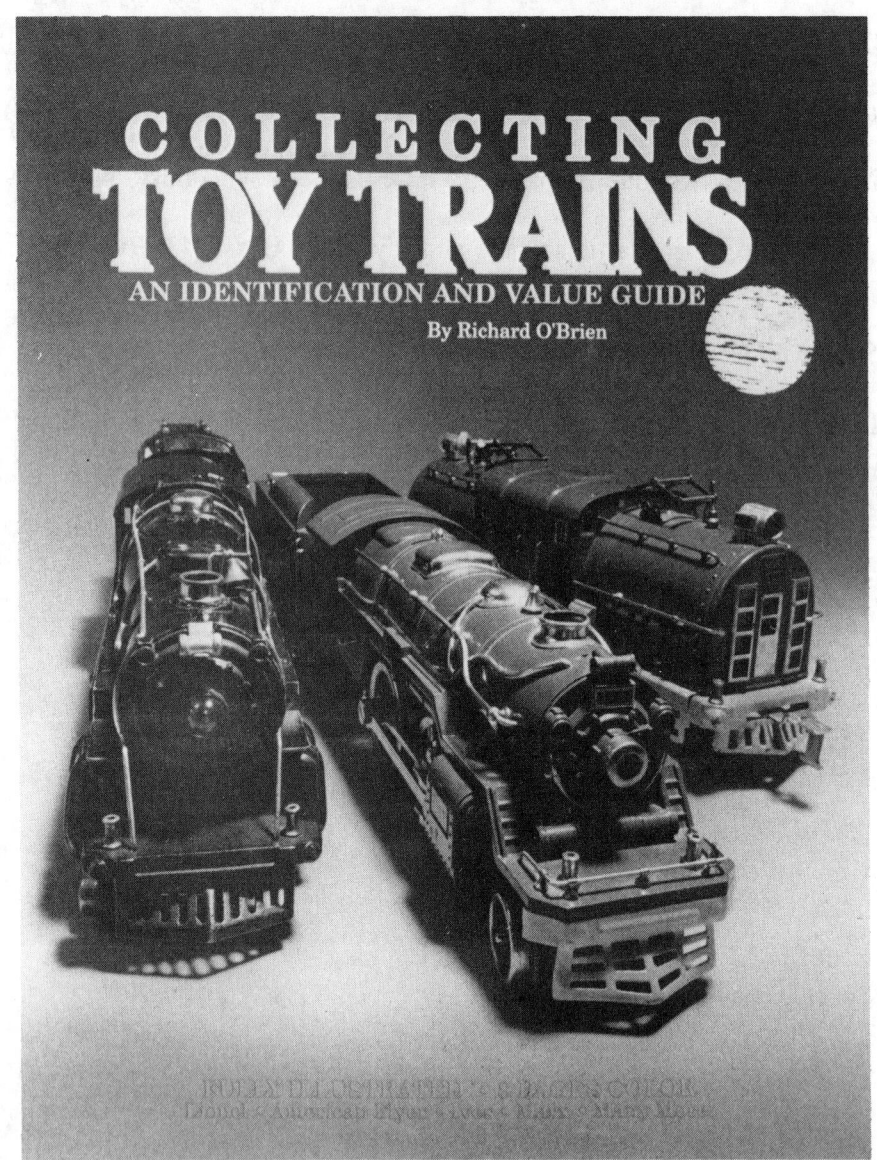

Collecting Toys No. 6
A Collector's Identification & Value Guide
by Richard O'Brien

Due September '92

A COLLECTOR'S IDENTIFICATION & VALUE GUIDE

Collecting no.6 TOYS

Richard O"Brien

**NEW LISTINGS INCLUDE:
MATCHBOX, JAPANESE TIN, ACTION FIGURES, AURORA FIGURE KITS**

This is the most comprehensive book on toys ever published. A complete revision and update of the fantastic 5th edition. Thousands of new listings and photos have been added to the existing information. This book is the favorite of toy collectors worldwide, but whether you are a collector or not, this book is just plain fun reading. 520 pages loaded with illustrations, many in full color, softcover. 8½"x11". ISBN 0-89689-094-5.

$22.95